P9-AQR-216

VOTE

IN THEIR FOOTSTEPS

THE *AMERICAN VISIONS* GUIDE
TO AFRICAN-AMERICAN
HERITAGE SITES

HENRY CHASE
TRAVEL EDITOR,
AMERICAN VISIONS MAGAZINE

HENRY HOLT AND COMPANY · NEW YORK

Henry Holt and Company, Inc.
Publishers since 1866
115 West 18th Street
New York, New York 10011

Henry Holt ® is a registered
trademark of Henry Holt and Company, Inc.

Published in Canada by Fitzhenry & Whiteside Ltd.,
195 Allstate Parkway, Markham, Ontario L3R 4T8.

Library of Congress Cataloging-in-Publication Data
Chase, Henry.
In their footsteps : the *American Visions* guide to African-American heritage sites / Henry Chase. —1st ed.
p. cm.
Includes bibliographical references and index.
1. Historic sites—United States—Guidebooks. 2. United States—Guidebooks. I. American visions. II. Title.
E159.C45 1994
917.304'929—dc20 94-2965
CIP

ISBN 0-8050-3246-0
ISBN 0-8050-2089-6 (An Owl Book: pbk.)

Henry Holt books are available for special promotions and premiums.
For details contact: Director, Special Markets.

First Edition—1994

Designed by Jessica Shatan

Maps by Jackie Aher

Printed in the United States of America
All first editions are printed on acid-free paper. ∞

1 3 5 7 9 10 8 6 4 2

1 3 5 7 9 10 8 6 4 2
(pbk.)

Frontispiece: 1965: The 100th anniversary of both the 13th Amendment to the United States Constitution, which abolished slavery, and the end of the Civil War. Participants in the Selma-to-Montgomery Voting Rights March prepare for the latest round of the black struggle to share the fruits of American liberty.
Courtesy National Civil Rights Museum

To *American Visions'* loyal subscribers,
who make all things possible

HIS DREAM - OUR DREAM
DR. MARTIN LUTHER KING JR.

CONTENTS

FOREWORD

Sometimes as I look back over the course of this nation's history as a black man and as a professional historian, it seems as if destiny had a special mission in mind for African Americans. The mass migration of blacks to these shores began in 1619—before the Pilgrims landed at Plymouth Rock. Unlike others who were drawn to America by the promise of freedom and opportunity, Africans came as slaves in shackles and chains. Denied what others could take for granted, the black community committed itself to the quest for freedom and dignity.

Ironically, out of this struggle blacks became preservers of the founding fathers' dream of a new republic where all were equal in the eyes of the law. *American Visions*, the magazine, records the dreams, the aspirations, the culture of a people who faithfully tended a garden that was sown in 1776. It is this garden that is now beginning to blossom into a modern, multicultural democracy.

American Visions and American Visions Inc. are products of serendipity. About a decade ago, while a tenured history professor at Rutgers University, I spent a sabbatical year as a fellow of the Smithsonian Institution's National Museum of American History working on a project in the history of classical medicine. During that time Roger Kennedy, then director of the museum and now the head of America's National Park Service, raised the idea of my staying at the museum and asked me what I might like to do. I promptly declared that I would like to launch a journal that explored the range of African-American culture. And so with the Smithsonian's assistance, I gave up my faculty position and plunged into the bottom-line business of publishing a magazine.

When I made my declaration I did not fully appreciate that culture is a commodity that can be bought and sold in the same fashion as diamonds and automobiles. Here I speak of culture as artifacts, works of art, literature, music, cuisine, and the performing arts. All of these can be commodities that have market value.

Viewed from this vantage point, African-American culture has historically been undervalued, and the devaluing of our culture is directly related to notions of race. For many it was a simple formula. Blacks were inferior, thus incapable of producing works of great value. Gallery owners interested in exhibiting works of rare beauty, to cite one example, could comfortably categorize the works of African-American artists as a single genre. The result of this stereotyping was to keep African-American culture out of the mainstream marketplace. In the process, our art and literature were devalued.

American Visions flies in the face of the tradition that discounts the value of the black experience. In ways both direct and subtle, it proclaims that African-American culture is a precious commodity worthy of studying, collecting, and promulgating. In so doing, it challenges old formulas and builds self-esteem in our community. Thus I found myself in the struggle. We at *American Visions* have war stories, which I will save for another time; however, I cannot fail to thank the tens of thousands who, through their subscriptions, have supported *American Visions* and its goal of promoting an understanding of African-American culture. I must also mention my partners in this venture, Joanne Harris and Timothy Jenkins, who understood the vision and had the courage to dare to succeed.

In Their Footsteps is an outgrowth of others sharing our vision of the richness of black culture. In 1990, with the assistance of Greyhound Lines, Inc., we published a special issue of our magazine on black historic sites in the lower 48 states. This issue was well received, and Theresa Burns, a senior editor at Henry Holt and Company, contacted us, suggesting that we had the kernel of a book.

The task of cultivating this kernel fell to our travel editor, Henry Chase, who brought to it several years of postgraduate study in Britain, a decade's worth of tramping around Africa, a keen interest in history, and a skeptical mind. From this kernel he has created a full garden, something vastly different—and far better—than the issue we published in 1990. He has, in fact, written the most comprehensive and compelling guide to African-American heritage sites in this country and Canada ever published.

This work *is American Visions*. *In Their Footsteps* reminds us that we are linked together in a seamless web, each generation contributing and advancing the common good and producing its share of humanly flawed heroes.

—GARY PUCKREIN, President and Editor in Chief,
American Visions Magazine

September 10, 1993

ACKNOWLEDGMENTS

The best part about book projects is writing the acknowledgments page. Not only does it mean that you've almost got the monkey off your back, it allows you to offer thanks for assistance and encouragement received and to record debts that cannot adequately be repaid. When I returned from a decade in Africa and joined *American Visions*, I remarked to its founder, Gary Puckrein, that I was very impressed by the magazine, the more so for having come from a hard news environment in which the creative arts and "visuals" were rarely featured. Gary replied that although the magazine looked very slick, the operation that produced it was not so much lean as bare bones, and that my experience in the Third World would serve me well. He spoke truly. In hardship, camaraderie and resourcefulness are vital. I've found both common to my colleagues at the magazine. Michelle, Ed, Mel, Margaret, Diane, Sheronda, Sam, and Jam have eased my path through this endeavor.

In addition to my managing editor at the magazine, Joanne Harris, who during the book project has borne the burden of my reduced role as editor/writer, I'm particularly grateful to my editorial assistant, Anthony Murphy, who usually managed to find what I wanted and always found what I needed. At Henry Holt, I am greatly indebted to my editor, Theresa Burns. Not only is *In Their Footsteps* far better for her interventions, I'm a better editor as a result of watching her work. I am also grateful for her "good cop" colleague at Holt, Tracy Sherrod. As I note in my introduction, it's been a pleasure to work with *Footsteps*' essayists. For years Gloria Naylor, Amiri Baraka, Gayle Pemberton, Ishmael Reed, and Frederick Ivor Case have in their different ways explored the diaspora's ordeal in and contribution to Babylon. They have all, of course, done much more than merely that, creating from that experience and their lives mirrors that reveal ourselves. I thank them for contributing to *American Visions*' first book. Most important, I thank Mike, Nancy, Tim, Andrew, Marie, and Joanna—my brother, sister-in-law, nephews, and nieces, respectively—in whose home I lived during the book project. Living with them, like researching and writing this book, has been an arduous pleasure.

Captain Mac Ross, Tuskegee airman, was killed in combat in the skies over Italy in 1944.
Courtesy USAF Museum

INTRODUCTION

Although she feeds me bread of bitterness,
And sinks into my throat her tiger's tooth . . .
I love this cultured hell that tests my youth!
Her vigor flows like tides into my blood,
Giving me strength against her hate.
Her bigness sweeps my being like a flood.

Three centuries before the African-American poet and novelist Claude McKay penned the above poem, "America," John Rolfe's Jamestown journal of August 20, 1619, recorded that "there came in a Dutch man-of-warre that sold us 20 negars." Traditionally, the Jamestown episode is considered the opening chapter both of slavery in the United States and of the African-American story.

On both counts, tradition deceives. Rather than enslaved, the Africans who arrived at Jamestown were compelled into a period of indentured servitude—after which they became land-owning members of the community. Nor were they North America's first black arrivals. Fifteen years before Rolfe's Jamestown entry, the mulatto Mathieu da Costa served as an interpreter of the Mic Mac Indian tongue during Samuel de Champlain's exploration of Canada. And almost a century before Rolfe's entry, Estevanico, a Moor, arrived in Florida as part of Narváez's expedition. Following the expedition's collapse and his capture and years of enslavement by Indians, Estevanico would embark on one of the great sagas of escape, endurance, and adventure, walking across the uncharted territory from the mouth of the Mississippi to Culiacán on Mexico's Pacific coast. Soon thereafter Estevanico would *precede* Coronado as an explorer of our Southwest, dying in 1539 at the hands of the Háwikuh Zuni, just south of modern-day Gallup, New Mexico. Between Estevanico and McKay—and beyond—African-American blood would flow like tides into this land, adding vigor and sweep to North America's epic tale—and leaving enough evidence for the modern traveler to trace its impact.

With this book, *American Visions* welcomes you on a journey into largely unexplored territory, into a past that is at once black and American, unknown and important, pleasurable and enlightening; a journey on which it is as joyful to travel as to arrive. The only preparation for the exploration is to open your eyes—and mind. The true portrait of North America—particularly the United States—cannot be painted without the color black and without African Americans in the foreground as protagonists. This is not an Afrocentric claim; it's descriptive truth. The ethnic history of the founding of the United States and Canada is aboriginal Indian, English, Welsh, Scottish, and African, mixed with dollops of French, Dutch, Spanish, and German. (More than three centuries after Estevanico's death, fewer than 5,000 Italian immigrants had stepped ashore in America. Far fewer Greeks, Poles, or Chinese had arrived. Yet for the preceding century and a half, about one in six of every being walking the land of the United States was black; and as the Confederate force under P.G.T. Beauregard opened fire on Fort Sumter, heralding a civil war that would slay hundreds of thousands and partially scour slavery's stain from the nation, fully 90 percent of America's black folk had been born here.) Phillis Wheatley, Prince Hall, Benjamin Banneker, Richard Allen, Horace King, Martin Delany, Frederick Douglass, Harriet Tubman, Booker T. Washington, W.E.B. Du Bois, Colonel Charles Young, A. Philip Randolph, and Zora Neale Hurston are *representative* of America—except insofar as they achieved greatness in the face not merely of the odds but of white supremacy, contempt, and violence.

Fortunately, travelers who wish to walk in the footsteps of the African-American founders and builders of this nation can still *see* this truth about our past—as will be evident in this book. They can also see an 1870 former-slave wedding; the men and women who toiled for Nathaniel Burwell—son-in-law of Robert "King" Carter, the largest slaveholder in colonial Virginia; the Canadian cabin that housed in freedom Josiah Henson, a model for Harriet Beecher Stowe's Uncle Tom; the wharf site where Harriet Tubman landed during her expedition to free her sister, who was being sold at a nearby slave auction; the home of Colonel Charles Young, America's first black military attaché and a victim of President Woodrow Wilson's virulent racism; and the home of Monroe Trotter, an ardent black activist who challenged President Wilson to his face, leading Wilson to remark that Trotter was the only American citizen to have come to the White House and addressed the President in such a tone.

In Their Footsteps takes travelers to these and almost 1,000 other black heritage sites in the United States and Canada. Battlefields crucial to African-American freedom—and to that of the nation—monuments to black achievement, museums chock full of African and African-American art and artifacts, clubs where the blues and jazz gave birth to America's most original contributions to the arts, homes of illustrious men and women who championed the struggle for black advancement, historic churches that housed congregations of believers (in God and in the struggle for equal rights), cemeteries where a people's heroes lie, forts that headquartered black men in blue, cultural centers that exist to tell our tales, and parks and streetcorners where black men and women stood up, spoke out, were beaten down, and bore witness to the truth that they were subjects rather than objects of history will all be found inside these pages. Also found within are remnants of everyday living, the surest signs that African Americans were common to the making of this land. Black cattle punchers, homesteaders, sailors, whaling men, doctors, coal miners, prospectors, tinkerers, and inventors left their mark on America—as they do in these pages.

Although there are many more African-American heritage sites listed in *In Their Footsteps* than in any other source, and although the historical interpretation that fleshes out the sites is a great deal deeper than will be found in other guidebooks, this work is far from exhaustive. The constraint of space required excluding many sites and curtailing the description of all the entries. Thus readers will find few entries locating in America's cities the many statues of Martin Luther King, Jr. (They will, however, find the addresses and telephone numbers of tourist commissions and the titles of the local pamphlets that identify the locations of additional black heritage sites.) Though Dr. King is certainly present in these pages, our intention at *American Visions* has been to highlight the many African-American contributions that have been slighted, to help rescue from relative oblivion the work of Isaac Myers, Garrett Morgan, Dr. Charles Drew; the determination of Lewis Hayden, William Still, Mary Ann Shadd; and the sacrifice of the black crewmen of Perry's fleet, the Revolutionary War African-American patriots who sloped muskets next to Thomas Paine during the depressing and disastrous winter retreat across New Jersey into Pennsylvania—a crisis that led Paine to pen "these are the times that try men's souls"—and that of the U.S. Army's Seminole-Negro Scouts, who tracked a band of Mescalero Apache for 34 days across 1,260 miles of wasteland and won in return for their service a segregated graveyard.

At least till the mid-20th century, both the United States and Canada were composed of regions in more than simply a geographical sense—as anyone who was born in Georgia, as I was, and sat on porch swings sipping iced tea and listening to grandparents, aunts, and uncles, as I did, can attest. Certainly the black experience in the United States had distinctly regional flavors, primarily, of course, because slavery, Jim Crow, and segregation, while common throughout America, were absolutely central to and longer lived in the South. Though the African-American story has a common theme, it comes with regional accents, and we've organized *In Their Footsteps* to reflect this truth. The book divides the United States into four regions—the South, the North, the Midwest, and the West—and, to make its use by travelers easier, organizes the states alphabetically within each region. Each part of the country is introduced by a prominent African-American writer whose connection to the region is long standing and whose work in some measure reflects that connection. Canada, which from the perspective of black history is broadly reducible to Nova Scotia and Ontario, we have treated as a whole—quite possibly to the reasonable displeasure of Canadians. Finally, in addition to identifying, locating, and describing the sites themselves, *In Their Footsteps* incorporates information critical to travelers (particularly those who may have children in tow). Days and hours of opening, admission fees, general directions for those sites located in out-of-the-way places, and telephone numbers are provided. The last is perhaps the most crucial: It is always wise to call ahead to confirm times, prices, and exhibits on view.

In the 1970s and '80s I spent more than a decade living in Africa, primarily working as a journalist. It was an arduous and rewarding time, and in that sense only mirrors my experience researching and writing *In Their Footsteps*. It's been a joy to get reacquainted with old heroes of mine (Randolph, Rustin, Du Bois, Johnson, Beckwourth, Banneker) and to find new ones (particularly the 18th-century divines Richard Allen, Absalom Jones, George Liele, but also Still, Myers, and Colonel Young). Certainly it's been a pleasure to work with the essayists who grace *In Their Footsteps* and introduce the regions of North America. I first read Baraka's *It's Nation Time* and *The Dutchman* in my 20s; the same period in which I followed the clash between the Loop Garoo Kid and Drag Gibson in Reed's *Yellow Back Radio Broke-Down*. I first came across Naylor's *Linden Hills* and the mortician/landlord Luther Nedeed more than a decade later, in a crumbling paramedical hut on the edge of the civil war combat zone in southern Sudan. Pemberton's *The Hottest Water in Chicago*, an account of (among other things) the intersection of family, the Midwest, and race, was a discovery on my return to the States. In none of the instances did it occur to me that I would ever be other than a distant admirer of these authors' creative power. Only through working on this book have I gained a knowledge of Afro-Canadian heritage—and of Fred Case; both more than repay the labor *Footsteps* has entailed. Finally, having spent more than a decade covering Africa's wars, famines, and hall-of-fame corruption—a true bacchanalia of folly and depravity—it's a pleasure to turn my focus toward a people's transformation and triumphs. And it is these that *In Their Footsteps* celebrates.

Our black past is not only the story of America, it's an American story. Though the transformation and the rise of the diaspora in North America are uniquely African American, in broad outline they are also typically American. (Paradoxically, this appreciation is grasped more readily by those outside the culture, by Africans—frequently to the consternation of those who think a journey to Africa is the journey home. In a country that embodies change, all elements of the ethnic mélange—but particularly African Americans—are unfinished peoples, busy writing the next chapter of their collective story. What the next African-American chapter will be is seen only through a glass darkly, but the black past shines forth brilliantly. Tracing this past is of value not simply because it gives us pride, but because it gives us true perspective—and joy.

Now more than four centuries old, the African-American epic will endure. Word. ("But be ye doers of the word, and not hearers only, deceiving your own selves.") *American Visions* invites you on a journey of joyful discovery.

SURVEY OF AFRICAN-AMERICAN HISTORY

Though no brief summary of the black experience in North America could possibly contain the full range of the diaspora's contributions here, the following survey at least illustrates that African Americans have marched to the farthest boundaries of the American epic. With rare exceptions, this survey is keyed to individuals whose contributions to America and Canada have been *visibly* commemorated, and enables visitors to black heritage sites to place what they are observing within a larger historical framework. It bears repeating, however: The time line is merely illustrative. Far from being a comprehensive overview of black history, it does not even include all the individuals and events that *In Their Footsteps* records.

1539 Estevanico, a Moor, guides Friar Marcos from Mexico City through Arizona into New Mexico, becoming the first known explorer of the American Southwest.

1604 Mathieu da Costa serves as an interpreter of the Mic Mac Indian tongue for Champlain's exploration of Canada and the Great Lakes.

1619 John Rolfe's Jamestown journal records that on August 20 "there came in a Dutch man-of-warre that sold us 20 negars." The 20, who labored as indentured servants, were the first known black settlers in the English colonies of North America.

1642 Mathias de Sousa becomes first black member of a colonial legislature.

1739 Cato leads the Stono River slave revolt in South Carolina, one of three slave outbreaks in the state this year.

1745 Jean Baptist DuSable, the black explorer and founder of the settlement that becomes Chicago, is born in Haiti.

1753 Phillis Wheatley, the most significant 18th-century African-American poet, is born in Africa.

1770 Crispus Attucks is killed in the Boston Massacre.

1775– The American Revolution sees widespread black participation in both the colonial and British ranks.

1787 Prince Hall and Boston's black community petition for financial aid for an African colonization scheme and for access to the public school system for black children.

1791 Benjamin Banneker's first almanac is published, and he is appointed to assist in surveying the nation's new capital of Washington, D.C.

1793 In Philadelphia, Richard Allen and Absalom Jones organize the Mother Bethel African Methodist Episcopal Church.

1800 Gabriel Prosser plans one of the three great 19th-century slave revolts and is executed upon the plan's betrayal.

Led by Absalom Jones, one of the greatest 18th-century African-American divines, the black community of Philadelphia petitions the U.S. Congress for the gradual abolition of slavery. By a 85-to-1 vote, Congress decides that such petitions should receive "no encouragement or countenance."

1804– The Lewis and Clark expedition, accompanied by Clark's slave, York, explores America's Northwest, reaching the Pacific Ocean.

1808 In New York, the Reverend Thomas Paul organizes a congregation that evolves to become Abyssinian Baptist Church.

1809 Joseph Jenkins Roberts, the future first president of Liberia, is born to free black parents in Virginia.

1813 Oliver Hazard Perry wins fame with his Lake Erie naval victory. One in four of his fleet's crew is black.

1815 At the Battle of New Orleans, General Andrew Jackson secures America's one major victory on land during the War of 1812. His force is substantially augmented by black troops, whose courage he praises after the battle.

1816 The National African Methodist Episcopal Church is organized.

1822 Denmark Vesey's slave conspiracy is exposed. He and 34 comrades mount the gallows.

1827 John Russwurm and Samuel Cornish edit *Freedom's Journal*, the first black newspaper in the United States.

1830 The first free black national convention is held in Philadelphia and rejects African emigration in favor of the abolition of slavery and equal rights in the United States.

1831 Nat Turner's Rebellion explodes in Southampton County, Virginia.

William Lloyd Garrison's abolitionist journal, *Liberator*, is first published.

1833 The American Anti-Slavery Society is formed; Samuel Cornish is one of three African Americans on its executive committee.

Oberlin College, the principal antebellum institution of higher education for African Americans, is founded.

The white abolitionist newspaper publisher Elijah Lovejoy is martyred by a mob.

1838 Frederick Douglass, the most prominent black abolitionist of the 19th century, escapes from slavery.

1839 The Liberty Party, the first American political party to open up leadership positions to African Americans, is founded, receiving support from black abolitionists Henry Highland Garnet and Samuel Ringgold Ward.

A group of abducted Mende tribesmen, led by their headman, Cinque, seize *La Amistad,* the slave ship carrying them into bondage, slay their captors, and sail into the deep waters of the U.S. Supreme Court.

Robert Smalls, who will become the only African-American U.S. Navy captain during the Civil War and subsequently a five-term U.S. congressman from South Carolina, is born in slavery.

1840 The escaped slave Josiah Henson, who will serve as a model for Uncle Tom in Harriet Beecher Stowe's novel, founds the British-American Institute in Canada as the nucleus of a black community.

1843 Isabella, a former slave in New York, assumes the name Sojourner Truth and begins her career as a peripatetic advocate of abolitionism and feminism.

Martin Delany publishes his Pittsburgh newspaper, *The Mystery*.

1844 Elijah McCoy, African-American inventor and the source for the expression "the real McCoy," is born in Canada.

1847 Frederick Douglass and Martin Delany publish the abolitionist newspaper, *North Star*.

1848 Lewis Temple invents the toggle harpoon, one of the key instruments of the whaling industry.

1849 Harriet Tubman, who will gain fame for her forays into slave territory to rescue her brethren, escapes from slavery.

1850 Congress passes the Fugitive Slave Law and the Missouri Compromise.

1851 James Beckwourth, the noted black explorer of the far West, discovers a pass through the Sierra Nevadas into California.

1852 Harriet Beecher Stowe's *Uncle Tom's Cabin* is published and sells 300,000 copies in its first year of print.

Sojourner Truth's "Ain't I a woman" address arouses the National Women's Suffrage Convention and quiets male hecklers.

1854 The Kansas-Nebraska Act supercedes the Missouri Compromise on the issue of permitting slavery in U.S. territories.

Lewis Hayden and the Boston Vigilance Committee are unsuccessful in their attempt to rescue Anthony Burns, a fugitive slave being returned to Virginia.

1855 J. M. Langston becomes the first elected black official in the United States.

The first statewide convention of California's African Americans meets.

1856 T. T. Fortune, the late 19th century's most influential African-American publisher, is born in slavery.

Wilberforce University in Ohio and Berea College in Kentucky are founded to provide higher education to African Americans.

1857 The Supreme Court's Dred Scott ruling declares that the U.S. Congress cannot exclude slavery from American territories seeking admission to the Union.

1858 Probable year Booker T. Washington is born in slavery.

1859 John Brown leads the raid on the government arsenal at Harpers Ferry in an attempt to spark a slave uprising. Five African Americans ride with Brown.
The *Clotilde*, the last known illegal slave ship to land a cargo in the United States, is chased into Mobile Bay by a U.S. patrol boat.

1861 The Civil War begins. African Americans seeking to join the army are rejected, though the U.S. Navy enlists them under discriminatory terms of service.
W. C. Nell, pioneering 19th-century black historian, becomes the first African American to hold a civilian U.S. government job.

1862 Following the Battle of Antietam, Lincoln announces Emancipation Proclamation.

1863 First regiments of the United States Colored Troops are inducted into service. In combat at Port Hudson, Louisiana, and Battery Wagner in Charleston, South Carolina, black soldiers convincingly demonstrate their merit, encouraging wider recruitment of African Americans.

1864 At Fort Pillow, Tennessee, Confederate troops commanded by Nathan Bedford Forrest massacre captured and wounded black troops in the best-documented but far from unique racial atrocity of the war.
Probable year George Washington Carver is born in slavery.

1865 The 13th Amendment, abolishing slavery, is adopted.
The Freedmen's Bureau is formed and Reconstruction begins in the South.

1866 Isaac Myers forms the black National Labor Union.
Six black army regiments are formed, two of cavalry and four of infantry. This marks the inception of troops that will gain fame as the "buffalo soldiers."

1868 W.E.B. Du Bois, the outstanding African-American intellectual of the first century of Emancipation, is born in Great Barrington, Massachusetts.

1870 Hiram Revels, appointed to fill the unexpired term of Jefferson Davis, becomes the first African American to serve in the U.S. Senate.

1871 James Weldon Johnson, poet, novelist, diplomat, and executive secretary of the NAACP, is born in Florida.

1872 Paul Laurence Dunbar, the first African-American poet to gain national recognition, is born in Ohio.

1873 W. C. Handy, the "Father of the Blues," is born in Alabama.

1874 Blanche K. Bruce becomes the first African American elected to serve a regular term in the U.S. Senate.

1875 James Augustine Healy is ordained the first Catholic bishop of African descent.

1877 Traditional year assigned to the collapse of Reconstruction, which had been faltering almost from its inception under the twin pressures of white violence in the South and extremely limited white support in the North.
Black "Exoduster" movement brings large numbers of African Americans to the Midwest and gives birth to Nicodemus, Kansas, and other all-black communities.
Henry O. Flipper becomes the first African-American graduate of West Point.

1881 Booker T. Washington assumes leadership of Tuskegee Institute.

1886 Augustine Tolton is ordained the first Catholic priest of full African descent.

1890 Claude McKay, leading light of the Harlem Renaissance, is born in Jamaica.
George Dixon becomes first official black boxing champion.

1893 Dr. D. H. Williams performs the first successful open-heart surgery.

1894 Blues great Bessie Smith is born in Tennessee.

1896 The Supreme Court's *Plessy v. Ferguson* ruling accepts as constitutionally defensible the "separate but equal" doctrine, codifying and protecting segregation.

1897 Scott Joplin, the "Father of Ragtime," publishes his first rag.

1898 Paul Robeson, black activist, actor, and singer, is born.

1900 W.E.B. Du Bois attends the first Pan-African Congress in London and is elected vice president.
Louis Armstrong is born.

1905 Led by W.E.B. Du Bois and Monroe Trotter, the militant Niagara Movement is formed to promote full African-American equality.
The first issue of *The Chicago Defender* is published.

1908 Richard Wright, arguably the most significant African-American novelist of the 20th century, is born the son of Mississippi sharecroppers.

1909 The NAACP is formed and W.E.B. Du Bois serves as its only African-American senior official.
Matthew Henson and Robert Peary reach the North Pole.

1915 Booker T. Washington dies.

1916 Carter G. Woodson founds the Association for the Study of Negro Life and History and edits its publication, the *Journal of Negro History*.

1917 Lieutenant Colonel Charles Young, America's senior African-American officer, a combat veteran, and a West Point graduate, is forced from the active-duty roster, nominally on grounds of health, as America enters World War I.
In Houston, Texas, men of the all-black 24th Infantry Regiment, aroused by a policeman's mistreatment of one of their unit, assault and kill more than a dozen civilians. Ensuing trials yield 19 death sentences and the U.S. Army curtails its planned World War I expansion of black military service.

Marcus Garvey arrives in New York and founds the Universal Negro Improvement Association's journal, *Negro World*.

1918 Two black combat divisions see service in World War I.

1919 From Chicago, Illinois, through Washington, D.C., to Elaine, Arkansas, white America goes on one of its periodic rampages against African Americans, producing the worst upsurge of racial assaults in the 20th century.

1921 The black neighborhood of Tulsa, Oklahoma, is leveled in a race riot.

1923 Marcus Garvey, for some time a target of FBI surveillance, is convicted of mail fraud and sentenced to five years in jail.

1924 Garrett Morgan invents the tricolor traffic light, making motorists everywhere see red.

1925 Malcolm X is born.

1926 Carter G. Woodson introduces Negro History Week.

1927 Marcus Garvey is released from prison and deported to Jamaica.

1929 Martin Luther King, Jr., is born.

1930 W. D. Fard, founder of the Nation of Islam, begins preaching his message on Detroit's streets.

1931 The "Scottsboro Boys"—nine young African-American men arrested on rape charges after sharing a railroad freight-car compartment with two white women—are tried, found guilty on extraordinarily dubious evidence, and sentenced to death.

1934 Elijah Muhammad assumes leadership of the Nation of Islam after the disappearance of W. D. Fard and moves the group's headquarters to Chicago.

1935 Mary McLeod Bethune forms the National Council of Negro Women.

1936 Jesse Owens wins four gold medals at the Berlin Olympics in Nazi Germany.

1937 Joe Lewis wins the world heavyweight boxing championship.

1940 Benjamin O. Davis becomes the first African-American general in the U.S. Army.

Dr. Charles Drew directs wartime Britain's blood plasma bank.

1941 A. Philip Randolph organizes a march on Washington, D.C., in response to the refusal of America's burgeoning defense industries to employ African Americans in any roles other than janitorial. The march is canceled when President Roosevelt issues an executive order to fulfill Randolph's demand and creates the Fair Employment Practices Commission to implement the order.

1942 The "Tuskegee Experiment" trains African-American pilots for World War II combat.

John H. Johnson starts *Negro Digest*, the foundation of a publishing empire that later includes *Ebony* and *Jet*.

1943 Black fighter pilots from the "Tuskegee Experiment" enter combat in Europe.

1945 Adam Clayton Powell, Jr., enters the U.S. Congress.

1947 Jackie Robinson breaks professional baseball's color barrier.

1948 Segregation in the U.S. armed services is barred by presidential order. The last segregated unit, the 24th Infantry Regiment, is disbanded in 1951.

1954 The U.S. Supreme Court's ruling in *Brown v. Board of Education of Topeka* unanimously declares school desegregation unconstitutional.
Benjamin O. Davis, Jr., becomes the first black general in the U.S. Air Force.

1955 In Montgomery, Alabama, Rosa Parks is arrested for refusing to surrender her seat at the front of a city bus to a white man who wanted it. Her arrest sparks the historic Montgomery Bus Boycott and brings Martin Luther King, Jr., his first prominence as a civil rights activist.
Roy Wilkins assumes the leadership of the NAACP.

1957 President Eisenhower sends paratroopers from the 101st Division to enforce school desegregation in Little Rock, Arkansas.
The Southern Christian Leadership Conference is founded and Dr. King emerges as its principal exponent.

1960 A lunch counter sit-in organized at a Greensboro, North Carolina, Woolworth store gains national recognition and signals the shift in the civil rights movement from a courtroom strategy to one of direct action.
SNCC, the Student Nonviolent Coordinating Committee, is founded.

1963 W.E.B. Du Bois dies in exile in Ghana.
A. Philip Randolph promotes the historic March on Washington, the highlight of which is Dr. King's impassioned "I have a dream" address.
In Birmingham, the 16th Street Baptist Church is bombed; killed are four young African-American girls.

1964 Three young civil rights activists, two white and one black, are murdered in Mississippi in a case that briefly seizes the nation's attention.
Malcolm X announces his separation from the Nation of Islam.
Dr. King receives the Nobel Peace Prize.
Cassius Clay wins the world heavyweight boxing championship, promptly announces his adherence to Elijah Muhammad's Nation of Islam, and takes the name Muhammad Ali as a sign of his faith and allegiance.

1965 The Selma-to-Montgomery Voting Rights March meets first with violence, most notably during the notorious confrontation on the Edmund Pettus Bridge in Selma, Alabama, and then with success, as Congress passes the 1965 Voting Rights Act, the 20th century's most significant civil rights legislation.
Malcolm X is assassinated.

1966 Huey P. Newton and Bobby Seale form the Black Panther Party.
Bill Russell is appointed the coach of the Boston Celtics, becoming the first African American to manage a major professional sports team.

1967 Edward Brooke of Massachusetts becomes the first African-American U.S. senator since the collapse of Reconstruction.

Thurgood Marshall becomes the first black Justice of the U.S. Supreme Court.

Muhammad Ali is stripped of his boxing title and receives a five-year prison sentence for refusing to serve in the U.S. Army.

Congressman Adam Clayton Powell, Jr., is barred from the U.S. House of Representatives by his colleagues because of his alleged improprieties.

1968 Martin Luther King, Jr., is assassinated in Memphis, Tennessee.

1969 Dr. Clifton R. Wharton, Jr., is elected president of Michigan State University, becoming the first African American to direct a major public (and predominantly white) university.

1971 The Congressional Black Caucus is formally established.

1975 General Daniel "Chappie" James becomes the first black four-star general.

1977 After tracing her descent from the Revolutionary War soldier William Hood, Karen Farmer becomes the first black member of the Daughters of the American Revolution.

1983 Jesse Jackson becomes the first African American to seek the presidential nomination of a major political party.

1986 First national holiday honoring Dr. Martin Luther King, Jr.

1989 Ron Brown becomes the first African American selected to chair a major political party.

1989 General Colin Powell becomes the first black Chairman of the Joint Chiefs of Staff of the U.S. Armed Forces.

1993 Carol Moseley Braun takes a seat in the U.S. Senate, becoming the first black woman ever to do so.

THE SOUTH

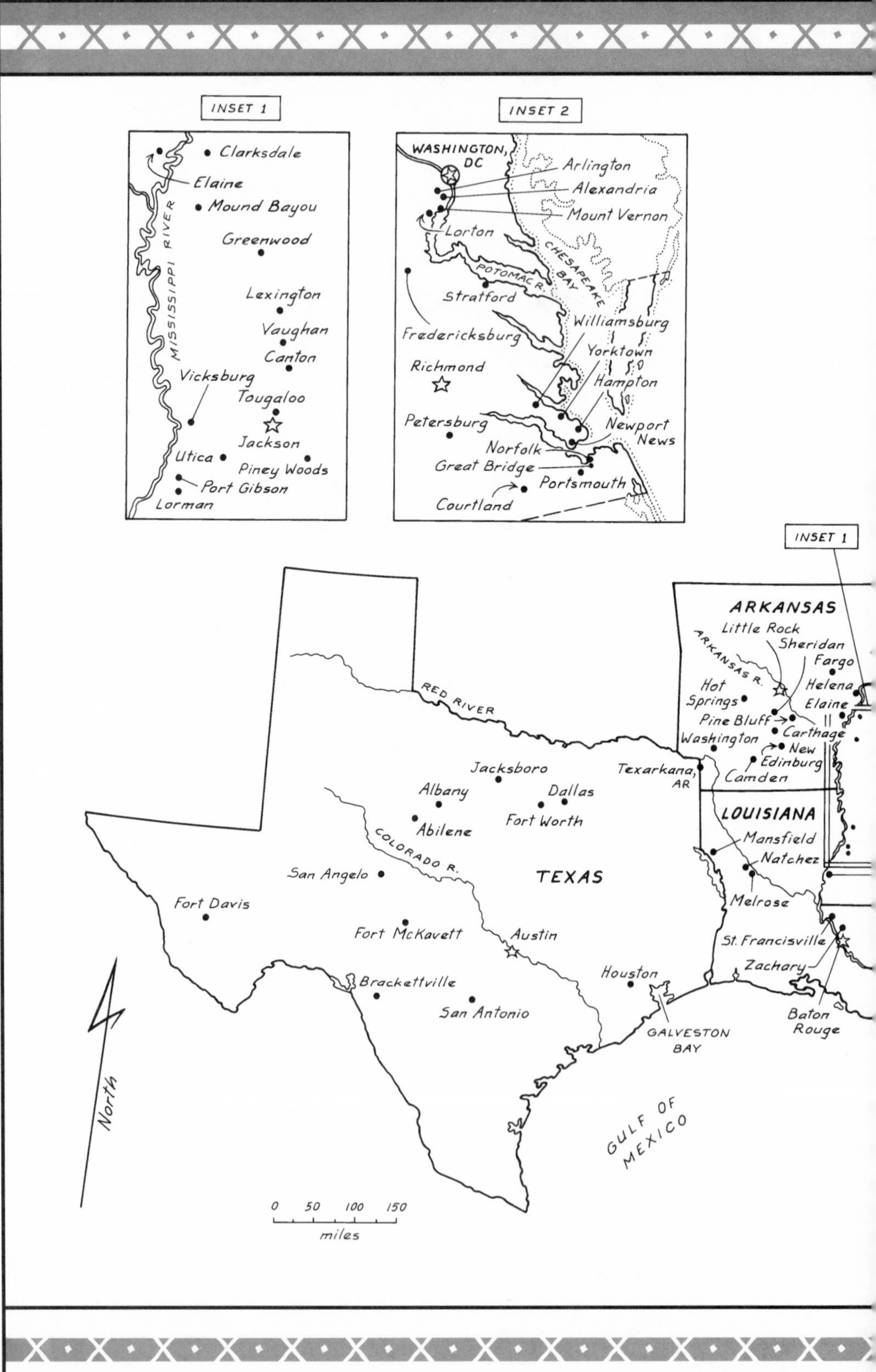
INSET 1
Clarksdale
Elaine
Mound Bayou
MISSISSIPPI RIVER
Greenwood
Lexington
Vaughan
Canton
Vicksburg
Tougaloo
Jackson
Utica
Piney Woods
Port Gibson
Lorman
INSET 2
WASHINGTON, DC
Arlington
Alexandria
Mount Vernon
Lorton
CHESAPEAKE BAY
POTOMAC R.
Stratford
Fredericksburg
Williamsburg
Yorktown
Richmond
Hampton
Petersburg
Newport News
Norfolk
Great Bridge
Portsmouth
Courtland
INSET 1
ARKANSAS
Little Rock
Sheridan
ARKANSAS R.
Fargo
Helena
Hot Springs
Elaine
Pine Bluff
Carthage
Washington
New Edinburg
Camden
Texarkana, AR
RED RIVER
Jacksboro
Albany
Dallas
Abilene
Fort Worth
LOUISIANA
Mansfield
Natchez
COLORADO R.
San Angelo
TEXAS
Melrose
Fort Davis
Fort McKavett
Austin
St. Francisville
Zachary
Houston
Brackettville
San Antonio
Baton Rouge
GALVESTON BAY
North
GULF OF MEXICO
0 50 100 150
miles

BLUE RIDGE MOUNTAINS
Charles Town
Harpers Ferry
INSET 2
Institute
Lewisburg
Kimball
Blue-field
WEST VIRGINIA
Frankfort
Washington
Simpsonville
Ceredo
OHIO RIVER
Charleston
Malden
Clifftop
Louisville
Paris
Lexington
Richmond
Talcott
Owensboro
CHESAPEAKE BAY
Charlottesville
Appomattox
Lynchburg
Halifax
Hardy
KENTUCKY
Berea
Hazard
Roanoke
VIRGINIA
Creswell
Hickman, KY
Mammouth Cave
Rocky Mount
Milton
Manteo, Roanoke Island
Hodgenville
Guilford
Durham
Raleigh
Greensboro
Sedalia
Dover
Greenville
Winston-Salem
Jamestown
MISSISSIPPI RIVER
Knoxville
Henning
Nashville
N. CAROLINA
PAMLICO SOUND
Memphis
TENNESSEE
Salisbury
TENNESSEE R.
Asheville
Charlotte
Fayetteville
Jackson
Florence
Chattanooga
Corinth
Decatur
Greenville
S. CAROLINA
Oxford
Holly Springs
Normal
Leesburg, AL
Atlantic Beach
Columbia
Mayesville
Oakville
Atlanta
Beech Island
Georgetown
Tupelo
Tuscumbia
Orangeburg
Birmingham
Eatonton
Okolona
Carrollton
Augusta
Denmark
Charleston
Rantowles
Talladega
Phenix City, AL
Philadelphia
Macon
Sheldon
St. Helena Island
Tuscaloosa
Columbus
Selma
Alberta
Beaufort
Andersonville
Montgomery
Savannah
Meridian
Tuskegee
GEORGIA
Carlton
Darien
Natchez
ALABAMA
Albany
MISSISSIPPI
Mobile
Jacksonville
Plateau
Lake City
New Orleans
Bay St. Louis
Marianna
St. Augustine
Olustee
MOBILE BAY
Pensacola
Gainesville
Daytona Beach
ATLANTIC OCEAN
Tallahassee
Eatonville
Dauphin Island
Sumatra
Bushnell
Orlando
FLORIDA
Fort Pierce
Tampa
LAKE OKEECHOBEE
Fort Lauderdale
Miami
Marathon
FLORIDA KEYS

OF FATHERS AND SONGS: A DAUGHTER REMEMBERS

GLORIA NAYLOR

My parents were married in 1949 on the front porch of my mother's house in Robinsonville, Mississippi. My father wanted to stay in Mississippi and he wanted my mother to give him sons. When the newlyweds boarded the train in Memphis for New York City six months later, my mother had already conceived the first of the three daughters to be born into this marriage.

I've always known that to trace my connections back to the South through my father would mean going *between* the lines of these three sentences into deceptively small spaces. Spaces that contain a lifetime of silences, on his part, about what he left behind. His ambivalence, the dreams denied. Perhaps he had dreamed of a South that exists today: a region where his sons would be more likely to hold public office and wield true power than in New York, where he ended up spending the next 43 years of his life. And then again, they could have been more modest dreams: his own plot of land instead of sharecropping someone else's? his own tractors and barns? Because who would have dreamed that Mississippi, of all places, the Mississippi that Nina Simone asked God to damn and that many felt had damned itself with the blood splattered on the backroads of Meridian and the campus of Jackson State, would be the toothless tiger that it is today?

I can only imagine what my father's dreams were, because it was my mother's dreams—of the horizon beyond those endless rows of cotton holding a better world for her children—that were given voice throughout my childhood. We heard her story so often it became the stuff of family legend: the young girl who went to the limits of hiring herself out in someone else's fields to get the pocket money she needed to send away to book clubs to obtain her reading material because she was denied access to the public libraries; the young bride who was so adamantly against raising a child in Mississippi that she told her waffling young husband, "They'll sell me a ticket for that train with or without you, and this baby I'm carrying rides free." With its inherent pathos and humor, it's the type of "life material" that almost writes itself. And how easy it's been for me over the years to write about it, write from it, shape it into a metaphor for my own personal history. Mother to daughter. Woman to woman. Dreamer to dreamer.

But my father did not have such drama in his "life material." And for me to have captured the boy that he was, the man that he turned out to be—all shaped in those same cotton fields—would have been to have to journey into his silence, to poke and prod; and perhaps, to be afraid of the answers. And I've felt, why bother? But then I reflect on the South, knowing that there is no one South, not even for my parents who grew up side by side, worked side by side, in just one tiny corner of one state. The South is to itself what the 50 states are to America: sprawling, diverse in its landscapes, idiosyncratic in its people, divided in its politics. (Southerners know—and rightfully resent—that America has been self-serving in using their region as a national metaphor for racial injustice. He who is without sin, cast the first stone.)

Just as there is no one South, there is no one side to any story, including my own. And the debt I owe, if for nothing but my base existence, is double fold. And with all that I do not know, all that he has not said, I do know that I have never thanked my father for getting on that train. I have not given credence to his fears or his courage in overcoming them. My life would have been vastly different if he had not, since I was the unborn child that my mother was carrying. And if, indeed, I can only imagine what my father's dreams were, then my imagination should be good enough. I have built quite a career on that alone. And if I am to break my own silence to him, I imagine myself sitting down at my scarred roll-top desk in the quiet of early morning when I think the best and composing a letter to my father that might begin:

> I'm sorry that I was not the firstborn son that you wanted, but I am writing to thank you for your determination to make me into the proud and strong woman that I am. I am writing to acknowledge the pain in your eyes at the growing revelation that New York *was* Mississippi when a black man went looking for respect. I am writing you a song of the longing for respect. I am writing you a song of the longing for the feel of rich earth under your hands, of the sweet pull of muscles lifting, of backs stretching, of sweat bathing sun-toughened skin—of redemption through work well done. Of mellow nights thick with the salt of fried catfish, the strum of a blues guitar, the slow thighs of fast women. Of the freedom in dense green woods, the first taste of dewberries, the rush of muddy waters by the levee. Of youth lost. Of morning breaking. Daddy, as a small token of my appreciation, I am writing you home.

Editor's note: Ms. Naylor's father passed on September 17, 1993, several weeks after this essay was written.

X·X·X

Although GLORIA NAYLOR was born and raised in New York, she was conceived in Robinsonville, Mississippi, and says because of this the South has become "a kind of spiritual place for me." Later in life, this recipient of the American Book Award for First Fiction in 1983 for *The Women of Brewster Place* traveled throughout the South for seven years. Naylor, also the author of *Linden Hills*, *Mama Day*, and, most recently, *Bailey's Cafe*, makes frequent references to this region in her literature. She is a graduate of Brooklyn College and Yale University, where she received a master's degree in Afro-American studies.

ALABAMA

Bureau of Tourism and Travel
401 Adams Avenue, Suite 126, P.O. Box 4309, Montgomery, AL 36103-4309
(800) ALABAMA
Hours: Mon.–Fri., 8 A.M.–5 P.M.

Ask for the "Alabama's Black Heritage" pamphlet to discover more than 130 Alabama sites connected with the African-American past.

ALBERTA

Freedom Quilting Bee
Route 1, Box 43-A, Alberta, AL 36720
(205) 573-2225
Hours: By appointment only
Admission: Free

Spawned by the fervent civil rights protests of the era, an all-black women's cooperative was formed in 1966 in one of Alabama's poorer counties. Then one of the very few women's cooperatives in the United States, the sisters of the Freedom Quilting Bee have since gained nationwide recognition for the quality of their quilts, which embody designs that come out of a 140-year-old tradition.

BIRMINGHAM

Birmingham Convention and Visitors Bureau
2200 Ninth Avenue North, Birmingham, AL 35203
(800) 962-6453
Hours: Mon.–Fri., 8:30 A.M.–5 P.M.

Ask for the "Birmingham's Black Heritage Tour" pamphlet.

16th Street Baptist Church
Sixth Avenue and 16th Street North, Birmingham, AL 35203
(205) 251-9402
Hours: By appointment only
Admission: Free. Voluntary donations requested

Birmingham's reclaimed past can be found at the 16th Street Baptist Church, which has been at the center of black Birmingham for more than a century.

Organized in 1873 as the First Colored Baptist Church, the congregation moved to its current site at Sixth Avenue and 16th Street North in 1884. The present structure, designed by Alabama's sole African-American architect and constructed under the supervision of a leading black contractor, was raised in 1911 and served as a center of segregated black Birmingham society. W.E.B. Du Bois, Booker T. Washington, and Mary McLeod Bethune all spoke here in the early decades of this century.

COURTESY OF THE ALABAMA BUREAU OF TOURISM AND TRAVEL

The 16th Street Baptist Church: The heart of black Birmingham and the site of the notorious 1963 Ku Klux Klan bombing.

The church's prominence in the community and its central location close by Kelly-Ingram Park—gathering point for the protest marches of the 1960s—naturally led to its seeing service as a local headquarters of the civil rights movement. It was from here that Dr. Martin Luther King, Jr., and the church's Reverend Fred L. Shuttlesworth provided inspirational leadership to a citizenry challenging segregation. It was here too that one of the era's most horrific racial crimes occurred: the September 15, 1963, Ku Klux Klan bombing that claimed the lives of four young black girls who were preparing to serve at the Sunday morning worship. Today a stained glass window dominated by a crucified black Christ looks out over the sanctuary and serves as a memorial to the slain girls. Outside the church, a statue is being raised to commemorate the martyrs of a community that was unyielding in its nonviolent resistance to segregation and in its demands for social justice.

Birmingham Civil Rights Institute
Sixth Avenue and 16th Street North, Birmingham, AL 35203
(205) 328-9696
Hours: Mon.–Sat., 9 A.M.–5 P.M.; Sun., 1 P.M.–5 P.M.
Admission: Free

Visitors to the Civil Rights Institute journey through more than half a century of Alabama's black history. In the Barriers Gallery, the environment of segregation, circa 1920 to 1940, still flourishes. A whites-only snack bar beckons to those who qualify and resonates with the message from Martin Luther King's "Letter from Birmingham Jail": "One day the South will recognize its real heroes. . . . One day the South will know that when these disinherited children of God sat down at lunch counters, they were in reality standing up for what is best in the American dream. . . ."

Here too we see another side of segregation, a black response to the opportunities and challenges of separation. Barred by law and tradition from most white commerce, Birmingham's black businessmen organized their own enterprises along the Fourth Avenue corridor. Hotels, restaurants, nightclubs, and the offices of doctors, dentists, and architects, among others, stood as mute testimony to black achievement.

Also on view here are the fruits of that separation rooted not in segregation but in alternative, though not rival, cultural perspectives. Visitors to the institute listen to the music of the black church and of the popular black entertainers of the 1930s and 1940s. A video jukebox transports patrons back to a time when black achievement was legally circumscribed, a chalk-white line limiting advancement for individuals and a people.

From barriers visitors move to conflict. Entering the Confrontation Gallery one sees the price paid not to achieve the victory of the Supreme Court's decision in *Brown v. Board of Education* but in consequence of it. Not for nothing did King's "Letter from Birmingham Jail" record that "There have been more unsolved bombings of Negro homes and churches in Birmingham than in any other city in the nation. These are the hard, brutal facts of the case."

The African-American response to these hard, brutal facts is presented in the Movement Gallery, which highlights the impact of individual acts of courage and the moral force and social power of a mass protest that sundered the 20th-century bonds of disenfranchisement, broke the back of segregation, and forcibly changed the course of American history. Lunch counter sit-ins, the Freedom Bus Rides, mass demonstrations in Birmingham's streets, the march in Selma, the March on Washington, voter registrations in county after county, the bombing of the 16th Street Baptist Church, madness and martyrdom, a nation in ferment, and a people who said "Enough!" All this and more—most of it shallowly known, if at all, by the youth of this nation—is found in the Civil Rights Institute.

Alabama Penny Savings Bank Building
310 18th Street North, Birmingham, AL 35203
Hours: Daily until sunset
Admission: Not open to the public. Exterior viewing only

Formed in 1890, the Alabama Penny Savings Bank was the largest black bank in the United States. Alabama's first black-owned bank financed the construction of homes and churches for thousands of Birmingham's African Americans, who otherwise would have been unable to secure a mortgage. Today the original bank has long since disappeared, though the building still stands.

Alabama Sports Hall of Fame
2150 Civic Center Boulevard, P.O. Box 10163, Birmingham, AL 35202-0163
(205) 323-6665
Hours: Mon.–Sat., 9 A.M.–5 P.M.; Sun., 1 P.M.–5 P.M.
Admission: Adults, $5; seniors, $4; students, $3

The careers of Alabama's most famous athletes, including Joe Louis, Jesse Owens, Hank Aaron, and Willie Mays, are displayed via films, videos, and memorabilia.

Fourth Avenue Business District
1600–1800 blocks of Fourth Avenue and the 300 blocks of 17th and 18th Streets North, Birmingham, AL 35203
Hours: Daily, 24 hours
Admission: Free

The Fourth Avenue Business District was the center of Birmingham's early 20th century African-American commercial response to segregation. Black doctors, dentists, lawyers, architects, publishers, businessmen, and bankers dwelt within a narrow corridor that mirrored the narrow band of opportunity open to black achievement. Today some of the shells of these achievements still stand along Fourth Avenue, sterile architectural remains of a vibrant and self-confident black community.

Kelly-Ingram Park
Fifth Avenue North at 16th Street, Birmingham, AL 35203
Hours: Daily, 24 hours
Admission: Free

At 16th Street and Fifth Avenue North lies Kelly-Ingram Park, which in the past served as the central assembly point for civil rights demonstrators who were preparing to march to downtown, white Birmingham. On more than one occasion, they were not able even to leave the park, which was the site of the most notorious of Birmingham Public Safety Commissioner Bull Connor's attacks on the marchers with police dogs and firehoses. Today the park has been "planted" with four statues that symbolically recall the African-American struggle against white supremacy and the violence with which it was met: "Firehouse Attacks," "Child Marchers," "Kneeling Ministers," and "Leaping Police Dogs" remind onlookers that segregationist domination did not expire; rather it was defeated by a determined and courageous people.

Tuxedo Junction
1728 20th Street, Birmingham, AL 35203
Hours: Daily until sunset
Admission: Free

Tuxedo Junction, named for the streetcar line crossing the black community of Tuxedo Park, recalls both the second-floor dance hall of the Nixon building—

the centerpoint for the social life of black Birmingham in the 1920s and '30s—and the 1939 hit song of that name written by Birmingham-born trumpeter and composer Erskine Hawkins. Tuxedo Junction should appeal to lovers of big band music, those interested in American cultural history of the Roaring '20s and the depression, and those intrigued by the southern black response to segregation. Unfortunately, however, today there is little to recommend the site even to those already in Birmingham. Now old Tuxedo Park is a less than flourishing, peripheral neighborhood, and the small building that housed the dance hall is a dental clinic, outside of which the intrepid tourist will find his or her trek rewarded by a historical marker.

CARLTON

Effigy Cemetery/Mt. Nebo Baptist Church
Near Hal's Lake off Clark County Road 19, Carlton, AL 36515
Hours: Daily until sunset
Admission: Free

The "Effigy Cemetery" at Mt. Nebo Baptist Church underscores the diaspora's cultural link to Africa, in this case in the form of burial customs. In the late 1800s the local African-American artisan Isaac Nettles cast iron masks of the deceased, which he then placed on their gravestones. The effigy mask motif is common to much of Africa and serves to ease the deceased person's passage to the afterlife by misleading evil spirits into thinking that the mask is the person, who must therefore still be alive. Effigy cemeteries are far from common in the United States, and the one at Mt. Nebo is among the best preserved. Nettles failed to prepare for his own demise, and as a consequence his likeness is not to be found—indeed, he lacks even a gravestone.

CARROLLTON

Pickens County Courthouse
County Courthouse Square, Carrollton, AL 35447
(205) 367-2053
Hours: Mon.–Fri., 8 A.M.–4 P.M.
Admission: Free

Etched into an attic windowpane of the Pickens County Courthouse is a figure of a human face. Legend has it that "The Face in the Window" belonged to Henry Wells, a former slave who was the object of the fury of a white mob, which believed him guilty of having burned down the courthouse two years earlier. As a storm brewed on a sultry afternoon in the spring of 1878, the mob gathered outside the new courthouse, demanding that Wells be brought forth. Just then a violent electrical storm broke out, illuminating the fear-filled face of Wells, who was peering out the window at the approaching mob. Accounts vary as to Wells's ultimate fate. Some say that a lightning bolt struck him dead, others that he died at the hands of the lynch mob or as a result of wounds sustained in an escape attempt. All agree, however, that his fear-distorted face was left behind and to this day remains visible on the attic windowpane.

DAUPHIN ISLAND

Fort Gaines Historic Site
P.O. Box 97, Dauphin Island, AL 36528
(205) 861-6992
Hours: Daily, 9 A.M.–5 P.M.
Admission: Adults, $2; seniors and ages 6–15, $1

In a move the federal government would soon regret, $160,000 was appropriated in 1858 to complete the fortifications at Fort Gaines, which—with Fort Morgan—guarded the entrance to Mobile Bay. In 1864 Mobile remained one of the Confederacy's few secure ports, a situation Union admiral David Farragut was ordered to rectify. In the course of the August naval battle that immortalized Farragut's command "Damn the torpedoes; full speed ahead," John Lawson, who refused medical attention and continued to serve his gun despite his wounds, became the first African-American sailor to win the Medal of Honor. Confederate cannons actually fired in the battle, tunnels and bastions that served the fort's defenders, and special Civil War reenactments can be seen by visitors to the fort.

DECATUR

Morgan County Courthouse
302 Lee Street, Decatur, AL 35601
(205) 351-4600
Hours: Mon.–Fri., 8 A.M.–4 P.M.
Admission: Free

From 1933 through 1937, the Old Decatur Courthouse, which is now the Morgan County Courthouse, was the scene of three of the four trials arising from the historic case of the "Scottsboro Boys," nine African-American males, ages 13 to 21, who were hauled off an Alabama freight train in 1931 and charged with the rape of two white women who were riding in the boxcar with them. Despite the extremely questionable evidence, the first trial, held in Scottsboro, resulted in guilty verdicts and death sentences for eight of the defendants. However, the U.S. Supreme Court overturned the verdicts, ruling that the defendants unconstitutionally had been deprived of adequate legal counsel. In the course of the second trial, the defense argued that the systematic exclusion of blacks from Alabama's jury pools deprived the defendants of constitutionally guaranteed due process. Despite the fact that one of the alleged victims recanted her accusation, the all-white jury again found the accused guilty. However, the presiding judge, J. F. Horton (who in Jim Crow Alabama was, of course, white), overturned the jury's decision and ordered a retrial, ruling that the evidence presented did not support a guilty verdict. Not surprisingly, a subsequent Democratic Party primary election saw Horton defeated. With a new judge and another all-white jury, the third trial again produced guilty verdicts and death sentences. Once again the U.S. Supreme Court intervened, issuing an unprecedented ruling that the systematic exclusion of black citizens from Alabama's jury pools did indeed unconstitutionally deprive the defendants of due process of law. Five of the defendants were brought to a fourth trial and found guilty after blacks had been included formally in the jury pool and then excluded from the trial by peremptory prosecutorial challenge. Guilty verdicts and death sentences were handed down yet again, but—probably because of the widespread publicity concerning the dubious evidence—all the death sentences were commuted. Not until 1950 was the last defendant paroled from prison.

FLORENCE

W. C. Handy Birthplace, Museum and Library

620 West College Street, Florence, AL 35630
(205) 760-6434
Hours: Tue.–Sat., 9 A.M.–12 P.M. and 1 P.M.–4 P.M.
Admission: Adults, $2; under 18, 50 cents

In the last decade of the 19th century, 18-year-old William Christopher Handy, son and grandson of ministers and convert to the "blues," set forth from Florence, Alabama, for fortune—and after serious struggle found both that and fame. An entire era of music spilled forth from W. C. Handy's prolific mind. Beginning with a 1909 campaign song for the notorious Boss Crump of Memphis, which when reworked emerged as the classic "Memphis Blues," moving through the plaintive "Beale Street Blues," the nonpareil "St. Louis Blues," and 150 other tunes, and culminating with his performance at President Eisenhower's inaugural ball, Handy took the despair, hopes, and longings of the common people, elevated them to art, and thus secured them immortality.

The two-room log cabin in which Handy was born, the W. C. Handy Museum (housing the most complete collection of Handy memorabilia, including his famous trumpet, his personal piano, handwritten sheet music, and photographs), a library (which serves as a resource center for black history and culture), and an annual W. C. Handy Music Festival in the first week of August are all to be found in Florence.

St. Paul A.M.E. Church

121 South Cherokee Street, Florence, AL 35630
(205) 760-6434
Hours: Thu.–Fri., 1:30 P.M.–3:30 P.M.
Admission: Free

COURTESY ALABAMA BUREAU OF TOURISM AND TRAVEL

W. C. Handy, "The Father of the Blues," was born in a cabin in Florence, Alabama.

W. C. Handy's father and grandfather both pastored the St. Paul A.M.E. Church and fully intended William Christopher to do the same, but the blues intervened. Still to be seen in the church is an original stained glass window donated by the father of "The Father of the Blues."

LEESBURG

Moses Hampton Memorial Marker
Cedar Hill Church, Embros Island Road, P.O. Box 296, Leesburg, AL 35983
(205) 526-8697
Turn west off of La Rue Finie Street; church is first right, on top of hill
Hours: Memorial marker: Daily until sunset. Tours of church: By appointment made 2 to 3 weeks in advance
Admission: Free

In the 1820s, immigrants from Georgia and the Carolinas settled around Weiss Lake in northwestern Alabama. There, one Sunday morning at outdoor worship services, Moses Hampton stood up from the "colored section" and testified that God had revealed to him that a church should be built atop the cedar-covered hill, where no harm would befall it. Though a slave, Mose, as he was commonly called, was widely respected in the new settlement for his Biblical knowledge, and shortly after his testimony the congregation found themselves busy at a "log rolling." Logs were hand-hued, pegs were whittled, and a church soon stood atop the hill. Cedar Hill Methodist Church was the first church erected in present-day

Cherokee County and attracted more settlers to the area, even though in those days there were only lay preachers here. Among those preaching at Cedar Hill was Moses Hampton, who also later preached at First Methodist of Centre and St. Mary's Methodist in Possum Trot. In 1851, with the proceeds of the earnings made when he hired himself out as a skilled craftsman, Moses Hampton purchased his freedom. Years later, long after the first settlers had been buried on the hill near their church, the congregation moved into new quarters in Leesburg. The new church, though, was first hit by a fire, then struck several times by lightning, before being leveled by a cyclone. Upon reflection, the congregation decided that Hampton's original revelation was still valid, and they moved back to Cedar Hill, where today's visitors will find not only a Methodist church but also a Moses Hampton Memorial Marker honoring a man of vision.

MOBILE

Mobile-Fort Conde Welcome Center
150 South Royal Street, Mobile, AL 36602
(800) 252-3862; (205) 434-7304
Hours: Daily, 8 A.M.–5 P.M.

Ask about Mobile's Black Mardi Gras Celebration. Held annually in February, this tradition began fully a century before its better-known counterpart in New Orleans.

Fine Arts Museum of the South
4850 Museum Drive, Mobile, AL 36689
(203) 343-2667
Hours: Tue.–Sun., 10 A.M.–5 P.M.
Admission: Free

In its 4,000 objects, the Fine Arts Museum of the South encompasses 2,000 years of cultural history. Prominently included in this survey are works of art and craft from Africa. Masks, figures, ritual pieces, and items of everyday use created by the craftsmen of the Yoruba, Dogon, Senufo, and Bambara peoples form the bulk of the museum's African material, which is periodically complemented by the more modern creations of the diaspora that figure in the temporary art exhibitions hosted by the museum.

Magnolia Cemetery
Ann and Virginia streets, Mobile, AL 36603
(205) 434-7307
Hours: Daily until sunset
Admission: Free

When the advanced skirmishers of General Hawkins's all-black First Division tested the Confederate line guarding Mobile's Fort Blakeley in April 1865, they met with unexpected success. Encouraged, the division launched a spontaneous attack against its foes, driving the Confederates from their breastworks just moments before a scheduled general Union assault. Once they commanded the battlefield, Hawkins's soldiers mirrored the notorious behavior of Confederate general Nathan B. Forrest's troops at Fort Pillow (see entry on p. 146), massacring the wounded and surrendered southerners. By the last year of the Civil War, African-American executions of Confederates had become so common that black chaplain Henry M. Turner voiced public criticism of the atrocities. Black and white Union casualties of the battle at Fort Blakeley are buried at Mobile's Magnolia Cemetery.

Slave Market Site Historical Marker
St. Louis and Royal streets, Mobile, AL 36602
(205) 434-7304 (Visitors Bureau)
Hours: Daily until sunset
Admission: Free

The wharfside slave market site at the intersection of St. Louis and Royal streets was but one of Mobile's venues for the public auction of slaves. Today a Slave Market Site Historical Marker recalls the trade in human beings.

MONTGOMERY

Montgomery Convention & Visitors Center
401 Madison Avenue, Montgomery, AL 36104
(205) 262-0013
Hours: Mon.–Fri., 8:30 A.M.–5 P.M.; Sat.–Sun., 9 A.M.–4 P.M.

Alabama Department of Archives and History
State Capitol Complex, 624 Washington Avenue, Montgomery, AL 36104
(205) 242-4361
Hours: Mon.–Fri., 8 A.M.–5 P.M.; Sat.–Sun., 9 A.M.–4:30 P.M.
Admission: Free

The Alabama Department of Archives and History is notable not only for the eight museums it houses, but also for its role in tracing the geneology of the diaspora. In addition, it displays portraits and sculptures of prominent Afro-Alabamians, such as W. C. Handy (see entry on p. 14) and Nat "King" Cole, and other African Americans who found in Alabama a venue for their genius, such as Booker T. Washington (see entries on pp. 177 and 206) and Dr. Martin Luther King, Jr.

Alabama State Capitol
One Dexter Drive, Montgomery, AL 36130
(800) ALABAMA
Hours: Daily, 9 A.M.–4 P.M.
Admission: Free

On the front portico of Alabama's State Capitol in February of 1861, Jefferson Davis was inaugurated as the provisonal president of the Confederacy. Little over a century later, and standing on the same spot, George Wallace was first sworn in as Alabama's governor, promising "Segregation today, segregation tomorrow, and segregation forever." It proved a short forever—only two years later on the same steps, Dr. Martin Luther King, Jr., addressed the concluding rally of the Selma-to-Montgomery Voting Rights March. Two years, two visions: one outcome.

Walk through the Capitol's 19th-century front doors and you will find your eyes drawn to a massive, three-story spiral staircase, utterly lacking external support. This unflinching confidence and faith might well serve as a metaphor for a people's determination to lift themselves up—with or without support from outside their community. The staircase is the work of the noted black bridge-builder Horace King, who began life a slave and ended it after a career in the Alabama House of Representatives. (See Horace King Historical Marker entry on p. 24; and Dillingham Street Bridge entry on p. 70.) Near to the Capitol is the first Confederate White House, from which Jefferson Davis initially directed the secessionist struggle.

Alabama State University
809 South Jackson Street, Montgomery, AL 36104
(205) 293-4100
Hours: Mon.–Fri., 8:30 A.M.–4:30 P.M.
Admission: Free

Alabama State University was founded in 1866 in Marion—the hometown of Coretta Scott King—as a black private school but moved to Montgomery a little more than a decade later due to racial tensions. The university served as a major intellectual resource for Montgomery's civil rights activists of the 1950s and '60s. Today ASU houses the E. D. Nixon Collection, which presents an unprecedented look into the life and career of the principal activist of the Montgomery Bus Boycott of 1955–1956.

Centennial Hill Historic District
Jackson and High streets, Montgomery, AL 36104
Hours: Daily until sunset
Admission: Free

Montgomery's most prominent black residential area from the 1870s through the 1960s, Centennial Hill Historic District is now listed on the National Historic Register. Among its most interesting buildings is the now-closed Ben Moore Hotel, which was the sole first-class lodging for African Americans in segregated Montgomery. On its roof, early in 1955, local black leaders met with and questioned the white candidates running for the Montgomery City Commission. The perceived presumption of blacks questioning white candidates about their stands on issues of concern to the black community aroused considerable white animosity, which soon expressed itself in the electoral victory of an extreme segregationist as city police commissioner. He, in turn, was the precipitating factor in the 1955 bus boycott. Rosa Parks was the third person within nine months to be arrested for rejecting the segregated seating requirements on public transport. Rather than treating these incidents as isolated episodes, the ultra-segregationist police commissioner insisted on seeing them as an explicit challenge to white rule, which he heavy-handedly enforced, thus provoking that which he feared.

Civil Rights Memorial
c/o Southern Poverty Law Center, 400 Washington Avenue at Hall Street, Montgomery, AL 36104
(205) 264-0286
Hours: Daily, 24 hours
Admission: Free

Honoring Dr. Martin Luther King, Jr., and the host of lesser-known martyrs killed in the civil rights struggle of the 1950s and '60s, the Civil Rights Memorial is an extraordinarily powerful expression of conviction, both of principle and of sin. The monument meets the test of true art: It is at once enlightening and cathartic, as was the movement it celebrates. Its juxtaposition of the content of passion—hate, ignorance, confusion, murder, and martyrdom—and the restraint and firmness of the form—cool, dark granite, with its simple listing of representative deaths—all bathed in the low soothing murmur of running water, calling to mind the washing away of sin, well supports the burden of pain, struggle, and invincible resolution that the memorial commemorates.

Assuring herself of artistic immortality for a second time, Maya Lin designed the memorial in 1988, less than a decade after she had created an equally moving monument to another American experience that mixed courage, pain, and sacrifice in equal measure. Like the Vietnam Memorial in the nation's capital, with its long rising and falling wall of black granite inscribed with the names of the dead, the Civil Rights Memorial is meant to be touched. Thus the martyr's table, whereon are inscribed the names of representative fallen, is only 31 inches high—aptly within the reach of children, who have inherited a world made better by the men and women honored here.

Court Square and Rosa Parks Historical Marker
One Court Square, Montgomery, AL 36104
Hours: Daily until sunset
Admission: Free

Stand inside the Capitol and look out through its 19th-century doors down the sweep of Dexter Avenue. In the distance, past the church and the Supreme Court, down the town's principal street, which bears the name of the city's founder, sits Court Square (antebellum site of land, cotton, and slave auctions) and the nearby Empire Theater. Here, on the afternoon of December 1, 1955,

Rosa Parks's brief bus ride into the history of the civil rights movement came to an abrupt halt. (Without Parks's two-block ride, the Empire Theater would be best remembered as the stage on which the young Hank Williams made his country music debut in an amateur talent contest.) A historical marker in Court Square commemorates the lady's refusal to yield to segregation and the bus boycott sparked by her arrest in front of the Empire. An intriguing counterpoint lies close at hand: A marker commemorates the telegraph office, then located on the square, from which was sent the Confederate government's telegram ordering the firing on Fort Sumter. Thus, arguably, the opening of both the Civil War and the civil rights movement lie within a block of each other in Montgomery. And you wanted to go to Disneyland?

Dexter Avenue King Memorial Baptist Church
454 Dexter Avenue, Montgomery, AL 36104
(205) 263-3970
Hours: Mon.–Thu., 10 A.M. AND 2 P.M.; Fri., 10 A.M. only. One week's notice for groups
Admission: Free. Voluntary donations encouraged

Dexter Avenue King Memorial Baptist Church, which served as Martin Luther King, Jr.'s base during the Montgomery Bus Boycott of 1955–1956, is more than a century old. The church's struggle dates to its inception in 1887, when many of Montgomery's citizens resisted having a black church located on the town's most fashionable street. Though the pews are original, most of the windows are not—having been smashed at different times over the years by white mobs that viewed the church as a source of the black community's strength. The pulpit and the Bible are the same as used by Dr. King.

COURTESY ALABAMA BUREAU OF TOURISM AND TRAVEL

Dexter Avenue Baptist Church was Dr. King's base during the historic Montgomery Bus Boycott.

On the lower floor of the church is the now-famous mural depicting the intersection of Dr. King and the civil rights movement, particularly his journey from Montgomery to Memphis and martyrdom. Among the scenes and individuals shown are Dr. King and Coretta Scott King and their children, the Selma and Birmingham marches, President Lyndon Johnson, Thurgood Marshall, the Reverend Ralph Abernathy, Andrew Young, Roy

Wilkins, the Reverend Jesse Jackson, Elijah Muhammad, J. Edgar Hoover, James Earl Ray, Adam Clayton Powell, W.E.B. Du Bois, Frederick Douglass, Malcolm X, Whitney Young, President John Kennedy and his brother Robert, and Judge Frank Johnson of the Federal Court's Central District of Alabama.

When leaving the church, stand in the doorway for a moment and look around. Immediately across the street from you is the Alabama Supreme Court, which for a century upheld the validity of the segregationist policy laid down at the State Capitol, which itself is in sight no more than 100 paces to your right. This intimate proximity of rival racial camps aptly mirrors the history of white and black in the South, a history of peoples often in conflict but always closely bound together.

Old Alabama Town Historic District
310 North Hull Street, Montgomery, AL 36104
(205) 263-4355
Hours: Mon.–Sat., 9:30 A.M.–3:30 P.M.; Sun., 1:30 P.M.–3:30 P.M.
Admission: Tape tours: adults, $5; ages 6–18, $2

Old Alabama Town Historic District lies within easy walking distance of the Capitol. Here, within a three-block area, more than 30 preserved buildings reveal the life of 19th-century Alabama. The oldest building, Lucas Tavern, dates to 1818 and underscores Alabama's largely forgotten past as a settler outpost on the frontier—a frontier "shared" with an aboriginal population (Creek, Choctaw, Chickasaw, Cherokee) that by 1835 had largely been driven west or deported en masse. Most of the buildings, though, date to the latter half of the 19th century, when a more refined existence flourished—based on an enslaved population of African Americans.

Old Alabama Town's 1880s "Shotgun House" exemplifies the urban homes of Alabama's freed slaves. In this house in the 1890s lived Grant and Viney Fitzpatrick; he a railroad worker, she a washerwoman. Their landlord was Willis Willington, an enterprising young black entrepreneur who in 1894 had paid $610 to acquire a two-house property from a bankrupt realty firm headed by a former mayor of Montgomery.

A few brief steps from the "Shotgun House" sits the First Colored Presbyterian Church, constructed in 1890 by a congregation that traced its inception back six decades. From 1829 through 1885 this congregation, black and white, worshipped together—with the black members segregated in a horseshoe balcony constructed specifically to accommodate them. In 1885 black members began to worship in the building by themselves in hours set aside for them. Sermons were preached by Henry Sheppard, a student at Stillman Institute, one of Alabama's few black colleges. Five years later this group requested permission from the biracial congregation to organize their own church. Permission and financial aid being granted, the First Colored Presbyterian Church soon arose at the corner of Cleveland Avenue and Stone Street.

Less joyful reminders of life for 19th-century African Americans in Alabama can be found in the 1848 Ordeman-Shaw House. The Ordeman's rented rather

THE ASSOCIATED PRESS

The Reverend Martin Luther King, Jr., speaking about his arrest for leading the Montgomery, Alabama, Bus Boycott in 1955–56.

than owned slaves, who fared well compared to fieldworkers. Sleeping over the kitchen—in a room with a solid roof and a balcony porch complete with hand-me-down furniture and utensils—had much to recommend it in winter, but nothing attractive about it come the hot, muggy summer months. The Ordeman's were clearly well-to-do: The house had not wardrobes but real closets, which counted as separate rooms in the tax assessments based on the number of rooms in a house.

Old Alabama Town also includes a one-room school, a log cabin, a corner grocery, a country doctor's office, and much more. Visitors will see working craftspeople replicating their 19th-century tasks, though except for special events, none of these reenactors is African American.

Old Ship A.M.E. Zion Church
483 Holcombe Street, Montgomery, AL 36104
(205) 262-3922
Hours: By appointment
Admission: Free

The Court Street Methodist Church, built in 1834, was given in 1852 by its white congregation to its black members, who then rolled it on logs to its present location. In the course of seating the church on its new foundation, a passerby questioned what it would be named. After a moment's reflection, a congregation member replied, " 'Tis the Old Ship of Zion." This church is Montgomery's oldest African-American house of worship.

World Heritage Museum
119 West Jeff Davis Avenue, Montgomery, AL 36104
(205) 263-7229
Hours: By appointment
Admission: Voluntary donations requested

The World Heritage Museum consists of three small rooms in a Montgomery house, the most interesting of which holds material that records in some detail the history of the city's principal civil rights group of the 1950s, the Montgomery Improvement Association (MIA). Photographs, newspaper clippings, and portraits and memorabilia of the lesser-known stalwarts of the struggle, such as Zecozy Williams, the MIA's secretary, make this a particularly valuable stop for those interested in Alabama's black heritage.

NORMAL

Alabama Agricultural and Mechanical University
4900 Meridian Street, Normal, AL 35762
(205) 851-5000
Hours: Mon.–Fri., 8:30 A.M.–4:30 P.M.
Admission: Free

While no southern state during Reconstruction explicitly required racially segregated schools, they were the norm everywhere but Louisiana and South Carolina. Though freedmen resolutely opposed placing segregation in state *constitutions* and viewed school integration as a desired goal, they pragmatically accepted the existence of racially separate schooling, in part so as not to drive all white voters into the Democratic Party that threatened black gains and in part because of their urgent desire to see themselves and their children educated. For freedmen, black schools were more important than white pupils. In 1873 the Alabama legislature established Alabama Agricultural and Mechanical University for the education of black teachers, a move that came none too soon for the future of black education in the state. A year later the violence- and fraud-filled 1874 elections brought Democrats to control of the major state offices and both houses of the General Assembly—and Reconstruction to a bloody end.

OAKVILLE

Jesse Owens Monument
Jesse Owens Park, County Road 187, Oakville, AL 35619
Near Danville and Molton
Hours: Daily until sunset
Admission: Free

The son of an Oakville-area sharecropper, Jesse Owens worked the Alabama cotton fields as a young boy before his family migrated to the North. His four gold medals in track events at the 1936 Berlin Olympics won him national

COURTESY OHIO STATE UNIVERSITY ARCHIVES

Despite four Olympic gold medals in track, Jesse Owens could not outrun segregation.

acclaim (see Joe Louis Arena entry on p. 400) but not the right to use whites-only drinking fountains, rest rooms, and lunch counters in his native state. In the autumn of 1983, three years after Owens's death, this long-overdue monument was dedicated in the town of his birth.

PHENIX CITY

Horace King Historical Marker
Dillingham and Broad streets, Phenix City, AL 36867
Hours: Daily until sunset
Admission: Free

From slave, to artisan, to architect, to freedom, to service in the Alabama State Legislature, Horace King (1807–1877) led a life that underscores the 19th century as a time of revolutionary transformation in America. Barely a decade after Alabama's admission to the Union, King, while still a slave, was the foreman of a construction project that raised the first bridge spanning the stretch of Chattahoochee River that separates Alabama from Georgia. King (see Dillingham Street Bridge entry on p. 70) and his owner, John Godwin, went on to introduce the "Town Lattice" bridge design into the Chattahoochee River Valley, building most of the bridges along the river that runs half the length of

Alabama's eastern border. In 1846 King was freed by Godwin, a move that required and received the endorsement of the Alabama legislature. A few years later he designed the three-story spiral staircase that graces the entrance hall to the Alabama State Capitol. A slave-owning free black who repaired bridges for the Confederates during the Civil War, King later served in the Alabama legislature, representing the county that four decades earlier had benefited from having the first bridge access to Georgia.

After Godwin's death, the now well-to-do King financially supported his widow. He also placed a memorial on Godwin's grave, gratefully remembering his "lost friend and former master." Today, not far from the site of his first bridge, visitors to Phenix City will find the Horace King Historical Marker.

PLATEAU, EAST MOBILE

Cudjoe Lewis Memorial
506 Bay Bridge Road, Plateau, East Mobile, AL 36610
(205) 456-6080
Hours: Daily until sunset
Admission: Free

Plateau Cemetery
c/o Union Baptist Church, Bay Ridge Road, Plateau, East Mobile, AL 36610
(205) 456-6080
Hours: Daily until sunset
Admission: Free

In 1859, more than five decades after the African slave trade was declared illegal by the U.S. Congress, the Mobile-based ship *Clotilde* arrived in its home port with more than 100 abducted African men, women, and children on board. Slipping past the alerted federal authorities, the illegal slave ship was able to land its human cargo but not sell it. Eventually turned loose in a strange land, the seized but never enslaved Africans remained together, most of them forming a community that retained their native language and customs and settled in the nearby area of Plateau. Their descendants still inhabit the Africatown settlement on Happy Hill, Plateau, and Magazine Point. The last survivor of the *Clotilde*'s cargo, Cudjoe Lewis, died in 1935. Today the Cudjoe Lewis Memorial stands at the heart of Africatown, the Union Baptist Church. Close by lies the Plateau Cemetery, where Lewis and many others of the *Clotilde*'s final voyage rest.

SELMA

Selma-Dallas County Chamber of Commerce
P.O. Drawer D, Selma, AL 36702
(205) 875-7241
Hours: Mon.–Fri., 8:30 A.M.–5 P.M.

Ask for the "Selma 1865–1965: A Legacy of Black Heritage" brochure, which mentions a number of African-American heritage sites—including Concordia College, First Baptist Church, Old City Hall, and Selma University—that space precludes detailing herein.

Brown A.M.E. Chapel
410 Martin Luther King Street, Selma, AL 36703
(205) 874-7897
Hours: By appointment
Admission: Free

Founded in 1867 by the first A.M.E. congregation in Alabama, the Brown A.M.E. Chapel was the starting point of the famous 1965 Selma-to-Montgomery Voting Rights March. Today in front of the church is a monument to martyrs of the civil rights struggle, two black and two white: Dr. Martin Luther King, Jr., killed in Memphis; Jimmy Lee Jackson, shot by a state trooper during a 1965 march in Marion, which lies close to Selma and is the hometown of Coretta Scott King; the Reverend James Reeb of Boston, beaten to death in Selma during a spring demonstration; and Mrs. Viola Liuzzo of Detroit, shot to death by a carload of Klansmen, including an FBI informant, in the course of the Selma-to-Montgomery march.

Old Depot Museum
Foot of Water Avenue, Selma, AL 36701
(205) 875-9918
Hours: Mon.–Fri., 10 A.M.–12 P.M. and 2 P.M.–4 P.M.
Admission: Free

With the collapse of Reconstruction and the advent of Jim Crow, Selma's African Americans turned inward and focused their energies on self-development. By the first decades of the 20th century, Selma's large black community had developed commercial and professional breadth, with a balanced business sector, its own newspaper (the *Selma Advocate*), a black-staffed and administered hospital (Burwell Infirmary), local private schools for black youth (Knox Academy, Payne Academy, East End Academy), and two church-affiliated colleges (Alabama Lutheran College and the Baptist's Selma University).

A visit to Selma's small Old Depot Museum uncovers the 20th-century dimension of this hidden history, primarily through a one-room display of newspaper clippings and photographs. These images of the people of Knox, Burwell, Alabama Lutheran, and Selma University, as well as of other prominent local African Americans, reveal that black life in central Alabama was far more textured and vibrant than is generally appreciated. The photographs also offer clues to another aspect of the city's hidden black history—a civil rights struggle that predated, and indeed formed the foundation for, Selma's inclusion in the famous 1965 Selma-to-Montgomery Voting Rights March. Selma's African-American doctors, professors, businessmen, and craftsmen did not depend financially on the white economy. They enjoyed—and earned—an autonomy that expressed itself in the Dallas County Voters League's push for black rights. (Throughout the South, the critical measure for judging the success of civil rights actions was the participation of those African Americans who *did* depend on the white economy, whose livelihoods fell under the hammer of white supremacist rule.)

Regrettably, the full richness and complexity of Selma's 20th-century black community is only partially revealed in the museum's artifacts and exhibits. Even fewer artifacts survive to interpret the days of slavery and Reconstruction in Selma, which are respectively represented by the odd handbill announcing a slave sale and by paintings, of no artistic power, of black Reconstruction-era politicians.

However, these limitations of material and interpretation are more than compensated for by the museum's possession of the Kepp Collection: 45 photographs that date back more than a century and capture the lives of Selma's 19th-century black laborers. Anyone interested in Alabama's black heritage will want to see Selma; while there do not neglect the Old Depot Museum.

Edmund Pettus Bridge and Historical Marker
Highway 80, Selma, AL 36703
Hours: Daily until sunset
Admission: Free

As Birmingham's image is stereotyped by hoses and dogs, so too is Selma's by the Edmund Pettus Bridge. It was here, on a Sunday in March of 1965, that the

ALABAMA BUREAU OF TOURISM AND TRAVEL

The historic Selma-to-Montgomery Voting Rights March over the Edmund Pettus Bridge, Selma, March 7, 1965.

struggle for voting rights reached its "imaged" culmination, with mounted Alabama state troopers, clad in blue helmets and armed with shotguns and clubs, striking out right and left and riding down peaceful demonstrators amid the swirl of tear gas in a scene that recalled the "dispersal" of the crowd approaching the Winter Palace in 1905 in Eisenstein's *Potemkin*. So powerful was the moment that television networks interrupted their regular broadcasts to convey the police assault, shocking anew a nation that was finding it harder and harder to "see no evil." As with the 1957 Little Rock Central High School incident, which featured a howling white mob threatening black children, the image overwhelmed all explanatory frameworks and left in its wake the instantaneous moral sense that something was gravely *wrong*. Though very far from the most brutal clash of the civil rights struggle, the segregationist cause never recovered from this encounter, and a week later President Johnson addressed a special joint session of Congress to propose a Voting Rights Act. Today, a historical marker recalls the encounter of 1965.

Benjamin S. Turner Grave and Monument
Live Oak Cemetery, 110 West Dallas Avenue, Selma, AL 36701
(205) 874-2160
Hours: Daily until sunset
Admission: Free

With its rich, dark soil (the soil rather than slaves giving rise to the term "the black belt"), Dallas, the county seat of which is Selma, was antebellum Alabama's leading cotton-producing county, and hence "slave-heavy." (Although slightly less than one-sixth of the county's white population possessed slaves, the average slaveholder in Dallas owned 17 human beings, while his counterpart in Montgomery County owned but 10.) As the era of Reconstruction opened, the county was 80 percent black. Thus Selma's African-American community contributed the first black Alabamian ever elected to the U.S. House of Representatives, Benjamin S. Turner; the first black judge in Alabama's history, Roderick B. Thomas; and the area's last black congressman of the Reconstruction era, Jeremiah Haralson.

Of the three, Turner was far and away the most substantial figure. A native of North Carolina, he was brought to Alabama at the age of six. Three decades later he was literate and the manager of his master's Saint James Hotel. (The hotel still stands and can be viewed within a block of the Edmund Pettus Bridge—see p. 27—the site of the infamous attack on the Selma-to-Montgomery Voting Rights March in 1965.) Turner's accomplishments did not alter his legal status—he remained a slave and thus could not prevent his wife's being purchased away to serve as the mistress of a white Alabamian.

After the Civil War and Emancipation, Turner entered politics in 1868 as a member of Selma's City Council, from which he resigned in indignation when members (all of whom were Republicans) voted themselves handsome salaries from the war-debilitated city's limited tax revenues. Two years later, amid a

Republican debacle that cost the party a governor, a U.S. senator, and control of the state legislature, the widely respected Turner easily won election to the U.S. House of Representatives as a Republican. In Washington, he again confounded some of his Republican colleagues. A strong supporter of both "universal suffrage and universal amnesty," his first act was to introduce a bill to grant amnesty to the approximately 20,000 former Confederates who were disenfranchised. "Let the past be forgotten," he told Congress in his maiden speech, "and let us all, from every sun and every clime, of every hue and every shade, go to work peacefully to build up the shattered temples of this grand and glorious republic." Turner's incorruptibility, courage, and vision did not serve him well politically: He was defeated in the next election after Alabama's Republican power brokers, resentful that he had not deferred to them in appointments to offices that fell within his power of official patronage, nominated another African American, split the black vote, and threw the election to the Democrats. Turner never again held public office. His Selma admirers commemorated his life with a monument above his grave, which lies in Live Oak Cemetery.

TALLADEGA

Talladega College
627 West Battle Street, Talladega, AL 35160
(205) 362-0206
Hours: Mon.–Fri., 9 A.M.–4 P.M.
Admission: Free

> Some years before emancipation my master signed $900 to be paid in work toward building a Baptist College where we lived. He sent me to work out his subscription. I thought it was hard for me to work out his $900 when I could have no privilege of educating my own children . . . but God has turned things about so . . . when I worked out this subscription of my master, I was building a college for myself and my family.
>
> —AMBROSE HEADEN, ex-slave, bricklayer, trustee of Talladega College

In the winter of 1865 William Savery and Thomas Tarrant, from Talladega, and other freedmen from across the state gathered in Mobile to consider their free future, resolving that "the education of our children . . . [is] vital to the preservation of our liberties." Upon their return to Talladega, Savery and Tarrant, aided by Ambrose Headen and other local freedmen, opened a one-room school within sight of the Baptist College building that Headen and other enslaved carpenters, plasterers, and bricklayers had helped construct in 1852. Within a year, and with the support of the commissioner of Alabama's Freedmen's Bureau, General Wager B. Swayne, and of the American Missionary Association, Savery, Tarrant, Headen, and the other freedmen had purchased that building. In the winter of 1867, two years from the original Mobile meeting, the deed to the newly named Swayne Hall was transferred to the newly created Talladega College, on the board of trustees of which sat Savery and Headen.

Swayne Hall, for many years the only college facility, is still in use, with its original brickwork laid by Headen and its original woodwork, including an unsupported three-story spiral staircase reminiscent of Horace King's work in the State Capitol. Talladega College, now a National Historic Landmark, still flourishes; in 1992 Bill Cosby addressed its 125th anniversary commencement. For more than a century the product of Headen's finest labor has gone forth to the state and the nation, emulating and honoring the contributions to the African-American community of Savery, Tarrant, Headen, and the other Talladega freedmen.

The college's most famous feature—not to be missed—adorns the walls of Savery Library: Hale Woodruff's 1939 mural commemorating the 100th anniversary of the Amistad Incident, in which Mende villagers who had been abducted from Sierra Leone seized control of the ship carrying them into slavery and slew most of their captors. Eventually, the ship ended up in U.S. waters and the Mende in a U.S. Supreme Court case. (See Foone's Grave entry on p. 224.) Woodruff's powerful and beautiful mural resonates with African and American history (all but four of the faces were painted from contemporaneous portraits, sketches, and etchings of the figures in the events portrayed) and contains a special bonus—look carefully at the audience in the trial scene (panel two), for among the faces gazing at the Mende's leader, Cinque, is that of Hale Woodruff.

TUSCALOOSA

Stillman College
3600 15th Street, Tuscaloosa, AL 35405
(205) 349-4240
Hours: By appointment through Admissions Department
Admission: Free

Founded in 1876 by the Presbyterian Church and later named after its chief organizer and first director, Stillman College, then Tuscaloosa Institute, was originally an "Institute for Training Negro Ministers." Both the Reverend C. A. Stillman and the institute's first teacher, the Reverend A. F. Dickson, originally were members of the Second Presbyterian Church of Charleston, South Carolina, which in the 1830s and '40s was pastored by the Irish native Dr. Thomas Smythe, one of the antebellum South's principal promoters of black churches.

TUSCUMBIA

Alabama Music Hall of Fame
P.O. Box 709, Tuscumbia, AL 35674
(800) 239-2643; (205) 381-4417
Hours: Mon.–Sat., 9 A.M.–5 P.M.; Sun., 1 P.M.–5 P.M.; tours by appointment
Admission: Adults, $6; seniors and students 13–18, $5; children 6–12, $3; under 6, free

From W. C. Handy through Sun Ra, and including Nat "King" Cole, Erskine Hawkins, Martha Reeves, Wilson Pickett, Lionel Richie, and others, Alabama pays tribute to its musical greats at the Alabama Music Hall of Fame. Costumes, awards, musical instruments, and memorabilia of these and other stars are on display.

TUSKEGEE

Tuskegee University
317 Kresge Center, Tuskegee, AL 36083
(205) 727-8011
Hours: Campus visits: Mon.–Fri., 9 A.M.–5 P.M. Tours by appointment, arranged 1 week in advance.
Admission: Free

Undoubtedly the best-known historically black college in the United States, Tuskegee University was not founded by Booker T. Washington but by Lewis Adams, a former slave politically influential among African Americans in rural Macon County in the decades after the Civil War, and George W. Campbell, a former slave owner who needed black votes to secure election to the state legislature. In exchange for black electoral support, Campbell offered to introduce legislation appropriating funds to pay the salaries of the staff of a privately funded black normal (that is, teacher training) school. Upon the recommendation of the founder of Hampton Institute, Washington was recruited in 1881 to run the school in Tuskegee. It was Washington's passionate commitment to moral instruction and practical education and his drive, particularly regarding fund-raising among northern whites, that secured the school its renown and its resources. Though Washington's success as an African-American spokesman was aided by his social pragmatism in the face of the onset of Jim Crow—symbolized by his famous 1895 "Atlanta Compromise" speech ("In all things that are purely social, we can be as separate as the fingers, yet one as the hand in all things essential to mutual progress")—his concern was not racial accommodation to white supremacy but rather the establishment of black economic self-sufficiency.

Washington's most influential Tuskegee appointment was made in 1896, when he hired George Washington Carver (see entries on pp. 365 and 414) to direct the school's new agricultural department. Like Washington, Carver had been born a slave and was never certain of the year of his birth; indeed, if not for the Civil War, both men almost certainly would have lived out their lives as uneducated laborers. Carver, whose real love was painting, spent almost five decades at Tuskegee, achieving fame as the "Peanut Man" after testifying before Congress in the 1920s about the hundreds of uses for one of the South's rising cash crops. Both Washington and Carver were a publicist's dream: intelligent African-American achievers with humble, apparently apolitical demeanors. As a consequence the identities of both men—who were truly giants—were quickly subsumed within public relations myths. Carver never made a scientifically significant contribution to agronomy and never developed a single commercially viable product; indeed, after achieving fame in the 1920s, Carver stopped both teaching and research, spending most of his time on the lecture circuit or in dispensing free advice to farmers. His deepest contribution, essentially immeasurable and largely unappreciated by the public, was the alleviation of the stark rural poverty of black sharecroppers, who were the prime beneficiaries of his practical research, which encouraged the shift from soil-depleting cotton to alternative crops and offered substitutes for expensive commercial fertilizers.

Campus visitors will wish to see the Founder's Marker, located at the shanty that served as Tuskegee's original classroom; the Booker T. Washington Monument; the Daniel "Chappie" James Center for Aerospace Science, named for the Tuskegee graduate and Vietnam veteran who became America's first African-American four- star general; and the university library, which houses the Booker T. Washington Collection of archival material and other African-American artifacts.

Tuskegee Institute National Historic Site
Carver Museum, 1212 Old Montgomery Road, Tuskegee, AL 36087
(205) 727-6390
Hours: Daily, 9 A.M.–5 P.M. Tours of the Carver Museum and the Oaks: On the hour; last tour at 4 P.M.
Admission: Free

LIBRARY OF CONGRESS

More than a century ago, black voters in post-Reconstruction Alabama transformed their ballots into a school.

Appropriately, the Tuskegee Institute National Historic Site is mainly a tribute to Booker T. Washington and George Washington Carver, though its 5,000 acres contain more than 100 buildings. Visitors will want to stop at the Orientation Center, where an ancient recording of Washington reading from his 1895 Atlanta Compromise address can be heard; at the Oaks, Washington's restored home; and at the George Washington Carver Museum and Research Center. Also of great interest is Moton Field, the "Home of Black Aviation" and the scene of the operational training for the black crews who broke America's World War II air-combat color barrier.

ARKANSAS

Arkansas Department of Parks and Tourism
One Capitol Mall, Little Rock, AR 72201
(800) 628-8725; (501) 682-7777
Hours: Mon.–Fri., 8 A.M.–5 P.M.

CAMDEN

Poison Springs Historical State Park
Highway 76, Camden, AR 71701
(501) 685-2748
Poison Spring is located 12 miles northwest of Camden by way of Arkansas 24, then Highway 76
Hours: Daily until sunset
Admission: Free

The success in 1863 of Grant's siege of Vicksburg made possible and the establishment in 1864 of the pro-Confederate regime of Emperor Maximilian in Mexico made urgent a Union presence in Texas. Toward this end, in the spring of 1864 General Steele's Little Rock–based Union force was ordered to link up at the Red River with federal troops moving north from Louisiana. In the course of the Red River campaign three battles were fought in south-central Arkansas. In the first encounter, fought at Poison Springs, Confederate troops (including a Choctaw contingent; see Fort Towson Historical Marker and Five Civilized Tribes Museum entries on pp. 453 and 455) thrashed an outnumbered Union element guarding a supply train heading toward Steele in Camden. Prominent in the fighting was the 1st Kansas Colored Regiment, which suffered its heaviest casualties of the war (182 of the regiment's 438 men) and whose wounded or surrendered soldiers were massacred on the field of battle by Confederate troops. According to black survivors who crawled off the field of battle after feigning death, Confederate troops scoured the field calling (with considerable justification regarding the last clause) "Where is the First Nigger now? All cut to pieces and gone to hell by bad management." The *Washington Telegraph*, the Arkansas Confederate newspaper (see Ethnic Minorities entry on p. 41), reported that the Choctaw buried the white men and then used the half-buried black corpses for grave markers. Historical markers in the park commemorate this Civil War encounter.

CARTHAGE

Hampton Springs Cemetery
County Road 244, Carthage, AR 71725
(501) 254-2463 (Carthage City Hall)
The cemetery is about 4 miles east of Carthage and ½ mile off of Highway 48
Hours: Daily until sunset
Admission: Free

Particularly in days gone by, the hill ranges that segmented the Arkansas frontier encouraged social isolation and yielded distinct population clusters. These distinct clusters were especially notable among slaves, first because they frequently arrived on the frontier in "tribal" batches and second because once on the frontier, they lacked the freedom to move about. Thus, over time, their particular African heritage was preserved, largely unaffected by a process of erosion and adaptation that elsewhere transformed abducted Africans into African Americans. The Hampton Springs Cemetery, which dates to the 1800s, offers a rare example of preserved traditions, in this case the common African burial custom of placing clay plates, bowls, and jugs on the grave of the departed. Today researchers are studying the pottery shards found at grave sites here to determine the specific tribal and clan affiliation of a group of Africans who obviously shared a common heritage—and who ended up together at this frontier outpost.

ELAINE

Elaine
Elaine, AR 72333
25 miles south of Helena by way of Arkansas 20
Hours: Daily, 24 hours
Admission: Free

World War I may have yielded to the "Roaring Twenties" for the rest of America, but for African Americans it yielded to major urban riots, as wartime labor shortages had drawn large numbers of blacks into previously predominantly white communities, exacerbating racial tensions. (For the labor movement—which, though white, was largely led by non-WASP immigrants—yielded to the "Red Scare," which saw widespread police raids on socialist and trade union organizations.) Though the Chicago race riot of 1919, sparked by the crossing of an unofficial race boundary at a Lake Shore beach (see 1919 Race Riot Site entry on p. 350) is the most notorious, it was far from unique. Outside the orbit of the mass media, rural America also experienced one of its periodic upsurges in racial violence. In this Mississippi River Delta town, the race and labor challenges to the "old ways" merged—with deadly results. Black sharecroppers saw in a union some protection from white overlords who unilaterally judged the value of their crops and the terms of credit offered to African Americans. Determined to prevent any challenge to established custom (white rule), a white mob shot up a crowded union meeting. Their gunfire was returned, leading to the death of a sheriff's deputy. This, in turn, led to a posse's rampage and at least a dozen black deaths, a weeklong back-country communal war and more deaths, the intervention of 500 army troops, arrests, trial and death sentences for 12 African Americans and long prison sentences for another 67. The trial was a model of Jim Crow: Prospective defense witnesses were beaten and compelled to testify for the prosecution; the court-appointed defense attorney called no witnesses and neglected to ask for a change of venue; the trial of 79 men took less than an hour; the jury took less than five minutes to find everyone guilty; and throughout the brief encounter a white mob milled outside the court demanding prompt "justice." Nothing in the proceedings offended the Arkansas Supreme Court, which endorsed the trial and the sentences.

At this juncture the U.S. Supreme Court entered the picture. Speaking for the Court, Oliver Wendell Holmes declared: "If the case is such that the whole proceeding is a mask; that counsel, jury and judge were swept to a fatal end by an irresistible wave of public passion . . . neither perfection in the machinery for correction nor the possibility that the trial court and counsel saw no other way of avoiding an immediate outbreak of the mob can prevent this court from securing to the petitioners their constitutional rights." All the sentences were overturned and the defendants freed. Today Elaine remains a small Delta town. Though the events of 1919 are not commemorated, travelers through the Mississippi Delta may want to stop in and do their part to keep the folk-history chain alive.

FARGO

Fargo Agricultural School Museum
c/o Arkansas Land & Farm Development Corporation, Route 2, Box 291,
Fargo, AR 72021
(501) 734-1140
Hours: Mon.–Fri., 9 A.M.–5 P.M.
Admission: Free

In 1919 Floyd Brown arrived in Fargo with $2.80, the equivalent of a fifth-grade education, a couple of years' exposure to Booker T. Washington and the Tuskegee Institute in Alabama, and true grit and purpose. He borrowed $20, used it as down payment on 20 acres of land, and opened Fargo Agricultural School, one of the few private, nonsectarian schools for black children ever established in the Delta. Sharing Washington's passionate belief in the values of education and labor, Brown demanded and received from his charges—most of whom were sharecroppers' children—decorum, application, practical skills, as well as formal education. Surely his charges had not only a mentor but an exemplar: Throughout the depression, this small private school was kept afloat by Brown's unceasing summer travels "up North" to solicit funds and materiel from black and white folks alike. Failing health and the slight widening of public education opportunities for African Americans led Brown to sell the property to the state in 1949. The frame buildings were torn down; the new brick buildings housed the Fargo Reformatory for Negro Girls. Tied to the sale was Brown's donation of 40 percent of his proceeds to the state in return for its erecting and maintaining in situ a museum to the old school. Today a small, simple building lacking heat and cared for by alumni pays tribute to the virtues of work and vision.

HELENA

Phillips County Museum
623 Pecan Street, Helena, AR 72342
(501) 338-3537
Hours: Tours: Mon.–Fri., 1:30 P.M.–4:30 P.M.; Sat., 10 A.M.–12 P.M. and 1 P.M.–4 P.M.
Admission: Free

In the course of the siege of Vicksburg, the decisive battle of the decisive theater of operations in the Civil War, Union forces seized all the Mississippi River ports, including Helena, Arkansas. Here, in the summer of 1863, Confederate forces attempted to break the Union blockade or at least draw off federal forces surrounding Vicksburg. Among the defenders at Helena were troops of the 2nd Arkansas Infantry, African Descent Regiment. Historical markers around Helena commemorate battle sites, while an exhibit at this museum chronicles both the battle and the town's Civil War history.

HOT SPRINGS

Hot Springs National Park
Visitor Center, Number 1 Reserve Street, Hot Springs, AR 71902
(501) 624-3383
Hours: Daily, 8 A.M. to 5 P.M.
Admission: Free

Hot Springs National Park is a park of a different sort, one revealing the life of early 19th-century bathhouses (which were of the traditional, steamy rather than seamy nature). By the early 20th century, Hot Springs had become a major health resort and playground for the wealthy—which meant employment for African Americans. In addition, segregation ensured opportunities for black health and resort businesses, particularly in the neighborhood of Malvern

Avenue, which was lined with beauty parlors, the offices of dentists and doctors, and laundry and dry-cleaning establishments. Photographs on permanent exhibit at the park yield a portrait of the black workforce of the bathhouses, while a film on the area's black heritage is available by special request.

LITTLE ROCK

Little Rock Convention & Visitor Information Bureau
7 Statehouse Plaza, Markham and Broadway, Little Rock, AR 72201
(501) 376-4781
Hours: Mon.–Fri., 8:30 A.M.–5 P.M.

Central High School
1500 Park Street, Little Rock, AR 72202
(501) 376-4751
Hours: Historical marker: daily until sunset
Admission: Free

In the autumn of 1957, amid the prosperity and propriety of the Eisenhower era, nine black schoolchildren found themselves day after day surrounded by an overtly threatening white mob as they attempted to attend Little Rock's hitherto segregated Central High School. While the mob cursed and spat its hatred, Arkansas's governor used the state's National Guard to block black students

COURTESY ARKANSAS HISTORY COMMISSION

Mrs. Daisy Bates (foreground), leader of the black struggle in Little Rock, Arkansas, and Thurgood Marshall, champion of the NAACP's legal team, leave a federal courtroom with students seeking entry into Little Rock's segregated Central High School.

from entering the school grounds. When a federal court order finally forced the troops' removal, local police escorted the nine children to class. The mob responded by attacking first black and then white journalists covering the incident. As the mob grew more threatening, the nine students were removed from the school under police protection. President Eisenhower then responded by federalizing the Arkansas National Guard and sending in paratroopers of the 101st Airborne. Protected by the bayonets of an elite U.S. Army division, the children exercised a right recognized three years earlier in the Supreme Court's *Brown v. Board of Education* decision. Photographs of the intense confrontation—which underscored the disparity between the few and the small and the feral mob—shocked the nation. Obscured by these events was the clear, if legally compelled, willingness of both the city's political establishment and a majority of its citizenry to accept the formalities, if not the spirit, of integration. (In a special meeting called days after the Supreme Court's 1954 Brown decision, the Little Rock School Board had voted unanimously to comply with the ruling.) By 1959 Little Rock's schoolchildren would begin confronting face to face in integrated classes the past they had inherited. Today a majority of Central High School's student body is African American. On the school grounds there is a historical marker recalling the events of 1957 and 1958.

Dunbar Junior High School
1100 Wright Avenue, Little Rock, AR 72206
(501) 324-2440
Hours: Historical marker: daily until sunset
Admission: Free

From 1930 through 1955 Paul Laurence Dunbar was Little Rock's sole public junior high and high school for African Americans and the centerpiece of Arkansas's segregated public school system. Named for the famous poet (see Dunbar entry on p. 493), the school (which in 1931–32 also attained accredited junior college rating) was the fourth in a series of five all-black public high schools in the state capital, the first of which opened in 1867 through the combined efforts of the Freedmen's Bureau and the Society of Friends (Quakers) and the last of which existed until 1971. In 1943 Dunbar was involved in a controversy concerning equal pay for black and white teachers that was resolved in a landmark U.S. Circuit Court of Appeals decision establishing the principle of "equal pay based on professional qualifications and services rendered." Today the integrated Dunbar Junior High School is on the National Register of Historic Places. A historical marker at the school recalls its role in the education of the city's African Americans.

First Missionary Baptist Church
Seventh and Gaines streets, Little Rock, AR 72201
(501) 372-2705
Hours: Mon.–Fri., 9 A.M.–1 P.M.
Admission: Free

The First Missionary Baptist Church is home to one of the oldest black congregations in Arkansas. Constructed in 1882 with all the conveniences of the day—steam heat, lights, and mechanical fans—this is the third building to house parishioners originally brought together in 1845 by the Reverend Wilson Brown. Brown, a slave, received assistance from the white Missionary Baptist Church of which he was a member to form a black congregation, which outgrew two successive frame buildings.

Miflin Gibbs Grave
Oakland Fraternal Cemetery, 21st and Barber streets, Little Rock, AR 72206
(501) 372-6429
Hours: Daily, 8:30 A.M.–4:30 P.M.
Admission: Free

Following a successful career as a merchant in gold-rush California and in Canada, the free-born Miflin W. Gibbs arrived in Little Rock in 1871. Two years later Gibbs became the first black man ever to win a municipal judgeship in America. He later served President McKinley as U.S. consul in Madagascar. Today his grave is found in the Oakland Fraternal Cemetery.

Philander Smith College
812 West 13th Street, Little Rock, AR 72202
(501) 375-9845
Hours: Mon.–Fri., 9 A.M.–4 P.M.
Admission: Free

Philander Smith College dates to 1877, opening its doors just as Reconstruction had its doors slammed shut. This historically black college, one of whose buildings is listed on the National Register of Historic Places, was the first educational institution of the Southwest Annual Conference of the Methodist Episcopal Church. Today Philander is best known for having provided one of the choirs that graced the inauguration of President Clinton.

Taborian Hall
800 West Ninth Street, Little Rock, AR 72202
(501) 375-7633
Hours: Daily until sunset
Admission: Exterior viewing only. Now houses a private business

Taborian Hall is one of the few surviving buildings of what was once the hub of Little Rock's black business and social community. As with its segregated counterparts across the country, this hub prominently featured the black fraternal organizations, such as the Knights and Daughters of Tabor, that bound a people together and provided basic insurance protection. Taborian Hall housed business and professional offices, while its ballroom was graced by performances by Louis Armstrong, Count Basie, Cab Calloway, Duke Ellington, and others. This building now houses a commercial enterprise with no connection to the Knights and Daughters of Tabor.

NEW EDINBURG

Marks' Mill Battle Monument
Marks' Mill Battleground Historic Park, Highway 8, New Edinburg, AR 71660
(501) 463-8555
Hours: Daily, 24 hours. Open pavilion with monument
Admission: Free

The second of the battles of the Red River campaign, fought at Marks' Mill near New Edinburg, again witnessed both a successful Confederate attack on a Union supply train and the Confederate's battlefield massacre of all black soldiers. "No orders, threats, or commands," recorded one Confederate commander, "could restrain the men from vengeance on the Negroes and they were piled in great heaps about the wagons, in the tangled brushwood, and upon the muddy and trampled road." The loss of the supply train compelled Steele's retreat from Camden and set in motion the third and final battle of the campaign. Today a monument recalls the bloody encounter of 1864.

PINE BLUFF

Isaac Hathaway Fine Arts Center
University of Arkansas at Pine Bluff, 1200 North University Drive, Pine Bluff, AR 71601
(501) 543-8236
Hours: Mon.–Fri., 8:30 A.M.–4:30 P.M.; weekends by appointment
Admission: Free

Primarily a black institution, the University of Arkansas at Pine Bluff and its Isaac Hathaway Fine Arts Center host "Persistence of the Spirit," an exhibit of interpretive panels that chronicle the experiences of black Arkansans since 1803. The central themes of this interpretive project are the strength and sacrifices of African Americans and the enduring tension between black hopes and the constraints of the larger society.

SHERIDAN

Jenkins' Ferry State Park
Arkansas 46 (Leola Highway), Sheridan, AR 72150
(501) 844-4176
Hours: Tue.–Sat., 9 A.M.–5 P.M. Open pavilion with historical markers
Admission: Free

The final encounter of the Union's disastrous Red River campaign found General Steele's Union force in retreat from Camden. The Confederates caught up with him as he attempted to extricate his troops across the Saline River at Jenkins' Ferry. His river crossing under fire succeeded in large measure because the enraged survivors of the 1st Kansas Colored Regiment and their comrades of the 2nd Kansas Colored Regiment charged the field artillery that was shelling Union troops. Shouting "Remember Poison Springs" (see Poison Springs entry on p. 33), the Afro-Kansans killed about 150 of their enemy, enabling themselves and the rest of Steele's force to reach Little Rock without further difficulty.

TEXARKANA

Scott Joplin Commemorative Marker
831 Laurel Street, Texarkana, AR 75502
(501) 772-9551
Hours: Daily until sunset
Admission: Free

Scott Joplin, the "Father of Ragtime Music," was born in 1868 and grew up in the border town of Texarkana, the son of an ex-slave father and a free woman from Kentucky. Intensely musical, he quickly picked up the rudiments of the guitar, bugle, and piano. Still in his teens, Joplin (see Joplin House entry on p. 424) took the only road open to a Mississippi Valley black musician of his era: itinerant player in saloons, bordellos, and tent shows. It was a rough but vibrant life, and Joplin transformed its patois into a new and vital musical expression. Though his musical career is more associated with St. Louis and Sedalia, Missouri, and New York City, Joplin never forgot his roots: His opera *Treemonisha,* which obsessively absorbed the last decade of his life, was set in the Texas-Arkansas border area of his youth. Joplin is the most famous alumnus of the local Orr Grade School, which honored him with a commemorative marker erected by the Association for the Study of Afro-American Life and History. Today that school is a day-care center, but the marker remains.

WASHINGTON

Ethnic Minorities Memorabilia Association Museum
Franklin Street, P.O. Box 55, Old Washington Historic State Park,
Washington, AR 71868
(501) 983-2891
Hours: By appointment
Admission: Voluntary donation requested

Located on the Southwest Trail, Washington welcomed such travelers as Sam Houston, Davy Crockett, and Jim Bowie and later served as Arkansas's Confederate capital from 1863 to 1865. Today Old Washington State Park interprets the town's history from 1824 to 1875. The restored 19th-century town includes the Confederate Capitol, the 1874 Courthouse, a tavern, a blacksmith shop, a print museum, and a turn-of-the-century business building that now serves the Ethnic Minorities Memorabilia Association as a museum of regional black history and culture.

FLORIDA

Florida Division of Tourism
126 West Van Buren Street, Tallahassee, FL 32399-2000
(904) 487-1462
Hours: Mon.–Fri., 8 A.M.–5 P.M.
Ask for the "Florida Black Heritage Trail" booklet.

BUSHNELL

Dade Battlefield State Historic Site
County Road 476, Bushnell, FL 33513
(904) 793-4781
15 miles south of Wildwood near I-75
Hours: Grounds: daily, 9 A.M.–sunset. Museum: daily, 9 A.M.–5 P.M.
Admission: $2 per vehicle

As 108 cold and weary soldiers gathered in a Florida pine forest on the morning of December 28, 1835, their commander, Major Francis L. Dade, spoke words of encouragement: "Have a good heart; our difficulties and dangers are over now, and as soon as we arrive at Fort King you'll have three days to rest and keep Christmas gaily." Before the sun fell only four of those gathered would remain alive, one of whom was Dade's slave interpreter and guide, Louis Pacheco. The rest fell in the first real battle of the Second Seminole War, a white-Indian conflict whose critical component was African Americans.

(Florida's Seminole Indians had come to Colonial America's attention earlier not only for their raids into Georgia, but particularly for the sanctuary they offered to runaway slaves, some of whom were incorporated into Seminole bands and some of whom were bound to subordinated black sharecropping communities. By the time of President Washington's inauguration, a century of contact between two races under the dominion of whites had led to a broad unity of purpose and considerable interbreeding—and the Seminoles still raided into Georgia and still offered a haven to runaways. (See Fort Gadsden entry on p. 56.) As soon as Spain ceded Florida to the United States in 1819, a campaign was begun to crush the Seminoles, who by 1823 had been forced to accept a reservation system in Florida. This campaign was directed by General Andrew Jackson, who later, when President of the United States, attempted to move the Seminoles west of the Mississippi, provoking the war that opened with the annihilation of Dade's command.)

The Second Seminole War's outstanding figure was Oscela, whose principal wife was at least partially of African extraction, as were 52 of his 55 bodyguards. African Americans figured in less subordinate roles as well: The African Americans Cohia (or John Horse) and Negro Abraham led black Seminole bands allied with Oscela and Wild Cat in the seven-year war that cost the U.S. government $40 million and about 1,500 lives. The critical role of blacks in the war was acknowledged by Sidney T. Jesup, one of a series of the generals sent to command the American forces: "Throughout my operations I found negroes the most active and determined warriors; and during the conferences with the Indian chief I ascertained that they exercised an almost controlling influence over them. . . . This, you may be assured, is a negro not an Indian war."

Blacks were not only central to the war, they were also central to its conclusion. Despite pressure from white slaveholders who wished to reenslave runaways and their descendants, the 1837 treaty (which did not end a war that continued until 1842) acknowledged that the Seminoles' "negroes, their bona fide property, shall accompany them to the West." As Jesup explained, "The negroes rule the Indians, and it is important that they should feel themselves secure; if they should become alarmed and hold out, the war will be resumed."

Eventually, about 3,000 Seminoles, including 500 blacks, were removed to Oklahoma. (See Five Civilized Tribes Museum entry on p. 455; and Fort Clark entry on p. 159.) Today the Dade Battlefield State Historic Site is one of the few remnants of one of America's most costly "Indian" wars. The site includes a museum, monuments, and reproductions of the log breastworks used in the battle.

DAYTONA BEACH

Bethune-Cookman College
640 Second Avenue, Daytona Beach, FL 32114
(904) 255-1401
Hours: Cookman Home: Mon.–Fri., 9 A.M.–11:30 A.M. and 1:30 P.M.–4 P.M.
Admission: Free

Mary McLeod Bethune's drive, aided by the luck that accompanies pluck and perseverance, took this 15th child of former slaves to the White House as a national advisor to four presidents on issues of black education and racial equality. Of more lasting significance, Bethune—then a 29-year-old graduate of Scotia Seminary in North Carolina and of Moody Bible Institute, and a widow with one child and only $1.50 to spare—founded in 1904 the Daytona Normal and Industrial Institute for Girls. The first school in the state established for and by blacks that offered an education beyond the elementary level began with a single, unheated room and five pupils. Within two years there were 250 students and Bethune's work was on its way to making her nationally prominent. Merged in 1923 with Cookman Institute—a Methodist school for black males that opened in 1872—her work endures as Bethune-Cookman College.

COURTESY BETHUNE-COOKMAN COLLEGE

Mary McLeod Bethune, for five decades a champion of the African-American struggle.

In many ways, Bethune's outlook mirrored Booker T. Washington's: She stressed Christian morals and proper manners, followed by domestic skills and teacher training. Like Washington, she was a fierce fund-raiser, particularly among wealthy whites. From Coolidge and Hoover, through FDR (she was the New Deal's director of the Division of Negro Affairs in the National Youth Administration), Truman, and Eisenhower, Bethune (see entry on p. 140) marshaled her influence to advance black progress. Founder of the National Council of Negro Women, whose *Aframerican Women's Journal* advocated "that Negro History be taught in the public schools of the country," Bethune was perhaps the 20th century's most influential African-American woman.

Visitors to the Bethune-Cookman campus can tour the home in which Mrs. Bethune lived from 1920 until her death in 1955. Filled with her memorabilia, the home stands near her grave.

Museum of Arts and Sciences
1040 Museum Boulevard, Daytona Beach, FL 32114-4597
(904) 255-0285
Hours: Tue.–Fri., 9 A.M.–4 P.M.; Sat.–Sun., 12 P.M.–5 P.M.
Admission: Adults, $3; students and children, $1.50

With a permanent exhibition of 160 works of African art from 30 cultures and the long-term loan of 135 pieces of Ashanti goldwork, the African collection in the Museum of Arts and Sciences justly wins rave reviews. From the Gurunshi cat mask through the Baule mouth oracle used in divination ceremonies, and from the *Sande* (a women's secret society of the Mende) initiation ceremony item through the cloak of a Fulani *kahasa* (king), the museum gives Florida something other than sun and beaches about which to brag. The Yoruba, Guriama, Senufo, Touba, Baule, Wee, Fon, Asen, and other peoples are represented with ritual, status, and utilitarian objects—all of which are crafted with skill and an eye for beauty.

EATONVILLE

Eatonville, Zora Neale Hurston Memorial Park and Marker
Marker: 11 People Street, Eatonville, FL 32751
(407) 647-3307
Hours: Daily until sunset
Admission: Free

Twenty-seven black men gathered in August 1887 and incorporated the all-black community of Eatonville, which claims to be the oldest such town in America. Its fourth mayor, John Hurston, was a former slave, a master carpenter, and a Baptist preacher. History knows him better as the father of Zora Neale Hurston, a major contributor to the Harlem Renaissance, a master storyteller who died penniless in a welfare home, and the author of *Their Eyes Were Watching God, Tell My Horse*, and *Dust Tracks on a Road.* This last is autobiographical and describes her hometown: "I was born in a Negro town. I do not mean by that the black back-side of an average town. Eatonville, Florida, is, and was at the time of my birth, a pure Negro town—charter, mayor, council, town marshal and all." Today Eatonville remains virtually all black and offers each January a Zora Neale Hurston Festival that celebrates the author's life and works, the latter of which were rescued from obscurity by the praise of novelist Alice Walker. A marker is located in the Zora Neale Hurston Memorial Park.

MOORLAND-SPINGARN RESEARCH CENTER, HOWARD UNIVERSITY

Noted novelist Zora Neale Hurston was born in "a pure Negro town—charter, mayor, council, town marshal and all."

Zora Neale Hurston Museum of Art
227 East Kennedy Boulevard, P.O. Box 2586, Eatonville, FL 32751
(407) 647-3307
Hours: Mon.–Fri., 9 A.M.–4 P.M.
Admission: Voluntary donations requested

Featuring a portrait of Hurston executed by Arthur Rayford, the Zora Neale Hurston Museum of Art each year hosts six shows of the works of local artists.

FORT LAUDERDALE

African-American–Caribbean Cultural Center
BankAtlantic Building, 1601 South Andrews Avenue, Fort Lauderdale, FL 33316
(305) 467-4056
Hours: Tue.–Sat., 10 A.M.–4 P.M.
Admission: Free

In Fort Lauderdale, which has a significant population of black Americans and Caribbean immigrants, the various broadly related cultures of the diaspora are preserved and promoted at the African-American–Caribbean Cultural Center through temporary exhibits of arts, crafts, and history.

Museum of Art
One East Las Olas Boulevard, Fort Lauderdale, FL 33301-1807
(305) 763-6464; (305) 525-5500
Hours: Tue., 11 A.M.–9 P.M.; Wed.–Sat., 10 A.M.–5 P.M.; Sun., 12 P.M.–5 P.M.
Admission: Adults, $4; seniors over 65, $3; students with I.D., $2; members and children under 12, free; groups of 10 or more, $3 per person. Free highlight tours: Tue., 1 P.M., 6:30 P.M.; Thu.–Fri., 1 P.M.

The Yoruba *Egungun* society crocodile is eight feet long. During ceremonies commemorating the death of a loved one, three or four elaborately costumed society members dance about with the wooden carving—inside of which is a boy working the croc's mouth open and shut. The crocodile, like most of the African objects in Fort Lauderdale's Museum of Art, was created not as an object for aesthetic appreciation but as an object of spiritual power and purpose. But the Yoruba—also represented here by a pair of *oba* (chief) sanctuary doors—bring an aesthetic appreciation to everything they do. That they are not unique in this regard is evident from the museum's holdings of creations of the Mende, Guro, Bambara, Baule, Dogon, Ibo, Pende, Kuba, and Yaka, among others. Surely this museum is a must stop for all the college kids who flock here during spring break?

FORT PIERCE

Zora Neale Hurston House
1734 School Court Street, Fort Pierce, FL 33450
Hours: Daily until sunset
Admission: Not open to the public. Exterior viewing only

This *private residence* is the only known extant dwelling in which Zora Neale Hurston lived and worked. It was here in the mid-1950s that she wrote *Herod the Great*. The rejection of her manuscript completed a long slide down from the 1943 publication of her award-winning *Dust Tracks on the Road*. Though she continued to write, it was as a reporter and columnist for the *Fort Pierce Chronicle*, rather than as a novelist.

GAINESVILLE

Josiah Walls Historical Marker
University Avenue between First and Second streets, Gainesville, FL 32601
Hours: Daily until sunset
Admission: Free

The Josiah Walls Historical Marker commemorates Florida's first black congressman. Born a slave, Walls was impressed into the Confederate army and later joined the Union ranks voluntarily. First elected to the U.S. House of Representatives in 1870, Walls served three terms, being denied renomination in 1876 by white Republicans in Florida who sought to combat growing anti-Reconstruction sentiment by nominating an all-white, moderate ticket. Walls is best remembered for his concentration on issues of black education, including his sponsorship of a bill that led to the college now known as Florida Agricultural and Mechanical University.

JACKSONVILLE

Jacksonville Convention & Visitors Bureau
6 East Bay Street, Suite 200, Jacksonville, FL 32202
(800) 733-2668; (904) 798-9148
Hours: Mon.–Fri., 8 A.M.–5 P.M.

Minority Convention and Tourism Division
6 East Bay Street, Suite 200, Jacksonville, FL 32202
(904) 798-9105
Hours: Mon.–Fri., 8 A.M.–5 P.M.

American Beach
On Amelia Island, about 40 miles northeast of Jacksonville by way of Florida A1A, between Fernandina Beach and the Amelia Island Plantations
Hours: Daily, 24 hours
Admission: Free

From the 1930s to the early 1960s, carloads of folk from as far away as Tupelo, Mississippi, church buses from Jacksonville filled with local children and hoards of fraternity brothers and sorority sisters from Morehouse and Spelman headed for American Beach, *the* Atlantic Ocean social hub for African Americans in a South so segregated that it would deny the ocean's waves to black folks. American Beach was the product of the remarkable A. L. Lewis, founder of the Afro-American Life Insurance Co. of Jacksonville and one of the Jim Crow South's few black millionaires. By the 1920s, his firm had become a staple of southern black existence, its 10-cents-a-week policies securing burials and tiny annuities for all but the desperately poor. After the depression forced the closing of the city's sole black beach, Lewis purchased several hundred acres on Amelia Island as a recreation center for his employees. Soon middle-class blacks from Alabama and Georgia began buying lots from Lewis, happy to have a summer home for their families away from the omnipresent "whites-only" signs (and doubtless, away from whites as well). Working-class African Americans then began day-tripping to American Beach; soon they were followed by small black businesses, and in no time the area was jammed and jammin'. What the pressure of segregation created, integration destroyed, as black folks headed toward that which for so long had been denied them. Today American Beach is under a new pressure: escalating taxes and condos. But locals who remember the glory days when a black beach community lived without the necessity of asking whites for anything are seeking to secure listing on the National Register of Historic Places so as to limit development and gentrification.

Centennial Hall, Edward Waters College
1750 Kings Road, Jacksonville, FL 32209
(904) 355-3030
Hours: Mon.–Fri., 8 A.M.–5 P.M.
Admission: Free

Established in 1866 by the African Methodist Episcopal Church as Florida's first independent institution of higher learning for African Americans, Edward Waters College features the three-story Centennial Hall, built in 1916 to commemorate the 100th anniversary of A.M.E.'s founding. A. Philip Randolph (see entries on pp. 202 and 267), the nation's foremost spokesman for black labor and the first president of the all-black International Brotherhood of Sleeping Car Porters, graduated from Waters.

Kingsley Plantation
Fort George Island, 11676 Palmetto Avenue, Jacksonville, FL 32226
(904) 251-3537
15 miles northwest of Jacksonville
Hours: Grounds: daily, 9 A.M.–5 P.M. Tours: Thu.–Mon., 9:30 A.M., 11 A.M., 1:30 P.M., and 3 P.M.
Admission: Grounds, free; tours, $1

Florida's oldest example of a slave-based plantation system dates to 1792, when the king of Spain granted Fort George Island to John McQueen, who had fled Charleston to escape his creditors. In 1804 the island, still a Spanish possession, was sold to J. H. McIntosh, whose involvement in the "Patriot's Revolt," an unsuccessful attempt to free east Florida from Spanish rule, forced him to flee to Georgia in 1814. The island then became the possession of Zephaniah Kingsley, who had made his money in the African slave trade. The Kingsley Plantation—about 750 acres of land, of which perhaps 500 were cleared for cultivation—was principally under Sea Island cotton, though rice, sugarcane, corn, and beans were also planted.

Kingsley, whose total Florida holdings eventually included 30,000 acres, four major plantations, and more than 200 slaves, held unconventional views about most everything, scorning organized religion, supporting (and practicing) common-law interracial marriages, and defending a patriarchal and paternalistic form of slavery that included refusing to separate family members and permitting slaves the opportunity to purchase their freedom. He had ten children by three different women, all of whom had started life in slavery. (Kingsley provided liberally in his will for all his children and their mothers.) His acknowledged wife was Anna Madgigne Jai. Originally purchased in Havana as a slave for Kingsley's mother, she bore him four children and ultimately helped him run his plantations. Alarmed by the escalating constraints against free people of color, Kingsley in the 1830s urged his children to move to Haiti to protect their freedom. In 1839 Kingsley took 53 slaves, his three "wives," and eight mulatto children to Haiti. There he ran a small farming colony from which his slaves either ran away or served an indentured apprenticeship before being freed. After Kingsley's death, Anna returned to Florida, where she strove for ten years to receive her share of his estate, the inheritance of which was challenged by Kingsley's sister, Martha K. Whistler (the model for the famous painting of "Whistler's Mother"), who could not believe her brother would leave his fortune to a black woman. Anna died in 1870 in Florida, where she had continued to work her land, though now with sharecroppers rather than slaves.

At Kingsley, the "task"—as distinct from "gang"—system of slavery was used. White overseers and their slave "drivers" assigned, on a daily basis, specific work to individual slaves. A typical daily task was ginning 20 to 30 pounds of cotton or, for a cooper, making three barrels; field tasks were measured in units of a quarter of an acre (105 feet square). Upon completion of the task, the slave was free to spend the remainder of the day (typically, from 2 P.M. on) as he or she wished. This system was common on the rice and cotton plantations of the Sea Islands, of which Fort George is the southernmost. (The far more tightly supervised—and sunup to "cain't see"—gang labor was common on tobacco and sugar plantations as well as the cotton plantations of Virginia and the middle and western South.)

Between 35 and 100 slaves labored at Kingsley. Their 32 cabins, arranged in a semicircle, 16 on either side of the road, were constructed of "tabby," a primitive type of concrete made of sand, limestone, water, and crushed and whole oyster shells, and had roofs composed of cedar shingles.

Today's visitor to Kingsley can tour the remains of 23 of these cabins as well as the main house, the kitchen house, the barn/carriage house, and the nearby McQueen House, which was Anna Jai's residence.

LAKE CITY

Florida Sports Hall of Fame
201 Florida Sports Hall of Fame, Lake City, FL 32055
(904) 758-1310
Hours: Daily, 9 A.M.–6:45 P.M.
Admission: Adults, $2; under 12, free with adult

Althea Gibson, Willie Gallimore, and Paul Warfield are but a few of the many African-American sports legends whose careers are traced at the Florida Sports Hall of Fame. Exhibits and video displays, including game footage, compete with computerized games that let children (and their parents) test their skills against those of the greats.

MARATHON

Pigeon Key Historic District
Off U.S. Highway 1 at Mile Marker 45, Marathon, FL 33050
Hours: Daily until sunset
Admission: Not open to the public. Exterior viewing only

A railroad construction work camp in the Pigeon Key Historic District includes a 1912 "Negro Workers Cottage" whose exterior can be viewed and offers insight into the life and conditions of unorganized black labor in the Jim Crow South of the early 20th century.

Adderlyville and Adderly House

c/o Florida Keys Museum of Natural History, 5550 Overseas Highway, Marathon, FL 33050
(305) 743-9100
Hours: Museum: Mon.–Sat., 9 A.M.–5 P.M.; Sun., 12 P.M.–5 P.M.
Adderlyville/Adderly House: tours by appointment
Admission: Free

A 63-acre preserve, owned by the Florida Keys Land and Sea Trust, contains Adderlyville and the Adderly House, which will become a living history museum once restoration is completed in the summer of 1994. Adderly House, on the National Registry of Historic Sites, is believed to be the only structure of its kind in the Florida Keys. Of a "tabby" construction traced back to Africa, the house is built of limestone, crushed rock, and coral "mortared" by a crushed oyster shell mixture. The home was built by Bahamians George and Olivia Adderly, who occupied it from 1903 to 1948. The museum has a wall that discusses Adderlyville, a turn-of-the-century black settlement that is not yet fully restored.

MARIANNA

T. T. Fortune Birthplace

Joseph Russ, Jr. House, 310 West Lafayette Street, Marianna, FL 32446
Hours: Daily until sunset
Admission: Not open to the public. Exterior viewing only

Born a slave to a skilled slave father who during Reconstruction proved so effective an advocate for African Americans that the family was driven from their Florida home by the Ku Klux Klan, Timothy Thomas Fortune became the most radical and influential black journalist and publisher of the late 19th century. His *New York Age* (1887), the most widely read black newspaper in America, was secretly funded by Booker T. Washington, who publicly maintained a far less militant posture. In addition to propagating the use of the term "Afro-American," Fortune (see entry on p. 287) was also the driving force behind the formation of the National Afro-American League (1889), the country's first civil rights organization, which predated the NAACP by 20 years. Fortune's later years were far from blessed: Financial failure, conflicts with Washington, condemnation by W.E.B. Du Bois, and a nervous breakdown were his fate before recovery and a partial conversion to the Garvey movement, whose journal, *Negro World*, Fortune edited, closed out his life in 1928.

That life began in 1856 in Marianna, near what is now the Joseph Russ, Jr. House, a *private residence* that was then the main plantation house of the family who owned Fortune and his parents. So violently determined to maintain white supremacy was Marianna that the Fortunes and other local African Americans were not emancipated until 1868, when the Freedmen's Bureau sent a troop of black soldiers from Philadelphia to enforce the law of the land.

MIAMI

Greater Miami Convention & Visitors Bureau
701 Brickell Avenue, Suite 2700, Miami, FL 33131
(305) 539-3000
Hours: Mon.–Fri., 8 A.M.–5 P.M.

Call the bureau or the following numbers for information about these African-American–related festivals: Arabian Nights Festival (three days in May); Black Heritage Month Celebration (305 347-3007; February); Black Music Festival (June); Carib-Fest Miami (September); Haitian Festival (May); Jamaica Awareness Day Reggae Festival (August); Martin Luther King Parade & Festival (January); Miami Bahamas Goombay Festival (305 445-8292; May and June); Miami Jazz Festival (five days in June); Sunstreet Festival (November).

Miami-Dade Chamber of Commerce
9190 Biscayne Boulevard, Suite 201, Miami, FL 33138
(305) 751-8648
Hours: Mon.–Fri., 9 A.M.–5 P.M.

Ask about its "Visitors' Guide to Black Miami."

Black Archives History and Research Foundation
Joseph Caleb Community Center, 5400 NW 22nd Avenue, Miami, FL 33142
(305) 638-6064; (305) 638-6375
Hours: Mon.–Fri., 10 A.M.–5 P.M.
Admission: Voluntary donation requested

The cross-cultural fertilization of southern black and Caribbean, particularly Bahamian, experiences of the diaspora (to mention nothing of the Hispanic input) makes southern Florida a fascinating mélange. The mixture—which is not without friction—is explored at the Black Archives, History and Research Foundation of South Florida through documents, manuscripts, photographs, field trips, and works of art.

Black Heritage Museum
Box 570327, Miami, FL 33257-0327 (*Formerly Miracle Center Mall, 3301 Coral Way, Miami, FL 33131. Operations disrupted by Hurricane Andrew*)
(305) 252-3535
Hours: Call for appointment
Admission: Free. Tours: $1 per person

Masks, carvings, and utilitarian objects created by the craftsmen of the Pende, Ashanti, Kuba, Yaka, Baluba, Akan, Dan, Bayuka, Chokwe, Baule, Senufo, and other African peoples can be found at the Black Heritage Museum. Complementing the continent's profusions are works of art by the Haitian diaspora, including paintings by Pierre Toseth, Florestant, and Berjo.

Coconut Grove
Charles Avenue, Miami, FL 33133
Hours: Daily, 24 hours
Admission: Free

Until Henry Flagler pushed his railroad south from Palm Beach in 1895, Miami was but an undistinguished grouping of small, tin-roofed houses and one hotel. Not long before Flagler's enterprise, Miami's first black community took shape in an area now known as Coconut Grove. Many of its pioneers were from the Bahamas and brought their celebrations with them. By 1915 Coconut Grove's residents enjoyed a midwinter break with their Magic Knights of Dade Festival, the forerunner of the now-famous Orange Bowl Festival. Many of the original frame houses built in turn-of-the-century Coconut Grove still stand, yet more testimony to the contributions of America's immigrants.

The Miami Times
900 NW 54th Street, Miami, FL 33127
(305) 757-1147
Hours: By appointment only
Admission: Free

In 1923 the Bahamian immigrant Henry E. S. Reeves launched the *Miami Times*. Through the 1930s depression, world war, hurricanes, financial losses, and mundane mechanical problems, Reeves kept afloat the South's most influential black newspaper. Today the *Times* enters its seventh decade of family ownership. Its files are a primary source of information on the black experience in Florida and other southern states.

OLUSTEE

Olustee Battlefield State Historic Site
P.O. Box 40, Olustee, FL 32072
(904) 752-3866
2½ miles east of Olustee, on U.S. 90
Hours: Park: 8 A.M.–5 P.M. Center: Thu.–Mon., 9 A.M.–5 P.M.
Admission: Free

Early in 1864, the Union, utilizing its command of the seas, sent an expedition under General Seymour from Hilton Head Island, South Carolina, to Jacksonville, Florida, from whence Seymour was to advance and disrupt the Confederacy's supply route from central Florida; recruit black troops; seize stored cotton, turpentine, and timber; and induce Unionists in east Florida to form a loyalist government. Marching his 5,500 men and 16 cannons due west from Jacksonville, Seymour ran into 5,200 Confederate troops near Olustee and began what proved to be Florida's largest battle of the Civil War. Within four hours, almost 3,000 men fell dead or wounded. As Union casualties were twice that of the Confederates and as Seymour retreated back to Jacksonville, the battle is reckoned a clear Union defeat. Of the Union casualties, one-third were black, most prominently from the 8th Regiment of the United States Colored Troops and the 54th Massachusetts regiments. Unlike the 54th, the troops of the 8th entered combat largely untrained and unblooded. As one of its officers wrote home about his men: "We have had very little practice in firing, and, though they could stand and be killed, they could not kill a concealed enemy fast enough to satisfy my feelings." Sergeant Swails from the 54th became that regiment's first black officer, for the coolness and valor he displayed in this battle. Visitors to the Olustee Battlefield State Historic Site can view the monument to the participating troops, walk the battlefield, which is marked with interpretive signs, visit the interpretive center, and, during February, watch historical re-enactors bring the battle to life . . . and death.

ORLANDO

Orlando Museum of Art
2416 North Hills, Orlando, FL 32803
(407) 896-4231
Hours: Tue.–Fri., 10 A.M.–5 P.M.; weekends, 12 P.M.–5 P.M.
Admission: Free

The Orlando Museum of Art houses a small collection of West African sculpture. The carvings of the Yoruba, Dan, Baule, Ibo, and Dogon and some Benin bronzes make up the bulk of the material. Recently, however, this material was taken off display. It has been replaced with the loan of portions of the Paul and Ruth Tishman Collection. Bronze heads, armlets, and salt cellars from Benin and house posts, divination trays, and *Shango* figures of the Yoruba permit comparisons of two of the African continent's major art-producing cultures.

PENSACOLA

Daniel "Chappie" James Birthplace
1606 North Alcaniz Street, Pensacola, FL 32503
Hours: Daily until sunset
Admission: Free

Though only the front steps that led to the house in which he was born in the segregated Pensacola of 1920 remain, the Daniel "Chappie" James Birthplace recalls an African-American hero. After 179 combat missions in two wars, decorations for valor, and a face-to-face confrontation with Libya's Muammar Qadhafi when the Libyan leader sought to seize the U.S. air base in his country, Daniel "Chappie" James became the first African-American four-star general in the history of the American armed forces. A small shelter covers the still-extant front steps, which are painted white and labeled "Chappie's First Steps." In the house James's mother ran a school for black children.

Julee Cottage Museum
201 East Zaragoza Street, Pensacola, FL 32501
(904) 444-8905
Hours: Mon.–Sat., 10 A.M.–4 P.M.; also, from Memorial Day to Labor Day, Sun., 10 A.M.–4 P.M.
Admission: Tour (includes other sites): adults, $5.50; military and seniors, $4.50; children 4–16, $2.25; under 4, free

Built in the first decade of the 19th century, the wood-frame building once owned by Julee Panton, a free woman of color who tradition records as having been dedicated to purchasing the freedom of enslaved African Americans, is now the Julee Cottage Museum. The cottage serves as a black history museum, concentrating on the African-American heritage in west Florida. It has been rehabilitated rather than restored and is Pensacola's sole surviving example of "to the sidewalk" construction, a form that is reminiscent of the Creole cottages of New Orleans' French Quarter.

ST. AUGUSTINE

Castillo de San Marcos National Monument
One Castillo Drive East, St. Augustine, FL 32084-3699
(904) 829-6506
Hours: Labor Day–Memorial Day: daily, 9 A.M.–5:15 P.M. Rest of year: daily, 9 A.M.–5:45 P.M.
Admission: Adults, $1; seniors and under 13, free

Though formally discovered by the Spanish in 1513, Florida was not settled by Europeans and their African property for half a century. Typically, settlement became an issue because of foreign intrusion. In 1564, near what became St. Augustine, the French established Fort Caroline, from which they were expelled the following year after land and sea battles that saw the losers summarily executed. Upon victory, the Spanish formally established St. Augustine, the oldest city in what would become the United States. Sparse settlement in Florida (which then extended into what is now Georgia) and South Carolina during the next century left little imprint. However, as the British replaced the French as the local threat, Florida's proximity to the slave-based South Carolina rice and sugar plantations loomed larger and larger on the horizon of enslaved black labor. Gingerly attempting to undermine the recent British colony in Carolina, a Spanish royal proclamation in 1686 promised freedom to runaway slaves who converted to Catholicism, and in the same year a Spanish slave raiding party attacked Port Royal. The following year eight men, two women, and a child are recorded as seeking sanctuary in Florida, the first of hundreds on what would prove to be America's original Underground Railroad.

In fact, however, the hoped-for refuge with the Spanish would prove to be ambiguous, if not illusory. For some decades, the Spanish were uncertain how to handle the runaways, their British masters, and the British crown. Very infrequently, the slaves were returned to their former masters. Somewhat more frequently, the runaways found themselves reenslaved, though Spanish slavery at least offered them access to the courts, the right to preclude family separation, and the right to own property (which by extension implied the right to purchase oneself from slavery). Others found themselves in a status of indentured servitude, particularly regarding their obligation to serve in the Spanish militia; still others found themselves ambiguously free.

In 1733 two more royal proclamations were issued, one ending the intermittently observed policy of reimbursing the runaways' masters, the other commending the black Spanish militia composed of runaways for their staunch defense of St. Augustine against a 1728 British colonial attack and reinforcing the promise of freedom in return for four years of royal service. Even after 1733, Florida's Spanish governor, supported by the auxiliary bishop of Cuba residing in Florida, declined the appeals of Melendez, the black commander of the black militia, to act fully on the crown's decree. Finally, in the spring of 1738, the new Spanish governor, Manuel de Montiano, released from slavery those who had fled for freedom only to find new masters. Montiano organized the newly free into a militia and settled them two miles from St. Augustine in a thatched hut village he named Santa Teresa de la Gracia Real de Mose, which thus became the first legally sanctioned free black community in what is now the United States (and, by no means incidentally, the first line of defense against the English to the north). Montiano went so far as to request the governor in Havana to secure the return of those runaways sold to slavery on the island, whom he also wished to settle in Mose. Montiano's underlying message quickly percolated north and within six months of his original emancipation, 23 men, women, and children fleeing South Carolina arrived in St. Augustine and were settled at Mose.

In 1739 Mose was fortified to protect the former slaves from Indian attack. In 1740 an invading English colonial force from the newly settled Georgia attacked St. Augustine, ravaged Mose (whose inhabitants had been withdrawn for safety within Castillo de San Marcos, St. Augustine's fortress), and were defeated in battle and driven back to Georgia by a Spanish force that included 20 freedmen. After the battle, the freedmen were reluctant to return to Mose, which they ultimately did in 1752 only under compulsion and after it had been refortified. Mose was abandoned by its inhabitants, who moved to Cuba, in 1763, when Spain ceded Florida to England. While Spanish rule returned to Florida in 1784, Mose's former inhabitants did not.

Though there is no permanent exhibit on America's first free, armed black community, the Castillo de San Marcos National Monument in St. Augustine has an exhibit on the history of free blacks during Spain's period of rule of

Florida. The Florida Museum of Natural History also has a traveling historical and archaeological exhibit on Fort Mose.

SUMATRA

Fort Gadsden Historic Site
Florida 65, P.O. Box 157, Sumatra, FL 32328
(904) 670-8988
6 miles south of Sumatra, about 26 miles north of Apalachicola
Hours: Mon., Thu.–Sun., 8 A.M.–5 P.M.
Admission: Per vehicle (8 or fewer), $3.25; per person and buses (more than 8 people), $1 each; school groups, free

Spanish rule in Florida during the first decades of the 19th century found itself pressed on all sides: War with Britain in 1804 brought the threat of English ships and soldiers, while the new American republic looked south longingly and was determined to prevent the return of the British. Less than a decade later, Britain was allied with the Spanish royalty dispossessed by Napoleon—and the new American republic still looked south longingly. From 1810, President Madison's administration maintained discreet contact with the so-called Patriots Revolt, American settlers in Florida who sought to detach at least part of the territory and annex it to the United States.

With the onset of the War of 1812, the rivalries of three nations came to a head in Florida. The British built and provisioned a fort on the lower Apalachicola River in northwestern Florida, which they staffed with a force composed of runaway slaves, Seminole Indians, and Afro-Seminoles and from which they raided into southern Georgia. Following the war, the British abandoned the fort; the multiracial troops remained, however, and what had been known as the "British Fort" gained the name "Fort Negro." By whatever name, it remained a haven and a lure for escaped slaves—and hence an open wound to the slaveholders in Georgia and the Carolinas. It was also a base from which the Seminoles raided north. (See Dade Battlefield entry on p. 42.) These attacks provided the grounds for the First Seminole War—and the excuse to seize Florida from Spain.

In 1816 Andrew Jackson, fresh from his trouncing of the Creeks and his triumph at the Battle of New Orleans and still in command of U.S. military forces along the southern border, ordered General Gaines to take a force of regular U.S. troops, marines, and a detachment of Creek mercenaries into Spanish Florida, destroy Fort Negro, and "restore the stolen negroes . . . to their rightful owners." Gaines's river boats shelled the fort. In the course of the battle, a shell landed in the fort's ammunition dump, causing a massive explosion that destroyed the fort, killed 270 of its defenders, wounded 64, and left but three men uninjured. The fort's black commander was summarily executed, the fatally injured were ignored, and the surviving men, women, and children were marched back to slavery in Georgia. Three years later, after Jackson had captured Pensacola, the Spanish conceded their inability to hold onto their possession and ceded Florida to America in exchange for $5 million.

Today's visitor to the Fort Gadsden State Historic Site can trace the network of trenches and breastworks that guarded an armed and free black/Indian community.

TALLAHASSEE

Black Archives, Research Center and Museum
Carnegie Library, Florida A&M University, Tallahassee, FL 32307
(904) 599-3020
Hours: Mon.–Fri., 8 A.M.–5 P.M.; weekends, by appointment only
Admission: Free

Harriet Tubman's eyeglasses, leg irons worn by a slave, handbills offering a reward for runaway human property, 300-year-old maps of Africa, original copies of *The Liberator,* "Coon" memorabilia, African art and artifacts, the correspondence of Mary McLeod Bethune and of Dr. Martin Luther King, Jr., "whites-only" signs, skin lighteners, and a great deal more that touches on the history of the diaspora in this land can be found at the Black Archives, Research Center and Museum. Located on the campus of Florida Agricultural and Mechanical University, a school that traces its roots to a bill offered in the U.S. Congress by the state's first black congressman, the museum is the black highlight of Tallahassee.

Florida Agricultural and Mechanical University
South Adams Street, Tallahassee, FL 32307
(904) 599-3000
Hours: Daily until sunset
Admission: Free

Florida's oldest historically black university, established in 1887 as the Florida State Normal and Industrial School for Negroes and first presided over by the Sierra Leone–born Thomas DeSaille Tucker, Florida A&M is home to a Carnegie Library, the first to be built on a black land-grant college, and to the Black Archives, Research Center and Museum.

Gibbs Cottage
Florida A&M University, South Adams Street, Tallahassee, FL 32307
(904) 599-3413
Hours: Daily until sunset
Admission: Not open to the public. Exterior viewing only

Thomas Gibbs, perhaps Florida's most influential black politician of the late 19th and early 20th centuries, was a member of the state legislature in 1887 and introduced the bill that resulted in the founding of Florida Agricultural and Mechanical School, the state's oldest historically black college. The Gibbs Cottage, constructed in 1894, is on the Florida A&M campus and its exterior can be viewed.

Frenchtown
Bounded by Park Avenue, MLK Boulevard, West Brevard Street, and Dewey Street, Tallahassee, FL 32304
Hours: Daily, 24 hours
Admission: Free

Frenchtown, an 18-block area so named because it was the center of European settlement during the territorial period, became the primary residential area for emancipated slaves and has remained a continuously black neighborhood since 1865. Though commercial development has changed the appearance of the area, it retains notable examples of the early 20th-century vernacular architecture popular with African Americans.

John G. Riley House
419 West Jefferson, Tallahassee, FL 32302
(904) 224-0697
Hours: Mon.–Fri., 9 A.M.–5 P.M.
Admission: Free

Largely self-taught, John G. Riley (1857–1954) became the principal of Lincoln Academy, the only source of secondary education for African Americans in Tallahassee following the Civil War. The John G. Riley House, built in 1890 and located but a few blocks from the state Capitol, now serves both as a cultural center preserving local black heritage and as the Tallahassee headquarters of the NAACP.

Tallahassee Museum of History and Natural Science
Museum Drive, Tallahassee, FL 32310
(904) 576-1636
Hours: Mon.–Sat., 9 A.M.–5 P.M.; Sun., 12:30 P.M.–5 P.M.
Admission: Adults 16–61, $5; seniors 62 and older, $4; children 4–15, $3; under 4, free

The Tallahassee Museum of History and Natural Science has two structures appealing to those interested in black heritage. The Bethlehem Missionary Baptist Church, built in 1937 by a congregation that dates to the 1850s, was restored by Florida A&M and now offers exhibits that explore the role of religion as a bond among slaves and the role of religious leaders in black political activity dating back to the 1870s. The Concord Schoolhouse was built in the 1870s for the children of former slaves. This one-room structure was used as a Tallahassee public school until 1968.

Tallahassee Old City Cemetery
MLK Boulevard and Park Avenue, Tallahassee, FL 32301
(904) 891-8712
Hours: Daily until sunset
Admission: Free

Established in 1829 by the Florida Territorial Council as the capital's public burying ground, the Tallahassee Old City Cemetery was segregated, with slaves and free blacks being buried in the western half of the grounds. Though the original dividing fence has been removed, the furrow it has left in the ground offers evidence of its former presence.

TAMPA

Busch Gardens
3000 East Busch Boulevard and 40th Street, Tampa, FL 33674
(813) 988-5171
Hours: Daily, 9:30 A.M.–6 P.M. Extended summer hours and selected holidays, 9 A.M.–7 P.M.
Admission: $20.95 (includes all sites); under 2, free

Busch Gardens' 300 acres offer visitors a look into the wildlife and the social life of the Mother Continent. This African theme park has opened a three-acre habitat featuring gorillas and chimpanzees in a tropical forest environment, which complements seven other distinctly themed slices of Africa that include more than 3,000 animals, marketplaces, village life, and the rapids of the Congo River.

Museum of African-American Art
1308 North Marion Street, Tampa, FL 33602
(813) 272-2466
Hours: Tue.–Sat., 10 A.M.–4:30 P.M.; Sun., 1 P.M.–4:30 P.M.
Admission: Suggested donation, $2

Much of wartime Washington, D.C., may not have noticed, but in 1943 what shortly thereafter became the first chartered collection of African-American art in the United States opened at the Barnett-Aden Gallery. This collection, arguably the foremost artistic representation of the diaspora's achievement in North America, now permanently resides at the Museum of African-American Art in Tampa. More than 100 paintings and 30 sculptures from 81 artists—including Hale Woodruff, Romare Bearden, and Laura Wheeler—give the visitor a black perspective on this nation's culture and history from the late 1800s to the present.

GEORGIA

Georgia Department of Tourism
P.O. Box 1776, 285 Peachtree Center Avenue, Suite 1000, Atlanta, GA 30301-1776
(800) 847-4842; (404) 656-3590
Hours: Mon.–Fri., 8 A.M.–5 P.M.

Ask for the "Georgia Black Heritage" brochure.

ALBANY

Albany Museum of Art
311 Meadowlark Drive, Albany, GA 31707
(912) 439-8400
Hours: Tue.–Sat., 10 A.M.–5 P.M.; Sun., 2 P.M.–5 P.M.
Admission: Adults, $3; seniors, $2; students, $1

The Albany Museum of Art has a permanent collection of more than 1,500 objects of art and craft from 18 sub-Saharan African cultures. While the bulk of its holdings is West African (for example, Ashanti, Dan, Yoruba, Gola, Mende), the museum is notable for its Ethiopian Coptic crosses and votive pieces. East Africa is also represented; since many of these cultures are nomadic, though, the pieces tend to be small and utilitarian, with jewelry and basketry predominating.

ANDERSONVILLE

Andersonville National Historic Site
Highway 49 North, Route 1, Box 800, Andersonville, GA 31711
(912) 924-0343
Hours: Daily, 8:30 A.M.–5 P.M.
Admission: Free

With more than 30,000 Union prisoners of war crowded into a facility designed for 10,000 and with the Confederacy struggling to feed its own troops toward the war's end, the Andersonville Prison Camp became little more than a way station on the path to the grave. Fully a quarter of the camp's population wasted and died in the camp's year of operation, including Corporal James Henry Gooding of the black 54th Massachusetts Volunteers. In the autumn of 1863, Gooding had written to President Lincoln denouncing the discriminatory pay that black troops received: African Americans of all ranks received $7 monthly, while white pay ranged through the ranks from $13 to $30. Gooding joined his comrades in the 54th Massachusetts in a unique protest—they continued to serve the Union but refused to accept second-class wages, preferring instead to fight without pay. Wounded and captured at the Battle of Olustee in Florida (see Olustee Battlefield State Historic Site entry on p. 52) in February 1864, Gooding died in Andersonville before the U.S. Congress later in 1864 authorized pay by rank rather than by race.

ATLANTA

Atlanta Convention & Visitors Bureau
223 Peachtree Street, NE, Atlanta, GA 30303
(404) 521-6600
Hours: Mon.–Fri., 8:30 A.M.–5:30 P.M.

APEX Museum
135 Auburn Avenue, NE, Atlanta, GA 30312
(404) 521-2739
Hours: Tue., Thu., Fri., Sat., 10 A.M.–5 P.M.; Wed., 10 A.M.–6 P.M.; in Feb., June, July, Aug.: Sun., 1 P.M.–5 P.M.
Admission: Adults, $2; seniors and children under 12, $1

"Sweet Auburn," black Atlanta's main artery, was the home turf of young Martin Luther King, Jr., who was born in the home of his grandfather, the Reverend A. D. Williams, pastor of the Ebenezer Baptist Church. (See entry on p. 64.) Churches, banks, insurance companies, doctors' and dentists' offices, beauty and funeral parlors, a business college, and a newspaper testified to the drive of an emerging business class that arose a generation after the Civil War and that has continued its expansion to the present day. APEX, the African-American Panoramic Experience, celebrates this local heritage with audio-visual presentations, displays of artifacts, and art exhibits.

Trevor Arnett Library
Clark Atlanta University, 111 James P. Brawley Drive, Atlanta, GA 30314
(404) 880-8000
Hours: Daily, 9 A.M.–11 P.M.
Admission: Free

Original manuscripts by and personal papers of Arna Bontemps, Countee Cullen, Claude McKay, and other prominent literati of the Harlem Renaissance, a signed poem by Phillis Wheatley, and antebellum publications relating to slavery are held at the Trevor Arnett Library on the campus of the historically black Clark Atlanta University. The library's Waddell Art Gallery houses works by Henry O. Tanner, Elizabeth Catlett, John Biggers, and leading modern black artists.

Atlanta Life Insurance Headquarters
100 Auburn Avenue, NE, Atlanta, GA 30312
(404) 659-2100
Hours: Mon.–Fri., 10 A.M.–6 P.M.
Admission: Free

The headquarters (1920–1980) of the Atlanta Life Insurance Co., the nation's second largest African-American-owned insurance firm, has a lobby display tracing the company's history and that of its founder, the prominent black entrepreneur Alonzo Herndon. (See entry on p. 65.)

Atlanta University Center
James P. Brawley Center, SW, Atlanta, GA 30314
(404) 522-8980
Hours: Library: Mon.–Thu., 8:30 A.M.–midnight; Fri., 8:30 A.M.–5 P.M.; Sat., 10 A.M.–6 P.M.; Sun., 2 P.M.–10 P.M.
Admission: Free

The Atlanta University Center defines synergy, bringing together six of the country's most important historically black colleges: Clark Atlanta, Morris Brown, Morehouse, Morehouse School of Medicine, Interdenominational Theological Center (an amalgam of Gammon Theological and five other predominantly black seminaries), and Spelman. For more than a century, these institutions have provided the intellectual underpinning for a people's advance. The center itself is largely an administrative entity; the one site of interest is the library, which is shared by all the affiliated colleges and which houses substantial African-American archival material.

Birth Home of Martin Luther King, Jr.
501 Auburn Avenue, NE, Atlanta, GA 30312
(404) 331-3920
Hours: June–Aug.: daily, 10 A.M.–7 P.M.; Sept.–May: daily, 10 A.M.–5 P.M.
Admission: Free

On the 15th of January, 1929, a nine-room, two-story house presided over by the pastor of Atlanta's Ebenezer Baptist Church echoed with the first cries of a child whose voice would later be heard around the world. It was an apt birthplace for the "young M.L.," as the child was commonly called. Son and grandson of preachers, Martin Luther King, Jr., was born in, nurtured by, and died in the black church, historically the principal outlet for expression of the African-American people.

For 12 years King and his brother and sister, parents, and grandparents shared the Queen Anne residence in the midst of Atlanta's black middle-class Auburn neighborhood. Here King's childhood centered upon family (his grandfather

COURTESY OF CHRISTINE KING FARRIS

and father sequentially pastored Ebenezer Baptist Church), the Baptist faith (the five-year-old King and his sister, Christine, joined the church in 1934 at a revival held by a visiting evangelist), and the thriving segregated Auburn neighborhood (a few blocks from King's childhood home was a black business district that included banks, insurance companies, offices of doctors and dentists, a newspaper, a library, and a business college). In 1944 the young teenager, not yet out of high school, passed a special examination and entered Atlanta's historically black Morehouse College, from which he graduated in 1948. That same year Ebenezer Baptist Church ordained him to the Christian ministry. He appeared set on his life's path, and spent the next seven years earning theological degrees, first at the Baptist Crozer Seminary in Pennsylvania and then at Boston University, which awarded him a doctorate in 1955. Two events in these years of schooling stand out: King's 1953 marriage to Coretta Scott and his 1954 acceptance of the pastorate of Montgomery, Alabama's black Dexter Avenue Baptist Church.

The Dexter appointment, ironically the result of the upscale congregation's unease with the militant civil rights posture of King's predecessor, the Reverend Vernon Johns, was the start of Dr. King's renown and of his public involvement in the civil rights struggle that he would come to personify. Little more than a year after King's accession, Rosa Parks, a 43-year-old seamstress and former secretary of the Montgomery NAACP, refused to vacate her seat on the city bus to a white man, as Jim Crow law demanded. Her refusal sparked the famous Montgomery Bus Boycott, whose leading spokesman the eloquent King became. Though King's arrest, trial, and conviction (his first) for conspiring to boycott, and the firebombing of his home were by no means unique to black Montgomery, they brought him to the attention of the national media, which he used with masterful skill.

A year after the boycott's conclusion in 1956, King played a leading role in founding the Southern Christian Leadership Conference (SCLC). The SCLC provided him with an autonomous vehicle to promote his newly acquired political leverage in the nation's black community. Staying out of the embrace of the NAACP and other established civil rights groups, and accenting direct action, resolute nonviolence, and the moral right to disobey immoral laws, King symbolized the shift of the black struggle from the courts to the streets. With an independent organizational base in the SCLC, King's civil rights career never looked back; indeed, it took such a prominent place in his life that he resigned the pastorate of Dexter Avenue in 1960 and returned to Ebenezer Baptist Church. There he shared pastoral duties with his father.

Throughout the 1960s King seemed to embody the southern civil rights struggle, a struggle rooted in the nonviolent, mass rejection of segregation and its legal underpinnings. Aiding the formation of the Student Nonviolent Coordinating Committee (SNCC) in 1960; leading the antisegregationist struggle in Albany, Georgia, in 1961; taking a prominent role in the Birmingham movement of 1963; dominating the famous 1963 March on Washington with his "I have a dream" address; moving on to St. Augustine, Florida, and the struggle there in 1964; and returning to Alabama in 1965 for the historic Selma-to-Montgomery Voting Rights March, Dr. King garnered not only a Nobel Peace Prize for his advocacy of nonviolent resistance to injustice but also continued media coverage—and continued threats against his life. In 1966 Dr. King took his campaign north, to Chicago and its Cicero suburbs, where housing discrimination was rife. A year later he was prominent in the anti–Vietnam War campaign. A year after this he was dead, gunned down in Memphis, Tennessee, where he was aiding striking garbage collectors.

Neither the most brilliant strategist nor organizer of the black struggle, Dr. King was far more than simply the most eloquent civil rights spokesman of his time. Rather, he both conveyed and inspired in others the moral passion of the campaign for social justice, the demand that America recognize and realize its better self. King shared with John Winthrop and the Puritan divines—America's founding ideologues—the view that America's purpose was to redeem itself and the world, to be "a city upon a hill, the eyes of all people . . . upon us." Nothing less would suffice either for America or for the man whose life was his sermon.

Today visitors to the Birth Home of Martin Luther King, Jr., will find the late-19th-century house restored to its appearance during the years 1929–1941, years when the "young M.L." played in its rooms not knowing that he had a destiny and an appointment in Memphis, from which he would not run.

Clark Atlanta University
111 James P. Brawley Drive, Atlanta, GA 30314
(404) 880-8000
Hours: Mon.–Fri., 10 A.M.–3 P.M. (Tours through Admissions Office, 404 880-8917)
Admission: Free

Into devastated Atlanta in 1865 the American Missionary Association sent a railroad boxcar that became the first schoolroom of Atlanta University. Four years later Clark College was founded to further the education of freedmen. Their 1988 merger formed one of the components of the Atlanta University consortium.

Ebenezer Baptist Church
407 Auburn Avenue, NE, Atlanta, GA 30312
(404) 688-7263
Hours: Tours: Mon.–Fri., 9:30 A.M.–12 P.M.; 1:30 P.M.–4:30 P.M.
Admission: Free

The descent is direct: From the Reverend A. D. Williams, a noted activist for African-American advancement in early-20th-century Atlanta, to his son-in-law, the Reverend Martin Luther King, to King's son, Martin Luther King, Jr., three generations of one family have pastored Ebenezer Baptist Church. From sermon and song, from prayer and politics, from triumph and tragedy (in 1974 Dr. King's mother was fatally shot by an assassin as she sat at the church organ), Ebenezer Baptist has been at the center of Afro-Atlanta's turbulent history.

Hammonds House
503 Peeples Street, SW, Atlanta, GA 30310
(404) 752-8730
Hours: Tue.–Fri., 10 A.M.–6 P.M.; weekends, 1 P.M.–5 P.M.
Admission: Voluntary donations requested

From the earliest datable work of the 19th-century painter Robert S. Duncanson through the post-1960s collages, prints, and paintings of Romare Bearden; from African sculpture to Haitian paintings; from ideological constructs depicting derogatory stereotypes of African Americans to contemporary efforts of local artists, black and white—Hammonds House has it all. The mid-19th-century Victorian-style house in Atlanta's historic West End and much of the collection it contains belonged to the late Dr. Otis T. Hammonds.

Herndon Home
587 University Place, NW, Atlanta, GA 30314
(404) 581-9813
Hours: Tue.–Sat., 10 A.M.–4 P.M. Tours begin on the hour. Groups scheduled in advance
Admission: Free

Less than four decades after his 1858 birth as a slave in Social Circle, Georgia, and after a youth of heavy field work as a sharecropper's son, Alonzo Herndon was Atlanta's wealthiest African American. His rise may have been anomalous; his path was not: a few months of schooling, migration to the big city, the opening of a barbershop catering to whites (the primary occupation of free black entrepreneurs even in antebellum days) and subsequent investment in real estate. Though a participant in the founding meeting of W.E.B. Du Bois's Niagara Movement and simultaneously a supporter of Booker T. Washington's National Negro Business League, Herndon was never particularly active in the struggle for racial justice. This did not, however, protect him from racial enmity: In

COURTESY HERNDON HOME

Alonzo Herndon *(right)*, constrained but not crushed by segregation, achieved commercial success in Jim Crow Georgia.

the 1906 Atlanta Race Riot, his Peachtree Street barbershop was attacked and three of his employees were killed. Along with his brethren he was deprived of his right to vote in 1907 by the Georgia legislature. Beginning in 1905, Herndon entered the insurance business, gradually purchasing several small enterprises, which he united to form the Atlanta Life Insurance Co. (See entry on p. 61.) Herndon's first wife, Adrienne, whom he married in 1893, joined the faculty of Atlanta University in 1895, becoming with W.E.B. Du Bois and George Towns the only African-American faculty members. Adrienne died in 1910, the year that saw the completion of Herndon Home, which is now a memorial to a remarkable black family and a museum chronicling African-American achievement.

Martin Luther King, Jr. National Historic Site
526 Auburn Avenue, NE, Atlanta, GA 30312
(404) 331-3919
Hours: June–Sept.: daily, 9 A.M.–8 P.M. (tours every half hour, 10 A.M.–5 P.M.); Oct.–May: daily, 9 A.M.–5 P.M. (tours every half hour, beginning at 9 A.M.)
Admission: Free

The centerpieces of the Martin Luther King, Jr. National Historic Site are King's birthplace (see Birth Home of Martin Luther King, Jr. entry on p. 62), the museum and research center named after Dr. King (see following entry), and the Ebenezer Baptist Church (see entry on p. 64). The National Historic Site is run by the National Park Service, whose address and telephone number noted above are an excellent starting point for further information.

Martin Luther King, Jr. Center for Non-Violent Social Change
449 Auburn Avenue, NE, Atlanta, GA 30312
(404) 524-1956; (404) 331-3919
Hours: Daily, 9 A.M.–5:30 P.M.
Admission: Free

Conceived by his widow, Coretta Scott King, as a memorial both to preserve and to advance his legacy and his vision, the Martin Luther King, Jr. Center for Non-Violent Social Change is housed in the Freedom Hall Complex on the Martin Luther King, Jr. National Historic Site. Dr. King is buried on the mall between the center and Ebenezer Baptist Church. The King Library and Archives holds his personal papers; manuscripts, documents, and oral histories about the civil rights movement of the 1950s and '60s; and the records of the Southern Christian Leadership Conference.

Morehouse College
830 Westview Drive, SW, Atlanta, GA 30314
(404) 681-2800
Hours: Tours given Mon.–Fri., 9 A.M.–4 P.M. with 2 weeks' notice
Admission: Free

Morehouse, the nation's sole historically black, all-male, four-year liberal arts college, whose alumni range from Dr. King to Spike Lee, was born in the basement of Springfield Baptist Church (see entry on p. 68) in Augusta, Georgia, in 1867 as Augusta Institute. Its founders were a former escaped slave from Augusta, an Augusta Baptist minister, and the organizer of a school for freedmen in Washington, D.C. In the ensuing years, the school moved to Atlanta, came under the direction of its first black president, the renowned educator John Hope, and changed its name to Morehouse.

Morris Brown College
643 Martin Luther King, Jr. Drive, NW, Atlanta, GA 30314-4140
(404) 525-7831; for tours call 220-0309 or 220-0152
Hours: Mon.–Fri., 9 A.M.–4 P.M.
Admission: Free

Founded in 1881 by the African Methodist Episcopal Church, Morris Brown is unique in Georgia for being the only college founded for African Americans by African Americans.

Spelman College
350 Spelman Lane, SW, Atlanta, GA 30314
(404) 681-3643; (800) 241-3421
Hours: Tours given Mon.–Fri., 10 A.M., 11 A.M., 2 P.M., 3 P.M., with 2 weeks' notice
Admission: Free

Eleven students, most of them illiterate former slaves, and two remarkable white women, Sophia Packard and Harriet Giles—products of the Women's American Baptist Home Mission Society of New England—"gathered in a damp, dark basement" of Atlanta's Friendship Baptist Church in April 1881, little knowing that they were the foundation of what is now Spelman College, the nation's premier African-American women's college. Financial support from the black community and from the Rockefeller family and the continuing effort of Packard and Giles secured Spelman's future into the 20th century. By 1930 Spelman was one of only six black colleges to hold membership in the American Association of Colleges.

Underground Atlanta Visitor Center
65 Upper Alabama Street, Atlanta, GA 30303
(404) 577-2148
Hours: Mon.–Sat., 9:30 A.M.–9 P.M.; Sun., 12 P.M.–6 P.M.
Admission: Free

Walking around town and uncertain what to do or where to go? Check in with the Underground Atlanta Visitor Center for recommended African-American (and other) points of interest.

AUGUSTA

Augusta Convention & Visitors Bureau
32 Eighth Street, Augusta, GA 30901
(706) 823-6600
Hours: Mon.–Fri., 8:30 A.M.–5 P.M.

Paine College
1235 15th Street, Augusta, GA 30910-2799
(404) 821-8200
Hours: Mon.–Fri., 9 A.M.–5 P.M.
Admission: Free

Paine Institute's origins in 1882 testify to the painful changes and progress forced upon southern Methodists of both races after the Civil War. Prior to the war, more than 200,000 African Americans were members of the Methodist Episcopal Church, South (MEC,S). (With the Methodist Episcopal Church, its northern counterpart, it was the product of an 1844 schism that turned on whether slave owners should be precluded from positions of ecclesiastical authority, if not communion.) By 1866 only 78,000 black members remained in the MEC,S. Most of the departed either affiliated with independent black Methodist churches in the North that predated the war or with the Methodist Episcopal Church. In either event, the departed were sharply critical of their brethren who remained in the southern church, and by 1870 the remaining members had split off to form the wholly independent Colored Methodist Episcopal (CME) Church in America. Severing ties, however, did not solve the problem of obtaining trained ministers for the new church. After a decade of struggle, leaders of both the CME and MEC,S churches joined together to establish a school for the training of black ministers and teachers in the South, which they located in Augusta, Georgia, center of the CME's congregation. Though many southern whites opposed educating African Americans, and though most freedmen placed no trust in those who had acquiesced in their enslavement, Paine slowly prospered and fulfilled its mission. Like most black "colleges" formed in the decades immediately following the war, Paine limited its education to elementary and secondary levels well into the 20th century. Until 1926 the first through the sixth grades were taught; not until 1944, with the opening of the first black public school in Augusta, did Paine College eliminate its secondary education. Historically biracial in establishment and leadership, and predominantly black in enrollment, Paine is one of 41 member colleges of the United Negro College Fund and retains an affiliation to its two founding churches.

Springfield Baptist Church
114 12th Street, Augusta, GA 30910
(706) 724-1056
Hours: Daily, 9 A.M.–3 P.M. Tours by appointment
Admission: Free

The "Great Awakening," a revivalist ferment beginning in the late 1730s and continuing until the 1760s, not only confirmed a distinctly American accent to what had originally been an imported European Protestantism, it also opened the gate to incorporating African Americans into Christian churches. The Baptists and Methodists, in particular, licensed black men to preach, and by the 1770s some African-American ministers led their own congregations. The Virginia-born George Liele, one of the first American missionaries to foreign lands, was active in the Deep South. In South Carolina, just across the Savannah River border with Georgia, he preached at the Silver Bluff Baptist Church (an established white church that in 1773 passed into the hands of the predominantly black congregation and was then pastored by David George; see Shelburne County Museum entry on p. 544), arguably the oldest black Baptist church in America. The Revolutionary War brought church activity to a halt as many of the congregation fled to Savannah or Augusta. In the latter town, Liele and a colleague founded in 1787 the Springfield Baptist Church, which four years later was officially organized. (The 1787 founding and its connection to the Silver Bluff Baptist congregation provide the basis for the church's claim to be the oldest black Baptist church in America.) Almost 80 years later, the church's basement served as the first classroom of what is now Morehouse College.

The present church building includes at its rear a wooden, New England meeting house–style predecessor raised in 1801. One of the few church structures of this style in the South, it is congregation-centered in distinction to (actually, in revolt against) the typical, altar-centered liturgical style of most churches.

COLUMBUS

Convention & Visitors Bureau
801 Front Avenue, Columbus, GA 31901
(706) 322-1613
Hours: Mon.–Fri., 8:30 A.M.–5 P.M.

Ask for the "Columbus' Black Heritage" brochure for directions to a number of sites—including the childhood home of Alma Thomas, America's foremost black female painter; a marker commemorating Eugene Bullard (see U.S. Air Force Museum entry on p. 441), a black World War I pilot who flew for the French since he was racially barred from flying for America; and the assassination site of Dr. T. H. Brewer, the founding father of Columbus's NAACP who was gunned down in 1956 (space constraints preclude their mention below).

Blind Tom Marker
6 miles north of Columbus, on U.S. 27A
Hours: Daily until sunset
Admission: Free

Born blind and a slave in 1849, Thomas Wiggins gained international fame for his ability to replicate musical compositions, of any complexity, upon only one hearing. The Blind Tom Marker commemorates his achievement.

Bragg Smith Monument
Fourth Street and Seventh Avenue, Columbus, GA 31901
Hours: Daily until sunset
Admission: Free

The Bragg Smith Monument, one of the first in the South to commemorate an African American, honors the memory of a city employee who was buried alive in an attempt to save the life of a city engineer caught in a building cave-in.

Columbus Times Newspaper
2230 Buena Vista Road, P.O. Box 2845, Columbus, GA 31993-2999
(706) 324-2404
Hours: By appointment
Admission: Free

Founded in 1924 by Joseph Clark, the *Columbus Times* newspaper (circulation 20,000) has been the voice of the city's black community. In its files, seven decades of struggle can be followed.

Dillingham Street Bridge
Dillingham Street at Chattahoochee River, Columbus, GA 31901
Hours: Daily, 24 hours
Admission: Free

In 1832 Horace King (see entry on p. 24) and his master constructed the Dillingham Street Bridge, the first of a series of bridges spanning the Chattahoochee River that divided Georgia and Alabama.

Ma Rainey House
805 Fifth Avenue, Columbus, GA 31901
(706) 571-4700
Hours: Daily until sunset
Admission: Not yet open to the public. Exterior viewing only

Born in Columbus, Georgia, to parents who were tent-show minstrel performers, Gertrude Pridgett "Ma" Rainey (1886–1939) put her stamp on the blues—and the blues' stamp on America—long before Bessie Smith hit the scene. The professional career of the woman who would reign unchallenged as the "Mother of the Blues" opened at the age of 14, when she appeared locally in the production of "The Bunch of Black Berries." She soon hooked up with Will Rainey, who led the Rabbit Foot Minstrels troupe. Married in 1904, the pair billed themselves as "Rainey and Rainey, Assassinators of the Blues." Ma Rainey's powerful evocation of black life in secular and spiritual song kept minstrelsy alive past World War I. Indeed, even as the "Jazz Age" and the "Roaring '20s" opened, three large minstrel companies toured America, offering jubilee singers, plantation songs, revival camp meeting songs, work songs, and field-

DUNCAN SHEIDT

Ma Rainey brought the blues north.

hollers that all shared an African rhythmic heritage. Rainey won a national following as a gospel and blues performer long before her 1920 recordings preserved her sound. She retired in 1934, about a decade after her successor, Bessie Smith (see Chattanooga African-American Museum entry on p. 144) cut her first record, "Down Hearted Blues."

Rainey retired to her hometown, which had seen little of her in the last quarter of a century and which listed her in the 1937 Columbus City Directory as "Rainey, Gertrude, colored, 805 5th Avenue." She became active in the Friendship Baptist Church and sang there—in a style very different from her professional one. (Following "See that spider crawling up the wall / He's goin' up there to get his ashes hauled; / Oh it's tight like that, / Be De Um Bumm, / I say it's tight like that," the last chorus of Rainey's "It's Tight Like That," the singer would pull up her skirt and dance to the raucous applause of the audience.) Ma Rainey died in 1939 and is buried in the Porterdale Cemetery in Columbus. Her death certificate listed her occupation as "housekeeping." Today in Rainey's hometown, the retirement residence of the woman who first transported the blues from its southern setting is listed on the National Register of Historic Places. Inscribed in the sidewalk outside the house is the name of Rainey's brother, Thomas Pridgett, who lived there from Rainey's death in 1939 until his own in 1975.

St. James A.M.E. Church
1002 Sixth Avenue, Columbus, GA 31901
(706) 322-8043; (706) 687-3521
Hours: By appointment
Admission: Free

Wooden doors hand-carved by slaves grace the present structure of St. James A.M.E. Church, which was built in 1875 on land donated by the Georgia legislature.

DARIEN

St. Andrew's Episcopal Church
301 Washington Street on Vernon Square, P.O. Drawer 929, Darien, GA 31305
(912) 437-4562
16 miles north of Brunswick, on U.S. 17
Hours: Daily until sunset
Admission: Free

A marker at the St. Andrew's Episcopal Church recalls the 1863 burning of the building and most of the rest of Darien at the hands of the 54th Massachusetts Regiment, one of the Civil War's first all-black units. According to the outraged testimony of the regiment's colonel, Robert Gould Shaw (see entry on p. 263 and Battery Wagner entry on p. 135), the torching of the town was explicitly ordered by the expedition's commander, Colonel James Montgomery, who afterward turned to Shaw with a "sweet smile" and told him: "Southerners must be made to feel this is a real war, and that they are to be swept away by the hand of God like the Jews of old." Shaw's protests that his troops were more worthy of combat than of pillage were heeded. Shortly thereafter they were sent into the attack on Fort Wagner in Charleston, during which Shaw and a third of his regiment fell.

EATONTON

Uncle Remus Museum
Turner Park, Eatonton, GA 31024
(706) 485-6856
Hours: Mon.–Sat., 10 A.M.–12 P.M., 1 P.M.–5 P.M.; Sun., 2 P.M.–5 P.M.
Admission: Adults, 50 cents; students, 25 cents

The Uncle Remus Museum is as much a monument to African-American folk tales as it is to the tales' preserver and promoter, Joel Chandler Harris. Harris grew up around Eatonton and first heard the now famous folk tales on the steps of slave cabins, in mule-drawn carts, and in fields of corn and cotton. As passed on by "Uncle" Remus, an elderly former slave on Mr. Turner's plantation, the delightful tales that Harris transcribed celebrate the triumph of the underdog's opportunistic wit over the brute force of the powerful. Derived from a West African oral tradition that flourished in America as a form of resistance "literature" among generations of slaves, the tales cheerfully recount how the trouble-prone but wily Br'er Rabbit evades the clutches of Br'er Fox and Br'er Bear.

While the real Uncle Remus is largely lost in the mist of the past, Joel Chandler Harris's character and beliefs are better known: Though a "New South" advocate and a proponent of civil rights for African Americans, Harris was never a believer in racial equality. Still, he viewed the tales as genuinely insightful and amusing, and he promoted them without the thought that the dialect and characters defined a people. Today visitors to the log-cabin museum see objects and furnishings that date to Harris's youth and that are mentioned in the tales, as well as paintings and wood carvings of Uncle Remus's characters. Visitors to Eatonton (also the hometown of Alice Walker) should be sure to stop by the courthouse in the center of the town—for there stands a statue of Uncle Remus's most famous character, Br'er Rabbit.

MACON

Macon Convention & Visitors Bureau
200 Cherry Street, Macon, GA 31208
(912) 743-3401; (800) 768-3401
Hours: Mon.–Sat., 9 A.M.–5 P.M.

Ask for the "Macon Black Heritage" brochure, which features a self-guided tour of 21 sites of interest, including the bridge over the Ocmulgee River named after Macon native Otis Redding. Also ask whether the Georgia Music Hall of Fame (featuring Macon natives Lena Horne, Little Richard, and Otis Redding, as well as the Allman Brothers, James Brown—whose first hit, "Please, Please, Please," was recorded here in 1956—and others) has opened yet.

Douglass Theatre
Intersection of Broadway and Martin Luther King Boulevard, Macon, GA 31201
Hours: Daily until sunset
Admission: Not open to the public. Exterior viewing only

Now being restored, the Douglass Theatre was the focal point for black entertainment in Macon for 60 years. Bessie Smith, Cab Calloway, and Count Basie played on the stage, which also served as the starting point for the careers of Lena Horne, Little Richard, James Brown, and Otis Redding.

Little Richard's Childhood Home
1437 Woodcliff, Macon, GA 31201
Hours: Daily until sunset
Admission: Not open to the public. Exterior viewing only

Little Richard Penniman and Lena Horne both grew up in the black Pleasant Hill district of Macon. Today Little Richard's Childhood Home, where one of the weirdest and wildest musical forces of the modern age first let loose his piercing screams, is a *private residence*, which can only be viewed from the sidewalk. One day, when justice triumphs, Graceland will be rivaled by the birthplace of the man who gave America "Good Golly, Miss Molly," "Tutti Frutti," and so much, much more.

Harriet Tubman Historical and Cultural Museum
340 Walnut Street, P.O. Box 6671, Macon, GA 31208
(912) 743-8544
Hours: Mon.–Fri., 10 A.M.–5 P.M.; Sat., 2 P.M.–5 P.M.
Admission: Free. Voluntary donations accepted

Named for the boldly determined woman who championed the Underground Railroad (see Harriet Tubman entry on p. 249), the Harriet Tubman Historical and Cultural Museum displays a massive mural that traces the journey of African Americans from the homeland of yesteryear to modern America. Complementing "From Africa to America" is a permanent exhibit of art and artifacts from Africa and traveling exhibitions of African-American artists.

Washington Avenue Presbyterian Church
939 Washington Avenue, Macon, GA 31201
(912) 743-3345
Hours: By appointment
Admission: Free

Founded in 1838 in a building donated by the First Presbyterian Church of Macon, the Washington Avenue Presbyterian Church is the oldest black Presbyterian congregation in Georgia. The original wooden Gothic Revival church built on the current site was remodeled in brick in 1904.

SAVANNAH

Savannah Convention & Visitors Bureau
222 West Oglethorpe Street, Savannah, GA 31499
(912) 944-0456; (800) 444-2427
Hours: Mon.–Fri., 8:30 A.M.–5 P.M.

Savannah Visitors Center
301 Martin Luther King Boulevard, Savannah, GA 31402
(800) 444-2427
Hours: Mon.–Fri., 8:30 A.M.–5 P.M.; Sat.–Sun., 9 A.M.–5 P.M.

Beach Institute
502 East Harris Street, Savannah, GA 31401
(912) 234-8001
Hours: Daily, 12 P.M.–5 P.M.
Admission: Adults, $1.50; children, 75 cents

Established in 1865 by the American Missionary Association to educate freedmen, Beach Institute is the oldest surviving black educational center in

Georgia and now serves primarily as a facility for the African-American arts. Its permanent exhibit centers on the work of the woodcarver Ulysses Davis.

First African Baptist Church
23 Montgomery Street, Savannah, GA 31401
(912) 233-6597
Hours: Walk-ins: Mon.–Fri., 9 A.M.–2 P.M. Tours scheduled Mon.–Thur. by appointment
Admission: Free

Prior to the American Revolution, the Virginia-born George Liele was sold South. Hearing the preaching of a white Baptist church in Georgia, Liele was convicted of sin, reborn in Christ, and began preaching to whites and blacks on both sides of the Savannah River. Freed to preach and ordained in 1775, Liele in December 1777 formally organized a black congregation that dated to his pre-licensed preaching of 1773. The First African Baptist Church thus claims to be the oldest continuously active, autonomously developed black church in America. Liele sided with the British during the Revolution (as they promised freedom to slaves who fled their masters) and left Savannah with the evacuating British forces. Arriving in Jamaica, he converted 400 souls and began an organized mission to Africa. Early in 1788 Andrew Bryan, who had earlier been converted by Liele, was ordained and became the second pastor of First African. Within a decade the congregation had purchased a lot and built a church. Growth led the congregation (which soon exceeded 2,500) in 1832 first to move and then to splinter. The splinter congregation, the First Bryan Baptist Church, returned to the original site, which it still occupies. Visitors to First African can view a historical museum that details the development of the black Baptist church in America.

First Bryan Baptist Church
559 West Bryan Street, Savannah, GA 31401
(912) 232-5526
Hours: By appointment
Admission: Free

White ministers preaching the brotherhood of man had a hard row to hoe in Savannah in 1832. Alexander Campbell, preaching the new doctrine of the Church of Christ, found himself unwelcome in white churches but invited to preach at First African Baptist Church. His views caused some controversy in a congregation that, except in church, was largely under the authority of white masters. When the controversy refused to subside, the white First Baptist Church of Savannah was invited to mediate. When its reconciliation efforts failed, it offered three suggestions: Give letters of dismissal to the unsatisfied; let those departing form a new church; and since the departing would have no building in which to worship, let them have the original building and lot of First

COURTESY SAVANNAH CONVENTION & VISITORS BUREAU

Andrew Bryan, colleague of the renowned George Liele (note variation of surname spelling), was one of the pioneering black preachers of the 18th century.

African. Thus was formed the Third African Baptist Church, which after the Civil War changed its name to First Bryan. On its grounds is a monument to George Liele, from whose original proselytizing efforts the congregation of First Bryan traces its descent.

King-Tisdell Cottage
514 East Huntingdon Street, Savannah, GA 31401
(912) 234-8000
Hours: Mon.–Fri., 12 P.M.–4:30 P.M.; Sat., Sun., 1 P.M.–4 P.M. Negro History Trail: Mon.–Sat., 10 A.M. and 1 P.M. and by appointment
Admission: Adults, $1.50; children, 75 cents. Negro History Trail: adults, $10; children $5

King-Tisdell Cottage, a restored 1896 Victorian home noted for its intricate gingerbread ornamentation, preserves the African-American heritage of Savannah and the Sea Islands. Furnished as a middle-class, turn-of-the-century black residence, the facility displays original documents (including the first issue of the *Liberator,* William Lloyd Garrison's abolitionist newspaper), artifacts (slave ship inventories, slave auction handbills, and basketry) and yellowed newspapers that chronicle a people's culture. The cottage also offers a Negro History Trail tour that takes one to the birthplace of the black Baptist church in America; the spot where General Sherman promised newly freed slaves "40 acres and a mule"; the school attended by Robert S. Abbott, founder of the *Chicago Defender*; and the place where Haiti's Henri Christophe fought for American Independence.

St. Phillips Monumental A.M.E. Church
1112 Jefferson Street, Savannah, GA 31401
(912) 233-8547
Hours: Archives: Mon.–Fri., 9:30 A.M.–2:30 P.M.; Sun., after worship
Admission: Free

"Extermination or re-enslavement is only a question of time . . . it's a white man's government . . . they mean at all hazards to keep the negro down." Henry M. Turner, one of the 19th century's most outspoken critics of white supremacy, offered this jeremiad in 1876 on becoming the vice president of the American Colonization Society, to whose African settlement schemes he dedicated the last four decades of his life. His words were mild compared to his response when the U.S. Supreme Court in 1883 nullified the Civil Rights Act of 1875: "[the Constitution is] a dirty rag . . . and ought to be spit upon by every negro in the land." Turner's bitterness with the betrayal of Reconstruction marked a turning point in his life. Born to poor free black parents in South Carolina in 1834, Turner learned to read and write while working as an office boy for a local attorney. Moving North, he was ordained in the A.M.E. Church and attended two years of college before arriving in Washington, D.C., during the Civil War, where he pastored the town's largest black congregation. After serving as a Union chaplain (where he denounced black atrocities against captured and wounded Confederate soldiers) and briefly with the Freedmen's Bureau in Georgia, Turner settled down to denominational proselytizing (from 1870 to 1874 pastoring Georgia's first A.M.E. church, St. Phillips Monumental A.M.E. Church) and working to construct Georgia's Republican Party. In politics he earned a reputation for moderacy in policy (supporting a literacy test for electoral rights) and militancy in defense of his person and race ("I am here to demand my rights, and to hurl thunderbolts at the men who dare to cross the threshold of my manhood"). With the collapse of Reconstruction, Turner turned his attention to the church and its publications, to issues of black education (serving as president of Atlanta's Morris Brown College from 1880 to the close of the century), and to African colonization. Today visitors to St. Phillips Monumental A.M.E. Church have access to an archives that includes photographs of Bishop Turner as well as records of his tenure as pastor. There are also memorial tablets listing the names and dates of service of all of Georgia's A.M.E. bishops and of all pastors of St. Phillips. Finally, on Turner Boulevard in Savannah, there is a Bishop Henry M. Turner Historical Marker.

Second African Baptist Church
123 Houston Street, Savannah, GA 31401
(912) 233-6163
Hours: Tours by appointment
Admission: Free

Where better than a church to proclaim the good news? Late in 1864 General Sherman mounted the steps of the Second African Baptist Church, read the Emancipation Proclamation to Savannah's citizens, and promised newly freed slaves "40 acres and a mule." Almost a century later, inside the church founded in 1802 by Andrew Bryan to accommodate a black urban congregation that disliked trekking to the outskirts of town to worship at First African Baptist Church (see entry on p. 75), Dr. King preached his "I have a dream" sermon preparatory to giving it as an address during the famous 1963 March on Washington, D.C.

KENTUCKY

Department of Travel
Capital Plaza Tower, Frankfort, KY 40601
(800) 225-8747
Hours: Mon.–Fri., 8 A.M.–4:15 P.M.

BEREA

Berea College
CPO 2316, Berea, KY 40404
(606) 986-9341
Hours: Tours: Sept.–May: Mon.–Fri., 9 A.M.–2 P.M.; Sat., mornings only
Admission: Free

In 1855, as the nation spiraled toward secession and civil war, two of Kentucky's most ardent white abolitionists, Cassius Marcellus Clay and John Fee, opened the first college in America specifically founded for the purpose of multiracial education. Their goal was not simply to admit a few black students, but rather to actively recruit a student body that was more or less equally white and black. This would have been a novel idea in the North—in a border state where slavery remained in force, the notion was heretical. Few heresies go unpunished . . . and Berea College was no exception. Closed during the Civil War (though Kentucky never joined the Confederacy), the biracial college reopened in 1866, only to have the state legislature in 1904 exclude by law the admission of African Americans. Not until 1950 were African Americans readmitted to a school founded to serve them. Even in 1950 Kentucky only *amended* the 1904 law, permitting private institutions to admit blacks.

Visitors to the historic campus can take advantage of free tours, view Lincoln Hall, built in 1887 and a National Historic Site, check out the African art at the Dorish Ulmann Galleries, and stop by the Black Cultural Center.

FRANKFORT

Kentucky Military History Museum
Capitol Avenue at U.S. 60, Frankfort, KY 40601
(502) 564-3265
Hours: Mon.–Sat., 9 A.M.–4 P.M.; Sun., 1 P.M.–5 P.M.
Admission: Free

A border slave state that never joined the Confederacy and was occupied by Union forces early in the Civil War, Kentucky proved fertile ground for the recruitment of black Union troops, whose experiences are explored in a special section of the Kentucky Military History Museum. It has Civil War photographs of black troops; reproductions of documents relating to William H. Graham, a slave turned soldier; a photograph of Charles Young, the second black graduate of the Military Academy at West Point (see Greene County Historical Society Museum entry on p. 451 and Fort Duchesne entry on p. 518); and a World War II exhibit that occasionally includes material on the Tuskegee flyers (see U.S. Air Force Museum entry on p. 441 and National Museum of the Tuskegee Airmen entry on p. 403).

HAZARD

First Baptist Church Town Mountain
Town Mountain, Highway 451, Hazard, KY 41702
(606) 439-5169
3 miles outside of town, in the Brownsfork area
Hours: Exterior viewing: Daily until sunset. Tours by appointment
Admission: Free

In 1893 a tiny two-room plank church was raised by a largely black congregation in the Kentucky hills. The church stood on top of Town Mountain on land donated by former slaves. Though most of the congregation were children of former slaves, First Baptist Church Town Mountain has been interracial from its inception, even in the days when its services were held under a tree and the congregation sat on logs supported by rocks. Over the last century, the church's ministers have been African American, Caucasian, Haitian, Indian, and Jamaican. In 1920 the original plank building was covered in stone hand-cut by church members. Today that 1920 building still proudly stands in Hazard.

HODGENVILLE

Abraham Lincoln Birthplace National Historic Site
2995 Lincoln Farm Road, Hodgenville, KY 42748
(502) 358-3874
Hours: June–Labor Day, 8 A.M.–6:45 P.M.; Sept.–Oct., Apr.–May, 8 A.M.–5:45 P.M.; rest of year, 8 A.M.–5:45 P.M.
Admission: Free

The centerpiece of the Abraham Lincoln Birthplace National Historic Site is the log cabin in which was born Kentucky's most famous native, the author of the Emancipation Proclamation and the 16th president of the United States. The cabin is incongruously encased in an ornate granite-marble memorial building that serves to remind viewers that not everyone had Lincoln's sense of proportion. In the visitor center there is a Lincoln family Bible, a bust of the president, interpretive panels, and a relief map that shows how the Lincoln farm must have looked when he was born.

LEXINGTON

Kentucky Horse Park
4089 Iron Works Pike, Lexington, KY 40511
(606) 233-4303
Hours: Apr.–Oct.: daily, 9 A.M.–5 P.M. Nov.–Mar.: Wed.–Sun., 9 A.M.–5 P.M.
Admission: Adults, $6.50; children ages 7–12, $4.50; under 7, free

More famous even than its bourbon and its colonels are Kentucky's horse races. Aptly, the Kentucky Horse Park commemorates with honored burial places the two greatest names in horse racing—Man o' War and Isaac Murphy. The horse is renowned, the African-American jockey but little known. Equally unappreciated by the general public is the early black role in the "Sport of Kings": 14 of the 15 jockeys in the first running of the Kentucky Derby were black. African Americans remained prominent throughout 19th-century horse racing, when more than half the Derby winners were ridden by black jockeys. Murphy was not merely prominent but dominant, winning almost half of the races he entered in his 20-year (1875–1895) career. His record of three Kentucky Derby victories was not equaled until 1930 and not broken till 1948—not bad for a man who died at the still competitive age of 36.

The park has a museum, pony rides, and horse shows twice daily. Murphy's grave is to the left of the main gate and can be viewed from the parking lot without paying the park entrance fee, though a $1 parking fee is collected.

LOUISVILLE

Convention & Visitors Bureau
400 South First Street, Louisville, KY 40202
(800) 626-5646
Hours: Mon.–Fri., 8:30 A.M.–5 P.M.

Ask for "A Closer Look: Louisville's African-American Historic and Cultural Guide" for several additional black heritage sites that space precludes detailing below.

Kentucky Derby Museum
704 Central Avenue, Box 3513, Louisville, KY 40201
(502) 637-7097
Hours: Daily, 9 A.M.–5 P.M.
Admission: Adults, $3.50; seniors, $2.50; ages 5–12, $1.50; children under 5 and members, free

Adjacent to historic Churchill Downs, the Kentucky Derby Museum has a new permanent exhibit, "African-Americans in Thoroughbred Racing," that traces the role of black jockeys, trainers, handlers, grooms, and owners in the "Sport of Kings." Paintings and photographs of 19th- and 20th-century riders such as Isaac Murphy, James Winkfield, and Willie Simms (generally considered the three greatest African Americans ever to ride competitively) jockey for attention with Isaac Murphy's original tombstone and other memorabilia. Murphy (see Kentucky Horse Park entry on p. 80) was a three-time Derby champion and triumphed in an incredible 44 percent of the races he entered. In addition to his tombstone, Murphy is represented at the museum by a tobacco trading card that features him in his riding costume, by several photographs (including one that shows him 20 pounds over his riding weight), by a rare portrait studio tintype, and by the silk purse presented to him for his 1891 Kentucky Derby victory.

Louisville Free Public Library, Western Branch
604 South 10th Street, Louisville, KY 46203
(502) 584-5526
Hours: Mon.–Tue., Thu., 12 P.M.–8 P.M.; Wed., Fri., Sat., 10 A.M.–5 P.M.
Admission: Free

When Louisville's Free Public Library opened in 1905, its plans called for ten branch libraries, two of which were for the town's "colored" citizens. This concern for black welfare was, to say the least, rare in a southern border state, and the Colored Department of the Louisville Library, as it was then known, became the first library system in America established for and staffed by black folks. (In 1952 Louisville became the first southern city to permit African Americans to use its main library.) A 1905 Carnegie Grant enabled the library to build a permanent structure in 1908, to which it moved from the three rented rooms in a house that till then constituted its facilities. That structure, now the Louisville Free Public Library, Western Branch, is on the National Register of Historic Places and houses an extensive collection of African-American cultural and historical information.

Muhammad Ali's Boyhood Home
3302 Grand Avenue, Louisville, KY 40211
Hours: Daily until sunset
Admission: Not open to the public. Exterior viewing only

Boxing master and amateur poet, fast with hands and wit, Muhammad Ali is Kentucky's most famous African American—and was even in the days when he won the 1960 Olympic gold medal for heavyweight boxing and his first professional world heavyweight title (thrashing Sonny Liston) under the name with which he was christened, Cassius Clay. The day after his ring victory over Liston, Clay adopted a Muslim name as a sign of his commitment to Islam. Today Muhammad Ali's Boyhood Home is visible from the street. It is a *private residence, not open to the public.*

J. B. Speed Art Museum
2035 South Third Street, Louisville, KY 40208
(502) 636-2893
Hours: Tue.–Sat., 10 A.M.–4 P.M.; Sun., 12 P.M.–5 P.M.
Admission: Voluntary donations requested

Ceremonial axes from Zaire, carved Yoruba panels from Nigeria, and an outstanding antelope crest worn by the Bamana of southern Mali are but some of the remarkable works of African artists and artisans on display at the J. B. Speed Art Museum. This permanent exhibition of African art, which ranges in time from the 1600s to the early 1900s, is complemented by interpretive material that locates the objects within their culture.

MAMMOTH CAVE

Mammoth Cave National Park
Mammoth Cave, KY 42259
(502) 758-2328
Hours: Daily, 9 A.M.–4:30 P.M.
Admission: Prices vary widely depending on the length of the tour

The longest known cave system in the world, Mammoth Cave National Park has more than 300 miles of explored passageways—which directly connect to the African-American experience. Mammoth's preeminent explorer was Stephen Bishop, a slave who first became acquainted with Mammoth in 1838. Bishop, the first man to discover that the cave did not end with "Bottomless Pit," won national renown for his explorations—renown that finally secured him his freedom in 1856. Bishop's goal remained neither exploration nor renown but rather earning sufficient money to purchase the freedom of his wife and son, with whom he planned to emigrate to the independent African republic of Liberia. His death a year later meant yet another black dream unfulfilled. Though he may have considered it scant compensation for his lost dream, Bishop's death means that the grave of a great American underground explorer is, properly, in America; more properly still, Bishop's grave can be visited at the Old Guides Cemetery, located just off the Heritage Trail above the Historic Entrance.

OWENSBORO

Josiah Henson Trail
U.S. 60, Owensboro and Maceo, KY
U.S. 60 parallels the Ohio River. Maceo and the Hancock County line lie to the east of Owensboro
Hours: Daily, 24 hours
Admission: Free

Shipped from the Maryland home of his slave birth to his owner's brother in Kentucky, Josiah Henson (see Uncle Tom entries on pp. 253 and 549) learned the rudiments of reading, was ordained a minister in the Methodist Episcopal Church, and served as an overseer on the Riley Plantation near Maceo. After unsuccessfully attempting to purchase his freedom, Henson in 1830 fled with his wife and child, crossed the Ohio River into Indiana, and, with the assistance of the Underground Railroad, finally reached Canada. In fact, he reached further—all the way into America's mass consciousness, for his autobiography and his later interviews with Harriet Beecher Stowe provided the novelist with the central character of her powerfully influential *Uncle Tom's Cabin*.

The Riley Plantation has long since passed to dust and is recalled only by a marker on U.S. 60 near Maceo. From the Ohio River port of Owensboro toward the Hancock County line, U.S. 60 has been designated the Josiah Henson Trail. The trail, which passes by the site of the old Riley Plantation, commemorates rather than interprets Henson's life and the struggle against slavery.

PARIS

Garrett A. Morgan Historic Marker
Winchester Road and Vine Street, Paris, KY 40361
Hours: Daily until sunset
Admission: Free

Born 17 miles northeast of Lexington in the small town of Paris, Garrett A. Morgan (see African-American Museum entry on p. 436) went on to invent the gas mask, the now ubiquitous tricolor traffic signal light, and the first hair-straightening solution. Only the last would have led white America to assume anything other than that the successful inventor must have been of European descent. Today, at the intersection of Winchester and Vine, Paris honors its most prominent African-American native son with a historical marker.

RICHMOND

White Hall State Historic Site
500 White Hall Shrine Road, Richmond, KY 40475
(606) 623-9178
Hours: Apr. 1–Oct. 31: Tue.–Sun., 9 A.M.–4:30 P.M.; closed Mon. until Labor Day
Admission: $3.50

Touring the White Hall State Historic Site, once home to the ardent and irascible abolitionist Cassius Marcellus Clay, offers insights into the man who defied his father by founding a militantly abolitionist newspaper; founded the nation's first deliberately multiracial college (see Berea College entry on p. 78); served as America's minister (ambassador) to Russia; refused a major-general's rank in the Union army, offered by his friend President Lincoln, because Lincoln would not then emancipate slaves; and suffered—within the limits of being a wealthy and socially prominent white man in a slave state—for his abolitionist commitment. Though an abolitionist without being an advocate of racial equality, Clay's reputation was sufficiently respected by black Kentuckians that parents in the 20th century named their children after him. That the boxer born Cassius Marcellus Clay, Jr. (see Muhammad Ali entry on p. 81) would reject this name and choose in its stead the name of a European (Albanian by birth) Muslim, Muhammad Ali, who, as the audacious and ruthless ruler of Egypt, was the 19th century's single greatest slaver and mass murderer of Africans, says much for the amusing ironies of ideological and religious orthodoxy.

SIMPSONVILLE

Whitney M. Young, Jr. House and Historical Marker
U.S. 60 West, on the grounds of the Whitney Young Job Corps Center, Simpsonville, KY 40067
(502) 585-4733
Hours: Tours by appointment
Admission: Free

In the town of his birth, the Whitney Young, Jr. House and Historical Marker honors the author, former executive director of the National Urban League from 1961 until his death in 1971, advisor to three presidents, recipient of this nation's highest civilian award, and the man who turned down a cabinet appointment in 1968 because he believed he could accomplish more for his people and his country by staying with the League.

WASHINGTON

Slave Market Historic Marker
Washington Visitor Center, Washington, KY 41096
(606) 759-7411
Hours: Visitor Center: Apr.–Dec.: daily, 11 A.M.–5 P.M.
Admission: Free

In 1835, three years after moving to Cincinnati and three years before she would marry Calvin Stowe, the 24-year-old Harriet Beecher visited a friend's family just across the Ohio River in Washington, Kentucky. Her friend's house, which still survives, looked out upon the town's slave market, where Beecher observed the despair and torment of African Americans being sold within miles of the river—and the freedom that lay across it. Years later, after writing *Uncle Tom's Cabin* (1852) under her married name, Harriet Beecher Stowe (see First Parish entry on p. 236 and Stowe entries on pp. 226 and 434) noted that the trauma of that day had never left her and was one of the motivating images that drove her emotional and religious abolitionist sentiment. Though the slave market has long since ceased operation and her friend's house is now a private residence, a historical marker notes the site on which, aptly enough, the old courthouse stood and from which nearby the traffic in human beings was conducted.

LOUISIANA

Louisiana Office of Tourism
P.O. Box 94291, Baton Rouge, LA 70804-9291
(504) 342-8119
Hours: Mon.–Fri., 8 A.M.–4:30 P.M.

BATON ROUGE

Convention & Visitors Bureau
P.O. Box 4149, Baton Rouge, LA 70821
(800) 527-6843
Hours: Mon.–Fri., 8:30 A.M.–5 P.M.

Southern University
Harding Boulevard, Baton Rouge, LA 70813
University: (504) 771-4500; library: (504) 771-2841
Hours: Campus tours: Jan.–June: Mon.–Thu., 8 A.M.–5 P.M. (Self-guided tours allowed at other times. Contact Campus Security first.) Library: Mon.–Fri., 8 A.M.–5 P.M.

Opened in New Orleans in 1880 as a technical high school for African Americans, what is now Southern University moved to the state capital in Baton Rouge in 1914. In addition to serving as the parent campus of the largest predominantly black university system in the United States, Southern hosts the Black Heritage Exhibit Series in its library. The exhibit consists of 9,000 noncirculating volumes on black history, photographs of leading black Louisianans of the 19th and 20 centuries, and a painting by Clementine Hunter, Louisiana's preeminent primitive artist.

MANSFIELD

Mansfield Battlefield Park

Mansfield State Commemorative Area, Route 2, Box 459, Mansfield, LA 71052
(318) 872-1474
Hours: Wed.–Sun., 8 A.M.–4:30 P.M.
Admission: Adults, $2; ages 6–12, $1

In both Arkansas and Louisiana, the Union's 1864 Red River campaign (see Poison Springs, Marks' Mill, and Jenkins' Ferry entries on pp. 33 and 40) proved an unmitigated disaster. Near Mansfield, Louisiana, General Nathaniel Banks's advance toward Shreveport ran into the forces of Confederate general Richard Taylor, the son of the former Mexican War commander and later U.S. president Zachary Taylor, and the son-in-law of Confederate president Jefferson Davis. In a series of encounters over several days, the Union forces, including Colonel Dickey's brigade of about 1,500 black troops, which was detailed to guard the main wagon train, were driven back toward Alexandria in a retreat that threatened to become a rout. As the Red River dropped to an unusually low level, Banks looked likely to lose his gunboats. Then an engineering officer, Colonel Joseph Bailey, devised a scheme to build wing dams, raise the river's level, and float the gunboats over the rapids. The 96th and 97th U.S. Colored Engineer regiments and 400 troops from Dickey's brigade built the dams that saved the boats that protected Banks's retreat. Today the Mansfield Battlefield Park has a self-guided walking tour, artifacts, documents, and an interpretive center that touch upon the role of Banks's African-American troops, including those who were enrolled in largely white regiments, such as the 165th New York.

MELROSE

Melrose Plantation

Highway 119, Melrose, LA 71542
(318) 379-0055
Hours: Daily, 12 P.M.–4 P.M.
Admission: Adults, $4; children 13–18, $2; children 6–12, $1; children under 6, free

Born a slave in the middle of the 18th century, Marie Therese Coincoin passed to her third master, the Cane River French planter T. P. Metoyer, at the age of 26. To him she bore ten children and by him she and their offspring were freed and given land along the river near Natchitoches. This was the start of an Afro-Creole family that employed initiative and slavery to build several large estates before the close of the 18th century. The largest of these became over time the 2,000-acre Melrose Plantation and employed 50 enslaved African Americans. Here was built first Yucca House, constructed of river bottom mud, Spanish moss, and deer hair, then African House, constructed as a joint storehouse and jail and taking its name from its overhanging second story reminiscent of Congolese huts, and last the main mansion.

Passing through a series of white hands after 1847, Melrose languished until the turn of the century. At that point the Henry family repaired the estate and turned Melrose into a well-known writers' and artists' refuge, lodging writers in Yucca House. Four decades later the Henrys discovered that their former field hand and present cook, Clementine Hunter, who had spent most of her 60 years working on the estate, had a remarkable talent for painting. Encouraging Hunter to forgo the kitchen for the studio, Melrose's masters proved to be the patrons of Louisiana's preeminent primitive artist, whose works recorded a rural black life that was disappearing even more rapidly than she painted. Many of Hunter's works are displayed at Melrose, particularly in African House, and make the trip to Louisiana's Cane River backcountry an enlightening joy for those interested in black heritage or powerful paintings.

NATCHEZ

Magnolia Plantation
Highway 119, HC 66, Box 1040, Natchez, LA 71456
(318) 379-2221
Hours: Sun.–Sat., 1 P.M.–4 P.M.
Admission: Adults, $4; college students, $3; students 7–18, $2; children under 7, $1; adult groups of more than 20, $3.50 each

An early Federal-era plantation burned during the Civil War, Magnolia Plantation was rebuilt on its original foundations and today is a working farm that may be toured by visitors. Some of its antebellum outbuildings and implements still stand, including a row of brick cottages that housed slaves, the overseer's house, a chapel, a blacksmith's shop, and a mule-drawn cotton press.

NEW ORLEANS

Greater New Orleans Tourist & Convention Commission
529 St. Ann Street, New Orleans, LA 70116
(504) 566-5011
Hours: Daily, 9 A.M.–5 P.M.

Ask for the "Black Heritage of New Orleans" brochure, which details several sites that space precludes mentioning below.

Greater New Orleans Black Tourism Network
Greater New Orleans Tourist/Convention Commission, Inc.
1520 Sugar Bowl Drive, New Orleans, LA 70130
(504) 523-5652
Hours: Mon.–Fri., 8:30 A.M.–5 P.M.

Ask about New Orleans' Minority Tourism Month (January).

New Orleans Jazz & Heritage Festival
1205 North Rampart Street, P.O. Box 53407, New Orleans, LA 70153-3407
(504) 522-4786; (800) 535-8747; (504) 561-8747
Hours: Last week in April
Admission: Weekend fair: $7; evening concerts, $10 to $25; group discounts available

A ten-day celebration of a unique culture, the New Orleans Jazz & Heritage Festival offers great music—from Afro-Caribbean through zydeco, and touching on every letter of the alphabet in between—splendid regional food (alligator sauce piquante, for instance), and African-American crafts and performances. If you can't enjoy yourself here, call Marie Laveau for help—for you, sir, are dead!

Amistad Research Center
6823 St. Charles Avenue, Tilton Hall, Tulane University, New Orleans, LA 70118-5698
(504) 865-5535
Hours: Daily, 8:30 A.M.–5 P.M.
Admission: Free

From 1841 onward, the American Missionary Association (AMA) has played a central role in this nation's unfinished racial business, from campaigning for the abolition of slavery and aiding the Underground Railroad through establishing schools, churches, and hospitals for freedmen. In 1966 the AMA formed the Amistad Research Center at Fisk University (see entry on p. 155)—which it had helped establish a century previously—to preserve and expand the documentary record of the African-American travails and triumphs in America. Continued growth led the center to move repeatedly, and it is now housed at Tulane University. The center is the world's largest repository of primary source material on African-American history. The personal papers of Mary McLeod Bethune, Fannie Lou Hamer, Countee Cullen, and others; the records of groups such as the American Committee on Africa, the Federation of Southern Cooperatives, Operation Crossroads Africa; the paintings of Henry O. Turner, Romare Bearden, Elizabeth Catlett, Jacob Lawrence, Hale Woodruff, and others; 250,000 photographs; and several collections of African art ensure that the center is the unmatched resource for tracing the trajectory of black heritage in America.

Louis Armstrong Park
901 North Rampart Street at St. Anne Street, New Orleans, LA 70116
Downtown, in front of Municipal Auditorium
Hours: Daily until sunset
Admission: Free

A young black boy in trouble behind a gun is an old story—and jail is the punchline. Having pulled the trigger in public during the excitement of Mardi Gras, the 13-year-old Louis Armstrong found himself off the streets, in the Colored Waifs Home for Boys, and headed toward a career that would take him around the world and make his work immortal. The bandmaster at the Waifs Home knew the magic of music and introduced the young Armstrong to the cornet and the trumpet. When Louis departed 18 months later he was leading the band, not a gang. Then 15, Armstrong sold newspapers and worked in a dairy by day in order to hang out at night in club-laden Storyville, New Orleans' licensed brothel district, near his idol, Joe "King" Oliver of the Kid Orys band. Sensing a kindred spirit, Oliver taught Armstrong much more about the cornet and trumpet. When the King left to play Chicago in 1917, Armstrong took his place in the Kid Orys. From there it was a 2,000-mile, two-year trip up the Mississippi with the band, then his first recordings with Oliver's Creole Jazz Band, then New York and Fletcher Henderson's orchestra, his own band, the Vendome, the Sunset Cafe, and musicals such as *Hot Chocolates* and *Ain't Misbehavin'*. Never his favorite drink, water did not stop Armstrong. England and a command performance before King George VI, France, Holland, Italy, and elsewhere fell before his musical genius. His Paris residence must have seemed a long way from the Waifs Home, if not from New Orleans, but it too could not long hold Armstrong. Hollywood called him home and revealed yet another of his facets. Previously he had brought people to his culture; now *Pennies from Heaven*, *Every Day's a Holiday*, and *Going Places* (how apt!) brought him into popular culture.

New Orleans has not forgotten Armstrong. Louis Armstrong Park, complete with a sculpture of the "World's Greatest Trumpeter" by the black sculptor Elizabeth Catlett, is located on the edge of the French Quarter. Its location could not be more appropriate, for in colonial and antebellum times the southwestern corner of the park was "Congo Square," a weekend gathering place for slaves. Here the diaspora enjoyed and transformed the music, dance, and social rituals of the Mother Continent, free for the moment from masters. A few blocks to the west of the park was Storyville, where the youthful Armstrong hung around the clubs soaking up the atmosphere and the music. Just to the east of the park is Preservation Hall, which rescued from oblivion the early 20th-century New Orleans jazz style that had first entranced young Louis.

Cabildo

Chartres and St. Peter streets, New Orleans, LA 70130

(504) 568-6968

Hours: Scheduled to reopen Feb. 27, 1994. Call ahead for hours of operation and admission fees

Scheduled to reopen in the spring of 1994, the Cabildo, constructed in 1794 as the city hall building for then Spanish town of New Orleans, will serve as the element of the Louisiana State Museum that focuses on the African-American perspective of the state's history. Louis XV's 1724 Code Noir, which prescribed the treatment of slaves in the then French colony; French and Spanish judicial documents relating to slavery, including acts of resistance, suits for mistreatment, and testimony concerning the 1795 Pointe Coupee conspiracy; copies of *L'Union*, the South's first black newspaper; the Oath of Allegiance to the Spanish government, signed in 1769 by the Free Black Militia; black Union soldiers' enlistment and discharge papers; and numerous slave sale documents are but some of the artifacts that touch upon a people's heritage in this unique state.

Chalmette Battlefield
423 Canal Street, New Orleans, LA 70130
(504) 589-4428; 589-4430
Hours: Daily, 8 A.M.–5 P.M.
Admission: Free

As with the Revolutionary War, the War of 1812 brought blacks into combat on both sides; and as with the Revolutionary War, the aftermath of the War of 1812 saw African Americans once again cast out of the nation's organized military forces. After Congress in 1792 passed legislation authorizing the creation of a militia composed of white men between the ages of 18 and 45, only three states interpreted the law as not automatically banning African Americans. Oddly, all were in the South. North Carolina permitted free blacks to bear arms in its militia, while Georgia and South Carolina allowed them to serve as laborers or musicians. As the "Indian problem" that gave rise to the 1792 law receded and the militias took on more of an aspect of social clubs, and as the example of Haiti's black insurgence gripped men's minds, the chances of a multiracial military grew still more remote. The United States Armed Forces followed the militias' lead toward black exclusion. Thus at the end of the first decade of the 19th century, America's Army was all white; service in the navy, however, was so uninviting that recruiters and captains turned a blind eye to the ban on "Negroes and Mulatoes," with the result that perhaps one in five of America's sailors was black.

During the War of 1812, British commanders emulated Lord Dunmore's tactic from the Revolutionary War, encouraging slaves to escape and either serve in their ranks or be transported as free people to Canada or the West Indies. This tactic both undermined the economic well-being of America (about 5,000 African Americans—ironically the same number as fought for American independence three decades earlier—fled Chesapeake Bay plantations) and yielded a new supply of troops. In the Chesapeake region, Britain's General Cockburn organized 200 escaped slaves into a detachment of colonial marines, which participated in combat in Virginia and Maryland before taking part in the attack on Washington, D.C., that led to the burning of the Capitol and the White House and in the attack on Fort McHenry in Baltimore that led observer Francis Scott Key to write "The Star-Spangled Banner." The British example did not lead to widespread American emulation, though in 1814 New York state authorized both free black and slave enlistment, the latter only with their owner's consent, of course.

Only in Louisiana did the American side utilize black combatants in land battle, and this anomaly was a function both of desperation and of the state's unique heritage. Indeed, the strength of these factors underscores the role of racialist considerations: It proved extremely difficult to win white authorization for black troops *even* in Louisiana. Free men of color, many of whom were offspring of prominent French, Spanish, and Creole planter families, had fought in the local militia before the Spanish and then French possession passed into American hands in 1803 as a consequence of the Louisiana Purchase. The new American governor of the territory welcomed their offer of military service, but his Anglo-American constituents—and still more the many refugee planter families that had just flowed into New Orleans from Santo Domingo in flight from the Haitian rebellion—compelled him to exclude blacks from the militia. In April 1812 Louisiana was admitted to the Union; less than two months later the War of 1812 commenced, and the state's government decided to recruit a free blacks-only militia unit based on tax-paying property owners. Though initially this unit was officered only by whites, this too changed under the twin exigencies of war and the social standing of many free blacks in Creole-dominated Louisiana. By 1814 the state was aware of an impending British invasion, for which it was ill prepared. General Andrew Jackson, in command of American forces along the gulf coast, arrived in New Orleans and promptly urged free men of color to enlist in his ranks, promising them equality of pay, rations, and bounty with white volunteers. Jackson's invitation took account of white (and probably free black) sensibilities by organizing racially distinct units, but did not address the fact of already existing, trained black militiamen, whom the state then called up. The two new black units that formed had senior black officers, and by the Battle of New Orleans one of the units was under black command.

The battle itself, fought at Chalmette plantation on January 8, 1815—ironically in ignorance that two weeks earlier the Treaty of Ghent had formally ended the war—proved a dreadful slaughter of British troops, who though twice as numerous as the Americans lacked effective artillery support and were attacking a defended rampart well supplied with cannon. The 36-year-old British commander, Sir Edward Pakenham, sent Gibbs's brigade against Jackson's left wing. Artillery and small-arms fire devastated the British brigade, killing Gibbs and most of his officers. Seeing the main attack falter, Keane took his 93rd Highlanders to its aid. Bagpipes playing, the Scots marched diagonally across the field of battle, murderously raked particularly by the free black brigade and the Americans' largest cannon. Recognizing that his men had expended their heroism and stood poised to fall back, Pakenham raced to the front, rallied his forces, and though wounded personally organized another attack, losing his life as the British lost the battle. While the Americans reported but 13 casualties, the British acknowledged more than 2,000. Jackson's report on the battle paid gracious tribute to the black volunteers, who "have not disappointed the hopes that were formed of their courage and perseverance in the performance of their duty." This tribute, however, and the service it applauded, did not balance the weight of white supremacy: In 1834 Louisiana again revised its militia law, excluding blacks.

Interestingly, Pakenham's force also included black troops, the 1st and 5th West Indian regiments, which lost about half their strength prior to the battle due to exposure and disease. These regiments saw little action, though their light companies were mixed in with the British skirmishing screen at Chalmette. Ironically, the origin of the 1st West Indian Regiment, formed in 1781, lay in the American Revolution. It was then composed of escaped slaves to whom the British promised freedom in exchange for service. Following the war the unit was withdrawn to the West Indies. Of course, by 1812 it is unlikely that any of the original soldiers were still active, though it is quite possible that some sons of the unit's founding members were following in their fathers' footsteps and again fighting against slave owners—such as Andrew Jackson, future president of the United States.

Today's visitors to the Chalmette Battlefield, which is part of the Jean Lafitte National Historical Park, can avail themselves of a self-guided auto tour, a video presentation at the visitor center, the Chalmette Monument—which stands less than 100 yards from the battle position of the free black brigade—and the nearby Chalmette National Cemetery. Apropos the last: The cemetery was established to hold the Union dead from the Civil War; only four veterans of the War of 1812—only one of whom fought in the Battle of New Orleans—are buried here. (For the African-American naval role in the War of 1812, see the Put-in-Bay entry on p. 446; for black participation in the American Revolution, see the Bunker Hill entry on p. 260; the Monmouth Battlefield entry on p. 282; the Butts Hill entry on p. 325; and the Battle of Great Bridge and Yorktown entries on pp. 173 and 191.)

A. L. Davis Park
Third and La Salle streets, New Orleans, LA 70113
The park is 1 block from the church

New Zion Baptist Church
2319 Third Street, New Orleans, LA 70113
(504) 891-4283
Hours: Mon.–Fri., 9 A.M.–4 P.M.
Admission: Free

In the 1960s many of the city's civil rights rallies, including the historic September 1963 Citizens Council of New Orleans' march to City Hall, assembled in what is now the Reverend A. L. Davis Park. Davis was the pastor of New Zion Baptist Church in 1956, when it served as the founding site of the Southern Christian Leadership Conference. A noted civil rights activist, he was also New Orleans' first black councilman.

Tomb(s) of Marie Laveau, Voodoo Queen(s)
St. Louis Cemetery Number 1 and/or 2, North Claiborne Avenue at Bienville Street, New Orleans, LA 70112
(504) 861-9521
Hours: Daily until sunset
Admission: Free

Be forewarned that there are (at least) two Tombs of Marie Laveau in different cemeteries, both of which purport to be the burial site of New Orleans' most famous voodoo queen(s). Voodoo (Vodun to its proponents) gained ground in New Orleans because of the city's close connection to Santa Domingo/Haiti, where it flourished as a melding of Christianity and an African spiritualism with ancestor worship at its base. Its use of communication by trance with spirits and its common employment of spells, hexes, charms, and potions brought it a following among the city's black residents, as did its close identification with the hemisphere's sole independent black state. On the New Orleans' streets in the 19th century, Marie was widely reputed as the most powerful practitioner of the conjuring arts. Her grave (or their graves, since some say her daughter also had voodoo powers and is buried in one of these tombs) can be found in St. Louis Cemetery No. 1 and/or No. 2. The St. Louis cemeteries are one of New Orleans' most intriguing sites, for the high underground water table and the frequency of flooding over the low-lying city demand that the dead be buried in tombs aboveground. The tombs, resembling small windowless houses, are built close together, row on row, yielding the impression of a miniature city—of the dead. The graves are located as follows: Cemetery No. 1, Alley No. 2-L, Tomb No. 7, facing St. Louis Street, close to the cemetery's Basin Street entrance (this Laveau tomb is close to the tomb of Paul Morphy, the 19th century's most brilliant chess champion) and Cemetery No. 2, Square No. 3.

Musee Conti Museum of Wax
917 Conti Street, New Orleans, LA 70112
(504) 525-2605
Hours: Daily, 10 A.M.–5:30 P.M.
Admission: Adults, $5; seniors, $4.50; ages 4–17, $3

Prominent aspects of the African-American presence in 18th- and 19th-century New Orleans are highlighted in life-size wax figures at the Musee Conti Museum of Wax. From the auction block and Congo Square gatherings through the hexes of "Voodoo Queen" Marie Laveau and the licks of early New Orleans jazz, the city's black heritage comes almost to life. Laveau (see preceding entry), Armstrong (see Louis Armstrong Park entry on p. 88), and unnamed black soldiers who fought at the Battle of New Orleans (see Chalmette Battlefield entry on p. 90) are among the figures portrayed.

Xavier University
7325 Palmetto Street, New Orleans, LA 70125
(504) 483-7568
Hours: Mon.–Fri., 9 A.M.–5 P.M.
Admission: Free

The sole historically black Roman Catholic college in the United States, Xavier University is renowned for the number of graduating students it sends on to medical careers. The campus itself has little to recommend it in the way of architectural distinction—indeed, until recently its main science building was an old World War II barracks, and even today the campus is hedged in by a drainage canal, a low-income housing project, and a highway. However, for those concerned with expanding the pool of black science graduates, Xavier remains the exemplar.

ST. FRANCISVILLE

Cottage Plantation
U.S. 61, St. Francisville, LA 70775
(504) 635-3674
6 miles north of St. Francisville, which is 50 miles south of Natchez, Mississippi
Hours: Tours may be arranged
Admission: $5 per person. Groups of 15 or more, $4 per person

Though the complete plantation setting is not interpreted—and thus the African-American component does not fully emerge—Cottage Plantation remains of interest, not so much for its surviving slave quarters, though these are rare and merit a reflective appraisal, but because it is one of the few antebellum sugar plantations to survive in something approximating its working form. The nexus between sugar and slavery developed more slowly in the United States than in the Caribbean, largely due to differences in climate, production, and resulting profitability. Ironically, a slave's son, Norbert Rillieux, discovered in the 1840s a process by which sugar crystals were more easily extracted from sugarcane, reducing refining costs and revolutionizing the industry and—much like the cotton gin—increasing the demand for slaves. In 1934 the Louisiana State Museum honored Rillieux with a plaque—perhaps by then enough time had passed to make his achievement outweigh its irony in the eyes of his fellow slave descendants. Cottage Plantation's mansion now serves as a hotel, but tours of the great house and the grounds (which include the smokehouse, a schoolhouse, a carriage house, and the detached kitchen as well as the slave quarters) may be arranged.

ZACHARY

Port Hudson State Commemorative Area and Museum
756 West Plains, Port Hudson Road, Zachary, LA 70791
(504) 654-3775
Hours: Apr.–Sept.: museum, Wed.–Sun., 9 A.M.–5 P.M.; grounds, Wed.–Sun., 9 A.M.–7 P.M. Oct.–Mar.: Wed.–Sun., 9 A.M.–5 P.M.
Admission: Adults 13 and older, $2; children 12 and under, free

May 1863 saw the first large-scale employment of black troops in Civil War combat. At this time, Port Hudson, Louisiana, and Vicksburg, Mississippi, were the last Confederate bastions on the Mississippi River. Without them the South would be separated from Louisiana, Arkansas, Texas, and its allies in Missouri. While General Ulysses S. Grant was assigned Vicksburg, General Nathaniel P. Banks was ordered toward Port Hudson, where his 30,000 to 40,000 troops confronted General Franklin Gardner's 7,000 dug-in Confederates. Among Banks's troops were two black regiments, the 1st and 3rd Louisiana Native Guards (later the 73rd and 75th U.S. Colored Infantry regiments, respectively). The 1st was composed of free blacks, many of them the illegitimate offspring of the male heads of the finest families in the state, and though led by a white colonel had black captains and lieutenants in command; the 3rd was composed of former slaves and only white officers. Together they comprised about 1,000 men and were stationed on the far right of the Union line. About 7 A.M. on May 27 they were ordered forward, through a cane brake and across a creek, to launch a diversionary attack—effectively without artillery support—against Confederate troops safely ensconced on bluffs that overlooked their advance. Shelled as they crossed the creek and struggled up its banks, they formed their ranks and began their advance in the face of intense rifle fire. As they closed to within 200 yards they came under a withering enfilade fire. Canister fire then ensued and the black troops fell in large numbers, many of the 1st's survivors falling back in disorder upon the 3rd, which was then just crossing the creek, while others struggled onward to their slaughter. Though not a single Confederate was lost in this action, there were 308 African-American casualties, about half of whom were listed as wounded. Since the 3rd saw but limited action, these casualties amounted to about 60 percent of the actual attacking force. The unsupported attack against one of the strongest natural positions of the Confederate line drew praise from Union generals who until then had doubted the combat utility of black troops, and was the prelude to the widespread employment of African Americans at the sharp end on the field of battle.

Not until a month later, and then only following the fall of Vicksburg, did Gardner surrender. Today visitors to the battlefield can take advantage of outdoor exhibits, guided tours, and a museum that interprets the 45-day siege during which African Americans won the opportunity to spill their blood to hasten the day of their compatriots' liberation.

MISSISSIPPI

Mississippi Division of Tourism
P.O. Box 22825, Jackson, MS 39205
(800) 647-2290

BAY ST. LOUIS

St. Augustine Seminary

199 Seminary Drive, Bay St. Louis, MS 39520
(601) 467-6414
Hours: Daily, 9 A.M.–5 P.M. Group tours by appointment
Admission: Free

Lying on the Gulf of Mexico roughly midway between the first French regional settlement (1699) in Biloxi and the later settlement of New Orleans, Bay St. Louis has long been one of the few Catholic oases in a deeply Protestant area. In 1923 a three-year-old seminary that had been based in Greenville moved to Bay St. Louis, where it still operates as St. Augustine Seminary, America's first institute for the training of black Catholic seminarians. Today the seminary serves as a retreat center and retirement home. In front of its chapel visitors will find a historical marker outlining the seminary's deep connection to the history of Catholicism in the African-American community.

CANTON

Black Confederate Memorial

East Academy Street at Howcott Memorial Park, Canton, MS 39046
(800) 844-3369
Hours: Daily until sunset
Admission: Free

Underscoring the depth of Confederate despair, black Confederate troops were training on the grounds of Richmond's hospitals in April 1865 as Lee abandoned the town and headed toward Appomattox. As late as the autumn of 1864, the desperate secessionist government—which then was compelled to end military exemptions for plantation overseers—had rejected the idea of recruiting black combat troops, largely because of its fear of the long-term consequence of placing weapons in the hands of *trained and organized* bands of black men.

Long before 1865, however, individual African Americans accompanied their slave masters into battle. This was part and parcel of one of the more peculiar aspects of the "peculiar institution": the perception of masters (frequently internalized by their possessions) that their close body servants were members of their families—who nonetheless could be bought and sold. Among the slaves who served alongside their masters in combat was Willis, property of William Hill Howcott and with his master a member of Harvey's Scouts, a Mississippi irregular unit that operated behind Union lines. Killed in one of the countless minor clashes that characterize war, Willis was honored by his owner and—in the context of slavery—friend with a 20-foot-high monument. The Black Confederate Memorial recalls Willis's "rare loyalty and faithfullness whose memory I cherish with deep gratitude." Next to the monument an inscription commemorates all the black members of Harvey's Scouts.

CLARKSDALE

Blues Alley
Fourth Street, Clarksdale, MS 38614
Crossing Ashton and Harrison streets
Hours: Daily until sunset
Admission: Free

Clarksdale was ground zero for the blues explosion, the shock wave of which, after a slow start, has traveled around the world. Blues Alley, now a business district, once boasted W. C. Handy's residence—which is now graced with a historical marker (between 309 and 317 Issaquena Street)—Wade Walton's barbershop, and the plaintive wails of a score of now-famous bluesmen such as Robert Johnson, Muddy Waters, and John Lee Hooker.

The Delta Blues Museum
Carnegie Public Library, 114 Delta Avenue, P.O. Box 280, Clarksdale, MS 38614
(601) 624-4461
Hours: Mon.–Fri., 9 A.M.–5 P.M.; Sat. 10 A.M.–2 P.M.
Admission: Free

Clarksdale and the surrounding Coahoma County were home to illustrious black men/bluesmen W. C. Handy (see entry on p. 14), Robert Johnson, Son House, Muddy Waters, Howlin' Wolf, John Lee Hooker, and sundry others—none of whom would ever have imagined themselves the subject of doctoral dissertations, full-scale biographies, or a museum. Juke joints, urban black clubs, backcountry honky-tonks, shacks, and bordellos were the expected world—at least while in white Mississippi. Inclusion in the Delta Blues Museum, housed in the main library of Clarksdale and dedicated to these and other practitioners, was a respectability beyond the imagining of the pre–World War II blues giants. Indeed, they could not have even entered the library! Today the museum fosters an appreciation of the blues and its connection to American culture, offering videotapes, recordings, photographs, memorabilia, performances, and a blues archive.

Rooster Blues Records
232 Sunflower Avenue, Clarksdale, MS 38614
(601) 627-2209
Hours: Mon.–Sat., 11 A.M.–6 P.M. Blues tours by appointment
Admission: Free

If the Delta Blues Museum has whetted your appetite, Rooster Blues Records is your next stop in Clarksdale. Rooster Blues offers a blues tour, a guide to local blues clubs, and access to some truly obscure blues recordings. It's amazing how cheerful a long time spent listening to sad songs amid the rural isolation of Delta poverty can leave one.

CORINTH

Corinth National Cemetery
1551 Horton Street, Corinth, MS 38834
(601) 286-5782
Hours: Daily, 8 A.M.–4:30 P.M.
Admission: Free

Corinth, where the Mobile & Ohio Railroad crossed the Memphis & Charleston (the Confederacy's sole east–west cross-country link), was one of the few genuinely critical junctions in the Civil War. Here, in April 1862, A. S. Johnston gathered the 45,000 troops he would hurl at Ulysses S. Grant during the Battle of Shiloh. Located in the northwest corner of Mississippi not far from where the Tennessee River shifts from a southerly to an easterly course, the city is now home to the Corinth National Cemetery, in which are buried some of the fallen from the Federal 14th, 40th, 106th, 108th, and 111th Colored Infantry regiments. Like their white counterparts, most of these dead, who fell in battles late in the war in Mississippi, Alabama, and Tennessee, originally were buried near the field of battle in mass trenches and only later formally interred. (Though it is not often mentioned at the 80 National Civil War cemeteries, more than half the graves are filled with those whose names are unknown.)

GREENWOOD

Cottonlandia Museum
U.S. 82W bypass, Greenwood, MS 38930
(601) 453-0925
2½ miles west of town
Hours: Tue.–Fri., 8 A.M.–5 P.M.; Sat.–Sun., 2 P.M.–5 P.M.
Admission: Adults, $2.50; ages 6–18, 50 cents

Despite its name, the Cottonlandia Museum does more than merely highlight the workings of an economic system whose cash crop was as white as its labor was black. Mississippi came late to cotton production; by far the greatest part of the state's story falls under the rubric of pre-Columbian Indian history, while most of its postdiscovery history reflects frontier clashes among jostling Indian, Spanish, French, and Anglo-American empires. From its pre-Columbian beginnings through the post–Civil War continuing exploitation of African-American labor, Mississippi's past is on display at the museum.

Florewood River Plantation
Fort Loring Road, Greenwood, MS 38930
(601) 455-3821
2 miles west of town and south of U.S. 82 and U.S. 49E
Hours: Tues.–Sat., 9 A.M.–12 P.M. and 1 P.M.–5 P.M.; Sun., 1 P.M.–5 P.M. (early Mar. to early Dec.); scheduled tours available
Admission: Adults, $3.50; seniors, $3; ages 5–18, $2.50

Florewood River Plantation re-creates the life and workings of a late-antebellum cotton plantation, complete with demonstrations of the appropriate 19th-century crafts and trades that were performed by skilled slaves. Slave quarters and two African-American living history interpreters in period dress convey a sense of slavery days and ways. A Cotton Museum is also open to visitors.

HOLLY SPRINGS

Ida B. Wells Post Office

365 Highway 178 West, Holly Springs, MS 38635
(601) 252-3631; (601) 252-2943
Hours: Mon.–Fri., 9 A.M.–5 P.M.
Admission: Free

Born a slave in the north-central Mississippi town of Holly Springs, Ida B. Wells became one of the nation's preeminent crusaders for African-American rights and women's suffrage. After graduating from the local Shaw (now Rust) College, actually a high school and industrial school, Wells traveled 40 miles northwest to Memphis, where she taught school and continued her education at Fisk University. There, in 1891, she co-founded the militant journal *Free Speech*, in whose pages she denounced local whites for the lynching of black men. While she was away lecturing in the North on this subject, a white mob burned her printing press. She responded by launching an international antilynching campaign and by intensifying her social protest against racial discrimination. Not marriage, nor motherhood, nor a career as a prominent journalist and, later in Chicago, a municipal court probation officer forestalled her efforts for racial and gender equality. Her struggle brought her into conflict both with the NAACP, which she judged insufficiently militant, and with the National American Woman Suffrage Association, which deprecated—or found tactically difficult—a close association with black issues. Although her hometown has no historical marker to commemorate the woman who surely was its most significant inhabitant, it does have the Ida B. Wells Post Office.

Hiram Revels' Burial Site

Hillcrest Cemetery, Market Street, Holly Springs, MS 38635
(601) 252-2943
Hours: Daily until sunset
Admission: Free

After study at Knox College in Illinois and ordination as an A.M.E. minister, the free black North Carolinian Hiram Revels taught school, recruited black troops for the Union army, founded a freedmen's school in Missouri, and joined the Union ranks as a chaplain of a African-American regiment in Mississippi. At war's end he remained in Mississippi, entered politics, and became the first African American to serve in the U.S. Senate, where he filled the seat previously held by Jefferson Davis and where he supported the removal of sanctions against former Confederates. Revels later served as president of Alcorn University (in 1871 named after the white, Old Whig "scalawag," Republican governor of Reconstruction Mississippi against whom the state's black Republicans mobilized in 1873 in a successful effort to acquire more state offices), which was established as a black-run school so as to prevent integration of the state university. Revels also served as Mississippi's secretary of state. Hiram Revels' Burial Site is yet another reason to visit Holly Springs.

Rust College
150 Rust Avenue, Holly Springs, MS 38635
(601) 252-8000
Hours: Mon.–Fri., 8 A.M.–5 P.M.
Admission: Free

Shaw University was established in 1866 by the Freedmen's Aid Bureau and the Methodist Episcopal Church (North) to educate black children and train black teachers. Mississippi's first facility for black higher education was renamed Rust College in 1890 to honor a prominent Methodist clergyman and abolitionist. Today its most notable features are the Leontyne Price Library, named after the Mississippi-born soprano who was the first black singer to have an opening-night lead role at the New York Metropolitan Opera Company, and Oak View, the sole extant 19th-century building on campus.

JACKSON

Convention & Visitors Bureau
921 North President Street, Jackson, MS 39202
(601) 960-1891
Hours: Mon.–Fri., 8:30 A.M.–5 P.M.

Farish Street Historic District
c/o Convention & Visitors Bureau, Box 1450, Jackson, MS 39215
(601) 960-1891 (c/o CVB)
Hours: Daily, 24 hours
Admission: Free

More than 800 buildings in the 125-acre Farish Street Historic District testify to the strength and self-sufficiency of the black professional community created under the compulsion of Jim Crow. The Farish community was the entire state's hub of black political, economic, and social development. Giants such as Louis Armstrong, Duke Ellington, and Cab Calloway walked its streets in the 1930s and '40s, while in the 1950s and '60s Martin Luther King, Jr., Stokely Carmichael, Medgar and Charles Evers, and others spoke here. Today Jackson offers both an annual September Farish Street Festival, which celebrates and partially re-creates the street's "glory days," and a brochure for a Farish Street walking tour.

James D. Lynch Grave and Monument
Greenwood Cemetery, North West and George streets, Jackson, MS 39202
(601) 960-1131
Hours: Daily until sunset
Admission: Free

Above his grave, the James D. Lynch Monument honors Mississippi's first (1869–1872) black secretary of state (a slot that southern white Republicans often offered to black colleagues as it was a ceremonial rather than substantive post) and one of Reconstruction's most vibrant, effective, interesting, and admired figures. Lynch (1839–1872) was freeborn in Baltimore to a free mulatto merchant and A.M.E. minister and a slave woman whom his father had purchased in order to free and marry. Lynch early decided upon the ministry, first choosing the Presbyterians, although at the age of 21 he transferred his allegiance to the A.M.E. Church. During the Civil War, Lynch organized congregations in Union-held territory in South Carolina and Georgia. In Georgia he took part in the 1865 Savannah meeting between General William Sherman and a group of black ministers, during which he forcefully dissented from his colleagues' contention that African Americans wished to separate from whites. After the war Lynch assumed the comfortable and useful post as editor of a Philadelphia newspaper, which he soon abandoned to move to the South ". . . and unite my destiny with that of my people." Simultaneously, he left the A.M.E. Church, to demonstrate his belief and declare that the time for separatism had passed.

After moving to Mississippi, Lynch established Methodist Episcopal (North) churches, which immediately led him to schools, which led him to the Freedmen's Bureau, which led him to the Republicans, at whose 1867 founding convention he played a leading role. The sole black candidate on Alcorn's Republican ticket in 1869, Lynch advocated good relations with the "master" class (including opposition to disenfranchising former Confederates) while simultaneously refusing to compromise on black civil rights and economic advancement. Dying early, before "Redemption," Lynch became the first black man to be buried in a white cemetery in Jackson. This situation was rectified at the turn of the century, when the state legislature—evidently rejecting his view that the time for black separatism had passed—had him disinterred and transferred to a black cemetery.

Jackson State University
1400 John R. Lynch Street, Jackson, MS 39217
(601) 968-2272
Hours: Call for appointment
Admission: Free

Perhaps best known today as the site of the 1970 nighttime confrontation that provided the excuse for white police to launch a fusillade of shots at a dormitory that killed two students, Jackson State University (JSU) began life in

1877 in Natchez, Mississippi, as the Natchez Seminary. A product of abolitionist sentiment in northern Protestant churches, which after the Civil War was renewed as a missionary commitment to aid and educate freed African Americans, the school was established by the American Baptist Home Mission Society of New York for the training of black teachers and preachers, who were seen as the core of a new community's leadership. Six years of success underscored the need to move to larger facilities in a more central location, and Jackson, the state's capital, was selected. Two decades later, recognizing that population shifts in the town were separating the school from the community it was designed to serve, Jackson College moved to its present location. In the midst of the depression, financial difficulties forced the American Baptist Home Mission Society to cease its support for the college. Dedicated efforts of the black and white communities saved the school, which was brought within the state's (segregated, of course) education system in 1940. Today JSU is the sixth largest of the nation's 116 historically black colleges.

Mississippi State Historical Museum
Old State Capitol Building, North State and Capitol streets, Jackson, MS 39201
(601) 359-6920
Hours: Mon.–Fri., 8 A.M.–5 P.M.; Sat., 9:30 A.M.–4:30 P.M.;
Sun., 12:30 P.M.–4:30 P.M.
Admission: Free

The South's first comprehensive, permanent exhibit on the civil rights movement can be found at the Mississippi State Historical Museum. Aptly, it occupies the Old State Capitol, in which the Ordinance of Secession was passed, Hiram Revels was elected to serve out Jefferson Davis's U.S. Senate term, and two state constitutional conventions (in 1868 confirming black political rights and in 1890 denying them) were held. Today slavery, Reconstruction, and Jim Crow precede an examination of the 1950s and '60s. Twelve minutes of television news film highlight sit-ins, marches, speeches, Freedom Rides, police wagons, and James Meredith's entry onto the Ole Miss campus, while artifacts from the period—remnants of bombed buildings, a charred cross, a voting booth, banners, and buttons—complete the story.

Mt. Helm Baptist Church
300 East Church Street, Jackson, MS 39202
(601) 353-3981
Hours: Mon.–Fri., 9 A.M.–5 P.M.
Admission: Free

The oldest black church in Mississippi's capital, Mt. Helm Baptist (1835), can be found at the intersection of Lamar and Church streets.

Smith Robertson Museum, School and Cultural Center
528 Bloom Street, P.O. Box 3259, Jackson, MS 39207
(601) 960-1457
Hours: Tue.–Fri., 9 A.M.–5 P.M.; Sat., 9 A.M.–12 P.M.; Sun., 2 P.M.–5 P.M.
Admission: Adults, $1; seniors and under 19, 50 cents

Located in the center of Jackson's historic black community, occupying the site of what was the city's first black public school and named after the former slave who rose to become Jackson's first black alderman and convinced the city's white elite to educate black youth, the Smith Robertson Museum interprets the history and culture of Afro-Mississippians.

LEXINGTON

Booker-Thomas Museum
Highway 12 (Tchula Road), Route 2, Box 314-P, Lexington, MS 39095
(601) 834-2672
Hours: Open all year by appointment
Admission: Voluntary donation requested

The Booker-Thomas Museum gives visitors a rare portrait of early-20th-century black, rural Mississippi life. It exhibits "anything your grandmother ever used," from 19th-century farming equipment to kitchen utensils and the furnishings of former slaves. This homegrown museum is set up like an old-fashioned rural general store; as recently as the 1950s such stores were common in the deep South.

LORMAN

Alcorn State University
Highway 552 at U.S. 61, Lorman, MS 39096
(601) 877-6100
Hours: Oakland Chapel: Mon.–Fri., 8 A.M.–4 P.M.; or by appointment
Admission: Free

Reconstruction era politics was a wild affair in Mississippi, and no one loomed larger on the scene than James L. Alcorn, owner of the largest plantation in the Yazoo-Mississippi Delta. This former Whig served briefly in the Confederate army before retiring to his plantation, whereupon he began smuggling his contraband cotton in exchange for sound Union currency. Guided by a keen political sense unencumbered by even the pretense of moral scruple, Alcorn in 1865 advocated a limited black suffrage and the following year supported ratification of the 14th Amendment as steps to his political ascendancy. Alcorn won control of Mississippi's Republican Party by virtue of his former Whig connections, his money, and his recognition (and adamant determination) that while the guarantee of freedmen's civil and political rights would be imposed by the occupying Union forces, whites could retain control of state government. In 1871, in an effort to meet black demands for higher education without integrating the state university, Alcorn and his supporters endorsed the creation of a black-run agricultural college. Despite the honor of having the university named after him, within four years Alcorn allied himself with the state Democratic Party's successful effort to smash Reconstruction and force the resignation or deposition of all black officeholders.

Alcorn Agricultural & Mechanical College, now Alcorn State University, opened with former U.S. Senator Hiram Revels (see entry on p. 99) as its first president. It was America's first black college funded under the Civil War's Morrill Land Grant Act of 1862, which provided for the sale of public lands to fund agricultural schools in each state. Appropriately, it was built on the grounds and took over the facilities of then-suspended Oakland College, a Presbyterian school dating to 1830 whose staunchly Unionist president was stabbed to death in 1851 in front of his campus home by a secessionist. Today the school's Oakland Memorial Chapel, a National Historic Site, remains an outstanding example of southern Greek Revival architecture. In addition, nine period buildings comprise the Alcorn State University Historic District.

MERIDIAN

Convention & Visitors Bureau
721 Front Street Extension, Suite 800, Meridian, MS 39302
(601) 483-0083
Hours: Mon.–Fri., 8 A.M.–5 P.M.

Ask for its "African-American Heritage: Historic Sites of Meridian & Lauderdale County, Mississippi" brochure.

Carnegie Library
2721 13th Street, c/o St. Paul's United Methodist Church, Meridian, MS, 39301
(601) 482-3753
Hours: Daily until sunset
Admission: Not open to the public. Exterior viewing only

As the second decade of the 20th century opened, a local group of black Methodists initiated a drive for a library for "the colored citizens" of Meridian. An $8,000 grant from the Carnegie Foundation gave this east-central Mississippi town the Carnegie Library. It is believed in Mississippi that Meridian was the only city ever given a black library by the Carnegie Foundation as part of an original grant. What is certain is that in the early 1900s, this was the only library Meridian's African Americans could enter for any purpose other than sweeping.

Wechsler School
1415 30th Avenue, Meridian, MS
c/o 1327 30th Avenue, Meridian, MS 39301
(601) 485-8882; (601) 483-3130
Hours: By appointment only
Admission: Free. Voluntary donations encouraged

Constructed in 1894, this school—Mississippi's first brick public school for blacks financed by state bonds—originally housed only the primary through the eighth grades. Not until 1921 did Wechsler offer a high school diploma. At the time, it was the only school in all of east-central Mississippi to do so for African Americans.

MOUND BAYOU

Mound Bayou City Hall
Green Street, Box 680, Mound Bayou, MS 38762-0680
(601) 741-2193

I. T. Montgomery House
302 South West Main Street, Mound Bayou, MS 38762
(601) 741-2193
Hours: Daily until sunset
Admission: House: Not open to the public. Exterior viewing only. Sculpture: Free

In 1887 Isaiah T. Montgomery, born near Vicksburg on the Davis Bend plantation as the property of Jefferson Davis's brother, founded the town of Mound Bayou for freed slaves so that he and his companions could enjoy self-government in an independent black community. Montgomery's belief in the necessity and possibility of black land ownership and self-government owed much to his experiences in Reconstruction Mississippi. There, from 1867 through 1885, he helped run the Davis Bend property his father had purchased after the war. In 1885 the land was reclaimed by the Davis family in a court suit following the death of the senior Montgomery and the family's financial ruin after the depression of the 1870s. While some accounts suggest that the Davises used the white courts crudely to seize the property that the elder Montgomery had legally purchased, Mound Bayou African-American folk memory holds that Montgomery had purchased two plantations on long-term credit; they reverted to the Davises when the loan's terms could not be met.

In either event, I. T. Montgomery's rise was aided by the fact that, after being taught to read by a Davis slave, the ten-year-old boy trained as Joseph Davis's private secretary, in which capacity he served until freed in 1863 when Admiral David Porter's fleet ran the Vicksburg blockade. Montgomery thereupon entered the service of the U.S. Navy, witnessing Ulysses S. Grant's attack on Port Gibson. Then, in Montgomery's words, "With the first return of peace, correspondence between Mr. J. E. Davis and my father was resumed, which resulted in the sale of the Davis estate, some 4,000 acres, to us in 1867."

Mound Bayou owed its existence not only to Montgomery's vision and tenacity, but also to the development of a railroad, whose managers believed that only African Americans could adapt to the area's semitropical climate, which was conducive to malaria. The town, carved out of wilderness and swampland, attracted settlers from Louisiana, Alabama, and Georgia, who were drawn by the high yields of fertile soil, the ease of transporting their cotton by rail to market, and most of all, of course, by black self-government and the absence of white overlords. Under Montgomery's leadership, the town flourished. By 1920 the largest enterprise of its kind in the state, the Mound Bayou Oil Mill and Manufacturing Company, was erected at an investment cost of $100,000. Years before this the community had focused on education, opening with the assistance of the American Missionary Association a school taught by Montgomery's sister, Mary, a former pupil at Oberlin College. For a long time the Mound Bayou Normal and Industrial Institute was the only school in the county for African-American children. In 1910 the I. T. Montgomery House, now a National Historic Landmark, was constructed in what today still claims to be the largest all-black municipality in the country. Not far from the house is the Mound Bayou city hall, in front of which stands a large wooden sculpture that depicts the contributions of famous African Americans.

NATCHEZ

Convention & Visitors Bureau
P.O. Box 1485, 311 Liberty Road, Natchez, MS 39121-1485
(800) 647-6724
Hours: Mon.–Fri., 8 A.M.–5 P.M.

Ask for the "Historic Natchez on the Mississippi: The African-American Experience" brochure for additional black heritage sites not mentioned below.

Angelety House
125 St. Catherine Street, Natchez, MS 39120
(601) 442-5448
Hours: Tour of unfurnished interior: Sept.–May: Wed.–Sat., 1 P.M.–5 P.M. Exterior: Daily until sunset
Admission: Voluntary donations requested

Bearing the name of the African-American family whose home it was at the turn of the century, the Angelety House, a restored antebellum Greek Revival structure with Gothic Revival overtones, now houses the Mostly African Market, in which the arts and crafts of Africa and its diaspora are exhibited or sold.

Proceeds from sales support Project Southern Cross, a three-year summer enrichment program for some of Natchez's public school students.

Dunleith
84 Homochitto Street, Natchez, MS 39120
(601) 446-8500
Hours: Mon.–Sat., 9 A.M.–5 P.M.; Sun., 12:30 P.M.–5 P.M.
Admission: Adults, $4; ages 6–17, $2

In this Greek Revival–style house the young John R. Lynch—the son of an Irish immigrant plantation manager and a slave woman, and a future U.S. congressman—fanned dinner guests before being freed by Union troops and attending the Freedmen's School in Natchez. Lynch entered the state legislature in 1870, becoming its speaker in 1872 at the age of 24. Winning a congressional seat in the 1872 election, he served in the 43rd session of U.S. House of Representatives in 1873. He and other black officeholders fell victim to the 1875 white Democratic Party "Redemption," which overturned Reconstruction in Mississippi amid massive voter intimidation and fraud and the murder of several hundred African Americans statewide by armed bands of whites who did not even bother to shield their identities with hoods.

Like his colleague Blanche K. Bruce (see Bruce House entry on p. 193), Lynch supported President Hayes's southern policy and gained federal patronage when Republican opportunities in the South disappeared entirely. (Lynch was a telling example of southern Republican marginalization: He, a black man, served as the state party chairman from 1881 through 1892.) Lynch was a noted, if impotent, Republican Party figure, regularly attending national conventions. Indeed, he was the first African American to deliver a keynote address at a Democratic or Republican national convention—he did not have a successor until 1968. Thanks to the still-open local opportunities for African Americans following the collapse of Reconstruction and prior to the turn-of-the-century imposition of rigid and comprehensive Jim Crow, Lynch was admitted to the Mississippi bar in 1890 and held city and plantation property in Mississippi valued at more than $100,000.

Lynch later moved to Chicago and in the first decades of this century used the pages of Carter G. Woodson's *Journal of Negro History* (see Woodson House entry on p. 204) to rebut the then-dominant historiography of Reconstruction, which portrayed the period as a monstrosity forced upon the South by, in the words of Bowers's best-selling *The Tragic Era*, "emissaries of hate." Unfortunately, Dunleith house does not interpret Lynch's career.

William Johnson House
Natchez National Historical Park, 210 State Street, P.O. Box 1208, Natchez, MS 39120
(601) 442-7047
Hours: Temporarily closed for renovation

The William Johnson House was home from 1841 to 1851 to one of Natchez's more prosperous free black antebellum residents. Johnson was born a slave in 1809 and released from slavery in 1820 after his master, William Johnson, who presumably was his father as well, petitioned the legislature to grant freedom to "the mulatto boy named William." A successful barber, land speculator, money lender, and slave owner, the freed Johnson kept a diary that offers virtually unprecedented access into the experience of the South's small free black community. Johnson was murdered in 1851 by a neighboring landowner; his house stayed in his family until the 1970s.

Natchez Museum of Afro-American History and Culture
307A Marker Street, Natchez, MS 39120
(601) 445-0728 or 442-6822
Hours: Summer: Wed.–Fri., 1 P.M.–5 P.M.; Sat., 11 A.M.–4 P.M. Oct.–May: Wed., 1 P.M.–5 P.M.; Sat., 11 A.M.–4 P.M. Other times by appointment
Admission: Free. Voluntary donations encouraged

As the Natchez Museum of Afro-American History and Culture says, "We exist to tell our story." That story principally concerns the struggles and accomplishments of southwestern Mississippi's African Americans from 1890 through the 1960s and is detailed with the aid of more than 500 artifacts.

Slave Market Site
St. Catherine Street, Natchez, MS 39126
(800) 647-6724 (CVB)
Hours: Daily until sunset

Shamefully bare of any historical marker, the junction of St. Catherine and Liberty (!) Road was a major Slave Market Site. Coupled with sales at Cotton Square and the river landing on Silver Street, this site made Natchez the sole rival of New Orleans as the busiest slave-trade town in 19th-century America and reflected the spread of cotton production from the soil-depleted southern seaboard states.

Richard Wright Marker
Bluff Park at Broadway, Natchez, MS 39120
Near the bandstand and the Rhythm Club fire marker
Hours: Daily until sunset
Admission: Free

Richard Wright (1908–1960), arguably the most influential African-American literary figure of the 20th century, was born near Natchez. Like the vast majority of his compatriots born in the early years of the 20th century in Mississippi, Wright was the son of sharecroppers whose ancestors were raised in bondage. Today the author of *Native Son* and *Black Boy* is honored in his hometown with a historical marker. (Visitors to Natchez may also wish to view Wright's boyhood home, *now a private residence and not open to the public*, at 20 East Woodlawn.)

LIBRARY OF CONGRESS

Richard Wright, perhaps the greatest 20th-century African-American writer, was born the son of Mississippi sharecroppers.

Zion Chapel A.M.E. Church
338 Martin Luther King Street, Natchez, MS 39126
(601) 442-1396

In 1868, two years before he was elected to fill the unexpired term of Jefferson Davis in the U.S. Senate, the freeborn black Hiram Revels (see entry on p. 99) was minister of the Zion Chapel A.M.E. Church of Natchez. During his pastorate, the present church building was purchased.

OKOLONA

Civil War Marker
U.S. 45S, Okolona, MS 38860
On the city's southern limits
Hours: Daily until sunset
Admission: Free

Located in the northeast corner of Mississippi directly south of Tupelo, Okolona changed hands more than once in the course of the Civil War, largely as a consequence of whichever side happened to have its troops in the area. In 1864, shortly before what would prove to be the unhappiest Christmas in the town's history, the third Union raid of the war virtually destroyed it. Among the units involved in this raid was the 3rd Colored Cavalry Regiment ("thought by good judges to be about as good cavalry as we have," in the words of Major General N.J.T. Dana), which had to its credit the audacious triumph at the Big Black River railroad bridge that had cut off Confederate Lieutenant General John Bell Hood's supply route just as he began his last invasion of Tennessee.

Twenty-one of the 3rd Regiment's line officers later gained notoriety in Mississippi when they summarily tried and hanged a civilian who had threatened to cut the throat of a black sentinel for talking to a black woman. The verdict was doubtless speeded by the fact that the defendant, a cotton speculator whose business was protected by the black troops of the regiment, earlier had told the officers and troops that Confederate General Nathan B. Forrest—who in the course of the war had once recaptured Okolona from Union forces—had been right to massacre black troops after the spring of 1864 battle at Fort Pillow, Tennessee.

A Civil War Marker on the southern outskirts of the city describes the actions fought in and around Okolona. (Also see Brices Cross Roads entry on p. 114; Battle of Oxford entry on p. 110; Tupelo Battlefield entry on p. 115; the Fort Pillow entry on p. 146; and the Poison Springs entry on p. 33.) Okolona also is the birthplace of William Raspberry, whose coverage of the Watts riot in 1965 won him Journalist of the Year honors from the Capital Press Club in Washington, D.C.

OXFORD

Battle of Oxford Marker
State Highway 6, Oxford, MS 38655

A marker recalls the Union army's 1864 destruction of Oxford, during which only the buildings of the University of Mississippi were spared. Involved in this action were troops of the 55th Colored Infantry Regiment, who earlier in the year had taken part in the Battle of Brices Cross Roads, in which Union forces once again were thrashed soundly by General Nathan B. Forrest. While Mississippi's fate was sealed with Ulysses S. Grant's victory at Vicksburg in the summer of 1863, it was Lincoln's spring 1864 appointment of Grant as Supreme Commander of all Union forces, and Grant's appointment of General William Sherman to command the western theater of operations, that brought home to central Mississippi the price of defeat. The fighting in Mississippi in the summer of 1864 had but one aim: to affect the supply lines that kept Sherman's troops on the march in Alabama and Georgia. At Brices Cross Roads, Tupelo, Okolona, and Oxford, Confederate forces under the command of Forrest confronted the larger number of Union troops under the command of a number of generals who proved no match for Forrest. As occurred in northern Virginia, Georgia, and South Carolina, Mississippi learned the harsh meaning of total war. Active in this campaign were several African-American units, including the 55th, 59th, 61st, and 68th Colored Infantry regiments, the 3rd Colored Calvary Regiment, and the 2nd Colored Light Artillery Regiment. At this stage of the war all black troops were well aware of the Fort Pillow massacre (see entry on p. 146) and the peril of falling into the hands of Confederate forces.

Blues Archives
University of Mississippi, Farley Hall—Room 340, Oxford, MS 38677
(601) 232-7753
Hours: Mon.–Fri., 8:30 A.M.–5 P.M.
Admission: Free

It is difficult to decide who would be more shocked by the existence of the Blues Archives of the University of Mississippi: Robert Johnson and other blues giants of the 1920s and '30s or Governor Ross Barnett, Congressman Theodore

Bilbo, and Senator James Eastland, all of whom bore such manifest contempt (and in Bilbo's case, psychopathological fear and hatred) of African Americans that any museum other than an anthropological one devoted to black heritage would have seemed even more absurd than vile. Yet on the Ole Miss campus, where in the autumn of 1962 3,000 federal troops were required in order for James Meredith to break the color barrier, today's visitors will find a collection of B. B. King memorabilia and recordings; books, periodicals, and recordings focusing on southern folklore and music; photographs, posters, and taped interviews of major bluesmen; and collections highlighting Ma Rainey, Percy Mayfield, and others.

Museums of the University of Mississippi
5th Street and University Avenue, Oxford, MS 38677
(601) 232-7073
Five blocks east of campus
Hours: Tue.–Sat., 10 A.M.–4 P.M.; Sun., 1 P.M.–4 P.M.
Admission: Free

Folk art of the South, much of it African-American in origin, and African art comprise part of the holdings of the Museums of the University of Mississippi, which are a five-minute walk east of the Ole Miss campus.

PHILADELPHIA

Mount Zion United Methodist Church
Route 2 (Highway 747), Philadelphia, MS 39350
(601) 656-8277
5 miles northeast of Philadelphia, via Highway 482
Hours: Memorial marker: Daily until sunset

Neshoba County Courthouse
401 Beacon Street, #201, Philadelphia, MS 39350
(601) 656-6281
Hours: Mon.–Fri., 8 A.M.–5 P.M.
Admission: Free

Though four decades ago African Americans constituted 45 percent of Mississippi's population, only 5 percent of them were registered to vote, the highest and lowest percentages respectively in the nation. Linked to both ends of this disparity was white racial violence, in which Mississippi also led the nation, and the state's extreme (and biracial) poverty, again unrivaled in the nation. Neither violence nor disenfranchisement—which were common to the deep South—accounts for the severity of white dominance and black oppression in Mississippi. The explanation lies in black rural isolation and the absence of a black professional class. In the decade after World War II, Selma, Alabama, alone had more black attorneys, dentists, and almost as many doctors as the entire state of Mississippi.

To this anomalous and violent state there came in 1964 the "Freedom Summer," which differed from the previous voter-registration efforts by the NAACP and SNCC (Student Nonviolent Coordinating Committee) in that the bulk of its troops were white, middle-class university students, many of them female. This difference, particularly in the context of a presidential election year in which the right to vote might be exercised with immediate impact, focused the attention of the news media on Mississippi. But it was white supremacist murder that assured that "Freedom Summer" became and remained for months one of the country's lead news stories.

In the east-central Mississippi county of Neshoba, near the inaptly named town of Philadelphia, three young civil rights workers, two white and one black, were murdered by members of the Ku Klux Klan with the complicity of local police and their bodies secretly buried.

For six weeks, as hundreds of unarmed U.S. troops searched for the missing men and hundreds of FBI agents roamed the state seeking leads in the case, as racial violence continued in Mississippi, as the 1964 Civil Rights Act came to a vote on the U.S. Senate floor, and as the Democratic Party presidential convention approached, America's newspapers and television news shows kept alive the story of the presumed dead. Early in August presumption became confirmed fact as the bodies of James Earl Chaney, Michael Schwerner, and Andrew Goodman were unearthed on a farm not far from the Philadelphia jail from which six weeks earlier they had been released into the waiting arms of Klan killers.

In December the FBI arrested a score of men in Philadelphia, including the sheriff, the six-foot two-inch, 250-pound Lawrence Rainey, who in the course of his career had killed two African Americans in "self-defense"; his deputy, Cecil Price, who had brought the three victims to the local jail in the Neshoba County Courthouse hours before their deaths; and Sam Bowers, the Klan Imperial Wizard. Soon the arrested themselves sat in the Neshoba County Courthouse as a grand jury considered murder indictments. Photographs of the accused, smug smiles on faces distended by plugs of tobacco, offended a country that had turned a blind eye to decades of racial violence against black Mississippians. The accused men's smugness proved as justified as black Mississippians' lack of faith in the state's justice. No indictments were returned and no one was ever convicted of the murders. However, three years later in a federal court trial in Meridian, Mississippi, an all-white jury convicted Price, Bowers, and five other men of conspiracy to deprive the three slain men of their civil rights.

Today, at the Mount Zion United Methodist Church, which was burned to the ground in the summer of 1964 because it served as a local base for the "Freedom Summer" civil rights workers, there is a memorial marker to Chaney, Schwerner, and Goodman. Nearby, the county courthouse still stands as mute reminder of the ironic observation—frequently voiced in Alabama, Georgia, and elsewhere in the deep South—of the more respectable sort of segregationists of those years, "Thank God for Mississippi."

PINEY WOODS

The Piney Woods Country Life School
Highway 49 South, Piney Woods, MS 39148
(601) 845-2214
Hours: Mon.–Fri., 8 A.M.–5 P.M.
Admission: Free

Located in Rankin County—which shares its name with Mississippi's former congressman John Rankin, one of the most vituperative racists ever to disgrace the halls of the U.S. House of Representatives—the Piney Woods Country Life School was founded by Dr. Laurence C. Jones in 1910 and directed by him until 1975. A black boarding institution typical of the Jim Crow–era industrial schools that constituted the pinnacle of education for all but an infinitesimal few African Americans in the deep South of the early 20th century, Piney Woods continues to embody an explicitly Christian ethic and a commitment to physical labor and personal responsibility.

PORT GIBSON

Grant's March Through Claiborne County Marker
U.S. 61, Port Gibson, MS 39150
In front of St. James Episcopal Church, corner of Church (U.S. 61) and Jackson streets
Hours: Daily until sunset
Admission: Free

In Port Gibson is the first in a series of markers that commemorate Grant's March Through Claiborne County. In April 1863, after the failure during the 1862–63 winter of a series of amphibious operations (often referred to as the Bayou Expeditions) aimed at reducing Vicksburg, General Ulysses S. Grant took his 45,000-man army, which included numerous African-American regiments, down the Louisiana side of the Mississippi, crossed the river well south of Vicksburg, and marched toward Port Gibson, where he overwhelmed an element of General John C. Pemberton's Confederate forces. Grant then marched northeast and took Jackson, the state capital, before turning due west and driving Pemberton's forces back into Vicksburg's fortifications.

TOUGALOO

Tougaloo Mansion House and Tougaloo College
500 County Line Road, Tougaloo, MS 39174
(601) 977-7700
Hours: Mansion House: Exterior only; currently houses college offices
Admission: Free

In 1869 the Tougaloo Mansion House, the home of J. W. Boddie, a successful planter who died at the end of the Civil War, became the nucleus of Tougaloo College. Founded by the American Missionary Association, Tougaloo aimed to educate freedmen to partake in the new society opened up by the destruction of slavery. A small school (its first A.B. degree was awarded to the only member of the class of 1901 and today's enrollment is less than 1,000), Tougaloo's black rights heritage shone through in the civil rights struggles of the 1950s and '60s.

TUPELO

Brices Cross Roads National Battlefield Site
Natchez Trace Parkway, Rural Route 1, NT-143, Tupelo, MS 38801
(601) 842-1572
6 miles west of Baldwyn on I-370
Hours: Daily until sunset
Admission: Free

In north Georgia from May through September of 1864 General William Sherman doggedly fought the Confederate forces of Joseph E. Johnston in an attempt to capture Atlanta. Sherman's supplies depended on the one-track railroad from Nashville to Chattanooga. From Tupelo, Mississippi, General Nathan B. Forrest sought to sever that supply line. Sherman ordered General S. D. Sturgis, whose command included an element of the 2nd Colored Light Artillery Regiment and the 55th and 59th Colored Infantry regiments, to move from Memphis into northern Mississippi to forestall Forrest and to destroy the Confederate rail line running between Corinth and Tupelo. Early in June Forrest's 3,500 men and some of Sturgis's 8,100 clashed at Brices Cross Roads near Baldwyn north of Tupelo. Unable to bring all his weary forces into battle, Sturgis was forced to retreat. A botched river crossing led to panic, and the retreat turned into a rout that led to Forrest's capture of 1,500 Union troops. The 59th Colored Infantry Regiment covered the rear of the disorderly retreat, either fighting with bayonets and clubbed muskets as its ammunition ran out or picking up weapons cast aside by fleeing Union troops. An Illinois artillery officer, Lieutenant John Merriles, praised the black troops both for preventing an even greater Confederate victory and for marching uncomplainingly though their clothes were sodden with blood from their wounds. That wounded black troops did not fall out and surrender owed more to the memory (reinforced by federal propaganda) of the Fort Pillow (and other) Confederate massacres of black Union captives than to exceptional courage.

Today, about ten miles north of Tupelo, the Brices Cross Roads National Battlefield Site offers a view of much of the battleground and interpretive markers with text and maps. **Note:** There are no facilities or personnel at Brices; however, park interpreters at the Tupelo visitor center of the Natchez Trace Parkway can answer questions about the battle.

Tupelo National Battlefield Site
Natchez Trace National Parkway Rural, Route 1, NT-143, Tupelo, MS 38801
(601) 680-4026
1 mile west of crossroads of I-6 and U.S. 45, ½ mile east of Natchez Trace Parkway
Hours: Daily until sunset
Admission: Free

Though General Nathan B. Forrest's victory at Brices Cross Roads had no immediate strategic consequence—with far greater resources of men and material, General William Sherman could, and repeatedly did, order small commands into northern Mississippi to protect his supply line—the Union commander could not rest secure. He therefore ordered his commander in Memphis to "follow Forrest to the death, if it cost 10,000 men and breaks the Treasury." Toward this end about 20,000 Union troops, supported by 24 cannon, marched into Mississippi. Forrest fortified Okolona in an attempt to get his far more numerous opponents to attack a strongly defended position. Instead the Union forces marched toward Tupelo—from which Confederate troops had been withdrawn to help Forrest in Okolona—and the railhead there. Recognizing that he would lose his rail line and be forced with inferior numbers to attack a fortified Union-held Tupelo, Forrest left his fortifications and attacked the Union troops on their march. Two days of attacks saw the outnumbered and outgunned Forrest worsted. But on the third day, the federal forces, short on ammunition, food, and water, and with many prostrated by the heat, abandoned both their own and the Confederate wounded and began an orderly retreat toward Tennessee. Again Forrest attacked and again he was repulsed; and again the integrity of Sherman's supply line was maintained. Not until September would Forrest raid Tennessee, by which time Atlanta had fallen and Sherman no longer depended on the Nashville-to-Chattanooga rail line.

Fighting at Tupelo were the 59th, 61st, and 68th Colored Infantry regiments and a unit of the 2nd Colored Light Artillery Regiment. Today the Tupelo National Battlefield Site has markers, maps, and monuments that recall the battle and honor its participants, and National Park Service interpreters to answer questions.

UTICA

Utica Junior College
c/o Hinds Community College—Utica Campus, Box 3, Utica, MS 39175
(601) 885-6062
About 35 miles southwest of Jackson, on Highway 18
Hours: By appointment through the Admissions Office
Admission: Free

W. H. Holtzclaw founded the Utica Normal and Industrial Institute (now Utica Junior College) in 1903 and later helped found the Mississippi Association of Teachers in Colored Schools and the Farmers Conference in Mississippi, all in an endeavor to provide a better future for the black sharecroppers and small farmers who constituted the great bulk of the slave descendants in one of the country's most economically undeveloped and socially isolated areas. The William H. Holtzclaw House on the Utica campus was his residence from its construction in 1925 until his death in 1943.

VAUGHAN

Casey Jones Museum
P.O. Box 605, Vaughan, MS 39179
(601) 673-9864
Just off I-55, 35 miles north of Jackson
Hours: Tue.–Sat., 9 A.M.–5 P.M.
Admission: Adults, $1; children, 3–11, 50 cents

What distinguished the spring 1900 collision in central Mississippi of the *Cannonball Express* with a parked freight train was not the death of the Cannonball's engineer, Casey Jones, but the creative virtuosity of Wallace Saunders, a black engine wiper. Saunders's mournful song of railroad courage captured the public's fancy—and little else. Saunders was a far better tunesmith than businessman—he sold the rights to the song for a bottle of gin!

Today, in the Casey Jones Museum, housed in an old railroad station, visitors will find memorabilia of the crash and of Saunders's composition.

VICKSBURG

Convention and Visitors Bureau
P.O. Box 110, Vicksburg, MS 39181
(601) 636-9421; (800) 221-3536

U.S.S. CAIRO Museum
3201 Clay Street, Vicksburg, MS 39180
(601) 636-0583
Hours: June–Aug.: daily, 8 A.M.–7 P.M. Rest of year: 8 A.M.–5 P.M.
Admission: $3 per car; $1 per person by bus; seniors and under 16, free; Visitor Center, free

In the course of General Ulysses S. Grant's winter 1862 attempt to capture Vicksburg, he sent the ironclad gunboat *Cairo*, along with several other vessels, to destroy Confederate batteries and clear the river of enemy obstructions. On December 12 *Cairo* was sunk, history's first victim of electronically detonated mines. With her to the bottom went most of the crew, including four African Americans. A century later the gunboat was raised from its riverbed grave and yielded a wealth of artifacts that shed light on naval life during the Civil War.

The U.S.S. CAIRO Museum displays these artifacts and the remains of the gunboat and interprets the naval aspects of the Vicksburg campaign.

Old Court House Museum
1008 Cherry Street, Vicksburg, MS 39180
(601) 636-0741
Hours: Mon.–Sat., 8:30 A.M.–4:30 P.M.; Sun., 1:30 P.M.–4:30 P.M.
Admission: Adults, $2; over 65, $1.50; students, $1; under 6, free. No credit cards. Group rates available

When the American flag was raised at Vicksburg's Old Court House on Independence Day of 1863, it was a particularly significant moment in U.S. history: On that day, following nine months of resistance to General Ulysses S. Grant, the city President Lincoln called "the key" to the Confederacy officially surrendered. Today's visitors to the Old Court House Museum will not only view artifacts that help explicate the city's history, they will also see a small exhibit on local black achievements.

Vicksburg National Military Park and Cemetery
3201 Clay Street, Vicksburg, MS 39180
Park: (601) 636-0583; museum: (601) 636-2199
Hours: Visitor Center, 8 A.M.–5 P.M.; museum, 9 A.M.–5 P.M., daily
Admission: Driving tour with guide: cars, $15; vans, $20; buses, $30; cassette rental, $4.50.
National Park: cars, $3; buses/vans, $1; under 16, over 62, free

In the Vicksburg National Military Park and Cemetery more than 1,200 markers and monuments commemorate the most decisive campaign of the Civil War. Black regiments played a crucial role in it, particularly from General Ulysses S. Grant's spring 1863 river crossing south of the city through the formal siege that lasted from May 18 until July 4, and many of their dead lie here. The visitor center has exhibits, electric maps, and a recorded lecture describing the campaign.

NORTH CAROLINA

Travel and Tourism Division
430 North Salisbury Street, Raleigh, NC 27603
(800) 847-4862; (919) 733-4171
Hours: Early spring–mid-October: Mon.–Fri., 9 A.M.–9:30 P.M. Rest of year: Mon.–Fri., 9 A.M.–5 P.M.

ASHEVILLE

Young Men's Institute Cultural Center
39 South Market Street, Asheville, NC 28801
(704) 255-4614
Hours: Daily, 9 A.M.–5 P.M.
Admission: Free

Asheville's most enduring African-American cultural institution dates from 1892. The Young Men's Institute, now the YMI Cultural Center, was commissioned by George Vanderbilt in gratitude to the local black workers who spent five years building his Biltmore Estate, a French Renaissance chateau with 250 rooms and 35 acres of formal gardens. Declared a National Historic Landmark in 1976, the center has been renovated and now includes a museum and an auditorium. The nearby Biltmore Estate, which is open to the public, is also a National Historic Landmark, and its great house remains the largest private residence in the United States.

CHARLOTTE

Afro-American Cultural Center
401 North Myers Street, Charlotte, NC 28202
(704) 374-1565
Hours: Tue.–Sat., 10 A.M.–6 P.M.; Sun., 1 P.M.–5 P.M.
Admission: Free; some ticketed events

Art and artifacts—masks, wooden sculpture, bronze castings, drums, doors, and furniture—from the Benin, Dogon, Ibo, Ashanti, and other African cultures—and African-American creativity in the musical, theatrical, and visual arts are on view at the Afro-American Cultural Center. The center also has on site two "shotgun houses"—shallow frame structures that were the typical residential building style for African Americans in the South in the century following Emancipation. Soon one of these shotgun houses will serve as a walk-through period museum interpreting early 20th-century African-American everyday life, while the other will house a black history and culture archives.

CRESWELL

Somerset Place
P.O. Box 215, Creswell, NC 27928
(919) 797-4560
Hours: Apr.–Oct.: Mon.–Sat., 9 A.M.–5 P.M.; Sun., 1 P.M.–5 P.M.
Rest of year: Tue.–Sat., 10 A.M.–4 P.M.; Sun., 1 P.M.–4 P.M.
Admission: Free

Eighty West African slaves arrived at this antebellum coastal plantation in 1786. Eventually 21 slave families would coalesce here. Today the restored Somerset Place is the scene of an annual reunion of the descendants of the slaves and freedmen who once labored here. Guided tours of the mansion, small museum, garden, and outbuildings provide glimpses into the 19th century. Though remains of the slave chapel and quarters can be seen by visitors, the site's interpretive framework is oriented toward the Great Family and the Great House.

DURHAM

Durham Convention & Visitors Bureau
101 East Morgan Street, Durham, NC 27701
(919) 687-0288; (800) 446-8604
Hours: Mon.–Fri., 8:30 A.M.–5 P.M.

Hayti Heritage Center
804 Old Fayetteville Street, Durham, NC 27702
(919) 683-1709
Hours: Mon.–Fri., 9 A.M.–5 P.M.; weekends, 10 A.M.–2 P.M.
Admission: Free

St. Joseph's A.M.E. Church was founded in 1869, one of the first autonomous black churches in Durham and the oldest such structure still standing. Its sanctuary, which dates to 1891, today sees service as the Hayti Heritage Center and houses the William Tucker African-American Archive—a collection of the works of authors and illustrators of children's books—and an art gallery and a dance studio.

North Carolina Central University
Fayetteville and Lawson streets, Durham, NC 27707
(919) 560-6100; Library: (919) 560-6473; Museum: (919) 560-6211
Hours: Library: Mon.–Fri., 8:30 A.M.–4:30 P.M.
Museum: Tue.–Fri., 9 A.M.–5 P.M.; Sun., 2 P.M.–5 P.M.
Admission: Free

Chartered by the state in 1909 as a "Colored Race" religious training school, North Carolina Central University (NCCU) is home to the James E. Shephard Memorial Library, which houses many materials on African-American life and culture, and to the NCCU Art Museum, which contains a collection of African-American art.

North Carolina Mutual Life Insurance Company
114–116 Parrish Street (National Historic Site); 411 West Chapel Hill Street (Heritage Room tours), Durham, NC 27701
(919) 682-9201
Hours: Mon.–Thu., 8:30 A.M.–5 P.M.; Sat., 8:30 A.M.–12 P.M.
Tours by appointment: 9:30 A.M.–11:30 A.M.; 2 P.M.–4:30 P.M.
Admission: Free

North Carolina was once home to the wealthiest and most fully developed black business class in America, much of it centered in Durham on Parrish Street, which was known throughout the Southeast as "Black Wall Street." Here, in 1898, John Merrick and other African-American businessmen founded the North Carolina Mutual Life Insurance Company, once the largest black-owned business in the United States. Today the company still grosses more than $1 billion annually. Its original home office building (which also housed the black-owned Mechanics & Farmers Bank) has been declared a National Historic Site, and its current home office offers tours of a Heritage Room filled with company memorabilia.

Stagville Preservation Center
P.O. Box 71217, Durham, NC 27722-1217
(919) 620-0120
Roxboro Road (U.S. 501) to Old Oxford Highway
Hours: Daily, 9 A.M.–4 P.M.
Admission: Free

Daily life on an early Federal era tobacco plantation is portrayed at the Stagville Center on the grounds of the former Bennehan Estate. Begun in 1787, the estate grew to almost 30,000 acres worked by 900 slaves at the outset of the Civil War. Stagville was but one of the working plantations on the huge estate and itself quartered several slave communities. A slave-built barn, artifacts, and four original slave dwellings of the Horton Grove slave quarters, which housed perhaps 100 slaves in four-room, two-story cabins, are on view for visitors. The center periodically offers programs on African-American history and the material culture of the enslaved.

FAYETTEVILLE

Evans Metropolitan Methodist Church
301 Cool Spring Street, Fayetteville, NC 28301
(919) 483-2862
Hours: Tours by appointment
Admission: Free

On the site of Fayetteville's first Methodist Church, founded in 1795 by the free black minister Henry Evans, is the Evans Metropolitan Methodist Church. Evans, a shoemaker and a native of Virginia who converted at an early age to Methodism, was licensed to preach by his home state congregation and moved to North Carolina, where he preached to both blacks and white. After overcoming initial opposition from Fayetteville's town council, Evans built a small, rough-sawn church building on a leased lot for his racially mixed congregation. He died in 1810 and was buried under the church; the present structure stands on top of the remains of that church.

Fayetteville State University
1200 Murchison Road, Fayetteville, NC 28301-4298
(919) 486-1111
Hours: Tours: Mon.–Fri. by appointment, 9 A.M.–3 P.M.
Admission: Free

In 1867 A. J. Chesnutt and six other local African Americans purchased a lot and persuaded General O. O. Howard of the Freedmen's Bureau to finance the construction of a school for black children. Ten years later Governor Zebulon Vance, the strikingly large, rough-hewn, populist small farmer who had served as the Confederate governor of North Carolina and who had subsequently been selected, after an international search, to represent the Caucasian race in a geography textbook, transformed the Howard School into the state's first teacher-training institute. The Fayetteville State Colored Normal School, now Fayetteville State University (FSU), was the first training facility in the South for teachers of any race. One of FSU's former principals was Charles W. Chesnutt, the preeminent turn-of-the-century African-American author and one of the first novelists to treat black life from a black perspective. A tablet on the school's grounds commemorates Chesnutt; another pays tribute to Dr. E. E. Smith, a former U.S. minister to Liberia who headed the school from 1899—when it was still a three-room frame building—through 1933, when the school's ten buildings stood on 50 acres of land.

GREENSBORO

Greensboro Convention & Visitors Bureau
317 South Green Street, Greensboro, NC 27401
(800) 344-2282; (919) 274-2282
Hours: Mon.–Fri., 8:30 A.M.–5:30 P.M.; Sat., 10 A.M.–4 P.M.; Sun., 1 P.M.–4 P.M.

Greensboro Cultural Center Art Gallery
200 North Davie Street, Greensboro, NC 27401
(919) 333-6885
Hours: Tue.–Sat., 11 A.M.–5 P.M.; Sun., 3 P.M.–6 P.M.
Admission: Free

The African-American Atelier of the Greensboro Cultural Center Art Gallery highlights the creative energies of black artists from the local community.

Greensboro Historical Museum
130 Summit Avenue, Greensboro, NC 27401
(919) 373-2043
Hours: Tue.–Sat., 10 A.M.–5 P.M.; Sun., 2 P.M.–5 P.M.
Admission: Free

The Greensboro Historical Museum interprets the city's history from its colonial foundation through the 1960s' civil rights struggle. Though First Lady

Dolley Madison and short-story writer O. Henry are the featured local citizens, the most interesting display is a re-creation of the historic February 1960 sit-in at the Woolworth lunch counter in Greensboro. (See Woolworth entry on p. 123.) The sit-in began with four black students of North Carolina Agricultural and Technical State University, who sat down and ordered food at Woolworth's segregated lunch counter. They were refused service and requested to leave. Instead, they took out their books and began to study. As the store would soon close, they were simply ignored. The following day 20 North Carolina A&T students entered Woolworth's, purchased goods there, and then sat down and ordered a meal. They too were refused service. The next day there were 70 students at the counter. Within a week, all of Greensboro's chain-store lunch counters were closed and all of the chain stores' northern corporate headquarters were trying to evade responsibility by claiming that they deplored but could not prevent the Jim Crow customs of the South. Within a month, similar sit-ins spread throughout the South, sparking a new militancy in the civil rights movement and putting Jim Crow on the run. (See North Carolina Agricultural and Technical State University entry on p. 123.)

Mattye Reed African Heritage Center
North Carolina A&T University, 200 Nocho Street, Greensboro, NC 27411
(919) 334-7874
Hours: Mon.–Fri., 9 A.M.–3:30 P.M.

Satellite Gallery (Reed Center affiliate)
Greensboro Cultural Center, 200 North Davie Street, Greensboro, NC 27411
(919) 334-7108
Hours: Tue.–Fri., 10 A.M.–4 P.M.; weekends, 1 P.M.–4 P.M.

H. C. Taylor Art Gallery
North Carolina A&T University, Art Department, Greensboro, NC 27411
(919) 334-7993
Hours: Mon.–Fri., 9 A.M.–5 P.M. The Taylor Gallery is currently closed for renovations and is scheduled to reopen in 1994. Call ahead to confirm status
Admission: Center and galleries, free

The Mattye Reed African Heritage Center and the H. C. Taylor Art Gallery, both of which are on the campus of North Carolina Agricultural and Technical State University, contain more than 3,500 artifacts and works of art from more than 30 African nations. From a metalwork Dogon granary shutter to carved masks, from woven cloth to bronze, ivory, and wooden sculptures, from weapons to jewelry, these holdings are among the finer African collections in the nation.

North Carolina Agricultural and Technical State University
1601 East Market Street, Greensboro, NC 27401
(919) 334-7500; (919) 334-7946
Hours: Tours: large groups: Mon.–Fri., by appointment with one-month's notice; individuals: Mon.–Thu., 10 A.M., 2 P.M.; Fri., 10 A.M.
Admission: Free

The Agricultural and Mechanical College for the Colored Race, now North Carolina Agricultural and Technical State University, started operations in 1890 in Raleigh in association with Shaw University. (See entry on p. 128.) The school moved to Greensboro after its citizens contributed 14 acres of land and $11,000 for construction costs. In 1891 the state legislature added $2,500 and established the school as one of its two federally mandated Morrill Act land grant colleges.

Today the school is best remembered as the alma mater of Jesse Jackson and of the four young students who, on their own initiative, conceived and executed the February 1960 Greensboro lunch counter sit-in that kick-started the 1960s-era civil rights activism. Within a month, sit-ins were being held in every southern state, and soon the traditional civil rights organizations were under pressure from a new, younger, more vocal group, the Student Nonviolent Coordinating Committee.

Woolworth's Lunch Counter Sit-in
Woolworth's, 220 South Elm Street, Greensboro, NC 27401
(919) 272-8331
Hours: Daily until sunset
Admission: Free

On the outside wall of a downtown Greensboro department store that otherwise would attract only customers is a Woolworth's Lunch Counter Sit-in Historical Marker. The marker locates the store in which four young black men in 1960 helped launched an era of civil rights direct-action campaigns, campaigns that challenged not only white supremacy but also the established civil rights organizations such as the NAACP and the Urban League. (See Greensboro Historical Museum entry on p. 121.)

GUILFORD

Levi Coffin Historical Marker
560 West Friendly Avenue, Guilford, NC 27419
Hours: Daily until sunset
Admission: Free

Born in North Carolina, Levi Coffin, a Quaker and the so-called president of the Underground Railroad, was one of the outstanding white abolitionists. Notable for his zeal, Coffin (see entry on p. 361) left North Carolina and settled in southern Indiana, from there helping more than 3,000 African Americans escape the bonds of slavery. Today, outside Guilford, a historical marker recalls his nearby birthplace.

HALIFAX

Historic Halifax
P.O. Box 406, Halifax, NC 27839
(919) 583-7191
Hours: Apr. 1–Oct. 31: Mon.–Sat., 9 A.M.–5 P.M.; Sun., 1 P.M.–5 P.M.
Nov. 1–Mar. 31: Tue.–Sat., 10 A.M.–4 P.M.; Sun., 1 P.M.–4 P.M.
Admission: Free

With the adoption of the "Halifax Resolves" in April 1776, North Carolina became the first American colony formally to declare that independence from Britain rather than reform of British-American relations should be the goal of the Continental Congress. Today, one of the earliest river port towns of the Roanoke Valley retains much of its colonial foundation. Halifax's 18th-century origin and the slave-based plantation economy that flourished until the railroad passed it by in the late 1830s can be seen on a walking tour of "Historic Halifax." Though little of the interpretive framework has an African-American focus, the Burgess Law Office and the Sally-Billy House touch upon the lives of free blacks and slaves respectively.

JAMESTOWN

Mendenhall Plantation
603 West Main Street, Jamestown, NC 27282
(919) 454-3819
Hours: Mid-Mar.–Dec.: Fri.–Sat., 10 A.M.–4 P.M.; Sun., 2 P.M.–4 P.M. Rest of year: Sun., 2 P.M.–4 P.M.
Admission: Voluntary donations requested

Mendenhall Plantation, an early 19th-century Quaker plantation, houses a small museum, an art gallery, and—most notably—one of two existing false-bottomed wagons used to transport runaway slaves along the Underground Railroad.

MANTEO, ROANOKE ISLAND

Pea Island Coast Guard Station, North Carolina Aquarium
P.O. Box 967, Manteo, NC 27954
Aquarium, (919) 473-3493; Pea Island, (919) 987-2394
Aquarium: U. S. 64, east of bridge from mainland. Pea Island: N.C. 12, 15 miles southeast of aquarium
Hours: Aquarium: weekdays, 9 A.M.–5 P.M.; weekends, 1 P.M.–5 P.M. Pea Island Refuge: Daily until sunset
Admission: Both free

Fifty years before African Americans were invited to enlist in the U.S. Navy, the U.S. Coast Guard maintained an all-black rescue station on dangerous North Carolina shoals. Pea Island Station, built in 1878, was one of 18 stations on the Outer Banks run by the U.S. Lifesaving Service, then a division of the Treasury Department. In 1879, after the survivors of the sinking *Henderson* reached shore and found the first Pea Island crew sound asleep, Richard Etheridge—"a colored man . . . strong, intelligent and able to read and write [and] one of the best surfman on this part of the coast" in the words of the investigator sent out to report on the incident—was appointed as Pea Island keeper. He recruited six black surfmen, and from then until the station's closing in 1947, the keeper (with one brief exception) and his crew were black. For 20 years, Etheridge ran what was widely recognized as one of the Service's best stations. Like other such stations, Pea Island's isolated existence was one of the boredom of constant training interrupted by episodes of incredible moonless-night rescues amid gale-driven waves and treacherous surf. If a ship was in desperate danger, the weather was almost certainly horrendous; more certainly still, the Pea Island rescue boat rowed through waves that towered above it in an attempt to close on a ship of several tons, which would have sent it straight to the bottom should the sea fling one against the other. In the 1930s, shoaling left Pea Island no longer an island, though the dune peas that provided its name still flourished and attracted thousands of birds. Now devoid of inhabitants, Pea Island is a wildlife preserve. But on nearby Roanoke Island, the North Carolina Aquarium has an exhibit on the Pea Island station, while just outside the aquarium entrance the graves of Richard Etheridge and his family remain in their original location as a memorial. Close by lies a commemorative stone marker honoring the men of Pea Island station.

MILTON

Milton Presbyterian Church
Highway 62, Milton, NC 27305
(919) 234-7215
Hours: Tours by appointment
Admission: Tours: $4 per person

Union Tavern/Thomas Day House
P.O. Box 1996, Milton, NC 27305
(919) 234-7215
Hours: Under renovation; phone ahead for times and admission

Milton's most famous building and its most renowned citizen combine in the Union Tavern/Thomas Day House. Day, born about 1801 in Virginia to a free black mother and hence free himself, moved to North Carolina in 1823 and within a decade established himself as the state's preeminent furniture craftsman and entrepreneur. His creative work was widely recognized as outstanding, securing him the custom of two of North Carolina's governors and a commission to furnish the interior woodwork for the first major extant building of the University of North Carolina in Chapel Hill. Day trained white and slave apprentices, but the latter in particular were withdrawn by their masters once they became proficient. Day's solution was to purchase slaves in order to secure a reliable labor force for his expanding business, which by the mid-19th century was the state's largest furniture workshop measured both by volume of production and number of apprentices employed. His work was in demand from Virginia to Georgia, and Day properly viewed himself as a man not only of property but of merit and stature. When he married a free black woman of Virginia and confronted North Carolina's law forbidding the immigration of free blacks, he responded by suggesting that he would move himself and his shop to Virginia. Prominent citizens of Milton, including the state's attorney general, had the North Carolina legislature pass a special bill exempting Mrs. Day from the provisions of the 1827 law. Similarly, Day executed handsome pews of walnut, yellow poplar, and pine with gracefully curved arms for the Milton Presbyterian Church—in exchange for the privilege of his family's sitting in the section reserved for whites. Day's career and social achievements rested not on monopoly—in fact he had many competitors—but on the aesthetic vision, inventive decorative motifs, and precise craftsmanship of his work. In 1848 Day purchased the Union Tavern, which was then 30 years old and is today the sole remaining of the 13 structures that existed when the town of Milton was laid out in 1819. Known locally as Yellow Tavern, this served as Day's workshop and residence until shortly before his death in 1861. The tavern, a National Historic Landmark, was partially destroyed in a fire in 1989. It has since undergone restoration with the aim of establishing a museum celebrating Day's extraordinary talents. His work is on display at the North Carolina Museum of History in Raleigh. (See entry on p. 127.)

RALEIGH

Greater Raleigh Convention & Visitors Bureau
P.O. Box 1879, Raleigh, NC 27602
(919) 834-5900
Hours: Mon.–Fri., 8:30 A.M.–5 P.M.

John Chavis Memorial Park
East Lenoir at Worth Street, Raleigh, NC
Hours: Daily, 24 hours
Admission: Free

In the first half of the 19th century, John Chavis was the most influential free black in North Carolina. A Presbyterian preacher and a teacher of both white and black pupils, Chavis was also the most politically active free black in the state. By tradition, Chavis is believed to have studied at the College of New Jersey—later known as Princeton University—though there is no record of his presence there. Certainly he was a regularly enrolled student at what is now

Washington and Lee University in Lexington, Virginia. Affiliated with the presbyteries of Lexington and Hanover, Virginia, Chavis briefly rode the circuit as a missionary before moving to North Carolina in the first decade of the 19th century. For the next three decades he served as a preacher and a teacher, gaining public respect particularly in the latter role because prominent white families permitted him to instruct their sons. Though he originally sought to include black students in his classes, Chavis deferred to white sensibilities and instead taught black children separately in evening classes. In 1831, after several minor slave conspiracies in the preceding years, North Carolina tightened its restrictions on the activities of free blacks, who were thought likely to involve themselves, on the basis of racial solidarity, with any general slave revolt. In fact, this judgment was undoubtedly unsound, at least as applied to those free blacks of means. Thomas Day, one of the state's wealthiest free blacks, was considered reliable by whites. Chavis—who on a number of occasions received financial assistance from prominent whites—opposed immediate general emancipation, and even the three free blacks actually charged in an abortive local uprising in 1831 were found innocent by the county superior court. But white fear was implacable, and the 1831 tightening of the Black Codes meant the end of Chavis's intermittent preaching career and the curtailment of his teaching. Shortly thereafter Chavis—with almost three decades of service to North Carolinian communities—received from a Presbyterian church financial support for himself and his wife for the remainder of their lives. Later North Carolinians also looked favorably on Chavis: In 1938 the city of Raleigh placed a commemorative marker near John Chavis Memorial Park.

North Carolina Museum of Art
2110 Blue Ridge Boulevard, Raleigh, NC 27607
(919) 833-1935
Hours: Tue.–Sat., 9 A.M.–5 P.M.; Fri., 9 A.M.–9 P.M.; Sun, 11 A.M.–6 P.M.; guided tours with reservations (visually/hearing-impaired, and French, German, and Spanish: Tue.–Sun., 1:30 P.M.)
Admission: Free; accessible by wheelchair and stroller

In 1947 North Carolina became the first state to use public funds to establish an art museum. Today five millennia of artistic heritage can be explored at the North Carolina Museum of Art, including the creative representation of Africa's military might, religious symbolism, and social rituals.

North Carolina Museum of History
1 East Edenton Street, Raleigh, NC 27601
(919) 715-0200
Hours: Tue.–Sat., 9 A.M.–5 P.M.; Sun., 1 P.M.–6 P.M.
Admission: Free

Among the more interesting features of the North Carolina Museum of History is the collection of furniture and interior woodworking of Thomas Day, the antebellum South's most distinguished free-black craftsman and a man who literally carved his own path through the legal thicket constraining free black existence. (See Union Tavern entry on p. 125.)

Shaw University
118 East South Street, Raleigh, NC 27602
(919) 546-8200
Hours: Call ahead for appointment through Admissions Office
Admission: Free

Even before the close of the Civil War, the Reverend H. M. Tupper of Massachusetts received a commission to educate freedmen in North Carolina. Starting with a single class, Tupper's work eventually yielded Shaw University, the oldest historically black college in the South and the first African-American coeducational institution in the United States. Today, among other sights, visitors to the campus will see Estey Hall, the first (1873) building constructed for the education of African-American women.

St. Augustine's College
1315 Oakwood Avenue, Raleigh, NC 27611
(919) 828-4451
Hours: By appointment through the Admissions Office. Call in advance
Admission: Free

In 1867 the Freedmen's Commission of the Protestant Episcopal Church founded St. Augustine's Normal School and Collegiate Institute for the purpose of "normal training," or teacher education. Realizing that there would never be enough white teachers willing to move into black communities to educate all freedmen, 95 percent of whom were illiterate, the college's founders, who never contemplated other than segregated education, determined to provide a corps of African-American teachers. By 1884 the typical entering student was on the fourth- or fifth-grade level, and if he or she stayed through the preparatory, normal, academic, and collegiate courses, the student would leave St. Augustine's with the equivalent of a first-year education at a traditional college. In fact, many of St. Augustine's students left after a year or even a semester of instruction and embarked on teaching careers in black schools. In 1927 the school changed its name to St. Augustine's College, and in 1931 it awarded its first baccalaureate degree. Today's visitors to the school, which remains private and affiliated to the Episcopal Church, will gain insight into the early limits and the dedication of America's first institutions devoted to African-American education. Though several of the campus buildings have been declared National Historic Landmarks, most of the original structures were destroyed in an 1883 fire, in part because the white fire company did not cover black blazes and the black fire company was poorly equipped.

SALISBURY

Livingstone College
701 West Monroe Street, Salisbury, NC 28144
(704) 683-5500
Hours: Heritage Hall: Mon.–Sat., 10 A.M.–4 P.M. during school year. Tours available on Thursday
Admission: Free

In 1879 the noted African-American orator J. C. Price and the A.M.E. Church founded the Zion Wesley Institute in Concord, North Carolina. Two years later the school moved to Salisbury and changed its name to Livingstone College to honor the memory of David Livingstone, the noted missionary and explorer of Africa and an ardent abolitionist. During the Civil War Livingstone's son, Robert, enlisted in the Union ranks under an assumed name, was captured in battle, and died in a Confederate prison camp outside Salisbury. Today visitors to Livingstone's campus, which in 1892 was the site of the first black intercollegiate football game, can view Price's tomb, African artifacts, African-American art and historical memorabilia, and an archive tracing the development of the A.M.E. Church.

Salisbury National Cemetery
202 Government Road (U.S. 52), Salisbury, NC 28144
(704) 636-2661
Hours: Daily until sunset
Admission: Free

Robert Livingstone and 10,000 fellow Union captives were crowded into a Confederate prison camp designed to accommodate 2,000 men. As the North's stranglehold on the South intensified, conditions for prisoners of war deteriorated sharply. In the course of the war, about 5,000 captive Union soldiers, including Livingstone and many African Americans, perished in the Salisbury camp. They and their comrades who fell in battles in North Carolina are buried in the Salisbury National Cemetery.

SEDALIA

Charlotte Hawkins Brown Memorial State Historic Site
Drawer B, 6135 Burlington Road, Sedalia, NC 27342-0190
(919) 449-4846
Hours: Apr. 1–Oct. 31: Mon.–Sat., 9 A.M.–5 P.M.; Sun., 1 P.M.–5 P.M.
Nov. 1–Mar. 31: Tue.–Sat., 10 A.M.–4 P.M.; Sun., 1 P.M.–4 P.M.
Admission: Free

Following the Civil War, the brief window of "Jubilation" and Reconstruction was quickly closed by "Redemption" and Jim Crow, forestalling the growth of educational opportunities for African Americans in the South. In 1883, less than a decade after the old South was "redeemed," Charlotte Eugenia Hawkins was born in North Carolina. After her family moved to Massachusetts and she attended Salem State Normal School, the 18-year-old Hawkins accepted an offer by the American Missionary Association to return to her home state and teach rural black children in a church school in Sedalia. The school closed after one term, but Hawkins resolved to stay on and establish her own school. After securing northern benefactors, of whom the most significant was Alice Freeman Palmer, first female president of Wellesley College in Massachusetts, Hawkins opened Palmer Memorial Institute in Sedalia. Almost single-handedly she built Palmer into one of the most respected black schools in the South—one of the few to receive full accreditation from the Southern Association of Colleges and Secondary Schools. Her 50 years as Palmer's head brought Brown national recognition as an educator and African-American spokeswoman. Her associates included Mary McLeod Bethune, Nannie Helen Burroughs, Booker T. Washington, W.E.B. Du Bois, and Eleanor Roosevelt.

Married in 1911, Charlotte Hawkins Brown died in 1961. Ten years and three administrations later, Palmer closed its doors. Today the old Palmer campus hosts the Charlotte Hawkins Brown Memorial State Historic Site, which features exhibits on Dr. Brown and her work, tours of historic campus buildings, and audio-visual presentations highlighting black history.

WINSTON-SALEM

Delta Art Center
1511 East Third Street, Winston-Salem, NC 27101
(919) 722-2625
Hours: Mon.–Fri., 10 A.M.–5:30 P.M.
Admission: Free

The Delta Art Center, run by Winston-Salem's oldest nonprofit African-American cultural organization, hosts exhibits and programs that foster knowledge of the black contribution to the arts and humanities.

SOUTH CAROLINA

South Carolina Division of Tourism
P.O. Box 71, Columbia, SC 29202
(803) 734-0235
Hours: Mon.–Fri., 8:30 A.M.–5 P.M.

Ask for the pamphlet on the state's African-American heritage, "To Walk the Whole Journey."

ATLANTIC BEACH

Black Pearl
Atlantic Beach, Horry County, SC 29582
(803) 448-7166
Hours: Daily, 24 hours
Admission: Free

South Carolina and Mississippi are the only states that ever had a black majority population. In Jim Crow South Carolina, when African Americans wanted to go to the beach, they headed for Black Pearl, the equivalent of Jacksonville, Florida's American Beach, and The Inkwell on Martha's Vineyard. Located not far from Myrtle Beach, one of the state's major tourist draws for decades, this strip of primarily black-owned coastal property annually hosts "Afro-Fest" during the Labor Day weekend.

BEAUFORT

Beaufort Chamber of Commerce
Charles and Bay streets, P.O. Box 910, Beaufort, SC 29901
(803) 524-3163
Hours: Visitor Center: Mon.–Sat., 9:30 A.M.–5:30 P.M.; Sun., 10 A.M.–5 P.M.

Baptist Tabernacle Church
907 Craven Street, Beaufort, SC 29902
(803) 524-0376
Hours: Daily until sunset
Admission: Free

On the grounds of the Baptist Tabernacle Church are the grave and a memorial bust of Robert Smalls, black Civil War hero and political master of South Carolina's low-country Reconstruction. Smalls's story is arguably more dramatic than that of any of his African-American contemporaries. Born a slave in Beaufort, Smalls was rented out by his master and moved to Charleston, where he worked as a waiter before being pressed into service as a pilot on the Confederate steamer *Planter*, which plied Charleston Harbor. A year into the war, Smalls smuggled his family on board and, with its white officers ashore, sailed the craft and its black crew into the ranks of the Union navy blockading Charleston. Rewarded with a pilot's rank in the Union navy, Smalls rose to a

PHOTOGRAPHY BY PATTY LANGLEY

Robert Smalls, Civil War hero, United States congressman, African American.

captaincy (the only one to be held by an African American) due to his coolness and valor in combat.

After the war Smalls returned to Beaufort, where he had purchased in a direct-tax sale of Union army–confiscated property the McKee home, in which he had served as a slave in his youth. One day the elderly, widowed, and somewhat confused Mrs. McKee entered the house, thinking it was still her home. Smalls installed her in her old room and thereafter took care of the widow of his former master, without ever feeling diminished as a man. He also entered Reconstruction-era politics in the one of the South's most interesting states, one in which African Americans constituted a majority of the populace and in which the struggle between white and black Republicans during the first years of Reconstruction was particularly acute. After participating as a delegate to the 1868 State Constitutional Convention (48 of the delegates were white, of whom 15 were from the North, and 76 were black; adoption of the resulting constitution enabled the state to be readmitted to the Union), Smalls served either in South Carolina's House of Representatives or its Senate from 1868 through 1874, representing and dominating a low-country black constituency that already controlled the police force, the magistracy, and many mayoralities. With this base, Smalls was elected to the U.S. House of Representatives in 1875. Though Reconstruction collapsed shortly thereafter, Smalls served five terms, longer than any other 19th-century black congressman. Ten years after his congressional career ended, Smalls was a delegate to South Carolina's 1895 State Constitutional Convention, where he labored unsuccessfully to prevent the disenfranchisement of African Americans. From the convention, Smalls returned to Beaufort, where he served as customs collector until his death in 1915.

Gullah Festival
c/o Gullah Festival, Inc., P.O. Box 83, Beaufort, SC 29901
(803) 525-0628
Hours: Thu. evening–Sun. on the weekend preceding Memorial Day
Admission: Free

Gullah is a creole language (and by extension a people) that extends along the Atlantic coast roughly from Jacksonville, North Carolina, to Jacksonville, Florida, and centers on the 15 sea islands near Beaufort. A merger of English (particularly regarding vocabulary) and the languages (especially the grammatical and intonational features) of the West African slave belt, including Yoruba, Mandinka, Ibo, and Kongo, the language anchors a culture shaped by slavery, geographical isolation, marginal contact with speakers outside the sea island communities, and economic independence. Long viewed as a corrupted and backward dialect of English, Gullah is today coming into its own as a language and authentic American subculture, even as the power of mass communications, economic integration and consumerism erode its foundations. Beaufort annually celebrates a Gullah Festival.

Robert Smalls House
511 Prince Street, Beaufort, SC 29902
(803) 524-0376
Hours: Daily until sunset
Admission: Private residence is not open to the public. Exterior viewing only

The Robert Smalls House, now a National Historic Landmark, was home for decades to the Beaufort native who served longer in the U.S. House of Representatives than any other 19th-century African American. In this house the youthful Smalls (see Baptist Tabernacle Church entry, on p. 131) labored as a slave. Upon his return from the Civil War, he purchased the house and took care of the impoverished widow of his former master until her death. Though it is a *private residence not open to the public*, the house is readily visible from the street.

BEECH ISLAND

Silver Bluff Baptist Church
Highway 28, Beech Island, SC 29841
(803) 827-0706
As you head off the island toward Jackson, South Carolina, the large Kimberley-Clark Company plant is just west of the church
Hours: By appointment
Admission: Free

A white church organized in 1750 on the South Carolina side of the Savannah River, Silver Bluff Baptist Church passed into the hands of its black slave members in 1773. George Liele, an early licensed black Baptist preacher, pastored the congregation.

CHARLESTON

Charleston Convention & Visitors Bureau
375 Meeting Street, Charleston, SC 29403
(803) 853-8000
Hours: Mon.–Fri., 8:00 A.M.–5 P.M.

Some of Charleston's heritage sites are still under renovation following the devastation of Hurricane Hugo, so call ahead to the sites or to the visitors bureau to confirm their status, hours of operation, and so on.

African-American Gallery
43 John Street, Charleston, SC 29403
(803) 722-8224
Hours: Daily, 10 A.M.–6 P.M.
Admission: Free

The African-American Gallery is Charleston's premier showcase for African and African-American art, with new exhibits organized every two months. From the works of Bruce Onobrakpeya, one of contemporary Africa's leading artists, through paintings and sculpture that reflect the low-country heritage of South Carolina's Gullah culture (see Gullah Festival entry on p. 132), to wearable one-of-a-kind cloth art for sale, the gallery covers it all.

Avery Research Center for African-American History and Culture
125 Bull Street, Charleston, SC 29424
(803) 792-5742; (803) 727-2009
Hours: Small group walk-in tours: Mon.–Fri., 2 P.M.–4 P.M. Large group tours: by appointment. Research Room: Mon.–Fri., 1 P.M.–4:30 P.M.
Admission: Voluntary donations requested

Born in antebellum Charleston to a Jewish father and a free woman of mixed but largely black ancestry, Francis L. Cardozo was decidedly an outsider. Following an education in Europe and a brief stint as a Congregationalist minister in New England, Cardozo returned to the town of his birth in the summer of 1865. There he replaced his brother Thomas as the education director of the American Missionary Association. (Thomas had been dismissed upon the discovery of his seduction of one of his pupils in New York City.) That autumn he established the Avery Normal Institute "for the education of colored children." Though proclaiming that he gave up "all the superior advantages and privileges of the North" in order to train black teachers, Cardozo spent considerable time on larger Reconstruction issues—and on his political career. These twin concerns dated at least as far back as his participation in the October 1864 national black convention held in Syracuse, New York. There Cardozo, Frederick Douglass, and the rest of the mulatto and black elite rejected Henry Highland Garnet's "Negro nationality" perspective and a focus on the economic interests of poor and illiterate freedmen, emphasizing instead political rights and legal equality with whites. In South Carolina, Cardozo attended the state black convention of 1865. He served as South Carolina's secretary of state from 1868 through 1873 and then as state treasurer from 1873 through 1877. In office, Cardozo staunchly advocated black civil rights and the continued curtailment of the power of the deposed white planter elite. He fell victim in 1876 to the Democratic "Redemption" that restored white rule except at the local level within the state. Once out of office, Cardozo was indicted and convicted on charges of corruption and malfeasance (though his record in this regard never matched that of his brother Thomas, who was shameless in his venality). Cardozo would escape the consequences of his conviction on fraud charges as part of a political deal whereby other charges against white Democrats were quietly buried. His South Carolina career in tatters, Cardozo headed north undaunted. In Washington, D.C., he secured a federal appointment, administered a black high school, assumed his place among the ranks of the city's black elite, and died.

Today the grounds of what was the Avery Normal Institute host the Avery Research Center for African-American History and Culture, a repository for materials on the African-American history and Gullah culture of South Carolina's low country. Composed of the present-day counties of Beaufort, Berkeley, Charleston, Dorchester, and Georgetown, the rice- and indigo-producing low country contained one of the densest concentrations of African Americans in the United States throughout the 18th and 19th centuries. Visitors to the institute have access to an archive of books, photographs, art, and videotapes that pays tribute to the black heritage of this region. As for Cardozo, other than establishing Avery Institute and serving as a Reconstruction-era state official, his claim to fame is through his granddaughter, who was once married to Paul Robeson. (See entry on p. 284.)

Battery Wagner
Morris Island, c/o Fort Sumter, 1214 Middle Street, Sullivans Island,
Charleston, SC 29482
(803) 883-3123
Hours: Tours (alternating from the city marina and Patriots' Point, respectively): 9:30 A.M., 10:45 P.M., 12 P.M., 1:30 P.M., 2:30 P.M., and 4 P.M.
Admission: Adults, $9; ages 6–12, $4.50; under 6, free

Battery Wagner on Morris Island was the scene of one of the first combat uses of black troops in the Civil War. In storming the fort, the black 54th Massachusetts Volunteer Infantry Regiment (see Robert Gould Shaw and 54th Regiment entry on p. 263) proved its valor, with its commander, Robert Gould Shaw, and more than one-third of its troops killed in the action. Though the fort did not fall to assault, the performance of the black Union troops confirmed the wisdom of the North's recruitment of African Americans and encouraged Union commanders to commit their black troops to battle. The battery no longer stands and Morris Island is not accessible to the public, but the island can be seen during tours of the harbor conducted from the Fort Sumter National Monument on Sullivans Island.

Boone Hall
U.S. 17, Charleston, SC 29407
(803) 884-4371
Hours: Apr.–Labor Day: Mon.–Sat., 8:30 A.M.–6:30 P.M.; Sun., 1 P.M.–5 P.M. Rest of year: Mon.–Sat., 9 A.M.–5 P.M.; Sun., 1 P.M.–4 P.M.
Admission: Adults, $6; seniors, $5; ages 6–12, $2

Cotton, rice, and indigo plantations in South Carolina required a massive labor force of enslaved African Americans. At Boone Hall, where once 1,000 slaves worked 17,000 acres, there still stands the only extant "slave row" in the southeastern United States. Nine tile-roofed slave cabins that sheltered the "house servants" are open to the public, as are the mansion house, some outbuildings, and the gardens.

Catfish Row
91 Church Street, Charleston, SC 29401
Hours: Daily until sunset
Admission: Free

George Gershwin's *Porgy and Bess*, an operatic transformation of DuBose Heyward's 1925 novel (or more probably, of Heyward's wife's 1927 play based on the novel) about life in Charleston's waterfront Gullah ghetto, proved yet again the power of art to triumph over reality. The musical enjoyed worldwide success and was later filmed, combining the extraordinary talents of Gershwin, Sidney Poitier, and Dorothy Dandridge. Playing off this success, the real (and run-down) Cabbage Row—Catfish Row in the musical—was renovated and renamed. Rather than Gullah patois and vibrancy amid dilapidation, today's visitors to Catfish Row will find a sun-dappled red-brick alley adorned with a plaque.

Charleston Museum
360 Meeting Street, Charleston, SC 29403-6297
(803) 722-2996
Hours: Mon.–Sat., 9 A.M.–5 P.M.; Sun., 1 P.M.–5 P.M.
Admission: Adults, $3; seniors, $2.70; ages 3–12, $1.50

The Charleston Museum, founded in 1773, is America's oldest museum and principally interprets the social and natural history of Charleston and low-country South Carolina. Though the museum's social history concentrates on the politically dominant planter culture, there is a permanent exhibit on slavery and the material culture of South Carolina's African Americans. There are also transitory exhibits, which increasingly seek to interpret the lives and cultural expressions of the historically disenfranchised.

Emmanuel A.M.E. Church
110 Calhoun Street, Charleston, SC 29401
(803) 722-2561
Hours: Mon.–Fri., 9 A.M.–4 P.M.
Admission: Free

Responding to tightening restrictions placed on them during 1817 and 1818 by the white-led Methodist Church, 4,000 African Americans in Charleston affiliated with the newly organized African Methodist Episcopal Church. The Emmanuel A.M.E. Church, one of the first black churches founded south of Baltimore, and three congregations emerged from this mass influx. Denmark Vesey, organizer of one of the three major planned slave insurrections of the 19th century, was a leading member of one of these congregations. Following his failed uprising, the church's building was destroyed by outraged whites and, with 1834 passage of a state law closing black institutions, not rebuilt. This led members to worship in secret until the close of the Civil War, when the church was rebuilt at its present site. There is a historical marker at the church proclaiming its deep involvement with Charleston's black community.

Drayton Hall
Route 4, Box 276, 3380 Ashley River Road, Charleston, SC 29407
(803) 766-0188
9 miles northwest of downtown
Hours: Tours on the hour. Mar.–Oct.: daily, 10 A.M.–5 P.M. Rest of year: daily, 10 A.M.–3 P.M.
Admission: Adults, $6; children 6–18, $3; under 6, free

The confluence of the Ashley and Cooper rivers defines the peninsula of Charleston, one of the antebellum South's preeminent cities. Only one of the plantation mansions that then graced the Ashley today survives, but it does so in splendid form. Drayton Hall, with its Georgian Palladian architecture, is essentially in its original circa 1740 condition—indoor plumbing, central heating, and electricity never marred its colonial purity. Of equal interest, Drayton's interpretation of the plantation in the colonial and antebellum periods, and its special events, reflect its concern with the African-American contribution to the plantation setting.

DuBose Heyward House
76 Church Street, Charleston, SC 29401
Hours: Daily until sunset
Admission: Not open to public. Exterior viewing only

The DuBose Heyward House, a National Historic Landmark that is *not open to the public,* was the home of the socially prominent white Charlestonian whose 1925 novel was the basis for George Gershwin's inimitable opera *Porgy and Bess.*

Middleton Place
S.C. 61, Charleston, SC 29403
(803) 556-6020
Northwest of Charleston on S.C. 61, 14 miles from junction with U.S. 17
Hours: Gardens and outbuildings: daily, 9 A.M.–5 P.M. House tours: Mon., 1:30 P.M.–4:30 P.M.; Tue.–Sun., 10 A.M.–4:30 P.M.
Admission: Gardens and outbuildings: Adults, $8, ages 6–12, $4. House: $4 extra. Admission slightly higher mid-March to mid-June

Middleton Place is typical of the antebellum plantations of the Ashley River—the mansion house did not survive the Civil War and the outbuildings visible today are restored. In these buildings visitors witness demonstrations of the crafts that kept plantations afloat, crafts that were the daily labor of enslaved African Americans. More uniquely, Middleton is home to America's oldest landscaped gardens, which were the product of ten years of labor by 100 slaves. At Middleton, little of the lives of these laborers is left—except the beauty of the gardens. Associated with Middleton is Eliza's House. Built by freed slaves who wished to remain at Middleton, the house recently has been restored.

Denmark Vesey House
56 Bull Street, Charleston, SC 29401
Hours: Daily until sunset
Admission: Not open to the public. Exterior viewing only

Born about 1767, Denmark Vesey became the protégé of his owner, Captain Vesey, a slaver from Charleston, South Carolina, and sailed with him for two decades. After winning a lottery in 1800, Denmark purchased his freedom and set himself up as a carpenter. Though successful in his new, free career, the epileptic Vesey remained deeply resentful of slavery, preaching rebellion to Charleston area slaves. His planned insurrection, half a year in the making, was betrayed at the last moment, and Vesey and about three dozen of his comrades met their ends on the gallows. The detail of Vesey's planning was sufficiently thorough and his goal—the killing of all whites—sufficiently stark as to terrify the white minority of South Carolina, which responded by limiting the movements and occupations of free blacks; by precluding slaves from purchasing their freedom except with the specific-to-the-individual consent of the state legislature; by limiting the gathering together of African Americans, free or enslaved; and by limiting the education that slaves could receive. Today the Denmark Vesey House, in which he lived during the planning of the insurrection, is a National Historic Landmark. Readily visible from the street, it is *not open to the public*.

COLUMBIA

Columbia Metropolitan Convention & Visitors Bureau
1012 Gervais Street, Columbia, SC 29201
(803) 254-0479
Hours: Mon.–Fri., 9 A.M.–5 P.M.; Sat., 10 A.M.–4 P.M.

Allen University
1530 Harden Street, Columbia, SC 29204
(803) 254-4165
Hours: Mon.–Fri., 8 A.M.–5 P.M.
Admission: Free

Established in Cokesbury, South Carolina, in 1870 by the A.M.E. Church, Payne Institute was renamed Allen University in honor of A.M.E.'s founder (see Allen entry on p. 230), the ex-slave and charismatic lay preacher the Right Reverend Richard Allen (1760–1831), when it was moved to Columbia in 1880. Four buildings on campus, including three designed by J. A. Lanford (1874–1946), "the dean of black architects" and the official architect of the A.M.E. Church, are on the National Register of Historic Places.

Mann-Simons Cottage
1403 Richland Street, Columbia, SC 29201
(803) 252-1450
Hours: Tue.–Fri., 10:15 A.M.–4:15 P.M.; Sat., 10:15 A.M.–1:15 P.M.
Admission: Adults, $1; seniors, students, and children, 50 cents

The Mann-Simons Cottage, originally the antebellum home of Celia Mann, a free black woman who had purchased herself out of slavery, today serves as a museum of African-American culture, offering period furnishings, 19th-century documents, and the works of local black artists. On the last Saturday of September, it sponsors the Jubilee Festival of Heritage.

Randolph Cemetery
Elmwood Avenue Extension, Columbia, SC 29403
(803) 771-6417
Hours: Daily until sunset
Admission: Free

Over the opposition of white South Carolinian Republicans, northern-born white and black Republicans in post–Civil War South Carolina, joined by South Carolinian African Americans, put northern-born Benjamin Franklin Randolph at the head of the state Republican committee in 1868. A state senator, Randolph was assassinated later in the year while running for office, reportedly at the behest of D. Wyatt Aiken, a South Carolinian agricultural reformer who bemoaned the rising political and economic power of African Americans, the spread of sharecropping (which implied black quasi-proprietorship of former plantations), and the related reduced number of blacks still willing to labor on white farms. In 1871 a score of African Americans founded Randolph Cemetery as a final resting place for and memorial to the senator. Joining Randolph are eight other African Americans who served in the state legislature during Reconstruction.

South Carolina State Museum
301 Gervais Street, P.O. Box 100107, Columbia, SC 29202-3107
(803) 737-4921
Hours: Mon.–Sat., 10 A.M.–5 P.M.; Sun., 1 P.M.–5 P.M.
Admission: Adults, $3; seniors, $2; ages 6–17, $1.25; under 6, free

The South Carolina State Museum offers the state's most comprehensive collection of art, history, and science exhibits. Its history hall has a permanent exhibit on slave life and the material culture of disenfranchised African Americans. Particularly notable are the displays of pottery and sea islands' basketry.

DENMARK

Voorhees College
Voorhees Road, Denmark, SC 29042
(803) 793-3351
Hours: By appointment, through the Admissions Office
Admission: Free

Like Floyd Brown (see Fargo entry on p. 35), Elizabeth Evelyn Wright was transformed by her exposure to Booker T. Washington and Tuskegee Institute. After graduating from Tuskegee, she came to South Carolina zealously determined to pass on her passion for learning and for uplifting the race. In 1897 she founded the Denmark Industrial School. Though sickly, she walked many miles—frequently without the benefit of shoes—to raise funds for the school. Shortly before her death at the age of 30, she found a northern benefactor who financially secured the newly renamed Voorhees College. Today's visitors can trace the college's development through photographs that grace the turn-of-the-century buildings on campus.

GEORGETOWN

Prince George Winyah Church
Highmarket and Broad streets, Georgetown, SC 29440
(803) 546-4358
Hours: Mar.–Oct.: Mon.–Fri., 11 A.M.–4:30 P.M.
Admission: Free

Stained glass windows from the abandoned St. Mary's Chapel for Negroes, located on the nearby DuPont Plantation, grace the red-brick Prince George Winyah Church, built in 1746.

GREENVILLE

Greenville Cultural Exchange Center
P.O. Box 5482, Station B, Sumner Street, Greenville, SC 29606
(803) 232-9162
Hours: Tue.–Sun., by appointment and varied hours; call ahead
Admission: Free

The Greenville Cultural Exchange Center highlights local African-American heritage and includes the Jesse Jackson Hall of Fame, which honors the Greenville native, among others. One room of the center is devoted to an exhibit on the formerly segregated black schools of the city and features the annual yearbooks of the schools. The center features photographs of the Neptune Fire Department, a turn-of-the-century all-black fire brigade; photographs and memorabilia of Peg-Leg Bates (see entry on p. 295), a native of the area whose career as a dancer missed neither a beat nor a step despite the absence of a leg; the Reverend Jackson's high school football helmet, his uniform from his days as an employee of the Poinsett Club, and other memorabilia; and African, Haitian, and early African-American art.

MAYESVILLE

Mary McLeod Bethune Birthplace Historical Marker
U.S. 76 at Lafayette Street, Mayesville, SC 29104
(800) 688-4748
Hours: Daily until sunset
Admission: Free

Born near Mayesville, South Carolina, the 15th child of former slaves, Mary McLeod Bethune played a pivotal role in the history of African-American women, spanning the eras of black self-improvement and political protest. In 1904 the 29-year-old widow founded the Daytona Normal and Industrial Institute for Girls, which—typically for the period—emphasized moral virtues and domestic arts. Two decades later this school merged with Cookman Institute, a Methodist school for black males, to form Bethune-Cookman College. (See entry on p. 43 and Bethune Museum entry on p. 193.) Her endeavors in the field of black education brought her national attention, and beginning with the Coolidge administration she served several presidents as an advisor on African-American affairs. She founded the National Council of Negro Women, was director of the Division of Negro Affairs of the National Youth Administration during the New Deal, and helped draft the United Nations Charter. A historical marker in Mayesville commemorates her life.

ORANGEBURG

Clafin College
700 College Avenue, Orangeburg, SC 29115
(803) 534-2710
Hours: Daily, 8:30 A.M.–5 P.M.
Admission: Free

Founded in 1869 by the philanthropist Lee Clafin; his son, the governor of Massachusetts; and the Methodist Episcopal Church, Clafin College is South Carolina's oldest historically black college. A photographic and archival exhibit in the Tingley Building traces Clafin's early history as an agricultural school for freed African Americans.

I. P. Stanback Museum and Planetarium
South Carolina State College, 300 College Street, Orangeburg, SC 29117
(803) 536-7174
Hours: Sept.–May, Museum: Mon.–Fri., 9 A.M.–4:30 P.M.
Planetarium: Mon.–Thu., by appointment only; shows 9 A.M., 10 A.M., 11 A.M.; First Sun., 3 P.M.–4 P.M.
Admission: Museum: free. Planetarium: Adults, $1; seniors and students, 50 cents

The I. P. Stanback Museum and Planetarium is best known for its 40-foot domed planetarium and a 4,000-star projector that can display the sky for any time, place, or date. But visitors will also enjoy the museum's West African sculpture from Benin and Cameroon; the works of African-American artists Romare Bearden, Jacob Lawrence, William Johnson, and others; and a collection of 19th- and 20th-century photographs that highlight South Carolina's black heritage.

RANTOWLES

Stono River Slave Rebellion Historical Marker
U.S. 17, Rantowles, SC
12 miles west of Charleston
Hours: Daily until sunset
Admission: Free

In the first half of the 18th century, South Carolina was England's most anomalous North American colony. With only 40 percent of its small population (between 120,000 and 150,000) white, it generated more wealth and distributed it less equally than any other mainland colony. The threat to minority white rule was not only internal. Until the settling of Georgia in the mid-1730s, South Carolina found itself with an aggressive foreign neighbor, Spain, that offered safe haven to runaway slaves. The year 1739, when England and Spain were at war and the new Mose settlement for runaways was available in Florida (see Castillo de San Marcos entry on p. 54), proved a particularly bad year for the state's white masters, with three bloody, if minor, slave uprisings allegedly provoked by the false expectation of deliverance raised in slaves' minds by the preachings of Spanish missionaries. From Charleston, from Berkeley County, and from the Stono River area, three bands of slaves tried to make their way to St. Augustine in Spanish Florida, slaying whites along the way. More than 50 whites were killed; at least twice that many slaves died in their bids for freedom. The following year South Carolina passed its consolidated Slave Act, which made for more prohibitions and even more severe penalties for transgressing the intense restrictions on the disenfranchised. A historical marker commemorates the uprising led by the slave Cato.

ST. HELENA ISLAND

Penn School
Box 126, Martin Luther King Drive, St. Helena Island, SC 29920
(803) 838-2432; (803) 838-2235
Hours: Mon.–Fri., 9 A.M.–5 P.M. Bailey Museum: Tue.–Fri., 11 A.M.–4 P.M.
Admission: Museum: $2 per person

Even before South Carolina became a colony, St. Helena Island was a desired landing for Spanish, French, and English seafarers because of its protected port. Early in the Civil War, the Union utilized its superior navy to seize the island and its adjuncts and dominate the Confederacy's southern Atlantic seacoast. In 1862 the Philadelphia Quaker missionaries Laura Towne and Ellen Murray—soon to be joined by Charlotte Forten Grimke, granddaughter of the wealthy African-American abolitionist James Forten (see entry on p. 316)—opened a school to educate the 10,000 African Americans formerly enslaved on the island. From that day to this, the Penn School on St. Helena Island has been the leading educational and cultural center for the Gullah people. Towne and Murray remained for 40 years, and not until 1948 did the Penn School affiliate with the county school system. With 50 acres and 18 buildings dating as far back as

1882 designated as a National Historic District, Penn Center is one of the oldest and most historically significant African-American educational and cultural institutions in North America. Its library and Bailey Museum provide a unique repository of Gullah artifacts and history and include hundreds of hours of taped oral histories in the Gullah language, sea islands' basketry woven from local rushes, and 19th-century tools and small machines that formed the material substratum of the school's industrial instruction.

SHELDON

Oyotunji African Village
U.S. 17-21, Sheldon, SC 29941
(803) 846-8900; (803) 846-9939
Sheldon lies just east of I-95. Highways 17 and 21 run west from Charleston and intersect I-95
Hours: Fall–Winter: daily, 9 A.M.–5 P.M. Spring–Summer: 9 A.M.–8 P.M.
Admission: Adults, $3.50; children, 6–16, $2.50; guided tours for groups of 10 or more

Midway between Charleston, South Carolina, and Savannah, Georgia, lies a replica of a Yoruba village. Living history interpreters, a small museum with art and craft objects from Yoruba and Benin cultures, an exploration of religious ideas and iconography of southeastern Nigeria, and monthly drum festivals compete for the visitor's attention. Among the festivals celebrated at appropriate times of the year are one that honors the patron god of the Yoruba village and another that honors the Yoruba *oba* (king).

TENNESSEE

Tennessee Department of Tourism
P.O. Box 23170, 320 Sixth Avenue North, Nashville, TN 37202
(615) 741-2158
Hours: Mon.–Fri., 8 A.M.–4:30 P.M.

Ask for "Roots of Tennessee: An African-American Guide."

CHATTANOOGA

Convention & Visitors Bureau
1001 Market Street, Chattanooga, TN 37402
(800) 322-3344
Hours: Mon.–Fri., 8:15 A.M.–5 P.M.

Chattanooga African-American Museum
730 MLK Boulevard, Chattanooga, TN 37403
(615) 267-1076
The continuation of 9th Street at I-124
Hours: Mon.–Fri., 9:30 A.M.–4:30 P.M.; other times by appointment
Admission: Free

Born in a one-room shack in the "Blue Goose Hollow" section of Chattanooga in 1894, Bessie Smith rose from singing on street corners for pennies to touring the country with the famed Ma Rainey Rabbit Foot Minstrels (see Ma Rainey House entry on p. 70) before she was 19. By World War I Smith was a headliner on the black T.O.B.A. (Theatre Owners Booking Association, known to its rank-and-file performers as Tough On Black Actors) circuit. By the 1920s she was one of the most popular African-American entertainers of the day—and her "race records" brought her a still wider audience in the black community. In her ten-year recording career, from "Down Hearted Blues," "St. Louis Blues," "Careless Love," through "Nobody Knows You When You're Down and Out" and about 160 other songs, the "Empress of the Blues" defined for all time the ultimate interpretation of a major African-American art form. Smith died in an automobile accident in 1937, appropriately enough in Clarksdale, Mississippi, a city which was considered ground zero for the blues movement. (See all Clarksdale entries on p. 97.) Contrary to popular myth, perpetuated by everyone from Langston Hughes (*Black Magic*) to Edward Albee (*The Death of Bessie Smith*), Smith did not die because she was refused entrance to a whites-only hospital. Rather she was immediately taken in an ambulance, driven by the black George Miller, to G. T. Thomas Hospital—the local black hospital—where she succumbed to injuries so massive that even today she probably could not have been saved. Smith's piano and sundry memorabilia are the highlights of the Chattanooga African-American Museum. The museum also interprets the history of the local African-American community, particularly the role of three black newspapers during the era of Jim Crow, and offers two brief pamphlets, "African-American Historic Sites in Chattanooga" and "African-American Presence in Chattanooga, 1900–1940," of interest to visitors to the city.

Mary Walker Museum
3031 Wilcox Boulevard, Chattanooga, TN 37411
(615) 629-7651
Hours: Mon.–Fri., 10 A.M.–4 P.M.; Sat.–Sun., by appointment
Admission: Adults, $2; children under 12, $1

The small Mary Walker Museum, named after a former slave who in the 1960s, at the age of 117, learned to read, has a replica of a slave cabin on its premises that is used to educate the public about "slavery days."

Roland Hayes Historical Marker
New Monumental Baptist Church, 715 East 8th Street, Chattanooga, TN 37403
(615) 267-6106
Hours: Daily until sunset
Admission: Free

The Georgia native Roland Hayes moved to Chattanooga at the age of ten and began singing in choir. Upon entering Fisk University, he joined the famed Fisk Jubilee Singers. Rated by some as the "greatest tenor of the era," Hayes became the first African American to perform at Carnegie Hall. Today his old church hosts a historical marker.

DOVER

Fort Donelson National Military Park
Route 1, Box 346, Dover, TN 37058
(615) 232-5706
West of town square on Highway 79
Hours: Daily, 8 A.M.–4:30 P.M.
Admission: Free

Early in the Civil War, the Confederates constructed several forts along Tennessee's border with the neutral state of Kentucky in order to prevent access to the South via the Tennessee River. Among these forts, which were constructed with slave labor, were Fort Henry and Fort Donelson. The latter was captured early in 1862 by Ulysses S. Grant and, though a minor engagement, it was the Union's first strategically significant victory. Thereafter Grant's career never faltered. Later in the war African-American troops were stationed at the fort and recruited from the surrounding area—without much regard as to their legal status, much to the discomfort of slave-owning Kentuckians. Today at the cemetery at Fort Donelson National Military Park the graves of black Union troops who fell in battles in the vicinity can be found, while the slave-built Confederate earthwork defenses are still visible.

GREENEVILLE

Andrew Johnson National Historic Site
College and Depot streets, Greeneville, TN 37743
(615) 638-3551
Hours: Daily, 9 A.M.–5 P.M.
Admission: Adults, $1; under 18, free

Born into a North Carolina family of most modest means, Andrew Johnson at the age of ten was indentured to a tailor, from whom he ran away to settle in Tennessee. Affiliating himself with the state's Jacksonian Democrats, Johnson rose to become governor and U.S. senator. The only senator from a seceding state to remain loyal to the Union, Johnson served as military governor of Tennessee and then as vice-president in Lincoln's second term. Assuming the presidency upon Lincoln's assassination, Johnson soon found himself in deep political waters. While Lincoln may have possessed the credibility to pursue a reconciliationist policy toward the South, Johnson did not, more especially as he was justly seen as unconcerned with promoting the advancement of—or indeed even protection for—freedmen. His veto of the Freedmen's Bureau and civil rights bills, his opposition to the 14th Amendment, and his unsuccessful attempt to purge his congressional and cabinet opponents ultimately led to his impeachment by the House of Representatives and his trial before the U.S. Senate. Probably only the few months left to his administration prevented his being convicted by the Senate; as it is, he escaped conviction—which requires a two-thirds vote—by the narrowest possible margin. The Andrew Johnson National Historic Site preserves the home and memorabilia of America's most controversial president.

HENNING

Bethlehem Cemetery

Durhamville Road, Henning, TN 38041
(901) 738-5055 (City Hall)

In the Bethlehem Cemetery lies "Chicken George," grandson of the abducted and enslaved Kunta Kinte and progenitor of Alex Haley (see entry on p. 147), whose *Roots* would justly commend both men.

Fort Pillow State Park

Route 2, Box 109, Henning, TN 38041
(901) 738-5581
Located 17 miles west of Henning via TN. 87
Hours: Park: daily, 8 A.M.–10 P.M.; Interpretive Center: 8 A.M.–4:30 P.M.
Admission: Free

Returning from a raid into Kentucky, Confederate general Nathan B. Forrest brought his 1,600 men to the outskirts of the Union-held Fort Pillow in April 1864. The fort, named after a Tennessee Confederate general of scant talent who had been appointed early in the war on the basis of his Mexican War fame, was located about 40 miles north of Memphis and was intended to guard against Union invasion of the South via the Mississippi River. In Union hands since mid-1862, Fort Pillow in 1864 was held by about 560 men, half of them African American (a battalion of the 6th Heavy Artillery and a battalion of the 2nd Light Artillery of the United States Colored Troops). Upon the refusal of the Union commander to surrender, Forrest's troops assaulted the fort and, after limited fighting interrupted by a brief parley, were victorious. Confederate losses were 14 killed and 87 wounded, while the Union casualties were about

220 killed and 130 wounded. The sharp disparity between white (36 percent) and black (nearly two-thirds) Union deaths, coupled with accounts of the survivors, led to charges that the Confederates had simply slaughtered every African American who fell into their clutches. A joint congressional committee interviewed survivors (including Private George Shaw, who testified that he saw three young black males shot out of hand as they pleaded for their lives, and Private John Jacob, who testified that several black sergeants were nailed to logs and set afire) and reported in May of 1864 that this is indeed what happened. The Confederates denied these accounts, maintaining that the racial disparity in deaths reflected the unwillingness of African Americans to surrender. While the Fort Pillow incident will never be delineated precisely, the burden of contemporary scholarship clearly upholds the outline if not all the details of the charge of deliberate racial massacre—and certainly subsequent battles underscored that Confederate ferocity toward black prisoners was not uncommon. Black Union troops, most of whom were recruited from runaway slaves, had no difficulty believing the charges; nor did they need (though they surely received) the encouragement of federal propaganda to cry "Remember Fort Pillow!"

Today's visitors to Fort Pillow State Park can walk among the remains of the fort, which are maintained, visit the park's interpretive center, and enjoy the recreational grounds beside tributaries of the Mississippi River. **Note:** The state park is resolutely determined to maintain a "neutral" position on the massacre charges.

Alex Haley House Museum
200 South Church Street, P.O. Box 500, Henning, TN 38041
(901) 738-2240
Hours: Tue.–Sat., 10 A.M.–5 P.M.; Sun., 1 P.M.–5 P.M.
Admission: Adults, $2.50; students, $1

From the village of Juffure and the slave ship *Lord Ligonier* to Will Palmer's house in Henning, Tennessee, six generations prepared the way for Alex Haley to discover and promulgate his *Roots*. Sitting on his grandparents' porch in the 1920s and listening to the tales of his progenitors, Haley was borne up by a story of tribulation, initiative, and success repeated generation after generation. Today the old Palmer residence, built by Haley's grandfather, a successful businessman and community leader, serves as the Alex Haley House Museum. An excellent interpretation of rural small-town life in early 20th-century Tennessee, the house still retains many of the furnishings and possessions that surrounded Haley when he came to visit his grandparents, while also displaying memorabilia from the life and career of a writer who, failing *Roots*, would nonetheless be a prominent figure in African-American life for his co-authorship of *The Autobiography of Malcolm X*.

JACKSON

Casey Jones Home and Railroad Museum
c/o Casey Jones Village, Jackson, TN 38315
(901) 668-1222
Hours: Sept.–June: daily, 8 A.M.–8 P.M. Rest of year: Mon.–Sat., 9 A.M.–5 P.M.; Sun., 1 P.M.–5 P.M.
Admission: Adults, $3; ages 6–12, $2

On that spring morning in 1900, John Luther ("Casey") Jones should never have gotten out of bed in his Jackson home and boarded *Old 382*, the train that would carry him to fame. Plowing into the back of a parked freight train near Vaughan, Mississippi, Jones would enter American legend—but never again his home. You, however, still can; when you visit the Casey Jones Home and Railroad Museum, you will see an engine and tender identical to that of *Old 382* and sundry railroad artifacts. Also in Jackson, at the Calvary Cemetery in which the railroad hero lies, is a historical marker recalling Casey Jones, whom "all the switchmen knew by the engine's moans." (Also see Casey Jones Museum entry on p. 116.)

KNOXVILLE

Beck Cultural Exchange Center
1927 Dandridge Avenue, Knoxville, TN 37915
(615) 524-8461
Hours: Tue.–Sat., 10 A.M.–6 P.M.
Admission: Free

Two centuries of black heritage in eastern Tennessee are traced in the Beck Cultural Exchange Center, formerly the home of James Beck, the first African-American clerk employed by the U.S. Postal Service (in addition to barring blacks from serving in the militia and becoming naturalized citizens, the first congress after the adoption in 1887 of the U.S. Constitution barred African Americans from serving as mail carriers) and subsequently a wealthy real estate entrepreneur and philanthropist. Eastern Tennessee's regional history, including its black component, is unusually interesting: It had the largest concentration of free blacks in the Deep South, and a clear majority of its white population was pro-Union (and suffered for it) throughout the Civil War.

MEMPHIS

Memphis Convention & Visitors Bureau
40 South Front Street, Memphis, TN 38103
(901) 543-5300
Hours: Mon.–Fri., 9 A.M.–4:30 P.M.

Visitors Information Center
340 Beale Street, Memphis, TN 38103
(901) 543-5333
Hours: Mon.–Sat., 9 A.M.–6 P.M.; Sun., 12 P.M.–6 P.M.

Beale Street Historic District
168 Beale Street, Memphis, TN 38103
(901) 526-0110 (Beale Street Management)
Hours: Mon.–Sat., 9 A.M.–5 P.M.
Admission: Free

After three decades as a more or less lawless river port, Memphis had the good fortune to fall to Union assault early in the Civil War, thus escaping the perils of siege and sack. The first decade after the war was not so fortunate, however, as cholera and yellow fever epidemics killed a tenth of the population, forced half to flee, and drove the city into bankruptcy. With the 1890s, however, a new city emerged based on the trade in cotton and timber. Black professionals educated in the North returned to the South and many settled in Memphis, particularly along Beale Street, which stretched from the river eastward. Beale Street soon offered every legal and illegal entertainment imaginable and swarmed with gamblers, loggers, boatmen, and the city's respectable-by-day white business elite. It also swarmed with musicians—and would do so for the next six decades, even as the city and the street gradually became less raw, vibrant, and seductive. W. C. Handy settled on Beale Street in 1912 and quickly gave America its first original musical form, the blues. ("Another night my brother and I sat in a Beale Street barber shop till midnight. 'When will you close up?' Charlie asked, yawning and stretching his arms. 'Humph?' The barber answered surprised. 'I never close up till somebody gets killed.' That was my cue to write the 'Beale Street Blues.' ")

Two world wars later, Sam Phillips, owner of the 18-by-30-foot Sun Studio, would be the first to bring the bluesmen of Beale Street to national prominence, recording Howlin' Wolf, Muddy Waters, and B. B. King, and then would virtually start the crossover of black music into the mainstream by producing the wild elixir of rock 'n' roll. Elvis Presley, Jerry Lee Lewis, Carl Perkins, and Johnny Cash jumped straight from Sun Studio into the mass subconsciousness of America. Beale Street today is a National Historic Landmark—which is to say a helluva lot less raucous and more respectable than when W. C. Handy told America: "The seven wonders of the world I have seen, and many are places I have been. Take my advice, folks, and see Beale Street first." Though less wild, the Beale Street Historic District is still worth a walk, during which one can see the Center for Southern Folklore, the W. C. Handy House and Museum, Sun Studio, the Daisy Theater—on whose stage several generations of black entertainers performed—a number of clubs (check in with the Beale Street Information Center for details on current attractions and hours), and many historical markers that will at once enlighten and entertain.

Center for Southern Folklore
152 Beale Street, P.O. Box 226, Memphis, TN 38101-0226
(901) 525-3655
Hours: Mon.–Sat., 9 A.M.–5:30 P.M.; Sun., 1 P.M.–5:30 P.M.; evenings by appointment; research and media presentations, by appointment
Admission: Free

Brushing up on the heritage of the South is easy to do at the Center for Southern Folklore. Exhibits, photographs, tours, festivals, and films explore the folklore of Dixie, prominently including its African-American component.

W. C. Handy House and Museum
352 Beale Street, Memphis, TN 38103
(901) 522-8300; (901) 527-2583 (the Blues Foundation)
Hours: Tue.–Sat., 10 A.M.–5 P.M.; Sun., 1 P.M.–5 P.M.
Admission: $2 per person

A small house filled with his wife and six children was home to W. C. Handy (see entry on p. 14 and Beale Street entry on p. 149) during the most creative and prolific years of his career. Today the W. C. Handy House and Museum is filled with memorabilia from a career that spanned a log cabin in rural Alabama and the White House.

LeMoyne-Owen College
807 Walker Avenue, Memphis, TN 38126
(901) 774-9090
Hours: Call to arrange tours
Admission: Free

Shortly after Union forces captured Memphis in 1862, the American Missionary Association (AMA) arrived to begin educating the 16,000 slaves who swarmed into the city in search of freedom, food, and employment. By 1866 the AMA was teaching 2,000 pupils in schools and black churches. Then a minor collision between two carriages, one driven by a black man and the other by a white, the former arrested and the latter not, sparked off several days of racial rioting. After a crowd of recently discharged black veterans attempted to prevent the arrest, white mobs, mainly composed of the city's recently arrived Irish-American immigrants, who dominated the police and fire forces, rampaged through the city's black shantytown, killing about 50 people and burning black churches and schools. In 1867 the AMA began anew, this time with a 150-person, six-classroom building that within two years held 2,000 students. In 1871 a gift from a white philanthropist, Dr. F. J. LeMoyne, secured the school's future. Over the years the LeMoyne Normal and Commercial School went through several transitions, including a 1968 merger with Owen College, to emerge as LeMoyne-Owen College, one of the South's oldest historically black colleges.

Memphis Music & Blues Museum
97 South Second Street, Memphis, TN 38103
(901) 525-4007
Hours: Sun.–Thu., 11 A.M.–6 P.M.; Fri.–Sat., 11 A.M.–9 P.M.
Admission: Adults, $5; under 12, free

Vintage posters and advertisements, rare recordings, photographs, artifacts and instruments, unusual film footage (including of Bessie Smith, Furry Lewis, Sleepy John Estes, and others) and a re-creation of Prohibition-era Pee Wee's Saloon can all be found at the Memphis Music & Blues Museum.

National Civil Rights Museum
450 Mulberry Street, Memphis, TN 38103
(901) 521-9699
Hours: Sept.–May: Wed.–Sat., 10 A.M.–5 P.M.; Sun., 1 P.M.–5 P.M.
June–Aug.: 1 P.M.–6 P.M.
Admission: Adults, $5; seniors and students, $4; ages 6–12, $3

A quarter of a century ago, Dr. Martin Luther King, Jr., was gunned down on the balcony of the Lorraine Motel by one in a long line of white supremacists who believed that the African-American quest for full equality could be forestalled by terror. Though his status afforded him privilege unavailable to his fellow blacks, in death King shared the southern black experience of resistance to white supremacy. The story of this resistance in the 1950s and '60s, from the Supreme Court's 1954 *Brown v. Board of Education of Topeka* decision through King's martyrdom in Memphis in 1968, is the centerpiece of the National Civil Rights Museum, which aptly is erected on the site of the motel where Dr. King was assassinated. From the courts to the streets, the decisive civil rights epoch is captured through vignettes, with exhibits highlighting the *Brown* decision; the attempt to prevent school desegregation in Little Rock; the Montgomery Bus Boycott; the lunch-counter sit-ins; the Freedom Rides; the battle to integrate Ole Miss; the March on Washington; black Birmingham's clash with Bull Connor; Freedom Summer and voter registration drives; the march from Selma to Montgomery; the Chicago Freedom Movement and the civil rights movement's shift from an exclusive focus on the Deep South; and a biographical review of the life and philosophy of Dr. King. The emotional climax of the museum's attempt to "never forget" is Rooms 306 and 307 of the Lorraine Motel. Here Dr. King's room can be viewed as it was on the day of his death.

Sun Studio
706 Union Avenue, Memphis, TN 38103
(901) 521-0664
Hours: Daily tours on the half hour of every hour, 10:30 A.M.–5:30 P.M.
Admission: Adults, $4; children 4–12, $3; children under 4, free

Sun Studio, the birthplace of rock 'n' roll, is a museum by day and a recording studio at night. Blues greats B. B. King, Muddy Waters, and Howlin' Wolf (see

Beale Street entry on p. 149), among many others, launched their recording careers here, as did several white kids, including Elvis Aron Presley, heavily influenced by a black musical idiom that had yet to find its way into the mainstream market.

Ida B. Wells Plaque
First Baptist Church, 379 Beale Street, Memphis, TN 38103
(901) 527-4832
Hours: Daily until sunset
Admission: Free

On the site where Ida B. Wells published her crusading newspaper, *Free Speech,* a plaque can be found. Wells (see entry on p. 99) moved to Memphis from Mississippi and in 1891 co-founded the newspaper whose scathing denunciations of lynchings led to death threats and a mob's destruction of her press.

NASHVILLE

Convention & Visitors Bureau
161 4th Avenue North, Nashville, TN 37219
(615) 259-4700
Hours: Mon.–Fri., 8 A.M.–5 P.M.

Ask for the "African-American Historic Sites of Nashville, Tennessee" brochure published by the Metropolitan Historical Commission (400 Broadway, Suite 200, Nashville, TN 37203; 615 862-7970).

Battle of Nashville Historical Markers
c/o Metropolitan Historical Commission, 400 Broadway, Suite 200, Nashville, TN 37203; (615) 862-7970
Hours: Commission: Mon.–Fri., 8:30 A.M.–4:30 P.M. Markers: Daily until sunset
Admission: Free to Historical Commission and to markers

Following General William Sherman's capture of Atlanta in September 1864, his Confederate opponent, General John B. Hood, took his forces into Tennessee in an effort to link up with Nathan B. Forrest's cavalry before passing through Kentucky and, ideally, falling on the rear of Grant's forces in Virginia. Sherman sent 65,000 troops under General George H. Thomas to bring Hood to battle. On the last days of November, in a series of initial encounters with a detachment of the Union command, the impetuous Hood committed his troops to a frontal assault across exposed ground, losing one-fifth of his total strength—and six generals—in the process. A few days later Hood's depleted force drew up before Nashville, where Thomas was hurriedly organizing his defenses.

On December 15 Thomas assaulted Hood's lines, initially sending a diversionary force of 7,600 men under Steedman's command against the Confederate right. The bulk of Steedman's assault force was black—the 12th, 13th, 14th, 17th, 18th, 44th, and 100th regiments of the United States Colored Troops

(USCT). The diversion did not fool Hood, nor did it meet with great success tactically; the men were driven back in confusion, enabling Hood to withdraw some of his own men in order to reinforce his left wing. Yet the black troops were back in battle the next day, attacking Peach Orchard Hill and Overton Hill. Their assaults were furious but unsuccessful. The Confederate commander on Peach Hill recorded that "Five color-bearers with their colors were shot down within a few steps of the works, one of which, having inscribed in its folds 'Eighteenth Regiment U.S. Colored Infantry; presented by the colored ladies of Murfreesborough,' was brought in." The 13th USCT assaulted strongly fortified Overton Hill, advancing uphill in the face of withering musket fire and losing a quarter of its ranks. Alabama's Brigadier General James T. Holtzclaw reckoned the Union's butcher's bill to be high indeed: "I have seen most of the battlefields of the West, but never saw dead men thicker than in front of my two regiments." Though the Confederate right withstood the attacks, which were supported by exceptionally fierce artillery fire, Hood was sufficiently apprehensive that at noon he transferred three brigades from Shy's Hill on his left wing to reinforce his right. Three hours later, overrunning the spot formerly occupied by those three Confederate brigades, Wilson's Union cavalry got to the rear of the Confederates just as McArthur's Union division seized Shy's Hill and precipitated Hood's defeat. At about the same time, the black Union troops on the Confederate right occupied the lines of their largely departed foes of that morning.

In two days of battle the Confederate Army of Tennessee was effectively destroyed, escaping annihilation only because of the skillful rear-guard action under Forrest's direction. Though Hood's force escaped back into Alabama, Thomas had ended organized Confederate operations in the western theater of operations. Today there are Nashville Battlefield Historical Markers located around the city. A map showing the location of battle sites and markers may be secured from the Nashville Metropolitan Historical Commission. Those interested in the role of the African-American troops will want markers N1–19 (4th Avenue South, at Peachtree Street), N1–20 (Hermitage Avenue, near entrance to City Hospital), N1–21 (Lafayette Street, at intersection with Claiborne Street), and N2–4 (State Route 6, north of intersection with Elysian Fields Road). **Note:** The markers make no mention of black (or white) troops, merely of the brigade, division, and corps commanders. (Look for references to Steedman and Peach Orchard Hill.) The Historical Commission also has produced and will supply a useful and interesting brochure outlining the city's black heritage locations, many of which are not mentioned herein because of space constraints. Ask for "African-American Historic Sites of Nashville, Tennessee."

National Baptist Publishing Board
6717 Centennial Boulevard, Nashville, TN 37209
(615) 350-8000
Hours: Call in advance to arrange tour
Admission: Free

Richard Henry Boyd was born a slave in Mississippi in 1843 and christened Dick Gray by his master. After service in the Civil War, he shed his slave name; worked as a cowboy in Texas, New Mexico, and Arizona; was ordained a minister in 1871; and later served as secretary of the Home Mission Board of the Negro National Baptist Convention. A fervent advocate of black self-help, Boyd moved from Texas to Nashville in 1896 to establish the National Baptist Publishing Board, which produced denominational literature that touched upon the African-American experience. Initially aided by the loan of the white Baptist Publishing Board's printing presses, Boyd's endeavor flourished, becoming one of the largest black-owned and operated enterprises in America. Still in family hands, it now produces more than 14 million books and periodicals a year.

Citizens' Bank
401 Charlotte Avenue, Nashville, TN 37219
(615) 256-6193
Hours: Mon.–Thu., 8:30 A.M.–3:30 P.M.
Admission: Free

Beginning in 1904 as the One Cent Savings Bank (a typical commercial exaggeration as in fact ten cents was the minimum balance required), Citizens Bank survived the Great Depression thanks to its conservative lending practices and is now the oldest continuously operated black-owned bank in America. Today the bank's lobby has the original streetcorner clock that stood outside the old bank building and portraits of the bank's founders, while the president's office has documents that highlight the original bank building.

Country Music Hall of Fame
4 Music Square East, Nashville, TN 37203
(615) 256-1639; (615) 255-5333; (800) 255-2357
Hours: June–Aug.: daily, 8 A.M.–8 P.M. Rest of year: 9 A.M.–5 P.M.
Admission: Adults, $6.50; ages 6–11, $1.75; under 6, free

Country music (the commercialization of authentic Anglo-American folk music or, alternatively, "white girls' blues," in the critical appraisal of P. M. Thomas) has never been solely a white phenomenon. Long before Charley Pride there was Deford Bailey, whose harmonica graced both the white country bands with whom he played and radio station WSM's Saturday Barn Dance (otherwise known as the Grand Ole Opry) between 1925 and 1941. The Grand Ole Opry—surely outside the church and the Confederacy, the main culturally unifying experience of the white South—frequently headlined Bailey, who in the 1930s had a regular 15-minute slot following the Fruit Jar Drinkers and preceding the blackface team of Jamup and Honey. Then, in 1941, his career crashed amid copyright restrictions facing all radio performers, who were caught up in the rivalry between the stations and the American Society of Composers, Authors, and Publishers. Bailey's repertoire, which WSM had not encouraged him to expand, was largely limited to traditional tunes, which nonetheless were

ASCAP copyrighted and thus barred from the radio waves. WSM let Bailey go at the height of the stations' battle with ASCAP; when the battle was resolved, he was not brought back. Although formerly well known throughout Dixie, Bailey became a largely obscure figure for the remaining four decades of his life. Today Bailey's Grand Ole Opry appearances are recalled at the Country Music Hall of Fame, which displays his harmonica amid the memorabilia of other country stars. (Other than a suit of Pride's and the banjo player in Thomas Hart Benton's "The Sources of Country Music" mural, nothing else in the place pertains to African Americans.) There also is a Deford Bailey Historical Marker at the corner of 12th Avenue, South Street, and Edgehill Avenue, near where Bailey's shoeshine shop stood, and one at Greenwood Cemetery (1428 Elm Hill Pike; 615 256-4395), where Bailey is buried.

Aaron Douglas Gallery
Fisk University Library, 17th Avenue North at Jackson Street, Nashville, TN 37208
(615) 329-8720
Hours: Tue.–Fri., 12 P.M.–4 P.M.
Admission: Suggested contributions: adults, $4; students, $2

Aaron Douglas was the illustrator for *Crisis* magazine (W.E.B. Du Bois called him the maker of visual images for "the New Negro Movement"), one of the important painters of the Harlem Renaissance (though James A. Porter found his work a crude appropriation of African motifs and an overly exotic portrayal of African-American life) and the founding chairman of Fisk's Art Department, which he served with distinction from 1937 until his death in 1979. Today Fisk's Aaron Douglas Gallery displays the work of prominent African-American artists, such as Porter, Alma Thomas, and Walter Williams, and a collection of African art, including Dogon and Kota figures, Yaure and Baule masks, and Bambara "Chiwara" and Male headdresses.

Fisk University
1000 17th Avenue North, Nashville, TN 37208-3051
(615) 329-8500
Hours: Mon.–Fri., 8 A.M.–12 P.M., 1 P.M.–5 P.M.; 3–4 days' advance notice
Admission: Free

In 1866 Fisk School opened its doors—the doors of a temporary Civil War barracks—to a student body of former slaves. Named after General Clinton B. Fisk, the head of Tennessee's Freedmen's Bureau and an early benefactor, the school raised funds to move from the barracks to its present site by forming the Fisk Jubilee Singers. The singers toured America and Europe, introducing the "spiritual" as an American art form and serving notice that at least one of the cultural contributions of African Americans to this country was worthy of preservation and study. Winning worldwide acclaim, including praise from Queen Victoria, their concerts raised $150,000 and financed Fisk's oldest permanent structure,

Jubilee Hall. Now a National Historic Landmark, Jubilee Hall, the Little Theatre—a barracks building relocated from the original campus—the Carl Van Vechten and Aaron Douglas art galleries, and the university library (which holds original manuscripts by Langston Hughes, C. W. Chesnutt, W.E.B. Du Bois, and others) all make a visit to the campus worthwhile.

James Weldon Johnson Home Historical Marker
911 D. B. Todd Boulevard, Nashville, TN
Hours: Daily until sunset
Admission: Free

James Weldon Johnson (see entries on pp. 228 and 271), poet, editor of the *New York Age*, U.S. Consul to Venezuela and Nicaragua, field secretary of the NAACP, and author of "Lift Every Voice and Sing," which when set to music by his brother won renown as the "Negro National Anthem," taught creative writing at Fisk University (see preceding entry) from 1931 until his death in 1938. The James Weldon Johnson Home Historical Marker locates his Nashville residence during his last years.

Meharry Medical College
1005 D. B. Todd Boulevard, Nashville, TN 37208
(615) 327-6000
Hours: Write to Office of Student Services for information on campus tours
Admission: Free

Founded in 1876 as the medical department of the now-defunct Central Tennessee College, an institution established by the Freedmen's Aid Society of the Methodist Episcopal Church, and subsequently named for the family that provided much of its initial financial support, Meharry Medical College was the nation's first medical education program established for African Americans. Today the school is the largest private institution for the training of black medical professionals. On its grounds it offers a compelling historical exploration of the production of African-American physicians during the long night of segregation. Meharry also publishes an excellent medical newsletter, "Journal for the Poor and Under-Served."

Tennessee State University
3500 John A. Merritt Boulevard, Nashville, TN 37209
(615) 320-3131
Hours: Mon.–Fri., 10 A.M. and 2 P.M., by appointment
Admission: Free

In 1909, five years after it prohibited integrated university education, the Tennessee legislature established a teacher training institution for the state's 473,000 "colored people." What was then Tennessee Agricultural and Industrial State Normal School is now Tennessee State University, on whose campus are a historical marker commemorating the founding of the first chapter of Alpha Kappa Mu, a black honorary society, and a small African-American museum in the main library.

Carl Van Vechten Gallery
Fisk University, Jackson Street at D. B. Todd Boulevard, Nashville, TN 37208
(615) 329-8720
Hours: Tue.–Fri., 10 A.M.–5 P.M.; Sat.–Sun., 1 P.M.–5 P.M.; group tours, by appointment
Admission: Suggested contributions: adults, $4; children, free

African sculpture from Zaire, Gabon, and the Ivory Coast can be found in the Carl Van Vechten Gallery at Fisk University and provides an interlude from the gallery's other marvelous holdings, which include the works of Cézanne, O'Keeffe, Renoir, Rivera, Picasso, and others.

TEXAS

Texas Travel & Information
P.O. Box 5064, Austin, TX 78765-5064
(512) 462-9191
Hours: Mon.–Fri., 8 A.M.–5 P.M.

ABILENE

Fort Phantom Hill
No phone
10 miles northeast of Abilene via Texas Farm Road 600
Hours: Daily until sunset
Admission: Free

In the summer of 1866, General Philip Sheridan, commander of the Military Division of the Gulf, was authorized to raise a regiment of "colored troops." Designated the 9th Cavalry and recruited from freedmen in Louisiana and later Kentucky, the regiment's first barracks in New Orleans were empty cotton presses and its rations were cooked over open fires. Within a year, the white-officered regiment under the command of Colonel Hatch was ordered into Texas and directed to open and protect the mail and stage route from San Antonio to El Paso, combat marauding Indian bands, and establish law and order along the Rio Grande frontier. The 9th Cavalry spent eight years in Texas, during which time it won a reputation for speed, toughness, and valor. Among its many engagements was an autumn 1869 battle at Fort Phantom Hill, a brutal hand-to-hand encounter with 500 Comanche and Kiowa braves. (Also active in the fight was a detachment from the justly renowned, white, 4th Regiment.) Though the fort, in operation only from 1851 to 1854, today lies in ruins, with only the stone guardhouse, powder magazine, and commissary offering a sense of frontier existence a century and a half ago, there are interpretive signs to guide visitors.

ALBANY

Fort Griffin State Historical Park
Route 1, Highway 283 North, Albany, TX 76430
(915) 762-3592
Hours: Daily, 8 A.M.–10 P.M.
Admission: Per car, $2

In 1866 the U.S. Congress authorized the establishment of six African-American regiments, four infantry (the 38th, 39th, 40th, and 41st, which three years later were consolidated as the 24th and 25th) and two cavalry (the 9th and 10th), all of which proved to be first-class fighting troops and a vital component of the force that secured the West for settlement by winning the wars against the Plains Indians. Collectively these black troops came to be known as buffalo soldiers. Tradition ascribes the name to the Indian perception that the soldiers' hair resembled the fur of the buffalo, the staple upon which Plains Indian societies depended. The name may well have been first applied to the troops of the 10th Cavalry (recruited primarily from among free blacks in the north), who shortly after arriving on the plains adopted the buffalo image for their battle crest. Led by Colonel Grierson, who like the 9th's Hatch had an outstanding Civil War record and had been personally selected for command by President Ulysses S. Grant, the 10th spent some of the 1870s stationed at Fort Griffin, from which they sortied against Comanche raiders, arguably the finest and certainly the fiercest horsemen in the world. Today the interpretive programs at Fort Griffin State Park highlight the impact of the buffalo soldiers on the settlement of the Texas frontier. The park also occasionally conducts living history reenactments that include or focus on the African-American contribution to the Texas frontier.

AUSTIN

Black Arts Alliance
1157 Navasota Street, Austin, TX 78702
(512) 477-9660
Hours: Mon.–Fri., 9 A.M.–5 P.M.
Admission: Free

A richly diverse palate of artistic programs—ethnic dance, music and theater productions, film and video shows, painting and sculpture exhibitions—make the Black Arts Alliance one of Austin's delights.

George Washington Carver Museum
1165 Angelina Street, Austin, TX 78702
(512) 472-4809
Hours: Tue.–Thu., 10 A.M.–6 P.M.; Fri.–Sat., 12 P.M.–5 P.M.
Admission: Free

Housed in what in 1933 was Austin's first "colored" library, the George Washington Carver Museum pays tribute to the "peanut doctor" whose work aided black sharecroppers and small farmers throughout the South in the early decades of the 20th century (see Tuskegee University entry on p. 31; Carver Museum entry on p. 370; George Washington Carver Monument entry on p. 414) and documents local and county black heritage. The museum also hosts changing exhibitions, special programs, and classes that explore the African-American experience.

BRACKETTVILLE

Old Fort Clark Guardhouse Museum
c/o Fort Clark Springs, Highway 90, Box 345, Brackettville, TX 78832
(210) 563-2493
Hours: Museum: Sat.–Sun., 1 P.M.–4 P.M.; other times by appointment with the Fort Clark Springs Information Center
Admission: Free

Associated with the 24th and 25th Infantry during their years in Texas was an extraordinary unit, the Seminole-Negro Indian Scouts, who ended up in Texas after more than a half century of migration. Their ancestors were runaway slaves of the early 19th century who had fled to Florida and allied themselves, frequently by marriage, to the Seminoles. From Florida they had been sent with the Seminoles to the Indian Territory (Oklahoma) after the Second Seminole War (see Dade Battlefield entry on p. 42), there to meet with persecution from Creek Indians and slave hunters. (See Five Civilized Tribes entry on p. 455.) Fleeing the threat of reenslavement, they and many Seminoles moved to Mexico. In 1858, when the Seminoles returned to the United States, the black Seminoles remained south of the Rio Grande, where they had adapted the survival skills they'd learned in the Florida swamps to the austere desert borderland of northern Mexico. When the U.S. Army began to match wits with the Apache and Comanche after the Civil War, it discovered a need for such men. In the summer of 1870, after being recruited by Major Zenas Bliss of the 25th Infantry, the first volunteers crossed the Rio Grande and began operating out of forts Clark and Duncan.

Serving on both sides of the U.S.-Mexican border against Apache, Kickapoo, and Comanche warriors, the Seminole-Negro Indian Scouts proved themselves to be superb trackers and outstanding combat troops. Never numbering more than 50 men at a time, they won four Medals of Honor, three of them for saving the life of a white officer of the 24th, Lieutenant John Bullis. In one incredible feat of tracking, 39 scouts led by—or rather commanded by—Lieutenant Bullis tracked Mescalero Apache raiders for 34 days across 1,260 miles. Their postwar fate can doubtless be guessed: No written record of any possible oral promises made to these men existed, so although many of their officers endorsed the Seminole-Negro Scouts' claim of land offered in exchange for service, no land came their way. Ironically, the rolls of the Seminole tribe had closed in 1866, so the Seminole-Negroes who crossed from Mexico were ineligible for land on Indian reservations.

Insult was added to injury when the scouts were written out of the history of the Indian wars of the Southwest; of course, this fate, like Indian wars themselves, they shared with the men of the 9th, 10th, 24th, and 25th regiments. The scouts were based at Fort Clark, a rugged outpost near the Texas-Mexico border, and were buried in a segregated plot on the grounds of the fort. Their unit name says much for the times and the intricacies of bureaucratic regulation: They could not be scouts without being Indian; being Negro, they could not be buried with whites and Indians.

DALLAS

Dallas Black Chamber of Commerce
2838 MLK Jr. Boulevard, Dallas, TX 75215
(214) 421-5200
Hours: Mon.–Fri., 9 A.M.–5 P.M.

Knights of Pythias Temple
2551 Elm Street, Dallas, TX 75226
No telephone
Hours: Daily until sunset
Admission: Closed to the public. Exterior viewing only

The Knights of Pythias Temple, completed in 1916, was for more than three decades the social, cultural, and professional center of a black community living under the constraints of Jim Crow white Texas. The building's eclectic, Beaux Arts style can be traced to its designer, W. S. Pittman, Dallas's first black architect and the son-in-law of Booker T. Washington. The temple remains one of the most visible landmarks of the black presence in Dallas.

Museum of African-American Life and Culture
1620 First Avenue, at the Dallas Fair Park, Dallas, TX 75226
(214) 565-9026
Hours: Tue.–Sat., 9:30 A.M.–5:30 P.M.; Sun., 12:30 P.M.–5:30 P.M.
Admission: Free

Artifacts and fine and folk art of Africa and its diaspora are on display at the Museum of African-American Life and Culture. Lectures, exhibits, and festivals that celebrate black heritage are also held intermittently.

FORT DAVIS

Fort Davis National Historic Site
Highways 17 and 118, Fort Davis, TX 79734
(915) 426-3225
Located on the stretch of highway where the two routes are joined, Fort Davis is adjacent to the town of the same name, 207 miles southeast of El Paso by way of I-10 and Texas 118
Hours: June–Aug.: daily, 8 A.M.–5 P.M. Sept.–May: daily, 8 A.M.–6 P.M.
Admission: $1 per person, not to exceed $3 per family

Drawing the attention of Confederate Texas toward the conflict with the Union, the Civil War opened up the state's interior to intensified Indian depredations, the cumulative effect of which was to destroy Texas's frontier defense system. Fort Davis, to the west of which lay Mescalero Apache territory and to the east of which was the "Great Comanche War Trail," was wrecked by Apaches after its abandonment by Confederate troops in 1862. Five years later, four companies of the recently organized 9th Cavalry rode into its ruins and began to rebuild the fort. Over the next 20 years, all four buffalo soldier regiments, the 9th and 10th Cavalry and the 24th and 25th Infantry, would spend time at Davis—or more frequently in the surrounding wasteland threatened by Apache and Comanche warriors. For African Americans, Fort Davis is perhaps best known as Lieutenant Henry Ossian Flipper's Cavalry.

Flipper, born a slave in Georgia in 1854, was the first black graduate of the United States Military Academy at West Point. He joined the 10th Cavalry at Fort Concho in Texas and distinguished himself in the 1879–80 campaign against the Apache chief Victorio. Soon after Flipper's company transferred to Fort Davis, the young lieutenant was accused of embezzling government funds. After a controversial court-martial, Flipper was found innocent of embezzlement but guilty of "conduct unbecoming a gentleman" and was dismissed from the army. Only in 1976, after a 94-year struggle to clear Flipper's name, did the army review the transcripts of the trial and change Flipper's service discharge from dishonorable to honorable.

That the army found Flipper less than a gentleman, and that Flipper felt himself racially persecuted, should come as no surprise. The buffalo soldiers' service never secured them anything but the formal equality of equal pay with their white counterparts, rank by rank. Their service was always west of the Mississippi, in the most arduous environments and far from settled white populations. White officers usually avoided the all-black regiments, even if it meant serving at a lower rank. F. W. Benteen (see Fort Duchesne entry on p. 518), who declined major's rank in the 10th to serve as a captain in a white regiment, and George Armstrong Custer, who declined a lieutenant colonelcy in the 9th, would later meet their fate—the former to survive in some disgrace and the latter to die in "glory"—with the 7th Cavalry at the Battle of the Little Big Horn. (See entry on p. 497.) Those white officers who did accept command of black regiments were generally excellent. Indeed, the prerequisites for such command were more severe than for leading white troops: two years of active Civil War service and an examination before a board of officers selected by the secretary of war. Excellence, however, did not secure these officers much in the way of career advancement. Nor did it secure them or their troops first-class equipment or rations. At Fort Sill in Oklahoma in 1873, for example, 45 of the 48 horses of the 10th's F Company were more than 15 years old, while the Fort Concho surgeon reported that the food for black troops was below even the army's normally unappetizing standard. Moreover, in conflicts with white civilians black troopers were at a decided disadvantage, their assailants rarely being brought to trial and still more rarely being found guilty.

Despite all this, the buffalo soldiers had an exemplary record for service. In 1867, when more than 20 percent of the U.S. Army deserted, only 4.2 percent of black soldiers were among the missing. A decade later, the famous 4th had 184 deserters and the 7th 172, while the 10th had 18 and the 9th but 6. Finally, the incidence of drunkenness, suicide, and venereal disease was also lower among black troops than white.

No one exhibited this capacity to staunchly endure harsh conditions (and treatment) more than Flipper. While spending the rest of his life attempting to clear his name, he settled in El Paso, where he was a successful engineer, served as a translator for the U.S. Senate, and helped build a railroad through the Alaskan wilderness. In 1978, two years after the army reversed Flipper's dishonorable discharge, his body was reinterred in Thomasville, Georgia, with full military honors.

Visitors to Fort Davis National Historic Site view interpretive displays, a diorama, and a slide show that include information on the role of the buffalo soldiers.

FORT McKAVETT

Fort McKavett State Historic Site
Texas Farm Road 864, Fort McKavett, TX 76841
(915) 396-2358
Hours: Daily, 8 A.M.–5 P.M.
Admission: Free

Originally in operation from 1852 through 1859, Fort McKavett provided protection to travelers on the Upper El Paso Road—an important artery to the California goldfields—and partially deterred raids by the Lipan Apaches and nomadic Comanches. As Indian raids declined and civilian traffic shifted to the Lower El Paso Road with its more dependable water supply, the fort was abandoned. Increased Indian activity during and after the Civil War, and increased western immigration, necessitated the fort's reopening, which was undertaken in 1868 by the 4th Cavalry. In the 1870s, the peak years of the fort's activities, the black troopers of 9th and 10th Cavalry were periodically based here. (In a battle near the fort, the 9th's wiry five-foot 23-year-old ex-slave, Sergeant Emanuel Stance, formerly of Charleston, South Carolina, became the first

African-American to win the Medal of Honor in the years after the Civil War.) Fort McKavett also served for some time as the regimental headquarters of the 24th Infantry.

Today's visitor to Fort McKavett State Historical Park can wander through the restored post headquarters, officers' quarters, barracks, hospital (now the interpretive center), and morgue, and can view the remains of other buildings. The fort's interpretive displays include information on the buffalo soldiers.

FORT WORTH

Cattleman's Museum
1301 West Seventh Street, Fort Worth, TX 76102
(817) 332-7064
Hours: Mon.–Fri., 8:30 A.M.–4:30 P.M.
Admission: Free

Though you'd never know it from John Wayne's westerns, the West was full of black folk. By 1890, when the West was essentially secure from Indian trouble, half a million African Americans lived in Texas and Oklahoma alone. In the years following the Civil War, many made their living punching cattle along the Western, Chisholm, and Goodnight-Loving trails. The last trail, which led to New Mexico and later to Colorado and Wyoming, was opened in 1866 by cattle barons Charles Goodnight and Oliver Loving. Goodnight's closest paid "hand" was Bose Ikard, a former slave from Mississippi, of whom Goodnight said, "I trusted him farther than any living man. He was my detective, banker, and everything else in Colorado, New Mexico, and any other wild country I was in." A little of the West's black cowboy history is on display at the Cattleman's Museum.

HOUSTON

Convention & Visitors Bureau
3300 Main Street, Houston, TX 77002
(713) 227-3100
Hours: Mon.–Fri., 8:30 A.M.–5 P.M.

Museum of Fine Arts, Houston
1001 Bissonet Street, Houston, TX 77265-6826
(713) 639-7300
Hours: Tue.–Sat., 10 A.M.–5 P.M.; Thu., 5 P.M.–9 P.M.; Sun., 12:15 P.M.–6 P.M.
Admission: Adults, $3; seniors and students, $1.50; under 19, free

Fine and folk art of the Mother Continent and paintings, photographs, and sculpture by some of its diaspora make up a substantial portion of the many extraordinary pieces on view at the Museum of Fine Arts, Houston. Its African Collection includes work from the Ndebele (Zimbabwe), Bamileke (Cameroon), Ibo, Yoruba and Chamba (Nigeria), Kuba (Zaire), and Baule (Ivory Coast) cultures, among many others. African-American artists in the museum's permanent collection include John Biggers, Jacob Lawrence, Romare Bearden, and many others. In addition, the museum hosts temporary exhibits of work of well-known and emerging African-American artists.

Taylor-Stevenson Ranch
11822 Almeda Street, Houston, TX 79045
(713) 433-4441
Hours: By appointment, daily, 10 A.M.–sunset
Admission: Tours, including the museum, hayrides and other activities: $3 per person. Specialty group bookings, such as barbecues and zydecos: $5 per person

The Taylor-Stevenson Ranch is one of the first and still one of the few black family-owned working cattle ranches in America. Ranch tours, kids' birthday parties, and horseback riding are available on the property, as is the American Cowboy Museum. Exhibits and artifacts at the museum highlight the African-American, Hispanic, and Native American aspects of America's cowboy past.

JACKSBORO

Fort Richardson State Historical Park
Highway 281 South, Jacksboro, TX 76458
(817) 567-3506
Hours: Museum: Wed.–Sun., 8 A.M.–12 P.M.; 1 P.M.–5 P.M. Tours: prearranged. Recreational facilities and grounds: daily, daylight hours
Admission: $3 per vehicle; $1 per walker or biker; 65 and older, free

Not far from the Red River that separates Texas and Oklahoma is the Fort Richardson State Historical Park. At what once was a base of operations for the African-American buffalo soldiers, seven original buildings still stand, including an enlisted men's barracks that now serves as a museum of military history. Here one will find a scouting map of the 10th Cavalry and a list of the buffalo soldiers once stationed at the fort.

SAN ANGELO

Fort Concho National Historic Landmark and Museum
213 East Avenue D, San Angelo, TX 76903
(915) 657-4441
Hours: Tue.–Sat., 10 A.M.–5 P.M.; Sun., 1 P.M.–5 P.M.
Admission: $1.50

Fort Concho was located at the confluence of the three Concho rivers and guarded the territory through which passed the San Antonio–El Paso Upper Road, the old Butterfield Trail, the Goodnight-Loving Trail, and an eastern branch of the Comanche War Trail. The fort was well placed—particularly if you liked spending time chasing through desolate lands after Comanche and Kiowa warriors who, if you caught up with them, would settle for killing you quickly but would much prefer to do so at length and amid laughter. Regimental headquarters of the 10th from 1875 to 1882, the fort was home at various times to companies from all four of America's black regiments. Today Fort Concho National Historic Landmark and Museum is one of the nation's best-preserved frontier forts and Texas's premier showcase for interpreting the role of African-American regiments in the winning of the West. Sculptures of black Indian scouts, a brief biography of Lieutenant Flipper (see Fort Davis entry on p. 161), a display on the 10th Cavalry, mannequins of black troopers, Fort Concho reenactment units (including one portraying Company A of the 10th), 20 restored buildings—including an enlisted men's barracks, officers' quarters, and a hospital—and a 35,000-item museum compete for visitors' attention.

SAN ANTONIO

Institute of Texas Cultures
801 South Bowie, San Antonio, TX 78294
(210) 226-7651
Hours: Tue.–Sun., 9 A.M.–5 P.M.
Admission: Voluntary donations requested

The good news of Texas's ethnic heritages is spread by the Institute of Texas Cultures. Permanent and traveling exhibits, collections of artifacts and photographs, demographic and statistical data, original ethnic newspapers, and ethnic festivals trace and celebrate the heritage of African Americans (and many others) in Texas. Prime among the black contributions to the state is the Juneteenth celebration, which recalls the belated announcement in Texas of the manumission of slaves. Far from the main battlegrounds of the Civil War, Texas slaves knew little of Lincoln's 1863 Emancipation Proclamation (not that knowledge would have availed them anything beyond hope); nor indeed did many know of the war's conclusion and its consequences. Not until two months after the formal Confederate surrender did the Union army reach even east Texas. Then, on June 19, 1865, in the east Texas port of Galveston, General Granger proclaimed a world turned upside down. This was the first news African Americans had of their freedom. Since that time they have held annual celebrations in remembrance of their deliverance from captivity, if not from Babylon.

VIRGINIA

Virginia Division of Tourism
1021 East Cary Street, Richmond, VA 23219
(804) 786-4484
Hours: Mon.–Fri., 8:15 A.M.–5 P.M.

Ask for the state's guide to its African-American historical sites and cultural events: "Virginia: The Presence of the Past."

ALEXANDRIA

Alexandria Black History Resource Center

638 North Alfred Street, Alexandria, VA 22314
(703) 838-4356
Hours: Tue.–Sat., 10 A.M.–4 P.M.
Admission: Free

The Alexandria Black History Resource Center, housed in what was the African-American community's first public library, uses paintings, photographs, books, and other memorabilia to interpret the black contribution to the city's history and has produced a brochure outlining a "Black Historic Sites Walking Tour."

Fort Ward Museum and Historic Site

4301 West Braddock Road, Alexandria, VA 22304
(703) 838-4848
Hours: Museum: Tue.–Sat., 9 A.M.–5 P.M.; Sun., 12 P.M.–5 P.M. Historic site: daily, 9 A.M.–sunset
Admission: Free

The responsibilities of black and white Union troops in the defense of Washington, D.C., are compared at Fort Ward Museum and Historic Site. At Fort Ward, the fifth largest of the 162 Union earthwork forts and batteries constructed to defend Washington against a Confederate onslaught, a photo-essay exhibit complemented by a small selection of objects chronicles the role of African-American soldiers in the northern army, with an emphasis on black troops who served or are buried in Alexandria.

Franklin and Armfield Office

1315 Duke Street, Alexandria, VA 22314
Hours: Daily until sunset
Admission: Not open to the public. Exterior viewing only

While the 1830s are typically treated as the era of Jacksonian democracy, for Virginia they were preeminently the years of the massive trade in slaves occasioned by declining agricultural yields in the original southern colonies and the vast expansion of cotton production in the lands of the Louisiana Purchase, particularly in the Mississippi Delta. With importation of slaves to the United States forbidden since 1809, new labor came only from the natural increase of those who by this period were already African Americans. This internal trade in slaves, or "slave-farming," was led by Virginia, America's oldest colony and one whose tidewater land was worn from the rigors of more than a century of tobacco planting. Indeed, Virginia's slave population actually declined in these years rather than grew. The explanation lies neither in declining slave birth rates nor in manumission, but in massive sales. During the administration of Andrew Jackson (1829–1837), himself of course a slave owner, the Alexandria firm of Franklin and Armfield was the South's largest slave-trading enterprise, an achievement the more memorable because throughout this period Alexandria was part of the District of Columbia. With America's largest slave-trading firm operating within the nation's capital during the reign of one of its most progressive (or in any event, populist) antebellum presidents, slavery was clearly central to the nation's experience. Today the Franklin and Armfield Office is a National Historic Landmark and is closed to the public.

Gadsby's Tavern Museum
134 North Royal Street, Alexandria, VA 22314
(703) 838-4242
Hours: Tue.–Sat., 10 A.M.–5 P.M.; Sun., 1 P.M.–5 P.M. Tours at quarter before and quarter after the hour. Last tour begins at 4:15 P.M. each day
Admission: Adults, $3; ages 11–17, $1; under 11, free

George Washington, John Adams, Thomas Jefferson, James Madison, and the Marquis de Lafayette were among the patrons of slave-trader John Gadsby's tavern in Alexandria. Today patrons of Gadsby's Tavern Museum see the workaday side of this late 18th-century tavern—and particularly the sundry responsibilities of free and enslaved African Americans employed there. At least once a week, history reenactors, including African-American interpreters of various roles, slave and free, can be found strolling about the tavern.

Stabler-Leadbeater Apothecary Museum and Shop
105–107 South Fairfax, Alexandria, VA 22314
(703) 836-3713
Hours: Mon.–Sat., 10 A.M.–4 P.M. Group tours must be prearranged
Admission: Donations ($1) encouraged. Small fee for group tours

When you enter the Stabler-Leadbeater Apothecary Shop, founded in 1792 by the Quaker Edward Stabler, you walk in the footsteps of former patrons such as George Washington, Daniel Webster, Henry Clay, John Calhoun, and Robert E. Lee. You also enter a museum devoted in part to the related subjects of the manumission of slaves and the education of African Americans in Alexandria. Quakers were the principal founders of the city's emancipation societies. Organizations such as the "Society for the Relief of People Illegally Held in Bondage," formed by Edward Stabler around 1796, operated freely until the white fallout from the Nat Turner Rebellion of 1831 (see Nat Turner entry on p. 171) restricted their activities.

APPOMATTOX

Appomattox Courthouse National Historical Park
State Route 24, Box 218, Appomattox, VA 24522
(804) 352-8987
Hours: June–Aug.: daily, 9 A.M.–5:30 P.M. Rest of year: 8:30 A.M.–5 P.M.
Admission: Adults, $1; seniors and under 17, free

The surrender ceremony between General Ulysses S. Grant and General Robert E. Lee at Appomattox Courthouse is justly portrayed as embodying, and as the beginning of, genuine reconciliation following the most destructive conflict in this nation's history. The continuing centrality of the color line in U.S. history is underscored by the fact that although almost 180,000 of the Union's troops were black—of whom more than one-third died by war's end—including the 25th Corps, which pursued Lee from Richmond to Appomattox in April of 1865, to date no equivalent racial reconciliation has been recorded.

Visitors to the Appomattox Courthouse National Historical Park view the village as it looked on April 9 almost 130 years ago. The reconstructed courthouse sees service as visitor center and museum, complete with detailed audiovisual programs. If you come in the summer months, you'll find yourself surrounded by living history reenactors, including African Americans in various free black roles.

ARLINGTON

Benjamin Banneker Boundary Stone
18th and Van Buren streets, Arlington, VA 22205
Hours: Daily until sunset
Admission: Free

Descended from a Welsh grandmother who had married a slave, Benjamin Banneker was freeborn on his father's tobacco farm in Maryland. From an early age, he showed promise of mechanical and scientific skill, though not until late in life would this promise be gloriously fulfilled. Just short of his 60th birthday and with only a limited education, Banneker by self-study from books and astronomical devices borrowed from a Quaker neighbor fully comprehended the principles of calculus and spherical trigonometry, a feat if not of true genius at least of truly staggering proportions. His accomplishment was seized upon by abolitionists, most of them Quakers, as proof that "the powers of the mind are disconnected with the colour of the skin." A few years later Charles Ellicot, the Quaker surveyor laying out the boundaries of the nation's new capital, employed Banneker as his assistant, and he was again used as an exemplar of the black race's potential. Shortly thereafter Banneker published his first almanac, which, with a letter rebutting Jefferson's deprecatory observations about the intellectual capacity of African Americans, he sent to the then U.S. Secretary of State. Though politely phrased, as from one scholar to another, Banneker drew Jefferson's attention to the fact that the future president and past author of a justly renowned document that confidently declared the natural law equality of all humankind detained "by fraud and violence so numerous a part of my brethren under groaning captivity and cruel oppression."

Though the charmingly heroic tale that Banneker assisted Pierre L'Enfant in developing the master plan of Washington, D.C.; that L'Enfant departed the U.S. in a huff, taking the sole copy of the new city's plan with him; and that

Banneker then reconstructed from his capacious memory the entire design, thus saving the new capital, enjoys wide currency in the lower reaches of popularized black history, it is false in every detail. Rather, Banneker (see entry on p. 238) performed the astronomical calculations necessary to site the city's cornerstones. One of these stones, now known as the Benjamin Banneker Boundary Stone and declared in 1976 a National Historic Landmark, defined the southwestern border of the District of Columbia until a portion of donated Virginia was returned to the state in 1847.

Charles R. Drew House
2505 1st Street South, Arlington, VA 22204
Hours: Not open to the public. Exterior viewing only

The Charles R. Drew House, a National Historic Landmark *not open to the public*, commemorates the life and work of the Howard University (see entry on p. 198) faculty member who developed the nation's first blood bank, an achievement that rested on Drew's prior research into the practicality of storing blood plasma. His achievement was timely indeed, coming shortly before the outbreak of World War II, which offered unprecedented scope to test the clinical application of his work. With war imminent and Drew the world's recognized authority, Britain invited him to establish its national blood bank system, following which he did the same for the American Red Cross. He then returned to Howard to head its medical school's surgery department, a post he retained until killed in an automobile accident in 1950.

CHARLOTTESVILLE

Charlottesville/Albemarle Convention & Visitors Bureau
Highway 20 South, P.O. Box 161, Charlottesville, VA 22902
(804) 977-1783
Hours: Daily, 9 A.M.–5:30 P.M.

Ash Lawn–Highland
Highway 795, Route 6, Box 37, Charlottesville, VA 22901
(804) 293-9539
Hours: Daily, 9 A.M.–6 P.M.
Admission: Adults, $6; seniors, $5.50; ages 6–11, $2; under 6, free

President Monroe was no stranger to slavery, growing up on a 500-acre tobacco farm. Eleven slaves were included in the 1744 final estate inventory of his father, one of whom, a "Negro boy Ralph," passed to the 16-year-old James as a provision of his father's will. Three decades later, Monroe's Highland Plantation was essentially a village unto itself, a largely self-contained community of 45 to 50 souls—about 35 of them enslaved. Later still, Monroe was Virginia's governor at the time of the 1800 slave uprising known as Gabriel's Rebellion.

Led by Gabriel Prosser (to give him the surname of his owner), a skilled and literate slave blacksmith, the Richmond-area rebels planned to raid the state arsenal, seize the state capital and the governor, and kill or hold hostage all whites (excepting antislavery Quakers and Methodists). At the last moment, with many of the rebels already armed and in the field, the insurrection was betrayed. At the resulting trial, Monroe realized that many of the accused had been intimidated into giving dubious and incriminating testimony, and he called for clemency in their cases. Despite his pleas, about 35 slaves were executed for their alleged roles in the planned uprising. Convinced that manumission followed by integration was neither desirable nor possible as public policy, ("[Slaves] can never here enjoy all the advantages, social and political, of freemen. If the Constitution and the laws were even to proclaim them entitled to these advantages, such is the force of habit and prejudice, that the constitution and the laws would in this respect be altogether inoperative"), Monroe saw in colonization in Africa the solution to what still remains as America's major piece of unfinished business. His support as President of the United States of the American Colonization Society's establishment of Liberia led that new nation to name its capital Monrovia.

Today's visitors to Monroe's plantation, now named Ash Lawn–Highland, still approach the mansion house through fields and pasture in which graze cattle and horses, though the rude dwellings of the field slaves have vanished. The service yard still bustles with activity, and the original smokehouse and overseer's cottage still stand. The well and the quarters for the house slaves have been reconstructed and see service in demonstrations of open-hearth cooking, candlemaking, and other crafts that in Monroe's day were the daily lot of dispossessed African-American labor. Finally, an exhibit of relevant artifacts and illustrations addresses the subject of Monroe and slavery, while on the 4th of July weekend living history reenactors, including an African-American interpreter in first and third person, re-create life on Monroe's plantation.

Monticello
P.O. Box 316, Charlottesville, VA 22902
(804) 295-8181
Hours: Mar.–Oct.: daily, 8 A.M.–5 P.M. Rest of year: 9 A.M.–4:30 P.M.
Admission: Adults, $8; seniors, $7; ages 6–11, $4. Group rates available

Thomas Jefferson's house at Monticello dominated his 5,000-acre holding in Albemarle County. From his mountaintop, Jefferson overlooked the farms that composed his plantation. Of its 170 members, 120 were enslaved. Most of the physical evidence of the plantation and its residents has long since disappeared. The wheat fields and sheep pastures have fallen to forests; the tobacco barns and slave cabins have vanished. Relics of the community survive only on Mulberry Row, a 1,000-foot-long road on the Monticello mountaintop.

Two centuries ago Mulberry Row was a hive of activity—more than a dozen nailmakers banged hammers on anvils near the forge's fire, axes and planes scattered wood chips and shavings, milk pans banged together as dairy workers jumped to avoid mule-drawn carts that trotted along a row overlooked by 17 buildings. At the end of the day the shops grew quiet and the laborers returned home, the slaves to five log-cabin dwellings that lined the lane. For visitors eager to travel back in time, a self-guided tour brochure offers a sense of the 18th-century lives, free and slave, that were played out here.

One other source provides glimpses of the lives of Monticello's disenfranchised black laborers and their families. Artifacts from recent archaeological excavations—ceramics, decorative objects such as pierced coins and cowrie shells, and products of craft labor such as tin cups and nails—illustrate the material culture of the dispossessed.

COURTLAND

Nat Turner Insurrection
Courtland, VA
55 miles west of Norfolk, on U.S. 58
Hours: Daily until sunset
Admission: Free

In the summer of 1831 a literate slave preacher and mystic, after almost a decade of seeing violent visions written across the sky, became convinced that God had chosen him to lead his people out of bondage. With faith but without a plan, with five followers but without a prayer, Nat Turner marched from farm to farm across Southampton County killing every white person God placed in his path—and gathering followers as he did so. After threescore deaths, God evidently lifted His sanction and the white community, whose terror exceeded even its wrath, wreaked its revenge not only on the rebellious but on the race. For weeks Turner remained at large—a deadly threat to every black on whom white eyes fell—before being captured, interrogated, tried, and executed.

The aftermath of this affair was so exceedingly strange that Turner's belief in divine inspiration seemed not without support. Concerned about the large black presence in the state, Virginia's legislature debated a proposal to abolish slavery gradually, a proposal that came tantalizingly close to passage before losing on a 65-to-58 vote. (This proposal had nothing to do with black civil rights—all the freed were to be deported. Rather it was motivated by racial fear and by the commercial and political interests of the small farmers and businessmen of the western part of the state, who used the issue to challenge the dominance of the Tidewater, slave-owning aristocracy.) Thereafter events followed a more normal course: repression and intensified restrictions on slave autonomy, including further limiting African Americans' freedom of movement and prohibitions both against slaves holding religious services in the absence of a white and against instructing slaves to read. These restrictions reflected a deeper appreciation of the history of slave rebellions (and of the power of the Bible) than today is found among America's populace, black or white: Each of the major antebellum African-American uprisings—Prosser in 1800 and Turner in 1831 in Virginia, and Vesey in 1822 in South Carolina—was led by skilled, literate, and relatively privileged black men from outside the plantation belt, and each drew significantly on biblical injunctions and imagery. (See Ash Lawn–Highland entry on p. 169 and Denmark Vesey entry on p. 138.)

Today the state has neither historical markers nor museums devoted to this uprising, but if you drive south from Courtland you will pass through the countryside briefly dominated by Turner and his adherents.

FREDERICKSBURG

Fredericksburg Tourist Bureau
706 Caroline Street, Fredericksburg, VA 22401
(800) 678-4748; (703) 373-1776
Hours: Daily, 9 A.M.–5 P.M.

Stop in here and ask for the "Black History of Fredericksburg, Virginia" pamphlet, which is full of information on local sites that connect to the city's black heritage.

Fredericksburg and Spotsylvania National Military Park
120 Chatham Lane, Fredericksburg, VA 22405
(703) 373-1776
Hours: Park: daylight hours. Visitors' centers: 8:30 A.M.–6:30 P.M.
Admission: Free

The ground that is now Fredericksburg and Spotsylvania National Military Park was the scene of some of the most intense, deadly, and strategically significant combat of America's most intense, deadly, and strategically significant war. The Fredericksburg ("A chicken could not live on that field when we open on it"), Chancellorsville ("our men went down before them like trees in a hurricane"), Wilderness ("Bushwhacking on a grand scale"), and Spotsylvania ("chiefly a savage hand-to-hand fight across the breastworks") battlefields *each* bore at least twice as many American dead or wounded than were killed in the entire course of the Revolutionary War. By the time of the last two battles, which were fought by the same two forces after only two days' rest, African-American units were an integral part of the Union army. Today the National Park Service maintains almost 6,000 acres of land, two visitors' centers, and on-site historians to interpret the four battles. During the summer months special programs re-create Civil War scenes.

Fredericksburg Area Museum & Cultural Center
904 Princess Anne Street, Fredericksburg, VA 22401
(703) 371-3037
Hours: Nov.–Mar.: Mon.–Sat., 10 A.M.–4 P.M.; Sun., 1 P.M.–4 P.M. Apr.–Oct.: Mon.–Sat., 9 A.M.–5 P.M.; Sun., 1 P.M.–5 P.M.
Admission: Adults, $3; with student ID, $1; under 6, free

African Americans arrived in the Rappahannock River Valley long before Fredericksburg was officially founded in 1728. Before long they comprised roughly half the population: From the end of the 18th century until the middle of the 19th there were about 14,000 whites and 13,000 blacks, slightly fewer than 1,000 of the latter being free, in the valley. Fredericksburg itself had a population of about 3,000 whites, 1,200 enslaved, and 350 free African Americans. The Fredericksburg Area Museum & Cultural Center interprets local African-American history, including the deterioration in status of free black farmers and artisans, the growth of direct importation of slaves from Africa to service an expanding tobacco economy, the resistance of the enslaved, and the impact of their transplanted African culture on everything from their masters' musical tastes to their dialect. The museum occupies the old Town Hall, in which from 1866 to 1869 the Freedmen's Bureau had its offices.

Kenmore
1201 Washington Avenue, Fredericksburg, VA 22401
(703) 373-3381
Hours: Mar.–Nov.: daily, 9 A.M.–5 P.M. Dec.–Feb.: daily, 10 A.M.–4 P.M.
Admission: Adults, $5; under 19, $2.50; families, $10

Kenmore, which today offers tours that incorporate the house's African-American heritage, was the home of George Washington's sister, Betty, and her husband, Fielding Lewis, who between them owned 40 or 50 slaves. Colonel Lewis also owned a firearms factory that supplied guns to the Revolutionary army and ships that saw service in the war. Upon the latter there served a number of enslaved African Americans, several of whom were freed as a consequence of their service and thereafter prospered as free blacks in the Fredericksburg area. Prior to the war, Lewis administered a school, sponsored by the Propagation of the Gospel in Foreign Parts and the Bray Associates of England, that taught slave children ages five to eight to read, but the school closed after five years as its purpose met with scant support from most slave owners.

Slave Block
Charles and Williams streets, Fredericksburg, VA 22401
(703) 373-1776
Hours: Daily until sunset
Admission: Free

Thousands of African Americans were led from nearby warehouses, where they were stashed prior to sale, to the circular sandstone Slave Block at which they were inspected and auctioned.

GREAT BRIDGE

Battle of Great Bridge Memorial
City of Chesapeake Municipal Center, 306 Cedar Road, Great Bridge, VA 23320
(804) 547-6241
Hours: Daily until sunset
Admission: Free

From its inception, the American Revolution involved black voices and lives. Indeed, at the Battle of Bunker Hill, a dozen or so African Americans fought in the rebel ranks. George Washington, who first sought to reduce the role of blacks when he took up his command in July 1775, quickly recanted and by December of that year welcomed African Americans into his forces. By the time of Lord Cornwallis's defeat at Yorktown in Virginia, 5,000 to 8,000 African Americans—some free but most enslaved—had associated themselves with the colonial army or navy. More participated in the ranks of the British forces; in either case the choice was usually made on the basis of which side offered freedom from slavery in return for service.

The royal governor of Virginia, Lord Dunmore, for example, offered freedom to enslaved African Americans who fled their masters, provided—and only provided—that those masters were in rebellion. Dunmore's proclamation declared "all indented servants, Negroes, or others, *appertaining to Rebels* free, that are able and willing to bear Arms" for King George. From the ablest men of the 20,000 men, women, and children who reached his lines, he formed several regiments. Thus at the Battle of Great Bridge, fought near Norfolk, Virginia, in December of 1775, African Americans found themselves in both combatant forces. On the British side were Dunmore's "Ethiopian" regiments, while in the Third Virginia Regiment, Major Thomas Marshall and his son John (later U.S. Secretary of State under John Adams, and then America's most significant Chief Justice of the Supreme Court) fought alongside several black men, including most notably William Flora of Portsmouth. Today, about 20 miles south of Norfolk, this encounter is commemorated with a Battle of Great Bridge memorial.

At the war's end, the surviving 19,000 Afro-Virginians freed by Dunmore's proclamation were settled in the West Indies, Canada, and England—many of them ultimately resettling in Africa in the new Sierra Leone colony created for them. Those promised freedom for their service in the colonial ranks met differing fates. After many of Virginia's slave owners reneged on their promises, Governor Benjamin Harrison enlisted the assistance of the legislature to secure freedom for the veterans.

Of greater significance, however, the new federal Constitution of 1787 recognized the legal status of slavery. Moreover, the new Congress barred blacks from serving in the militia, from becoming naturalized citizens, and from serving as mail carriers. The limited gains African Americans secured in the Revolution and the continued functioning of chattel slavery were incitements to rebellion.

HAMPTON

Hampton Convention & Tourism
Two Eaton Street, #106, Hampton, VA 23669
(804) 722-1222
Hours: Mon.–Fri., 8:30 A.M.–4:30 P.M.

Fort Monroe and Casemate Museum
Fort Monroe, P.O. Box 341, Hampton, VA 23651
(804) 727-3973
Hours: Daily, 10:30 A.M.–4:30 P.M.
Admission: Free

While in the Hampton Roads area be sure to stop in briefly at Fort Monroe, where, isolated deep in the Confederacy, the largest stone fortress ever built in the United States guarded the junction of the James River and the Chesapeake Bay. Here, in what would become Jefferson Davis's postwar prison, African-American slaves found their first Union refuge. In the earliest days of the Civil War, the commanding officer, Major General Benjamin Butler, unilaterally took action that anticipated by 18 months Lincoln's Emancipation Proclamation. Rather than turn away escaping slaves or—as some Union commanders did in the spring of 1861—permit their owners to enter Union lines and repossess them, Butler declared them "contraband of war." Butler's action emboldened the black populace of the surrounding countryside, many thousands of whom fled to the fort's sanctuary. Two years before African Americans would be permitted to enlist in the Union army (though they were permitted to do so in the navy as early as the summer of 1861), these refugees served Butler's forces as cooks, stevedores, carpenters, teamsters, and general laborers.

Today, although it lacks a tour program emphasizing African-American themes, the Casemate Museum of Fort Monroe is in the process of installing a new exhibit on an old subject: the "contraband" that within three years composed a substantial element of the Union forces that crushed the Confederacy.

Hampton Roads History Center
c/o Virginia Air and Space Center, 600 Settlers Landing Road, Hampton, VA 23669
(804) 727-0800
Hours: Mon.–Wed., 10 A.M.–5 P.M.; Thu.–Sat., 10 A.M.–7 P.M.; Sun., 12 P.M.–7 P.M.
Admission: Adults, $6; seniors and military, $5.50; ages 4–17, $4.25

Located within the Virginia Air & Space Center is the Hampton Roads History Center, which interprets the African-American experience in Virginia from colonial days to the present. From Jamestown to the moon, from Virginia's first black indentured servant to Guion Bluford, Jr., member of the 1983 Space Shuttle *Challenger* crew and the first African American in space, it's all in one building.

Hampton University
Queen Street, Hampton, VA 23668
(804) 727-5000
Hours: Hampton Museum: Tue.–Fri., 9 A.M.–5 P.M.; weekends, 12 P.M.–4 P.M.
Admission: Free

In 1868 a 27-year-old Hawaiian-born son of missionaries and former Union commander of an African-American regiment, Samuel Chapman Armstrong, with the encouragement of the Freedmen's Bureau and the aid of the American Missionary Association, founded what now is arguably the most renowned historically black college in the United States, Hampton Normal and Agricultural Institute (now University). Beginning with a 120-acre farm, few buildings, little equipment, 15 students, two teachers, and a strong commitment to linking Christian ethics, income-generating skills, and intellectual achievement, Armstrong and his successors turned a vision into a university. Four years after opening its doors, Booker T. Washington (see entries on pp. 177 and 206) walked across the breadth of Virginia to Hampton, a journey that would culminate in Tuskegee, Alabama. (See Tuskegee University entry on p. 31.) Ten years after opening its doors to African Americans, the school began a pioneering program to educate American Indians. Today, in addition to the five National Historic Landmark buildings on campus, visitors are drawn to the 98-foot-diameter Emancipation Oak, already an ancient tree when it served as the site where Lincoln's Emancipation Proclamation was read to Hampton Roads residents; to the Booker T. Washington statue; to the Huntington Memorial Library, which holds personal papers of Booker T. Washington, George Washington Carver, Mary McLeod Bethune, Martin Luther King, Jr., and others; and to the annual jazz and African-American festivals, both held in June.

COURTESY HAMPTON UNIVERSITY MUSEUM

The Mukenga mask of the Kuba people of Zaire is but one of many outstanding African pieces at the Hampton University Museum.

In the year of its inception Hampton opened its museum, which is thus one of the oldest in the state. Today's visitor to the Hampton University Museum will find not simply the largest (9,000 works of art) and strongest collection of its kind in the southeastern United States, but a museum whose African and American Indian collections are truly remarkable. With 2,700 pieces representing 87 ethnic groups and cultures, the African Collection is outstanding by any measure. At its heart are 400 objects gathered at the turn of the century by a Hampton student of the 1880s. Rivaling the African Collection in quality and significance is the American Indian Collection, of 1,600 pieces from 93 tribes.

This collection began with the 1878 arrival of the first representatives of the culture. Hampton, which had a multicultural appreciation more than a century before the issue became topical, also has a fine Oceanic Collection—600 objects from the cultures of Melanesia, Micronesia, Polynesia, and Aboriginal Australia. This is the museum's oldest collection, having its origin in Armstrong's request to his mother, who still lived in Hawaii, for "specimans of coral, lava and curiosities of all kinds found in the Pacific."

Also of keen interest in the museum is a fine arts collection that is particularly strong in works by Harlem Renaissance–inspired artists. Hale Woodruff, Richmond Barthé, Claude Clark, and a number of others are represented by some of their finest work. The museum also has nine paintings by the most renowned 19th-century African-American artist, Henry O. Tanner.

Virginia Air & Space Center
600 Settlers Landing Road, Hampton, VA 23669
(804) 727-0800
Hours: Mon.–Wed., 10 A.M.–5 P.M.; Thu.–Sat., 10 A.M.–7 P.M.;
Sun., 12 P.M.–7 P.M.
Admission: Adults, $6; seniors and military, $5.50; ages 4–17, $4.25

Hampton, birthplace of America's space program and the training site for the original *Mercury* astronauts, is also home to the Virginia Air & Space Center. The center features artifacts from NASA's space missions (including a three-billion-year-old moon rock), more than a dozen aircraft and space capsules, historical exhibits, an IMAX Theater, and a photo exhibit in the Air Force Gallery of the famous black Tuskegee flyers, many of whom first earned their wings in Hampton's War Training Service Program.

HARDY

Booker T. Washington National Monument
Route 3, Box 310, Highway 122, Hardy, VA 24101
(703) 721-2094
Hours: Daily, 8:30 A.M.–5 P.M.
Admission: Families, $3; ages 17–62, $1; others, free

The Booker T. Washington National Monument is a reconstruction of the Burrough's farm on which Washington spent the first nine years of his life. The facility is run by the National Park Service, which means it is well researched, maintained, and explained. Guided tours are offered around the reconstructed small farm of the 19th century, which includes the kitchen cabin birthplace of Washington. "The cabin was without glass windows," Washington recalled, "[and] had only openings in the side to let in light and also the cold, chilly air of winter." Here Washington and his brother and sister slept on the dirt floor bundled in rags. The newly freed Washington left the farm in 1865, nine years old and illiterate. When he returned for a visit in 1908, he was a college president

COURTESY BOOKER T. WASHINGTON MEMORIAL, NATIONAL PARK SERVICE

African-American historical interpreters bring to life the childhood environment of the young slave Booker T. Washington.

and influential statesman. Today you need be neither to visit the birthplace of an American giant.

LORTON

Gunston Hall

10709 Gunston Road, Lorton, VA 22079
(703) 550-9220
Hours: Daily, 9:30 A.M.–5 P.M.; last tour at 4:30 P.M.
Admission: Adults, $5; seniors, $4; children, $1.50; under 6, free

In 1755 George Mason, author of the Virginia Declaration of Human Rights and progenitor of the U.S. Constitution's Bill of Rights, built Gunston Hall, the centerpiece of a community of 100 people, most of them enslaved. As Mason's son John recalled in his old age, "My Father worked four plantations with his own Slaves, each under an overseer, and containing 4 or 500 acres of open Land. . . . The west Side of the [mansion's] Lawn was skirted by a wood, just far enough within which, to be out of sight, was a little village called Log-Town, so called because most of the houses were built of hewn pine logs, here lived several Families of the Slaves, serving about the Mansion house."

Today Gunston Hall is surrounded by 550 acres of the original 5,000-acre plantation. Little remains of the slaves' story, though the reconstructed kitchen yard is a mundane reminder of the African-American presence. The 30 or more outbuildings of Mason's day, including slaves' quarters and workshops, are to be found only in the documentary record, though Mason's beautiful gardens and house still stand and please even the most jaundiced eye.

LYNCHBURG

Lynchburg Museum
901 Court Street, P.O. Box 60, Lynchburg, VA 24505
(804) 846-1459
Hours: Daily, 1 P.M.–4 P.M.
Admission: Adults, $1; students, 50 cents; preschoolers, free with adult

Although the Lynchburg Museum's current holdings are inadequate to interpret the city's antebellum slave community, the 20th-century African-American social and business presence is highlighted. Memorabilia of C. W. Seay, a Fisk University (see entry on p. 155) and Columbia University graduate who for 30 years served as principal of the city's segregated black high school before becoming Lynchburg's first African-American city councilman since Reconstruction, and of the nationally renowned Dr. R. Walter Johnson, mentor to Althea Gibson and Arthur Ashe and himself a six-time winner of national tennis championships, are the most prominent of the museum's modern-era black holdings.

Anne Spencer House and Garden
1313 Pierce Street, Lynchburg, VA 24501
(804) 846-0517
Hours: By appointment only
Admission: $2 per person

Shadowed by the Blue Ridge Mountains and surrounded by one of Virginia's most historic cities, Lynchburg, is the Anne Spencer House and Garden. Spencer, the only Virginian whose poetry is included in the first edition of the prestigious *Norton Anthology of Modern Poetry*, was a major influence within the Harlem Literary Renaissance and counted among her friends and admirers Dr. James Weldon Johnson, Langston Hughes, Claude McKay, Paul Robeson, Marian Anderson, W.E.B. Du Bois, and Mary McLeod Bethune. Founder of Lynchburg's NAACP chapter in the years after World War I, Spencer composed much of her most famous poetry in her garden and its small, one-room cottage, "Edankraal." Today's visitor, who must call ahead for an appointment, can enjoy both the beauty of the garden and the photographs and memorabilia that recall the commonwealth's most significant 20th-century literary figure.

MOUNT VERNON

Mount Vernon Estate
George Washington Memorial Parkway, Mount Vernon, VA 22121
(703) 780-2000
Hours: Mar.–Oct.: daily, 9 A.M.–5 P.M. Rest of year: 9 A.M.–4 P.M.
Admission: Adults, $7; seniors over 62 with ID, $6; ages 6–11, $3

Mount Vernon, the treasured estate of George Washington, had four outlying farms and was largely a self-contained community—one that included between 20 African Americans in 1758 and more than 300 in 1799. Little is known of their lives, though it is clear that family was an important source of stability for the unfree members of the community. The 1799 census reveals that two-thirds of the adults were married and that three-fourths of the children under the age of 14 had both a mother and father living on the estate.

Many of the slaves at the Mansion House Farm lived in the greenhouse complex, which was constructed in 1793. Today's visitors to the reconstructed greenhouse complex can view sleeping quarters, a shoemaker's shop, and a museum annex that contains artifacts that highlight the daily life of the enslaved. However, they can only imagine what life must have been like on the outlying farms, which were less rich in material resources than the mansion house. A Polish admirer of Washington remarked after his 1798 visit to Mount Vernon, "We entered one of the huts of the Blacks. . . . They are more miserable than the most miserable of the cottages of our peasants. The husband and wife sleep on a mean pallet, the children on the ground."

After a life of toil, death. At Mount Vernon's slave burial ground, on a wooded hillside 50 yards southwest of Washington's Tomb, are two memorials, perhaps the only slave memorials in the United States. Of the cemetery itself, little is known: Neither the names nor the number of slave and free black members of the Mount Vernon community buried here survive. The sole exception is William Lee, General Washington's personal servant during the Revolutionary War. Each September there is a tribute at the Slave Memorial that includes griot storytellers and music.

NEWPORT NEWS

Newsome House Museum and Cultural Center
2803 Oak Street, Newport News, VA 23607
(804) 247-2380
Hours: Mon.–Fri., 2 P.M.–5 P.M.; Sun., by appointment
Admission: Free

Newsome House in Newport News is an elegant Queen Anne structure that became the home of Joseph Thomas Newsome and his wife. Born in 1869, this son of former slaves educated himself in the law and journalism, becoming the editor of the *Newport News Star* and one of the first African-American attorneys licensed to practice before the Virginia Supreme Court. His restored home, in which Booker T. Washington was a frequent guest, now offers programs and exhibits highlighting black heritage.

War Memorial Museum of Virginia
9285 Warwick Boulevard, Huntington Park, Newport News, VA 23607
(804) 247-8523
Hours: Mon.–Sat., 9 A.M.–5 P.M.; Sun., 1 P.M.–5 P.M. Archives open by appointment
Admission: Adults, $2; seniors, military, and ages 6–16, $1

Black Americans have taken part in nearly all of this nation's wars, defending a country that denied them and their families equality. At Monmouth, one in 20 of Washington's troops was African American. America's major victories in the War of 1812 were naval, and in that navy one in five of the crews was black. Nearly 180,000 black combat troops (and another 300,000 laborers) served the Union in the Civil War, 23 of whom won Medals of Honor. Thirteen Medal of Honor winners during the Indian wars of 1870 to 1900 were African American. These stories and their 20th-century counterparts—including the post-Reconstruction trend to exclude African Americans from the fighting ranks and the use of mass punishments against black regiments for the alleged crimes of their individual members—are explored in "The Black Soldier" gallery of the War Memorial Museum of Virginia.

NORFOLK

Black Civil War Veterans' Memorial
238 East Princess Anne Road, Norfolk, VA 23510
(804) 441-2576 (Elmwood Cemetery)
Hours: Daily until sunset
Admission: Free

Just across the narrow body of water overlooked by Fort Monroe (see entry on p. 175) is the city of Norfolk, whose Elmwood Cemetery has the South's only black soldiers memorial honoring Union veterans of the Civil War. Gravestones of African-American soldiers and sailors who died in the Civil War and the Spanish-American War are found behind the granite monument atop which stands a black Billy Yank.

COURTESY NORFOLK CONVENTION AND VISITORS BUREAU

Norfolk pays tribute to black Union soldiers.

PETERSBURG

Petersburg Visitor Center
425 Cockade Alley, P.O. Box 2107, Petersburg, VA 23804
(804) 733-2400; (800) 368-3595
Hours: Daily, 9 A.M.–5 P.M.

First Baptist Church
236 Harrison Street, Petersburg, VA 23803
(804) 732-2841
Hours: By appointment, Mon.–Fri., 9 A.M.–4 P.M.
Admission: Free

The First Baptist Church traces its origins to a plantation congregation formed in 1756 and hence claims to be the earliest African-American church in the United States. Less than two decades after its inception, the congregation was organized as the First Baptist Church on the estate of Colonel William Byrd. After its building burned in 1820, the church moved to Petersburg. The present church structure dates back to 1870.

Gillfield Baptist Church
29 Perry Street, Petersburg, VA 23803
(804) 732-3565
Hours: Mon.–Fri., 9 A.M.–5 P.M.; groups should make appointments
Admission: Free; voluntary donations welcomed

Formally organized in 1803 as the Sandy Beach Baptist Church on Pocahontas Island, the Gillfield Baptist Church traces its history back to a racially mixed congregation in 1788. In 1818 the church assumed its present name, making it one of the oldest African-American congregations in the United States. The present church structure dates back to 1878.

Petersburg National Battlefield Park and Museum
Highway 36, Petersburg, VA 23804
(804) 732-3531
Hours: Park: daily, 8 A.M.–dark. Visitor Center: Summer: 8 A.M.–7 P.M. Rest of year: 8 A.M.–5 P.M.
Admission: $3 per automobile; $1 for bikers or walkers; seniors, children under 16, free.

At the Petersburg National Battlefield Park and Museum, visitors will gain a deeper understanding of the drama of the Civil War, particularly regarding black Union troops and the famous Battle of the Crater. To break the Confederate defense of the besieged city, the 48th Pennsylvania Infantry, many of whom were miners in civilian life (and, contrary to pop black history, were white), secretly dug a lengthy tunnel under the rebel breastworks, which were then thunderously blown up. The nine United States Colored Troops (USCT) regiments that composed the 4th Division of Burnside's 9th Corps were scheduled to exploit the resulting gap in the Confederate line. At the last moment, however, the Union high command, fearful of political repercussions if the black troops suffered severely in the vanguard of the attack, changed the order of battle and sent the (white) 1st, 2nd, and 3rd divisions into the line first. Ironically, strong Confederate resistance and the Union forces' difficulty negotiating the crater caused by the explosion trapped the last-into-battle 4th Division in the crater, where they suffered unmercifully. At the battle's conclusion the Union casualties were 654 (1st), 832 (2nd), 659 (3rd), and 1,327 (4th).

The park has site markers commemorating the USCT forces, and the museum's various displays acknowledge the contribution of the Union's African-American troops. Be sure to look for the USCT Monument at Confederate Battery #9, which commemorates the capture of the battery by Hinks's

USCT division on June 15, 1864. In the summer months, there are guided tours of the battlefield and living history reenactments of a Union siege encampment and a Confederate artillery battery—complete with cannon and mortar firing. Representatives of the USCT take part in the reenactments. Finally, be sure to ask for the free "African Americans at Petersburg" brochure.

Pocahontas Island
Petersburg, VA 23803
Joseph Jenkins Roberts Monument
Halifax and South Sycamore streets, Petersburg, VA 23803
(800) 368-3595; (804) 733-2400 (Convention and Visitors Bureau)
Hours: Monument: daily until sunset
Admission: Free

Petersburg is best known in African-American circles for its antebellum free black community (as the Civil War opened, half of the city's population was African American, of whom one-third were free) and for the ten-month Civil War siege that culminated in the bloody Battle of the Crater. Although no local museum focuses on the area's African-American experience, visitors can still wander about Pocahontas Island. Situated on the north side of the Appomattox River, this was an early 1800s free black community and the home from 1815 to 1829 of Joseph Jenkins Roberts, who served as chief justice, lieutenant governor, and governor of the colony of Liberia, before becoming its first president in 1848, when Liberian independence was granted.

Virginia State University
One Hayden Drive, Petersburg, VA 23806
(804) 524-5000
Hours: Mon.–Fri., 8 A.M.–4 P.M.
Admission: Free

The first state-supported African-American college in the country was chartered in 1882 as the Virginia Normal and Collegiate Institute. Now Virginia State University, the school opened with a black faculty, a seven-man board of visitors with but one white member, and John Mercer Langston as its first president. Langston and his brother Charles were the sons of a white Virginia planter who freed their mother, Lucy Langston. After both were educated at Oberlin College, a hotbed of abolitionist sentiment, John became the dean of Howard University Law School, while Charles married the widow of a man killed on John Brown's raid on Harpers Ferry and became the grandfather of Langston Hughes.

PORTSMOUTH

Virginia Sports Hall of Fame
420 High Street, P.O. Box 370, Portsmouth, VA 23705
(804) 393-8031
Hours: Tue.–Sat., 10 A.M.–5 P.M.; Sun., 1 P.M.–5 P.M.
Admission: Free

Arthur Ashe leads a contingent of well-known black Virginia athletes whose feats are commemorated with photographs, biographical summaries, and personal memorabilia at this hall of fame.

RICHMOND

Metro Richmond Convention & Visitors Bureau
300 East Main Street, Richmond, VA 23219
(800) 365-7272; (804) 358-5511
Hours: Mon.–Fri., 8:30 A.M.–5 P.M.

Black History Museum and Cultural Center of Virginia
00 Clay Street, Richmond, VA 23261
(804) 780-9093
Hours: Tue., Thu., Fri., Sat., 11 A.M.–4 P.M.
Admission: Adults, $2; children 12 and under, $1

In the mood for a place where black predominates? Richmond—Holy City of the Lost Cause of the Confederacy, whose Monument Avenue hosts a series of statues of the Confederacy's paladins of war and a memorial to the troops they led—can accommodate you. The Black History Museum and Cultural Center seeks to become a central repository for the memoirs, documents, oral histories, artifacts, and memorabilia of central Virginia's African-American community. Housed in a building utilized in the 1920s by the Council of Colored Women, an organization led by Richmond's Maggie Walker, founder of the state's first black bank, the Black History Museum displays two small exhibits, "Historic Jackson Ward: Personalities and Places" and a "Voting Rights Exhibit."

Jackson Ward
Bordered by Fourth, Marshall, and Smith streets, and I-95, Richmond, VA
Hours: Daily until sunset
Admission: Free

Richmond's Jackson Ward district, which is on the Register of National Historic Places, was the centerpiece of urban black America at the close of the 19th century. Today's visitors can stroll about and examine the district's historic black sites, which include a statue commemorating the Jackson Ward–born Bill "Bojangles" Robinson; a park commemorating John Mitchell, Jr., founder in 1884 of the *Richmond Planet*, forerunner of the *Richmond Afro-American Newspaper*; and the "Wall Street of Black America," the site of Consolidated Bank and Trust Company, which was created by merger of four black-operated banks.

Museum of the Confederacy
1201 East Clay Street, Richmond, VA 23219
(804) 649-1861
Hours: Mon.–Sat., 10 A.M.–5 P.M.; Sun., 12 P.M.–5 P.M.
Admission: Per person, $4 ($7 includes White House of the Confederacy on the same day)

African Americans—few of them free—comprised one-third of the population of the Confederacy. The Museum of the Confederacy increasingly is interpreting their lives within its walls—and outside its walls too, in school programs, in living history presentations on its steps during the summer months, in family reunions, and in summer camps. In 1991, for example, "Before Freedom Came: African-American Life in the Antebellum South, 1790–1865" started out as a museum exhibition, before branching out, reaching out, and transforming itself into "African Legacies: American Traditions," a weeklong day camp complete with living history interpreters, storytelling, authentic craft instruction, African dance, and games, food, and frolic. While the exhibit changed in 1992, to "Sun-up to Sun-up: African American Daily Life, 1800–1865," the summer African-American History Day-Camp remains; as does the museum's annual Down Home Family Reunion in Richmond's historically black district, Jackson Ward. This festival features games, storytelling, music, African dance, food, and drama, and underscores the tragic dispersal of slave families that produced their pale image—the post–Civil War reunions of plantation communities that had come to know each other as kin. Finally, the White House of the Confederacy, from which Jefferson Davis guided the secessionist struggle, is the scene for the museum's exploration of the urban experience of southern African Americans, slave and free, during the Civil War.

Lee, Jackson, Davis, and their kin continue to dominate the museum—as they did the Confederacy—but more and more the dispossessed black populace is given its due.

Virginia E. Randolph Cottage Museum
2200 Mountain Road, Glen Allen, Richmond, VA 23060
(804) 261-5029, (804) 262-3363
Hours: Mon., Wed., Fri., Sun., 1 P.M.–4 P.M.
Admission: Free

Virginia Randolph was instrumental in fostering black vocational training in Virginia, particularly for women. The small Virginia E. Randolph Cottage Museum explores the development of one of the few educational, and subsequent career, paths open to African-American women during the era of segregation.

Richmond National Battlefield Park
Chimborazo Visitor Center, 3215 E. Broad Street, Richmond, VA 23223
Fort Harrison Visitor Center, at the battlefield, Richmond, VA 23231
(804) 226-1981
Hours: Chimborazo Visitor Center: daily, 9 A.M.–5 P.M. Fort Harrison Visitor Center: daily, 9 A.M.–5 P.M. Battlefield Park: daily, sunrise to sunset
Admission: Free

"On to Richmond!" was the rallying cry and primary objective of Union troops throughout the Civil War. Seven military drives headed for the Confederate capital, but only two (McClellan's 1862 Peninsula Campaign and Grant's 1864 assault) came within sight of the city. Richmond National Battlefield Park was the site of battles that yielded, amid carnage, 14 Medals of Honor to African Americans. In the 1864 campaign federal forces finally seized Fort Harrison—and held it against vigorous counterattacks personally directed by Lee. A mile and a half north of the fort, Union troops initially were repulsed at New Market Road. In a war that saw, particularly after 1863, significant African-American participation, perhaps the outstanding achievement of black troops was the charge on the Confederate fortifications on New Market Heights by the Third Brigade (composed of the 4th, 6th, and 10th regiments of the United States Colored Troops) and Second Brigade (5th, 36th, and 38th USCT regiments) of the 3rd Division of Ord's 18th Corps.

Today you can enter Fort Harrison bloodlessly, as you can Richmond's other Civil War battlefield sites. Should you come in the summer for the living history reenactments, you will get a good sense of how your ancestors, black or white, spent their time in uniform.

Valentine Museum
(Wickham-Valentine House)
1015 East Clay Street, Richmond, VA 23219
(804) 649-0711; group tours, (804) 225-8730
Hours: Mon.–Sat., 10 A.M.–5 P.M.; Sun., 12 P.M.–5 P.M.
Admission: Adults, $3.50; seniors, $3; ages 7–12, $1.50

An urban history museum with holdings in paintings, prints, manuscripts, textiles, costumes, photographs, furniture, and industrial artifacts, the Valentine Museum interprets Richmond's African-American experiences as strands inextricably woven into the true fabric of the city's communal history. The museum's exhibitions regularly reflect Richmond's African-American presence: Whether at the thematic center or on the periphery, black is treated as a constant, of varying intensity, in the chiaroscuro of southern life.

Virginia Museum of Fine Arts
2800 Grove Avenue, Richmond, VA 23221-2466
(804) 367-0844
Hours: Tue.–Sat., 11 A.M.–5 P.M.; Thu., until 10 P.M.; Sun., 1 P.M.–5 P.M.
Admission: Donation: adults, $4; others, $2

The Virginia Museum of Fine Arts is arguably the finest museum in a city of its population in the United States. Its holdings range in scope from pharaonic Egypt to 20th-century masters. Sculpture, paintings, drawings, and objects from five continents across five millennia demand your attention. If you've only a few hours and an urge to open yourself to the power of African art, you must be strong! Avert your eyes from the art of Asia and ancient Greece. Snub Monet, Renoir, and van Gogh. Spurn the seductions of Georgia O'Keeffe. Turn instead to an African Collection that includes some 60 sculptures, sundry pieces of jewelry, and 35 textiles, all of which are of West African origin. The sculpture is bold and accessible, and ranges from the lost-wax bronze casting plaque of a Middle Kingdom (1590–1650) Benin chief to the masterful wooden neck rest by a 20th-century Yaka sculptor. The textiles, of Nigerian—primarily Yoruban—origin, are also 20th century. Particularly striking is the narrow-band weave, embroidered, indigo agbada (man's robe). Of the jewelry, perhaps the most impressive piece is the 19th-century, gold Ashanti necklace. Its cast disks and bells are arranged symmetrically, separated by small cross-shaped beads; a live cast solid gold pendant of a small land crab is suspended to fall on the center of the wearer's breast. You must see it to appreciate its beauty.

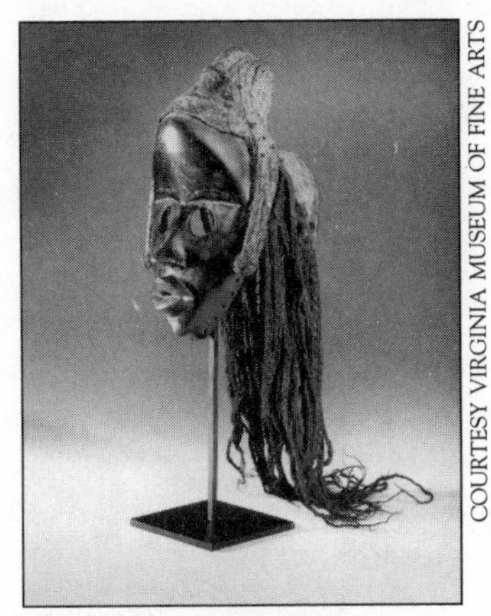
COURTESY VIRGINIA MUSEUM OF FINE ARTS

This Dan mask, probably used during initiation dances by the males of the Poro society, graces the Virginia Museum of Fine Arts.

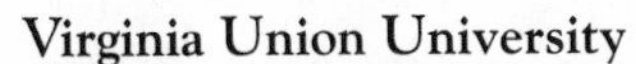

Virginia Union University
1500 North Lombardy Street, Richmond, VA 23220
(804) 257-5600
Hours: Mon.–Fri., 8:30 A.M.–4:30 P.M.
Admission: Free

Founded in 1865 by the American Baptist Home Mission Society to educate young black men and women, what is now Virginia Union University took its name from the 1899 merger of Wayland Seminary and Richmond Theological Institute. Visitors to the school, which is the alma mater of L. Douglas Wilder, Virginia's governor from 1989 through 1993 and the first person of African descent popularly elected as governor of a state, are most often drawn to those old buildings that were constructed with granite blocks hand-hewn by newly freed black men determined to see their children well educated.

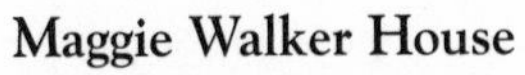

Maggie Walker House
110 Leigh Street, Richmond, VA 22323
(804) 780-1380
Hours: Wed.–Sun., 9 A.M.–5 P.M.
Admission: Free

Born near the close of the Civil War to former slaves, Maggie Walker rose to be one of the most significant forces in Richmond's black community, particularly through her affiliation with the black fraternal organization, the Independent Order of St. Luke. After establishing and editing the *St. Luke Herald*, Walker founded the St. Luke Penny Savings Bank, becoming the first female bank president in the country. Several mergers later, her institution survives and asserts itself to be the oldest continually black-operated bank in the United States. A leading figure nationally in the NAACP, Walker also served in a leadership capacity of the National Association of Colored Women and the Virginia

Industrial School for Girls. Today the Maggie Walker House, the 22-room red-brick home in which she lived from 1904 to 1934, is a National Historic Site run by the National Park Service. Visitors to the house get a rare glimpse into African-American life in the first three decades of this century.

ROANOKE

Harrison Museum of African-American Culture
523 Harrison Avenue, NW, Roanoke, VA 24016
(703) 345-4818
Hours: Mon.–Fri., 10 A.M.–5 P.M.
Admission: Free

The Harrison Museum of African-American Culture in Roanoke is the sole black cultural museum in southwest Virginia. Located on the ground floor of what was formerly the first public high school for African Americans in western Virginia, this small museum documents the achievements of the black community and provides a forum for the presentation of art exhibitions and the performing arts.

ROCKY MOUNT

Franklin County Courthouse
108 East Court Street, Rocky Mount, VA 24151
(703) 483-3030
Hours: Mon.–Fri., 8:30 A.M.–5 P.M.
Admission: Free

The Franklin County Courthouse owes its historical importance to the ownership of a 1861 inventory of James Burroughs's estate. The inventory makes reference, amid a lengthy list of farm implements and household goods, to "one negro boy, 'Booker.' Value $400." "Booker," the son of Burroughs's slave Jane Ferguson and an unnamed white man, later spontaneously adopted the surname Washington upon his entry into school. Still later as Booker T. Washington, he became the preeminent black educator and power broker of his day. While his accommodationist social views did not long dominate the black community after his death in 1915, the value he placed on black financial independence enjoys an increasing vogue.

STRATFORD

Stratford Hall Plantation
Highway 214, Stratford, VA 22558
(804) 493-8038
Hours: Daily, 9 A.M.–4:30 P.M. First tour begins at 9:30 A.M.
Admission: Adults, $5; ages 6–18, $2; under 6, free

Stratford Hall Plantation is best known today as the birthplace and home of the General in Chief of the Confederate Armies, Robert E. Lee. Built in the late 1730s by Thomas Lee, Stratford passed into the hands of Revolutionary War hero "Light Horse Harry" Lee. This Lee fathered the future Confederate commander, who was born at Stratford in 1807. All of these Lees grew up amid the laughter, cries, and song of slaves: Tom Limerick, Kajah, and Rippon, who survive in the records because of their alleged thievery; Titus and Caesar, both postilions; Congo, a bricklayer; Anthony, a gardener; Tom, a weaver; and Harry the fiddler all loved, labored, and died, and kept Stratford and themselves afloat, before the future Confederate paladin (whose crib still rocks in its place) ever drew breath.

Of these lives and labor little is left. Only the Great House, the southwest dependency (plantation office and indentured servants' common room), and the kitchen building are interpreted. The reconstructed slave dwellings and kitchen yard are posted with signs for a self-guided tour. Finally, there is the ultimate reminder that the shared fate of both halves of the community found, from birth through death, unequal expression: the ubiquitous slave cemetery.

WILLIAMSBURG

Williamsburg Area Convention & Visitors Bureau
P.O. Box Drawer GB, Williamsburg, VA 23187
(804) 253-0192; (800) HISTORY; (800) 368-6511, U.S. and Canada
Hours: Mon.–Fri., 8:30 A.M.–5 P.M.

Colonial Williamsburg
P.O. Box 1776, 1 Visitor Center Drive, Williamsburg, VA 23185
(804) 220-7645; (800) HISTORY
Hours: Visitor Center: 8:30 A.M.–8 P.M. Exhibits: 9 A.M.–5:30 P.M.
Admission: Value and peak-season costs vary. Value seasons: Mar. 1–Apr. 2; May 31–Sept. 10; Oct. 25–Nov. 24

Carter's Grove
Route 60 East at Pocahontas Trail, Williamsburg, VA 23185
(804) 220-7452; (800) HISTORY
Hours: Tue.–Sun., 9 A.M.–5 P.M.
Admission: Adults, $10; children under 13, $6

Plantations were laboring communities that strove for self-sufficiency—little was purchased that might be produced, and little was produced by labor that was free. The core of a plantation was not the mansion, or even the mansion's service yard containing the well, laundry, icehouse, and smokehouse that served the Great Family's immediate needs. Rather, the core was the outlying farms, each with a quarters area where the overseer and the enslaved laborers lived with their families. Here African Americans, many of them skilled craftsmen and a few even overseers, built houses, barns, and stables; made plows, harrows, chains, and nails; made the hogsheads that tobacco was "prized in"; distilled the plantation's cider and liquors; tanned and dressed the leathers that became the shoes they then made; spun, wove, and knitted all of their own and much of their masters' clothes; and produced the food and commercial crops that fed the plantation community and brought the Great Family its wealth.

Nowhere is this portrait of plantation life better revealed than at Colonial Williamsburg, Virginia's capital from 1699 to 1780 and a city half of whose population was black. For more than a decade now, bringing to the fore the history of "the other half" has been the central impulse of Colonial Williamsburg.

The centerpiece of Williamsburg's African-American interpretation is Carter's Grove plantation. Here one crosses a footbridge spanning a deep ravine—and two centuries—and enters a scene that is already becoming a textbook classic in African-American history. Reconstructed in the foreground are the only pre-Revolutionary slave quarters to be seen anywhere in the country. Against a backdrop of orchards and cultivated fields stands a cluster of slave houses; in the distance rises the 1755 brick mansion of Nathaniel Burwell, son-in-law of Robert "King" Carter, the largest slaveholder in Virginia.

The 20 or so African Americans who lived at Carter's Grove tended the orchards, raised the cereal crops, and made the cider that Burwell sold to hungry and thirsty Williamsburg down the road. Today living history interpreters, dressed in the clothes and employing the locutions of the colonial period, bring to life the reality of those days, demonstrating African Americans' contributions to the plantation economy and dramatizing the African traditions they retained and the Afro-American culture they created when their labors were done.

Williamsburg's summer season is notable for highly dramatic tours, conceived and presented especially for families—stories of runaways, of families separated at auction block, of perfidy and loyalty; stories about free, unfree, white, black, good, and bad people; stories about Americans, Afro-Virginians, and Anglo-Virginians.

These stories scarcely exhaust the African-American presentation at Colonial Williamsburg, which includes "The Other Half," a two-hour walking tour that embraces the slave trade, the middle passage, urban and rural slavery, religion, and music; "The Storyteller," a one-hour program that combines African and African-American tales that impart survival knowledge to the unfree; an African-American Music Program that underscores the surviving remnants of the African homeland; and still more.

Jamestown Settlement
Highway 1 at Colonial Parkway, Williamsburg, VA 23081
(804) 229-1607
Hours: Daily, 9 A.M.–5 P.M.
Admission: Adults, $7; ages 6–12, $3.50; under 6, free

In 1607, long before the Pilgrims landed on the Massachusetts shore, 104 Englishmen settled along the banks of the James River in Virginia. Their story, and that of the American Indians they encountered, is told at Jamestown Settlement in gallery exhibits and through living history interpretations in three outdoor re-created settings: a Powhatan Indian village, James Fort, and full-scale replicas of the three ships that landed in 1607.

Life in the earliest Virginia settlement was grim and dominated by hunger, disease, and labor—most of the last provided by white, and soon black, indentured servants. Particularly after the introduction of tobacco as a cash crop in 1613, the demand for labor soared. Within a generation of the first arrival of indentured black servants in 1619, lifetime black slavery had become an established custom, though one still lacking explicit legal foundation. By midcentury there were probably fewer than 500 slaves in the entire colony, almost all of whom arrived as slaves from the Spanish Caribbean. However, the expansion of a labor-intensive tobacco economy, the beginning of slave importation directly from Africa in 1672, and the advent of legal framework for chattel slavery produced a sharply different picture by the century's close. This process is treated in a small exhibit at Jamestown Settlement—and is yet another sound reason to visit Virginia.

YORKTOWN

Yorktown National Historic Park and Victory Center
Route 238 at Colonial Parkway, Yorktown, VA 23690
(804) 887-1776
Hours: Daily, 9 A.M.–5 P.M.
Admission: Free

From colonial America's beginning in Virginia to its close, also in Virginia, is a matter of almost two centuries—or of 25 minutes, the driving time that separates Jamestown Settlement and Yorktown, Virginia.

From Bunker Hill in 1775 to Cornwallis's defeat at Yorktown in 1781, between 5,000 and 8,000 free or enslaved African Americans served the Revolution, on the field of battle, on the high seas, or—most commonly—behind the lines in noncombatant roles. Many, perhaps more, served the British. In either case the motivation was the promise of freedom. The impact of the American Revolution on the lives of the half-million African Americans in the 13 rebellious colonies is examined at the Yorktown National Historic Park and Victory Center. In "Witnesses to Revolution," an African-American patriot, a Loyalist, a Quaker pacifist, two Continental army soldiers, and a Virginia planter's wife tell their stories in words drawn from diaries, correspondence, and legal documents of the years 1775 to 1781. A Revolutionary War encampment, an 18th-century farm, "The Road to Yorktown" documentary film, artifacts from the opposing armies and navies, and an exploration of the two Virginia towns on opposite sides of the York River that were drawn into the Revolution's last major battle complete a day's adventure in our nation's past.

WASHINGTON, D.C.

Convention & Visitors Association
Visitor Center: 1455 Pennsylvania Avenue, NW, Washington, D.C. 20005
(202) 789-7038
Hours: Visitor Center: Mon.–Sat., 9 A.M.–5 P.M.; Sun., 11 A.M.–3 P.M.
Admission: Free

Ask for the "CECE Africentric Visitor's Guide"; the "Washington, D.C.: Attractions & Tours Highlighting African-American History" brochure; and the "Washington, D.C. Black History National Recreation Trail" brochure.

Anacostia Museum
1901 Fort Place, SE, Washington, D.C. 20020
(202) 287-3369
Hours: Daily, 10 A.M.–5 P.M. Guided tours (35 or fewer): Mon.–Fri., 10 A.M., 11 A.M., and 1 P.M.
Admission: Free

Black history and urban issues of the upper South—the Carolinas, Virginia, Maryland, and Washington, D.C.—are the core concerns of the exhibitions mounted by the Anacostia Museum. This branch of the Smithsonian Institution began as a neighborhood museum and cultural center in 1967—the year before the riots that erupted following the assassination of Dr. Martin Luther King, Jr., devastated the commercial heart of the area and accelerated the neighborhood's decline—but has long since grown into a major player in the institutional interpretation of African-American culture.

Benjamin Banneker Memorial
L'Enfant Plaza, Washington, D.C. 20024
East side of Tenth Street, NW, south of the Mall
Hours: 24 hours
Admission: Free

Though lacking a formal education, the outstanding black mathematician and scientist Benjamin Banneker (see entry on p. 238) published an almanac in 1791. In the same year, he was selected as an assistant by his friend and neighbor, Major Andrew Ellicott, who had been appointed to survey the boundaries of the new nation's new capital. Though failing health limited his contribution to this task, the presence at the creation of the capital city of an African American who forcefully had assailed the vileness of slavery and skillfully had defended the intellectual equality of Africa's children was symbolically potent. Today in the nation's capital, the man is honored with a memorial.

Bethune Museum and Archives
1318 Vermont Avenue, NW, Washington, D.C. 20005
(202) 332-1233; (202) 332-9201
Hours: Mon.–Sat., 10 A.M.–4 P.M.
Admission: Free

Mary McLeod Bethune's pioneering success as an educator of young black women (see Bethune-Cookman College entry on p. 43) brought her both national recognition and into the orbit of white financial donors—though the order was rather the reverse. Her gender and her emphasis on good manners and domestic virtues facilitated her absorption as a racial spokeswoman and gave her the opportunity to advise presidents of the United States, from Coolidge to Eisenhower, on racial matters. Bethune was scarcely naive; she understood the necessity of marshaling political power, necessarily white, on behalf of African Americans, and she knew how to leverage her national influence to enhance her weight within her community. Having been invited to the White House by Coolidge, Hoover, and F. D. Roosevelt, she founded in 1935 the National Council of Negro Women, whose president she remained until 1949. From 1936 through the close of World War II, she served as the director of the Division of Negro Affairs in the New Deal's National Youth Administration. During these years of influence, she lived much of the time in Washington, D.C. Her home in the national capital is now the Bethune Museum and Archives, where visitors will find photographs, artifacts, documents, and exhibits on a woman who used her friendship with Eleanor Roosevelt quietly to press for black voting rights, the abolition of the poll tax, and an antilynching law. The museum's permanent exhibits are two: One centers on the public career of Mrs. Bethune, which is marked largely through photographs (including ones of her with Walter White, W.E.B. Du Bois, Eleanor Roosevelt, and President Eisenhower); the other explores African-American women's commitment to social change as expressed in the suffragette and temperance movements of the 19th and early 20th centuries. The Bethune Archives is the world's largest repository for information on black women and their organizations.

Blanche K. Bruce House
909 M Street, NW, Washington, D.C. 20001
Hours: Daily until sunset
Admission: Not open to the public. Exterior viewing only

Blanche K. Bruce was the only African American to serve a full term in the U.S. Senate in the 19th century. (To date, he has but one counterpart in the 20th century.) Born into slavery in 1841 in Virginia, he was probably the son of his owner, who employed Bruce as the body servant of his legitimate son, with whom he was educated by a private tutor. Taken to Missouri at the age of nine,

Bruce escaped slavery in 1861 and spent the Civil War years and their immediate aftermath teaching in African-American schools in Kansas and Missouri.

Bruce arrived in Mississippi in 1868 with 75 cents to his name. Before long he was a political force; not long thereafter, wealthy. By 1870 he was the tax collector, sheriff, and school superintendant of Bolivar County. Politically moderate as an advocate and implementer of Reconstruction, Bruce already had secured white planter support in the form of the $125,000 bond required to assume the sheriff's office. By 1874 Bruce was the owner of a 1,000-acre plantation in the Delta. A year later the Mississippi legislature appointed him to the U.S. Senate, just prior to the Democratic Party "Redemption" that, amid blood, terror, and fraud, overturned Reconstruction in the state. Though on his way to being wealthy, a U.S. senator, and *contextually* acceptable to Bolivar County's white planters, Bruce was still black. Upon his arrival for his senatorial swearing-in, Mississippi's senior senator, James Alcorn (see Alcorn State entry on p. 103), refused to present Bruce. Stepping forward in his stead was Roscoe Conkling, New York senator and a Republican Party wheelhorse for the next two decades. (Bruce would not forget the courtesy—nor would he forget Conkling's power: He named his son Roscoe Conkling Bruce.)

During his Senate term, Bruce backed both minority rights—including those of Indians and Chinese—and the return of the franchise to former Confederates. In this last regard, he was square in the mainstream of African-American congressmen; and he, like them, would be drowned in the deluge that followed, as those whose causes he had supported jeered on the banks. Wise enough not to return to Mississippi, Bruce stayed on in Washington and parlayed his Republican connections into a series of government jobs, finally dying—and leaving an estate in excess of $100,000—during the administration of William McKinley.

A quarter of a century later, six years before Faulkner's *Sartoris* would introduce Yoknapatawpha County, Bruce's grandson, Roscoe Conkling Bruce, Jr., would be refused residence in Harvard's freshman halls—halls in which his father, Roscoe Conkling Bruce, had lived. Today the Blanche K. Bruce House, which is not open to the public, is a National Historic Landmark and pays tribute to the power of Lethe and to the eccentricities of official endorsement: Conkling, genuinely significant in American history in the latter half of the 19th century, is superceded by an anomaly.

Frederick Douglass House
1411 W Street, SE, Washington, D.C. 20020
(202) 426-5960
Hours: Daily, 9 A.M.–5 P.M. Last tour, 4 P.M.
Admission: Free. Donations encouraged

Much of Frederick Douglass's career after the Civil War was marked by a lust for official position, a compulsion that regularly overrode prudence—and on occasion, decency. Assuming the presidency of the Freedmen's Bank in 1874, when its financial condition was critical, Douglass attached his prestige to a foundering ship. Rather than captain this ship, he instead stood on the prow proclaiming to depositors smooth sailing and to his subsequent critics his ignorance of the shoals ahead and the holes below the waterline. More skilled in advocacy than administration—and more interested, too—Douglass divided his time between attempting to convince black depositors not to withdraw their money and attempting to convince white politicians to support unrelated civil rights legislation. Sadly, he was somewhat successful in the former, with the result that when he and his fellow trustees closed the bank, the savings of his brethren fell victim to the illusion that there were funds to match his protestations.

COURTESY NATIONAL PARK SERVICE

Frederick Douglass's home at Cedar Hill (Washington, D.C.) is now open to visitors.

Two years later, the Republican Rutherford B. Hayes assumed the presidency after a congressional commission, with the backing of southern Democrats, resolved in his favor the rival electoral claims of Democratic Party violence and Republican Party fraud in three southern states. The favor was returned—amid allegations of a quid pro quo—when Hayes withdrew federal military backing for black civil rights in the South. Hayes named Douglass to the post he had so long sought, marshal of the District of Columbia. Douglass's appointment was the first requiring Senate confirmation of an African American. Now loaded with honor, a substantial income, and the power of patronage that attended the post, Douglass stood mutely if metaphorically by Hayes's side as Reconstruction was buried. (Hayes, who had supported Radical Republican Reconstruction measures when he was in the U.S. Congress, responded to the loss of northern support for radical Reconstruction rather than promoted it. He also resolutely rejected legislation designed to curtail black voting rights, which on a local southern level remained in place until near the end of the century, and received notable support for his program from African-American leaders in the South.)

In September 1878 Douglass purchased Cedar Hill, a nine-acre hillside estate. (There is no evidence to support the allegation that the funds for this purchase originated with a Freedmen's Bank loan.) This would be his home for the remainder of his life, years in which he would serve as recorder of deeds for the District of Columbia, chargé d'affaires for Santo Domingo, and minister to Haiti. It was here that he brought his second wife and from here that he would in the last years of his life again vocally champion the African-American cause, whose most prominent 19th-century spokesman he was. Today visitors to the Frederick Douglass House tour the building's interior, which has been restored to its setting during Douglass's tenancy, and a museum dedicated to his life and career. The visitor center has a film on Douglass's life.

Duke Ellington Memorial Plaque
420 Elm Street, NW, Washington, D.C. 20001
Hours: Daily until sunset
Admission: Free

The composer of "Mood Indigo," "Solitude," "Satin Doll," and "Black and Tan Fantasy" composed his first song, "Soda Fountain Rag," on the job. Growing up in Washington's famous black neighborhood of Shaw, Edward "Duke" Ellington worked after school as a soda jerk and then in the evenings played with local bands at the Poodle Dog Cafe. In 1923 his band left for Harlem and the big time, the latter of which they achieved five years later with a permanent job at The Cotton Club. Legendary by 1943, when he became the first nonclassical musician to perform at Carnegie Hall, Ellington saw his popularity decline after the war as styles changed. His smash success at the Newport Jazz Festival in 1956 brought him front and center again, and he spent the bulk of his later years touring the world as a musical ambassador of goodwill. Today visitors to the nation's capital will find a memorial plaque, a Duke Ellington Bridge, a Duke Ellington School of Arts (3500 R Street, NW), and the Duke Ellington Home, (1212 T Street, NW) in which the young boy was raised.

Emancipation Proclamation
Library of Congress, Second Street and Independence Avenue, SE, Washington, D.C. 20540
(202) 707-5000
Hours: Exhibit areas: Mon.–Fri., 8:30 A.M.–9:30 P.M.;
Sat.–Sun., 8:30 A.M.–6 P.M.
Admission: Free

In the summer of 1862, President Lincoln read to his assembled cabinet a draft of the Emancipation Proclamation. (See Antietam entry on p. 256.) Today that draft, the first of three, is on permanent exhibit at the Library of Congress.

Evans-Tibbs Collection
1910 Vermont Avenue, NW, Washington, D.C. 20001
(202) 234-8164
Hours: By appointment only
Admission: Free

Lillian Evans-Tibbs, the great-great niece of Hiram Revels, the first black U.S. senator (see Hiram Revels' Burial Site entry on p. 99), paved the way for Marian Anderson. A graduate of Howard University, the lyric soprano performed under the name Madame Evanti (a contraction of her birth and married surnames) on the stages of Europe, America, Africa, and the Caribbean. Denied an audition at the Metropolitan Opera because of her race, she performed at the

White House in 1935 and helped found the Negro National Opera Company. Today her former home, a 1920s' beacon for black artists and intellectuals, is on the National Historic Register and houses the world-famous Evans-Tibbs Collection of 19th- and 20th-century African-American art. Henry O. Tanner, Romare Bearden, Richmond Barthé, Charles Alston, Jacob Lawrence, and Elizabeth Catlett are among the giants represented in the permanent collection. In addition, temporary exhibits are mounted in the house, which also is the repository for the largest and most comprehensive library on African-American art in the last two centuries. Only open by appointment, the collection can be viewed without the jostling of a large surrounding crowd. Finally, there is no admission fee charged for this experience. Do you have to be beaten over the head before you wake up to opportunity?

Marcus Garvey & Malcolm X Statue
1440 Belmont Street, NW, Washington, D.C.
Hours: Daily until sunset
Admission: Free

The Jamaican-born Marcus Garvey (1887–1940) was one of the first African-American leaders to tap into the urban transformation of black America, its rising economic power, and the political potential and developing class awareness of black businessmen. Apprenticed to a printer at the age of 14, he rose to become a printshop foreman and took part in Jamaica's first (and unsuccessful) printers' union strike before embarking on a career as an agitator-organizer and newspaper publisher dedicated to improving the lot of the island's black populace. His paper, *The Watchman*, was a financial failure, as were subsequent business ventures in Central and South America.

Returning to Jamaica in 1911, Garvey founded the Universal Negro Improvement Association (UNIA). This too was stillborn until Garvey came to America in 1917 and founded *The Negro World* as a voice for African-American aspirations and identification with the Mother Continent. Fortuitously timed to a period both of optimism and opportunity and of growing awareness of imperialist domination of people of color around the world, Garvey tapped into the reemergence of black assertion that (yet again) had been forcibly damped down by the late 19th-century imposition of rigid Jim Crow practices. Aiming to forge modern black polities in the western hemisphere and Africa (particularly in the former German colonies that briefly seemed open to some other fate than that which they found, alternative European masters), Garvey founded not only local UNIA chapters but also business enterprises. The business ventures failed, Garvey aroused opposition in other black organizations, and UNIA itself fell prey to its internal incoherence and rivalries.

Now vulnerable, Garvey was targeted by FBI director J. Edgar Hoover. Indicted and convicted of mail fraud in 1923 and imprisoned in 1925, Garvey was deported to Jamaica in 1927, neither the first nor the last in a line of victims of U.S. government surveillance and harassment. UNIA never recovered from its initial difficulties, despite Garvey's efforts, and he died in London, at the end largely a symbol of the diaspora's urge toward unity. That same urge toward unity, now reflected through the prism of black individuals' drive toward self-definition and affirmation, brought Malcolm X to the forefront in another period of African-American assertion. Creating nothing and leaving behind nothing beyond the powerful message, manifest in his life, of black redemption and purpose, Malcolm too was targeted by the FBI and ended up a symbol. Malcolm's pairing with Garvey is apt, for after his break with Elijah Muhammad and the Nation of Islam, Malcolm moved closer toward the pan-Africanism that had been his father's orientation. ("My father, the Reverend Earl Little, was a Baptist minister, a dedicated organizer for Marcus [Aurelius] Garvey's UNIA.") Today the Marcus Garvey & Malcolm X Statue, a 12-foot monument of steel and stained glass, commemorates the aspiration that too easily is simply labeled black nationalism.

Howard University
2400 Sixth Street, NW, Washington, D.C. 20059
(202) 806-6100
Hours: Mon.–Fri., 9:30 A.M.–4:30 P.M. Library archives open for research only
Admission: Free

The first student body of one of America's most prestigious historically black universities was composed largely of young white women, who were the daughters of faculty members. Howard University was not, as widely reported, conceived by the Freedmen's Bureau, but by the Missionary Society of the First Congregational Church of Washington, which recognized the need for freedmen's higher education. Enthusiastically supported by General O. O. Howard (see Bowdoin College, Peary-McMillan Arctic Museum entry on p. 235), then head of the Freedmen's Bureau, the school that soon bore his name opened as (and remains) a multiracial institution. Not until the turn of the century, when Jim Crow restrictions finally extinguished the surviving remnants of Reconstruction, did the school become a magnet for black youth shut out from higher education opportunities. By this time, 90 percent of the school's student body was black. Today the only remaining original structure is Howard Hall, built in 1869 as the on-campus residence of General Howard, who died in 1909, the last surviving Civil War general. The Founders Library houses the Moorland-Spingarn Research Center, one of the world's most comprehensive collections of material related to Africa and the diaspora. The Howard University Gallery of Art contains the Alain Locke African Collection and the work of a wide range of African-American artists (Horace Pippin, Henry O. Tanner, Aaron Douglas, Hale Woodruff, Archibald Motley, William Harper, Richmond Barthé, Elizabeth Catlett).

Lincoln Memorial
The Mall West, Washington, D.C.
(202) 426-6895
Hours: Daily, 24 hours
Admission: Free

Aside from stunningly representing the power and beauty of monumental art, honoring the author of the Emancipation Proclamation, and incorporating the words of the most compelling presidential inaugural address of American history, the Lincoln Memorial is of note as the site of the Easter 1939 concert of Marian Anderson and Dr. Martin Luther King, Jr.'s 1963 "I have a dream" oration.

The Anderson concert arose as a consequence of and protest against the singer's racial exclusion from Constitution Hall, whose owners, the Daughters of the American Revolution (DAR), explained that they were simply abiding by "local custom." (The local custom to which they referred was Washington's segregated status.) Anderson's Lincoln Memorial appearance was a major political event. Eleanor Roosevelt resigned from the DAR and 75,000 people appeared for the concert, which underscored the irony of America's condemnation of Nazi racial doctrines and pogroms. Within months, most of the public facilities in the nation's capital were desegregated.

Almost a quarter of a century later at the Lincoln Memorial, Dr. King directly challenged that which Anderson had implicitly condemned. Standing in front of a huge throng, King spoke words that elevated the African-American quest for equality to high art, words whose eloquence, anguish, power, truth, and mercy matched those of Lincoln's etched on the monument on whose steps King stood.

Lincoln Park
East Capitol Street, Washington, D.C. 20002
Between 11th and 13th streets, east of the Capitol
Hours: Daily, 24 hours
Admission: Free

The first memorial to Lincoln erected in Washington was paid for by the subscription of former slaves, one of whose descendants, Mary McLeod Bethune (see Bethune-Cookman College entry on p. 43 and Bethune Museum entry on

COURTESY WASHINGTON, D.C., CONVENTION & VISITORS ASSOCIATION

The statue of Mary McLeod Bethune, counselor to four presidents, incorporates a cane that belonged to President Franklin D. Roosevelt.

p. 193), is also honored with a statue at Lincoln Park. The Bethune statue was the first monument to an African American in the nation's capital. The statue's walking stick had belonged to FDR and was given to Bethune by Eleanor Roosevelt after the president's death.

National Air & Space Museum
Sixth Street and Independence Avenue, SW, Washington, D.C. 20560
(202) 357-1552
Hours: Daily, 10 A.M.–5:30 P.M. Summer: extended hours.
Guided tours: 10:15 A.M., 1 P.M.
Admission: Free. Charge for planetarium and theater

"Black Wings" at the Smithsonian's National Air & Space Museum traces the rising trajectory of the African-American contribution to aviation.

National Gallery of Art
Fourth Street and Constitution Avenue, NW, Washington, D.C. 20006
(202) 734-4215
Hours: Mon.–Sat., 10 A.M.–5 P.M.; Sun., 12 P.M.–6 P.M. Tours available
Admission: Free

Paintings by Joshua Johnson (see entry on p. 246), America's first black portraitist of note, are among the extraordinary works showcased at this gallery.

National Museum of African Art
950 Independence Avenue, SW, Washington, D.C. 20560
(202) 357-4860
Hours: Daily, 10 A.M.–5:30 P.M.
Admission: Free

The kingdom of Benin is renowned for its traditional court art. Crafted over half a century by guilds of artisans, Benin royal commemorative heads, figures, and plaques, most executed by the lost-wax process, are featured at the National Museum of African Art. Balanced by pottery crafted by women of Central Africa and by a broad range of personal objects that underscore the integration of aesthetics and daily life on the continent, the high art of Africa is comprehensively surveyed. Masks, carved figures, altars, divination objects, fetish pieces, baskets, and cloth from around the continent are displayed and interpreted. From the Asante to the Zande, African culture is covered, with the "i's" dotted (Igala, Ibo, Ibibio, et al.) and the "t's" crossed (Tswa, Teke, Turkana, Tiv, et al.).

National Museum of American Art
Eighth and G streets, NW, Washington, D.C. 20001
(202) 357-3176
Hours: Daily, 10 A.M.–5 P.M.
Admission: Free

The creative expressions of more than 100 black artists find an appropriate home at the National Museum of American Art. Almost 1,500 pieces, ranging from the 19th century to the present and encompassing virtually every medium, ensure a representative look. Particularly strong in 19th-century painters such as Bannister, Tanner, and Duncanson, the museum also embraces the paintings of the Harlem Renaissance (William H. Johnson, Palmer Hayden, Joseph and Beauford Delaney) and the New Deal's relief programs. Works by Edmonia Lewis, Elizabeth Catlett, Sargent Johnson, and Richard Hunt are highlights of the museum's sculpture collection, while its folk collection is highlighted by the works of William Edmondson, Mose Toliver, and Bill Traylor. Modern and contemporary paintings by Alma Thomas, Romare Bearden, Jacob Lawrence, and Sam Gilliam are complemented by their counterparts in the media of printmaking and sculpture.

National Museum of Natural History
Tenth Street and Constitution Avenue, NW, Washington, D.C. 20004
(202) 357-2700
Hours: Summer: daily, 9:30 A.M.–7:30 P.M. Rest of year:
daily, 10 A.M.–5:30 P.M. Guided tours available
Admission: Free

In Africa, as elsewhere, the presence of power is articulated through a panoply of symbolic and political regalia. Staffs, formal jewelry, accoutrements, and special dress convey status. Frequently the signs are scarcely noticeable to those outside the culture, differences being signified by degree or dimension. These distinctions of power and status in Africa, along with the continent's musical heritage and the traditional rural lifestyle of the Himba people, are explored in the African Hall of the National Museum of Natural History.

National Portrait Gallery
Eighth and F streets, NW, Washington, D.C. 20001
(202) 357-1300
Hours: Daily, 10 A.M.–5:30 P.M.
Admission: Free

Jean Toomer, Langston Hughes, James Weldon Johnson, Paul Robeson, Marian Anderson, and W.E.B. Du Bois are among the 40 African Americans portrayed at the National Portrait Gallery.

Phillips Collection
1612 21st Street, NW, Washington, D.C. 20009
(202) 387-2151
Hours: Tue.–Sat., 10 A.M.–5 P.M.; Sun., 12 P.M.–7 P.M.
Admission: Adults, $6; seniors and students, $3

Half of the 60 panels that compose Jacob Lawrence's "Migration of the Negro" (see Jacob Lawrence entry on p. 279) will be found in the Phillips Collection. Once—when free—the best-kept, tucked-away secret in the nation's capital, the Phillips is still a bargain.

COURTESY THE PHILLIPS COLLECTION

Jacob Lawrence's Migration Series, Panel No. 49: "They found discrimination in the North. It was a different kind."

A. Philip Randolph Bust
Union Station, 50 Massachusetts Avenue, NE, Washington, D.C. 20002
Hours: 24 hours
Admission: Free

In the modern world of African Americans, it is Asa Philip Randolph, not Ralph Ellison, who is the invisible man. In terms of accomplishment, stalwart courage, and persistence, no 20th-century African-American figure can stand comparison with him. Martin Luther King, Jr., Walter White, and Mary McLeod Bethune pale in comparison, while those beloved by intellectuals and purveyors of myth and movies—Malcolm X, Marcus Garvey, and W.E.B. Du Bois—are seen in their true light, symbols of angry protestation and hoped-for salvation. Despite his true historical weight, which arguably almost rivals Richard Allen's in the long course of the 400 years of oppression, Randolph has no monument. No movie will be made about him, nor will he grace sweatshirts as a statement of blackness and assertion. Randolph's aloof character, his admiration for dead white men from Marx to Shakespeare, his confidence that it was the black working class rather than the intelligentsia that was the engine for African-American advancement, and his belief that this engine would fail in the absence of links formed with inhabitants of the dominant and oppressing white world underscore his political coming of age in the era of World War I and the mass urbanization of African Americans.

Leaving the Florida of his birth for New York City at the age of 22, Randolph worked during the day and studied at City College in the evenings. Five years after his arrival in the city, he and Owen Chandler founded a newspaper called *The Messenger*, and Randolph's challenge to white supremacy and the power of capital began. Sentenced to jail during World War I for his article "Pro-Germanism Amongst the Negroes" (which he co-authored with Chandler, who was also sentenced), Randolph subsequently faced trouble because of his endorsement of the Bolshevik Revolution. The mid-1920s saw the beginning of his long struggle to win recognition and bargaining rights for the Brotherhood of Sleeping Car Porters. (See A. Philip Randolph and Pullman Porters entry on p. 267.) The nexus of African Americans and trade unionism was Randolph's field for the remainder of his life. He laborered long and productively in this vineyard, fearing to challenge neither business interests nor a union movement that acquiesced in, when it did not openly endorse, white supremacy. The Porters Union—which finally secured its first contract in 1937—was his greatest triumph and the institutional base from which he reached out to push forward the African-American struggle.

In 1936 Randolph played a prominent part in the founding and became the president of the National Negro Congress, from which he withdrew in 1940 because of the Communist Party's dominance within its ranks. That same year Randolph, Walter White, and Arnold Hill of the Urban League submitted a petition to F. D. Roosevelt for the desegregation of the armed forces. In 1941 Randolph organized the March on Washington movement, which resulted in a presidential directive banning discrimination in defense industries (in which African Americans rarely were hired except as janitors) and creating the Fair Employment Practices Commission to enforce the executive order. The same year the American Federation of Labor (AFL) National Convention rejected Randolph's antidiscrimination resolution as an interference in member unions' autonomy—as it had in 1934 and again in 1935.

In 1948 Randolph formed the League for Nonviolent Civil Disobedience Against Military Segregation and told members of Congress he would encourage black resistance to induction in the absence of an end to segregation. A month later President Harry S Truman signed the historic Executive Order 9981, barring the practice Randolph long had opposed. Still going strong more than a decade later, Randolph (ably assisted by Bayard Rustin) in 1963 was the originator and driving force behind the March on Washington, which brought national attention to Dr. Martin Luther King, Jr.

Randolph's place in history is secure, but his reputation following his death in 1979 continues to suffer because the molders of opinion came of age in and have not forgotten his biting dismissal of the black power movement, which he regarded as a disreputable, pathetic, and self-indulgent joke lacking both program and possibility. A dozen or more names come to mind who, when they die in the course of the next 30 years, will receive lengthier obituaries than did Randolph; a century from now, not one will figure in the history books, while Randolph will endure. Today, across a country that is in his debt, few markers note the man's passage through a century of change; one, the A. Philip Randolph Bust, aptly graces the appropriately named Union Railroad Station in America's capital.

Charles Sumner School Museum and Archives
1201 17th Street, NW, Washington, D.C. 20036
(202) 727-3419
Hours: Mon.–Sat., 10 A.M.–5 P.M.
Admission: Free

Eight decades before *Brown v. Board of Education*, Senator Charles Sumner of Massachusetts introduced a measure to ban segregation in education by declaring that "the separate school is not equivalent." His bill and his vision went down to defeat at about the same moment (1872) that Sumner School opened in Washington, where for more than a century it served as the cornerstone of black education in the city. Today the Charles Sumner School Museum and Archives has as its subject the public school system of the District of Columbia.

Carter G. Woodson House
1538 Ninth Street, NW, Washington, D.C. 20001
c/o (202) 667-2822
Hours: Daily until sunset
Admission: Not open to the public. Exterior viewing only

Born to former slaves in 1875 as the first of their nine children, Carter G. Woodson spent his teenage years laboring in the fields and coal mines of Buckingham County, Virginia. Not until his family moved to West Virginia when he was 20 did he attend high school. He finished four years of work in two and enrolled in Berea College (see entry on p. 78), graduating one year before Kentucky passed legislation precluding multiracial education. Following another bachelor's degree, and a master's degree in history from the University of Chicago, and graduate work at the Sorbonne in Paris, he earned a Ph.D. in American history from Harvard University, becoming after Du Bois the second trained African-American historian and the sole one to emerge from an immediate ancestry of slavery. An obsessively private man, Woodson devoted his life to challenging the canard that there was no African-American history and that the diaspora in America appears as objects of history—buffoons when not victims. In 1915 he founded the Association for the Study of Negro (now Afro-American) Life and History. The following year he began publishing the *Journal of Negro History*. The progenitor in 1926 of Negro History Week, Woodson is the father of the modern-era Black History Month. For years he ran the Association for the Study of Negro Life and History out of his home in the Shaw neighborhood of Washington, D.C. Today the Carter G. Woodson House, until recently the headquarters of *American Visions* magazine, is a National Historic Landmark not open to the public.

WEST VIRGINIA

Division of Tourism
2101 Washington Street, East, State Capitol Complex, Building 6, Room 564, Charleston, WV 25305
(800) 225-5982
Hours: Mon.–Fri., 8 A.M.–8 P.M.; Sat., 8:30 A.M.–4:30 P.M.; Sun., 12 P.M.–5 P.M.

BLUEFIELD

Bluefield State College
219 Rock Street, Bluefield, WV 24701
(304) 327-4000
Hours: Mon.–Fri., 9 A.M.–3 P.M.
Admission: Free

In 1895 Bluefield State College became West Virginia's second black land-grant college, initially concentrating on teacher training. Both its location and its concentration attested to the influx of black miners—and their children—into the state's recently opened coal fields. The 1954 Supreme Court decision in *Brown v. Board of Education* led to the school's admission of whites, who soon outnumbered blacks on campus. But the school's African-American heritage remains its strongest claim to fame, a claim that is documented in the archives exhibit in the Hardaway Library on campus.

CEREDO

Z. D. Ramsdell House
1108 B Street, Ceredo, WV 25507
(304) 453-2482
Hours: By appointment
Admission: Free

The Ceredo bootmaker and abolitionist Z. D. Ramsdell was an adherent of the view of the town's founder, Eli Thayer, that steam power could replace slave power. His house served as an Underground Railroad station for fleeing runaways, whose immediate destination was across the Ohio River to Burlington, Ohio. Today in Burlington there is a cemetery filled with the remains of escaped slaves who lived the latter part of their lives in freedom, while in Ceredo the small Z. D. Ramsdell House is open by appointment for those with an interest in the juncture of the abolitionist movement and the Underground Railroad.

CHARLES TOWN

Jefferson County Courthouse
100 East Washington Street, Charles Town, WV 25414
(304) 725-9761
Hours: Courthouse: Mon.–Thu., 9 A.M.–5 P.M.; Fri., 9 A.M.–7 P.M. Groups should call in advance. Marker: Daily until sunset
Admission: Free

A historical marker on the front lawn of the Jefferson County Courthouse notes that in this building John Brown was tried (for murder, treason, and conspiring with slaves to create insurrection), convicted, and sentenced to hang for organizing the attack on the federal arsenal at Harpers Ferry. Brown—to whom the terms fanatic, murderer, terrorist, zealous lover of liberty, and opponent of bigotry might be applied with equal accuracy—skillfully used his trial to create the image of a religiously inspired martyr for freedom and equality. On the day of his execution, Brown (see John Brown Museum entry on p. 386 and Harpers Ferry National Historic Park entry on p. 207) wrote a last testament: "I, John Brown, am now quite certain that the crimes of this guilty land will never be purged away but with blood. I had, as I now think, vainly flattered myself that without very much bloodshed it might be done." Sixteen months later, with the firing on Fort Sumter, Brown appeared both prophetic and martyred.

CHARLESTON

West Virginia State Museum

State Capitol Complex, 1900 Kanawha Boulevard, East, Charleston, WV 25305
(304) 358-0220
Hours: Mon.–Fri., 9 A.M.–8 P.M.; Sat.–Sun., 1 P.M.–5 P.M.
Admission: Free

The West Virginia State Museum traces the history of a state that owes its founding and its admission to the Union (1863) to the refusal of its residents to follow the lead of the Tidewater planter aristocracy that led Virginia into the Confederacy. The museum's exhibits scan the subjects of slavery, the 1859 raid on the U.S. arsenal at Harpers Ferry by the zealous abolitionist John Brown, and the role of African Americans in the Civil War.

Booker T. Washington Memorial

State Capitol Complex, 1900 Kanawha Boulevard, East, Charleston, WV 25305
Hours: Daily until sunset
Admission: Free

Shortly after the defeat of the Confederacy brought freedom to the nine-year-old Booker T. Washington, his family left for West Virginia to join his stepfather. There, in the Kanawha Valley town of Malden, Washington (see entry on p. 177) took a job working the salt wells. He chose the shift that began at 4 A.M. so that he could attend school in the afternoon. His longing to learn was encouraged by Viola Ruffner, his employer's wife, and was matched by his ability. At age 16, virtually as penniless and ill-clothed as in his slave youth, Washington walked the 400 miles between his West Virginia home and Hampton Institute in Virginia. (See Hampton University entry on p. 175.) There his ragged clothes and country ways gave rise to doubts that he belonged, but his evident willingness when told to sweep floors to earn his keep won him admission. In one sense, a life of labor had brought him back to his beginnings in menial work, an endeavor he never despised no matter how high he rose.

From Hampton, Washington went on to become the best-known and most influential African-American leader of his day. Emphasizing moral instruction, black self-reliance, and the acquisition of skills that would enable the masses rather than just the intellectual elite to survive and then prosper in a world dominated by whites (see Tuskegee University entry on p. 31), Washington became a target for blacks who were unaware of his covert support for the antisegregationist struggle but who were very aware of his dependence on white financial and political support. Today, on the grounds of the capitol of the first state in which he lived a free existence, there is a Booker T. Washington Memorial.

CLIFFTOP

Camp Washington-Carver Museum
HC 35, Box 5, Clifftop, WV 25831
(304) 438-3005
Adjacent to Babcock State Park
Hours: May–Oct.: daily, 9 A.M.–5 P.M.
Admission: Free

In a facility originally utilized as the nation's first State Negro 4-H Camp and now on the National Register of Historic Places, Camp Washington-Carver promotes black heritage through its folk life programs and exhibits. In the summer an African-American Heritage Arts Camp offers teenagers exposure to some of West Virginia's most talented artists and an opportunity to study the performing, visual, literary, and technical arts in a focused atmosphere, while throughout most of the year the camp's museum is open and uses photographs and artifacts to trace the early black years of the facility.

HARPERS FERRY

Harpers Ferry National Historic Park
P.O. Box 65, Harpers Ferry, WV 25425
(304) 535-6298
Hours: Daily, 8 A.M.–5 P.M.
Admission: Park entrance fee: vehicle, $5; individuals on buses or walking, $3

Harpers Ferry National Historic Park is one of the true wonders of the American heritage movement—the entire town is a museum and a living history interpretation of the events and tensions (free/slave, white/black, industry/agriculture) that exploded into the nation's most devastating conflict. Here four themes—the industrial revolution, John Brown's raid, African-American history, and the Civil War—structure an exploration of America's past.

Located at the juncture of two of the colonial era's major transport arteries and power sources, the Potomac and Shenandoah rivers, and not far from the new federal capital, Harpers Ferry was selected by President Washington as the site for a United States Armory. By 1810 the armory was turning out 10,000 muskets annually. Eventually it grew into a huge facility, including a 20-building weapons-producing complex, across from which was located the arsenal where the new guns were stored.

This arsenal was the immediate target of John Brown's raid of 1859. Brown (see entry on p. 374) was a man with a messianic mission—and with a past. The 59-year-old abolitionist had buried one wife and several children (four of whom had died of dysentery within a month of each other), repeatedly failed in his business ventures, and dedicated two decades to the destruction of slavery. He had founded the abolitionist "League of Gileadites" to forcibly resist the application of the Fugitive Slave Law, moved to Kansas to see that it joined the Union as a free state, led a guerilla band in "Bleeding Kansas" and there cold-bloodedly murdered five defenseless pro-slavery settlers. (See Brown entry on p. 386.)

In the late 1850s, as the Supreme Court's Dred Scott decision appeared to undermine the antislavery potential of the Compromise of 1850 and the popular sovereignty doctrine of the Kansas-Nebraska Act, Brown's violent approach to ending black bondage gained favor with peaceful abolitionists, many of whom contributed money to his design, the details of which they carefully refused to learn. Brown finally concluded that he should lead a force to seize the more than 100,000 weapons in the Harpers Ferry arsenal, distribute them to the slaves in the Virginia countryside—whom he imagined would swarm to the opportunity for freedom and then, somehow, transform the posited insurrection into a popular uprising that would send slavery crashing to the ground. This vision failed to garner support from the leading black abolitionists of the day, such as Frederick Douglass, who just as carefully stood aside from commitment to his action as they did wish his cause well.

Late in the evening of October 16, 1859, John Brown led 21 men (16 whites, including three of his sons, and five blacks) from a rented farm five miles north of Harpers Ferry (see Kennedy Farm entry on p. 257) and seized the U.S. armory and arsenal. Early the next morning the raiders stopped a train, and in the process killed the station baggage master, the free black Hayward Shepherd. As the workers arrived at the armory later in the morning, they were seized and held hostage. Before long the alarm was raised and the raid was played out to its inevitable conclusion. By 7 A.M. of October 17, townspeople were exchanging shots with the raiders. In the afternoon a party of U.S. marines commanded by Colonel Robert E. Lee arrived by train from Washington, D.C. Early the next morning Lee directed Lieutenant J.E.B. Stuart to secure the fire engine house in which Brown, all but two of the surviving raiders, and their hostages were holed up. Twelve marines smashed down the door, burst into the firehouse, and killed two raiders and captured the remainder. The following day Brown and the captured raiders were transported to Charles Town for trial. (See Jefferson County Courthouse entry on p. 205.)

Sixteen months later the opening shots of the Civil War erupted, eventually breaking the impasse of slavery. Harpers Ferry spent most of the war in Union hands, though officially control of the town shifted back and forth eight times. While in Union hands the town was a magnet for escaping slaves. When the town—and 12,500 Union troops—surrendered to Stonewall Jackson in the autumn of 1863, as many as 1,000 escaped slaves fell back into the hands of their oppressors and were marched southward to slavery again. Six months later, after African Americans were permitted to join the Union army, the 19th United States Colored Troops Regiment came the first of several times to Harpers Ferry on recruiting missions—perhaps sweet irony to the moldering John Brown (a man with scant use for either sweetness or irony): Less than five years earlier his attempt to arm African Americans brought him to the scaffold; now the federal government routinely armed black men and sought to bring Lee and Stuart to the scaffold.

As the Civil War drew to a close and Harpers Ferry swelled with those who would soon be termed freedmen, the Freewill Baptist Home Mission established a local grammar school to educate former slaves. A $10,000 donation by John Storer, which had to be matched with funds raised by the school's trustees and the church, enabled the newly christened Storer College to survive. The Freedmen's Bureau contributed four buildings, and in 1868 the school received a charter from the state. From the local citizens it mainly received abuse, to the point where the principal permitted students and teachers to go armed for their own protection. The two historical high points of Storer College were the 1881 address by one of the school's first trustees, Frederick Douglass (see Douglass Statue entry on p. 243), paying homage to John Brown, and the second meeting (1906) of the Niagara Movement, which was addressed by W.E.B. Du Bois. (See entry on p. 269.) One of the earliest integrated institutions of higher learning in the United States, Storer closed its doors in 1955, a year after the Supreme Court issued its ruling in the *Brown v. Board of Education* case. Today four of the school's buildings are on the park grounds. Interpretive markers in front of Storer's Lockwood and Mather houses detail the school's origin and purpose.

All (and more) of the history related here can be explored at Harpers Ferry National Historic Park. Highlights include the John Brown Museum, which is housed in the firehouse where he and his men were captured and which includes a biography of each of the raiders (daily, 8 A.M.–5 P.M.; free); the nearby John Brown Monument; and the Visitor Center museum (daily, 8 A.M.–6 P.M.; free).

Finally, the park will prove an enlightening joy for those who believe that African-American history must be viewed in its own right *and* as an integrated aspect of American history. "Black Voices from Harpers Ferry" uses photographs, special and permanent exhibits, documents, living history interpreters, artifacts, and video programs to bring to life documented black individuals whose stories convey the range of experiences of the half free and the enslaved. Included are stories about Isaac Gilbert, a slave allowed to purchase his own time for $110 a year; John Butler, a free black who served in the U.S. Navy during the War of 1812; John Gust, a slave-owning free African American; Joseph Blanham, a free black boatman who served three years in the Virginia penitentiary for aiding escaped slaves; Charles Stewart, a slave who ran to freedom during the Civil War; Frederick Douglass; and W.E.B. Du Bois. Though the African-American theme is integrated throughout the park's interpretation, the "Black Voices" exhibit is concentrated in a house located at the corner of High Street and Shenandoah.

INSTITUTE

West Virginia State College
Route 25, P.O. Box 1000, Institute, WV 25112-1000
(304) 766-3380
Hours: Campus tours by appointment
Admission: Free

West Virginia State College is one of 17 historically black land-grant institutions founded following passage in 1890 of the second Morrill Act. (See Delaware State College entry on p. 231.) In response to the act, the West Virginia legislature proposed Storer College near Harpers Ferry, at the time the sole school in the state training black teachers, as the institution to receive the mandated aid. However, the black leaders in Kanawha County convinced the legislature to establish a new school and to locate it in the Kanawha Valley. Like most black "colleges" of the day, the institute offered the equivalent of a high school education. Tuition was free; there was a matriculation fee of $1 per term, and board was $7 monthly. In 1915 the school was authorized to grant college degrees, and shortly thereafter Carter G. Woodson—a son of former slaves who took his doctorate at Harvard and then organized the Association for the Study of Negro Life and History and founded the *Journal of Negro History* (see Carter G. Woodson House entry on p. 204)—joined the faculty. With the *Brown v. Board of Education* decision in 1954, West Virginia State College proudly opened its doors to whites. Within a decade African Americans were a minority on the campus. But the school remains a center of black culture in the state and emphasizes that the most important element in its century-long history is its black heritage. This heritage is evident throughout the campus, particularly in East Hall, which prior to integration housed guests of the college who because of their race could not find lodging elsewhere. W.E.B. Du Bois, Mary McLeod Bethune, Benjamin Mays, George Washington Carver, and Roland Hayes, among others, stayed in the hall.

KIMBALL

Kimball War Memorial
East Main Street, Kimball, WV 24853
(304) 448-2118
On U.S. 52 as you enter town from the east
Hours: Daily until sunset
Admission: Free

When West Virginia's great Pocahontas coal seam was discovered in the mid-1880s, only a few hunters, trappers, and farmers were living in the area. One indication that the new coal fields of West Virginia were soon full of black miners (many recruited from North Carolina) can be found in the McDowell County records of returned World War I veterans. Fully 1,500 black men from the county served in the military in those years, joining more than 370,000 other African Americans in uniform. A decade later the political muscle of black miners secured $25,000 from the county's World War Memorial Fund to establish a "Memorial to the Soldiers and Sailors of the Colored Race." In 1928 G. E. Ferguson of Charleston, the only black captain from West Virginia to serve in the war, officially dedicated the Kimball War Memorial for Colored Soldiers of the World War, one of the country's few commemorations of the African-American contribution to that struggle.

LEWISBURG

John Wesley Methodist Church

209 East Foster Street, Lewisburg, WV 24901
Hours: Exterior viewing, daily until sunset. Group tours of church interior arranged through Lewisburg Visitors Center (304 645-1000)
Admission: Free

John Dunn, a white contractor, and his now-nameless crew of slaves in 1820 constructed out of handmade bricks the John Wesley Methodist Church, which passed into the hands of its black congregation after the Civil War. The original church, somewhat altered by a 1835 addition, still stands. Also still visible is the consequence of a cannonball's impact that dates to the Battle of Lewisburg in the summer of 1862.

Mount Tabor Baptist Church

200 Foster Street, Lewisburg, WV 24901
Hours: Exterior viewing, daily until sunset. Group tours of church interior arranged through Lewisburg Visitors Center (304 645-1000)
Admission: Free

In 1833 a congregation that dated to 1796 built Mount Tabor Baptist Church with a three-level bell tower. Hardships following the Civil War interrupted services. Eventually they were resumed by the black members of the congregation, in whose hands the church and the 1833 structure still remain.

North House Museum

101 Church Street, P.O. Box 884, Lewisburg, WV 24901
(304) 645-3398
Hours: Tue.–Sat., 10 A.M.–4 P.M.
Admission: Adults, $3; seniors, $2.50; children, $1

Following the decisive defeat of the Northern Confederacy of Indians and the murder of the Mequashake Shawnee chief Cornstalk (see Blue Jacket Drama entry on p. 450) at the hands of the forces of General Andrew Lewis (after whom Lewisburg was named), the Shawnee raided Fort Donnally in 1778.

About 200 warriors attempted to force the fort's partially opened gate, only to be met by a blast from a smooth-bore gun held by the slave Dick Pointer. The gun, loaded with nails and slugs fashioned from pewter tableware, plowed a furrow through the Indian ranks, killing nine warriors and seriously disconcerting the surviving attackers. It also knocked the burly Pointer flat on his back. The reprieve, however, enabled some 25 men and 60 women and children to hold out until the afternoon, when they were rescued by a relief column led by Matthew Arbuckle. Accounts differ as to Pointer's ultimate fate, with the most reliable suggesting that he was granted his freedom in 1801 and lived as a free man until his death in 1827. Today the 47-pound Dick Pointer gun and Pointer's wooden foot locker are the African-American highpoints of the North House Museum. Pointer's grave will be found in the historically black section of the Lewisburg Cemetery on Church Street, graced with a marker recalling the hero of the attack on Fort Donnally.

MALDEN

African Zion Baptist Church/Booker T. Washington Park
4101 Malden Drive, Malden, WV 25306
(304) 768-2635
Hours: By appointment only
Admission: Free

Booker T. Washington (see entry on p. 206) spent his newly freed youth in Malden, which for the rest of his life he regarded as his hometown. There he worshipped at the African Zion Baptist Church, whose 1852 founding in nearby Tinkersville led it to be viewed as the mother church for the state's black Baptists. Following graduation from Hampton Institute (see Hampton University entry on p. 175), Washington briefly returned to Malden, where he taught Sunday school lessons and a day school for black children at African Zion. In 1963, a century after the church moved to Malden, the town honored Washington with a monument, which has since

COURTESY OF THE NATIONAL PARK SERVICE; LIBRARY OF CONGRESS

From a childhood in Malden, West Virginia, Booker T. Washington developed a drive that took him to the forefront of the black struggle—and to the White House.

been moved to the grounds of the State Capitol. More recently, Malden honored Washington with a historical marker and a small pocket park, both of which are located on the site of a home he purchased for his sister after he had left for Tuskegee. (See Tuskegee University entry on p. 31.) Booker T. Washington Park is on Malden Drive east of the African Zion Baptist Church.

TALCOTT

Big Bend Tunnel/John Henry Statue, Marker, and Park
Talcott, WV 24981
In John Henry Park, near the juncture of W.V. 12 and W.V. 3
Hours: Daily until sunset
Admission: Free

In the 1870s, laborers for the Chesapeake and Ohio Railroad drove a tunnel nearly a mile through the hard red shale of West Virginia's Big Bend Mountain. The tunneling entailed hammering steel spikes by hand into hard rock and breaking it apart preparatory to blasting. Though arduous, it was even more dangerous, and reportedly one in five of the laborers died under the fall of rocks before daylight could be seen clear through the mountain. Legend ascribes the Big Bend Tunnel as the site of John Henry's competition with a steam drill: "The men that made that steam drill / thought it mighty fine; / John Henry drove his 14 feet / While the steam drill made only nine. . . . John Henry was a steel-drivin' man." Even if he was created by Luddite legend, John Henry is representative, for many of the project's laborers were African Americans—and though many may have welcomed a machine that reduced the intensity of their labor, few could have welcomed the resulting reduction of jobs made the more hard to come by because of their race. Today, near the entrance to the tunnel, a John Henry statue, a commemorative marker, and a park pay homage to the man—or in any event, to an authentic American folk song celebrating the physical prowess of a black man.

THE NORTH

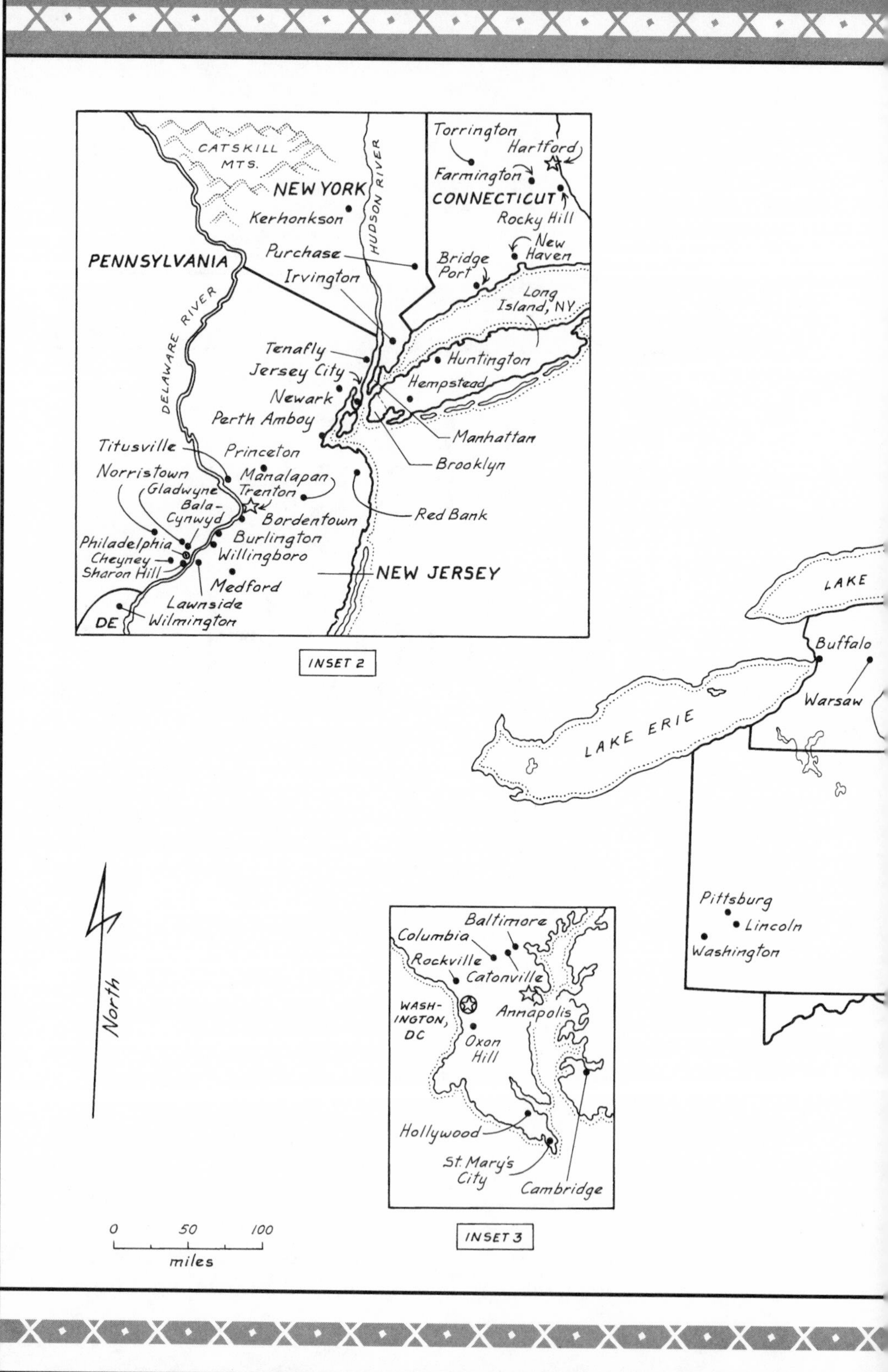
CATSKILL MTS.
NEW YORK
Kerhonkson
HUDSON RIVER
Torrington
Hartford
Farmington
CONNECTICUT
Rocky Hill
New Haven
Bridge Port
PENNSYLVANIA
Purchase
Irvington
DELAWARE RIVER
Long Island, NY
Tenafly
Huntington
Jersey City
Hempstead
Newark
Perth Amboy
Manhattan
Titusville
Princeton
Brooklyn
Norristown
Manalapan
Gladwyne
Trenton
Bala-Cynwyd
Bordentown
Red Bank
Burlington
Philadelphia
Willingboro
Cheyney
Sharon Hill
NEW JERSEY
Medford
Lawnside
DE
Wilmington
INSET 2
LAKE
Buffalo
Warsaw
LAKE ERIE
North
Pittsburg
Lincoln
Washington
Baltimore
Columbia
Rockville
Catonville
WASHINGTON, DC
Annapolis
Oxon Hill
Hollywood
St. Mary's City
Cambridge
INSET 3
0 50 100
miles

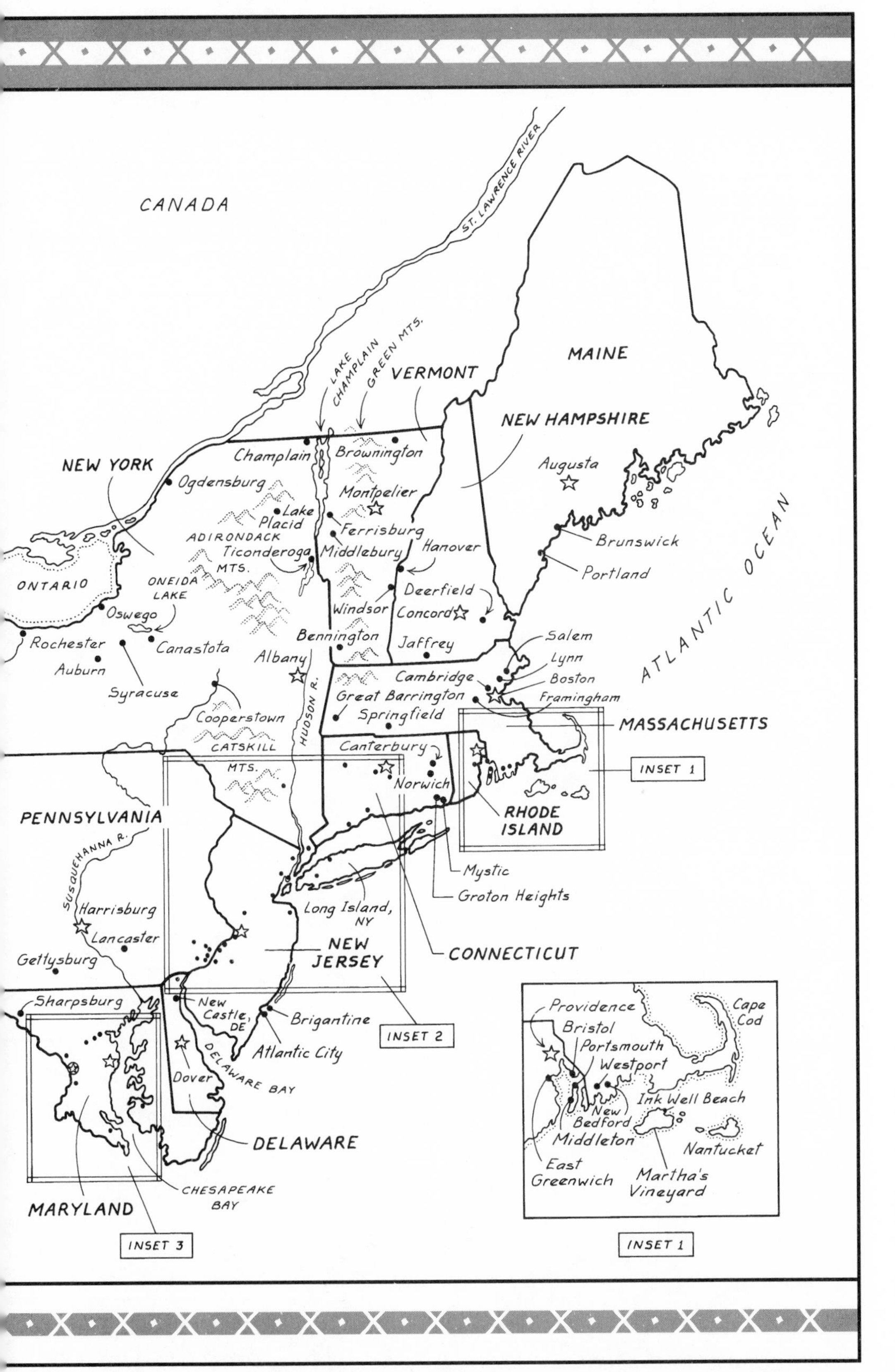

CANADA
ST. LAWRENCE RIVER
LAKE CHAMPLAIN
GREEN MTS.
VERMONT
MAINE
NEW HAMPSHIRE
NEW YORK
Champlain
Brownington
Ogdensburg
Augusta
Montpelier
Lake Placid
Ferrisburg
ADIRONDACK MTS.
Ticonderoga
Middlebury
Hanover
Brunswick
Portland
ATLANTIC OCEAN
ONTARIO
ONEIDA LAKE
Deerfield
Windsor
Concord
Oswego
Rochester
Canastota
Bennington
Jaffrey
Salem
Lynn
Auburn
Albany
Cambridge
Boston
Syracuse
Great Barrington
Framingham
Cooperstown
Springfield
MASSACHUSETTS
CATSKILL MTS.
HUDSON R.
Canterbury
INSET 1
Norwich
PENNSYLVANIA
RHODE ISLAND
SUSQUEHANNA R.
Mystic
Groton Heights
Long Island, NY
Harrisburg
Lancaster
NEW JERSEY
CONNECTICUT
Gettysburg
Sharpsburg
New Castle, DE
Brigantine
INSET 2
Atlantic City
DELAWARE BAY
Dover
DELAWARE
CHESAPEAKE BAY
MARYLAND
INSET 3
Providence
Cape Cod
Bristol
Portsmouth
Westport
Ink Well Beach
New Bedford
Middleton
Nantucket
East Greenwich
Martha's Vineyard
INSET 1

NEWARK'S "COAST": A CLASSIC TENDERLOIN

AMIRI BARAKA

When I was a kid, I never knew that it was called "the Coast." That name for Newark's red-light and black entertainment district—"the best place in the world to listen to black music," Duke Ellington once said—had long since passed on, at least out of my hearing. But when later I learned its name from Willie "the Lion" Smith, the great stride pianist and veteran of the Coast's bawdy houses and bars, I knew I had traversed the area many times. In fact I was born just west of it, though the old black entertainment district had already gone through changes that had all but erased it from the world by the time I got here.

I was born at Kinney Memorial Hospital, where my mother later worked as an administrator. Named after a black doctor, it still sits (now a rooming house) slightly above the heart of the oldest part of the Coast. Just around the corner from the hospital was the Howard University Alumni House. Next door Newark trombonist Graschan Moncur's mother had a beauty parlor. When I was a kid, there was still nearby a very heavy splash of black bars and nightclubs—the High Spot, Owl Club, and Little Johnny's Jumpin' Jive to name just to a few—though by the time of my teenage days, the area was also sprinkled with black doctors living in the former mansions of the rich white city fathers of another era.

I delivered groceries up and down these streets, when there were still white folks living in some of the upscale apartment buildings sprinkled among the mansions. This was a long time after the halcyon days of the Coast at its rawest and most raucous. Now the black petty bourgeoisie was edging in. Effa Manley, owner of the great Newark Eagles black baseball team, lived in a small house across from Mr. Pettigrew, president of the Postal Workers Alliance (the black postal workers union), who then lived in a "luxury" apartment. There was still the Young Men's & Women's Hebrew Association (which is now a sanctified church) on the corner of West Kinney and Washington, where I first saw Katherine Dunham and Talley Beatty perform. A few blocks north was the "Grand Hotel," a watering hole for the players and musicians and athletes and one of the most sophisticated spots in Black Newark. There, in a time when baseball—the "national pastime"—was not yet integrated, my father introduced me to Larry Doby (in 1948 he became the American League counterpart to Jackie Robinson) and Monte Irvin (who later joined Willie Mays in the New York Giants' outfield).

But the oldest Coast, with its roaring strip of "the life," had already gone through very heavy changes, from a bawdy blowout zone for mainly black workers, to a more established sendup of this, catering to the white tourists who wanted to check it all out (shades of Greenwich Village and Hell's Kitchen), to an early urban-renewed area where larger, white front establishments (Burlesque, Opera, the Flicks & Legit theaters) could co-opt and replace, as always. Then that was picked clean and it was time to vanish from the urbs. The old Coast was left a covered-over remnant of what it had been, now buried even from the memories of those who still lived there.

My interest in the old Coast was awakened by reading *Music on My Mind*, Willie "the Lion" Smith's autobiography. The Lion was one of the giants of Afro-American music, a two-fisted stride pianist who merits mention with Jelly Roll Morton, James P. Johnson, Fats Waller, and Duke Ellington, master jazz pianists of their times. The Lion (named because of his heroic feats in World War I, in France) arrived in Newark as a child shortly after the turn of the century and settled into "a four-room house with an attic at the edge of the tenderloin district." Rent was $12 a month and the tenderloin district was called "the Coast." Such districts were formed as floods of black immigrants from the South rushed north fleeing the destruction of the Reconstruction and the violence and intimidation that went with the so-called Redemption of the South.

The area that the Lion moved into around Academy Street is today the heart of the business and commercial downtown area. But at that time it was a sprawling area where Newark's poorest lived. Not just Afro-American, but Irish, Jewish, and Italian, all lived jumbled in this area, the streets' complexion or language changing from block to block.

Just to the south and east of this multinational working class area was the tenderloin. Full of bars and saloons and taverns, as well as those "Buffet Flats" as they were called, or sometimes just straight out "Cat Houses" or what were later called Ho houses, "Ho, Ho, Ho," named for the laughter therein, tenderloin districts naturally sprang up near the center of the working-class population. They were simply where working people hung out to "blow off steam," as the Lion says.

Newark's Coast was linked to three other essentially black tenderloin areas, by their grapevined fame: "Hell's Kitchen" or "the Jungle" on New York City's far west side, Chicago's "Levee" district, and San Francisco's "Barbary Coast." The Lion says these places were definitely hooked up (and quite a few others just like them, wherever the folks were) because they were the places "where the money, fun and excitement were found."

As well as magnets attracting black working people to entertain, groove, and pleasure themselves, these tenderloins were just about the only source of employment for black entertainers. The Lion learned his trade in Coast joints, wandering in and out, snatching a piano seat when the "ticklers," as they were called, dared to leave the piano, always afraid that somebody would come in, sit down in their still-warm seat, and beat them out of a job with a slightly slicker tickle on the keys than they had.

The Lion's first gig was at Bill Buss's saloon at Branford and Shipman Street. No wonder the vibes were still so strong years later when my wife, Amina, and Art Williams, Tom White, and a few others first formed The Loft, an arts center at that same spot.

The Coast also boasted James P. Johnson, one of the movers and shakers of the piano in the early 20th century. Though the Lion called James P. "the Brute," Johnson was one of the great ticklers and is still hailed as a giant today. He played at Kinney Hall (near East Kinney Street) with his wife, the singer Lillian Wright. In fact, Newark's Coast became widely known as a piano player's town, a tickler's paradise, where eventually the greatest piano players of Afro-American music would come to perform or just wail for after-hours kicks, for their own and their peers' edification. Plus to get down on the state of the art, if you could dig it.

No matter the wash of laughing houses and the red lights and bawdiness, one thing that should not be lost sight of was the heaviness of the artistic culture that was still going down. Serious dramatic productions—*The Way of the Transgressor, Willie Live*, and *The Boy Behind the Gun*, about the horrors of war—illuminated the world, even as the Lion, the Brute, and the Duke brought it joy. Those days have passed, but they left in their wake triumphs of Afro-American culture, contributions that serve not only as monuments to past achievement but as spurs to those who still hear the Coast's echo.

A group of us in Newark have submitted several proposals to reconstitute the old Coast neighborhood as a multicultural arts district embracing the music, theater, dance, and cuisine of all the diverse nationalities in the town. This is one way for the old cities of the North to rebuild—on the basis of their own cultural traditions, including the ethnic changes that define them today. This is not a poet's pipedream: The arts in New York City are an $8 billion source of revenue annually. All we have to do to rebuild the Coast is convince the politicians. The people have always dug it.

X·X·X

AMIRI BARAKA, born LeRoi Jones in Newark, New Jersey, is the author of *Dutchman*, which was awarded an Obie for Best American Play of the 1963–64 season. His other works, covering the areas of poetry, fiction, social criticism, and literary essays, include: *Blues People, The Slave, Home: Social Essays, Black Music*, and *Black Fire: Anthology of Afro-American Writing* (edited with Larry Neal). He has resided in "the Coast" for six decades.

CONNECTICUT

State Tourism
865 Brook Street, Rocky Hill, CT 06067
(203) 258-4355
Hours: Mon.–Fri., 8:30 A.M.–4:30 P.M.

BRIDGEPORT

Housatonic Museum of Art
510 Barnum Avenue, Bridgeport, CT 06608
(203) 579-6727
Hours: Mon.–Fri., 10 A.M.–3 P.M.; Wed., 10 A.M.–8 P.M.
Admission: Free

Named for the nearby river, the small Housatonic Museum of Art holds 300 to 400 ethnographic objects from West Africa. Masks, weapons, gold weights and scales, funerary statues, fertility objects, a carved granary door, and a most unusual puppet set greet the visitor. The collection at this small community college museum is an eclectic composition of various gifts, so unlike the experience at larger and richer museums, the visitor is exposed not only to "high culture" but also to what amount to African "tourist objects" of the early 20th century.

CANTERBURY

Prudence Crandall Museum
P.O. Box 58, Canterbury, CT 06331
(203) 546-9916
Intersection of Highways 14 and 169
Hours: Wed.–Sun., 10 A.M.–4:30 P.M.; closed Dec. 15–Jan. 15
Admission: Adults, $2; seniors and youth, $1; ages 5 and under, free

In January 1832 Prudence Crandall opened a girls' school in her house at the behest of Canterbury's citizens, whose sentiments changed when in the autumn she enrolled Sarah Harris, the 21-year-old daughter of a local free black family. Most parents withdrew their daughters; the few remaining girls had to be dismissed when the school closed under community pressure. Early the next year, after consultations with William Lloyd Garrison and other abolitionists, Crandall reopened her school, this time for the purpose of instructing "young ladies and misses of color," thus establishing New England's first black female academy.

Connecticut's response was swift: Within two months the General Assembly passed legislation outlawing the instruction of "colored persons who are not inhabitants of the state." This left open, of course, the issue of African Americans who *did* live in Connecticut, but nonjudicial community sanctions could be relied on in the North as in the South. Crandall's house was assaulted with eggs, mud, and stones; survived an attempted arson; and finally was sacked by a mob one evening. Fearing for the safety of her pupils, and already having been arrested, imprisoned overnight, tried three times, and convicted (though released on a technicality) for breaking the law that arose from her efforts to instruct African Americans, Crandall closed the school and departed the state. Half a century later, seeking to make amends, Canterbury initiated an annuity for Crandall (which received support from Mark Twain) and the Connecticut legislature granted her an annual pension. Today the state maintains in her old home, which was the region's first academy for black females, the Prudence Crandall Museum. Visitors view three period rooms and changing exhibits on Crandall and on local, black, and women's histories.

FARMINGTON

Farmington Historical Society
Village Library, 71 Maine Street, P.O. Box 1645, Farmington, CT 06034
(203) 678-1645
Hours: Tue., 10 A.M.–3:30 P.M.
Admission: Tours: $2

The slavers' terror would have been brief and cushioned by disbelief. Barely a moment's confusion of scuffles and a quick glimpse of the sun's reflection on the raised blades and it was over, for the shipboard uprising by the abducted Mende tribesmen of Sierra Leone was swiftly triumphant. Soon the corpses of the slain Spanish slavers bobbed in the wake of the vessel as its human cargo sailed for their distant homeland, little knowing that the journey would take years and would carry them into the deep waters of the U.S. Supreme Court—and then into the annals of American history.

COURTESY NEW HAVEN COLONY HISTORICAL SOCIETY

This idealized portrait of the Mende leader Cinque in "African" dress was painted in 1839.

The episode began in violence in 1839, when Portuguese and Spanish slavers raided the African coast and abducted scores of Mende men, women, and children. The victims of this violence were shipped to Cuba, a Spanish possession, and sold into slavery in violation of the (rarely enforced) laws and treaties of Spain. From the Cuban capital of Havana, 53 of the abductees were placed onboard *La Amistad* (which ironically means "friendship" in Spanish) for a brief coastal voyage to their place of bondage. Led by their headman "Cinque" (the now-traditional anglicization of Sengbe), the Mende revolted, seized the ship, slew most of their captors, and ordered the surviving Spanish to sail toward their homeland, "where the sun rises." By day the Spanish, keeping the sails flapping in the wind, stayed off the Bahamas, while at night, navigating by the stars, they turned the ship northward. For almost two months the dwindling band of deceived and desperate Mende sailed along the U.S. coast before the filthy and poorly crewed vessel attracted the attention of a U.S. Navy brig. The overjoyed slavers told the boarding American sailors a tale of mutiny and massacre, and upon landing in Connecticut, the Mende were jailed on charges of piracy and murder.

An international and domestic furor ensued. The Spanish—supported by the administration of American president Martin Van Buren—demanded the Mende's return, claiming they were indigenous and, hence, legal, Cuban slaves, while U.S. abolitionists demanded their release and return to Africa. After many a legal twist and turn, the matter ultimately reached the U.S. Supreme Court. There, in 1841, former president John Quincy Adams helped to defend Cinque and his comrades. The Court, led by Chief Justice Roger B. Taney, later author of the notorious Dred Scott decision (see Dred Scott Memorial entry on p. 410), ruled in favor of the Mende. They did indeed return to their homeland, though in many cases not to their families, who in the meantime had fallen into the hands of local slavers and been sold to who knew where.

During their long legal ordeal, Cinque and the Mende lived in the strongly pro-abolitionist town of Farmington. Today the Farmington Historical Society offers comprehensive tours of the town's *Amistad*-related sites, as well as of Farmington's Underground Railroad sites, most of both of which are private residences otherwise closed to the public. Tours include a visit to the dormitory where Cinque and his colleagues lived, and interpretation of public access sites that lack accompanying historical markers. The society's interpreters draw on extensive contemporary documentation concerning the Mende sojourners in Farmington to convey a detailed picture of the Africans' experience in Connecticut.

Foone's Grave
Riverside Cemetery, off Garden Street, Farmington, CT 06032
(203) 678-1645 (historical society); (203) 674-0280 (cemetery)
Hours: Daily until sunset
Admission: Free

While in the extended purgatory of Farmington, the Mende frequently expressed their longing for their African homeland and their doubts about ever returning. During their sojourn, one of their number, Foone, drowned, most probably as a suicide since the contemporary record speaks of his growing despondency, his indigenous African belief that death would reunite him with the loved ones he missed, and his capability as a swimmer who was unlikely to drown in the six feet of canal water in which he was found. Still visible today in the Riverside Cemetery is Foone's Grave and the marble headstone erected by the townspeople who had welcomed him and his comrades.

First Church of Christ, Congregational
75 Main Street, Farmington, CT 06032
(203) 677-2601
Hours: Mon.–Fri., 8 A.M.–4 P.M. Tours: advance notice
Admission: Free

During the two-year sojourn in Farmington of Cinque and his brethren, the center of their community life was the First Church of Christ, Congregational, where they were introduced to the English language and received schooling and religious instruction. This acculturation prepared the way for a mission station to be established with the 35 Mende who returned to Africa.

GROTON HEIGHTS

Fort Griswold Monument and Museum, Avery House Museum
Fort Griswold State Park, Groton Heights, CT 06340
(203) 445-1729
Hours: Monument House Museum: Memorial Day–Labor Day:
daily, 10 A.M.–5 P.M. Labor Day–Columbus Day: weekends only, 10 A.M.–5 P.M. Columbus Day–Memorial Day, closed.
Avery House Museum: Memorial Day–Labor Day, weekends only, 1 P.M.–5 P.M.
Park: daily, 8 A.M.–sunset
Admission: Park and both museums, free

In September 1781, shortly before the surrender at Yorktown, British troops under the command of the renegade Benedict Arnold launched a series of attacks on New England ports. At Groton a small colonial militia force ensconced in a hilltop fort unexpectedly stalled the advance of a British regiment, inflicting severe casualties. Among his Majesty's dead was Major Montgomery, a well-liked officer slain by Jordan Freeman, an African-American orderly. After prolonged and costly resistance, the American commander capitulated, formally offering his sword to an enraged British officer. The British officer took the proffered weapon and ran it through the American commander's body, killing Colonel William Ledyard; instantly thereupon another African-American orderly, Lambert Latham, attacked the British officer, setting in motion an eruption that resulted in the massacre of 84 Americans, most of whom already had surrendered their weapons. Two centuries later, a 135-foot memorial monument bearing the names of the massacre victims commemorates this Revolutionary War episode. Visitors to the Fort Griswold Monument will see the names of Freeman and Latham listed with their comrades. At the Monument Museum they will find a scale model of the fort and exhibits interpreting the Revolutionary War, while the Avery House Museum offers period rooms.

HARTFORD

Harriet Beecher Stowe House
73 Forest Street, Hartford, CT 06105
(203) 522-9258
Hours: June 1–Columbus Day, Dec. 1–31: Mon.–Sat., 9:30 A.M.–4 P.M.; Sun., 12 P.M.–4 P.M. Rest of year: closed Monday
Admission: Adults, $6.50; ages 6–12, $2.75. Admission covers Stowe and adjacent Mark Twain House

Harriet Beecher Stowe's *Uncle Tom's Cabin; or Life Among the Lowly* was the most provocative American novel ever written. It vehemently outraged both South and North, the one against the other. With sales of 3,000 copies on its first day of publication in 1852, 300,000 in its first year, and a million within seven years, the book made Stowe an unlikely celebrity in the abolitionist movement. She suddenly found herself courted by both William Lloyd Garrison and Frederick Douglass, whose differences she tried to mediate without success. Her failure here was inevitable: Serious issues of political strategy divided the two men, but Stowe's nature rejected both politics and compromise. Rather than struggles, Stowe supported causes and good works—as Garrison and Douglass should have known from a reading of *Uncle Tom*. The novel revealed Stowe truly: Emotional and moral fervor drove her denunciation of slavery, which she opposed more for its corrupting effect on Christians than for its treatment of the bound. This perspective accounted for her favored solution—which embarrassed her abolitionist friends: African colonization. Though ultimately a marginal figure as an abolitionist, Stowe (see First Parish entry on p. 236; Stowe House entries on pp. 226 and 434; and Slave Market entry on p. 84) was the most influential novelist in American history. Indeed, any author today would kill to have it said of him or her, as President Lincoln half seriously said of Stowe, that she bore some responsibility for the outbreak of the Civil War.

Visitors to the restored Harriet Beecher Stowe House view the memorabilia and furnishings of this influential author, whose passions were as intense as the objects thereof were ethereal. They also have the opportunity to tour the adjacent house of Mark Twain, whose perspective on slavery was somewhat different from Stowe's.

Wadsworth Atheneum
600 Main Street, Hartford, CT 06103
(203) 278-2670
Hours: Tue.–Sun., 11 A.M.–5 P.M.
Admission: Adults, $5; seniors and students, $2; under 13, free. Free all day Thursday, and Saturday, 11 A.M.–1 P.M.

More than three centuries of the African-American experience is explored through 6,000 objects at the Wadsworth Atheneum. Slave contracts and letters, photographs, sheet music, books, and utilitarian objects of the enslaved and of freedmen predominate, though the 20th-century triumphs of the diaspora are also interpreted.

MYSTIC

Mystic Seaport Museum
50 Greenmanville Avenue, Mystic, CT 06355
(203) 572-0711
Hours: Early Apr.–late Oct.: daily, 9 A.M.–5 P.M. Rest of year: 9 A.M.–4 P.M.
Admission: Adults, $12.50; ages 5–18, $6.25; children under 5, free

Unbeknownst to most Americans, black or white, the 19th-century maritime industry was far from devoid of color. Particularly prior to 1850, the traffic at sea involved a significant number of African Americans, who provided the most stable component of ships' crews. A family, coupled with limited alternative employment, kept black sailors at sea for life. On shore the picture was very different. Skilled white laborers resisted working with African Americans, as the escaped slave and caulker Frederick Douglass (see Douglass Statue entry on p. 243) discovered when he sought work alongside them. The ethnic diversity of the maritime community is integrated into the exhibits at the Mystic Seaport Museum. One of America's most acclaimed museums, Mystic is located on 17 acres and embraces scores of period homes, shops, and ships. The *Charles W. Morgan*, a whaler whose crew included African Americans, Cape Verdeans, and Azoreans, may be toured. The black American and African islands' contribution to the maritime culture is also reflected in the exhibits on the Atlantic trade's sea music and on blacksmithing, one of the trades most open to the African-American small-scale entrepreneur.

NEW HAVEN

Convention & Visitors Bureau
195 Church Street, New Haven, CT 06510
(203) 777-8550
Hours: Mon.–Fri., 8:30 A.M.–5 P.M.

Amistad Memorial
Whitney Avenue, New Haven, CT 06511
(203) 787-0120; (203) 787-5839
Directly across from New Haven Green, ½ mile from Museum of New Haven Historical Society
Hours: Daily until sunset
Admission: Free

The Amistad Memorial honors the abducted Mende tribesmen who seized *La Amistad*, the slave ship carrying them into bondage (see Farmington Historical Society entry on p. 223) and who, after sailing into American waters and being detained by a U.S. Navy brig, were tried for murder and mutiny in a New Haven courtroom. The court ruled that as the Mende had been enslaved illegally, they should not be extradited to Cuba to stand trial for killing most of the *Amistad*'s crew but instead should be returned to their African homeland. Though President Van Buren's administration appealed the verdict, the U.S. Supreme Court upheld the original ruling and the Mende joyfully departed for home, two years after being abducted.

COURTESY AMISTAD COMMITTEE

The Amistad Memorial recalls the efforts of the enslaved Mende to free themselves.

Connecticut Afro-American Historical Society
444 Orchard Street, New Haven, CT 06511
(203) 776-4907
Hours: Mon., 11:30 A.M.–1:30 P.M.; and by appointment
Admission: Free

The Connecticut Afro-American Historical Society primarily is a research center concerned with collecting and preserving objects and information that highlight the black contribution to New England. In its museum, the society displays the results of its efforts as well as exhibits on the national impact of African Americans.

James Weldon Johnson Memorial Collection of Negro Arts and Letters
Beinecke Library, Yale University, New Haven, CT 06511
(203) 432-2977
Hours: Mon.–Fri., 8:30 A.M.–5 P.M.; Sat., 10 A.M.–5 P.M. (closed Sat. in Aug.)
Admission: Free

Named after the prominent civil rights activist, author, and diplomat, the James Weldon Johnson Memorial Collection of Negro Arts and Letters (see Johnson entries on pp. 156 and 271) is a treasure trove—unfortunately one that is open only to scholars. Here one can find Johnson's papers, original manuscripts from Harlem Renaissance authors, correspondence between major figures in the African-American movements of the 19th and 20th centuries, and a comprehensive collection of spirituals and blues. The library's changing exhibits on black themes, however, are open to the public.

Museum of the New Haven Historical Society
114 Whitney Avenue, New Haven, CT 06510
(203) 562-4183
Hours: Tue.–Fri., 10 A.M.–5 P.M.; Sat.–Sun., 2 P.M.–5 P.M.
Admission: Museum: Wed.–Mon.: adults, $2; ages 6–16, $1; Tue., free. Library: $2

A portrait of Cinque (see Farmington Historical Society entry on p. 223), painted for the prominent black Garrisonian abolitionist Robert Purvis, hangs in the Museum of the New Haven Historical Society. The portrait, which poses Cinque in "African" garb with his stylized homeland in the background, was painted by Nathaniel Jocelyn, the son of Simeon Jocelyn, the pastor of Temple Street Church and an ardent abolitionist.

NORWICH

Slater Memorial Museum and Art Gallery
108 Crescent Street, Norwich, CT 06360
(203) 887-2506
Hours: Sept.–June: Mon.–Fri., 9 A.M.–4 P.M.; Sat.–Sun., 1 P.M.–4 P.M. Rest of year: Tue.–Sun., 1 P.M.–4 P.M.
Admission: Free

A Dogon granary door, Senufo helmet masks, Ashanti drums, Bambara carvings and Dan masks are but some of the holdings in the Slater Memorial Museum and Art Gallery. West African wooden objects of the late 19th and early 20th centuries predominate in the museum's African collection, which complements its Oceania holdings.

TORRINGTON

John Brown House Historical Marker
John Brown Road, Route 4, Torrington, CT 06790
Hours: Daily until sunset
Admission: Free

The babe who in adulthood believed himself God's providential agent for uprooting slavery—and thus fully justified both in hacking to death captive men who differed with him and in leading his sons and others on a suicidal and homicidal enterprise—was born in Connecticut. His parents, failing to apprehend God's design, neglected to supply him with an appropriate Old Testament name, instead christening him John Brown. (See Kennedy Farm entry on p. 257; Harpers Ferry entry on p. 207; John Brown Farm entry on p. 296; John Brown

Museum entry on p. 386; and John Brown Marker entry on p. 374.) Today the John Brown House Historical Marker recalls the first homestead of the fanatic who led the raid on the U.S. arsenal at Harpers Ferry as a prelude to arming those in bondage and overthrowing the blasphemous slave power that corrupted America.

DELAWARE

Tourism Office
99 Kings Highway, P.O. Box 1401, Dover, DE 19903
(800) 441-8846
Hours: Mon.–Fri., 8 A.M.–4:30 P.M.

DOVER

Richard Allen Historical Marker

Loockerman and Federal streets, Dover, DE 19901
Hours: Daily until sunset
Admission: Free

Richard Allen (1760–1831) first saw Delaware at the age of eight, when his family was sold by their owner in Philadelphia to a new master living near Dover. A decade later Allen was "saved" through the preachings of itinerant Methodists. Within three years he had purchased his freedom and begun a preaching career that would make him one of the most historically influential African Americans—indeed, Americans—of the 19th century. After supporting himself as an unskilled laborer and then a shoemaker, the 28-year-old Allen was called to Philadelphia by Methodists to preach to their black adherents. Within a few years he led the city's largest black congregation, but this was mere prologue to the story of his struggle with the white church, a struggle that led to the founding of the independent African Methodist Episcopal (A.M.E.) Church. Though Allen also deserves a place in history for his antislavery pamphlets and sermons and for his attempt to institutionalize through

COURTESY MOORLAND-SPINGARN RESEARCH CENTER, HOWARD UNIVERSITY

The 18th-century African-American preacher Richard Allen was the leading light in establishing autonomous black institutions.

mutual aid societies and schools a black existence not dependent on whites, it was the A.M.E. Church that is the foundation of his immense contribution to the nation. Decades after his death, and particularly following Emancipation, the A.M.E. Church was the guiding force in the creation of a self-referential African-American world, one that enabled former slaves to integrate into the larger society (insofar as that society permitted it) as autonomous subjects rather than as decultured objects. Today a historical marker recalls the life and work of an American giant.

Delaware State College
U.S. 13, Dover, DE 19901
(302) 739-4924
Hours: Mon.–Fri., by appointment
Admission: Free

Delaware State College is one of 17 historically black land-grant institutions founded in 1891 following passage in 1890 of the second Morrill Act. (Most of the more than 70 land-grant colleges founded under the first Morrill Act, which the U.S. Congress passed in 1862, were white, in part because the act mainly applied to the middle and western regions of the country, where few African Americans lived.) The second Morrill Act extended the provisions of the original act to 16 southern states and required beneficiaries of the original act to make provisions for the education of black citizens in the agricultural and mechanical arts—which in those states with segregated education meant the founding of black schools. A marker at the main entrance to the campus relates the history of Delaware State College's founding. Also of interest is Loockerman Hall, the campus's original building, which was donated by a former slave owner.

Old State House
Delaware State Visitors Center, 406 Federal Street, Dover, DE 19901
(302) 739-4266
Hours: Tue.–Sat., 10 A.M.–4:30 P.M.; Sun., 1:30 P.M.–4:30 P.M.
Admission: Free

No one gave more hostages to fortune than slave mothers, who at any moment might be sundered from the children they had suckled. Candace, who labored in bondage for Anna White, was freed outright in 1790. Even an event this joyful was tempered, however, as she thought of her four-year-old son, Zara, who was only conditionally freed. Zara's freedom would not take effect until his 21st birthday. Until then Candace was tied as tightly to her former mistress as she was bound in affection to her son.

Two centuries after Candace was freed, Delaware uses its Old State House as a vehicle to describe how the legal practices of the 18th century affected specific black residents, slave and free. Candace's history, for example, is traced through the 1790 manumission document registered at the Recorder of Deeds. Tours at the Old State House relate the fates of other African Americans, who doubtless would be surprised to learn that their lives, recovered from a paper trail, live on in the hearts of their descendants.

John Dickinson Plantation
Kitts Hummock Road, P.O. Box 273, Dover, DE 19901
(302) 739-3277
Hours: Tue.–Sat., 10 A.M.–3:30 P.M.; open Sun. (except during the winter months), 1:30 P.M.–4:30 P.M.
Admission: Free

In 1760 John Dickinson inherited land and slaves following his father's death. Influenced by Quaker teachings, Dickinson in 1777 conditionally freed his human property, offering freedom, food, shelter, and remuneration in exchange for 21 years of service. In 1785, two years before he signed the United States Constitution as a Delaware delegate, Dickinson unconditionally freed all his slaves. Many remained on his property, living in the same log dwellings and performing the same labors as before, though now under detailed rental agreements, while others established themselves as small farmers or tradesmen.

Today the John Dickinson Plantation interprets these 18th-century black lives, slave and free, as an integral aspect of plantation life. Dickinson's Georgian mansion, built by his father in 1740, still stands and can be toured, as can a one-room, reconstructed "log'd dwelling" typical of the residences of slaves, free blacks, and most whites. A granary, a feed barn, a corn crib, and a stable complete the colonial and Federal era atmosphere, which is intensified by the presence of costumed interpreters (black and white) strolling the grounds. Also available is a special-focus tour entitled "A World Apart," which highlights African-American life on Dickinson's plantation.

Woodburn Mansion
King's Highway and Pennsylvania Avenue, Dover, DE 19901
(302) 739-5656
Hours: Grounds open daily, 8 A.M.–4:30 P.M.; mansion open Sat., 2:30 P.M.–4:30 P.M. Group tours by appointment
Admission: Free

This Federal era house, which now serves as the official residence of the governor of Delaware, was owned by a Quaker family in antebellum times and served as a stop on the Underground Railroad. A historical marker on the front of the house attests to this use, while an old, large hollow tree in front of the building gave rise to the local tale that it was used to hide runaways.

MILFORD

Absalom Jones Historic Marker
About 2 miles southeast of Milford on the south side of Route 36, approximately ¼ mile west of the intersection of Routes 36 and 1
Hours: Daily until sunset
Admission: Free

Absalom Jones, one of America's greatest 18th-century black leaders and with Richard Allen one of the founders of an autonomous African-American social movement, was born a slave in 1746 on a Sussex County, Delaware, plantation called Cedar Town. Within the confines of slavery, which he ever opposed, Jones was blessed with opportunity, as he was by a character of initiative and determination. He learned to read as a child, spending the few pennies he managed to acquire on a speller and a New Testament. After moving to Philadelphia with his master in 1762, he studied in a night school. By 1784 Jones, now married, had purchased his freedom; not long thereafter he and his wife purchased two houses, which they rented out. Jones was an active member of St. George's Methodist Episcopal Church, where he and his black congregationists sat in a segregated section. To this church in 1786 came Richard Allen as a licensed preacher. With the addition of these two men, Philadelphia's African-American community achieved a critical mass and within a few short years burst forth in one of the most creative explosions of energy black America ever witnessed. In 1787 the Free African Society was established, with Allen's and Jones's prominence noted in the preamble of the group's Articles of Association. By 1792 an independent African-American Church—St. Thomas' African Episcopal Church—had been formed after Allen and Jones were, in the former's words, "dragged off our knees in St. George's church and treated worse than heathens." In 1794, after organizing local free blacks to assist Philadelphia during the yellow fever epidemic that killed a tenth of the city's population, the two men authored *A Narrative of the Proceedings of the Black People, During the Late Awful Calamity in Philadelphia*. That same year Allen opened Mother Bethel Church. In 1800 Jones and other of the city's leading African Americans authored a petition to the U.S. Congress calling for the gradual abolition of slavery—the petition was rejected on a 85-to-1 vote. In 1804 Absalom Jones was ordained the first African-American Episcopal priest, and from then until his death in 1818 he remained an active figure in a black community whose only rival for independence and initiative was its counterpart in Boston. Today, on the edge of the Cedar Town estate where he was born as property, a historic marker pays tribute to an African-American giant.

NEW CASTLE

Old New Castle Court House

211 Delaware Street, New Castle, DE 19720
(302) 323-4453
Hours: Tue.–Sat., 10 A.M.–3:30 P.M.; Sun., 1:30 P.M.–4:30 P.M.
Admission: Free

Samuel Hawkins and his family fled the bonds of slavery and made their way through Delaware with the assistance of the Underground Railroad in 1845. Thomas Garrett and John Hunn aided their escape. For their endeavors, they found themselves bound over for trial in the federal district court in New Castle three years later. Today the Old New Castle Court House offers tours that use the Hawkinses' escape and the Garrett-Hunn trial to explore the ways in which the antebellum legal system in Delaware affected the lives of the free (white and black) and the enslaved.

WILMINGTON

Convention & Visitors Bureau
1300 Market Street, Suite 504, Wilmington, DE 19801
(302) 652-4088
Hours: Mon.–Fri., 9 A.M.–5 P.M.

Cradle of African-American Political Leadership Monument
C Street and New Castle Avenue, Dover, DE 19801
Hours: Daily until sunset
Admission: Free

Black Delaware's 20th-century political groundbreakers—including William Winchester, the first African American elected to the State House of Representatives, Herman Holloway, the first African American to serve in the State Senate, and Henrietta Johnson, the first black woman elected to Delaware's House of Representatives—are featured in Wilmington's monumental Cradle of African-American Political Leadership.

Black Anthony Historic Marker/Fort Christina State Park Historic Marker
Seventh Street, Wilmington, DE 19801
(302) 739-4266
Hours: Daily until sunset
Admission: Free

The first permanent European settlement in the Delaware Valley dates back to the 1638 landing of Swedish settlers, who established Fort Christina. The following year a "Black Anthony" arrived from the West Indies aboard the Swedish ship *Vogel Grip*. Presumably Anthony was a slave, since later documents record his becoming a free man, adopting the name Antoni Swart (which is simply another version of his anglicized identity), and working for the colony's governor, Johan Printz. In the 1640s and '50s Anthony cut hay for Printz and sailed in the governor's sloop. Today Delaware's first recorded settler of African descent is commemorated with a historic marker in Fort Christina State Park.

Old Town Hall Museum
512 Market Street Mall, Wilmington, DE 19801
(302) 655-7161
Hours: Mar. 16–Jan. 18: Tue.–Fri., 12 P.M.–4 P.M.; Sat., 10 A.M.–4 P.M.
Jan. 19–Mar. 15: Sat. only, 10 A.M.–4 P.M.
Admission: Free

The Underground Railroad, the Civil War draft, and Delaware's late 19th-century development as they touched on African Americans are investigated through objects and exhibits on display at the Old Town Hall Museum. The museum's interpretation of the local abolitionist movement centers on Thomas Garrett, a Wilmington businessman who helped 2,700 slaves escape and who aided freedmen, going bankrupt in the process. A silver tea service presented to Garrett by the grateful black community is on display, along with Bass Otis's portrait of the man. Soon Wilmington will boast a statue of Garrett.

Peter Spencer Plaza
French Street, between Eighth and Ninth streets, Wilmington, DE 19801
Hours: Daily until sunset
Admission: Free

Freed from slavery, Peter Spencer in 1813 established the African Union Colored Methodist Protestant Church, which soon affiliated with and then split from Allen's A.M.E. movement. (See Richard Allen entry on p. 230.) Known today as the Mother African Union Methodist Protestant Church (812 North Franklin Street), Spencer's founding church stayed on its original site until 1970. That site is now part of Peter Spencer Plaza, which in addition to commemorating Spencer continues the story of the African-American struggle with a monument to the Underground Railroad. The monument honors the work of Harriet Tubman and Thomas Garrett, a Wilmington businessman and active abolitionist whose efforts resulted in the escape of 2,700 slaves. Spencer was also influential in fostering the "August Quarterly," an annual day of freedom for Delaware's slaves that permitted them to conduct religious services without the encumbrance of white overseers. Today the "August Quarterly" is still celebrated annually in Wilmington under the auspices of the Mother African Union Methodist Protestant Church and provides an occasion for festivals, food, and worship.

MAINE

Office of Tourism
189 State Street, Station 59, Augusta, ME 04333
(207) 287-5711
Hours: Mon.–Fri., 8 A.M.–5 P.M.

BRUNSWICK

Peary-McMillan Arctic Museum
Hubbard Hall Library, Bowdoin College, Brunswick, ME 04011
(207) 725-3416
Hours: Tue.–Sat., 10 A.M.–4 P.M.; Sun., 2 P.M.–5 P.M.
Admission: Free

In 1827 John Brown Russwurm and Samuel Cornish established *Freedom's Journal*, the first black newspaper in America. Two years later Russwurm became the first African American to earn an M.A., graduating from Bowdoin College, which today recalls his presence with a Russwurm Center, where facsimile copies of front pages of the *Journal* may be viewed. Upon graduating, Russwurm moved to Liberia, where he dedicated the rest of his life to establishing a black homeland, finally dying as governor of the Maryland colony in 1851. Bowdoin graduated two other men who tangentially figure in African-American history: Oliver Otis Howard (class of 1850), commissioner of the Freedmen's Bureau and the namesake and first president of Howard University (see entry on p. 198), and Robert E. Peary (1877), the polar explorer whose success was directly tied to the aid of his African-American colleague, Matthew Henson. (See entry on p. 239.) Today Bowdoin's Peary-McMillan Arctic Museum bears witness to the critical role played by Henson. Just off campus, on Maine Street, is a historical marker on the old home of General Joshua Chamberlain, who accepted Lee's surrender at Appomattox and who later served as the college's president.

First Parish Church
Maine Street, Brunswick, ME 04011
(207) 729-7331
Hours: By appointment
Admission: Free

On March 2, 1851, Harriet Beecher Stowe and her older children attended the morning service at First Parish Church, taking their accustomed place in pew 23 on the Broad Aisle of the nave. Two months earlier she had visited Boston—then the scene of a riot in opposition to the Fugitive Slave Act—where she had met and talked with Josiah Henson, who would serve as the model for Uncle Tom in her novel of that name. Stowe sat through the morning service and the subsequent communion service when, suddenly between noon and one o'clock, a vision struck. The scene of the death of Uncle Tom passed before her mind whole as her ears rang with Jesus' admonition "Inasmuch as ye have done it unto one of the least of these my brethren, ye have done it onto me." Thus was born *Uncle Tom's Cabin*. Today this epiphany is honored at First Parish Church with a bronze plaque in pew 23.

Stowe House Historical Marker
63 Federal Street, Brunswick, ME 04011
(207) 725-5543
Hours: Daily until sunset
Admission: Free

Immediately after her epiphany in the First Parish Church, Stowe returned home, locked herself in her room, and began writing down her vision. After she ran out of writing paper, she feverishly continued scribbling on the brown wrapping paper in which her groceries had been delivered the day before. Stowe later placed her short tale within a longer narrative, which appeared as a serial in the antislavery paper *The New Era* from June 1851 through April 1852. Before the serial's conclusion, the narrative was published as a book, which instantly became a best-seller. Today the home in which *Uncle Tom's Cabin* was written still survives in restored form and is attached to a hotel, which bears a historical marker commemorating the events of 1851.

PORTLAND

Cathedral of the Immaculate Conception
307 Congress Street, Portland, ME 04101
(207) 773-7746
Hours: Tours available by appointment
Admission: Free

The immensely talented Healy children were products of a common-law marriage between an Irish-Catholic small farmer in Georgia and his slave—and hence were legally slaves themselves, though they were never treated as such. The children gravitated to the church en masse. James Augustine Healy, born in a log cabin in Macon, Georgia, in 1830, studied in the North, in Canada, and then in France, where he was ordained in the Cathedral of Notre Dame in 1854. In the Cathedral of the Immaculate Conception in 1875, Healy was consecrated as the first African-American bishop of the Catholic Church. Today a 25-foot-high stained glass window in the cathedral recalls the man. Two of Healy's brothers also rose high in the church: At Georgetown University, Patrick Francis Healy, S.J., became the first African American in history to serve as president of an American college, while Sherwood Healy was rector of the Boston Cathedral. Three Healy sisters served God and the world as nuns.

MARYLAND

Maryland Office of Tourism Development
217 East Redwood Street, Baltimore, MD 21202
(410) 333-6611; (800) 543-1036
Hours: Mon.–Fri., 8:30 A.M.–5 P.M.
Ask for "Maryland's African-American Culture," a booklet that highlights the state's black heritage.

ANNAPOLIS

Annapolis and Anne Arundel County Conference & Visitors Bureau
One Annapolis Street, Annapolis, MD 21401
(410) 280-0445
Hours: Mon.–Fri., 9 A.M.–5 P.M.
Ask for the "Walking Tour of Annapolis Highlighting African-American Heritage Points of Interest" brochure.

Banneker-Douglass Museum
84 Franklin Street, Annapolis, MD 21401
(410) 974-2893
One block from Church Circle
Hours: Tue.–Fri., 10 A.M.–3 P.M.; Sat., 12 P.M.–4 P.M.
Admission: Free

Benjamin Banneker (see entry on p. 168), the 18th-century free-black farmer, scientist, and proponent of black equality, and Frederick Douglass (see Douglass Statue entry on p. 243), the 19th-century escaped slave turned militant abolitionist, were both Maryland born—the former to free-black, property-owning parents, the latter to a slave woman and a never-identified local white man. Their names now adorn Maryland's preeminent black heritage museum, which utilizes art, artifacts, documents, and photographs to interpret the transformation of African captives first into slaves and then into African Americans.

Maryland has a particularly interesting black background. The Chesapeake region's early experience with the labor-intensive tobacco cash crop economy stimulated a demand first for indentured servants—white and black—and soon after for slaves, most of whom initially were brought in from slave-stocked plantations of the West Indies. In the early years of settlement, those black indentured servants who survived their contracted period of labor gained freedom, and many soon became property owners and established citizens. Class, not race, determined social standing in a colony where most residents were indentured to servitude. But by the 18th century, Maryland's culture was defined by slavery.

A century later the ideals of the American revolution and the "equal in God's eyes" preachings of Quaker, Baptist, and Methodist ministers stimulated manumission, which joined with natural increase and immigration to yield a small but noticeable free black community. Indeed, by the 1790s the free black population steadily increased, while the slave population steadily declined. This trend continued throughout the 19th century. Neither legislation passed in 1827 and 1831, which required slaves freed after March 1832 to be removed from the state, nor the fact that free blacks faced greater abuse than slaves altered the trend: In 1790—the year before Banneker gained fame for his first *Almanac*—8,043 free blacks were swamped by 103,036 slaves; in 1830 Frederick Douglass languished as one of the state's 102,994 slaves, but he lived among 52,938 free black residents; a year before the outbreak of the Civil War, a free Douglass had 83,941 counterparts, who almost equaled the 87,189 African Americans still held in bondage.

From Africa to bondage to resistance to the perils and limitations of freedom, the story of Maryland's African Americans is interpreted at the Banneker-Douglass Museum. African art and utilitarian objects of the Dogon, Malinke, Bambara, Baule, and Guro cultures; documents and artifacts from the days of slavery and the abolitionist struggle; photographs and manuscripts touching upon the post–Civil War world of emancipation; and 20th-century items that detail the life of a community segregated because of race are on view here.

Kunta Kinte Marker
Main Street and Market Street, Annapolis, MD
Hours: Daily until sunset
Admission: Free

More than two centuries have passed since the line of the late Alex Haley (see entry on p. 147), represented by the newly enslaved Kunta Kinte, arrived in America aboard the slave ship *Lord Ligioner*. Stepping ashore in the harbor of Annapolis in 1767, Kinte survived bondage and prepared the way for his Haley descendant to write *Roots* and to co-author *The Autobiography of Malcolm X*.

Matthew Henson Memorial
Maryland State House, Annapolis, MD 21401
(410) 974-3400
In the lobby of the old section of the State House
Hours: Daily, 9 A.M.–5 P.M.
Admission: Free

From an early age Matthew Henson displayed an adventuring spirit. Born on a farm and former slave market site in Charles County a year after Lee's surrender at Appomattox, Henson ran away to Washington, D.C., before his 12th birthday and there spent some time working in his aunt's restaurant. At the age of 13, he walked to Baltimore, where he hung around the waterfront for a while before shipping out as a cabin boy on a schooner bound for China. During the voyage he learned the rudiments of mathematics and navigation. Subsequently Henson worked in a Washington, D.C., hat shop, where a chance meeting with then Lieutenant Robert E. Peary led to an offer of employment with a canal surveying expedition to Nicaragua. Henson sufficiently impressed Peary to be recruited for the latter's exploration of the Arctic region. Henson accompanied Peary on each of his seven Arctic and polar expeditions. Neither Peary nor any of his colleagues lacked courage and determination. But to these Henson added unusual endurance, a mastery of the Eskimo language, Arctic skills, and an easy rapport with the people. (One testament is the children he left behind with their Eskimo mothers.) Peary's view of him was straightforward: "He is my most valuable companion. I could not get along without him." Peary selected Henson to be one of the six men to make the final dash to the North Pole. More notably, with the exception of Peary, Henson was the only non-Eskimo included in what the explorer knew would be the honor of discovery. Strictly speaking, Henson was the first recorded human being to stand "atop" the North Pole; the exhausted Peary sent him ahead to make the final observation and calculations, which the explorer later confirmed when he was driven up on sled by the four Eskimos.

That was on April 6, 1909. Four years later Matthew Henson, explorer, was reduced to working at a New York City parking garage. Subsequently he worked as a messenger at the New York Customs House, retiring at the age of 70 and eking out the last 18 years of his life on a $1,000 yearly pension and his wife's earnings. Today the intrepid may visit Henson Bay in northwest Arctic Canada; those more pressed for time may choose instead to visit the Matthew Henson Memorial at the Maryland State House.

BALTIMORE

Baltimore Area Visitors Information Center
300 West Pratt Street, Baltimore, MD 21202
(410) 837-4636
Hours: Mon.–Fri., 9 A.M.–5 P.M.

Baltimore Museum of Art
Art Museum Drive, Baltimore, MD 21218
(410) 396-6310
Hours: Tue.–Fri., 10 A.M.–4 P.M.; Sat.–Sun., 11 A.M.–6 P.M.
Admission: Adults, $2; under 22, free; free to all on Thu.

More than 1,300 African art objects from the 12th through the 20th centuries grace the Baltimore Museum of Art. The creations of the Fang, Fante, Kuba, Yaka, Songye, Mbundu, Luba, Sapi, and many other peoples offer avenues of exploration into the cultural substratum of African Americans. They also offer the viewer the compelling, transcendent power of beauty—and a whiff of a world vanished, vanquished by tide of time and "progress."

The small stone figures of the Sapi, a people who occupied Sierra Leone in the mid-15th century, underscore both a cultural refinement noted by Portuguese explorers and traders of the day and the ephemeral nature of power: Within a century Sapi culture was destroyed by invaders from the African interior intent on securing control of the coastal trade. Today the figures are found neglected in the fields and streams over which their creators once exercised dominion.

Though some of the objects of African art were simple ornamentation, displays of wealth and social status, or commodities serving as items of trade or gift-giving, much of African art (like much of the Greek drama that defines High Culture for European civilization) was driven by a ritual function rather than unmediated aesthetic appreciation. Whether it marked a coronation, a harvest, a funeral, or the induction of young men and women into adult society, the object served to invoke the aid or comfort of spiritual forces at times of transition or anxiety.

African masks (from the Mossi, Mende, Dan, Kimba, Senufo, among others) are a prominent feature of the museum's collection. These masks are not whole, discrete objects but rather an element of a ritual "package." Masks represent the character of spiritual or personal forces, behind which the wearer/performer's identity is not so much hidden but obliterated. The mask's features, the costume of the performer, and the (usually, dance) movement employed collectively communicate to observers in the community ritual edifying messages: proper and improper social behavior, the role of ancestors, the power of spiritual forces, and so forth. The Baltimore Museum of Art uses interactive videos to highlight an embracing ritual complex, rescuing the masks from isolation by assembling them within a functional ensemble of associated objects, music, dance, architecture, and ritual participants. Once the masks are identified as fragments, both they and the whole of which they are a part become objects of appreciation—and their creators (and their creators' descendants) subjects of appreciation.

Black-American Museum
1769 Carswell Street, Baltimore, MD 21218
(410) 243-9600
Hours: Mon.–Fri., 9 A.M.–5 P.M.
Admission: Adults, $5; children, $3

The small Black-American Museum is primarily a contemporary art gallery specializing in works by local African-American artists, though the museum includes a few artifacts from Africa, such as a Twi sacred tribal pipe and an elephant tusk.

Eubie Blake National Museum and Cultural Center
409 North Charles Street, Baltimore, MD 21201
(410) 396-6442
Hours: Tue.–Fri., 12 P.M.–6 P.M.; Sat.–Sun., 12 P.M.–5 P.M.
Admission: Free

One of America's preeminent composers of ragtime and stage music was born the 11th—but only surviving—child to former slaves in 1883. Eubie Blake's musical talent was evident early on: At the age of six he climbed onto a organ stool in a store and began playing the instrument. The salesman urged Mrs. Blake to buy the $75 organ at a weekly rate of 25 cents, which she did. (Of course, this may have evidenced the salesman's skill more than young Eubie's.) Blake's talent blossomed under training, but—like his contemporary, W. C. Handy—he was drawn not to the church music favored by his parents but to the ragtime he heard in the local saloons. By 15, already an accomplished pianist, he was sneaking out of the house at night to play in a local bordello. By 19 he had left for New York, seeking work as a buck dancer. Before too long others would dance to *his* tunes. In addition to teaming up with Noble Sissle to form a successful vaudeville and song-writing duo that lasted until 1927, Blake wrote material for Josephine Baker, Sophie Tucker, Noel Coward, and other top stars. As styles changed, Blake's public success dimmed. Though he was never entirely without work in the 1940s and '50s, his career took off again only with the release of the Paul Newman/Robert Redford film *The Sting*, which brought a resurgence of interest in ragtime music. Blake emerged from retirement to please a whole new generation until well into his 90s, before dying five days past his 100th birthday.

The Eubie Blake National Museum and Cultural Center contains a panoramic pictorial essay of Blake's life and the origin of American musical theater. Memorabilia and video and audio presentations complement the photographs that trace Blake's life and his relationship with his show business partners. The center also boasts a gallery for local artists (with preference given to minorities) and for visiting exhibits (usually with a concentration on black artists or themes), a permanent exhibit on black Baltimore, and a recital theater for performing artists (again with a preference for minorities).

Cab Calloway Jazz Institute Museum
Coppin State College, 2500 West North Avenue, Baltimore, MD 21216
(410) 383-5926
In the Parlette Moore Library
Hours: Mon.–Fri., 9 A.M.–5 P.M.
Admission: Free

A teenager when his father died, Cab Calloway took a night and weekend job singing in a Baltimore speakeasy to help support his family. To please his mother, Calloway enrolled as a prelaw student at Crane College in Chicago. Perhaps tunes and tarts proved more compelling than torts, for soon the classroom was replaced by the ballroom, and he was leading the Alabamian Band at the Sunset Cafe on Chicago's South Side. Booked into Harlem's Savoy Ballroom, Calloway found his engagement canceled after opening night. Landing on his feet thanks to Louis Armstrong's assistance, Calloway secured the male lead in the Fats Waller revue *Connie's Hot Chocolates*. His rendition of "Ain't Misbehavin' " won him a following, and when the show closed he formed a new band. By 1930 he was a smash hit, playing in Harlem's top night spot, The Cotton Club, and touring London, Paris, and the United States. The following decade found him starring in films, such as *Stormy Weather* with Bill "Bojangles" Robinson and Lena Horne. The death of the big band sound following World War II left Calloway stranded . . . briefly. In 1950 he was offered the role of Sportin' Life in the revival of Gershwin's *Porgy and Bess*. A run of nearly four years ensued, as did another film (*St. Louis Blues* with Nat Cole, Eartha Kitt, Ella Fitzgerald, and Ruby Dee), leaving him well placed to enter his fifth decade of entertainment. In 1967 the return to Broadway of *Hello Dolly* with an all-black cast, featuring Calloway and Pearl Bailey, made it evident that Calloway was a mainstay of America's 20th-century entertainment world, a position he further secured in the succeeding decades. The John Belushi–Dan Ackroyd film *The Blues Brothers* brought him to the attention of yet another generation, quite possibly not the last he will conquer. The man gives every evidence of proving immortal in more than the term's usual Hollywood/Broadway sense. Today visitors to the Cab Calloway Jazz Institute Museum can follow his remarkable career through a series of photographs, posters, memorabilia, and film stills.

Coppin State College
2500 West North Avenue, Baltimore, MD 21216
(410) 383-5400
Hours: Tours: Mon.–Fri., 9 A.M.–5 P.M. by appointment only
Admission: Free

Coppin State College grew out of a turn-of-the-century teacher training course for black elementary school teachers offered at a local high school. Over time the course expanded and ultimately separated itself from the high school. In 1926 this teacher training facility took its current name from Fanny Jackson Coppin. Born a slave in the District of Columbia in 1837, Coppin was purchased out of slavery in her youth by an aunt, entered service for a family that permitted her an hour of study every other afternoon, graduated in 1865 from Oberlin College—one of the few colleges then open to African Americans—and thereafter spent 37 years as a teacher and then principal of the Institute for Colored Youth in Philadelphia. Her work during these years shaped the pattern of black education prior to World War I and earned her the respect of the community. The university's history can be traced through the Coppin Collection on the ground floor of the library.

Frederick Douglass Statue
Morgan State University, Hillen Road and Cold Spring Lane, Baltimore, MD 21239
(410) 319-3333
Hours: Daily until sunset
Admission: Free

Frederick Douglass, the most influential African American of the 19th century, was born Frederick Augustus Washington Bailey—and the wrong half white. Though his unknown father was free and white, he did not define his offspring—even if he had been willing to acknowledge him; as his mother was a slave, so was her son. A childhood of trauma ensued. Fatherless, the child was abandoned by a mother whom he rarely saw, though she lived nearby. He was nurtured instead by his grandmother Betsy, from whom he suddenly was torn at the age of six by the demands of slavery. The bright and inquisitive slave child then received unusually tolerant treatment in two succeeding white homes, resulting in confusion and presumption (of love, of acceptance, of near equality—of *belonging*) that required correction—a correction that shocked a child who sincerely had forgotten not so much his place, but that his place was a *life* sentence. As well, Frederick Bailey saw and suffered the mundane experiences of a slave world to which he felt certain he did not belong: the whipping of his young aunt Hester, the brutal and comprehensive kicking of his half brother Perry, the estate division that intentionally separated him (for the purpose of serving him) from his siblings whom life cruelly had made both strangers and inferiors.

From this childhood Frederick graduated to literacy, religion, rebelliousness, and the experience of field slavery under the rule of a man notorious for breaking the will of recalcitrant slaves. Unbroken by a system of slavery that could not easily accommodate exceptions, the teenage Frederick would not be broken by violence, which instead underscored his determination to make himself free. This he accomplished at the age of 20, shedding his slave name as he did so and tellingly replacing it with that of the hero of Sir Walter Scott's *The Lady of the Lake*.

Frederick Douglass spent the next six decades as one of the nation's leading abolitionists, social reformers, authors, and orators, creatively transforming trauma into three autobiographies and an adult life of commitment. One of the leading abolitionists in the two decades that preceded the Civil War, Douglass was an associate—and sometimes internal adversary—of the movement's greatest figures: William Lloyd Garrison, Wendell Phillips, John Brown, Martin Delany, Henry Highland Garnet, William Still, Sojourner Truth, Harriet Tubman, Maria Weston Chapman, Susan B. Anthony, and others. Publisher of the *North Star*, which broke with Garrison's strictly moralist abolitionism in favor of one tied to the political sphere; staunch supporter of the women's rights movement; Civil War recruiter of black troops; advisor to President Lincoln; president of postwar Freedmen's Bank (see Douglass House entry on p. 194); Republican Party supplicant for government positions; minister to Haiti; and, late in life, prompted particularly by Ida B. Wells, fervent critic of the lynching of African Americans, Douglass led a life of heroic achievement and personal complexity.

Frederick Douglass Historical Marker
500 South Dallas Street, Baltimore, MD
Fell's Point area
Hours: Daily until sunset
Admission: Free

Frederick Douglass (see preceding entry) was the 19th century's most prominent African American and the leading black figure in the abolitionist movement. The Maryland-born activist is honored with a historical marker.

Great Blacks in Wax Museum
1601 East North Avenue, Baltimore, MD 21213
(410) 563-3404
Hours: Jan. 15–Oct. 15: Tue.–Sat., 9 A.M.–6 P.M.; Sun., 12 P.M.–6 P.M.
Oct. 16–Jan. 14: Tue.–Sat., 9 A.M.–5 P.M.; Sun., 12 P.M.–5 P.M.
Admission: Adults, $4.50; seniors and college students, $4; ages 12–17, $3; ages 2–11, $2.50; group rates at 10 percent discount

From ancient Africa through the Middle Passage, from slavery through the Civil War and Reconstruction, from the Harlem Renaissance to the Civil Rights era, the black impact on world and American history—and vice versa—is traced at the Great Blacks in Wax Museum. Rather than entertainers and sports heroes, the museum emphasizes the contributions of black scientists, inventors, social activists, statesmen, explorers, and so forth. Beginning with Akhenaton, who struggled during his reign from 1379 to 1362 B.C. to shift Egypt toward monotheism, and continuing on to the modern-era leaders of the African Independence movement (Haile Selassie, Kwame Nkrumah, Jomo Kenyatta) and the struggle against apartheid (Nelson Mandela, Steve Biko), the Great Blacks in Wax Museum underscores Africa as the locus of civilization. The transformation of abducted Africans, who are seen in the Middle Passage exhibit, into African Americans, and the latter's contributions to the nation, are traced through a score of galleries, from the Colonial Period (Crispus Attucks and Phillis Wheatley), the Underground Railroad (Harriet Tubman), the Abolitionists (Sojourner Truth, Frederick Douglass), the legal (Dred Scott, Chief Justice Taney) and illegal (John Brown, Nat Turner) antislavery struggles, the Civil War (Martin Delany) and Reconstruction (Lieutenant Governor Pinchback), explorers (Matthew Henson), educators (Booker T. Washington, Mary McLeod Bethune), scientists (Charles Drew, George Washington Carver), writers (Richard Wright, Zora Hurston, James Baldwin), civil rights activists (Fannie Lou Hamer, James Weldon Johnson, Thurgood Marshall), to the leaders of the black consciousness movement (W.E.B. Du Bois, Marcus Garvey, El Hajj Malik, Elijah Muhammad). Black men and women of outstanding achievement are both celebrated and held up for emulation here. The figures may be in wax, but the achievements celebrated are immortal.

Billie Holiday Statue
Pennsylvania Avenue, Baltimore, MD
Between Lanvale and Lafayette streets
Hours: Daily until sunset
Admission: Free

Slipping if not already plunged into prostitution by the age of 12, Eleanora Fagan was the illegitimate daughter of a woman herself born out of wedlock to a teenage mother. It was scarcely an auspicious beginning—and the life that followed, though it had its highs in several senses, was an exercise in self-destruction redeemed only by her power to transform hard experience into plaintive song. Though her voice spanned little more than an octave, Eleanora, better known as Billie Holiday, seized an audience's attention with the force and persuasion of her interpretation, earning acclaim as the greatest jazz singer of her time. Drink, drugs, deceit, and a series of worthless men, many of them pimps and almost all exploiters, put paid to a life and career now recalled in the town where she grew up by a Billie Holiday Statue.

Joshua Johnson Historical Marker
Charles and Baltimore streets, Baltimore, MD
Hopkins Plaza, downtown
Hours: Daily until sunset
Admission: Free

Joshua Johnson, America's first black portrait painter of renown, lived and worked in Baltimore from 1765 to 1830 and received national acclaim for his portraits of prominent Marylanders. His paintings captured their likenesses in the colonial two-dimensional style. For a time, the painter's studio was located near the present-day Mechanic Theater at Charles and Baltimore streets, where there is currently a historical marker commemorating Johnson.

Thurgood Marshall Statue
Pratt Street at Hopkins Place, Baltimore, MD
Hours: Daily until sunset
Admission: Free

Perhaps the truest measure of Thurgood Marshall's greatness (and of the greater opportunities of his time) is that he superceded his mentor, Charles Houston, himself a giant. Houston, born just months before the *Plessy v. Ferguson* Supreme Court decision that he would spend his lifetime challenging, was raised in a black middle-class environment. His father was an attorney; his mother, a schoolteacher who shifted to hairdressing because its income was greater. (Some things never change.) Graduating Phi Beta Kappa from Amherst College as the only African American in his class, Houston served with the 368th Regiment during World War I. With the return of peace, Houston graduated Law Review from Harvard and followed in his father's footsteps before becoming vice-dean of Howard University Law School at the age of 34 and then special counsel to the NAACP.

Marshall grew up in a Baltimore black working class family. Turned away from the University of Maryland's School of Law because he was black, Marshall ended up at Howard under Houston's tutelage. Then he followed his mentor into the service of the NAACP, eventually replacing Houston when ill health forced his retirement in 1938. Within a decade of assuming Houston's mantle, Marshall won three landmark Supreme Court cases: *Smith v. Allwright* in 1944, outlawing the "white primary"; *Morgan v. Virginia* in 1946, prohibiting segregated seating in interstate transportation; and *Shelley v. Kraemer* in 1948, declaring racially restricted housing covenants to be legally unenforceable. (See Shelley House entry on p. 426.) In his 22 appearances before the Supreme Court, Marshall failed to carry the day only three times. One of his victories was in the most significant court decision of this century: the 1954 *Brown v. Board of Education* case. (Strictly speaking, Marshall did not argue this case but rather a related one; see Sumner Elementary School entry on p. 387.)

Brown represented the capstone of Marshall's career as a litigator. Following the rise of black activism in the late 1950s, which deprecated the legal struggle,

Marshall made a timely switch to the bench, being appointed to the Court of Appeals by President Kennedy. Following a stint (1965–1967) as solicitor general of the United States, Marshall again made history by becoming the first African-American Justice of the United States Supreme Court. During his quarter-century tenure on the Court, Marshall's piercing questions, provoked by a lifetime of real-world, front-line exposure to poverty and oppression, were readily evident—unlike his earthy wit, which he usually managed to constrain. Today one of the most influential and vibrant figures of black (and white) America in the 20th century is honored with a Thurgood Marshall Statue.

Maryland Historical Society Museum and Library
201 West Monument Street, Baltimore, MD 21202
(410) 685-3750
Hours: Library: Tue.–Fri., 10 A.M.–4:30 P.M.; Sat., 9 A.M.–4:30 P.M.
Museum: Tue.–Fri., 10 A.M.–5 P.M.; Sat., 9 A.M.–5 P.M.
Admission: Adults, $3.50; seniors and college students, $2.50; children, $1.50

Three and a half centuries of an African-American presence in Maryland is alluded to or directly explored at the Maryland Historical Society Museum and Library. Perhaps the most interesting feature—since the slave experience too often defines four centuries of black America—is the society's maritime museum, which highlights the 19th-century triumph of Isaac Myers. Born a free African American in 1835, Myers apprenticed as a ship's caulker—an important job in the days of wooden-hulled ships and one he shared with Frederick Douglass. Myers's skill was rewarded, and he rose to become a supervisor in one of the largest shipyards in Baltimore. After the Civil War, he watched as white America tried to eliminate black laborers from the ranks of shipyard workers. His response was to turn to his community for financial support to establish a black-owned cooperative shipyard. The Chesapeake Marine Railway and Dry Dock proved highly successful, paying off its outstanding debts and winning U.S. government contracts. It also provided the impetus for the establishment of the all-black Baltimore Caulkers Trade Society, an early craft union, and the Colored National Labor Union. Myers's success, like that of his comrades and of African Americans generally, for too long has gone unappreciated. A stop at the museum is a start to changing our understanding of the black past.

Morgan State University
Hillen Road at Cold Spring Lane, Baltimore, MD 21239
(410) 444-3333
Hours: Murphy Gallery, Soper Library: Mon.–Fri., during normal class hours; other times by appointment
Admission: Free

Among Morgan's attractions for visitors are the Beulah Davis Collections Room at the Soper Library, which holds manuscripts, artifacts, memorabilia, and pamphlets that reflect the struggles and accomplishments of African Americans;

a collection of manuscripts, early pamphlets, and books revealing the Quaker attitude toward slavery in the U.S.; artifacts from the life of Matthew Henson (see entry on p. 239); the papers of Dr. Emmett J. Scott (1873–1957), who served as Booker T. Washington's private secretary, then as special assistant to Secretary of War Newton Baker during World War I, and then as the assistant publicity director of the Republican National Committee from 1919 to 1939; and the unique Miscellaneous Negro Newspapers Collection, sporadic editions of 19th- and 20th-century black journals, such as *The Colored Patriot* of Topeka (1882), *The Crusader* (New Orleans, 1890), and *The Huntsville Star* (Alabama, 1900). Morgan's Art Gallery is a sure winner for those with an interest in African-American artists such as Beauford Delaney, Henry O. Tanner, and Robert S. Duncanson or in the artistic productions of Africa.

NAACP Henry Lee Moon Library and National Civil Rights Archives
4805 Mt. Hope Drive, Baltimore, MD 21215-3297
(410) 358-8900
Hours: Mon.–Fri., 9 A.M.–4:30 P.M., by appointment
Admission: Free

Housed on the first floor of the national headquarters of the NAACP is an information center and reference library that highlights the legacy of America's foremost civil rights organization. The NAACP Henry Lee Moon Library and National Civil Rights Archives has issues of *Crisis* from 1910 onward; rare volumes and first editions by James Weldon Johnson, W.E.B. Du Bois, Langston Hughes, and Carter G. Woodson, among others; photographs that trace the organization's roots, efforts, and leaders; and a wealth of other material that would enable visitors with serious inquiries to uncover the impact of an organization that has decades of heavy lifting and uplifting to its credit. The library also runs a lecture series, while the headquarters' Roy Wilkins Auditorium is the site of sundry activities that celebrate and explore the African-American heritage.

Orchard Street Church and Museum
512 Orchard Street, Baltimore, MD 21201
(410) 523-8150
Hours: Tours by appointment
Admission: Free. Voluntary donations encouraged

From 1837 to 1840, slaves and former slaves labored by torchlight to construct one of the first A.M.E. churches in Baltimore. The Orchard Street Church then erected housed a congregation that dated to 1825, when a former slave, the West Indian–born Trueman Le Pratt, began holding prayer meetings in his Orchard Street home. In 1882 the congregation finished the third church structure to occupy the Orchard street site; today that building has been restored and serves as the headquarters of the Baltimore Urban League. Soon it also will house an African-American cultural museum.

CAMBRIDGE

Harriet Tubman Historical Sites
c/o Harriet Tubman Coalition, 424 Race Street, Box 1164, Cambridge, MD 21613
(410) 228-0401
Hours: Tours of the four sites: Mon.–Fri., 10 A.M.–4 P.M., by appointment
The historical marker, church, and wharf are on view daily until sunset, free of charge
Admission: Guided tours: Adults 19 and older, $5; children 8–18, $3; under 8, free. Groups of 25 or more: adults, $4; children, $2.50

Bazzell Methodist Episcopal Church
Bucktown Road, Cambridge, MD 21613

Long Wharf
High Street, Cambridge, MD 21613

Stanley Institute
2365 Church Creek Road, Cambridge, MD 21613

Harriet Tubman Historical Marker
Bucktown Road, Cambridge, MD 21613
8 miles south of Cambridge, on Maryland 397

Harriet Tubman—slave; runaway; gun-toting, Dixie-raiding, slave-stealing Underground Railroad conductor; militant abolitionist and collaborator with John Brown, Union spy and scout—lived a life of drama by necessity and purpose by conviction. Had she not been black, short, squat, and missing several front teeth, and had she not spoken in a pronounced southern black dialect, she long ago would have been the subject of a Hollywood epic. Like so many of the 19th-century, slave-born African-American giants (Booker T. Washington and George Washington Carver come to mind), Tubman was never certain of the year of her birth. Of most everything else she was very certain indeed: God ruled the world, she must be free, her people must go free, and any slave who thought to back out of one of her freedom-bound expeditions and thus put it and her at risk would promptly meet his or her Maker. In 1849 Tubman ran to freedom, leaving behind her free husband (who refused to accompany her, preferring if not the restrictions of a slave state at least a new wife, which he shortly took), and her parents, sisters, and brothers. She viewed her freedom both as intrinsically necessary to her humanity and as a means and obligation to everyone shackled by slavery. Nineteen times or more Tubman hazarded her freedom—and her life—behind slavery's lines, bringing her family and hundreds of others out of bondage. Though the price on her head rose to $40,000, neither her courage nor her adamant determination faltered. Time and again, armed with a

Harriet Tubman escaped from bondage and then repeatedly returned to slavery's strongholds in order to free her brethren.

pistol and a fervent belief in God's protection, Tubman walked down country lanes, on paths through fields, and in small streams to rescue her brethren. For most abolitionists the opening of the Civil War offered hope and protection; for Tubman it offered more hazard, as the Union recruited her services as a spy and a scout for Colonel James Montgomery's Second Carolina Volunteers. Once again, though this time in unfamiliar terrain, Tubman forayed in Dixie.

Today, at no greater hazard than that offered every day on America's roads, you can make a pilgrimage to the site of the Brodas Plantation on which Tubman was born and where a historical marker stands; to the nearby Bazzel Methodist Episcopal Church, built on the site where Tubman worshipped in open-air services in the early 1800s; to Long Wharf, where Tubman arrived by boat and boldly freed her sister, who was being sold on the courthouse doorsteps a few blocks away; and to Stanley Institute, once one of Maryland's few African-American community schools and now the sole African-American museum on Maryland's Eastern Shore. The Harriet Tubman Coalition provides a slide show at the Dorchester County Library that not only places these sites in context but also offers enlightenment, inspiration, and enjoyment.

CATONSVILLE

Benjamin Banneker Marker
Mount Gilboa A.M.E. Church, 2312 Westchester Avenue, Catonsville, MD 21228
Hours: Daily until sunset
Admission: Free

Near the Mount Gilboa A.M.E. Church in the Oella neighborhood of Catonsville is a monument to Maryland's most historically significant African-American scientist, Benjamin Banneker. (See entries on pp. 168 and 238.)

COLUMBIA

Maryland Museum of African Art
P.O. Box 1105, 5430 Vantage Point Road, Columbia, MD 21044
(410) 730-7105; (301) 596-0051
Hours: Tue.–Fri., 10 A.M.–4 P.M.; Sun., 12 P.M.–4 P.M. Groups of 15 or more and other hours, by appointment
Admission: Voluntary donations encouraged

More than 200 objects of beauty and utility from the Mother Continent—including masks, textiles, ceremonial statues, household implements, body jewelry, weapons, funerary items, pottery, musical instruments, and woodworking tools—whet one's appetite for a second helping at the Maryland Museum of African Art. Cultures from the modern-day nation-states of Nigeria, Guinea, Mali, Burundi, Swaziland, and others are highlighted. A large (10 feet by 6½ feet) ceremonial mask of the Chewa people is among the museum's more notable—and certainly noticeable—attractions. Visitors are astounded to learn that the *kasiyamaliro* mask is worn by a Chewa dancer during certain male initiation and funeral ceremonies. As seeing is believing, the dancer's balance and skill are made manifest with the aid of a field video of an initiation ceremony.

Howard County Center of African-American Culture
1 Commerce Center, Columbia, MD 21044
(410) 715-1921; (410) 997-3685; (410) 730-6446
Opposite the Columbia Mall
Hours: Wed.–Fri., 10 A.M.–5 P.M.; Sat., 10 A.M.–1 P.M.; or by appointment
Admission: Voluntary donations encouraged

Columbia, Maryland, not only offers a slice of Africa, it also provides glimpses into local black heritage at the Howard County Center of African-American Culture. This new, small museum utilizes the donated artifacts of leading Howard County black families as an avenue to explore African-American achievement. It also holds a broad collection of black-oriented books, periodicals, and slides.

HOLLYWOOD

Sotterley
Sotterley Mansion Foundation, Box 67, Hollywood, MD 20636
(301) 373-2280
Hours: June–Sept.: Tue.–Sun., 11 A.M.–5 P.M.; Apr.–May and Oct.–Nov.: by appointment
Admission: Adults, $5; seniors, $4; ages 6–16, $2; admission to the grounds, $1

Almost three and a half centuries ago, Maryland's proprietor, Lord Calvert, issued a manorial grant of land along the Patuxent River. In time, Sotterley Plantation arose on this property, whose waterfront landing became a major port of entry in southern Maryland, witnessing the export of tobacco and the importation of Europe's manufactured goods. From 1729, when George Plater II acquired Sotterley along with the widow he married, generations of Platers supported their public careers—including delegate to the Continental Congress, president of the State Convention that ratified the U.S. Constitution, and an early Maryland governorship—on the wealth they derived as major landowners and merchants, wealth whose foundation was the labor of enslaved African Americans.

Today Sotterley remains a working farm and a private residence—but one that is also a public resource available to expand our knowledge of English colonization, African-American slavery, Maryland enterprise, and American democracy. In addition to strolling through Sotterley Mansion, which dates back to 1717, today's visitors can wander the grounds and gardens—which provide a somewhat clearer picture of what life was like for those who served the mansion's masters. The starkest contrast to the mansion, of course, is found at the extant 18th-century slave quarters, a plank one-room cabin. Complementing this portrait are sundry outbuildings where much of the (African-American) labor of a working plantation was performed: a spinning cottage, which began around 1780 as a small frame building; the 200-year-old corn crib, which now houses the farm exhibit of 19th- and 20th-century implements required to operate a plantation; the Necessary, which speaks for itself though without the effluvium of yesteryear; and the gardens, which still please the eye of the most critical visitor though they are no longer tended by the disenfranchised. Also on view are buildings somewhat more associated with the Great Family than with their human property: the 1757 customs warehouse, which underscored the Platers' connection to those who regulated colonial trade; the smokehouse, whose wares never graced—absent risky dexterity—the slaves' bowls; the gatehouses and the rolling road down which Sotterley's wares traveled to waiting ships and up which continental goods were hauled for the pleasure of the mansion house's residents. A good (and bad) bit of Maryland's colonial, federal, and antebellum history is embraced at Sotterley.

OXON HILL

Sojourner Truth Collection
Oxon Hill Library; 6200 Oxon Hill Road, Oxon Hill, MD 20745
(301) 839-2400
Hours: Mon.–Thu., 10 A.M.–9 P.M.; Fri., 10 A.M.–6 P.M.; Sat., 10 A.M.–5 P.M.; Sun. (Oct.–May), 1 P.M.–5 P.M.
Admission: Free

The six-foot, illiterate mystic who gained fame as the abolitionist and feminist advocate Sojourner Truth (see entries on pp. 392 and 432) was born with the slave name Isabella in 1797 in New York. Before the age of 30 she had borne five children to a fellow slave, at least one of whom was sold away from her. Escaping slavery one year before its mandatory emancipation in the state, she soon fell under the sway of evangelical religion, whose tenets she preached on New York City's streets before joining a utopian community. By the 1840s she was active in the abolitionist movement and had shed her slave name for one that clearly defined the rest of her life as a peripatetic orator. Before the war she campaigned for black and female liberties. During the war she campaigned to raise food and clothing for black regiments. After the war she campaigned for freedpeople.

Twenty-five years ago, at the height of the intersection of the black consciousness and civil rights movements, the Oxon Hill Branch Library was built. Realizing that too little research had been conducted in the field of black studies, the community decided that the library would house a special collection exploring the history, triumphs, and travails of African Americans. Today the Sojourner Truth Collection consists of more than 3,300 catalogued items, many of which are rare or out-of-print manuscripts and books, periodicals, posters, pictures, and pamphlets. The range of subject matter embraces slave narratives, the African-American presence in Maryland, slavery and antislavery tracts, and modern black literature. Not only the collection's name is apt; its location is too. In 1867 the blacksmith and former slave Henry Hatton started construction of the Oxon Hill school to educate freedmen—a subject dear to the heart of Sojourner Truth.

ROCKVILLE

Uncle Tom's Cabin
Old Georgetown Road, Rockville, MD
(301) 762-1492
Hours: Daily until sunset
Admission: Not open to the public. Exterior viewing only

Still standing in Rockville, Maryland, *attached to a private residence and not open to the public*, is a former home of Josiah Henson, whose life in, escape from, and deepening resistance to slavery made him one of the models for Uncle Tom in Harriet Beecher Stowe's hugely influential *Uncle Tom's Cabin*. (Stowe's 1852 novel sold 3,000 copies on the first day of its publication and 300,000 within the year, and was probably the most effective instrument of its day in portraying the horrors of slavery.) Henson (1789–1883) was slave-born on the Riley Plantation in Maryland in the first year of Washington's presidency, and as a child watched as his brothers and sisters were sold away to new masters. By his early manhood he was working as an overseer on the Riley estate. In 1825 he was placed in charge of his wife, two children, and 28 other slaves who were shipped to their master's brother in Kentucky. This journey crossed the free territory of Cincinnati, Ohio, where Henson refused to permit his charges to escape bondage. In Kentucky Henson again worked as an estate overseer, was ordained a minister in the Methodist Episcopal Church, and began to learn to read. His new opportunities permitted him to earn an income, with which he intended to purchase his and his family's freedom. But when his master raised freedom's price from $300 to $1,000 and then in 1830 looked likely to sell him south, Henson loaded his family on a boat and crossed the Ohio River, the start of a journey that would take him first to Canada and then into the mass consciousness of America.

Henson (see Uncle Tom's Cabin entry on p. 549) lived the rest of his life in Canada (and is buried there), where in 1841 he and the white Ohio abolitionist Hiram Wilson founded the all-black Dawn community in Colchester, near Chatham, Ontario. There they established a school to train escaped African Americans in the agricultural and mechanical arts. Around the school there soon grew a community of 500 souls, many of whom owned adjoining land and still more of whom heard the Reverend Henson preach in the wooden church on the 200-acre estate. In 1848 Henson published a biographical narrative, *The Life of Josiah Henson, Formerly a Slave, Now an Inhabitant of Canada*, and the following year he spoke with Harriet Beecher Stowe (see First Parish entry on p. 236 and Stowe entry on p. 226) in Boston, who later, in "A Key To Uncle Tom's Cabin," acknowledged Henson's book as a source of factual information for her fictional work. With the publication of Stowe's novel, Henson became forever identified as Uncle Tom—a mixed blessing. Henson's later life had its ups and downs, and included speaking tours of the United States and Great Britain and the collapse of the Dawn community amid charges of corruption leveled by the black journalist (and strong opponent of all-black communities) Mary Ann Shadd.

Henson's journey from slavery in Maryland to freedom in Canada was by no means unique: In the first six decades of the 19th century an estimated 40,000 runaway slaves started new lives north of the border, a journey made the more enticing following passage of the Fugitive Slave Act, which threatened the haven that northern states offered until then. What is unique, however, is the extant Maryland home of the man who came to symbolize the oppression of slavery.

SAINT MARYS CITY

Historic Saint Marys City
Saint Clements Island, P.O. Box 39, Saint Marys City, MD 20686
(301) 862-0960
Hours: Wed.–Sun., 10 A.M.–5 P.M.
Admission: Adults, $5; seniors, $4; children, $3; under 6, free

On a March day in 1634, the *Ark*, bound from England in the service of the Catholic peer Lord Baltimore, sailed up the Potomac River and landed the founding members of an experiment that became the state of Maryland. A son of Africa was among those who stepped from the ship onto soil previously untouched by people other than America's aboriginals. Mathias de Sousa, of African and Portuguese descent, arrived as one of nine indentured servants of Jesuit missionaries. His life in Maryland was almost stereotypically "American"—immigration, hard work on the frontier, advancement, and success. More interestingly, his life is evidence of what America briefly was, before it became defined by slavery and race. However much de Sousa's contemporaries noticed his blackness, it affected his status little if at all. Like white servants, de Sousa served out his indenture; like them he lived or died from disease, accident, or conflict as the fates willed; like them, once his indenture was served, he could vote, testify in court, and acquire land; like them he was a full member of the community. In fact, de Sousa prospered within his community. His ability was recognized and utilized: The Jesuits placed him in charge of the boat and the cargo (and the white crew) that sailed to trade with local Indians. Already the first black Marylander, de Sousa in 1642 became the first black member of the Maryland Assembly. Most intriguingly of all, de Sousa's color in a Maryland not yet defined by slavery is known only by historical accident. Had he a common English name, some further identification, ethnic or occupational, might have been appended. As he did not, only a lawsuit and the desire to supply a full range of corroborating detail tell us today that de Sousa was a mulatto.

Today there is a window through which we can see early Maryland, an America brutish but not yet corrupted by mass slavery. Where the *Ark*'s passengers stepped ashore, there they founded Saint Marys, the fourth permanent English settlement in America and Maryland's capital until 1695. Historic Saint Marys City is an 800-acre outdoor living history museum with three major exhibit areas. The Brentland Farm Visitor Center introduces visitors to the 17th century; the Governor's Field invites a walk through the reconstructed State House of 1676, Farthing's Ordinary (a re-created 17th-century inn), and the *Dove* (a square-rigged replica of *Ark*'s companion on that voyage of three and a half centuries ago); and the Godiah Spray Tobacco Plantation recalls a working farm of the 1660s—and the crop whose intense labor requirements and large profits spurred the mass enslavement of Africans. Throughout Historic Saint Marys, costumed interpreters, including on occasion African-American ones, portray the reality of what was then America's frontier, while on the grounds of the outdoor museum there stands a memorial to de Sousa.

SHARPSBURG

Antietam National Battlefield
P.O. Box 158, 5831 Dunbar Church Road, Sharpsburg, MD 21782
(301) 432-5124
Hours: Daily, 8:30 A.M.–5 P.M.
Admission: Free

Lee's victory at Second Bull Run in August 1862 drove the federal army from Virginia and placed the Union in peril of Confederate invasion. A southern triumph on a northern battlefield might have secured the secessionist government European recognition, or at least a widening of its ranks by the addition of slave border states that to date had remained neutral in the war. At the very least, a Confederate victory in the North might have brought in its wake a despondent Union's offer of peace negotiations. Maryland seemed the ideal target for Lee's aggression. A neighboring slave state, "allied to the States of the South by the strongest social, political and commercial ties"—in the words of the proclamation issued by Lee as he entered Maryland at the head of 45,000 troops—might well secede under the protection of a Confederate army that had just secured victory within its borders.

Thus, early in September, with regimental bands playing "Maryland, My Maryland," the Army of Northern Virginia forded the Potomac River north of Leesburg. Justly confident in the leadership of the man who in the last ten weeks had won resounding victories against superior forces in the Seven Days and Second Bull Run battles, the Confederates gathered at Frederick, Maryland. Less than a week later, almost 90,000 Union troops speedily reorganized by General George B. McClellan marched toward Lee. Lee's forces initially were depleted by the absence of Stonewall Jackson's troops—sent southeast to invest Harpers Ferry (see entry on p. 207)—and Longstreet's Corps, sent northwest toward Boonsboro. On September 17, near the town of Sharpsburg lying between the Potomac River and Antietam Creek, the two armies clashed in what is still the single bloodiest day of battle in U.S. military history. Though no precise casualty figures have ever been calculated, about 23,000 men were killed or wounded. Fighting began at dawn with Union general Joseph Hooker's attack on the reduced forces Jackson had night-marched from Harpers Ferry. It ended late in the afternoon when the remainder of Jackson's contingent, racing from Harpers Ferry, suddenly arrived on the left flank of General Ambrose Burnside's Union forces and drove them headlong into flight, back across an Antietam Creek that ran red that day. Though victorious, Lee's army suffered terribly, losing about a quarter of its strength, and was in no shape to continue its northern invasion against the larger Union forces. So Lee bid good-bye to Maryland—which had never rallied to his presence—and successfully slipped away south, back across the Potomac.

Though at this stage of the war African Americans were excluded from the Union army and hence did not take part in the battle southerners called Sharpsburg and northerners termed Antietam, the blood-sodden battlefield held enormous significance for them. The Confederacy's inability to wage war in the North, rally Maryland to the secessionist cause, or secure European recognition was a strategic defeat. More immediately and pertinently, Lee's tactical withdrawal enabled the Union to proclaim victory. And this claim of victory, however spurious, enabled Lincoln to issue the Emancipation Proclamation that for months had awaited something other than a context of defeat to define its purpose.

Though the Emancipation Proclamation was riven with irony—applying only to those places where it could not be enforced and quite calculatedly not applying to border slave states that remained loyal to the Union or even to those parts of the Confederacy occupied by Union troops prior to its effective date of January 1, 1863—it had a profound consequence: It turned the Civil War from a struggle to preserve the Union into a war against slavery. That transformation, that revolution, began on a Maryland field of battle where more than 12,000 Union soldiers fell in one day. Today visitors to the Antietam National Battlefield have access to a museum and markers that interpret the battle and its consequences for America.

Kennedy Farmhouse
2406 Chestnut Grove Road, Sharpsburg, MD 21782
(301) 432-2666
Hours: Sat.–Sun., 9 A.M.–5 P.M.; tours by appointment
Admission: Voluntary donations requested

LIBRARY OF CONGRESS

Determined to overthrow slavery, John Brown and his colleagues gathered at the Kennedy Farmhouse before raiding the government arsenal at Harpers Ferry.

In the summer of 1859 the zealous abolitionist John Brown, under the assumed name of Isaac Smith, arrived in Maryland, his penultimate step before mounting the gallows. On the Kennedy farm near Hagerstown, Brown found a base of operations from which he and his comrades could move on the federal arsenal at Harpers Ferry.

For three and a half months, Brown and his comrades (16 whites, including three of his sons, and five African Americans) gathered in the Kennedy Farmhouse, plotted their coup, hid from the neighbors either their presence or their identities, and grew increasingly testy as delay piled upon delay. Finally, late in the evening of October 16, 1859, Brown and his 21 men left the Kennedy Farm and rode into American history.

Today the Kennedy Farmhouse still stands—and is easily one of Maryland's most historically significant sites. Thanks to an ink drawing done within a month of the raid on Harpers Ferry and to detailed descriptions and drawings of Annie Brown, who as a 15-year-old spent part of the summer in the house with her father and brothers and the other raiders, the Kennedy Farmhouse looks as it did that summer before the world turned upside down. Four lifelike mannequins, including one of the austere Brown, now inhabit the house. The farmhouse's present owner, South Trimble Lynn, who is largely responsible for saving a piece of African-American history that had passed through the hands of the financially troubled Black Elks of America and onto the market, guides people through the house and conveys both the depth of his knowledge of the raiders and his conviction that "the Kennedy Farm is a pure piece of American history. The raid on Harpers Ferry set loose the lightning that changed this land. The American Civil War started in this living room, where the raid was planned."

MASSACHUSETTS

Office of Travel and Tourism
100 Cambridge Street, 13th floor, Boston, MA 02202
(800) 447-MASS; (617) 727-3201
Hours: Mon.–Fri., 8:45 A.M.–5 P.M.

BOSTON

Convention & Visitors Bureau
Box 490, Prudential Tower, Suite 400, Boston, MA 02199
(617) 536-4100
Hours: Mon.–Fri., 8:30 A.M.–5 P.M.

Boston National Historical Visitor Center
15 State Street, Boston, MA 02109
(617) 242-5642
Hours: Daily, 9 A.M.–5 P.M.

Ask for the "Black Heritage Trail" brochure, which outlines a 1½-mile walk that introduces the visitor to Boston's black past.

African Meeting House
8 Smith Court, Boston, MA 02114
(617) 742-1854
Hours: Mon.–Fri., 10 A.M.–4 P.M.
Admission: Free

Within most colonial and Federal era churches, members were segregated by race, with African Americans being restricted to balcony pews and denied voting privileges on matters of church policy and doctrine. Prominent in challenging this pattern was the black Baptist preacher Thomas Paul of New Hampshire. All along the northeastern seabord, Paul led African Americans into independent black churches. (See Abyssinian Baptist Church entry on p. 297.) In 1805 Paul and 20 members formed the First African Baptist Church in Boston. The following year they built a house of worship, which commonly was called the African Meeting House and which today is the oldest black church building standing in the United States. On the day they inaugurated their church, African Americans again sat in its balcony—*but this time by choice:* To honor others, they reserved the first-floor seats for those guests "benevolently disposed to the Africans." Two years later a school for black children opened in its basement, and the building began its long history of service as the center of Boston's black community.

Crispus Attucks Monument, Plaque and Burial Site
Boston Common
(617) 742-5415
Located in a park surrounded by Tremont, Park, Boylston, and Beacon streets
Hours: Daily until sunset
Admission: Free

Between the power of myth, the fog of the past, class prejudice, and the "diseased imagination" of racism, it is hard to get a real grasp on Crispus Attucks, who has entered history as an (African-) American martyr to American independence—but who may well have been principally an aggressive, intoxicated lout who made a major and irrevocable error of judgment. Attucks, of mixed African and Indian descent to judge by local lore, was one of the five men killed by British troops in the "Boston Massacre" of 1770. Brandishing a big stick but failing to foresee the other half of Teddy Roosevelt's admonition, he and companions intruded upon a developing confrontation between Boston citizens and British troops, adding fuel to the flames (which soon would consume him) by crying "Damn them, they dare not fire . . . kill the dogs, knock them over" and by clubbing a British soldier, whose comrades swiftly proved upon Attucks's body that they did indeed dare fire.

Though the fallen Attucks sooner was wrapped in the mantle of martyr than in a shroud, privately the "better sort" of proto-patriots were less certain of his merit. John Adams—the first in his family to attend college; theorist of the Anti-Stamp Act movement of 1765; key figure in the American Revolution; second president of the United States; husband of Abigail, a noted abolitionist; and throughout his long life a man who valued and embodied the virtues of the better sort—defended the principle that an accused person deserves a vigorous defense by defending the British troops in court. Attucks, he there said, was one of "a motley rabble of saucy boys, negroes and molattoes, Irish teagues and outlandish jack-tarrs . . . [who] happening to be here, shall sally out upon their thoughtless enterprises, at the head of such a rabble of negroes. &c., as they can collect together . . . to have this reinforcement coming down under the command of a stout mulatto fellow, whose very looks was enough to terrify any person, what had not the soldiers then to fear?"

Five years later the American Revolution erupted and Attucks's life would be justified by his death. To his memory a later generation would dedicate a plaque on State Street on the spot where he fell and a monument on nearby Boston Common. Also nearby at the corner of Tremont and Bromfield streets is the Granary Burial Ground, where Attucks and his fellow victims were interred in a common grave as Boston's church bells tolled a martyrs' farewell.

Bunker Hill Monument
Breed's Hill, Monument Square, Boston, MA 02128
(617) 242-5641
Hours: Daily, 9 A.M.–5 P.M.
Admission: Free

Close-quarter combat opened shortly after 3:00 P.M. on the afternoon of July 17, 1775, and closed less than three hours later. The Battle of Bunker Hill was no minor confrontation; it was a bloody engagement—made the more so by the six-hour delay in the British attack that enabled the Americans to organize and entrench. Of the approximately 1,500 colonial militia who actually saw combat, about 30 percent were killed, wounded, or captured. British troops displayed unbelievable courage in repeatedly attacking barricaded men whose (at least initially) disciplined fire in ranks prevented the attackers from closing with their bayonets. Of General Howe's British force of 2,500, the casualties totaled 1,150, among whom officers figured disproportionately. Peter Salem and Salem Poor, both of whom earned special distinction for their bravery, were among the score or so African Americans who fought in the colonial ranks and wreaked ruin especially upon his Majesty's grenadier and light infantry companies. Toward the close of battle, as the Americans' ammunition ran out, the surviving British scrambled over the last parapet, their officers in the forefront. There, as he stood atop the south wall waving his sword to encourage his men in their third assault, Major Pitcairn, who had led the British forces at Lexington, was slain by Peter Salem (and numerous others). Salem's shot knocked the major back over the wall but did not delay his men, who, in an intense hand-to-hand clash amid blinding dust, mortally bayoneted at least 30 Americans who had been reduced to fighting with musket butts and rocks. No other Revolutionary War battle was ever more desperately fought.

Today at the Bunker Hill Monument visitors view exhibits that interpret and an obelisk that commemorates the first major battle of the Revolution. Among the exhibits is the musket Peter Salem wielded that day and then later at the Revolutionary War battles of Saratoga and Stony Point. Visitors also may view the city from the top of the monument, but be forewarned: While there are 294 steps, there is no elevator.

Prince Hall Monument
Copp's Hill Burying Ground, Hull and Snowhill streets, Boston, MA 02112
Hours: Daily until sunset
Admission: Free

The background—year and place of birth, racial ancestry and legal status—and the Revolutionary War role of the most prominent late-18th-century black personage in Boston, Prince Hall, remain unclear. But whether freeborn in 1748 in Barbados of mixed English and mulatto ancestry or born more than a decade earlier in parts unknown and enslaved, whether participant at the Battle of Bunker Hill or simply small businessman making goods for the colonial army, Hall's repeated efforts to defend and advance the rights of African Americans shine forth clearly.

Shortly before the battles of Lexington and Concord in 1775, Hall and 14 other free blacks were enrolled in a British army lodge of the Freemasons in Boston. When the British troops abandoned the city a year later, Hall and his comrades received from their departing sponsors a provisional permit for their own African Lodge No. 1. For the next three decades, Prince Hall and this autonomous black lodge—arguably the first African-American institution in the United States—would be in the forefront of the black civil rights struggle in America, petitioning for an end to slavery, for the right of free black children to attend public schools, and for a black return to the African homeland. In the first (1787) formal, black-inspired proposal for a return to the Mother Continent, Hall and his comrades noted:

> We, or our ancestors have been taken from all our dear connections, and brought from Africa and put into a state of slavery in this country; from which unhappy situation we have been lately in some measure delivered by the new constitution [of Massachusetts]. . . . But we yet find ourselves, in many respects, in very disagreeable and disadvantageous circumstances; most of which must attend us so long as we and our children live in America.

A year after the submission of this petition, three free black Bostonians were lured aboard a ship and transported to slavery in the West Indies. Hall rallied the black Masons, who protested the abduction and secured the return of the three men. The black Mason–inspired publicity surrounding this case laid the foundation for the state court's decision denying slave ships the right to enter Massachusetts ports.

Until his death in 1807, Hall remained the leading figure in Boston's black community, ceaselessly struggling to expand the boundaries of black rights. His last years were brightened with the knowledge that in Haiti the diaspora forged what he in miniature had created in African Lodge No. 1, an autonomous black society. Today, on the Snowhill Street side of Copp's Hill Burying Ground, a cemetery dating back to 1659, visitors to Boston will find the grave of Prince Hall, founder of the oldest continuous black social organization in the United States. Nearby the Prince Hall Monument honors the man.

Faneuil Hall
Faneuil Hall Square, Merchants Row, Boston, MA 02109
(617) 242-5675
Hours: Daily, 9 A.M.–5 P.M.
Admission: Free

Once the colonial meeting place of anti-British agitators, Faneuil Hall is now a museum with a military focus. While Faneuil displays a painting of the shooting of Crispus Attucks and the other martyrs of the "Boston Massacre," it perhaps is more interesting as the site of the 1850 founding of the Boston Vigilance Committee. Inspired by the passage of the Fugitive Slave Act, Boston's black and white abolitionists came together in the committee to aid runaways and foil federal marshals intent on upholding the new law.

Among the many African Americans active on the committee was Lewis Hayden (1811–1889). Hayden's life was an epic: His mother beaten into insanity for refusing the advances of her owner and his family sundered on the auction block, Hayden was exchanged by his master for a pair of carriage horses. After learning to read from discarded newspapers and a Bible, Hayden ran to freedom in Canada with his wife and child, but returned to the U.S. to participate in the struggle against slavery. In addition to his work with the Boston Vigilance Committee, Hayden turned his home into a fugitive shelter, which he heavily fortified. The leader of Boston's black community, Hayden was utterly resolute and quite willing to stand outside the law: When slave catchers approached his home to seize one couple, they found him on his front porch heavily armed and surrounded by barrels of gunpowder and a torch. The leader of the 1851 rescue of Shadrach and of the failed 1854 attempt to free Anthony Burns, Hayden was a committed adherent of John Brown, an influential figure in the raising of the 54th and 55th Massachusetts Regiments, an active Freemason, a state senator (1873), a co-founder of the Boston Museum of Fine Arts, and a supporter of the women's movement.

Robert Gould Shaw and 54th Regiment Memorial
Intersection of Beacon and Park streets, Boston, MA 02133
(617) 522-2639 (National Park Service, Boston)
Hours: Daily until sunset
Admission: Free

Before motion pictures, heroes were honored with monuments. At the entrance to Boston Common is a bas-relief monument executed by Augustus Saint-Gaudens honoring the men and the commander of the 54th Regiment, one of the first and certainly the most renowned African-American unit in the Civil War. The 54th's renown predated its heroic efforts in the assault on Battery Wagner at Charleston, South Carolina. (See entry on p. 135.) Unlike its unknown predecessor, the 1st Kansas Colored Regiment (see Fort Scott entry on p. 379), the 54th was raised amid great publicity—its chief promoters were Frederick Douglass and John Andrew, the abolitionist governor of Massachusetts, both of whom had long advocated recruiting black troops—and carried in its black ranks the sons of the famous and in its white officer corps the sons of the prominent. Two of Frederick Douglass's sons (Lewis and Charles) were early recruits; they were joined by the grandson of Sojourner Truth (James Caldwell) and the son of Martin Delany (Toussaint). The 29 white officers of the 1,000 men eventually recruited were carefully selected, primarily from among the sons of socially and commercially prominent abolitionists. Robert Gould Shaw of the 2nd Massachusetts Infantry Regiment, then 25 and never to be 26, became the new regiment's colonel.

After shipping out to Hilton Head Island, South Carolina, the unit saw service at Darien, Georgia (see St. Andrew's entry on p. 72), and in the attack on Battery Wagner at Charleston, South Carolina. In the latter assault on July 18, 1863, the unit suffered casualties in excess of 40 percent, losing Shaw in the bargain. Though the assault was unsuccessful, the 54th's courage matched the performance of black troops at the contemporaneous Louisiana battle of Port Hudson (see entry on p. 94) and ensured both that African Americans would continue to be recruited and that they would see service in line regiments rather than solely in labor battalions.

While they were establishing their credibility as combat troops, the men of the 54th learned that they and other black soldiers would continue to be paid, regardless of their rank, at the flat rate of laborers, $7 to $10 monthly. Different black units took different approaches to protesting the pay inequality. (In addition to a clothing allowance, white privates and corporals earned $13; sergeants—such as William Carney, who won the Medal of Honor for his actions on July 18—$17; first sergeants, $20; master sergeants, $21.) The 3rd South Carolina Regiment, composed principally of liberated slaves, downed their guns and refused to fight. One of their sergeants, William Walker, judged the ringleader of the protest, was tried for mutiny and shot. The 54th, however, simply refused to accept the unequal pay and continued to serve, though without recompense. They also respectfully refused the Massachusetts legislature's offer to make up the pay differential, writing that they were unwilling "that the Federal Government should throw mud" at them, "even though Massachusetts stands ready to wipe it off." Not until June 1864 would the U.S. Congress end the racial disparity in pay—and then only for soldiers who had been free within a week of the war's outbreak. Finally, in September 1864, the 54th received its first pay since enlisting.

Though the Robert Gould Shaw and 54th Regiment Memorial was dedicated in 1897, the same year Carney received his Medal of Honor nomination, its origin may be said to date back to 1847, when Joshua B. Smith fled slavery in North Carolina. In freedom, Smith served in the Shaw household, before going on to become a caterer, the initiator of a fund to raise a memorial to the heroes of Battery Wagner, and a member of the Massachusetts legislature.

George Middleton House
5 Pinckney Street, Boston, MA 02114
Hours: Daily until sunset
Admission: Not open to the public. Exterior viewing only

Black, "intemperate and profane . . . ," George Middleton commanded an all-black unit, the "Bucks of America," in the Revolutionary War. According to the pioneer 19th-century African-American historian W. C. Nell, at the end of the war John Hancock reviewed the passing Bucks from his front doorstep and presented Colonel Middleton and his men with a silk banner bearing Hancock's and Middleton's initials, the figures of a buck and a pine tree, and the words "The Bucks of America." Today the George Middleton House, built in 1797, is the oldest extant home of an African American on Beacon Hill. It is a *private residence not open to the public*.

Abiel Smith School and Museum of Afro-American History
46 Joy Street, Boston, MA 02114
(617) 742-1854
Hours: Tue.–Fri., 10 A.M.–4 P.M.
Admission: Free

The year 1787 was a busy one for Prince Hall. He successfully petitioned the Mother Grand Lodge of the Free and Accepted Masons in England for formal acceptance of his decade-old, provisionally established black Masons lodge. (See Prince Hall Monument entry on p. 261.) Hall (and other local African-American colleagues) also penned petitions to the Massachusetts legislature seeking aid for an African colonization scheme and requesting permission for black children to attend Boston's public school system. These petitions were rejected. Eleven years later, still in search of an education for their children, black parents shifted their approach and petitioned for state support of a racially separate school. Upon this petition's rejection, a community grammar school was started in the home of Prince Hall's son, Primus. A decade later this school moved to the basement of the African Meeting House. (See entry on p. 259.)

Not until the 1820s did Boston open two (segregated) primary schools for black children. In 1834, with a bequest from Abiel Smith, the city opened a grammar and primary school that replaced the one run from the African Meeting House. For two decades the Abiel Smith School served Boston's black children, finally closing after a lengthy struggle to end school desegregation in antebellum Boston. This struggle was led by W. C. Nell, a former pupil at the African Meeting House School, who formed the Equal School Association and called for a black boycott of the Smith School. In 1848 a black parent who had to walk his daughter past five white schools in order to reach Smith sued the city under an ordinance prohibiting denial of school instruction to children. The parent's case was argued in court by Charles Sumner, the future Radical Republican leader in the U.S. Senate and martyr to the crippling beating inflicted on the Senate floor by South Carolina's congressman, Preston Brooks. Sumner was aided by Robert Morris, one of America's first black attorneys and a later participant in the 1851 rescue of Shadrach, an escaped slave who had fallen into the clutches of U.S. marshals. Despite Sumner's and Morris's pleas, the case was lost on the grounds that Smith's instruction was not inferior to that offered in white schools—an interesting commentary on the quality of the black school and a hint of the "separate but equal" doctrine pursued by later southern segregationists. Failing in the judicial sphere, the social issue perhaps more appropriately was taken to the state legislature, which finally in 1855 outlawed school desegregation—which at that time in Massachusetts was practiced only in Boston.

Today the Smith School houses the Museum of Afro-American History, which traces three centuries of African-American contributions to New England. Available at the museum are a "Black Heritage Trail" brochure, which outlines a 1½-mile walk that introduces the visitor to Boston's black past and tours of Boston's black heritage sites.

Museum of Fine Arts
Huntington Avenue and The Fenway, Boston, MA 02115
(617) 267-9300
Hours: Tue., 10 A.M.–4:45 P.M.; Wed., 10 A.M.–9:45 P.M.;
Thu.–Sun., 10 A.M.–4:45 P.M.
Admission: Adults, $7; seniors and college students, $6; ages 6–17, $3.50

African sculpture, particularly of the Egyptian and Nubian cultures, paintings by African Americans, and a drawing of the 54th Massachusetts Regiment (see Robert Gould Shaw and 54th Regiment entry on p. 263; and St. Andrew's entry on p. 72) marching into Charleston following the town's fall in February 1865 invite a stroll through the Museum of Fine Arts. The drawing was executed by Thomas Nast, America's most influential 19th-century political cartoonist and the man who effectively created the party symbols of the donkey and the elephant as Democrats and Republicans, respectively.

Museum of the National Center of Afro-American Artists
300 Walnut Avenue, Boston, MA 02119
(617) 442-8614
Hours: Daily, 12 P.M.–5 P.M.
Admission: Adults, $1.25; seniors and students, 50 cents

The culture and visual arts heritage of Africa and the diaspora are explored at the Museum of the National Center of Afro-American Artists. Its more than 4,000 works of African and Caribbean art are complemented by its permanent collection of drawings and prints of contemporary black artists and by changing exhibitions of works in various media.

Old South Meetinghouse
310 Washington Street, Boston, MA 02108
(617) 482-6439
Hours: Apr. 1–Oct. 31: daily, 9:30 A.M.–5 P.M. Rest of year: Mon.–Fri., 10 A.M.–4 P.M.; Sat.–Sun., 10 A.M.–5 P.M.
Admission: Adults, $2.50; seniors and college students, $2; ages 6–17, $1; under 6, free

"Some view our sable race with scornful eye, / 'Their colour is a diabolic die.' / *Remember, Christians, Negroes,* black as *Cain,* / May be refin'd, and join th' angelic train." While scarcely the most powerful poem of her short life, these words, penned by the young teenager Phillis Wheatley, not yet a decade out of Africa and into slavery, are the first black verse directly to confront the prevailing racist perception of Africans and African Americans. Wheatley, whose literary output was thought sufficiently refined as to challenge her authorship—necessitating a private examination and subsequent endorsement by a body of leading intellectuals of Boston, including the royal governor of Massachusetts, two future governors of the post-Revolutionary period, and several divines—was a child prodigy. Brought from Africa and bought in Boston at the age of seven, Phillis soon was treated more as a daughter than as a domestic. Quickly picking up the English language, Phillis went on to a competent command of sacred and secular literature (Gray and Pope being her favorite poets), before taking up the classics, science, and Latin. Her later life is a somber meditation on the perils—even for those whose talents were of a high order—of free black existence. Freed when her master's family went bankrupt, Wheatley married, cleaned and washed in a cheap boardinghouse while her husband languished in jail for failure to pay his debts, saw two of her three children die young, and herself died at the age of 31.

COURTESY LIBRARY, UNIVERSITY OF MASSACHUSETTS, AMHERST

The poet Phillis Wheatley challenged, both explicitly and by her accomplishments, the dominant racist nation of her day.

In the mid-18th century the Old South Meetinghouse welcomed John and Susannah Wheatley and their children. Included with the Wheatleys was the slave and future poet Phillis, whose third poem, written before she was 17, was an elegy on the death of her admired Old South pastor, the Reverend Joseph Sewall. (Sewall's father was best known then as a judge of the notorious New England witch trials, though perhaps to the adult Phillis he would be better remembered as the author of *The Selling of Joseph*, New England's first antislavery tract.) Today the meetinghouse displays an exhibit on Phillis Wheatley.

A. Philip Randolph Statue and Pullman Porters Memorial
Dartmouth Street, Back Bay Station/Orange Line T Stop, Boston, MA
Hours: Daily, 24 hours
Admission: Free

No one left his fingerprints on more 20th-century African-American initiatives than Asa Philip Randolph. (See entry on p. 202.) In 1925 he founded the Brotherhood of Sleeping Car Porters, instantly alienating the new union's employer, the Pullman Company, as well as many craft unions and the supporters of Booker T. Washington. More than a decade would pass before the Porters received a charter from the American Federation of Labor, one of whose affiliates, the Hotel and Restaurant Employees International, claimed jurisdiction over porters. (Randolph's difficulties with white unionists, though severe, did not rival the experience of Edward Dunn, founder of the Afro-American Flat Janitors Union in Chicago, who in 1926 was murdered by white unionists who declared his union illegal.) The Pullman Company strove hard to prevent unionization, in Kansas City in 1927 going so far as to demand that porters sign but not read a "petition for higher wages" that in fact was a paean of praise to the company and a denunciation of the Brotherhood. Randolph's long struggle for black unionism ultimately proved successful, enabling him to use the Brotherhood of Porters as a base from which to press for wider African-American rights. Today an A. Philip Randolph Statue and a memorial to the Pullman Porters, honoring Boston's black railroad workers, have been placed in a station junction of Boston's subway and railroad lines.

Monroe Trotter House
97 Sawyer Avenue, Boston, MA 02125
Hours: Daily until sunset
Admission: Not open to the public. Exterior viewing only

In 1900, W.E.B. Du Bois (see Du Bois entry on p. 269), Monroe Trotter—Harvard University's first black Phi Beta Kappa—and other militant African Americans rejected the Republican Party, which as the party of Lincoln had received black support for decades. Trotter, Du Bois, and the others backed the Democratic Party in the 1900 presidential campaign because of the Democrats' perceived opposition to imperialism and the acquisition of the Philippines. A year later Trotter (1872–1934) and George Forbes published *The Boston Guardian*, which championed immediate and unqualified racial equality. Trotter's uncompromising attitude expressed itself in his criticism of Booker T. Washington's accommodationist policies and in Trotter's affiliation with the Niagara Movement (the most militant African-American organization of the day), which he co-founded with Du Bois in 1905. In the 1912 presidential campaign, Du Bois withdrew from the Progressive Party to support Woodrow Wilson, because he believed the Virginia-born former president of segregated Princeton University, while not "our friend," would "not advance the cause of the oligarchy in the South." Trotter was doubtless amused at this judgment when in 1914 he was ordered out of the White House for speaking to Wilson in a fashion America's most racist president deemed insulting. (The *Chicago Defender* reported that "the president finally told him [Trotter] that if the organization he represented wished to approach him again it must choose another spokesman. The president told Mr. Trotter that he . . . was the only American who had ever come to the White House and addressed the president in such a tone and with such a background of passion.") By this time Wilson already had sent to Congress the greatest flood of discriminatory legislation ever to arrive on Capitol Hill. In 1934, two decades after challenging President Wilson, Trotter died on his birthday, apparently a suicide. Today the Monroe Trotter House, where the militant editor lived from 1899 to 1909, is a National Historic Landmark and bears a plaque commemorating the man who so annoyed Wilson.

Houghton Library
Harvard University, 1350 Massachusetts Avenue, Cambridge, MA 02138
(617) 495-2441
Hours: Mon.–Fri., 9 A.M.–5 P.M.; Sat., 9 A.M.–1 P.M.
Admission: Free

From the age of 14 until her death at 31, Phillis Wheatley (see Old South Meetinghouse, Boston, entry; p. 266) never stopped writing poetry. Some of her original manuscripts are to be found in the Houghton Library, along with some of her correspondence and a folio copy of Milton's *Paradise Lost*, which she was given during her visit to an admiring London in 1773.

FRAMINGHAM

Peter Salem's Gravesite
Old Burial Ground, Main Street, Framingham, MA 01701
(508) 620-4862 (Town Clerk)
Hours: Daily until sunset
Admission: Free

In the years before the African-American participation in the American Revolution was thought worthy of serious research, Peter Salem (and Salem Poor and a handful of others, such as Prince Whipple) stood in for the many black men who shouldered muskets and crowded their white comrades on

America's battlefields. Salem, a slave from Framingham, served as a private in Captain Simon Edgel's company and fought at Lexington, Bunker Hill, Saratoga, and Stony Point. Salem (among others, to be sure) is credited with the shot that slew Major Pitcairn, whom the colonials loathed, as the marine officer courageously led for the third time a charge upon the Patriot works. (See Bunker Hill entry on p. 266.) Salem's fame, though, derived not from his battlefield role, which was far from unique for African Americans, but from a long-standing misreading of John Trumball's renowned painting, "The Battle of Bunker Hill." The 1786 painting imaginatively re-creates the clash the artist had witnessed 11 years earlier from the far distance of Roxbury, across Boston's harbor. Trumball prominently portrays a Connecticut officer, Lieutenant Grosvenor, sword in hand, behind whom stands his musket-wielding black servant, traditionally identified as Salem. In fact, as noted above, Salem fought in Edgel's company of Framingham men. Possibly the largely hidden black man depicted in the painting beneath the colonial battle flag represents Peter Salem—or possibly the figure represents the free black Salem Poor of Captain Ames's company, whose courage that day led American officers to recommend Poor to the Continental Congress. Today Peter Salem's Gravesite is found in Framingham's Old Burial Ground, not far from the Minutemen Monument that pays tribute to the famous citizens' (and the not-so-famous noncitizens') militia.

GREAT BARRINGTON

Du Bois Memorial Marker
In Du Bois Park on Route 23 between Great Barrington and South Egremont streets, Great Barrington, MA 01230
Hours: Daily until sunset
Admission: Free

Armed with an incisive mind and a combative personality, W.E.B. Du Bois was the key figure bridging the 20th century's civil rights and black nationalist movements, playing a critical role in organizations as diverse as the Pan-African Congress and the NAACP. He was also the age's outstanding black intellectual. Born in 1868—the year the 14th Amendment was ratified and the year 2,000 persons (mainly African Americans) were killed or wounded by Klan violence in Louisiana election campaigns—Du Bois died on the eve of Martin Luther King, Jr.'s famous "I have a dream" address during the 1963 March on Washington.

In a long life dedicated to advancing the African-American cause, the event that most illumines Du Bois's activist career dates to the last decade of the 19th century. From 1890 through 1894, there were 879 Ph.D. degrees awarded in the United States. Only one was to an African American. William Edward Burghardt Du Bois had become an "endorsed" intellectual. He lived his life as such, managing to embrace and then spurn almost every tendency in the black movement, at each moment supremely confident in his shifting opinion. Though his views frequently placed him at odds with the African-American mainstream, he swam alone, uncaring. Who but an intellectual, confident that by standing on his opinion he was necessarily firmly grounded, would spurn the U.S. Communist Party during the depression, indeed during the year the party led the developing defense of the "Scottsboro Boys" (see Morgan County Courthouse entry on p. 13), only to embrace it at the height of its ill repute? After a lifetime of militancy, who else would have spent the early 1960s, as the civil rights movement shifted into an activist gear, in self-imposed exile in Africa?

COURTESY NATIONAL PORTRAIT GALLERY

W.E.B. Du Bois, the greatest African-American intellectual of the first century of Emancipation.

Harvard doctorate in hand, Du Bois emerged onto the public scene in London in 1900, aptly at the meeting of the African and New World Intellectuals, whose "Address to the Nations of the World" he composed. At the same juncture and reflecting what would prove to be a lifelong concern with freeing the Mother Continent from the shackles of European imperialism and uniting its diaspora, Du Bois attended the first Pan-African Congress, where he was elected vice president of the organization. Not content with leading a campaign critical of Booker T. Washington's accommodationist leadership of the burgeoning black movement and with authoring *The Souls of Black Folk,* the second of the 19 books he would publish, Du Bois in 1905 took the leading role in founding the Niagara Movement, which insisted upon full and effective legal equality and an end to segregation. Four years later Du Bois gave credence to the founding of the NAACP and emerged as that organization's sole African-American officer and the editor of its journal, *Crisis.* Though other African Americans earlier joined the white-inspired effort to aid the struggle for black equality, they lacked the stature—or more pertinently perhaps, the militant posture—of Du Bois. They also suffered the handicap of being either female or churchmen; thus their presence could not wrap the nascent organization with the needed no-nonsense, black masculine cachet embodied by the leader of the former Niagara Movement. Du Bois's keen mind and drive would have aided any group, but his presence was more critical to the NAACP because the group was opposed implicitly by Booker T. Washington (see Hardy, Virginia, and Charleston, West Virginia, entries on pp. 177 and 206) and explicitly by Monroe Trotter (see entry on p. 267), an independent African American who hitherto had frequently allied with Du Bois. (Trotter would later join and then leave the NAACP, attacking both Washington and Du Bois when he did so.)

Du Bois's militancy made for a stormy voyage with the biracial organization. (In any event, Du Bois never viewed his affiliation as a final definition; in 1911, for example, he joined the Socialist Party and in 1919 he formed a Pan-African Conference that throughout a decade of existence enjoyed, at best, lukewarm NAACP support.) Within a few years the NAACP's principal founder, Oswald Garrison Villard, resigned as executive chairman after a dispute with Du Bois over the handling of the *Crisis*. Two decades later, in another dispute, Du Bois resigned as the journal's editor and was replaced by Roy Wilkins. (See entry on p. 412.) This dispute centered on Du Bois's appraisal that, during the depression of the 1930s, African Americans should forgo the struggle for integration and legal equality and instead focus on economic advancement. Typically, Du Bois was not bothered in the least that his new position broadly mirrored that for which he had despised Washington at the turn of the century. In the 1940s Du Bois rejoined the NAACP, only to be dismissed within five years because of renewed disputes.

Roughly at the same time as his final break with the NAACP, Du Bois's attention was again drawn to Africa, where independence movements were challenging the old colonial overlords. These anticolonial struggles renewed Du Bois's attraction to socialism, which brought him closer to Moscow and, hence, to major trouble with the U.S. government. Drawn to leftist causes in the 1950s, and as usual unwilling to bend his stance under pressure, Du Bois was harassed by federal agencies and—like Paul Robeson (see entry on p. 284)—found his passport revoked. In 1961 Du Bois settled in Nkrumah's Ghana, where he became a citizen, joined the U.S. Communist Party, died, and is buried.

William Edward Burghardt Du Bois was born in Great Barrington, Massachusetts, where a marker recalls a life of scholarship, dissent, and passion, all centered on his people.

James Weldon Johnson Home

Great Barrington, MA 01230

In the village of Seekonk, within the town of Great Barrington

Hours: Daily until sunset

Admission: Not open to the public. Exterior viewing only

James Weldon Johnson (see entry on p. 302) emerged from a 19th-century black middle-class background to become an author, diplomat, and leader of the NAACP, in the last role sculpting both the early 20th-century black agenda in the legal and political spheres and a biracial strategy to advance that agenda. In the literary sphere, Johnson's openness to having the seamier/more exciting side of black life narratively explored/exploited without accompanying moral criticism places him squarely in the modern world—and separated him from both his political colleagues and the literary critics of his generation. In 1926, for example, Carl van Vechten's *Nigger Heaven* was published, rather luridly glamorizing lower-class Harlem life for its easy sex and violence. While most African-American intellectuals, including W.E.B. Du Bois, deplored what they saw as an affront and a travesty that played into prevailing white perceptions of the moral looseness of black America, Johnson offered his support for the white author and his work. History repeated itself a few years later with Claude McKay's *Home to Harlem*, which committed, in the eyes of some, the more mortal sin of having a *black* man rhapsodize about the attractiveness of Harlem's seamy street life and characters. Du Bois, who later would be caricaturized in a McKay novel, denounced the work. While younger black writers such as Langston Hughes welcomed McKay's novel, Johnson was the sole intellectual of the older generation to join in his younger colleagues' praise. The intrinsic value Johnson placed on artistic endeavor is suggested in his classic novel *The Autobiography of an Ex-Colored Man*, whose light-skinned protagonist settles for the easier path of passing as white at the expense of artistic and racial compromise. In Great Barrington, Johnson maintained a small country cottage, to which he retreated for relaxation and to write. Today the James Weldon Johnson Home is a *private residence not open to the public*.

LYNN

Matzeliger Monument
Pine Grove Cemetery, 25 Gentian Path, Lynn, MA 01905
Hours: Daily until sunset
Admission: Free

The paths of the mulatto inventors Norbert Rillieaux (1806–1894) and Jan Matzeliger (1852–1889) and the social conseqences of their inventions inversely mirror each other. Rillieux (see Cottage Plantation entry on p. 94), the son of a prominent planter, left the U.S. for Paris with his father's support. There he took an engineering degree, invented the triple-effect evaporator used in sugar refining—which intensified the demand for slaves on suddenly profitable sugarcane plantations—and died. Matzeliger arrived in the U.S. from Dutch Guiana, worked as a cobbler in Lynn, and there invented an automatic "sole machine" that held a shoe in place, pulled the leather around the heel, guided and drove the nails into place, and spat out a finished shoe. The device displaced thousands of skilled craftsmen and destroyed the industrial base of the town that has erected above his grave a monument to the memory of a not-quite-typical Yankee inventor. Matzeliger, who secured five patents, died before he could reap the financial rewards of his inventive mind.

MARTHA'S VINEYARD

Ink Well Beach

Oak Bluffs, Martha's Vineyard, MA 02539
Martha's Vineyard is a small island that lies southeast of New Bedford, just past the still smaller isles that compose the Elizabeth Islands chain. Oak Bluffs lies near the northeast tip of the island. Ink Well Beach is at the foot of Nashawena Avenue, south of the center of Oak Bluffs.
Hours: Daily, 24 hours
Admission: Free

Before Martha's Vineyard became an "in" spot for the socially and financially well-to-do, its Chappaquiddick, Edgartown, and then Oak Bluffs areas had substantial populations of African Americans and American Indians. The black community moved north on the island over time, particularly in response to the presence of a Baptist church centered on the "Highlands" neighborhood of Oak Bluffs and another Baptist church in town pastored from 1900 by the Jamaican immigrant Oscar Denniston. In time, with the resident black community as its base, Oak Bluffs metamorphosed into a primarily black summer resort and gave rise to Ink Well Beach at the foot of Nashawena Avenue. The Oak Bluffs area retains its African-American character and continues to draw veteran visitors who, today, could take their vacation dollars anywhere they wish.

NANTUCKET

African Baptist Church

York and Pleasant streets, Nantucket, MA 02554
c/o (617) 742-1854 (Afro-American Museum in Boston)
Nantucket Island lies south of the Massachusetts peninsula and east of the island of Martha's Vineyard
Hours: Under restoration until 1995. Call ahead for information
Admission: Free

The center of Nantucket's 19th-century black community was the African Baptist Church, where Frederick Douglass began his career as a public orator and antislavery critic. Raised in 1816, the original church building has been purchased and is being restored by the Afro-American Museum in Boston.

Nantucket Historical Association Research Center

Peter Folge Museum Building, Broad Street, Nantucket, MA 02554
(508) 228-1655
Hours: June 11–Aug. 31: daily, 10 A.M.–5 P.M. Rest of year: Sat.–Sun., 11 A.M.–3 P.M.
Admission: Research center: adults, $10 per 2-day visit. Museum: $3

Nantucket Whaling Museum
Broad Street, Nantucket, MA 02554, at the head of Steamboat Wharf
(508) 228-1736
Hours: June 11–Aug. 31: daily, 10 A.M.–5 P.M. Rest of year: Sat.–Sun., 11 A.M.–3 P.M.
Admission: Adults, $4; ages 5–14, $2

At the height of the whaling industry, perhaps 400 African Americans lived on Nantucket—and most would have made their living from the sea. Indeed, Nantucket boasted an all-black whaler, which was commanded by Absalom Boston. Though in a community that included black-owned businesses, black-run churches and schools, and black public officials, Boston was at least as well known for having led the drive to integrate the island's school system. Nantucket's black community also was noted for its support of the abolitionist movement, and the island served as the site of Frederick Douglass's first public address. Some of this abolitionist heritage, along with some (though little) of the African-American participation in the whaling industry, can be discovered at the Nantucket Historical Association Research Center and the nearby Nantucket Whaling Museum.

NEW BEDFORD

Liberty Bell Tablet
Bay Bank—Main Branch, 94 Williams Street at Purchase Street, New Bedford, MA 02740
Hours: Daily until sunset. Exterior wall mounting
Admission: Free

On the wall of a local bank is a reminder of the abolitionist sentiment that prevailed in New England. The Liberty Bell Tablet recalls that: "News of the passage of the Fugitive Slave Law was brought from Boston in 1851 by an express messenger who rode all night, and the bell on the old Hall was rung to give warning to fugitive slaves that U.S. Marshalls were coming."

Lewis Temple Statue
613 Pleasant Street, New Bedford, MA 02740
Hours: Daily until sunset
Admission: Free

As every student of *Moby Dick* knows (and as most readers who wade through its detailed description of the whaling industry surmise), Melville had researched his subject thoroughly; indeed, Melville had shipped out on a whaler from New Bedford, the greatest of New England's whaling ports. Small wonder, then, that aboard the *Pequod* we find African Americans. Aptly, Ishmael's shipmate Queequeg, the *Pequod*'s bones-throwing harpooner, was black—apt not only because harpooners disproportionately were African American, but also because the black metalsmith Lewis Temple invented an important tool of the trade, the Temple "toggle" iron (harpoon) that enabled whalers to securely fasten lines to their prey. Like many uneducated inventors, Temple was a better inventor than businessman: He never patented his creation and died destitute. Today a Lewis Temple Statue, crafted by the noted black sculptor James Toatley, stands in the town from which shipped more whalers, black and white, than any other in the nation.

Whaling Museum
18 Johnny Cake Hill, New Bedford, MA 02740
(508) 997-0046
Hours: Mon.–Sat., 9 A.M.–5 P.M.; Sun., 1 P.M.–5 P.M.
Admission: Adults, $3.50; seniors 59 and older, $3; ages 6–14, $2.50; under 6, free

Following the War of 1812, New Bedford replaced Nantucket as America's leading whaling port, an honor it retained until the industry went belly up. Visitors to the town's Whaling Museum will find the world's most comprehensive collection of industry artifacts—including Temple toggle irons, other whaling implements, ships' logs, and photographs. They also will find a detailed interpretation of the whaling enterprise, a major antebellum industry in which free African-American labor played a substantial role. Last, museum visitors are introduced to African Americans who participated in the industry as owners of ships and as merchant investors. Half-models of shipbuilder John Maslow's vessels and the papers of Paul Cuffe, sea captain and wealthy merchant, rebut the view of African Americans as objects rather than subjects of history.

SALEM

Salem Witch Museum
19½ Washington Square, Salem, MA 01970
(508) 744-1692
Hours: July 1–Aug. 31: daily, 10 A.M.–7 P.M. Rest of year: daily, 10 A.M.–5 P.M.
Admission: Adults, $4; seniors, $3.50; ages 6–14, $2

A fascinating example of an intracommunal clash masquerading as mass hysteria, the Salem witch trials of 1692–1693 managed to place one of the town's few black figures in peril of her life, superficially—and almost fatally—"empowering" the powerless. The Salem hysteria initially centered on the West Indian slave Tituba, whose scary (and probably African-derived) bedtime tales to the daughters of Reverend Parris so frightened the children that the village physician thought them bewitched. Under pressure, the bewildered children denounced Tituba and two other women, all of whom were sentenced to death after confessing. Their executions were postponed so that further investigations could be undertaken. Eventually, 19 men and women mounted the gallows for their dalliance with the Devil. Tituba, however, was not among them. She escaped by recanting her confession at a timely moment—a confession that was one stone in the path down which members of the master race went to their death—and was sold to pay the expenses of her upkeep in jail. It must have been an ironic experience for the slave, whose African heritage certainly incorporated mass hysteria, belief in possession by evil spirits, and witchcraft accusations and executions—the last most frequently without benefit of a formal trial (but, then, different cultures endorse their similar judgments and ease their doubts by different means). The events of three centuries ago—including Tituba's role—are interpreted at the Salem Witch Museum, which lies not far from the home of Judge Corwin (310½ Essex Street), who presided over many of the witchcraft trials.

SPRINGFIELD

Naismith Memorial Basketball Hall of Fame
1150 West Columbus Avenue, Springfield, MA 01105
(413) 781-5759
Hours: July 1–Labor Day: daily, 9 A.M.–6 P.M. Rest of year: daily, 9 A.M.–5 P.M.
Admission: Adults, $6; ages 7–15, $3; under 7, free

No American sport has evolved more dramatically under the fierce energy and style brought to it by African Americans than basketball. The evolution of the game and the emergence of the black titans who now dominate it are traced at the Naismith Memorial Basketball Hall of Fame.

WESTPORT

Paul Cuffe Monument
938 Main Street, Westport, MA 02790
Hours: Daily until sunset
Admission: Free

The son of an African who had purchased himself out of slavery in America and of an Indian woman, Paul Cuffe owned one ship, two brigs, and several smaller vessels—a minor merchant fleet—before he was 50 years old. His fleet had been hard won: Cuffe first went to sea at the age of 16 as a hand on a whaler, worked the hardscrabble land he had inherited from his father, and built a series of successively larger boats—many of which he lost to Tory privateers in the course of the Revolutionary War—before going into partnership with the seasoned seaman brother of his new Indian wife and graduating to the ownership of true ships. Though Cuffe's life may read as a prototypically American tale of hard work, entrepreneurial investment, and success, his repute rested on his Quaker humility and concern for others and his fame rests on his actions as an African American.

Cuffe never forgot his origins. At the age of 19, after his father's death, Paul shed the Slocum slave name he had inherited at birth and adopted as his surname his father's first name. In 1780, at the age of 21, Cuffe, his brother John, and others "chiefly of African extract" petitioned the Massachusetts legislature for relief from the payment of taxes on the grounds of their racial exclusion from the right to vote. Only a few years earlier, of course, "No taxation without representation" had echoed throughout New England. Cuffe's petition placed authorities in an awkward position, from which they extracted themselves by granting free blacks the same electoral rights and responsibilities as whites. In his later life Cuffe committed his time, energies, and money to African colonization schemes, making several voyages to the continent to lay the groundwork for future ventures. Cuffe viewed colonization as the most secure and most rapid means to eliminate the evil of slavery (because it reassured whites who were frightened that ending bondage would instantly create a large pool of free blacks, whom they did not wish in their midst) and as an opportunity to bring Christian enlightenment to a largely heathen continent. Cuffe lived long enough to learn that the American Colonization Society's program had been repudiated by the likes of Richard Allen (see entry on p. 230), Absalom Jones (see Jones entry on p. 232), and James Forten (see entry on p. 316), but not long enough to see the society plant its first colony on the continent from which his father had been stolen. On the grounds of the Friends Church, a monument pays tribute to Westport's most famous citizen, while nearby the Cuffe Farm (1504 Drift Road) has been designated a National Historical Landmark.

NEW HAMPSHIRE

Office of Vacation Travel
105 Loudon Road, Box 856, Concord, NH 03301
(800) 944-1117; (603) 271-2666
Hours: Mon.–Fri., 8 A.M.–4 P.M.

DEERFIELD

Captain Jonathan Longfellow Historical Marker
76 Nottingham Road, Deerfield, NH 03037
Hours: Daily until sunset
Admission: Free

Though never plentiful in colonial New England, slaves were a critical feature of the area's wider economy, serving as a medium of exchange. New England shippers traded the region's rum for slaves in Africa, who in turn were exchanged for sugar and molasses in the West Indies. In New Hampshire slaves accounted for less than 1 percent of the state's population at their height, though in absolute numbers their presence grew up until the Revolution. From the colony's beginning, Indian wars accelerated slavery. As early as the Pequot War of 1637, the victorious colonists shipped their war captives to the West

Indies and exchanged them for black slaves, who were thought less dangerous to maintain than vengeful warriors whose kin lived nearby. Indeed, by 1646, the New England Confederation decided as a matter of policy that Indians enslaved as war spoils should automatically "be shipped out and exchanged for Negroes." The Indian/African-American link took another form a century later. In 1743 Captain Jonathon Longfellow (a distant relative of the poet Henry Wadsworth Longfellow) erected a garrison near Deerfield as a defense against Indian predation. The garrison property was paid for with slaves, as the historical marker notes.

HANOVER

Hood Museum of Art
Dartmouth College, Hanover, NH 03755
(603) 646-2808
Hours: Tue.–Fri., Sun., 11 A.M.–5 P.M.; Sat., 11 A.M.–8 P.M.
Admission: Free

The African Collection of the Hood Museum of Art is especially strong in objects associated with male secret societies. Senufo *kpelie* masks utilized by the Poro society during initiation and funeral ceremonies; Baga *bansonyi* or serpent figures utilized by Simo, the male initiation society; Guro masks from a men's secret society; and a Widekum funerary mask used by members of the Nchiba warrior's (secret, of course) society are among the highlights of the museum's holdings. Also on display are statues, staffs, cultic fetishes, and other objects of the Bamana, Yoruba, Igbo, Suku, Tsogo, and other African peoples.

JAFFREY

Jaffrey Public Library
111 Main Street, Jaffrey, NH 03452
(603) 532-7301
Hours: Mon., Wed., Fri., 11 A.M.–5:30 P.M.; Tue., Thu., 1 P.M.–8 P.M.; Sat., 2 P.M.–5:30 P.M.
Admission: Free

Amos Fortune was aptly named, at least in his later days. In 1770 the 60-year-old slave purchased his freedom and began a new life—with a new bride, whom he also purchased out of slavery. Upon her death in 1775, he married again. Upon his second wife's death, the 69-year-old Fortune purchased another wife (and her daughter) out of slavery, moved to New Hampshire, opened a tannery, and later founded and funded the town's library. In 1801 Fortune died, leaving a legacy to the Quaker Meeting House and one to the local school district. Fortune and his third wife are buried in the Old Burial Ground next to the Meeting House. The Jaffrey Public Library, lineal descendant of his 1795 gift, has Fortune's freedom papers, newspaper clippings, and other reference materials relating to, in the words on his gravestone, "Amos Fortune, who was born free in Africa, a slave in America, he purchased liberty, professed Christianity, lived reputably, and died hopefully."

NEW JERSEY

Division of Travel and Tourism
20 West State Street, CN 826, Trenton, NJ 08625
(609) 292-2470
Hours: Mon.–Fri., 9 A.M.–5 P.M.

ATLANTIC CITY

Convention & Visitors Bureau
2314 Pacific Avenue, Atlantic City, NJ 08401
(609) 348-7100
Hours: Mon.–Fri., 9 A.M.–5 P.M. Summers, on boardwalk:
Sat.–Sun., 10 A.M.–6 P.M.

Chicken Bone Beach Historical Marker
Missouri Avenue at the Boardwalk, Atlantic City, NJ 08401
Hours: Daily until sunset
Admission: Free

Excluded from the beaches fronting the town's grand hotels, African Americans made the shoreline at Missouri Avenue their own. They called their black oasis Chicken Bone Beach. Despite the passing of segregation, the tradition of the black oasis lives on. Today the beach is overlooked by a historical marker that recounts the exclusion of an earlier time.

Jacob Lawrence Childhood Home
1522 Arctic Avenue, Atlantic City, NJ 08401
Hours: Daily until sunset
Admission: Not open to the public. Exterior viewing only

Located along one of the main arteries of Atlantic City's black community, Jacob Lawrence's Childhood Home (now a *private residence not open to the public*) witnessed the initial finger painting endeavors of one of 20th-century America's major painters. His monumental "Migration of the Negro" series captured in 60 panels (now equally divided between the Museum of Modern Art in New York City and the Phillips Collection in Washington, D.C.) one of America's greatest 20th-century social transformations, the mass movement of African Americans from the rural South to the major cities of the North. Lawrence achieved success early, perhaps because his work is readily accessible, and maintained it over five decades—as he did his thematic focus on and cultural allegiance to the lives and struggles of African Americans.

"Pop" Lloyd Baseball Stadium
Herron Avenue at Martin Luther King Boulevard, Atlantic City, NJ 08401
Hours: Daily until sunset
Admission: Free

To have played in the old Negro baseball leagues and to have gotten into the Baseball Hall of Fame in Cooperstown is compelling proof of extraordinary ability. John Henry "Pop" Lloyd's ability was never disputed. Though sports enthusiasts will never settle on just *how* good he (or anyone else) really was, Honus Wagner is the usual point of reference. After batting above .400 several times during his 27-year career, Lloyd in 1930 retired to Atlantic City, where he had made his winter home since 1919. There, in 1949, the "Pop" Lloyd Baseball Stadium was dedicated, one of the first ballparks named after an African-American participant in the national pastime. Inside the stadium, near third base, is a wall-mounted plaque honoring Lloyd.

BORDENTOWN

New Jersey Manual Training and Industrial School for Colored Youth
Burlington Street, Bordentown, NJ 08505
Until recently this facility on the southern outskirts of Bordentown was operated by the State of New Jersey as the Johnstone Training & Research Center.
Hours: Daily until sunset
Admission: Not open to the public. Exterior viewing only

Jim Crow lived north of the Mason-Dixon line—and continued to do so into the Eisenhower era. The New Jersey Manual Training and Industrial School for Colored Youth, the North's only state-supported segregated school, operated until 1955, when a NAACP lawsuit led the state to close it down. The school enjoyed an excellent reputation, due in large measure to the quality of its staff, numbered among whom was Judge William Hastie, the first African American appointed to the appellate level. After the segregated school was closed, the state used the building as a training and research center. Today the center too is closed. The building lacks any interpretive marker that would alert visitors to its restricted past.

BRIGANTINE

Brigantine Inn
1400 Ocean Avenue, Brigantine, NJ 08203
(609) 266-2266
Hours: Daily, 24 hours
Admission: Exterior viewing only

Like the other grand seashore hotels of Atlantic City, the Brigantine Inn once was off limits to African Americans, such as Madame Sarah Spencer Washington. Unlike most of those turned away from its doors, however, Madame Washington was worth a million dollars. Rather than protest angrily, black America's hair-products queen simply purchased the place—which she then turned over to Father Divine (see entry on p. 312), the charismatic African-American preacher whose Peace Mission Movement was one of America's few biracial groups led by a black man.

BURLINGTON

Oliver Cromwell Residence

200 block of East Union Street, Burlington, NJ 08016
Oliver Cromwell Society, P.O. Box 679, Burlington, NJ 08016
Hours: Daily until sunset
Admission: Closed to the public. Exterior viewing only

Oliver Cromwell, a member of the 2nd New Jersey Regiment, was a free black farmer who served for six years and nine months under Washington's immediate command, seeing action at Trenton, Princeton, Brandywine, and Yorktown. His discharge papers (now in the National Archives) bear Washington's handwritten signature. Cromwell's war service won him a pension and a warrant for 100 acres of Burlington County property. Surviving to the age of 100, Cromwell spent his last years living on East Union Street in Burlington City.

JERSEY CITY

Afro-American Historical and Cultural Society Museum

1841 Kennedy Boulevard, Jersey City, NJ 07305
(201) 547-5262
Hours: Mon.–Sat., 10 A.M.–5 P.M.
Admission: Free; donations encouraged

Though the dominant theme of the Afro-American Historical and Cultural Society Museum is an exploration of the lives of prominent New Jersey African Americans of the last 100 years, a typical black New Jersey household of the 1920s, African-American art, civil rights posters, quilts, lectures, and films also occupy the attention of museum-goers.

LAWNSIDE

Mount Pisgah A.M.E. Church

Warwick and Mouldy roads, Lawnside, NJ 08045
(609) 547-9895
Hours: Mon.–Sat., by appointment. Call ahead
Admission: Free

Mount Zion Methodist Church
White Horse at Charleston Avenue, Lawnside, NJ 08045
(609) 546-6334
Hours: By appointment
Admission: Free

Beginning early in the 19th century, independent black churches emerged in Camden County as outgrowths of existing biracial congregations. The First A.M.E. Church (now Mount Pisgah) and Mount Zion Methodist became the most prominent. With this black foundation, the abolitionist farmer Ralph Smith in 1840 purchased and donated land for the establishment of a black community, which first was known as Free Haven. Free Haven served both as a locus of black self-development and as a refuge for fugitive slaves, and was aptly named. Times have changed, as have names—Free Haven yielded to Snow Hill, the Maryland plantation from which many of the fugitives ran, and Snow Hill to Denton, then Launton and now Lawnside—but the place has remained a black community. In the graveyards of its leading churches, in Lawnside's cemeteries, and on the Warwick Road, markers to residents who died in America's wars can be traced a black presence in uniform, from the Civil War to Vietnam.

MANALAPAN

Monmouth Battlefield State Park
Route 33, 347 Freehold Road, Manalapan, NJ 07726
(908) 462-9616
Hours: Daily: Spring, 8 A.M.–6 P.M.; summer, 8 A.M.–8 P.M.; rest of year, 8 A.M.–4:30 P.M.
Admission: Free

Fought in the context of France's entry into the war, which necessitated a general British regroupment, the June 1778 Battle of Monmouth yielded a tactical draw between George Washington and Sir Henry Clinton. Clinton, who had replaced Sir William Howe in command of his Majesty's North American forces, achieved his fundamental defensive aim of successfully withdrawing from the captured colonial capital of Philadelphia into a New York enclave, though his abandonment of the Monmouth field of battle and of the sole British prize of the previous year's campaigning allowed Washington to proclaim victory. Perhaps the battle's largest significance was to consolidate the "new model" line of "Europeanizing" or professionalizing the American army—an approach advocated by Washington and his adherents and implemented by General Friedrich von Steuben, and opposed by advocates of a "republican army," who sought to fight a popular war of the masses. This consolidation was achieved as a consequence both of Washington personally rallying the retreating troops of Charles Lee and of the resulting court-martial of the "republican army" advocate Lee, who was tried by Washington's cronies.

Perhaps 7 or 8 percent of the colonial force engaged at Monmouth was African American. Significantly, this battle predated the widespread recruitment of black troops—the all-black First Rhode Island battalion had just been raised and did not see action until August. (See Butts Hill entry on p. 325 and Memorial to Black Soldiers entry on p. 325.) Colonel John Laurens of South Carolina advocated black recruitment in a letter to his kinsmen Henry, president of the Continental Congress, only four months before the Battle of Monmouth. The black presence in line brigades at Monmouth ranged approximately from 16 percent (Paterson's 3rd Massachusetts) and 13 percent (Muhlenberg's Virginia), through 8 percent (both Huntington's Connecticut and the North Carolina brigade), to as low as 0.4 percent (1st Pennsylvania).

The British, too, had their black adherents in the Monmouth area, notably "the brave Negro Tye," a Virginia veteran of Lord Dunmore's Ethiopian Regiment (see Battle of Great Bridge entry on p. 173) who in 1780 led a band of blacks, white Tories, and Queen's Rangers in a series of behind-the-lines raids on American outposts. Today's visitors to Monmouth Battlefield State Park have access to a groundbreaking pamphlet that outlines the respective black presences on the rolls of various Revolutionary units during the period when Monmouth was fought. In nearby Freehold, New Jersey, there is a Monmouth Battle Monument and a Monmouth Historical Association Museum (908 462-1466); neither reflects the African-American role in the battle.

MEDFORD

James Still Office

Church Road and Highway 541, Medford, NJ
Hours: Daily until sunset
Admission: Not open to the public. Exterior viewing only

A self-taught physician noted for his herbal remedies, James Still (1812–1882) practiced medicine for three decades in Burlington County and was the brother of William, a leader and chronicler of the Underground Railroad. (See William Still entry on p. 319.) Today Dr. Still's office—in which his son, the first black graduate of Harvard Medical School (1871), watched his father work—still stands, though it is now *a private residence not open to the public.* (James Still's grave will be found in nearby Mount Laurel, New Jersey, at the Jacob's Chapel A.M.E. Church Cemetery.)

NEWARK

Newark Museum

43–49 Washington Street, Newark, NJ 07102
(201) 596-6550
Hours: Tue.–Sun., 12 P.M.–4:45 P.M.
Admission: Free

The African Collection of the Newark Museum spans the continent from the Mediterranean to the Cape of Good Hope. Perhaps the most interesting holdings touch upon the cultures of North Africa, which figure only infrequently in many collections representing the Mother Continent. More rarely still, the museum's possessions enable visitors to compare the creations of urban and rural cultures within a region: Indigenous Berber pottery and weaving traditions, for example, sharply contrast with the richly textured arts of Mediterranean cities that trace their heritage back to Carthage's clash with Rome. Ethiopian baskets and crosses offer insight into an African Christian tradition that predates St. Augustine, while the more commonly collected cultures of Africa—including the Senufo, Kota, Kuba, Yoruba, and Bamileke—are by no means neglected. Reliquary guardians, masks, charms, stools, jewelry, beadwork, ironwork, courtly regalia, and textiles abound, seizing the attention of visitors to a city better known for urban blight.

Paul Robeson Center of Rutgers University at Newark
175 University Avenue, Newark, NJ 07102
(201) 648-5568
Hours: Mon.–Fri., 8 A.M.–10 P.M.
Admission: Free

The range of Paul Robeson's talents, interests, and courage was prodigious. Four-sport athlete and Phi Beta Kappa valedictorian of Rutgers University, Columbia Law School graduate, stage and screen star, renowned singer, civil rights militant, left-wing activist, and McCarthyite victim, Robeson (1898–1976) enjoyed more than a decade of being revered—then one of being reviled, followed by one of being forgotten. Seduced, abandoned, and forgotten: The process appeared cruelly to mirror Robeson's treatment of some of his benefactors and most of his lovers. Callously dismissive of individuals—such as his wife—who came between him and what he wanted, Robeson abandoned neither his causes nor his anger at racial slights and injustice. He refused to accept a racial servility in exchange for a position as a privileged black man in a white society. Robeson's support of the Soviet Union, his championing of Africa and African Americans, and his virtual abandonment of his African-American wife and son—who took fourth place in Robeson's life, behind his adulterous affairs, political concerns, and career—might have been overlooked by America if this son of a former slave had shown the slightest willingness to accept the charms of racial gradualism, propriety (read deference), and place. But Robeson was ever willful and would not conform. Assailed during the Cold War even by the NAACP; driven from radio, stage, and screen—and thus separated from the adulation he had grown to expect and need; physically and psychologically undermined by a prostate operation; and finally lost in a fog of depression and old age punctuated by electroshock treatments, Robeson paid in full measure for his temerity in challenging the dominant political and racial ideologies of his day. Today the centerpiece of the Paul Robeson Center of Rutgers University at

Newark is the famed 1920s Robeson bust sculpted by Antonio Salemme. Memorabilia from a life more heroic than tragic, a photographic survey of Robeson's career as activist and artist, and portraits and drawings of a man who became a symbol greet the visitor.

PERTH AMBOY

Grave of the First Black Voter
St. Peter's Church Cemetery, 183 Rector Street, Perth Amboy, NJ 08861
(908) 826-1594
Hours: Call in advance to arrange a free tour with the church's sexton
Admission: Free

As Ulysses S. Grant received the Republican Party presidential nomination in 1868, only eight of the northern states permitted African Americans to vote. Two years later the American Anti-Slavery Society disbanded, convinced its work was complete. In the interim, in a move that was widely viewed as the triumphal conclusion to decades of labor on behalf of the disenfranchised, Congress approved the 15th Amendment to the Constitution, which prohibited federal and state governments from depriving citizens of the vote on the basis of race. Though an event inconceivable only a few years before, black suffrage was purchased at a price. Casting aside the universalist language of the 14th Amendment and entirely ignoring the claims of women, the 15th Amendment permitted the states to determine voting rights provisions subject only to racial inclusion: property, literacy, political (regarding former Confederates), and other restrictions remained untouched. On March 31, 1870, the day after the 15th Amendment took effect, in a minor election revising Perth Amboy's city charter, Thomas Mundy Peterson became the first African American to cast a constitutionally protected vote. Today in Perth Amboy—along with Camden one of the state's two major slave ports—at the St. Peter's Church Cemetery, a memorial marker notes what colloquially is called the Grave of the First Black Voter.

PRINCETON

Historical Society of Princeton Library and Museum
Bainbridge House, 158 Nassau Street, Princeton, NJ 08542
(609) 921-6748
Hours: Tue.–Sun., 12 P.M.–4 P.M.
Admission: Donations encouraged

Local black heritage is illuminated in the holdings of the Historical Society of Princeton, which include 17th- and 18th-century cemetery records, the archives of the Friendship Club—a civic organization of black women—and the papers of Anna Bustill-Smith, author of *Reminiscence of the Colored People of Princeton 1800–1900*.

Paul Robeson Childhood Home
110 Witherspoon Street, Princeton, NJ 08542
Hours: Daily until sunset
Admission: Not open to the public. Exterior viewing only

In 1860 the 15-year-old slave William Drew Robeson fled the Roberson plantation in North Carolina. Eighteen years later, following graduation from Lincoln University in Pennsylvania, Robeson married Louise Bustill, a descendant of a prominent African-American family, and shortly thereafter began pastoring Witherspoon Street Presbyterian Church in Princeton. In 1898 their eighth child, Paul, was born. For the first three years of his life, Paul Robeson (see entry on p. 284) lived on Witherspoon Street in the parish house—*now a private residence not open to the public*—that today colloquially bears his name. Still standing just down the street is the Witherspoon Church.

Paul Robeson Green Street House
13 Green Street, Princeton, NJ 08542
Hours: Daily until sunset
Admission: Not open to the public. Exterior viewing only

Over the strenuous objections of his flock, the Reverend Robeson was forced out of his Princeton pastorate in 1901 by a church commission that was responding to the "dissatisfaction on the part of others [that is, white residents of Princeton] who have been the Church's friends and helpers." This dismissal entailed the Robesons' leaving their parish home and moving to a Green Street residence—*now a private residence not open to the public*—to which Robeson refers in his autobiographical *Here I Stand*. It was in this house in 1904 that the six-year-old's mother was fatally burned.

Witherspoon Street Presbyterian Church
124 Witherspoon Street, Princeton, NJ 08542
(609) 924-1666
Hours: By appointment
Admission: Free

Responding to years of pressure from local whites who wished them gone, black worshippers at the First Presbyterian Church of Princeton in 1840 established the First Presbyterian Church of Color. In 1848 the name was changed to Witherspoon Street Presbyterian Church; the following year the present structure—in which Paul Robeson's father preached for two decades—was raised.

RED BANK

T. Thomas Fortune's "Maple Hall"
94 West Bergen Place, Red Bank, NJ 07701
Hours: Daily until sunset
Admission: Not open to the public. Exterior viewing only

In the first decade of the 20th century, the nationally influential African-American agitator, author (*Black and White: Land, Labor, and Politics in the South*), journalist, and publisher of *The New York Age*, T. Thomas Fortune (see entry on p. 50), lived in "Maple Hall." From this house, now a *private residence not open to the public*, Fortune (1856–1928) rode back and forth to New York City on a tandem bicycle. His life ran less smoothly than his journey, for in these years the ironically named Fortune ("All along the way I have shaken the trees and others have gathered the fruit") slipped from alcoholism, condemnation by Du Bois and Monroe Trotter, and abandonment by Booker T. Washington into a nervous breakdown and years of destitution.

TENAFLY

African Arts Museum
23 Bliss Avenue, Tenafly, NJ 07670
(201) 567-0450
Hours: Daily, 9 A.M.–5 P.M.
Admission: Voluntary donations requested

Formed in Lyons, France, in the mid-19th century, the Roman Catholic Society of African Missions sent the bulk of its order to West Africa, especially Liberia. Today, with most of its missionaries hailing from the United States and Ireland, the society maintains its retirement home on an estate in Tenafly, New Jersey. Also on the estate is the African Arts Museum, New Jersey's only museum dedicated solely to the art and artifacts of the Mother Continent. In keeping with the locale of its missionary work, most of the society's art collection derives from West African cultures such as the Dogon, Ashanti, and Yoruba. Perhaps reflecting the society's deep involvement with the lives it pastors, most of the museum's pieces are 19th- and 20th-century utilitarian objects and folk art rather than of fine art. Masks, sculptures, musical instruments, fertility dolls, and other wooden artifacts predominate in the collection. Guided tours and programs are offered for children and adults, and there is always somebody nearby whose knowledge of the continent is far from merely academic.

TITUSVILLE

Washington Crossing State Park Museum
355 Pennington Road, Titusville, NJ 08560-1570
Museum, (609) 737-9304; park, (609) 737-0623
Hours: Museum: Wed.–Sun., 9 A.M.–4:30 P.M. Park: daily until sunset
Admission: Museum, free. Park: Memorial Day weekend–Labor Day weekend and holidays: cars, $3; New Jersey–registered buses, $40; buses registered out of state, $80

Swiftly descending from the high point of the Battle of Bunker Hill in June of 1775, America's struggling revolution saw one disaster after another in 1776.

With the collapse of the invasion of Canada, Washington's withdrawal from Boston, and his subsequent early-winter, full-scale retreat from New Jersey across the Delaware River into Pennsylvania—the colonial army dwindling with each step westward—the prospects were grim. Thomas Paine, who sloped a musket across his shoulders during the retreat, well caught the mood of the times in the famous opening lines of his aptly named pamphlet *The Crisis*: "These are the times that try men's souls: The summer soldier and the sunshine patriot will, in the crisis, shrink from service of his country; but he that stands it Now, deserves the love and thanks of every man and woman."

Among those joining the author of *Common Sense* in the painful retreat across New Jersey were several African Americans, the best known of whom, naturally, enter the historical record because they were owned or in the service of prominent white men. As Christmas approached, Washington could see little joy, particularly knowing that on the last day in December expiring enlistments would reduce his force to fewer than 1,500 men. Spurred by the prospect of losses without the recompense of battle and by reinforcements that brought his strength to 6,000 men, Washington planned a Christmas Day crossing of the Delaware River and an attack on Trenton, New Jersey. Despite the absence of two supporting divisions, Washington's attack on the Hessian troops in Trenton was a resounding success, restoring colonial morale and preparing the way for his victory a week later at the Battle of Princeton.

Washington's winter crossing of the Delaware is one of the highlights of American history in elementary school education, in part because there are two well-known paintings that symbolize America's triumph: Thomas Sully's "Washington's Passage of the Delaware" and Emanuel Leutze's famous "Washington Crossing the Delaware," which depicts the general standing in the bow of a small craft that is pushing aside floating chunks of ice as it draws near to the New Jersey shore. Both pictures offer very rare visual representations of the black component of the patriot army that wrested freedom from England. According to 19th-century tradition, the African American represented in both pictures is Prince Whipple, slave and bodyguard to General Whipple of New Hampshire. Our Whipple, who was sent from Africa by his wealthy parents to be educated in America and who was then betrayed and sold into slavery, was emancipated during the Revolutionary War and later settled and died in New Hampshire. Tradition, however, may be mistaken as to the individual. Possibly the black man in the paintings was William Lee, Washington's personal body servant and the only African American in the slave burial ground on Washington's Mt. Vernon estate whose name is known, or Oliver Cromwell, who is known to have participated in the retreat and advance across the Delaware and in the battles of Trenton and Princeton. Two things are certain: In Washington's army during the darkest days of the Revolution, African Americans—free and enslaved—slogged through the mud and freezing rain and stood on the field of battle in greater numbers than generally is appreciated; and in the Washington Crossing State Park Museum, visitors will see the copperplate engraving of Sully's painting. Visitors also may see posted a two-page summary of the secondary literature on the role of African Americans in the revolution, which must do service to balance the several hundred period artifacts and an interpretive framework that insufficiently incorporates America's people of color.

TRENTON

Mt. Zion A.M.E. Church
135 Perry Street, Trenton, NJ 08618
(609) 695-4475
Hours: By appointment
Admission: Free

The Free African Society of Trenton was six years old when it entered the ranks of the African Methodist Episcopal Church in 1817. Richard Allen (see entry on p. 230) conducted the first service of the reborn Mt. Zion A.M.E. Church, whose later history included—as was common with A.M.E. congregations—involvement with the abolitionist and freedmen movements. Visitors view the original building and stained glass windows in Trenton's oldest church structure. They also walk the floors that once were paced by Richard Allen, whose voice still echoes in the hall for those with imagination and enough historical knowledge to appreciate one of black America's most critical and decisive figures.

WILLINGBORO

Merabash Museum
c/o William Allen School, P.O. Box 752, Willingboro, NJ 08046
(609) 877-3177
Hours: By appointment
Admission: Voluntary donations requested

Exhibits on Dr. James Still, on the New Jersey Manual Training and Industrial School for Colored Youth, and on the black presence in New Jersey from the early 1600s are complemented by contemporary works of art by African-American painters at the Merabash Museum. The museum is in the process of establishing a new home and a new admission policy, so be sure to call ahead prior to a visit.

NEW YORK

Division of Tourism
One Commerce Plaza, Albany, NY 12245
(800) 225-5697
Hours: Mon.–Fri., 8:30 A.M.–4:50 P.M.

ALBANY

Israel A.M.E. Church

381 Hamilton Street, Albany, NY 12210
(518) 463-9290
Hours: Historical marker: daily until sunset
Admission: Free

In the 1820s, less than a decade after Richard Allen founded the African Methodist Episcopal Church, an Albany congregation affiliated with the first autonomous, national black church in America. Israel A.M.E. Church's original structure housed fugitive slaves headed north to Canada and freedom, a fact noted on a historical marker that stands near the present church sanctuary.

AUBURN

Harriet Tubman House

180 South Street, Auburn, NY 13901
(315) 252-2081
Hours: By appointment
Admission: Voluntary donations requested

The end of the Civil War brought no cessation of Harriet Tubman's work on behalf of her people. Moving into a former Underground Railroad station in Auburn, New York, where she lived until her death in 1913, Tubman turned her enormous energy toward several humanitarian causes, most particularly improving the life and lot of freedmen. Shortly before her death, she converted her house into a home for the aged. Aptly, Tubman (see entry on p. 249), whom John Brown called "General Tubman," received a military burial in Fort Hill Cemetery in Auburn. The following year a memorial plaque was unveiled at the Auburn Courthouse. Today, in addition to viewing the plaque and the gravesite, visitors may tour the restored Harriet Tubman House, which contains some of the mundane possessions of one of 19th-century America's least mundane figures.

BROOKLYN

Henry Ward Beecher Statue

Plymouth Church, Orange Street, Brooklyn, New York 11201
(718) 624-4743 (Plymouth Church)
The church is between Henry and Hicks streets
Hours: Statue: Daily until sunset
Admission: Free

In antebellum Brooklyn, Henry Ward Beecher was a more significant figure than his sister, Harriet Beecher Stowe. Though in 1852 his sister's *Uncle Tom's Cabin* had sold 300,000 copies, Henry Beecher had earlier made his name in the trading city that served as the intermediary between the cotton fields of the

South and the cotton mills of England by challenging his parishoners to break their complicitous links with products and commerce that were rooted in slavery. His compelling sermons brought an upsurge in parishoners and placed Plymouth Church in the forefront of the abolitionist struggle. Beecher prospered as a militant abolitionist, one who actively took part in arming the antislavery forces in Kansas. (See Beecher Bible and Rifle Church entry on p. 390.) At the end of the Civil War, Lincoln himself demanded that Beecher give the invocation at the raising of the Union flag at Fort Sumter, where the Civil War's opening shots had been fired. Beecher's days of prominence had years yet to run. But in 1871 the notorious women's rights activist and free-love proponent (and practitioner) Victoria Woodhull "outed" Beecher's heterosexual flings: "The immense physical potency of Henry Ward Beecher is one of the greatest and noblest endowments of this great and representative man." It was an endorsement he could have done without, especially since it led to the 19th-century's greatest sex scandal, the exposure of Beecher's adulterous relationship with the wife of the editor of his church's newspaper. Although a hung jury enabled Beecher to escape the legal consequences of the charge of "alienation of affection," and although he remained prominent in public affairs for more than another decade, the luster was gone from his shining moral armor. Today, in the courtyard next to Plymouth Church, a Henry Ward Beecher Statue stands erect, somewhat more upright than the minister's life. Visitors should note the nearby statue of the slave girl, Pinky, whom Beecher auctioned off from his pulpit to dramatize the evils of bondage and to raise funds to free the girl.

Brooklyn Museum
200 Eastern Parkway, Brooklyn, NY 11238
(718) 638-5000
Hours: Wed.–Mon., 10 A.M.–5 P.M.
Admission: Suggested donations: adults, $4; students, $2; seniors, $1.50; under 12, free with adult

In New York City African art is not restricted to Manhattan, as a visit to the Brooklyn Museum will reveal. Here, spanning six centuries, more than 3,000 African art and utilitarian objects, principally works of sculpture from the settled agricultural peoples of sub-Saharan Africa, demand attention. Ranging from headdresses used in planting and harvesting rituals by the Chiwara agricultural society through gold pendants from the Akan culture, and from painted wood houseposts of the Yoruba through bronze plaques from the royal palace of Benin, Africa figures prominently in Brooklyn.

Weeksville
1698 Bergen Street, Brooklyn, NY 11213
(718) 756-5250
Hours: Mon.–Fri., 9 A.M.–5 P.M. All tours by appointment
Admission: Free. Donations encouraged

Brooklyn—made famous by Jackie Robinson, Roy Campanella, and Don Newcombe (and also by "Pee Wee" Reese, "Duke" Snider, and Gil Hodges)—erupted with joy in October 1955 when the Dodgers baseball team won their first World Series. The joy was intensified because their vanquished foe was the loathed crosstown rival, the New York Yankees. It proved to be the Dodgers only World Series championship in Brooklyn—for a vile man moved the team to Los Angeles. But before African Americans brought Brooklyn 20th-century fame, they labored in 19th-century obscurity, particularly in the Weeksville community. Today the Society for the Preservation of Weeksville and Bedford-Stuyvesant History maintains four Hunterfly Road properties housing photographs and artifacts that yield a sense of 19th-century black urban life.

BUFFALO

Albright-Knox Art Gallery
1285 Elmwood Avenue, Buffalo, NY 14222
(716) 882-8700; weekends: (716) 882-8701
Hours: Tue.–Sat., 11 A.M.–5 P.M.; Sun., 12 P.M.–5 P.M.
Admission: Adults, $4; seniors, students, $3; family of four, $8; under 13 and members, free. Guided tours: adults, $4; seniors, students over 12, $3; members, $1; ages 12 and under, 50 cents

Recapitulating black history, Buffalo is frequently the final American stop for a contemporary exploration of the Canadian refuge offered fugitive slaves. While in the city, those interested in the Mother Continent and the diaspora may wish to stop in at the Allbright-Knox Art Gallery, which holds a handful of African and African-American creations. The continent is represented by a 16th-century Benin bronze bust and wooden sculptures or masks of the Yoruba, Babembe, and M'Pongwe peoples; 20th-century America is represented by a few paintings of Romare Bearden, Jacob Lawrence, and Horace Pippin and by the sculpture of Richard Hunt.

CANASTOTA

International Boxing Hall of Fame
One Hall of Fame Drive, Canastota, NY 13032
(315) 697-3451
Hours: Daily, 9 A.M.–5 P.M.
Admission: Adults, $3; seniors, $2.50; ages 9–15, $2; under 8 years, free

Brutal and basic, boxing's official black heritage predates Jack Johnson, whose victory over Tommy Burns in 1908 first gave the heavyweight world boxing crown to an African American. (Unofficially, of course, black men pounded each other for white men's pleasure from slavery days.) In 1890 George Dixon won the world bantamweight crown. Two years later Dixon was the featherweight champion. In that same year he entered the history books for something other than his physical prowess: Scheduled to fight in the segregated New Orleans Olympia Club, Dixon demanded and won 700 seats for African-American spectators, briefly breaking the club's color barrier. From Dixon forward, boxing has produced many black champions, whose careers can be traced at the International Boxing Hall of Fame.

COURTESY PHOTOGRAPH COLLECTION, PUBLIC ARCHIVES OF NOVA SCOTIA

In 1890 Canadian bantamweight George Dixon became the first African-American world boxing champion.

CHAMPLAIN

Jehudi Ashmun Birthplace Marker
Oak Street, Champlain, NY 12919
Hours: Daily until sunset
Admission: Free

In 1822 the American Colonization Society sent the Congregationalist minister Jehudi Ashmun to Liberia as its first agent. Ashmun organized the Monrovia colony of freedmen and until 1828 led its defense against the onslaughts of disease and attack from the indigenous population. Today, just south of the Canadian border that by 1822 represented freedom for the enslaved, a marker recalls both a heroic life of purpose and a path largely eschewed by Africa's American diaspora.

COOPERSTOWN

National Baseball Hall of Fame and Museum
Main Street, Cooperstown, NY 13326
(607) 547-9988
Hours: May 1–Oct. 31: daily, 9 A.M.–9 P.M. Nov. 1–Apr. 30: daily, 9 A.M.–5 P.M.
Admission: Adults, $8; ages 7–12, $3

Roughly paralleling the compelled conclusion of Reconstruction and the imposition of Jim Crow, America's national pastime drove African Americans from the diamond that was boys' (of all ages) best friend. Almost half the 20th century would pass before the African-American counterparts of Babe Ruth, Roger Hornsby, and Lefty Grove would be permitted to play major league baseball. Today a very few of the giants of the Negro Leagues—including "Satchel" Paige, Josh Gibson, and "Cool Papa" Bell—have been inducted into the National Baseball Hall of Fame and Museum, where they join the many African

Americans, such as Willie Mays, Hank Aaron, and Roy Campanella, who followed Jackie Robinson into the illustrious ranks at Cooperstown. As well as African-American stars, the museum contains an exhibit highlighting the many teams that played at different times in the various black leagues.

HEMPSTEAD

African-American Museum
110 North Franklin Street, Hempstead, NY 11550
(516) 485-0470
Hours: Tue.–Sat., 9 A.M.–4:45 P.M.; Sun., 1 P.M.–4:45 P.M.
Admission: Voluntary donations requested

Though concentrating on the black presence in and contribution to Long Island, the African-American Museum in Nassau County also offers changing exhibits that broaden its exploration into the black past.

HUNTINGTON

Joseph Lloyd Manor House
1 Lloyd Lane, Huntington, NY 11743
(516) 941-9444
Hours: Memorial Day–Columbus Day weekend: Sat.–Sun., 1 P.M.–5 P.M.
Admission: Adults, $1.50; seniors and ages 7–14, $1

Jupiter Hammon's name underscored his socially defined condition at birth: property. Like so many colonial slave owners, the man's master, Henry Lloyd, delighted in bestowing a classical name on his possession, perhaps because the classical world, too, was underpinned by slavery. Jupiter Hammon labored at the Joseph Lloyd Manor House, where in his spare time he composed the pietistic verses that made him our country's first published African-American poet. The 1760 publication of *Salvation by Christ with Penitential Cries* predates by six years *The University of Cambridge in New England* by the 14-year-old prodigy Phillis Wheatley, commonly considered America's first black poet. The house has a small exhibit on Jupiter Hammon and the existence of slavery on Long Island.

IRVINGTON

Villa Lewaro
North Broadway, Irvington, NY 10533
Hours: Daily until sunset
Admission: Not open to the public. Exterior viewing only

Born in Louisiana in 1867 to former slaves, Sarah Breedlove was orphaned at the age of six, married at 14, and a widowed washerwoman by the time she was 20. Little more than a decade later, Sarah was Madame C. J. Walker and on her way to becoming America's first black female millionaire. Her creation of a lotion that helped "relax" hair freed African-American women from the damaging ordeal of loosening tight curls by means of hot metal combs, though if anything it intensified the underlying pressure to change the natural order of one's appearance. To her discovery, Walker allied drive and marketing acumen, with the result that in 1917 she was able to have a 34-room mansion built on her Westchester estate. Designed by New York's first licensed black architect, Vertner Tandy, the neo-classical Revival-style mansion, dubbed Villa Lewaro by Walker's acquaintance, Enrico Caruso, is now a *private residence not open to the public*. However, a nearby marker on North Broadway identifies the marble-floored, painted-ceilinged retreat in whose "Gold Room" Madame Walker played her $25,000 organ.

Walker's home also served as a major salon for the early 20th-century African-American intelligentsia. As the Versailles Treaty negotiations opened in the aftermath of World War I, the National Equal Rights League (NERL), an all-black rival of the NAACP, sponsored a conference of black organizations so as to present to the international conclave the grievances of African Americans and to add to President Wilson's famous 14 Points a 15th: the "elimination of civil, political, and judicial discrimination based on race or color. . . ." (The black nationalist activist and journalist Monroe Trotter, denied a passport, worked his Atlantic passage as a ship's cook so as to present African-America's claims.) From the NERL conference a group, prominently including Marcus Garvey, A. Philip Randolph, and Adam Clayton Powell, Sr., gathered in Walker's home. They formed the International League of Darker Peoples to promote pan-Africanism and to ensure that defeated Germany's African colonies would be run by a consortium of peoples of color, including the Japanese and Chinese, rather than fall under the sway of a European colonial power. (All these men, as well as W.E.B. Du Bois, agreed that the principle of national self-determination could not be applied absolutely to semicivilized peoples, over whom some form of paternal guidance was required.)

KERHONKSON

Peg-Leg Bates Country Club

Route 2, Box 703, Kerhonkson, NY 12446
(914) 626-3781
Hours: Season: Apr.–Oct., daily, 8 A.M.–10 P.M. (dining room)

Still going strong at age 86, the tap dancer and vaudeville star Peg-Leg Bates opened a Catskills resort for African Americans more than four decades ago. Bates, who lost a leg at the age of 12, became known to a wider and whiter audience through his repeated appearances on the *Ed Sullivan Show*. Visitors to the Peg-Leg Bates Country Club dine in a room that has seen performances by the likes of Cab Calloway, Sarah Vaughn, Lena Horne, and Harry Belafonte. Photographs and plaques pay homage to these and other stars, whose brothers and sisters for decades were not welcome—except as menials—at other resorts in the area.

LAKE PLACID

John Brown Farm State Historic Site
2 John Brown Road, Lake Placid, NY 12946
(518) 523-3900
Hours: Late May–late Oct.: Wed.–Sat., 10 A.M.–5 P.M.; Sun., 1 P.M.–5 P.M.
Admission: Free

Born in Connecticut and raised in Ohio, John Brown's commitment to the abolitionist cause took him to New York's Adirondack Mountains before it took him to Kansas, Harpers Ferry, and martyrdom. In 1846 the noted New York abolitionist and philanthropist Gerrit Smith offered parcels of his vast landholdings in the Adirondack wilderness to free blacks. More than 2,000 deeds of land in eight counties were granted, and more than 400 African Americans settled "Timbucto," 17,000 acres near North Elba. Few of the grantees—for the most part cooks, waiters, barbers, and coachmen, interspersed with the rare minister and doctor—knew the fundamentals of farming. Brown, whose background included tanning, sheep and cattle raising, surveying, and farming, visited the struggling Timbucto in 1848. Soon he and his family moved there, where he aided his neighbors in surveying new plots, clearing land, building houses, and planting crops on ground that was far from productive. In 1851 Brown moved his family back to Ohio. He returned to live in North Elba in 1855, by which time only ten black families remained. Brown then felt the call of "bleeding Kansas," from which he periodically returned to his New York farm. Following Harpers Ferry and his execution, Brown's body was returned to his North Elba farm for burial, where it still lies. Also buried on what is now the John Brown Farm State Historic Site are his son Watson—whose body was taken from Harpers Ferry to the Winchester (Virginia) Medical College, where it was used as an anatomical specimen before being liberated by Union forces and then used in various lodge initiation ceremonies; his son Oliver, also killed at Harpers Ferry; and other associates killed in the raid on the arsenal. Visitors to the site see Brown's final home, restored to its 1855 appearance; the 244 acres he purchased in 1849 at $1 an acre; and the gravesites of men resolutely determined to overthrow the rule of southern slave masters.

MANHATTAN

New York Convention and Visitors Bureau
Two Columbus Circle, Manhattan, NY 10019-1823
(212) 397-8222
Hours: Mon.–Fri., 9 A.M.–6 P.M.; Sat.–Sun., 10 A.M.–6 P.M.

Harlem Visitors and Convention Association
One West 125 Street, Room 206, Manhattan, NY 10027
(212) 427-7200
Hours: Mon.–Fri., 10 A.M.–6 P.M.
Ask for the "Harlem Travel Guide."

Abyssinian Baptist Church
132 West 138th Street, Manhattan, NY 10030
(212) 862-7474
Hours: Tours by appointment
Admission: Free. Voluntary donations encouraged

A contemporary of Richard Allen (see entry on p. 230), Absalom Jones (see entry on p. 232), and John Chavis (see entry on p. 126), Thomas Paul led the movement to establish independent black Baptist churches in America. In 1808 Paul formed an autonomous congregation from which directly descends the Abyssinian Baptist Church, best known today as the base from which was launched the career of Adam Clayton Powell, Jr. In the 15 years between his college graduation and his entrance into the U.S. House of Representatives in 1945, Powell built a major Harlem following through his father's Abyssinian pulpit and through his own fervent advocacy of African-American rights and advancement—both of which had suffered during the depression. In Congress, Powell disdained the propriety of "to get ahead, go along." In fact, Powell disdained all proprieties. With a secure political and social base and considerable personal grace, Powell enjoyed flaunting social conventions (such as racial barriers and promptness), moral principles (such as financial and personal integrity), and the intersection of convention and moral behavior (such as marriage vows). Like many to whom conquests come easily and criticism rarely, Powell never deeply matured and toward the end of his days made something of a mockery of a life that for years had managed to combine self-indulgence with serious efforts to promote African-American advancement rather than himself. Indeed, for more than a decade, Powell represented in Congress not just his district, but any African American who sought his intervention in a political system that marginalized black voices and black votes. Today Abyssinian Baptist, the largest and best-known African-American church in the country, maintains a small Powell Museum dedicated to a U.S. congressman more controversial among his colleagues than in his community.

African Burial Ground Historical Marker
290 Broadway, Manhattan, NY 10278
(212) 432-5707
Hours: Daily until sunset
Admission: Free

Between 1712 and 1792 more than 20,000 enslaved and free blacks were interred—and forgotten—in the "Negros Burial Ground" at what is now the intersection of Broadway and Reade streets. Sharing this grave were the corpses of criminals and victims of epidemic diseases. In 1991, excavation on the site uncovered the intact skeletons of an estimated 450 souls, many of them among the first Africans brought onto colonial soil. Also uncovered were perhaps half a million artifacts that shed light on the lives and deaths of the dispossessed. Only the intervention of the African-American community prevented this hallowed ground from being promptly paved over. Today, an African Burial Ground Historical Marker notes the final resting place of those once thought fit to lie with felons. Soon a museum exploring the lives and culture of African Americans in the colonial period will be placed in the pavilion that has arisen on the site.

Afro Arts Cultural Center
2192 Adam Clayton Powell Jr. Boulevard at 130th Street, Manhattan, NY 10027
(212) 996-3333
Hours: Daily, 9 A.M.–5 P.M.
Admission: Voluntary donations requested

Complementing its African museum—in which Ethiopian religious paintings and bronze and terra-cotta figures predominate—and its holdings of contemporary African painters such as the Congolese artists Thango and Bella, the Afro Arts Cultural Center offers performances of jazz, opera, and classical music.

Apollo Theatre
253 West 125th Street, Manhattan, NY 10027
(212) 749-5838
Hours: Tours: Mon.–Sat., by appointment
Admission: Organizations, $4 per person. Individuals, $6

I may be wrong; but I think you're wonderful!
I may be wrong; but I think you're swell!
I like your style; say, I think it's marvelous!
I'm always wrong; so how can I tell?

COURTESY APOLLO THEATRE

The renowned Apollo Theatre, heart and soul of black entertainment in America for seven decades.

For nearly half a century the band would strike up this Harry Ruskin and Henry Sullivan tune, and everyone within earshot of Harlem's Apollo Theatre knew it was showtime. For entertainers it was the moment of truth. For Harlem audiences it was the hottest ticket in town.

Now famous as "black" landmarks, the Cotton Club and the Apollo began life (the latter under a different name) as whites-only clubs. African Americans—except menials, waiters, and performers—were unwelcome. Then, 20 years after its 1914 opening, the Hurtig & Seaman Theatre came under new ownership and a new name and opened its doors to all. From then through the 1960s, the Apollo beckoned to black performers and their audiences. Bessie Smith and Billie Holiday made the place wail, stomp, and shout; Duke Ellington and Count Basie made the place swing; and Charlie Parker and then Miles Davis brought new sounds to the Apollo's stage. After a decade of decline in the 1970s, the Apollo has returned to glory and regained its position as the acme of black entertainment. Perhaps the greatest draw is Amateur Night (Wednesday) at the Apollo, a showcase for the up-and-coming who are so far down the entertainment pecking order that they don't even have agents. One of the great audience participation spectacles on the planet, it unites severity, compassion, and passion. If you don't have it, don't bring it on the stage—for the audience certainly will let you know it!

Audubon Ballroom and Malcolm X Memorial
165th Street and Broadway, Manhattan, NY 10032
The ballroom and memorial will open in the spring of 1994
Hours, admission, and telephone number have not yet been determined

The shotgun blasts and pistol shots that shocked the throng gathered in Harlem's Audubon Ballroom on a February afternoon in 1965 did more than simply confirm Malcolm X's anticipation of his early and brutal death. They halted a series of personal and political transformations and redefinitions, a journey of growth that had brought the martyred black man back close to the pan-Africanist beliefs of his father.

Malcolm Little was born in 1925 (see Malcolm X entry on p. 405) and early on was exposed both to racial violence and racist indifference. Until he was six years old he had a father and a mentor. Earl Little preached the gospel—both the Baptist kind and that of Marcus Garvey, the early 20th-century's principal exponent of pan-Africanism. With his father's death and his mother's descent into madness, Malcolm's life came unmoored. Soon, with the help of mentors of a different sort, Malcolm Little had made himself over into "Detroit Red," a zoot-suited, "conked," teenage boy who spoke the patois of the streets and thought himself a man—and a sharp one at that. Before he could celebrate his 21st birthday, before he'd even begun to shave, a string of burglaries and a gun netted Malcolm a "dime"—ten years inside.

Detroit Red entered prison in 1946. Not quite seven years later, Malcolm X emerged in all but name, having again made himself over, though this time through hard work, hard-earned self-knowledge, and exposure to the teachings of Elijah Muhammad's Nation of Islam. (See Muhammad Temple entry on p. 397.) From the summer of 1952 through the fall of 1964, Malcolm found and served another mentor, the Honorable Elijah Muhammad, a man of his father's generation. In these years Malcolm emerged as an excoriating critic of white America and black moderates, the Nation of Islam's most forceful proslytizer and organizer, and the group's principal spokesman. His voice was heard on the streets, in the temples of the Nation of Islam, in the black press, and in the newspaper he founded for the organization, *Muhammad Speaks*. Soon he was heard on television, which propelled him to the media forefront of an African-American struggle that was entering a new phase of militance.

He also emerged as a challenger to his mentor, particularly as his exposure to the wider world led him to question the Nation of Islam's inward-looking and apolitical ideology and its downright bizarre theology. Driven by his growing doubts (and by his ambition) and proximately spurred by reports of Elijah Muhammad's adulterous proclivities (which paralleled those of his real father), Malcolm rebelled and in the spring of 1964 announced his break with the Nation of Islam. Less than a year later he was dead, gunned down as he addressed a rally of the Organization of Afro-American Unity, a group he had formed to promote the diaspora's solidarity.

The final year of Malcolm Little's life revealed yet another transformation. Following a pilgrimage of the holy city of Mecca and travel to Saudia Arabia, Egypt, and Lebanon, Malcolm adopted the name El Hajj Malik el Shabazz and conformed to the orthodox tenets of Sunni Islam. As El Hajj Malik, he acknowledged the need to reach out to black organizations and leaders he had previously condemned, disavowed the racialist perspective that he had propagated for more than a decade, and strove to promote a pan-Africanist perspective that politically challenged imperialist control of peoples of color all over the world. He also roundly condemned the Nation of Islam—which replied in kind. As tensions mounted between Elijah Muhammad and El Hajj Malik—tensions that were monitored, if not encouraged, by an FBI that spied on both—Malcolm's home in Harlem was firebombed as he and his family slept inside. A week later Malcolm addressed a rally at the Audubon Ballroom, a center of the Harlem scene for decades. According to testimony at the subsequent trial, just as he began to speak, and with his wife and daughters looking on, Norman 3X Butler, Thomas 15X Johnson, and Talmadge Hayer opened fire. None of his bodyguards, included among whom was Gene Roberts—an undercover New York policeman reporting to the FBI—could stay the assassins shots, and a journey of many twists and turns was brutally cut short.

Black Fashion Museum
155–57 West 126th Street, Manhattan, NY 10027
(212) 666-1320
Hours: Mon.–Fri., 12 P.M.–8 P.M. Tours arranged with 24-hour notice
Admission: Voluntary donations requested

From Elizabeth Keckley—slave, modiste to the wives of Jefferson Davis, Stephen Douglas, and Abraham Lincoln, companion to Mary Todd Lincoln, and author of *Behind the Scenes or Thirty Years a Slave, and Four Years in the White House*—to contemporary African-American dress designers, memorabilia, photographs, and work products of the fashion world are on display at the Black Fashion Museum.

Fraunces Tavern Museum
54 Pearl Street at Broad Street, Manhattan, NY 10004
(212) 425-1778
Hours: Mon.–Fri., 10 A.M.–4 P.M.
Admission: Voluntary donations requested

More plots have been hatched in taverns than in novels. At no time was this more true than during the American Revolution. Vital centers of community life, taverns provided a more secure meeting place than churches or town halls—or, in any event, more congenial ones. For 23 years Samuel Fraunces ran the Queen's Head, during which time its rooms were the scene of the founding of the first New York Chamber of Commerce, meetings of the Sons of Liberty, the launching of the so-called New York Tea Party, and the farewell party given to George Washington by his officers in 1783. In the days when New York City was America's capital, Fraunces Tavern housed the Department of Foreign Affairs, headed by John Jay, and then the Treasury Department and the War Department. Today Fraunces Tavern Museum interprets America's colonial history and culture, including its African-American component.

Though absolutely worth a visit, it should be noted that the tavern is *not* a black heritage site, though it is frequently identified as such. This misidentification turns on Fraunces's sobriquet, "Black Sam."

Mother Hale House
154 West 122nd Street, Manhattan, NY 10027
(212) 663-0700
Hours: Tours by appointment only
Admission: Free; donations encouraged

In 1969, as a heroin epidemic seized New York City, the 64-year-old Clara McBride Hale prepared to retire after 30 years as a licensed foster mother. Leaving Mrs. Hale's house one day, her daughter Lorraine saw a young woman nodding off even as she held a babe in her arms. Lorraine convinced the young woman to seek Mrs. Hale's help. Six months later 22 children of heroin-addicted mothers were living in Mrs. Hale's five-room apartment and "Mother" Hale's second career was taking off at an age when most folks are slowing down. More than two decades later Mother Hale was still growing strong—as was the incidence of children whose parents were lost in a fog of drugs and disease. All that had changed, except the numbers, was that now the *babies* were drug-addicted. Clara Hale, whom President Reagan hailed as "a true American hero," died in

1993. Before her death at the age of 90, Mother Hale had given her loving care to more than 500 infants in her second career. Her life's work, institutionalized as the Mother Hale House and run by her daughter, Dr. Lorraine Hale, is her memorial.

Harlem Renaissance Authors' Homes: Langston Hughes
20 East 120th Street, Manhattan, NY 10035
Hours: Daily until sunset
Admission: Not open to the public. Exterior viewing only

In the 1920s through the mid-1930s, the publication of *The Weary Blues*, *Fine Clothes to the Jew*, *The Ways of White Folks*, and *Mulatto* made Langston Hughes one of the driving forces of the Harlem Renaissance. Allied to his accomplishments as an artist (the preceding titles include verse collections, a novel, a collection of short stories, and a play) were a supportive attitude toward his literary colleagues and a deep devotion to the culture of his people. During these productive years, Hughes lived at 20 East 120th Street, which today is a *private residence not open to the public*.

Harlem Renaissance Authors' Homes: James Weldon Johnson
187 West 135th Street, Manhattan, NY 10030
Hours: Daily until sunset
Admission: Not open to the public. Exterior viewing only

Largely forgotten today, James Weldon Johnson (see entry on p. 271) embodies the perils of doing many things extremely well, rather than one thing brilliantly—or at least luridly. NAACP field secretary (1916–1920) and executive secretary (1920–1930), U.S. consul to Venezuela and Nicaragua (1906–1912), author (*Fifty Years and Other Poems*, *God's Trombones*, *The Autobiography of an Ex-Colored Man*, *Along This Way*), noted librettist and promoter of African-American writers and artists, Johnson's greatest impact probably lay in his work defining the early 20th-century black agenda in the political and legal spheres and in devising a strategy to advance that agenda biracially. Best known today for penning the poem "Lift Every Voice and Sing," which when set to music by his brother served unofficially as the "Negro National Anthem," Johnson's literary output and attendant long-term fame suffered from the rival claims on his time: Art is long, the political life is short. A giant of the Harlem Renaissance, Johnson's home during those years still can be seen from the street, though today it is a *private residence not open to the public*.

Harlem Renaissance Authors' Homes: Claude McKay
180 West 135th Street, Manhattan, NY 10030
Hours: Daily until sunset
Admission: Not open to the public. Exterior viewing only

Born in Jamaica, Claude McKay already had published two volumes of dialect poetry—*Songs of Jamaica* and *Constab Ballads*—by the time of his 1912 arrival in the States. Following a brief stay at Tuskegee, McKay found himself in Manhattan . . . Kansas. After two years of study in the Midwest, McKay headed for the Manhattan that even Toto would have recognized as not being in Kansas. Here his 1914 marriage quickly collapsed, floundering on the fact of McKay's bisexuality and the opportunities of New York City. While searching for a literary voice, he also sought a political avenue that challenged the racially (and sexually) repressive standards of the time, gravitating briefly toward both Cyril Briggs's African Blood Brotherhood and the founders of the Communist and Trotskyist movements in the United States. After World War I McKay traveled to the Soviet Union and Germany before settling for a decade in France. McKay's early 1920s publications brought him some renown—and aroused controversy in elite black circles because of his bitterly radical tone.

Ironically, McKay soon would arouse more controversy in the same circles with a far from bitter portrayal of Harlem life. His 1928 *Home to Harlem*, which put pimps and prostitutes, drug addicts and homosexuals, predators and prey at the center of Harlem's netherworld and thus appeared to endorse one of the dominant white conceptions of the rawness of black life, excited the younger African-American writers such as Langston Hughes as much as it antagonized the older black intelligentsia such as W.E.B. Du Bois. In 1934, after 12 years abroad, McKay returned to New York. Living not far from James Weldon Johnson, in a house still visible from the street though now a *private residence not open to the public*, McKay soon found himself out of step with the times. He rejected the NAACP's integrationist approach in favor of one that emphasized black communal cohesion. He also rejected the depression-era's black/Communist alliance because it bound African Americans not only to one political party but to a powerless and easily anathematized one at that. Underpinning both of these reasoned rejections were McKay's somewhat cantankerous personality and the tension between his urgent need to give himself to others and his dependency on favors from others. In the last year of his life, finally finding a means to combine dependency and a desired union, McKay joined the Catholic Church.

Mother A.M.E. Zion Church
140–146 West 137th Street, Manhattan, NY 10030
(212) 234-1545
Hours: By appointment
Admission: Free

Peter Williams was born a slave in a cowshed and as a youth was converted to Methodism. In the course of the Revolutionary War, the trustees of John Street Methodist Episcopal Church purchased him for £40 and made him sexton of the church, where he served for almost two decades. (Look carefully at the early 19th-century watercolor by Joseph Smith, "The First Methodist Episcopal Church in America," which is displayed at the Museum of the City of New York [see entry on p. 304]: Standing in the doorway of the John Street Church is Peter Williams.) In 1796 Williams—who had purchased his freedom—and other black congregationists requested permission to hold "meetings of their own, where they might have an opportunity to exercise their spiritual gifts among themselves and thereby be more useful to one another." Permission was granted and four years later the African-American worshippers had raised sufficient money to build their own church, which they named Zion. This is the origin of Mother A.M.E. Zion, the first church built by and for African Americans in New York City.

Museum of the City of New York
Fifth Avenue at 103rd Street, Manhattan, NY 10029
(212) 534-1672
Hours: Tue.–Sat., 10 A.M.–5 P.M.; Sun., 1 P.M.–5 P.M.
Admission: Free. Voluntary donations requested: adults, $4; seniors, children, and students, $2; families, $6

Three hundred years of black history in New York City are traced at the Museum of the City of New York, though in the permanent exhibits the visitor will see more of the world of black entertainment than he or she will of the state's slave past, the two 18th-century slave revolts, or the life of and restrictions on free blacks in 19th-century New York.

Museum of Modern Art
11 West 53rd Street, Manhattan, NY 10019
(212) 708-9480
Hours: Sat.–Tue., 11 A.M.–6 P.M.; Thu.–Fri., 12 P.M.–8:30 P.M.
Admission: Adults, $7.50; seniors, $4.50; under 16, free with adult

Among the works at the Museum of Modern Art are 30 of the 60 panels by Jacob Lawrence entitled "The Migration of the Negro." Painted in 1940–1941, when Lawrence was only 24 years old, "Migration" brought Lawrence fame—and commissions. His prior work, such as "Frederick Douglass" (1938–1939) and "Harriet Tubman" (1939–1940), underscored the young painter's allegiance to his African-American heritage, an allegiance strengthened by his Harlem Art Workshop acquaintance in his teenage years with Claude McKay, Countee Cullen, Alain Locke, Langston Hughes, Aaron Douglas, Richard Wright, Ralph Ellison, and other leading lights of the Harlem Renaissance.

Metropolitan Museum of Art, Rockefeller Wing
1000 Fifth Avenue (at 82nd Street), Manhattan, NY 10028
(212) 535-7710
Hours: Sun., Tue.–Thu., 9:30 A.M.–5:15 P.M.; Fri.–Sat., 9:30 A.M.–8:45 P.M.
Admission: Suggested donation: adults, $6; seniors and students, $3

The Metropolitan Museum of Art is a rare treasure trove. Other museums can rival its holdings of 19th- and 20th-century African-American artists, such as Horace Pippin, Jacob Lawrence, and Richmond Barthé. Still other museums may be able to match the more than 500 Central and West African objects displayed in its Rockefeller Wing, the highlights of which are wood sculptures of the Dogon and Bamana peoples of Mali, bronze and ivory sculptures from the Benin Kingdom, reliquary guardian figures from Gabon and the Congo, and power objects and royal regalia made by the Kongo, Luba, Chokwe, and Songye peoples. But unmatched is the collection of African musical instruments in the Mertens Gallery. *Kissars*—lutes made from the skulls of fallen foe—horns carved from elephant tusks, drums, gourd rattles, and thumb pianos are on display accompanied by listening devices that enable the viewer to hear the sounds that emanate from the instrument. Then, of course, there is the small matter that when one tires of Africa, the museum offers avenues of exploration into the art and culture of the world's other continents.

Arthur Schomburg Center for Research in Black Culture
New Public Library, 135th Street at Lenox Avenue, Manhattan, NY 10037
(212) 491-2200
Hours: Mon.–Sat., 10 A.M.–5:45 P.M.
Admission: Free

Puerto Rico was but one of the many Caribbean shores upon which the diaspora trod in chains, but few of the islands have given so prominent a figure in the preservation of the African-American legacy as Arthur Schomburg. He was born on the island in 1874 to a mother from St. Thomas, Virgin Islands, and a father of German Jewish descent. Schomburg moved to New York City in 1891 and shortly thereafter began collecting what today is the world's most comprehensive and priceless archive documenting the history and culture of the African diaspora. Bibliophile, art collector, and self-taught historian; supporter of Puerto Rican liberation from Spain; admirer of Caribbean independence figures ranging from Toussaint L'Ouverture to Rafael Cordero; Spanish-language teacher, law clerk, and head of the foreign mail division at Bankers Trust; participant in the 1911 formation of the Negro Society for Historical Research and President of the American Negro Academy from 1922 to 1926, Schomburg personally laid the groundwork for the rise of black studies. In 1926 the National Urban League convinced the Carnegie Foundation to offer $10,000 to the New York Public Library for the acquisition of Schomburg's holdings. Though worth far more, Schomburg's collection of more than 5,000 volumes, 3,000 manuscripts, 2,000 etchings, and several thousand pamphlets passed into the public domain—to the collector's immense satisfaction. The collection formed the foundation of the library's division of Negro literature, history, and

COURTESY SCHOMBURG CENTER, NEW YORK PUBLIC LIBRARY

Arthur Schomburg, a Puerto Rican of African descent, dedicated his life to the documentation of black history and culture.

prints, which today bears the title The Arthur Schomburg Center for Research in Black Culture. The center's holdings now date back to 8th- or 9th-century African artifacts and range forward through the Harlem Renaissance to the work of present-day African-American artists, writers, and filmmakers. The more than 250,000 photographs alone make the center an invaluable resource for those interested in the black presence in the western hemisphere. If Andrew Carnegie's money had done nothing else, the Schomburg grant alone would have justified Carnegie's foundation. Schomburg justified his own existence with passion and commitment—and without difficulty.

Studio Museum of Harlem
144 West 125th Street, Manhattan, NY 10027
(212) 865-2420
Hours: Tours: by appointment, Wed.–Fri., 10 A.M.–5 P.M.; Sat.–Sun., 1 P.M.–6 P.M.
Admission: Adults, $2; seniors, students, and children, $1

Working, talking, and hanging out in a studio above a liquor store in the late 1960s, a group of black artists gave birth to what is now one of America's most renowned institutions for the presentation of African-American, Caribbean-American, African, Hispanic, and Caribbean contemporary art. The Studio Museum in Harlem shows the world as perceived by artists of color. One of the best summaries of what's happening today in the universe of non-European art, the Studio Museum has moved from its original location, in the process gaining space for a concert hall, a lecture hall, and an assembly hall and losing only the convenience of the downstairs liquor store.

OGDENSBURG

Frederic Remington Art Museum
303 Washington, Ogdensburg, NY 13669
(315) 393-2425
Hours: May 1–Oct. 31: Mon.–Sat., 10 A.M.–5 P.M.; Sun., 1 P.M.–5 P.M.
Nov. 1–Apr. 30: Tue.–Sat., 10 A.M.–5 P.M.
Admission: Adults, $3; seniors and ages 13–16, $2; under 13, free

Prior to late 20th-century scholarship and to the earlier though not well-known writings of nonacademic African-American historians, the only widely accessible record of the black role in winning the wars against the western Plains Indians was the paintings, sketches, and writings of Frederic Remington. Remington spent some time on patrol with the 10th Cavalry in Arizona in 1888 and again a decade later, and was forthright in his defense of the capabilities and performance of America's buffalo soldiers. His paintings include one depicting a scene, based on a 1878 incident between troopers of the 10th's Company D and whites in San Angelo, Texas, wherein the buffalo soldiers shoot up Billy Powell's saloon to avenge a dead comrade killed in a racial attack. The Frederic Remington Art Museum includes many of the works in which buffalo soldiers figure.

OSWEGO

H. Lee White Museum

Foot of West First Street Pier, Oswego, NY 13126
(315) 342-0480
Hours: June: Sat.–Sun., 10 A.M.–5 P.M. July 1–Labor Day: daily, 10 A.M.–5 P.M.
Admission: Free; donations encouraged

The H. Lee White Museum maintains a permanent exhibit on the Underground Railroad. In addition to a replica of a hideyhole in which fugitive slaves were hidden, the exhibit includes the basic routes along which scores of thousands of African Americans made their escape from bondage into the perils of a freedom that, south of Canada, lacked legal status.

PURCHASE

The Neuberger Museum of Art

State University of New York, 735 Anderson Hill Road, Purchase, NY 10577-1400
(914) 251-6100
Hours: Tue.–Fri., 10 A.M.–4 P.M.; Sat.–Sun., 11 A.M.–5 P.M.
Admission: Adults, $4; seniors and students, $2

More than 100 objects grace the African Collection of the Neuberger Museum of Art. Whether originally serving spiritual or social purposes, the masks, headdresses, statues, divination figures, and utilitarian objects of the Luba, Dan, Mossi, Bamana, Bembe, Senufo, Fon, Mende, and other peoples of the continent now offer the opportunity to explore universes of meaning stranger but more immediately accessible than our own—which provides the unexamined, internalized framework from which we look *out* onto the world.

ROCHESTER

Frederick Douglass Grave and Monument

Grave: Mount Hope Cemetery, 1133 Mount Hope Avenue, Rochester, NY 14620
Monument: Highland Park Bowl, Highland Park, South and Reservoir Avenues, Rochester, NY 14605
(716) 473-2755 (Mount Hope Cemetery)
Hours: Grave and monument, daily until sunset
Admission: Free

The 19th century's most influential African-American abolitionist, Frederick Douglass (see Douglass Statue entry on p. 243), is buried in Rochester, the city to which he moved in the late 1840s and from where he published the *North Star*. Today's visitors to Rochester can view both the famous Frederick Douglass Monument, dedicated in 1899 by the state's governor, Theodore Roosevelt, and the grave site of an American giant. Aptly, the Frederick Douglass Grave is close to that of Susan B. Anthony, the 19th-century abolitionist and feminist advocate, whose cause he championed. The long-maintained association between Douglass and Anthony is also in evidence in Rochester, in the Susan B. Anthony Home (17 Madison Street; 716 235-6124).

LIBRARY OF CONGRESS

"The Great Emancipator," Frederick Douglass.

SYRACUSE

Everson Museum of Art

401 Harrison Street, Syracuse, NY 13202
(315) 474-6064
Hours: Tue.–Fri., 12 A.M.–5 P.M.; Sat., 10 A.M.–5 P.M.; Sun., 12 P.M.–5 P.M.
Admission: Free; suggested donation, $2

Though best known for its world-class collection of ceramics, the Everson Museum of Art also has a small holding of West African art and artifacts, including masks, fetish figures, and pottery.

TICONDEROGA

Fort Ticonderoga

Box 390, Fort Road, Ticonderoga, NY 12883
(518) 585-2821
Hours: July–Aug.: daily, 9 A.M.–6 P.M. May 10–June 30 and Sept. 1–Oct. 31: 9 A.M.–5 P.M.
Admission: Adults, $5; ages 10–13, $3. Includes admission to adjoining battle sites

Look closely at a map of New York state and you see a virtually direct water route from Canada to New York City. Beginning just east of Montreal, the Richelieu River connects to Lake Champlain, whose southern reaches near Ticonderoga include a stream that connects to Lake George, which in turn leaves but a short portage to the Hudson River. In colonial times, this was the quickest route connecting America's major seaboard city, New York, with

Britain's most secure North American territory. Fort Ticonderoga guarded this route. Its capture in 1775 by Ethan Allen and the Green Mountain Boys of Vermont (commissioned by Connecticut) and by Benedict Arnold, then an officer in the Connecticut militia but acting under the commission of Massachusetts, both secured the rebellion's northern flank and opened the possibility of invading Canada. More immediately significant, the raid secured some 60 much-needed cannons, which were laboriously transported 300 miles south.

More than Green and white boys were involved in the colonials' northern campaigning, for African Americans participated as well. Their participation scarcely makes Fort Ticonderoga an African-American heritage site—or in any event, any more of a site than virtually every Revolutionary battlefield, which also witnessed African-American participation. Rather, Fort Ticonderoga merits mention because one of the black combatants there was Lemuel Haynes. Haynes, who arrived after the fort's capture, would go on to become the first black minister of the Congregational Church in America. He was born in 1753 to a father he never knew ("of unmingled African extraction") and a mother ("a white woman of respectable ancestry") who abandoned her unlicensed issue. Haynes was bound out to and raised in the family of a deacon, where he early learned to read and to love books. At 21, Haynes enlisted as a minuteman and trained on the local green. From the siege of Boston he marched to Ticonderoga. Two years later he began to learn Latin and then Greek as stepping-stones to a career as a minister. In 1785, sponsored by the church deacons who a decade earlier had been his captain and colonel, Haynes was officially ordained. From then until his death in 1833, Haynes enjoyed a career as a divine and as an author of both religious and secular works. With the latter, he found himself in difficulty more often because of his Federalist political and social views than because of his singular explicit criticism of slavery.

Today's visitors to Fort Ticonderoga will find a well-marked battlefield, a restored fort, and a museum. The museum is well stocked with Revolutionary-era weapons, uniforms, and artifacts, though its exhibits lack anything specific about the black presence in the Revolutionary army. (Those interested in Haynes may pass by the house in which he lived in 1793, which is located along Route 149 in Washington County's South Granville.)

WARSAW

Warsaw Presbyterian Church (now the United Church)
22 South Main Street, Warsaw, NY 14569
(716) 786-3868
Hours: Mon.–Fri., 1:30 P.M.–5 P.M.
Admission: Free

America's first antislavery political party, the Liberty Party, was organized at the Warsaw Presbyterian Church in 1839 at a meeting of the Western New York Anti-Slavery Society. Particularly active in the party were New York abolitionists, led by Lewis Tappan, who had formed the American and Foreign Anti-Slavery Society when William Lloyd Garrison and his adherents took control of the American Anti-Slavery Society. Tappan's society had five African Americans on its executive committee, including Henry Highland Garnet, Samuel Cornish (editor of *Freedom's Journal*, in 1827 America's first black newspaper), and Samuel Ward (in 1850 first president of the American League of Colored Laborers). The Liberty Party never won many votes, though in the 1844 presidential election it secured enough New York support to deprive Henry Clay of the presidency, which instead went to James K. Polk. Its presidential candidate, James Birney, had a checkered past on African-American issues. (Its vice-presidential candidate, F. J. LeMoyne, had a rather more straightforward abolitionist record, though unlike Birney—who tried his hand in Kentucky and Alabama—LeMoyne spent his life in the less hazardous fields of Pennsylvania; see Washington, Pennsylvania, entry on p. 322.) But the Liberty Party is historically significant as the first political party to open leadership positions to African Americans.

PENNSYLVANIA

Bureau of Travel
Department of Commerce, Room 453, Forum Building, Harrisburg, PA 17120
(800) VISIT-PA
Hours: Mon.–Fri., 8 A.M.–4:30 P.M.
Ask for Pennsylvania's "African-American Guide" brochure.

BALA-CYNWYD

James Bland Grave
Merion Memorial Park, Bryn Mawr Avenue, Bala-Cynwyd, PA 19004
(215) 664-6699
Located in Merion Cemetery, north on Pennsylvania 23, across from an 18th-century Quaker school
Hours: Mon.–Sat., 8:30 A.M.–2:30 P.M.
Admission: Free

The African-American songwriter and minstrel performer James Bland was a smash hit in the 19th century, winning acclaim in America and England and for a short while annually earning a five-figure income. He could as little hold on to popularity as to money, and he died broke and forgotten. His later obscurity had an ironic consequence, hiding from most Virginians the fact that the state's official anthem, "Carry Me Back to Old Virginny," was not composed by Stephen

Foster but by a Yankee—moreover, by an African-American Yankee who neither had lived in Virginia nor ever expressed a sincere desire to do so. James Bland, whose father was one of America's first black college graduates, was freeborn in New York in 1854, graduated from Howard University, served as a page on the floor of the United States House of Representatives, is credited with composing 600 songs, and died impoverished in Philadelphia in 1911. So little remembered was he that his burial site (in a circa 1895 cemetery for African Americans and Chinese) was lost to memory for almost three decades, before the American Society of Composers, Authors and Performers located it in a cemetery in a Philadelphia suburb and erected a tombstone over his grave.

CHEYNEY

Cheyney University
Cheyney and Creed roads, Cheyney, PA 19319
(215) 399-2000
Hours: By appointment, through the admissions office
Admission: Free

The Institute for Colored Youth was established in 1837 to train African American teachers. Chartered in 1842, what is now Cheyney University prospered after the Civil War under the direction of the former slave Fanny Jackson Coppin, one of first African-American women to graduate from an American college. (See Coppin State College entry on p. 243.) Coppin served as the institute's principal into the 20th century and is honored with a historical marker on the campus. In 1920 Cheyney entered the state's educational system upon the promise that its graduates would be permitted to teach in white schools—a promise not kept for the next three decades.

GETTYSBURG

Gettysburg National Military Park
P.O. Box 1080, Gettysburg, PA 17325
(717) 334-1124
Hours: Daily, 8 A.M.–5 P.M.
Admission: Self-guided tours are free; guided tours are $20 per car and $50 per bus. The Electric Map fares are: adults, 62 and older, $1.50; 16–61, $2; 15 and under, free. Equivalent charges apply to the Cyclorama program

Though no substantial Union recruitment of African-American soldiers had occurred by July 1863 and though no black combat troops took part, the Battle of Gettysburg had at least one African-American connection: The clash's bloody climax—Pickett's immortal charge, which sent 12,000 Confederate troops across an open field savagely enfiladed by Union artillery on Little Round Top and Cemetery Hill and by the volleys of Stannard's Vermont regiments on their right and from Ziegler's Grove on their left—was fought partly on the property of Abraham Brien, a free black farmer. Seven thousand of the attackers never returned to the Confederate lines, and never again would Lee hope to invade Union territory. Today's visitors to Gettysburg National Military Park can take advantage of self-guided driving and walking tours, the Visitor Center's Electric Map detailing the course of the battle, a museum (which intermittently has exhibits on the Civil War role of United States Colored Troops regiments), the restored Brien farmhouse, a Cyclorama Center and film show, and for-hire guided tours of the battlefield. As well, lying close by are the Lincoln Museum Room, where the president completed his draft of the Gettysburg Address, and the Eisenhower National Historic Site, which details the life and career of the president in whose administration the Supreme Court handed down its *Brown v. Board of Education* decision.

GLADWYNE

Father Divine Shrine
Woodmont Estate, 1622 Spring Mill Road, Gladwyne, PA 19035
(215) 525-5598
Hours: Sun., 1 P.M.–5 P.M.
Admission: Free

From George Baker in Georgia to Father Divine up and down the eastern United States—what a long, strange trip and what a typically American transformation of self and status. A brilliant organizer (and self-promoter), Father Divine built up a major and almost uniquely multiracial following, whose adherents did indeed believe as Divine preached, "Father will provide." Today a shrine recalls the founder of the Peace Mission Movement, whose life began shortly after the defeat of Reconstruction and ended in the year the Voting Rights Act was passed.

LANCASTER

Thaddeus Stevens Grave
Concord (also called Shreiner's) Cemetery, West Chestnut at Mulberry streets, Lancaster, PA 17603
(717) 299-7730 (c/o Thaddeus Stevens State School of Technology)
Hours: Daylight or by appointment with Stevens School
Admission: Free

Thaddeus Stevens's life centered on the struggle for the abolition of slavery and the advancement of African-American rights. An outsider from birth—he was born with a clubfoot, then viewed as a sign of evil—he lived for years with a black housekeeper, deigning neither to confirm nor deny rumors of their sexual entanglement. A delegate to Pennsylvania's 1838 Constitutional Convention, he refused to sign the final document because voting rights were restricted to whites. The most severe of the Radical Republicans in the U.S. House of Representatives, Stevens opposed northern concessions to southerners during the winter 1860–1861 run-up to the outbreak of war; urged Lincoln to emancipate and arm slaves from the war's onset; opposed Lincoln's leniency regarding the readmission of secessionist states; demanded the disenfranchisement of Confederates and the distribution of their land to freedmen; guided through Congress the key pieces of Reconstruction legislation, including the 14th and 15th amendments, the Civil Rights Act of 1866, and the Reconstruction Act of 1867 (all of which he viewed as insufficiently rigorous); and was a leader of the impeachment movement against President Andrew Johnson. Determined to advertise his adamancy for racial equality beyond his life, he insisted on being buried in his constituency's sole integrated cemetery under an epitaph aptly (because it mirrored his psychological profile) self-composed: "I have chosen this that I might illustrate in my death the principals [*sic*] which I advocated through a long life, Equality of Man before his Creator." These words still can be read above his grave.

LINCOLN

Lincoln University
Lincoln, PA 19352
(215) 932-8300
Hours: Mon.–Fri., 8 A.M.–4:30 P.M.; closed 12 P.M.–1 P.M. Library's Special Collections: Mon.–Fri., 8:30 A.M.–5 P.M.; 7 P.M.–10 P.M.; Sat., 12 P.M.–5 P.M.
Admission: Free

Founded in 1854 as Ashmun Institute—its name honoring the first American Colonization Society agent sent to Liberia and underscoring the school's links to the society—what is now Lincoln University lays claim to being the first full university established for the purpose of educating African Americans. In 1859 its first three graduates all left for missionary work in Liberia, an African link Lincoln kept through the 20th century, when Kwame Nhrumah, leader of the Ghanian independence struggle and that country's first president, graduated from the school. Other 20th-century graduates include Langston Hughes and Thurgood Marshall.

NORRISTOWN

Valley Forge National Historical Park
Route 23 at North Gulph Road, Norristown, PA 19481
(215) 783-1000
Hours: Daily, 8:30 A.M.–5 P.M.
Admission: Free

Contrary to our shared American perception, not only white men shared the rigors of Valley Forge: Perhaps as many as 800 to 1,000 African-American troops, 1,500 women of various colors, and scores of Indian combatants joined the 10,000 white troops who suffered through a horrendous winter. Today's visitors can view a monument to the African-American contribution to the American Revolution that has been raised at Valley Forge through the efforts of the black sorority Delta Sigma Theta.

PHILADELPHIA

Philadelphia Convention & Visitors Bureau
1515 Market Street, Suite 2020, Philadelphia, PA 19102-2071
(215) 636-3300
Hours: Mon.–Fri., 8 A.M.–6 P.M.

Ask for its "African-American Historical & Cultural Guide" and for information on the following festivals: Martin Luther King Jr. Celebration (January); Presidential Jazz Weekend (February); Africamericas Festival (May); Odunde Festival (June); and Freedom Fest (October).

Philadelphia Visitor Center
1525 JFK Boulevard, Philadelphia, PA 19201
(800) 321-WKND; (215) 636-1666
Hours: Daily, 9 A.M.–5 P.M.

Afro-American Historical and Cultural Museum
Seventh and Arch streets, Philadelphia, PA 19107
(215) 574-0380
Hours: Museum: Tue.–Sat., 10 A.M.–5 P.M.; Sun., 12 P.M.–6 P.M. Heritage Tour: by appointment, Apr. 1–June 30 and Sept. 1–Nov. 30: Sat., 11 A.M., 1 P.M.; July 1–Aug. 31: Tue.–Sat., 11 A.M., 1 P.M.; Sept. 1–Nov. 30: Sat., 11 A.M., 1 P.M.
Admission: Museum: adults, $4; children, seniors, and students with ID, $2. Heritage Tour: By appointment

With four galleries, the Afro-American Historical and Cultural Museum is able to outline comprehensively the contours of black America's presence in the arts and life of this nation. Art galleries, performance spaces, multimedia presentations, changing exhibitions, and permanent historical collections portray the heritage and contributions of African Americans. In addition, the museum offers a 22-site African-American heritage tour of Philadelphia.

All-Wars Memorial to Black Soldiers
42nd Street and Parkside Avenue, Philadelphia, PA 19121
(215) 685-0001
Western edge of Fairmount Park
Hours: Daily until sunset
Admission: Free

An 18-foot column encircled by 12 life-size military figures being offered laurel wreaths by Columbia, the All-Wars Memorial to Black Soldiers pays tribute to three centuries of African-American veterans.

American Federation of Musicians, Union Local 274 Historical Marker
912 South Broad Street, Philadelphia, PA
Hours: Daily until sunset
Admission: Free

Racially excluded from Local 77 of the American Federation of Musicians, African Americans in 1935 formed Local 274, which remained in existence even after passage of the Civil Rights Act of 1964. Known for its integrated character, its democratic procedures, and the quality of its members—who included Dizzy Gillespie, John Coltrane, Nina Simone, and others—Local 274 refused to merge with Local 77 when the federation ended its dual union/single-race policy. Finally in 1971 the AFM revoked 274's charter, a decision upheld in a court ruling. Today a historical marker recalls the bad times and the big-time bad decision of a union local whose members probably couldn't even keep time—and certainly couldn't keep up with the playing of the musicians they excluded.

American Women's Heritage Society and Museum
Belmont Mansion Historic House, 2000 Belmont Drive, Philadelphia, PA 19131
(215) 878-8844
Hours: Tue.–Fri., 10 A.M.–5 P.M.; Sat.–Sun., by appointment
Admission: Tours: Adults, $3; children under high school age, $1.50

The contributions of African-American women in Philadelphia, in Pennsylvania, and across the nation are showcased at the American Women's Heritage Society and Museum.

Church of the Advocate
18th and Diamond streets, Philadelphia, PA 19121
(215) 236-0568
Hours: Group tours, by appointment
Admission: Free; donations encouraged

The Second Black Power Convention, the final Black Panther Party Congress, and numerous 1960s-era civil rights gatherings were held at the Church of the Advocate. Today a series of murals illustrate the fate of the diaspora in America, who allegorically are compared to the Jews in Egyptian bondage.

John W. Coltrane Home and Historical Marker
1511 North 33rd Street, Philadelphia, PA 19121
(215) 763-1118
Hours: Marker: Daily until sunset. Coltrane Home: By appointment and only in the summer months
Admission: Marker: Free. Home: Voluntary donations requested

Trane's music, memory, and former home are preserved in a context of Philadelphia's African-American musical heritage, while outside his former home a historical marker recounts the impact of the North Carolina–born saxophonist whose early death from liver cancer cut short a career that sent the music onto yet another new track.

Forten Home Historical Marker
336 Lombard Street, Philadelphia, PA 19147
Hours: Daily until sunset
Admission: Free

Outside James Forten's former residence, a historical marker recalls the black Revolutionary War ship's gunpowder boy, one of the founders of the Free African Society (see following entry), successful businessman, patriot who with the help of Richard Allen (see entry on p. 230) raised a 2,500-member free black militia unit to defend the city during the War of 1812, political activist, abolitionist, and organizer of the 1830 black convention that sought to unify the community on slavery and abolition issues.

Free African Society Historical Marker
Sixth and Lombard streets, Philadelphia, PA 19147
Hours: Daily until sunset
Admission: Free

In 1787, the same year Prince Hall received formal approval for African Lodge No. 1 in Boston, another autonomous black organization came into being in Philadelphia. The Free African Society, today commemorated with a historical marker, grew out of Richard Allen's and Absalom Jones's withdrawal from St. George's Methodist Episcopal Church, which did not offer equal treatment to all its members. The society was one of the earliest black self-help and protonationalist groups in America.

Billie Holiday State Historical Marker
1409 Lombard Street, Philadelphia, PA 19146
Between 15th and Broad streets
Hours: Daily until sunset
Admission: Free

Eleanora Fagan was born in Philadelphia and grew up in Baltimore. (See Billie Holiday entry on p. 245.) When she returned to Philadelphia it was to perform, and she always stayed at the Douglass Hotel, outside of which a Billie Holiday Historical Marker recalls the troubled life of a woman who could make "Strange Fruit," a song protesting the lynchings of African Americans, a commercial success.

Johnson House
6306 Germantown Avenue, Philadelphia, PA 19144
(215) 843-0943
Hours: Tours by appointment
Admission: Adults, $3; ages 12 and under, $1.50

Much of Pennsylvania's colonial, Federal, and antebellum history turned on the activity of nonconforming Christian sects such as the Friends Society (Quakers) and the Mennonites, which believed that politics should bear witness to Christian principles—and that included in the realm of these principles were Indians and African Americans. Bearing witness to these principles frequently placed their adherents on the wrong side of the law—particularly such laws as the Fugitive Slave Act. The attic and basement of the home of the Quakers Samuel and Jeanett Johnson hid slaves traveling the Underground Railroad north to freedom; the main floor of his home served as a gathering place for abolitionist activists, including Harriet Tubman and the Underground Railroad's leading East Coast figure and future chronicler, William Still. (See entry on p. 319.) Today the Johnson House is maintained in its abolitionist-era appearance by the Mennonites, who with the Quakers opposed slavery as a moral evil.

Liberty Bell
Market Street, Philadelphia, PA 19107
(215) 597-8974
Hours: Daily, 9 A.M.–5 P.M.
Admission: Free

As is so common in American history, the well-known Liberty Bell has a little-known connection to the struggle for African-American rights: Its name does not date to the American Revolution it symbolizes, but rather to 1839, when it was so first termed by The Friends of Freedom, one of America's numerous if small abolitionist groups.

Alain Locke Historical Marker
2221 South 5th Street, Philadelphia, PA 19148
Near Snyder Street
Hours: Daily until sunset
Admission: Free

The first black Rhodes scholar, Alain Locke promoted the Harlem Renaissance as a critic and as a chronicler and participated in it as an author. A historical marker notes the childhood home of a local boy who made—and did—good.

Most Worshipful Prince Hall Grand Lodge of Pennsylvania
Masonic Hall, 4301 North Broad Street, Philadelphia, PA 19140
(215) 457-6110
Hours: Mon.–Fri., 9 A.M.–5 P.M.
Admission: Free

America's oldest continuously active black fraternal order began in 1787 when the Revolutionary War veteran Prince Hall secured permission from Freemasonry's Mother Grand Lodge in England to establish an African-American lodge in Boston. (See Prince Hall entry on p. 261.) A decade later Richard Allen (see entry on p. 230) and Absalom Jones established the Most Worshipful Prince Hall Grand Lodge of Pennsylvania in Philadelphia. Allen's and Jones's involvement was typical of the men: Anything that brought the black community together and encouraged it to rely on and develop its own abilities was welcome and won their active support. Born in slavery in Delaware in 1746, Jones was almost 40 before he could purchase his and his wife's freedom. Thereafter he became a mainstay of Philadelphia's black community, participating in the Free African Society of Philadelphia, arguably the first independent black mutual aid society in the nation. He and Allen—aided by Benjamin Rush and other white Quakers—founded the African Church of Philadelphia, whose first minister he became. With Allen, he co-authored a series of pamphlets and petitions attacking slavery and propagating the contributions of the city's African Americans. Today, outside the lineal descendant of Allen's and Jones's endeavor, a historical marker makes mention of Hall and two of Philadelphia's African-American giants.

Mother Bethel African Methodist Episcopal Church
419 South Sixth Street, Philadelphia, PA 19147
(215) 925-0616
Hours: Museum tours: Tue.–Sat., 10 A.M.–2:30 P.M. and Sun. following church services
Admission: Free; donations encouraged

The oldest continuously black-owned property in America was purchased in 1787 through the efforts of Richard Allen, who in 1794 in protest against the segregated seating in white churches built on its ground the church that became Mother Bethel African Methodist Episcopal Church. Mother Bethel's claim to fame rests on more than the fact that it was conceived and dedicated by the founder and first bishop of the A.M.E. Church, for it was also the site of the first black convention in America. Held in 1830 and presided over by Allen, the convention sought to unify African Americans on antislavery matters, particularly on the position of rejecting Africa as a settlement site for freed slaves. Today, in the fourth church to occupy the corner of Sixth and Lombard streets, visitors to the Richard Allen Museum can trace the history of the A.M.E. Church and view memorabilia of both Allen and Jones.

COURTESY PHILADELPHIA CONVENTION AND VISITORS BUREAU

Organized by Richard Allen, Mother Bethel African Methodist Episcopal Church hosted the first national black convention and today has a small museum tracing Allen's contributions to America.

St. Thomas African Episcopal Church Historical Marker
St. James Place and Fifth Street, Philadelphia, PA 19139
(215) 473-3065
Hours: Daily until sunset
Admission: Free

A historical marker commemorates the original location of the church founded in 1794 by Absalom Jones, when he and Richard Allen withdrew from St. George's Methodist Church in protest against its segregated seating. St. Thomas received a state charter in 1796, becoming the first incorporated African-American institution in the United States.

William Still House Historical Marker
244 South 12th Street, Philadelphia, PA 19107
Hours: Daily until sunset
Admission: Free

William Still was born in New Jersey in 1821, the youngest of 18 children of Levin Steel, who had purchased his freedom and changed his name to protect his wife, a fugitive slave. By the age of 30, William Still—who legally remained a fugitive slave though born more than a decade after his mother fled bondage—was a leader of the antislavery movement in Philadelphia, which his drive and organizational skill reinvigorated. Still raised large sums of money, established a network of safe houses—through which almost 800 souls passed—and kept watch over the activities of slave catchers. Toward the latter end, Still carefully vetted fugitive slaves. In the course of an interview one day, Still suddenly realized that he was speaking to a brother, the 49-year-old Peter, whom he had never known.

Still's letter to J. M. McKim, a founding member of the American Anti-Slavery Society who had left the Presbyterian ministry to serve the abolitionist cause full-time, remains the best summary of the shocking encounter's background:

> My parents had four children, and the desire of freedom rested so heavily upon the mind of my mother, that she in concert with my father concluded that their only hope of enjoying each other's society, depended upon mother's making her escape. Their plans all being laid they soon found themselves in the State of New Jersey. But before mother had long enjoyed what she had so eagerly sought after, and what she prized so highly [liberty], she and all four of her children were pursued, captured and carried back to Maryland. . . . Before she had been back three months she made second flight, taking her two youngest, which were girls, and leaving her two oldest boys, Levin and Peter. I shall never forget hearing my mother speak of the memorable night when she fled. She went to the bed where her two boys were sleeping—kissed them—consigned them into the hands of God and took her departure again for a

land of liberty. My mother's efforts proved successful, though at the heartrending consideration of leaving two of her boys to the disposal of slaveholders. Those unfortunate boys were sold soon after my mother's escape. All that she ever heard of them afterwards was, that they had been sold far south.

Peter's life replicated that of his father: He purchased his freedom from his Alabamian master—though late rather than early in his life—and, after discovering his identity, sought to bring his family to freedom. Their escape, aided by the Underground Railroad, brought them to Indiana, where they were recaptured and returned to Alabama. With the backing of prominent abolitionists such as Harriet Beecher Stowe, Peter Still embarked on a fund-raising campaign to raise the $5,000 demanded to ransom his family, with whom he was reunited in 1854.

The William Still House Historical Marker locates the Philadelphia residence of the Underground Railroad conductor whose carefully maintained records of "passengers" both enabled relatives to locate each other once freedom was reached and served as the documentary foundation for his book *The Underground Railroad. Railroad*, the first significant history of the enterprise and still an invaluable resource, underscored the vital contribution of free blacks to 19th-century America's most extensive and significant clandestine operation.

Henry O. Tanner House Historical Marker
2908 West Diamond Street, Philadelphia, PA 19121
Hours: Daily until sunset
Admission: Free

A bishop's son who showed an early interest in painting, Henry O. Tanner became the most prominent and accomplished African-American artist of the late 19th and early 20th centuries. Encouraged in his childhood by his father, while studying at the Pennsylvania Academy of the Fine Arts by Thomas Eakins, and later while living in Paris by Benjamin Constant, Tanner's adult confidence and skill grew even as his thematic matter shifted toward biblical subjects with which he first had become acquainted in his childhood. Today a historical marker is located at the house, now a *private residence not open to the public*, in which the Tanner family lived while the young artist studied at the Pennsylvania Academy of the Fine Arts.

PITTSBURGH

Pittsburgh Convention & Visitors Bureau
4 Gateway Center, Suite 514, Pittsburgh, PA 15222
(412) 281-7711
Hours: Mon.–Fri., 9 A.M.–5 P.M.

African Heritage Classroom
University of Pittsburgh, Cathedral of Learning, Pittsburgh, PA 15260
(412) 624-6150
Hours: Mon.–Sat., 9 A.M.–3:30 P.M.; Sun., 11 A.M.–3:30 P.M.
Admission: Adults, $2; seniors, $1; ages 8–18, 50 cents

A portrayal that blends together different African civilizations to reveal the continent's cultural foundations, the African Heritage Classroom is organized around the concept of a courtyard because courtyards of various types are the focus of family activities in Africa, and the family is the basic unit of African society. The classroom is modeled on a central courtyard of an Ashanti royal residence, though the style broadly is found among the African cultures present in Nigeria, Ghana, Benin, Togo, and the Ivory Coast. To this model have been added symbols or artifacts from numerous other African peoples.

Martin R. Delany Historical Marker
5 PPG Place, Pittsburgh, PA
Between Third Avenue and Market Street
Hours: Daily until sunset
Admission: Free

Within the limits of race and place, Martin Delany was fortunate in his 1812 birth. The son of a slave father and a free black mother—and hence freeborn himself—Delany was raised with a deep and specific knowledge of his princely African heritage, which included Mandingan and Golah blood. Perhaps this accounts for his later advocacy of a black return to the African continent, one of the many examples and causes of his alienation from the majority sentiment of the 19th-century African-American movement. An early black nationalist, abolitionist, and propagandist, Delany married into the free black elite of Pittsburgh, where in the late 1840s he published a newspaper, the *Mystery*, and helped edit Frederick Douglass's *North Star.* Today his Pittsburgh publication is recalled by a historical marker located near his old *Mystery* office. Delany subsequently attended Harvard Medical School, where white protests compelled his withdrawal; scoured Africa for an appropriate African-American colonization site; authored an early black nationalist manifesto and a novel; was commissioned the first black field officer in the Union army; worked for the Freedmen's Bureau in South Carolina after the war; split with the Radical Republican Reconstruction and found himself in the unlikely position of supporting a white supremacist, former Confederate general for governor; returned to his African colonization efforts; and died in his 70s. Delany's awareness of his African grandfathers' high status in a hierarchical, slave-owning African culture, his sharp intellect, his favorable marriage, and his elitist perspective did not always win him friends. Frederick Douglass's famous observation, "I thank God for making me a man, but Delany thanks Him for making him a *black* man," reflected more than mutual gender gratitude: Delany was indeed confidently (and fully) black; Douglass was cast(e) adrift—a half-white slave abandoned by a father he never knew and, more agonizingly, by a mother he did.

SHARON HILL

Bessie Smith's Grave Site

Mt. Lawn Cemetery, 84th Street and Hook Road, Sharon Hill, PA 19079
(215) 586-8220
Hours: Daily until sunset
Admission: Free

Born in Tennessee and creatively tied to Delta Blues country, Bessie Smith, the "Queen of the Blues" (see Afro-American Museum, Chattanooga, Tennessee, and all Clarksdale, Mississippi entries) met her death in an automobile accident, in Clarksdale, Mississippi. Her marriage to a Philadelphia policeman accounts for the Pennsylvania location of her grave site. The present condition of her grave, which for years suffered from neglect, is due to the combined efforts of her former maid and the late Janis Joplin, an epigone who would have given much to have been an acolyte.

WASHINGTON

LeMoyne House

49 East Maiden Street, Washington, PA 15301
(412) 225-6740
Hours: Feb.–mid-Dec.: Wed.–Fri., 12 P.M.–4 P.M.; Sun., 2 P.M.–4 P.M.
Admission: Adults, $3; students, $1.50

Influenced by the state's nonconforming Christian sects, a Pennsylvania Anti-Slavery Society predated William Lloyd Garrison's 1833 American Anti-Slavery Society by many decades. Shortly after the founding of Garrison's group, a Washington County affiliate came into being, one of whose leaders was Dr. Francis J. LeMoyne. Three times in the 1840s LeMoyne ran for the governorship of Pennsylvania on the Liberty (abolitionist) Party ticket. The party, however, enjoyed scant electoral success, merging in 1848 with the Free Soil Party ("Free soil, free speech, free labor, and free men") and in 1856 with the newly organized Republican Party. Throughout these years, the Washington County abolitionists—who lived just north of Greene County, whose southern boundary was the Mason-Dixon line—did not restrict their efforts to the legal sphere. LeMoyne, too, was active in the Underground Railroad, sometimes hiding as many as 25 fugitives at one time in a secret third-floor room of his Maiden Street home. Today the LeMoyne House is maintained by the Washington County Historical Society, which there operates a small museum that traces one of the brighter moments of 19th-century American history.

RHODE ISLAND

Division of Tourism
Seven Jackson Walkway, Providence, RI 02903
(800) 556-2484
Hours: Mon.–Fri., 8:30 A.M.–4:30 P.M.

BRISTOL

Haffenreffer Museum of Anthropology
Brown University, Tower Road, Bristol, RI 02809
(401) 253-8388
Hours: June–Sept.: Tue.–Sun., 10 A.M.–5 P.M. Oct.–May: weekends only, 10 A.M.–5 P.M.
Admission: Adults, $2; seniors and children, $1

Wood, metal, ceramic, and fiber are the media; the subject is the real life of Africa, which is reflected in the 700 to 800 utilitarian objects from the continent displayed at the Haffenreffer Museum of Anthropology. Sculpture, masks, funerary objects, jewelry, textiles, and furnishings from the Yoruba, Afo, Ibo, Mende, Kran, Dan, Ashanti, Ewe, and other peoples elicit joy, recognition, and questions. Though most holdings date from the early 20th century, the museum displays Djenne ceramic pieces from the 9th and 10th centuries.

EAST GREENWICH

James Mitchell Varnum Home
1776 Revolution Street, East Greenwich, RI 02818
(401) 884-1776
Hours: June–Aug.: Tue.–Sat., 1 P.M.–4 P.M.
Admission: Adults, $2; children, $1

Brigadier General James Mitchell Varnum of Rhode Island saw extended action in the early years of the American Revolution, including at Valley Forge. There he suggested the unprecedented: the raising of an all-black regiment. (See Butts Hill Fort entry on p. 325.) The resulting 1st Rhode Island (Black) Regiment was the sole African-American unit in the Continental army whose exploits can be supported by a substantial documentary record. Varnum's link with Washington extended far beyond their shared rigors at Valley Forge: He was a member of the Society of Cincinnati—which was composed of Washington's closest senior colleagues—and a postwar founder of the Ohio Company, in which Washington was a major investor. Today the James Mitchell Varnum Home offers period rooms, portraits of the first proposer of a Revolutionary War African-American regiment, and memorabilia of a man who was closely acquainted with Washington, Lafayette, von Steuben, and Henry Knox.

MIDDLETON

Overing/Prescott House
2009 West Main Road, Middleton, RI 02840
(401) 847-6230
Hours: Apr.–Oct.: daily, 10 A.M.–4 P.M.
Admission: Farm: free. Museum and windmill: $1.50

The Revolutionary War episode in Rhode Island was fit for a historical novel of the more lurid and exciting sort. The cast of characters included a womanizing British general; one of his many conquests—a married American woman; the captured American general Charles Lee, Washington's second-in-command; Colonel William Barton, a militia commander; and Jack Sisson, an African American. The climax involved a daring commando raid by rowboat through the assembled British fleet and the kidnapping of the British general. In the summer of 1777, Colonel Barton, brooding on the British capture of Lee, who was a popular figure in Rhode Island if not with his colleagues, and learning that the local British commander, the roguish General Prescott, had headquartered himself at the home of his mistress, the wife of Henry Overing, resolved to kidnap Prescott and exchange him for Lee. Barton spoke to the members of his militia brigade, telling them that he needed volunteers for a mission the details of which he could not reveal. When all his men volunteered, Barton packed them aboard rowboats and, with oars muffled, rowed at night from Warwick Neck past three British frigates on the east side of Prudence Island, landed outside Middleton, and climbed the hill leading to the Overing House. After knocking out the British sentinel, Barton led his men to the bedroom, ordered Sisson to break down its door, and thereupon captured Prescott and Mrs. Overing in *flagrante delicto*. Lee soon thereafter returned to the Continental army, which may not have been to its—or his—benefit. (See Monmouth Battlefield entry on p. 282.) Sisson later joined the 1st Rhode Island (Black) Regiment. (See Butts Hill Fort entry on p. 325 and Memorial to Black Soldiers entry on p. 325.) Mrs. Overing's fate is unrecorded. Today visitors to the Overing/Prescott House wander 11 acres of farm, stroll through period rooms, have access to a restored 1811 windmill, and may tour a museum and the guardhouse to which Prescott rudely was transferred from the buxom embrace of Mrs. Overing. Visitors, however, will see nothing that directly ties Sisson to the raid.

PORTSMOUTH

Butts Hill Fort Historical Marker

(401) 683-9178 (Portsmouth Historical Society)
Off Sprague Street, at the northeast end of Aquidneck Island, overlooking the Sakkonet River and facing Tiverton, Rhode Island, and the Stone Bridge, Portsmouth
Hours: Daily until sunset
Admission: Free

The brutal winter of 1777 found Washington's army in desperate straits. Holed up in the snow of Valley Forge, many of the soldiers lacked shoes—and all of them lacked food and pleasant prospects for the future. On January 2, 1778, Brigadier General James Mitchell Varnum of Rhode Island proposed to Washington that his state's two understrength battalions be combined, and the officers thereby freed raise and train a "battalion of negroes." (A month later a similar proposal would be offered by a South Carolinian; see Monmouth Battlefield entry on p. 282.) Rhode Island's legislature endorsed the proposal, noting that since the British occupied the "greater part" of the state, it was "impossible . . . to furnish recruits" for the Continental army. Within a month of Varnum's proposal, the state enacted a law entitling slave and free black enlistees to "all the bounties, wages and encouragements" of other [white] soldiers. The act also provided that upon enrollment, each man would be "absolutely free, as though he had never been encumbered with any kind of servitude or slavery." Hurrying north from Valley Forge, Colonel Christopher Greene assumed command of the new unit, the 1st Rhode Island (Black) Regiment, which shortly thereafter saw action in the Battle of Rhode Island. At Butts Hill Fort, in the largest Revolutionary War encounter in the state, Sullivan's outnumbered Americans—unsupported by an intended French naval component delayed by storm at sea—were compelled to withdraw under attack by a superior British and Hessian force. The 95 former slaves and 30 free blacks in the 1st Rhode Island Regiment thrice repelled Hessian charges on Sullivan's right flank, earning, in Sullivan's report of the battle, "a proper share of the Honours of the day." Today, at the battle site, old redoubts worn by time are complemented by a historical marker that recounts the battle. Erected nearby, not far from the spot of the regiment's first blooding, is the Memorial to Black Soldiers.

Memorial to Black Soldiers of the Battle of Rhode Island

Patriots Park, Route 114 at Route 24, Portsmouth, RI 02871
Hours: Daily until sunset
Admission: Free

Following the Battle of Rhode Island, the Black Regiment saw further action in the war, most notably at Points Bridge near Croton in New York. There, in May of 1781, 40 of the regiment's men fell, like Anglo-Saxon housecarls around their king, dead to the man, in an unsuccessful attempt to protect Colonel Greene from the bayonets of 260 British soldiers. Today a memorial pays tribute to the courage of the free blacks and former slaves—the latter, men who ceased to be chattel only because of the state's desperation—who served America's cause.

PROVIDENCE

Civil War Monument

Kennedy Plaza, Washington and Exchange streets, Providence, RI 02903
(401) 331-8575 (Rhode Island Historical Society)
Hours: Daily until sunset
Admission: Free

Rhode Island's Union veterans are commemorated with a Civil War Monument. Among the names inscribed are those of the 14th Regiment Rhode Island Heavy Artillery (Colored). Raised in 1863, the regiment saw garrison duty in New Orleans in 1864 and '65. Despite missing the rigors of combat, the unit lost about 25 percent of its 1,452 men to disease.

Museum of Art

Rhode Island School of Design, 224 Benefit Street, Providence, RI 02903
(401) 454-6500
Hours: Sept. 1–June 15: Tue.–Wed., Fri.–Sat., 10:30 A.M.–5 P.M.; Thu., 12 P.M.–8 P.M.; Sun., holidays, 2 P.M.–5 P.M. Rest of year: Wed.–Sat., 12 P.M.–5 P.M.
Admission: Adults, $1; seniors, 50 cents; ages 5–18, 25 cents

Among the black artists whose work is displayed at the Rhode Island School of Design's Museum of Art is Edward Bannister, a Providence native noted for his seascapes. Bannister (1828–1901) was the first African-American painter to achieve national recognition, winning a medal at the Philadelphia Centennial Exposition in 1876. One of the founders of the famed Providence Art Club, he is represented at the museum by seven landscapes.

Old State House

150 Benefit Street, Providence, RI 02903
(401) 277-2678 (Rhode Island Historical & Preservation Commission)
Hours: Mon.–Fri., 8:30 A.M.–4:30 P.M.
Admission: Free

Though it was not a member of the New England Confederation, Rhode Island's experience with slavery broadly paralleled the region's. As elsewhere in New England, slavery provided large-scale employment—not of slaves but to the seaman, shipping and rum merchants, coopers, sailmakers, distillery workers, farmers, tanners, and others who serviced the triangular trade among the region (rum), Africa (slaves), and the West Indies (slave-produced sugar and molasses). By the 18th century Rhode Island displaced Massachusetts as a center of the trade, annually averaging 18 ships and 1,800 hogsheads of rum to Africa. The consequence was foreseeable: Though most of the Africans purchased ended up in the West Indies, the state's black population rose steadily, doubling between the close of the first decade and the middle of the century. Thereafter, at least as a proportion of Rhode Island's population, the African-American presence declined, so that when manumission was discussed in the state legislature in 1783, blacks comprised less than 5 percent of the population. Still, Rhode Island's shipping interests opposed attacks on the slave trade and succeeded in imposing on the legislature a compromise manumission proposal that provided for gradual emancipation but left the overseas slave trade untouched. Rhode Island's abolition debate, from the 1774 law prohibiting the importation of slaves through the 1784 act, and the debate over its subsequent legal constraints on African Americans, including exclusion from voting rights, took place in the Old State House. No longer the meeting place of the General Assembly, Old State House provides offices to government agencies and boasts but one historical marker interpreting its past. The marker makes no mention of the abolition debate, referring instead to the building being the site of the 1776 signing of the Rhode Island Declaration of Independence.

Rhode Island Black Heritage Society
One Hilton Street, Providence, RI 02905
(401) 751-3490
Hours: Mon.–Fri., 9 A.M.–4:30 P.M.; Sat.–Sun., by appointment
Admission: Free

The state's principal resource for discovering, interpreting, and promoting its African-American past, the Rhode Island Black Heritage Society also operates a small museum and offers black history tours of the area. Ask for a copy of the society's "Rhode Island's Freedom Trail," which details 50 locations that touch upon the state's black past.

VERMONT

Department of Travel and Tourism
134 State Street, Montpelier, VT 05602
(802) 828-3236
Hours: Mon.–Fri., 7:45 A.M.–4:30 P.M.

BENNINGTON

William Lloyd Garrison Historical Marker and Bennington Museum
West Main Street, Bennington, VT 05201
(802) 447-1571
Hours: Museum: Daily, 9 A.M.–5 P.M.
Admission: Museum: Adults, $5; seniors, $4; under 12, free

Driven by a moral absolutism worthy of Massachusetts' 17th-century theocracy, William Lloyd Garrison was America's leading abolitionist and moral reformer during the first half of the 19th century. Born in Massachusetts, Garrison was apprenticed to a newspaper printer at 13. A decade later, converted to "the cause of the slave" by the Quaker Benjamin Lundy, for whose paper, the *Genius of Universal Emancipation*, he labored, Garrison embarked on an abolitionist career that lasted until the passage of the 13th Amendment and the close of the Civil War. In 1831 Garrison founded the *Liberator*, an antislavery weekly he edited for the next 35 years. The same year he helped found the New England Anti-Slavery Society. Two years later he played a similar role in the founding of the American Anti-Slavery Society, which advocated—in a Declaration of Sentiments penned by Garrison—immediate emancipation, racial equality, and nonviolence. Probably Garrison's greatest significance in these early years was in undermining white antislavery support for the American Colonization Society, which viewed an African homeland as the end toward which abolitionism should aim.

In 1840 Garrison secured control of the American Anti-Slavery Society when his (mainly white) opponents—chary of his vigorous support for women's rights, his vituperative absolutism, and his rejection of political activism—split off to form the American and Foreign Anti-Slavery Society and the Liberty Party. (See Warsaw Presbyterian Church entry on p. 309.) African Americans, too, opposed Garrison and for the same reasons: Frederick Douglass because Garrison ignored the political realm, W. C. Nell (see Abiel Smith School entry on p. 264) because Garrison rejected illegal activity, and Samuel Cornish (see Peary-McMillan entry on p. 235) because Garrison supported anticlericalism and the women's movement. Garrison's American Anti-Slavery Society adopted advanced principles of such purity—moral suasion, feminism, pacificism, and the breakup of the Union—as to guarantee its marginalization. Like other radical absolutists, like John Brown in the last century or Lenin in this, Garrison was rescued from history's deep periphery by war. The Civil War made Garrison and Brown, who now were seen as prophetic, their reputations rising higher and higher in cadence with the body count.

Though the *Liberator* was published in Boston, Garrison's career as a newspaper publisher began in an office near the Bennington Common, where he published *The Journal of the Times*. Not far from his first office and the present location of the Bennington Museum is a William Lloyd Garrison Historical Marker. Visitors to the museum will find copies of the *Liberator* and *The Journal of the Times*, as well as a portrait of Lemuel Haynes (see Fort Ticonderoga entry on p. 308) preaching in the nearby First Congregational Church.

First Congregational Church
One Monument Circle, Bennington, VT 05201
(802) 447-1223
Hours: Call during office hours for appointment: Memorial Day–October: Mon.–Sat., 10 A.M.–12 P.M. and 1 P.M.–4 P.M.; Sun., 1 P.M.–4 P.M.
Admission: Free

In the gap that roughly bisects Vermont's Green Mountain range lies Rutland, to which Lemuel Haynes (see Fort Ticonderoga entry on p. 308) journeyed three years after his ordination. There, for the next three decades, the black minister and eloquent Christian apologist who secured a reputation for his defense of doctrinal orthodoxy labored to save souls. In addition to riding a circuit, Haynes journeyed south to Bennington. There he preached at the First Congregational Church often enough to have his service recorded in a painting now located next door in the Bennington Museum.

BROWNINGTON

Old Stone House Museum
c/o RFD 1, Box 500, Orleans, VT 05860
(802) 754-2022
Hours: July–Aug.: daily, 11 A.M.–5 P.M. May 15–June 30 and Sept. 1–Oct. 15: Thu.–Tue., 11 A.M.–5 P.M.
Admission: Adults, $3; under 12, $1

The Old House Museum and several other sites in the Brownington Village Historic District relate directly to the life and career of the first African American to earn a college degree in America, Alexander Lucius Twilight. Twilight, both of whose parents are listed in the 1800 federal census under the rubric normally assigned to free blacks, "All other free persons except Indians not taxed," was indentured to a local farmer. He purchased with his savings his last year of service and enrolled in a secondary school. Six years later he enrolled in Middlebury College, from which he graduated in 1823. In 1829, licensed to preach and married to the sister of a Middlebury classmate, Twilight arrived in Brownington, where he lived for the next three decades. First serving as minister of the village church and principal of the grammar school, Twilight went on to found and physically build a massive, four-story granite academy, "Athenian Hall," which for decades served as northeastern Vermont's principal educational resource. Twilight also served his community in Vermont's General Assembly in the 1836–1837 session, possibly being the first African American to sit in a state legislature. Today's visitors to the Old Stone House Museum walk the halls of Twilight's academy and view his signed Bible, his initialed trunk, his books, and his household wares. The cemetery of the nearby church in which he preached holds the remains and the gravestones of Twilight and his wife; also nearby are the first Brownington home of the Twilights and the frame buildings that served as the town's grammar school and church.

FERRISBURG

Rokeby
Highway 7, Ferrisburg, VT 05456
(802) 877-3406
Hours: Guided tours: May–mid-Oct.: Thu.–Sun., 11 A.M., 12:30 P.M., and 2 P.M.
Admission: Adults, $2; students and seniors, $1; under 12, 50 cents

Records of the Vermont Anti-Slavery Society, inflammatory broadsides of slaves being whipped, pamphlets denouncing slavery, the Anti-Slavery Society *Almanac*, and paintings and photographs of the abolitionist owners are on view at Rokeby, which served both as an Underground Railroad station and as the home of Rowland E. Robinson, the blind writer of Vermont folklore and romantic tales (for example, "Out of Bondage") of the antislavery struggle. The author's parents were Quaker stalwarts of the abolitionist movement, helping to establish both the Ferrisburg (1833) and Vermont (1834) Anti-Slavery societies.

MIDDLEBURY

Middlebury College
College Street, Middlebury, VT 05753
(802) 388-3711
Hours: Mon.–Fri., 8:45 A.M., 10:30 A.M., 12:30 P.M., and 2:15 P.M.
Admission: Free

Alexander Twilight, the first African American to earn a university degree, graduated from Middlebury College in 1823—two decades after the school had awarded an honorary degree to Lemuel Haynes. (See First Congregational Church entry on p. 328.) Middlebury's original building, in which Twilight studied, burned down. Its replacement is named Twilight Hall and bears a plaque commemorating America's first black college graduate.

Vermont Folklife Center
2 Court Street, Middlebury, VT 05753
(802) 388-4964
Hours: Mon.–Fri., 9 A.M.–5 P.M.; also Sat., 12 P.M.–4 P.M. in the summer and fall
Admission: Free; donations encouraged

In the course of the Civil War, a slave from Port Royal, Virginia, slipped across the Rappahannock River and entered the Union lines. Offering himself as an orderly to Ferdinand Dayton, a regimental surgeon, the man spent the rest of the war with the 1st New Jersey Cavalry. Following the war, he journeyed north and married. His daughter, Daisy Turner, was born in 1883 and spent much of the last decade of her long life recounting her family's and her own history to Vermont's state folklorist. Daisy Turner's life and recollections formed the basis for a National Public Radio series and the video *On My Own*. Today visitors to the Vermont Folklife Center, whose current director was Turner's interlocutor, can view the documentary and listen to the tapes of an African-American woman whose collective memory of her family spans slavery in Virginia and freedom in Vermont.

WINDSOR

Old Constitution House

North Main Street, Windsor, VT 05089
(802) 672-3773
Hours: Memorial Day weekend–Columbus Day weekend: Wed.–Sun., 10 A.M.–4 P.M.
Admission: Adults, $1; children under 14, free

Vermont effectively banned slavery at the same time it officially named itself, in its Constitution of 1777, Article 1 of which declared that no one "ought to be beholden by law to serve any person as a servant, slave, or apprentice after he arrives at the age of twenty one years." Strictly speaking, Vermont cannot claim pride of place in *U.S.* history for its constitutional prohibition of slavery, since it did not join the Union until 1791. The state's rugged independence on the issue of slavery perhaps was best typified by the State Supreme Court ruling in the first decade of the 19th century in a case brought by a New York slave owner who claimed that an African American residing in Middlebury was his runaway property. The court held that the plaintiff's evidence of title to the man was good as far as it went—but it did not go far enough, since the man's master could not show a bill of sale or grant from the Almighty, in the absence of which no man might own another. Today the Old Constitution House, where Vermont's founding fathers met (it was then a tavern) and placed a limit on servitude has been restored and is open to visitors.

THE MIDWEST

North
MINNESOTA
MISSISSIPPI RIVER
Minneapolis
St. Paul
IOWA
Ames
Des Moines
Grinnell
Iowa City
West Des Moines
Indianola
Tabor
Salem
NEBRASKA
Crawford
MISSOURI RIVER
Omaha
Lincoln
Nebraska City
KANSAS
Nicodemus
Bogue
Hays
Kanopolis
Ellsworth
Beeler
Larned
ARKANSAS RIVER
Wichita
Leavenworth
Wabaunsee
Ft. Riley
Topeka
Lawrence
Baldwin City
Osawatomie
Chanute
Ft. Scott
Baxter Springs
MISSOURI
Canton
Quincy, IL
Monroe City
Columbia
Kansas City
Sedalia
Jefferson City
Diamond
OKLAHOMA
Ponca City
Tulsa
Kingfisher
Langston
Muskogee
Boley
Oktaha
Oklahoma City
Lawton
Doaksville

LAKE SUPERIOR
MICHIGAN
WISCONSIN
LAKE MICHIGAN
LAKE HURON
LAKE ERIE
Milwaukee
Waukesha
Madison
Milton
Muskegan
Frankenmuth
Lansing
Augusta
Marshall
Battle Creek
Jackson
Cassopolis
Detroit
Dearborn
Adrian
Chicago
Davenport, IA
Princeton
Galesburg
ILLINOIS
Springfield
INDIANA
Fountain City
Indianapolis
Bloomington
Bedford
Put-in-Bay
Oberlin
Cleveland
Akron
Canton
Upper Sandusky
OHIO
Piqua
Westerville
Mt. Pleasant
Wilberforce
Columbus
Xenia
Dayton
Gallipolis
Cincinnati
Ripley
OHIO RIVER
Alton
East St. Louis
MISSISSIPPI RIVER
Junction
OHIO RIVER
0 50 100 150
miles

THERE'S NO PLACE LIKE HOME

GAYLE PEMBERTON

Forget Grant Wood's "American Gothic" painting of the farmer, the wife, and the pitchfork. Forget Carl Sandburg's "Chicago" poem celebrating stockyards and broad shoulders oiling the machinery of the industrial revolution. Forget the Blue Ox, Babe, and her owner Paul Bunyan; forget Billy Sunday and his famed inability to shut down Chicago; forget Lawrence Welk. *The Wizard of Oz*—MGM's 1939 extravaganza starring a 17-year-old Judy Garland—is the archetypal evocation of the Midwest.

With its dreamy adolescent among trusty farmhands, its kind aunt and uncle, its nasty schoolmarm complemented by good and bad witches, its tornado and enervating poppy field, and its philosophical snake-oil salesman and bumbling wizard, *Oz* is a cautionary tale with the axiomatic truth that what we so often believe must be in some distant place, beyond some rainbow, is literally right at our feet. Our dreams can come true in the metaphoric homes of our hearts, brains, spirits, and beliefs and, of course, in the very real places where families and friends live: on certain streets, in particular neighborhoods, in small towns as well as in big cities.

Bordered by Ohio in the east and the far western boundaries of Nebraska and Kansas, the Midwest is supposed to be the region of stability, moderation, and thrift—with a residual amount of pioneer spirit left over from the days when it was the West and our current West was a "beyond." Home to America's first people and later to millions of white immigrants who moved directly from northern Europe to the Plains, the Midwest became a distinct place—different from the West, which was demanding, volatile, and dangerous; different from the South, where the fundamental evil of slavery corrupted the American dream; and different from the East, where life was too highly classed, fast, crowded, and grim. After chasing his rainbow in New York, Nick Carroway, the disenchanted narrator of *The Great Gatsby*, feels the lure of his midwestern roots. After all was said and done, the East had too much a "quality of distortion" compared to his home.

Palpable and enduring, this version of the Midwest, like most visions, is only partly true—and the experiences of African Americans, while reinforcing the prescriptive scenario, offer clues to the contradictions and paradoxes embedded within. Nowhere is this more apparent than in the concept and construction of home.

For African Americans the Midwest offered a refuge from the violence of slavery and its aftermath. Black refugees before, during, and after the Civil War followed the northern star, creating the classic African-American journey to freedom. They were drawn to the cities, to the fertile land, to the promises of not merely a new life—which is what drew many European immigrants—but of the possibility of life itself. But just as one can hear, in 1994, a Germanic accent in the American speech of some midwesterners both young and old—who are separated from Germany by four or more generations—African Americans have created a midwestern home that still stands in the shadow of their predominantly southern past.

"Where do you stay?" a girl asked me on the first day of the fifth grade in Kansas City, Missouri, eons ago. "Stay?" I asked in some confusion. I told her I "lived" on Victor Street.

Though I now know it is a figure of speech, my schoolmate's question has lived with me, and over the years has suggested many things: first, impermanence and dislocation, as if I were an orphan, like Dorothy in *The Wizard of Oz*, staying with my aunt and uncle because I had no home. Or, I've thought, perhaps she meant that staying somewhere meant that movement and change were so commonplace that there was never time to set up a home and to live there. Perhaps she was religious, I figured, and secure in her belief that this earthly, temporary existence could never be the real home. In the last few years, though, I began to think that she pointed to the contested nature of the idea of an African-American home, and that no matter the region, where we live is as likely to be a symbolic space as it is a physical place.

I recall not long ago moving slowly on an Amtrak train leaving Chicago for parts west, looking intently—as I always do—out of the window. I had taken the route many times; I expected to see nothing out of the ordinary. But as the train rocked gently from side to side—gaining speed so slowly that I thought the engineer must have shared my view—I realized that the black neighborhoods that I saw from that window revealed a quality of Chicago life, perhaps midwestern life, that I had never noticed before. A man sat on a porch strumming a guitar; there were folding chairs, unoccupied, across the street in front of another house. I fully expected people to arrive to sit in them soon. It was a dusty street, despite its pavement. A few children were in the street playing a game. An older woman walked slowly toward one of the row houses, carrying her groceries in a reusable fabric shopping bag. This whole scene, I thought, belonged somewhere else, not in the big metropolis of Chicago. It divulged a secret of the windy city—a slower pace and a smaller world. I believed that I could hear a blues from the man's guitar that told me of the journey from some part of Mississippi or Alabama or Arkansas that he or his forebears had undertaken. Whether or not this was a home to him, where he lived—or stayed—I couldn't answer, but the street told me what it wanted to be, somewhere different than in the shadow of Bauhaus and other modernistic designs of Loop skyscrapers.

My father's family goes back five generations in Iowa. My mother was born in Nebraska, her parents in Oklahoma and Kansas; her parents' parents in Oklahoma and Kansas. I was born in Minnesota. I always felt that we lived in the Midwest—and we did, like millions of other black Americans who either have no ties to the South or who ignore them. But something about the street scene in Chicago—the precise feel, or poverty, or architecture of which is not duplicated in New York, Philadelphia, Los Angeles, Seattle, or Denver, but which can be seen in Cleveland, Kansas City, St. Paul, St. Louis, and Omaha—implied a reality about the Midwest and home, and about the United States. The Midwest, our most stable region, is more fragile and self-conscious than we might think. Like its changeable and extreme weather, the Midwest affirms itself frequently in attempting to define a home somewhere else. Doing so, it takes on all aspects of American identity and becomes the site of all regions and dreams, from the German-accented American teenagers; to adults on rollerblades, mimicking Venice Beach narcissists; to luxury apartment dwellers in Chicago or Cleveland, who might for a moment believe they were in Manhattan; to guitar players on a South-side Chicago street in a blues lament for a southern home they could no longer abide.

Judy Garland's great hit song from *The Wizard of Oz* was "Somewhere Over the Rainbow." Movie lore has it that the song was almost dropped from the show; it's hard to believe how we would remember the film—or Garland—without it. Years later, on Broadway, there appeared another version of the story. This time it was called *The Wiz*: an all-black cast, jazzier music, and the young Stephanie Mills as Dorothy. The hit song from *The Wiz* is called, appropriately, "Home." This is where the black Dorothy seeks to go, and the lyrics suggest the dual function of place and home for African Americans. Yes, she wants to go literally to her home, after having experienced the tornado, the journey to Oz, and the various witches, but she also longs for a place of security, somewhere overflowing with "love and affection." In the face of the precarious lives we, as African Americans, have lived in the United States, that may or may not be the physical home.

The world is right after all. The wisdom of both *The Wizard of Oz* and *The Wiz* is oddly affirmed; the quintessential midwestern experience shines forth in these stories. The answers to our questions are right at our feet, in the Midwest, where dreams of what we would like to be collide with the realities of the past and the present to create, for better or worse, not one kind of home, but the sum total of all our American homes.

X·X·X

Gayle Pemberton is the author of *The Hottest Water in Chicago* and is a 1993 Guggenheim Fellow. Born in St. Paul, Minnesota, she holds a Ph.D. in English and American literature from Harvard University. She has taught at Smith College, Columbia University, and Northwestern University, and is currently the associate director of Afro-American studies at Princeton. Pemberton is the offspring of a family that has for five generations lived in the Midwest, covering the states of Nebraska, Oklahoma, Kansas, Illinois, and Minnesota.

ILLINOIS

Tourism Council
629 East Washington Street, Springfield, IL 62701
(800) 822-0292
Hours: Mon.–Fri., 8:30 A.M.–5 P.M.

ALTON

Lincoln-Douglas Debate Historical Marker
Broadway and Market streets, Alton, IL 62002
Hours: Daily until sunset
Admission: Free

A largely unknown Abraham Lincoln introduced himself to the nation in the course of his now-historic 1858 debates with Senator Stephen A. Douglas of Illinois, debates that today are remembered for Lincoln's impassioned plea that "A house divided against itself cannot stand." (See Knox College entry on p. 356.) Lincoln's was a remarkable public relations triumph, but beneath his powerful denunciations of slavery lay several layers of cold political calculation.

The election debates were riven with irony. Though a Republican, Lincoln received the tacit support of the national Democratic Party in the course of his campaign for Douglas's Senate seat. (Douglas had angered the Democratic administration of President Buchanan by rejecting the admission of Kansas to the Union as a slave state—in consequence receiving the applause of Republicans.) This Democratic Party warfare and the knowledge that Douglas would seek the party's 1860 presidential nomination made the debates a media event, bringing nationwide newspaper coverage of a minor state election. Knowing that he would not win the election, Lincoln made the most of his opportunity. Though as late as 1854 he saw slavery as only a "minor question" politically, Lincoln made that issue the thrust of his attack on Douglas, in the process deliberately mischaracterizing the senator as a proponent of slavery's expansion. Douglas was nothing of the sort. He was simply a man who wanted to be president and did not intend to let slavery stand in his way. Though little appreciated today, Douglas held his own with Lincoln in the debates, both oratorically and analytically. He trounced Lincoln's claim that slavery was unconstitutional and in turn charged that Lincoln's views would provoke a civil war and lead to an unprecedented expansion of federal power. Douglas's reasoning was sound, even prescient—but Douglas never became president. Though the Democrats won the state elections and Douglas continued as senator, Lincoln's message—and the man—won favorable national attention. Three years later Lincoln was president and Douglas was dead. As the senator had forseen, civil war and a vast expansion of federal power ensued. In war's wake came doleful mourning cries, as hundreds of thousands of American men in uniform perished, partially scouring the country of slavery's stain.

One of the Lincoln-Douglas debates took place in Alton, through which ran a main line of the Underground Railroad. Today visitors to the town will find on the site of the 1858 debate a historical marker.

Elijah Lovejoy Monument and Grave
Alton Cemetery, Monument Avenue, Alton, IL 62002
(618) 462-2763
Hours: Daily until sunset
Admission: Free

The Presbyterian minister Elijah Lovejoy (1802–1837) lived a life as passionate as his name. An ardent abolitionist, he repeatedly published antislavery newspapers—briefly. The Mississippi River port of St. Louis was perhaps not the wisest choice for such a paper, but then passion and wisdom rarely go hand in hand—and in Lovejoy's case they never did. In St. Louis in 1836, a free black steamboat cook killed a deputy sheriff and wounded a constable before being taken to jail, whereupon he was dragged, burned to death, mutilated, and decapitated by a mob, none of whose members was ever indicted. Lovejoy's *Observer*, on which worked the escaped slave William Wells Brown, who later would become the first published African-American novelist, dramatist, and historian, excoriated the aptly named Judge Luke Lawless for his failure to pursue the lynch mob's members. For his efforts, Lovejoy was run out of town and had his office and press destroyed. Lacking the better part of valor, Lovejoy simply moved across the Mississippi River to Alton, Illinois, and started another abolitionist newspaper. Little more than a year later, a mob again came for his press. Having already seen three of his presses destroyed, Lovejoy unwisely resolved to defend his latest acquisition, which had yet to be installed. Thus Lovejoy and 20 of his supporters gathered at the Godfrey & Gilman warehouse, which soon was surrounded by a pro-slavery mob. First, rocks were hurled through the warehouse's windows. The press's defenders retaliated by bombarding the crowd with earthenware pots found in the building. An exchange of gunfire followed. Then began an attempt to burn the building. As Lovejoy ventured to the roof to put out the fire, he was killed by a blast from a shotgun. The mob wanted the lives of the rest of those in the warehouse but were persuaded instead to settle for sacking the place. The press itself was thrown from a window, smashed to pieces, and the remains thrown into the river. Lovejoy's body was left undisturbed and was claimed the following morning by his grieving friends. His murder by an Alton mob became a cause célèbre and Lovejoy the most prominent martyr of the abolitionist struggle. Today the town where he met his death has raised a monument to Lovejoy. It graces the cemetery in which his grave may be found. The monument, the tallest in the state, is topped by a winged victory; around the monument's base are bronze panels that tell of Lovejoy's life. In the center of Alton, the offices of *The Telegraph* contain the remains of Lovejoy's printing press, which was salvaged from the Mississippi River.

Museum of Art and History
121 East Broadway, Alton, IL 62002
(618) 462-2763
Hours: Thu.–Sat., 11 A.M.–3 P.M.; Sun., 1 P.M.–4 P.M.
Admission: Free

An 1830s-era printing shop similar to that operated by Elijah Lovejoy is displayed at Alton's Museum of Art and History, as are other exhibits on Lovejoy and his paper. Also on view is a Black Pioneers exhibit, which traces from the 1830s to the present the black farms, businesses, churches, and arts in the River Bend area. Among Alton's prominent 19th-century African Americans are William "Scotch" Johnston, who assisted in burying Lovejoy in an unmarked grave that the abolitionist's friends hoped would remain undesecrated, and Isaac Kelly, the first trustee of Lovejoy's reinterred and marked grave site.

CHICAGO

Convention & Tourism Bureau
McCormick Place, 2301 South Lake Shore Drive, Chicago, IL 60616-1497
(312) 567-8500
Hours: Mon.–Fri., 8:30 A.M.–4:30 P.M.

Muhammad Ali Residence
4800 block of South Woodlawn, Chicago, IL 60615
Hours: Daily until sunset
Admission: Not open to the public. Exterior viewing only

The young Cassius Clay repeatedly bore witness to his conversion to Elijah Muhammad's Nation of Islam. The day after he first won the world heavyweight boxing championship, Clay surrendered his birth name, taking in its stead the name Muhammad Ali. (See entry on p. 81.) After moving to Chicago to be near Elijah Muhammad, the greatest heavyweight boxer of the past four decades found more than one home. Though the true home of Muhammad Ali was the Nation of Islam, to which he committed his energies and for which he suffered persecution, his residence, now a *private residence not open to the public*, can be viewed from the street. Two doors down, at 4847 South Woodlawn, is the Chicago house in which lived his guide, Elijah Muhammad. (See entry on p. 348.)

Art Institute of Chicago
111 South Michigan Avenue, Chicago, IL 60603-6110
(312) 443-3600
Hours: Mon.–Fri., 10:30 A.M.–4:30 P.M.; Tue., 10:30 A.M.–8 P.M.; Sat., 1 P.M.–5 P.M.; Sun. and holidays, 12 P.M.–5 P.M.
Admission: Adults, $5; seniors and students, $2.50; free to all on Tuesday

You can't get more American than Grant Wood's "American Gothic." But there's more than merely great American and European (Monet, Degas, Renoir, van Gogh, Seurat, Magritte) art on view at the Art Institute of Chicago. In addition to the art of Asia, ancient America, and Oceania, the institute has a small but impressive collection of African material. Most of the pieces fall under the rubric of fine art rather than ethnographic objects, and hence sculpture (masks and standing figures) predominate over fetish objects, textiles, and jewelry. The cultures of the Dogon, Baule, Senufo, Yoruba, Benin, Kuba, Pende, Bamana, Waja, Hamba, Ashanti, and Nupe figure most prominently in the collection.

Chicago Daily Defender
2400 South Michigan Avenue, Chicago, IL 60616
(312) 225-2400
Hours: Mon.–Fri., 9 A.M.–5 P.M., by appointment only
Admission: Free

Robert S. Abbott (1870–1940) was born in Georgia and educated at Clafin Institute (see Clafin College entry on p. 141) and Hampton Institute (see Hampton University entry on p. 175), graduating from the latter as a skilled printer. After some years working for a Savannah, Georgia, newspaper, Abbott headed north. He graduated with a law degree from Kent College before establishing in 1905 the *Chicago Defender*. Arguably the most influential black newspaper in America for much of this century, the *Defender* gave the African-American community a nationwide sense of itself. It also was the principal institutional impetus toward the northern migration of black sharecroppers seeking economic advancement and an escape from Jim Crow. Today the *Defender* still serves both the black and the wider communities and is open *by appointment* to visitors, who will learn a great deal about the history of the paper, the city, and the nation.

Chicago Historical Society
Clark Street at North Avenue, Chicago, IL 60610
(312) 642-4600
Hours: Mon.–Sat., 9:30 A.M.–4:30 P.M.; Sun., 12 P.M.–5 P.M.
Admission: Adults, $1.50; over 65 and 6–17, 50 cents; free to all on Monday

Though the Chicago Historical Society takes note of the city's black presence—including, for example, Jean Baptiste DuSable, Chicago's founder, and John Jones, an abolitionist and tailor who became the city's first major black political leader—its American and African-American highpoint is its "House

Divided: America in the Age of Lincoln" exhibit. Involved in curating the exhibit is Eric Foner, whose record of scholarship in the field of 19th-century black (and other) history is exemplary. Though "A House Divided" embraces more than the issue of slavery, the Civil War, and its aftermath, these form the core of an interpretation of the social and political forces that tore apart the country. Slave trade and runaway broadsides, slave shackles and identification tags, material on the life of Frederick Douglass, abolitionist tracts, a printing press utilized by Elijah Lovejoy, John Brown's Bible, a manuscript letter from Lincoln to Senator Stephen A. Douglas outlining the terms for their 1858 debates, Civil War paraphernalia, a black soldier display, the table on which Lincoln signed the Emancipation Proclamation and the one on which Lee signed the surrender at Appomattox, and much more explicate the revolutionary transformation of 19th-century America—and do so for one-third the cost of a typical movie ticket.

DuSable Historical Marker
Pioneer Court, Michigan Avenue, Chicago, IL 60611
North end of Michigan Avenue
Hours: Daily until sunset
Admission: Free

The past of Chicago's black founder remains obscure. Probably from Haiti and probably of mixed ancestry, Jean Baptiste Pointe DuSable (the standard though by no means certain spelling of his surname) enters recorded history in 1779, by which time "the handsome negro, (well educated and settled in Eschecagou [Chicago]) but much in the French interest" had aroused the concern of British authorities prosecuting the Revolutionary War and worried about France's links to the Great Lakes Indians. The fur trader and general merchant managed to clear his name with British authorities, without permanently alienating the American government, which in the 1790s employed him in some capacity and rewarded him with several hundred acres of land. Precisely when DuSable first settled Chicago is unclear, but that he was the first nonaboriginal to establish more than a temporary foothold in the area is generally accepted by modern scholarship. His cabin there was luxurious by frontier standards and included a featherbed, mirrors, and candlesticks. (A replica may be seen in the Chicago Historical Society; see entry on p. 344.) Today these items may be taken for granted; the DuSable Historical Marker should not: Until recently few would have credited that a black man founded what became and remains America's second most famous city.

DuSable Museum of African-American History
740 East 56th Place (57th and Cottage Grove), Chicago, IL 60637
(312) 947-0600
Hours: Mon.–Fri., 9 A.M.–5 P.M.; Sat.–Sun., 12 P.M.–5 P.M.
Admission: Adults, $2; seniors and students, $1; under 13, 50 cents

The African-American experience in the Midwest serves as a principal theme of the DuSable Museum of African-American History, which begins with an exhibit on the 18th-century fur trader who first established a post on Lake Michigan and continues on through the life and career of Harold Washington, the only black man to serve as the mayor of America's second city. Though black history predominates in the museum, visitors also will find collections of African-American art from the 1940s through the 1960s and of African ethnographic objects and fine art.

Field Museum of Natural History
Roosevelt Road at Lake Shore Drive, Chicago, IL 60605
(312) 922-9410
Hours: Daily, 9 A.M.–5 P.M.
Admission: Adults, $5; ages 3–17, seniors and students with I.D., $3; maximum per family, $16; under 3, free; free on Thursday

More than 40 percent of Chicago's residents share African roots, and the city now has a comprehensive permanent exhibit that explores the culture and ecology of the Mother Continent. Employing a "You Are There" setting, the 15,000 square feet of "Africa" at the Field Museum of Natural History expose visitors to the contemporary urban life, art, animals, environments, and commerce of the continent, as well as to the experience of the diaspora. One exhibit explores community and family life in Dakar, and includes a bustling market and a suburban neighborhood celebrating the Muslim holy day of *Tabaski*. Another exhibit highlights the cultural settings of three major art-producing areas and consists of a reproduction of a room of the Palace Museum in Foumban in the northern grasslands of Cameroon, a re-creation of the BaKongo people's resolution of intergroup conflicts, and an exploration of the role of the divine ruler in the Kingdom of Benin. The animals of Africa's savannah environment and nature's adaptations in the Great Rift Valley that crosses Kenya, Tanzania, and Malawi are portrayed in still other exhibits. The interaction of human and environment in Africa is investigated through the medium of the commercial caravans of the Tuareg that ply the complex ecology of the Sahara down to the Sahel's major metropolitan trading city,

COURTESY FIELD MUSEUM

Among the BaKongo of Zaire, this *nkisi nkondi* figure is used to symbolize the resolution of conflict.

Kano in Nigeria. The Field's "Africa" offers a detailed and enlightening look at the diversity of a continent most commonly discussed for its famines. The museum then brings visitors full circle, back to themselves, as it were, by highlighting the African transformation of the Americas from slavery days to the present.

Vivian Harsh Collection of Afro-American History and Literature
9525 South Halsted Street, Chicago, IL 60628
(312) 747-6910
Hours: Mon.–Thu., 10 A.M.–8 P.M.; Fri.–Sat., 9 A.M.–5 P.M.
Admission: Free

At times her colleagues and assistants at the Chicago Public Library may have found her aptly named, but to researchers in the then little-cataloged field of black history, the Fisk University graduate Vivian Harsh was a revered figure. In 1924, after 15 years of service and following her postgraduate degree in library studies, she became the first black librarian of the city. Eight years later she became the head librarian of the branch library opened for Chicago's black South Side community. Harsh's special concern was the branch library's small Special Negro Collection, which she was determined to expand even though the library system's administration did not believe public funds should be spent on the project. Soon Harsh's branch library became a gathering point for black writers and artists. Arna Bontemps, Richard Wright, Langston Hughes, Zora Neale Hurston, Alain Locke, Gwendolyn Brooks, and others spoke there and donated materials to Harsh. Today the Special Negro Collection is the Vivian Harsh Collection of Afro-American History and Literature and consists of a book collection of some 70,000 volumes, a periodical collection from the first black newspaper in 1827 through the present, a microfilm research collection, and an archives and manuscript collection that includes original papers from Wright, Hughes, and many others.

Johnson Publishing Company
820 South Michigan Avenue, Chicago, IL 60605
(312) 322-9200
Hours: Lobby: Mon.–Fri., 9 A.M.–5 P.M.
Admission: Free

Perhaps distorted by the passage of time, the echo of Horace Greeley's admonition was heard by John H. Johnson as "Go black, young man." A man of vision, drive, and ingenuity, Johnson parlayed a part-time newspaper-clipping job and a $500 loan into a publishing empire. His vision was simple: Rather than clip black-related newspaper articles for an insurance company's free-to-its-black-clients reprint publication, why not do much the same thing for a new magazine modeled on *Reader's Digest?* And why not use the insurance company's mailing list, which he just happened to have in his hands, as a starting point for potential subscribers? And then, why not buy up much of the first run of *Negro*

Digest so as to convince a white distributor that it was a success and that he should stock it on newsstands? The only other question was: Where was a black entrepreneur in 1940s Chicago going to get a loan? From a bank? The question is rhetorical. Only from a small loan office in the South Side and then only after putting up his mother's furniture as collateral. The furniture was offered up only after considerable prayer by Mrs. Johnson and her son, but as the Bible (Matthew 7:7) says, ". . . knock, and it shall be opened unto you." Thereafter, her son's career took off and soared like an ebony jet. Johnson's head, however, was never in the clouds. He built his empire on the realistic proposition that black folks sought what white folks did: middle-class success, consumer consumption, an image of beauty and triumph, the piling up of treasure on earth, the satisfaction of their own and their people's success through hard work. Though Johnson today does not own every slick black commercial publication, he is their progenitor through his groundbreaking creation of *Ebony* and *Jet* magazines. Today, in the lobby of his office building, visitors will find outstanding examples of African and African-American art, both of which he supports with his patronage. However, visitors should note that the company no longer offers tours of the building.

Martin Luther King, Jr. Drive Historic Homes
Martin Luther King, Jr. Drive, Chicago, IL
Hours: Daily until sunset
Admission: Not open to the public. Exterior viewing only

Along Martin Luther King, Jr. Drive, visitors will pass several houses, all now *private residences not open to the public*, that in earlier times were the homes of key African-American figures. The Robert S. Abbott Home (4742 MLK Drive, 60615) recalls the founder of the *Chicago Defender* and its role in one of the century's major social transformations, the great African-American migration from southern soil to northern streets; in the Oscar Stanton De Priest Home (4536–4538 MLK Drive, 60653) lived the first black U.S. congressman elected from a northern state and a man whose journey from his Alabama birthplace to the halls of Congress was cut short in the depression because of his Republican Party affiliation; and in the Ida B. Wells-Barnett Home (3624 MLK Drive, 60653) lived the militant black civil rights advocate and social reformer who journeyed from rural Mississippi to the history books.

Elijah Muhammad Home
4847 South Woodlawn, Chicago, IL 60615
Hours: Daily until sunset
Admission: Not open to the public. Exterior viewing only

Recalling though not paralleling Muhammad's flight from Mecca to Medina, the Honorable Elijah Muhammad was driven from Detroit by envious rivals within the Lost-Found Nation of Islam (see Muhammad Temple No. 1 entry on p. 397), moving first to Chicago, where later he established his home and headquarters. There, and subsequently across the country, the Nation of Islam prospered under their guide's tutelage, eventually growing secure enough to survive Malcolm X's revelations of the elderly Elijah Muhammad's penchant for teenage schoolgirls. Malcolm, of course, did not long survive the revelations. Today visitors may view this the Elijah Muhammad Home, a *private residence not open to the public*.

Oak Woods Cemetery
1035 East 67th Street, Chicago, IL 60637
(312) 288-3800
Hours: Daily, 8:30 A.M.–4:15 P.M.
Admission: Free

The graves of Ida B. Wells (Barnett), militant black reformer of the late 19th and early 20th centuries (see Ida B. Wells entry on p. 99); her husband, Ferdinand Barnett, a civil rights activist; Jesse Owens, hero of the Berlin Olympics of 1936 (see Owens entry on p. 23); and Harold Washington, Chicago's sole African-American mayor, will be found at the Oak Woods Cemetery on Chicago's South Side. Baseball lovers will want to know that buried here also are Cap Anson and Judge Kenesaw Mountain Landis, both of whom contributed to the exclusion of African Americans from the national pastime. Also of interest is the cemetery's "Tower of Memories," which periodically provides the venue for major African-American heritage exhibits.

Provident Hospital
500 East 51st Street at Vincennes Avenue, Chicago, IL 60615
(312) 538-9700
Hours: Daily, 24 hours
Admission: Free

Williams Home
445 East 42nd Street, Chicago, IL
Hours: Daily until sunset
Admission: Not open to the public. Exterior viewing only

A black guy at death's doorstep bleeding internally from a stab wound to the heart garnered in some unsavory brawl is a stereotype—that is, an image codified through repeated occurrence. Far from banal, however, is the image of a doctor in 1893 taking the unprecedented step of slicing through the skin of the victim's breast, sawing through and levering open his rib cage, parting his scarcely quivering lungs, exposing the wounded heart, and suturing the wound with sufficient skill that the victim became medical history. Daniel Hale Williams, the 35-year-old African-American doctor who performed the world's first recorded open-heart surgery, was no stranger to "firsts," having two years previously opened Provident Hospital, Chicago's first training hospital for black nurses and doctors. Williams's institutional and surgical success led to his appointment as chief of surgery at the government-run Freedmen's Hospital in Washington, D.C., in 1894. A year later Williams organized the National Medical Association, an organization of African-American physicians. It would be delightful to report that his subsequent career fulfilled this immense promise, but such is not the case. Williams ran afoul of his own temper and ardent willfulness and faced charges of professional misconduct at Freedmen's. Though he was exonerated of the charges—and later in 1912 would become the sole black member of the newly chartered American College of Surgeons—he was tinged with disgrace. Returning to Chicago and to Provident wounded but unchastened, Williams on his way down met those he had passed on his way up. They were not inclined to forget or forgive the sharp words and short temper of his earlier residency—and Williams was too aloof and scornful to "network" and provide a safety net for his professional tightrope walk. In 1913 Williams left Provident after a dispute with the institution's third director and faded from view, dying in obscurity in 1931. Today's visitors to Provident will find in the main lobby an exhibit relating the hospital's history, prominently including Dr. Williams's career there and the hospital's role as a training institute for African-American nurses and doctors. Visitors to Chicago also may wish to drive by and view from the street the last home of Dr. Williams, which is located at 445 East 42nd Street. It is now a National Historic Site; it also is *not open to the public*.

Operation PUSH
930 East 50th Street, Chicago, IL 60615
(312) 373-3366
Hours: Mon.–Fri., 8:30 A.M.–5 P.M.; Sat., 8:30 A.M.–3 P.M.
Admission: Free

Operation PUSH, People United to Save (later changed to Serve) Humanity, was founded in Chicago on Christmas Day 1971 by the Reverend Jesse Jackson as a vehicle to promote human rights, notably including the right of black self-empowerment. Two decades later the national headquarters of Operation PUSH offers visitors year-round photo exhibits that focus on the civil rights movement of the past three decades, life-size statues of African-American heroes, and a civil rights library and audio archives.

1919 Race Riot Site
Lakefront at 27th Street, Chicago, IL 60616
Hours: Daily until sunset
Admission: Free

One's place, the knowing of which defined proper from uppity African Americans, is both hierarchical and geographical. On a hot July day in 1919, recent southern black immigrants to Chicago crossed the line—in this case an imaginary line in the waters of Lake Michigan that racially divided recreational space along the beachfront. Following an earlier flare-up on the beach, whites began to throw rocks at a black youth who had drifted across the line holding onto a railroad tie. Unable to reach the shore safely, Eugene Williams drowned. White police refused to arrest anyone for the incident—though they did arrest a black protestor, which provoked a black assault on the arresting officer. Things quickly spiraled out of control. Rumor fed rumor, and soon African Americans were being hauled off trolley cars and beaten, stabbed, and shot. Shortly all those of either race who had failed to get the word of the unfolding racial conflagration fell shocked victim to sudden attack. When the bloodshed and burning was halted a week later by the National Guard, casualties totaled 23 blacks and 15 whites killed, 342 blacks and 178 whites injured, and more than 1,000 homes burned to the ground, most belonging to Lithuanian immigrants huddled near Chicago's stockyards. Though the racial conflict in Chicago received the most news—and secured immortality in James Farrell's *Studs Lonigan*—it was not uncommon that year. From Millen, Georgia (seven black lodges and five churches burned and an African American lynched); Knoxville, Tennessee (six dead and 20 injured); and Elaine, Arkansas (where a full-fledged, back-country race war erupted; see Elaine entry on p. 34), to Washington, D.C., where the police chief called for the general questioning of all blacks found on the streets after dark and where marines and soldiers roamed the southwest district randomly shooting at and entering the homes of African Americans, the country embarked on one of its periodic generalized racial assaults on black people. The events in Chicago, which had been preceded in May by residents of the Hyde Park and Kenwood districts meeting to oppose the "negro invasion" of white neighborhoods and by the June bombing of the home in the area purchased by an African American, began at the beach area at 27th Street and Lakefront. Today no historical marker has been placed there to recall one of the worst summers ever to hit America.

Victory Monument
35th and State streets, Chicago, IL 60616
Hours: Daily until sunset
Admission: Free

As America entered World War I, the segregated U.S. army initially sought and expected substantial black enlistment, which indeed was forthcoming since America's color-blind draft provisions were overseen by all-white selective service boards by no means unwilling to ship large numbers of black men out of their communities. The army swiftly saw reason to reconsider, however. The operational difficulties of suddenly establishing a wide array of segregated training facilities were substantial. Added to the difficulties was a concern that the southern congressional powers would be less than thrilled to have large numbers of unified and militarily trained black men returning home. (See Black Confederate entry on p. 96.) But the deciding factor was the trauma that occurred in Houston, Texas, in August 1917, which ultimately led to the execution of 19 African-American soldiers and to grave doubts in the army's mind that black troops were worth the trouble aroused by their interaction with white communities.

Following Pancho Villa's March 1916 sack of Columbus, New Mexico (see Columbus Museum entry on p. 503), President Wilson authorized American troops to our southwestern border—and then into Mexico. The 3rd Battalion of the all-black 24th Infantry was dispatched to Houston, Texas. There the veteran soldiers refused to accept the Jim Crow obligations of the South, a refusal that provoked sharp white animosity. When the United States entered World War I in April 1917, the army withdrew many senior sergeants from America's four all-black regiments in order to train them for officers' responsibilities in the new segregated divisions they intended to establish. The withdrawal of sergeants from the 3rd Battalion proved disastrous—and paved the way for the cancellation of the new black divisions for which they had been withdrawn. In Houston, a black soldier's intervention into a white policeman's arrest/beating of a black woman led first to the soldier's being clubbed and arrested and then to another soldier being clubbed, shot at, and arrested by the same policeman. Though the battalion's white officers got the men released from police custody and the policeman suspended from duty, the men of the 3rd were not satisfied. Led by some of their remaining noncommissioned officers, the black soldiers distributed guns and ammunition, marched into town, cold-bloodedly murdered more than a dozen white and Hispanic civilians, wounded about as many, attacked a police station, and killed a white officer of the 8th Illinois National Guard, probably mistaking him for a policeman, and a member of their own mob, again probably mistaking him for a policeman. Investigation revealed that perhaps 156 men of the battalion had taken part in the mutiny. Enough evidence existed to charge 63 men with mutiny in time of war and premeditated murder. Of these, 54 were found guilty of both charges (of whom 13 were sentenced to death), four were found guilty of lesser charges, and five were found innocent. In December 1917, 13 African Americans mounted the gallows. Two further related trials of other defendants took place, resulting in death sentences for 16 men. In light of the protests from black America following the earlier executions, only six—each of whom had been found guilty of murdering a specific individual—of the 16 were executed.

The Houston incident led the army to reconsider the prospective establishment of 16 new black combat regiments. Instead, it chose to field four new black regiments as a division, which it quickly would ship overseas. (The army's four historically all-black regiments, the 9th, 10th, 24th, and 25th, were not selected for overseas service, remaining dispersed along the Mexican border or in Hawaii and the Philippines; the marines and navy had no use for African Americans except as laborers, cooks, and stewards.) The 92nd Division was organized in November 1917—a month later the army would hang the first 13 Houston mutineers and almost simultaneously decide to raise a second black division. The 92nd was composed of raw recruits who received little training, and that from largely inexperienced junior officers. Rather than a genuine fighting force, the War Department saw the 92nd as the price to be paid for African-American support of or at least acquiescence in the war effort. Shipped to France, it received less than a week's—and in some cases only hours—front-line indoctrination before being introduced into the trenches. The 92nd's participation with the French in the early autumn 1918 Meuse-Argonne offensive won it no plaudits. Its commander court-martialed for cowardice 30 of its recently commissioned black officers. Though under a new commander the division improved its performance a month later, in the closing days of the war it broadly lived up or rather down to the army establishment's racist expectations and associated lack of training.

The other black division, the 93rd, was composed principally of state National Guard units, prominently including the 8th Illinois/370th Infantry, which had been withdrawn from its Houston assignment following the mutiny, and the 15th New York, which was renumbered the 369th and gained fame, at least in the black community, as the "Harlem Hell-Fighters." It too received little training, but at least its men from the National Guard units had some prior experience working together. They also, particularly the 8th Illinois, had *experienced* black officers to whom to turn for leadership. Unfortunately, the 8th Illinois's black colonel, Franklin Dennison, was relieved of command because of ill health—soon after Charles Young, America's sole active black West Point graduate, suffered the same fate. (See Greene County Historical Society entry on p. 451.) Interestingly, and largely unknown to Americans, black or white, Dennison's replacement became the first white officer ever to command the black 8th Illinois. The 93rd's experience in Europe is instructive. Perhaps because its cadre of black officers inspired even less confidence than did white officers leading raw black recruits, the American commander in Europe, General Pershing, dumped the 93rd on the grateful French. (Oddly, earlier in his career Pershing had served with the famous, all-black 10th Cavalry, which he extolled for its competence and courage.) As the white commander of the 369th explained, "Our great American general [Pershing] simply put the black orphan in a basket, set it on the doorstep of the French, pulled the bell, and went away." The French had no cause to complain. The 369th, 371st, and 372nd fought during September and October 1918 in the Meuse-Argonne offensive, suffering 2,500 casualties, and the 370th fought from mid-September through war's end in the Oise-Ainse offensive, suffering 665 casualties. Perhaps because the French and the division's officers expected something of the men, they got it. This proved true even of the 371st, which was composed of raw draftees organized by white officers who had no particular sensitivity toward or belief in the equality of their African-American subordinates.

Of course, the roughly 36,000 men of the two combat divisions represented a little less than 10 percent of the African Americans who served in the wartime army and a little less than 20 percent of the black troops in Europe. The general black military experience in Europe and America was lifting, toting, hauling, and cleaning. Thus only about 750 of America's more than 50,000 combat deaths touched the African-American community and offered the hope of leveraging postwar racial gains. When the black veterans came home, the 369th got a victory parade up Fifth Avenue—but only because its commander, the son of a U.S. senator from Nebraska and himself a minor baron in New York's Republican Party establishment, pulled some political strings. The 8th Illinois/370th U.S. Infantry returned home to the notorious Chicago race riot of 1919 (see 1919 Race Riot entry on p. 350)—one of 30 across the country in the summer of that year. Not until 1927 and only after pressure from the black community was the Victory Monument, also known as "the Black Doughboys Monument," erected to pay homage to Illinois's black veterans.

Harold Washington Center
Chicago Public Library, 400 South State Street, Chicago, IL 60605
(312) 747-4300
Hours: Tue., 11 A.M.–7 P.M.; Wed., 9 A.M.–5 P.M.; Thu., 11 A.M.–7 P.M.; Fri.–Sat., 9 A.M.–5 P.M.
Admission: Free

Chicago, first settled by a black man and today a city 40 percent of whose residents share an African descent, has been served by 43 mayors, only one of whom, Harold Washington, was black. Washington's victory in the 1983 mayoralty election electrified the city; his reelection in 1987 calmed it. The first effect testifies to the resilient barriers of contemporary America, the second to Washington's impact on a urban populace sharply divided by race. Though a longtime politician, whose father served as a precinct captain in Chicago's Democratic Party machine, Washington's previous career as a state representative (1965–1977), state senator (1977–1981), and U.S. congressman (1981–1983) had never placed him in an executive office. Suddenly, in 1983, Chicago looked for direction to Washington, who now was in a position to deliver—or to fail to deliver without the protective cover of simply serving in a representative capacity. Though the job of big-city mayor in the 1980s offered little scope for much beyond heartache or—as happened to Washington—heart attack, and though Washington had his share of failures, the man did more than merely endure. His reelection testified to more than the electoral solidity of the black bloc, and his white support testified to more than that community's hope that Washington could pacify "his" people. Thus there was not just shock but concern at his sudden death seven months into his second term of office. Today visitors to the Harold Washington Center can explore the man's life and political career, examine the campaign paraphernalia of the 1983 and 1987 elections, and view traveling exhibits that detail the midwestern nexus of African Americans and electoral politics.

EAST ST. LOUIS

Katherine Dunham Museum
1005 Pennsylvania, East St. Louis, IL 62201
(618) 271-3367
Hours: By appointment
Admission: Free

The revolutionary transformation in the American theater's stage presentation of black dance from minstrelsy to a serious medium of communication, beauty, and cultural meaning began from anthropological field studies of Caribbean dance in the mid-1930s. Katherine Dunham, one of 20th-century black America's most potent creative powers, vividly expressed her appreciation for African and Caribbean culture in motion—in leaps, bounds, and swirls—as well as in scholarly monographs. In the process, she established the existence and validity of a black aesthetic.

COURTESY KATHERINE DUNHAM MUSEUM

Katherine Dunham spent a lifetime promoting African-American culture.

Returning in 1936 from her research into African-based culture, dance, and religious and secular rites, Dunham reassembled the company she had founded in her early 20s and began touring. With a strong narrative line, her sequences of dances riveted her audiences and led them to see the continuum from the primitive African movements through their West Indian modification to the blues and jazz of the diaspora in America.

Dunham's pride in and defense of her race was pronounced throughout her career. Hotels in Chicago and Cincinnati were sued for refusing accommodations to her company. And after a performance in Louisville during the height of World War II, at which African Americans were restricted to balcony seats, Ms. Dunham announced onstage that she would not return until equality prevailed. Dunham also was instrumental in helping to establish the slave-trade museum on Gorée Island off Senegal's coast. Though she never has stopped dancing, which in her words is only "rhythmic motion," Dunham has ceased performing. Those interested in the lady and her career may stop by the Katherine Dunham Museum, which contains artifacts and memorabilia that underscore the link between the dancer and Africa and the West Indies. Senufo, Dan, Baule, Ibibio, Benin, and other African peoples' masks and sculpture, percussive instruments from Africa and the West Indies—among them a Bata drum from Cuba—and contemporary artwork from Haiti, including macrame hangings, wooden statues, and paintings, fill the museum and begin to suggest the wide-ranging interests of one of the passionate sages of America.

GALESBURG

Knox College
2 East South Street, Galesburg, IL 61401
(309) 343-0112
Hours: Regular semester hours
Admission: Free

The Lincoln-Douglas debates opened with the former one-term congressman and future president of the United States attempting to establish the broad political framework within which he wished voters to locate the issue of slavery and his differences with Douglas. The debate took place at Knox College, where Lincoln proclaimed his "irrepressible conflict" thesis with a rhetorical force and a felicity of expression that ensured its being remembered: "A house divided against itself cannot stand. I believe that this government cannot endure permanently half-slave and half-free." Today only one structure associated with the historic debates still stands; the Old Main Building on the Knox campus is a National Historic Landmark.

JUNCTION

Crenshaw (Slave) House
Route 1, Junction, IL 62954
(618) 276-4410
9 miles west of Shawneetown, near the intersection of Highways 1 and 13
Hours: Apr.–Oct.: daily, 9 A.M.–5 P.M. Nov.: weekends, 9 A.M.–5 P.M.
Admission: Adults, $3.50; children, $2.50

Only two towns have been plotted and established by the federal government: Washington, D.C., on the Potomac River, and Shawneetown, Illinois, near the Saline River. In April 1810 the U.S. Congress authorized funds to plot two sections (two square miles) near one of America's most prolific salt springs, the water of which was 80 percent salt. Previously, the springs had been exploited by local Indians, the French, and the British, and now it was the turn of the U.S. government. In time, a 350-foot channel was dug, covered, and heated by a chimney placed at one end, boiling away the water and leaving the salt residue—and in the process releasing hydrogen sulfide, which rendered finding people to undertake the work difficult. Some sense of the springs' value can be gleaned from the fact that a local bank, capitalized at $300,000, opened in 1816—two years before Illinois became a state. By the mid-19th century, 7 percent of Illinois's total tax revenue came from the salt springs. More intriguingly still, so significant were the salt works that the Illinois State Constitution of 1818 effectively permitted—in a free-labor state that, as a territory, had entered the U.S. under the Northwest Ordinance of 1787, which forbade slavery—bondage within one small portion of the state. Article 6, Section 2, of that constitution read: "No person bound to labor in any other state shall be hired to labor in this state, except within the tract reserved for the salt-work near Shawneetown." The article continued by limiting the period of such servitude to one year at a stretch and by proscribing such servitude beyond 1825. Whether either of the two limits was enforced is uncertain, but at least for some time leased slave labor from nearby Kentucky toiled in the salt works. Today the Crenshaw House offers a (disputed) interpretation of Illinois's local slavery, which—it is contended—continued far beyond the constitutional termination date and which involved a prominent local businessman who, in addition to employing 746 slaves, used white employees to troll the nearby Ohio River border with Kentucky for fugitive slaves. Allegedly, the captured fugitives were held in his house under the local cover of his leased-slave salt-work operation and then sold back South for a handsome profit. Visitors to the area interested in the history of Old Shawneetown and the salt works that were the state's first industry should call (618) 269-3542 to arrange for a tour of the John Marshall Home Museum, where the letter authorizing the original town plotting and other memorabilia may be found.

PRINCETON

Owen Lovejoy Homestead
East Peru Street, Princeton, IL 61356
(815) 879-9151
Hours: May–Sept.: Thu. and Sun., 1 P.M.–4 P.M. or by appointment. Apr. and Oct.: by appointment
Admission: Adults, $2; seniors, $1.50; children, $1

A year after his brother Elijah's death in Alton (see Lovejoy Monument entry on p. 342), Owen Lovejoy went to Princeton, where he remained for 17 years. A fiery abolitionist, a Congregational minister, a known supporter of the Underground Railroad, and an acquaintance of Lincoln, Owen Lovejoy was indicted in 1843 for harboring two fugitive slave women but was acquitted at his trial. In 1854 he was elected to the Illinois state legislature, and then in 1856 to the U.S. House of Representatives, where he was a strong proponent of the antislavery struggle. Lovejoy served five terms in Congress and had the privilege of introducing on the House floor the enabling legislation to give force to Lincoln's Emancipation Proclamation. Today the restored Owen Lovejoy Homestead offers insight into the man and his beliefs. The secret hiding area above the stairs that harbored fugitive slaves is open to view to visitors, who may also wish to tour the nearby Colton Schoolhouse—erected in 1849 and a fine example of the old one-room schoolhouse—and the Red Covered Bridge, one of but six remaining covered bridges in a state that once was graced with 132. The 1863 bridge well recalls the 19th century, still being posted with a sign that warns of a "Five dollar fine for driving more than 12 horses, mules or cattle at any one time or leading any beast faster than a walk on or across this bridge."

QUINCY

Augustus Tolton Statue and Grave
St. Peter's School, 2600 Main Street 63201
Cemetery, 3300 Broadway, Quincy, IL 62301
(217) 222-3155
Hours: Daily until sunset
Admission: Free

Born in Missouri to slave parents, Augustus Tolton was carried by his mother to freedom in Quincy before the conclusion of the Civil War. There he entered St. Peter's School. Desiring to become a priest, Tolton sought admission to a seminary, but none was ready to accept African Americans. The Franciscan university in Quincy, however, did secure him a place at their order's missionary college in Rome, from whence he graduated fully expecting to serve in Africa. Instead he was returned to parishwork in Quincy, where he served as pastor of St. Joseph's Church, and later went on to establish a school for black children in Chicago and serve there as pastor of St. Monica's Church. Tolton's ordination as a Catholic priest in 1886 was the first of a wholly black American, though about a decade previously the mulatto James Augustine Healy had been ordained as a bishop. (See Portland, Maine, entry on p. 237.) Today visitors to St. Peter's School view a life-size, white marble statue of the school's alumnus, while a few blocks away in the local Catholic cemetery, Tolton's grave, over which stands a large, concrete cross, may be found.

SPRINGFIELD

Lincoln Home National Historic Site
413 South Eighth Street, Springfield, IL 62701
(217) 492-4150
Hours: Daily, 8:30 A.M.–5 P.M. Summers: Extended hours. Visitor Center: 8:30 A.M.–5 P.M.
Admission: Free tickets acquired on day of tour at Lincoln Home Visitor Center, 426 South 7th Street. For group tickets, contact the Springfield Convention and Visitors Bureau, (800) 545-7300

Lincoln's Tomb State Historic Site
Oak Ridge Cemetery, Springfield, IL 62702
(217) 782-2717
Hours: Daily, 9 A.M.–5 P.M.
Admission: Free

Lincoln-Herndon Law Offices
Sixth and Adams streets, Springfield, IL 62701
(217) 785-7289
Hours: Daily, 9 A.M.–5 P.M.
Admission: Free. Suggested donations: adults, $2; children, $1

Old State Capitol
Sixth and Adams streets, Springfield, IL 62701
(217) 782-4836
Hours: Daily, 9 A.M.–5 P.M.
Admission: Free. Suggested donations: adults, $2; children, $1

Lincoln Depot Museum
Tenth and Monroe streets, Springfield, IL 62703
(217) 544-8695
Hours: June–Aug.: daily, 10 A.M.–4 P.M.
Admission: Free

The 16th president of the United States may have been born in a Kentucky log cabin, but by the time the effective repeal of the Missouri Compromise—represented by the 1854 Kansas-Nebraska Act—again whetted the political interest and ambition of the former one-term U.S. congressman, he was a prosperous railroad attorney practicing in the state capital of Illinois. A man of raw ambition and tactical political acumen, of sharp distaste for slavery and scant liking for African Americans, of inordinate moral courage and still greater determination, Lincoln was prepared by his character to profit from his outrageously good fortune. Only the country as a whole profited more than the man from a guiding star that secured him three advantages over his Republican rivals for the 1860 presidential nomination. First, he was out of office during the crisis decade of the 1850s and was thus uncommitted by having previously cast votes on contentious issues. Second, he represented Illinois, a crucial swing state that the Republican Party absolutely needed to win in order to secure the presidential election, whereas his rivals from Ohio and New York represented states that were certain to vote Republican no matter who the nominee. Third, Lincoln was a moderate on the issue of slavery and thus acceptable if not devoutly desired by the abolitionist, nativist, and German wings of the still-fledgling Republican Party of 1860. Lincoln's guiding star continued after he secured his party's nomination. It placed him in competition against a divided Democratic Party—the northern and southern branches of which ran rival tickets in the 1860 election—before an electorate tired of southern intransigence and convinced that Lincoln's election would not *really* lead the South to secede.

The life and career of the man who when confronted by a cabinet united in opposition to one of his measures responded that only one vote counted, his, is nowhere better traced than in the only town in which Lincoln ever owned a home. Here in Springfield, the National Park Service and the state of Illinois maintain several sites that explore different aspects of Lincoln's life. The Great Western Depot (from which Lincoln departed for his inauguration in 1861), the Lincoln-Herndon Law Offices (where Lincoln and his partner practiced for many years), the Lincoln Home (purchased in 1844, two years after Lincoln married Mary Todd, and added on to as his family grew), Lincoln's Tomb, and the Old State Capitol (where Lincoln served four terms as a state legislator and where he argued more than 200 cases before the Illinois Supreme Court) all offer exhibits on the first president to invite African Americans to the White House. It was Lincoln's genuine humility, however, not his invitations, that is the core of his greatness as a leader. This humility left him uncorrupted by a presidential power that he pushed beyond constitutional limits in defense of the Union.

INDIANA

Indiana Department of Tourism
One North Capitol, Suite 700, Indianapolis, IN 46204-2288
(317) 232-8860
Hours: Mon.–Fri., 8:30 A.M.–5 P.M.

BEDFORD

Lick Creek (Little Africa)
c/o Hoosier National Forest Headquarters, 811 Constitution Avenue, Bedford, IN 47421
(812) 275-5987
5 miles east of Paoli, in Hoosier National Forest
Hours: Mon.–Fri., 8 A.M.–4:30 P.M.
Admission: Campsites: $4–$7 per site

The bloody Nat Turner uprising of 1831—under whose ax even young white children fell—terrified the white South, playing into its deepest fears that its hearths harbored black-hearted wretches who suddenly would slay those who maintained them. Broadened restrictions of states' Black Codes resulted and made life even more difficult for the South's free blacks, many of whom bid Dixie good-bye. The Indiana frontier beckoned, though as it was just across the Ohio River from Kentucky there was a danger from slave hunters. The Lick Creek settlement in Orange County was one of several congregations of African Americans that consolidated in Indiana in the 1830s. Drawn mostly from North Carolina, its population actively assisted the Underground Railroad, sent its menfolk into the Union army during the Civil War, and then subsequently declined as the lure of high-wage industrial jobs in burgeoning cities drew off the children of small farmers. By 1900 Lick Creek had seen the last of its black families depart—at which point the area became known as Little Africa. Ironically, our knowledge of this African-American community is a function of Indiana's Black Codes: In the 1850s a new state constitution, adopted by a majority of white voters, forbade "any negro or mulatto to come into, settle in, or become an inhabitant of the State." Enforcement legislation required all African Americans who were inhabitants of the state prior to 1851 to register with their county clerk. Names, ages, descriptions, residences, and places of birth were noted for each black individual.

Today, deep in the heart of Hoosier National Forest, the "Little Africa" cemetery contains the graves of these early Indiana settlers. There is also a plaque at the nearby site of the A.M.E. church built in 1846, the remains of the settlers' homes and wells, and—in springtime—a profusion of jonquils. Be forewarned: You must walk half a mile over a Forest Service road to reach the old settlement site—but then you probably have to walk that far in the city to get from your destination to your parked car, and the view is not nearly so nice.

BLOOMINGTON

Indiana University Art Museum
Fine Arts Plaza, Indiana University, Bloomington, IN 47405
(812) 855-5445
Hours: Wed.–Thu. and Sat., 10 A.M.–5 P.M.; Fri., 10 A.M.–8 P.M.; Sun., 12 P.M.–5 P.M.
Admission: Free

The 600 objects in the African Collection of the Indiana University Art Museum survey virtually all of sub-Saharan Africa, offering not only the typical examination of West Africa but also glimpses into areas usually unexplored, such as Madagascar and Somalia. Typically, the museum is strongest in wooden figures carved within the last century in West Africa; however, the decorative arts (cloth, glass, and metal jewelry) and utilitarian objects (pots, cups, the paraphernalia of the gold trade) also are on display and offer other avenues of exploration into the cultures that spawned the diaspora. In addition to the "roundup of the usual suspects"—the Dogon, Mossi, Bamana, Dan, Mende, Ashanti, Yoruba, Bale, Ibo, and Ibibio peoples—the collection's West African holdings include the art work of the Montol, Jaba, Igala, Idoma, Tiv, Nupe, and Mumuye. In Central Africa, in addition to the works of the Kongo, Luba, Kuba, Yaka, and Suku, the creations of the Pende and Bena Lulua can be seen. Most unusually for American museums, the Mahasaly and Saklava peoples of Madagascar Island are represented, in this case with graveposts. While no individual culture is explored in depth, the broad survey offers visitors a comprehensive view of a fascinating continent. And the price cannot be beat.

FOUNTAIN CITY

Levi Coffin House
North Main Street, Fountain City, IN 47341
(317) 847-2432
Hours: June–mid-Sept.: Tue.–Sun., 1 P.M.–4 P.M. Mid-Sept.–Oct.: Sat.–Sun., 1 P.M.–4 P.M.
Admission: Adults, $1; ages 6–18, 50 cents

Repelled by the tightening restrictions of the state's Black Codes and lured by the frontier and the future, whites as well as blacks left North Carolina in the 1820s and '30s—though in the former case, the emigrants principally were limited to Quakers with a rooted objection to slavery. Among the departing Quakers was Levi Coffin, who would go on to play a central role in the Underground Railroad. When Coffin and his wife arrived in Newport (now Fountain City) in 1826, they found a Quaker community that rejected rather than opposed slavery. Nearby they found an active Underground Railroad led by freed slaves who themselves were in constant danger of being abducted and resold into bondage. The Coffins committed themselves to the fugitives' cause, inviting whites to their home to meet with runaways and their local black champions. From this beginning, Levi Coffin built up a white support network that spanned several states. In 20 years of residence in Newport, Coffin helped perhaps 2,000 men, women, and children to freedom. He and his wife then moved to Cincinnati, Ohio, where they continued their efforts, helping another 1,100 souls to freedom. There they met and were admired by Harriet Beecher Stowe (see First Parish Church entry on p. 236 and Stowe House entry on p. 226), who incorporated Levi into *Uncle Tom's Cabin* as "Simeon Halliday" and one of those offered temporary sanctuary in his Cincinnati home as "Eliza." Today the restored Levi Coffin House is open to visitors, who tour period rooms, view the hidden quarters in which runaways were housed, and have the past brought to life for them by costumed history interpreters.

INDIANAPOLIS

Convention & Visitors Bureau
One Hoosier Dome, Suite 100, Indianapolis, IN 46225
(317) 639-4282
Hours: Mon.–Fri., 8:30 A.M.–5 P.M.

Children's Museum
3000 North Meridian Street, Indianapolis, IN 46208
(317) 924-5431
Hours: Summer: Mon.–Sat., 10 A.M.–5 P.M. Labor Day–Memorial Day: Tue.–Sat., 10 A.M.–5 P.M.; Sun., 12 P.M.–5 P.M.
Admission: Adults, $4; seniors and children 2–17, $3; children under 2, free

African-American inventors and scientists such as Charles Drew (see entry on p. 169) and Benjamin Banneker are highlighted in a permanent exhibit at the Children's Museum. For parents interested in black role models, this is the genuine article, the real McCoy—an expression deriving from the notable quality of the products of Elijah McCoy. McCoy, also featured in the "African-American Scientists and Inventors from A to Z" exhibit, was born in Canada to escaped slaves who had fled Kentucky via the Underground Railroad. After studies in Scotland, McCoy moved to Ypsilanti and Detroit and began a career based on his fascination with the lubrication of moving parts in engines. Forty-two patents resulted, as did an entry in the American lexicon. Realms other than lubrication are explored, ranging from the esoteric reaches of chemistry

(James Harris, co-discoverer of elements 104 and 105) to the mundane public mailbox (invented and patented in 1891 by Philip B. Downing).

Crispus Attucks High School and Museum Center
1140 MLK Drive, Indianapolis, IN 46202
(317) 226-4611
Museum is scheduled to open in May 1994. Phone ahead to confirm opening, hours, and admission fee

It's so nice to have people go out of their way—to do things for you, we mean. To honor the martyr traditionally referred to as the first man to die in the American Revolution—though the war itself began five years after his death—Indianapolis in 1927 opened Crispus Attucks as a black high school. Thanks to Indianapolis Public School Board policy, every other local high school promptly found itself all-white. Though the state passed a school desegregation law in 1949, Crispus Attucks remained segregated until the 1970s. Soon it will be one of the few high schools in America with a museum. The Attucks Museum will focus on African-American heritage and will prominently include, but not be limited to, the success of alumni such as Wes Montgomery, Slide Hampton, and Oscar Robertson.

Freetown Village Museum
Office and store: 860 West Tenth Street, Indianapolis, IN 46204
Performances: Indiana State Museum, 202 North Alabama Street, Indianapolis, IN 46202
(317) 232-8281; (317) 631-1870
Hours: Mon.–Sat., 9 A.M.–4:45 P.M.; Sun., 12 P.M.–4:45 P.M.
Admission: Free

When you enter Freetown Village you are surrounded by free black life in Indianapolis in the aftermath of the Civil War. Only one street is paved; candles, lard, or coal oil provide the street and home lighting. The local newspaper sells for two cents. And the wedding ceremony incorporates broom jumping, a slave-era ritual symbolizing leaving the old life of individualism behind and embarking on a new, joint life. Drift back in time. Drift back to a time when the 13th, 14th, and 15th amendments were vibrant, opening new lives characterized by the right to own land, legal sanction for marriages, the opportunity for schooling, the promise never again to mount an auction block. Costumed living history interpreters—including Mother Endura, a herbalist; the Reverend and Mrs. Strong; and Guinea Farnsworth, street peddler and gossip—re-create the life of Indianapolis's 3,000 African-American residents of 1870. Freetown Village is a touring program, and the breadth of its presentation depends on its location. But Freetown Village also maintains a permanent exhibit and performance space at the Indiana State Museum. There a porched area of a village residence serves as a gathering place for the Cuffee family and their neighbors, who reenact representative situations of a new and exciting era of African-American advancement.

Indianapolis Museum of Art
1200 West 38th Street, Indianapolis, IN 46208
(317) 923-1331
Hours: Tue.–Sun., 11 A.M.–5 P.M.
Admission: Free

More than 1,400 objects—at least a third of them on display—and 10,000 square feet greet the visitor to the African Collection of the Indianapolis Museum of Art. The museum's holdings range from pieces of personal adornment, masks, fetish figures, carved staffs, beadwork, textiles, and baskets through sculpture. Though the collection's strengths are centered on the cultural outpourings of the Yoruba, Benin, Mende, Dan, Ejaghan, and Cross Rivers peoples, the museum is especially interesting because of its holdings from areas other than West Africa. The creations of the Makonde, Giriama, Masai, and Turkana peoples in East Africa and the Ndebele, Shona, and Zulu from southern Africa are rarely found in American museums. The Indianapolis Museum of Art also has a small collection of early Egyptian pieces, which are the more welcome because if High Culture is not about the past, why do we learn about it in classrooms and museums rather than the streets?

Major Taylor Velodrome
3649 Cold Spring Road, Indianapolis, IN 46222
(317) 327-8356
Hours: Apr.–Nov.: Mon.–Fri., 9 A.M.–5 P.M.
Admission: Free

Before the advent of the automobile, competitive bicycle racing rivaled professional baseball in popularity—and in whiteness. In 1900 Marshall ("Major") Taylor not only broke the color barrier in the sport, he also was America's spring champion. His blackness did not make his success more welcome to his competitors, nor to many of the white fans, with the result that most of his professional career was spent in Europe. Before entering the competitive ranks, Taylor worked in a bicycle repair shop, earning a nickname and money on the side with deft performances of balancing tricks on a bike—during which he wore a major's uniform. Today the Major Taylor Velodrome honors a real race man with a plaque and a track.

Madame Walker Urban Life Center and Theatre
617 Indiana Avenue, Indianapolis, IN 46202
(317) 236-2099
Hours: Tours: 8:30 A.M.–5 P.M., with 2 weeks' notice
Admission: Tours: $2

Long before the Avon Lady, Madame C. J. Walker was knocking on doors. (See Villa Lewaro entry on p. 294.) On no door did she knock harder than that of opportunity. Parlaying $1.50, a hair-straightening formula, inimitable drive, and a sure sense of the power of vanity, Walker built up a million-dollar business, justly securing in 1992, long after her death in 1919, induction into the Junior Achievement National Business Hall of Fame. Walker established a correspondence course for beauticians and later opened a string of beauty schools across the United States, providing employment opportunities and a chance for economic independence to thousands of African-American women. Her daughter, A'Leila, paid tribute to her mother with the Walker Building. Erected on the main artery of the black community in the town Madame C. J. called home since 1910, it provided a base to Indianapolis's network of African-American professionals and entrepreneurs and a stage upon which the era's leading black entertainers proved their excellence. Today the Madame Walker Urban Life Center and Theatre remains a hub of the Indianapolis black community. Displays on local black history, an exhibit on Madame Walker, and a varying program of cultural events and performances can all be found at the center. Formal tours require advance notice.

IOWA

Tourism Office
200 East Grand Avenue, Des Moines, IA 50309
(800) 345-4692; (515) 242-4705
Hours: Mon.–Fri., 8 A.M.–4:30 P.M.

AMES

George Washington Carver Statue
Carver Hall, Iowa State University, Ames, IA 50011
(515) 294-4111
Hours: Mon.–Fri., 8 A.M.–5 P.M.
Admission: Free

George Washington Carver (see Tuskegee University entry on p. 31; see Carver entries on pp. 365 and 414) left Simpson College in 1891 after being convinced by his art instructor that his first love, painting, might prove an ardent mistress but surely not a reliable provider. Etta Budd's argument was persuasive—as perhaps subliminally was her name, for Carver shifted to agricultural science even as he transferred to Iowa State University. (For those of a more prosaic bent, Budd's father was chairman of Simpson's horticulture department.) Carver, the university's first African-American student, was welcomed on campus, befriended by the dean of agriculture, achieved the highest rank in the student military regiment, earned excellent marks, stayed on for graduate study, became the first black faculty member, and was placed in charge of the Agriculture Experiment Station greenhouse, before going on to Tuskegee and fame. His journey, however, was not without its racial indignities. He was refused service in the university dining hall, instead being relegated to the basement where the field hands ate. He was "honored" with the assignment of escorting the governor to a banquet, which avoided the situation of having him escort a white woman. He was heckled while serving as part of the military escort of the governor at the World's Fair in Chicago in 1893 (where two of Carver's paintings were hung). Despite these impediments, Carver enjoyed his years at Iowa State, where his fertile and varied artistic talents and his amiable personality won him many friends. As he departed for Tuskegee, the student newspaper remarked that "We know of no one who failed to be won to friendship by his genial disposition, and we are not guilty of meaningless praise when we wish him God speed." Today on campus visitors will find a George Washington Carver Statue in the lobby of Carver Hall and sundry Carver memorabilia and correspondence at the university library.

DAVENPORT

Davenport Museum of Art
1737 West 12th Street, Davenport, IA 52804
(319) 326-7804
Hours: Tue.–Sat., 10 A.M.–4:30 P.M.; Sun., 1 P.M.–4:30 P.M.
Admission: Free

With the virtual extinction of Haiti's aboriginal Arawak Indians early in the 16th century, African slaves began to be imported, first by the Spanish and then by their French supplanters. By the time Haiti in 1804 became the sole black republic in the western hemisphere, the island's unique culture already centered upon the syncretic mesh of Christianity and voodoo. Both the term and the function of the latter component derive from *vodun*, meaning "spirit" or "deity" among the Fon-speaking people of West Africa. Central to the voodoo pantheon are *loas*, spirits that personify mysterious or elemental forces in nature and human behavior. They are accessed by *houngans* (priests) and *mambas* (priestesses) in worship that frequently employs ash and flour symbols (*veves*) drawn on a dirt floor and subsequently erased by dancers' feet in accompanying ceremonies. Much of Haitian imagery entails voodoo symbolism, including the depiction of *veves*, the use of color as a signifier of specific *loas*, and the appearance of Erzulie, Ogùn, Agwe, and Hamedi, *loas* of love, war, the sea, and death/transformation, respectively. An exploration of the creative outpouring of Haiti begins with the Davenport Museum of Art, which in 1967 acquired the first substantial collection of Haitian works in the United States. More than 100 paintings, sculpture, and other objects produced by Hector Hyppolite, Sisson Blanchard, Serge Joulimeau, George Liautaud, and other Haitian artists can be found here. In addition to the consciously naive paintings that one associates with the island, the museum displays the works of "avance" artists such as Edourd Duval-Carrie, Paul Gardere, and Jacques-Enguerrand Gourgue, and the history and genre works of Cap Haitien school artists such as Philome Obin. If you don't go, you won't know—and you'll regret it should you some night run across a *zobop*.

DES MOINES

Convention & Visitors Bureau
Two Ruan Center, 601 Locust Street, Suite 222, Des Moines, IA 50309
(515) 286-4960
Hours: Mon.–Fri., 8:30 A.M.–5 P.M.

Buxton Heritage Museum
1226 Second Avenue, Des Moines, IA 50314
(c/o Buxton, Iowa Club Inc., Box 281, Johnston, Iowa 50131)
(515) 276-2252; (515) 260-0581
Hours: Fri., 12 P.M.–6 P.M.; Sat.–Sun., 8 A.M.–6 P.M.; other times by appointment
Admission: Free; donations encouraged

In the first decade of the 20th century, a coal seam was discovered in Iowa, soon giving rise to Buxton, a company town composed largely of African-American miners. The town lasted as long as the coal, and thus by 1920 Buxton was in a rapid and terminal decline. Today this evanescent black industrial town in America's heartland is recalled at the Buxton Heritage Museum primarily through photographs and personal artifacts of the miners. The museum, operated by *The Communicator,* a multicultural newspaper in Des Moines, also hosts other exhibits that explore aspects of African-American heritage in Iowa, such as Des Moines's black business corridor located along Center Street.

Des Moines Art Center
4700 Grand Avenue, Des Moines, IA 50312
(515) 277-4405
Hours: Tue.–Sat., 11 A.M.–5 P.M.; Sun., 12 P.M.–5 P.M.
Admission: Free

When you step through the door of the outstanding African collection of the Des Moines Art Center, you enter not merely another continent but another world, one that is hard to shake off even after you, like Dorothy, arrive safely back in the Midwest. The Yoruba have one of the world's highest rates of twin births. To twin births tradition ascribes either great fortune or great trouble. Frequently one or both infants dies. In the former case, the parents may have an *ere ibeji* carved and placed in the mother's sleeping room. Properly placated, the spirit of the deceased twin will bring its parents prosperity. The double-figured *kabeja* carving of the Hemba also offers protection, but with a rather different twist: In the world of magic it involves the sacrifice of infants. Traditionally, the Mangbetu bound the heads of their infants, and the corresponding elongated skulls of the tribe's largely secular sculpture identify the objects' origin. Salampasu masks have an entirely different mien: A bulging forehead and an open rectangular mouth, often with teeth, characterize these initiation ceremony accoutrements. Functioning both as ancestor images and divination elements, the carved figures of the Bijogo, who inhabit the islands off the coast of Guinea-Bissau, are rarely found in American museums—but then, the Des Moines Art Center is a rare museum that also offers the more commonly seen high art and ethnographic objects of the Bwa, Marka, Bassa, Dogon, Mossi, Senufo, Bambara, Baga, Mende, Dan, Guro, Baule, Ashanti, Atti, Fon, Bini, Igala, Mumuye, Mambila, Ibo, Ibibio, Ekoi, Kom, Fang, Kota, Azande, Lega, Bembe, Yaka, Kuba, Luba, Songye, Chokwe, and other African peoples. This collection is remarkable not only for its range, rarity, and location, but also for its admission charge. It costs you nothing to open your eyes and your mind to the other world explored at the center.

Fort Des Moines Historical Marker
South West Ninth Street and Army Post Road, Des Moines, IA 50315
(515) 281-5111 (Des Moines Historical Society)
Hours: Daily until sunset
Admission: Free

For America's leaders in World War I (and World War II, for that matter), black troops were not warriors, they were simply the political price of African-American support for the war. The black community also broadly shared the perspective that the crux of the matter was political. Educated black activists, in particular, saw in World War I much the same thing that Frederick Douglass saw in the Civil War use of black troops: "Once let the black man get upon his person the brass letters 'U.S.,' let him get an eagle on his button, and a musket on his shoulder and bullets in his pocket, and there is no power on earth which can deny that he has earned the right to citizenship in the United States of America." A committee of Howard University students, for example, echoed the views of W.E.B. Du Bois describing America's newly created black officer training program as "the greatest opportunity since the Civil War" for black advancement and urging their counterparts across the country to join them in flooding the training camps. In response to this enthusiasm if not for the war or military service at least for the chance to serve as an *officer,* the War Department in the summer of 1917 opened a black officer training school at Fort Des Moines. More than 1,000 men would hastily pass through this school. Many of its cursorily trained graduates would see service in European combat as platoon and company commanders in the 92nd Division, though their experiences there may have led them to regret their initial enthusiasm. (See Victory Monument entry on p. 351.)

Two decades later Fort Des Moines again saw African Americans training for wartime military service. Of the 4,000 black volunteers for the Women's Auxiliary Army Corps, 120 trained here, living in separate barracks and eating at segregated tables but sharing classroom instruction with their white counterparts.

Today the remnants of the Fort Des Moines barracks and parade ground and a historical marker are accessible to the public, though the fort essentially closed down following World War II. At the nearby Army Reserve Center there is a small exhibit on the fort's history, while the Des Moines Historical Society (600 East Locust, 50319) hosts temporary exhibits that touch on the fort's and Iowa's connection to black heritage.

State Capitol Building
1015 East Grand Avenue, Des Moines, IA 50309
(515) 281-5011
Hours: Mon.–Fri., 8 A.M.–4:30 P.M.; Sat.–Sun., 8 A.M.–4 P.M.; tours available
Admission: Free

Iowa's black Civil War troopers underscored a sad fact of war: A great deal of death and scant glory was their fate. The 1st Regiment of Iowa Colored Infantry was raised between the summer and winter of 1863 and passed into federal service the following spring as the 60th USCT Regiment. Garrison duty in Helena, Arkansas, a year after the Red River campaign brought few of combat's dangers, and by war's end only 12 of the regiment's 1,153 men had been killed in their one action at Wallace's Ferry in Big Creek, Arkansas. Yet when the men mustered out of service in the autumn of 1865, a total of 344 of their comrades had been buried, victims of the sundry diseases that carried off about half of the total casualties of the war. The veterans of the 60th, coming home to a state whose constitution deprived them of the vote, turned their attention to securing equal rights in law. Not until 1868, however, did Iowa's white male citizens amend their constitution to permit African-American men to vote. Today the Iowa State Capitol Building displays the regimental flags of its Civil War troops, including that of the 60th USCT.

GRINNELL

Grinnell Historical Museum
1125 Broad Street, Grinnell, IA 50112
(515) 236-3252 (Local Historical Society)
Hours: June–Sept.: Tue.–Sun., 2 P.M.–4 P.M. Rest of year: Sat., 2 P.M.–4 P.M.
Admission: Voluntary donations requested

Those with an interest in the white contribution to the abolitionist struggle may wish to stop in at this museum. The museum—like the town in which it resides and the college that lies nearby—is named for the New York City clergyman Josiah Bushnell Grinnell. After Grinnell's voice gave out and his health broke down, his friend and fellow temperance advocate Horace Greeley advised him to "go west; it's a healthy country." Grinnell not only went west, he did so astutely. He and a group of other clergymen, who became known as "the Iowa Band," learned where two railroad lines would cross, bought up all the surrounding land, and founded a town. Grinnell, who later served in the U.S. Congress, was an ardent abolitionist and offered shelter to John Brown in 1859 when the soon-to-be-martyr passed through the area at the head of a band of fugitive slaves seeking refuge in Canada. Though the Grinnell house in which Brown stayed is no more, the museum has photographs of it, as well as other memorabilia of a foot soldier in 19th-century America's most intense moral clash.

INDIANOLA

Carver Museum and Simpson College

Museum: Warren County Fairgrounds, Highway 92W, Indianola, IA 50125
College: 701 North "C" Street, Indianola, IA 50125
Museum: (515) 961-6031; College: (515) 961-6251
Hours: Museum: Sun., 1 P.M.–4:30 P.M.; and by appointment. College: daily, daylight hours
Admission: Museum and college, free

Sometime in his teens—as he did not know his date of birth, he could never assign a precise age to himself—George Washington Carver (see Tuskegee University and Carver entries on pp. 31 and 414) received a certificate of merit from a small black school located about eight miles from the farm of his former masters and current mentors, Moses and Susan Carver. Thereafter, the young man supported himself as he sought further education at schools across Missouri and Kansas. In 1885 Carver applied for admission to Highland University, which accepted him on the basis of his record and then suddenly rejected him when it discovered he was black. After an unsuccessful and unhappy career as a homesteader, Carver moved to Winterset, Iowa, where acquaintances encouraged him to apply to nearby Simpson College. Mindful of his earlier experience, he was reluctant to do so. But driven by a love of learning and of painting—neither of which passions were likely to be consumated on a small farm—Carver walked the 25 miles from Winterset to Indianola, where he was admitted following a conversation with the college president.

COURTESY SIMPSON COLLEGE

George Washington Carver left Simpson College, "paradise for me," and his ambitions for a life as an artist to embark on a career in agriculture.

It was 1890 and Carver was then between 25 and 30 years of age. At Simpson he entered the pivotal year of his life, finding not only acceptance and encouragement, but also recognition for his accomplishments as an artist and as a horticulturalist. There too he abandoned his dream, which largely was vanquished by a sense of duty. Carver only reluctantly decided to forgo an artist's life, and ever after painting remained the great passion of his existence. But, aside from its uncertainty, art was an exercise of limited utility, and Carver carried within himself as Protestant an ethic toward work and good works as ever drove America's Puritan founders. Carver's decision to pursue botany was the more painful because it entailed leaving Simpson ("paradise for me") and his art instructor there, Etta Budd—to both of which he returned a year later for a further term as a special student of Budd's.

The centerpiece of the George Washington Carver Museum is the shack that formerly sat about a block east of the campus and in which Carver lived and ran the one-man laundry that enabled him to eat and to pay his college fees. Upon enrollment, Carver paid $12, which left him 10 cents on which to survive for the week it took him to get his laundry service up and running. On the museum's walls are blown-up photographs of Carver taken during his stay at Simpson, including two that show the artist at work in Etta Budd's classroom and one that shows the African-American woman at whose house Carver and other students ate. Also on view is one of the 12 sets of weeds that Carver personally gathered, identified, and mounted while he was working on his M.A. at Iowa State University. For years the weeds were actively used in botany classes at Simpson. The George Washington Carver Historical Marker is in the lobby of Carver Hall. Other sites include the First United Methodist Church, at which Carver gave the college's commencement address in 1941, and the Art Room in which Carver and the other members of Budd's class painted.

IOWA CITY

University of Iowa Museum of Art
150 North Riverside Drive, Iowa City, IA 52242
(319) 335-1727
Hours: Tue.–Sat., 10 A.M.–5 P.M.; Sun., 12 P.M.–5 P.M.
Admission: Free

Unlikely as it may seem, Iowa not only has one of the country's best collections of Haitian art, it also has one of the most comprehensive, balanced, and outstanding collections of sub-Saharan African art in the nation. The matrilineal cultures of East Africa rarely receive extended consideration in American museums, but at the University of Iowa Art Museum more than 150 pieces explore these little-known peoples. The creative outpourings of the Kwere, Zaramo, Makonde, Pare, Leguru, Hehe, Nyamwzi, and other tribes are explored through their art—sculpture, masks, and staffs—as well as through their material objects such as snuff grinders. Rare objects, such as *mwana hiti*—small wooden figures associated with initiation ceremonies of young women—and more common creations such as dolls, staffs, and fetish objects abound at the museum. Stronger even than its East African holdings are the museum's Zairean pieces. From Lwalwa masks through the early 20th-century idealized carved portrait of the Kuba king Shamba Bolongogo (who reigned circa 1650), to the Chokwe king figure (one of only two in the U.S.), the museum's exploration of Central Africa extends far beyond the Salampasu, Bakongo, Legu, and Mangbetu. Not only are most of the continent's major styles represented with high-quality figures, the museum also serves as the central concentration of the university's African studies program, with the result that its exhibitions constantly shift focus, repaying repeated visits over the years.

SALEM

Lewelling Quaker House

401 South Main Street, Salem, IA 52649
No telephone. Visitors to the town may ask at the post office or the town hall for the names and telephone numbers of individuals who can arrange tours
Hours: May–Sept.: Sun., 1 P.M.–4 P.M. Weekdays, by appointment
Admission: Adults, $1; students, 50 cents; occasionally slightly higher for large groups touring by appointment

Founded in 1835, Salem was the first Quaker settlement west of the Mississippi. Four years later an advertisement with an accompanying reward appeared in *The Iowa Territorial Gazette* and mentioned Salem as the site at which runaway slaves had been seen. Four years later still, the town's Quakers split on the issue of opposition to slavery, with the more militant abolitionists withdrawing, establishing their own meeting, building, and cemetery. (A strip of land two feet wide divided the final resting places of the two groups.) Active among the abolitionists were Henderson Lewelling and William Henderson. The former's substantial home-office building was built with refuge in mind and included a hidden tunnel extending under the stone structure. In 1848, after recaptured slaves suddenly escaped their captors while being held in Justice Gibbs's law offices, Ruel Daggs, the well-known "slave owner from Missouri," appeared in town with armed men and threatened the building's owner. Daggs then sued 19 men of Salem for their part in the flight of his chattel. Henderson's frame house three blocks away also had a tunnel running out from his cellar, while the nearby "Beehive" building had a unique arrangement whereby the floor of one room could be lifted by a wheel and rope in the attic, opening the secret cellar hideaway. Today the Lewelling Quaker House provides grim reminders of those days in the form of the kitchen trapdoor, the basement tunnel, the attic wheel of the "Beehive," and the $200-reward advertisement for four fugitive male slaves. Visitors to Salem also will see the Quaker and abolitionist meeting houses and cemeteries, the Duvall-Henderson House, the "Beehive," and other aspects of a 19th-century Quaker village.

TABOR

Todd House
705 Park Street, Tabor, IA 51653
(712) 629-2675 (Tabor Historical Society)
Hours: By appointment only
Admission: Free

In 1852 the Reverend John Todd and others from Oberlin, Ohio, settled Tabor, bringing with them a commitment to the abolitionist cause. (See Oberlin entry on p. 445.) During the struggle to keep neighboring Kansas a free territory, the Reverend Todd permitted 200 Sharps rifles to be stored at his house prior to their introduction into "bleeding Kansas." Virtually the entire town enlisted in the abolitionist struggle. John Brown was a frequent visitor to Tabor, using the Todd house as his local headquarters in the mid-1850s. The town, however, eventually turned against his methods, and Brown was refused the right to speak at the local church in protest against his penchant for violence. As a result, though Brown continued in the late 1850s to pass through Tabor, he and his men camped on the outskirts of town. Today the Todd House looks much as it did in the mid-19th century with its native oak, black walnut, and cottonwood frame, adobe foundation, and hand-hewn beams and lath. The house is open to visitors by appointment. On view are the melodium, sewing table, Bible, furniture, photographs, and papers and correspondence of the Todds. Visitors also see other period furniture that did not descend directly from the family. Though there are no exhibits that interpret the era, the guide from the Tabor Historical Society provides an explanatory framework for the house. A John Brown Historical Marker is located in the park across the street from the Todd House.

WEST DES MOINES

Jordan House Museum
2001 Fuller Road, West Des Moines, IA 50265
(515) 225-1286
Hours: Tours: May 1–Oct. 31: Wed. and Sat., 1 P.M.–4 P.M.; Sun., 2 P.M.–5 P.M. Groups, by appointment
Admission: Adults, $2; school-age children, 50 cents; no additional charge for tours

Iowa, which had seen firsthand the violence of "bleeding Kansas," generally favored the abolitionist cause, though this did not imply a commitment to racial equality within its borders. West Des Moines (then known as Walnut Township), Grinnell, Iowa City, Tipton, Clinton, Lewis, Fontanelle, and Muscatine were but some of the Iowa towns known for their involvement in the Underground Railroad. John Brown himself was well known in the state and—despite the minor cloud that hung over him after the "Pottawatomie Creek massacre"—

could rely on assistance when he passed through. Indeed, he and his associates trained for their raid on Harpers Ferry at the Maxham farm in Springdale, Iowa, and earlier had stored guns and ammunition at the Reverend John Todd's home in Tabor. (See preceding entry.)

James Jordan, from an old line, slave-owning Virginia family, arrived in Iowa in 1846, founded Walnut Township, eventually built an impressive, 16-room, Italian Gothic house, served as a state senator, and actively assisted the Underground Railroad. A friend of Brown's, Jordan at least twice opened his home to the militant abolitionist during the last year of Brown's life. On one of these occasions, Brown was leading a group of fugitive slaves headed toward freedom in Canada. In those days, it is unlikely that the fugitives would have needed to hide themselves while at the remote Jordan farmhouse, which then was a good day's ride from Des Moines. These days the Jordan House Museum offers a general examination of Iowa's contribution to the Underground Railroad, including exhibits on the quilt designs that were hung out its windows as signals, the female antislavery sewing societies whose needlework raised funds for the abolitionist movement, the double meanings of spirituals, and on Brown and the various "railroad lines" that ran through the state. Also visitors view period rooms and the basement kitchen that housed runaways and are offered a guided, two-hour tour (which may be abbreviated to taste). Arranged group tours may avail themselves of a living history interpreter, who portrays Jordan, and taste a period meal prepared in the upstairs kitchen.

KANSAS

Department of Travel and Tourism
400 SW Eighth Street, Fifth Floor, Topeka, KS 66603
(800) 252-6727; (913) 296-2009
Hours: Mon.–Fri., 8 A.M.–5 P.M.

BALDWIN CITY

John Brown Historical Marker
Pearson (Black Jack) Park, KS 66006
3 miles east of Baldwin City on Highway 56, then south ¼ mile
Hours: Daily until sunset
Admission: Free

In the 1850s "bleeding Kansas" was full of federal troops and marshals trying to quell the increasingly violent encounters between antislavery and pro-slavery forces, each of which was attempting to determine the territory's political character before admission to the Union. In the view of the free-state militias, federal forces were pro-slavery and guilty of doing their own raiding and kidnapping. In 1856 a free-state militia band led by John Brown surrounded the troops of Missouri Deputy Marshal H. Clay Pate, who were camped in a grove of Black Jack oaks at a major crossing of the Santa Fe Trail. A daylong skirmish ensued, with the result that Pate surrendered and released the captives his men had seized in nearby Palmyra and Price City, among them two of Brown's sons. Today a historical marker in Pearson Park marks the spot of what commonly is called the first battle over slavery in the United States. The park also has a Sante Fe Trail historical marker. Directly across the road from the park is the Boyd Prairie Reserve, where visitors will see not only aboriginal prairie grasses but also the extant wagon ruts carved into the ground by the passage of Americans heading west along the Santa Fe Trail.

BAXTER SPRINGS

Baxter Springs Historical Museum and National Cemetery
Eighth Street and East Avenue, P.O. Box 514, Baxter Springs, KS 66713
(316) 856-2385
Hours: May–Oct.: Tue.–Sun., 10:30 A.M.–4:30 P.M. Nov.–Apr.: Sat., 10:30 A.M.–4:30 P.M.; Sun., 1 P.M.–4:30 P.M.
Admission: Free

Baxter Springs lies on the old Military Road that began in 1825 in Fort Snelling, Minnesota (see Dred Scott entry on p. 410), and ended at Fort Washita on the Red River in Texas. Not surprisingly, in the Civil War it saw considerable troop concentrations. The Union had four field camps or forts inside the city limits and one just across the Spring River that runs southeast of the town, while the Confederates had two camps nearby. During 1862 and 1863 Union troops from Ohio, Indiana, Wisconsin, and Colorado were stationed here, as were Kansas troops, including the 1st and 2nd Indian Home Guard and the 1st and 2nd Kansas Colored Infantry. In October 1863 William Clarke Quantrill's brutal and murderous raiders, who were notorious even by the standards of irregular warfare of the period, suddenly swooped down on Fort Blair at the dinner hour. The camp's defense mainly was undertaken by Company A of the 2nd Kansas Colored Infantry, which had to run back across a creek and some distance to their stacked guns through the milling Confederate forces. First Lieutenant James Pond, who won a Medal of Honor in this battle, credited his black troops with driving off Quantrill's men. Other Union forces, including General J. G. Blunt's men, who were on their way from Fort Scott to Fort Smith, Arkansas, were not so fortunate. Blunt himself escaped, but many of his men fell into Quantrill's hands and were massacred—shot in the back of the head after being captured—in part because irregular units lacked the means to imprison large numbers of their opponents and in part because the probably pathological Quantrill set the tone for his troops. Today, the Baxter Springs Historical

Museum has an 8-by-15-foot mural of the battle and massacre and can answer questions about the 1st and 2nd Kansas Colored Infantry Regiments. (See Fort Scott entry on p. 379 and Poison Springs entry on p. 33.) The nearby Baxter Springs National Cemetery (Route 166) once was a national cemetery and still has a special area in its center where the victims of these encounters are buried.

BEELER

George Washington Carver Homestead Site
3 miles south of Beeler on Highway 96, Beeler, KS 67518
Hours: Daily until sunset
Admission: Free

If at first you don't succeed, you may be in the wrong line of work. After being rejected for admission to Highland University in Kansas because of his race, George Washington Carver tried his hand at homesteading, living in a prairie dugout on 160 acres. His venture was not notably successful, perhaps because he spent much of his time as the assistant editor of a local literary society. Then in his 20s, Carver mortgaged his property and moved to Iowa, the first step on his journey toward higher education and a career as an agronomist. Today the George Washington Carver Homestead Site is noted by a historical marker deep in rural Ness County.

BOGUE

Nicodemus Colony Historical Marker
c/o Nicodemus Colony Historical Society, R.R. 2, Box 139, Bogue, KS 67625
(913) 674-3311
Marker is located on U.S. 24, 2 miles west of the Rooks-Graham County line
Hours: Daily until sunset
Admission: Free

"All Colored People that want to GO TO KANSAS Can do so for $5" promised the 1877 fliers that spoke of the black township of Nicodemus. In response to the flier—and to the fact that Reconstruction had been driven down more thoroughly than Ol' Dixie had been a decade earlier—a band of African Americans abandoned the glorious bluegrass country of Kentucky. They journeyed to the "Promised Land" of Kansas, a state settled by abolitionists in arms. Their hopes were high—which made their arrival all the more unsettling. A pioneer who witnessed their arrival later recalled: "They finally reached their goal, a prairie quarter section, just north of the Solomon River—just a plain prairie country—no horses, no wells, no shelter of any kind, and winter setting in." They were to live burrowed into the ground like animals, in dugouts carved four to six feet deep into the sod and measuring 14 by 15 feet wide. The sod roofs leaked and in summer the insects ravaged. A settler who arrived the following year later recalled the shout "There is Nicodemus!" and her response: "I looked with all the eyes I had. 'Where is Nicodemus? I don't see it.' My husband pointed out the various smokes coming out of the ground. . . . The families lived in dugouts. . . . I began to cry." Many turned right around and returned to Kentucky or to their other southern points of departure. Many more stayed, either in Nicodemus, though the nearest railroad was 30 miles distant, or, more frequently, elsewhere in Kansas. Indeed, in 1879 alone, the height of the so-called Exoduster movement, 15,000 black folk poured into Kansas, arousing the concern of white residents and leading Frederick Douglass to deplore the fact that African Americans were abandoning the South "as Lot did Sodom."

Barring the occasional white resident, Nicodemus remained a black town. Its promise, though, was never to be realized. The black township reached its height in 1878 with 700 residents. Many of these moved on once they had established themselves, so that by 1880 the town's population was only 300. In 1888 came the death knell of true prosperity: The railroad passed by—six miles away, through a town called Bogue. (Note the address of the Nicodemus Historical Society.) From that day forward, though Nicodemus remained a black oasis on the prairie, at one time complete with a bank, livery stables, law offices, schools, and a doctor, its population gradually declined.

Today perhaps 50 folk live in Nicodemus, though the town swells during the annual summer Homecoming-Emancipation Celebration. Visitors to this, the sole surviving all-black prairie township, pass by the Nicodemus Colony Historical Marker on U.S. 24 and have the chance to tour historic buildings—including the A.M.E. Church, the First Baptist Church, the town's one-room school, and the Fletcher House Hotel—that began as dugouts, progressed to sodhouses, and then emerged as native limestone structures, mute testimony of a determined people who forsook the beauty of Kentucky for the black autonomy of the Midwest prairie.

CHANUTE

Martin and Osa Johnson Safari Museum
111 North Lincoln, Chanute, KS 66720
(316) 431-2730
Hours: Mon.–Sat., 10 A.M.–5 P.M.; Sun., 1 P.M.–5 P.M.
Admission: Adults, $2.50; ages 13–17, $1; 12 and younger, free

In the 1920s and '30s much of what America knew of Africa—beyond the fertile and fervid effusions of Edgar Rice Burroughs, the creator of Tarzan—was a function of the photographs and films of Martin and Osa Johnson, native Kansans who journeyed to the infrequently traveled regions of East Africa, the South Seas, and Borneo. Though time has shifted the perspective through which primitive cultures are perceived, the Johnsons' work remains of interest and can be viewed at the Martin and Osa Johnson Safari Museum. Beyond the photographs of terrain even wilder than the now-endangered species that once crowded the Johnsons' photos, visitors can view a substantial collection of

African art and ethnographic objects, many of which derive from Mali. Two of the most notable pieces are Dogon *sirige* masks nearly 15 feet high. In addition, visitors will find here *n'tomo* society masks; *chiwara* antelope headdresses; circumcision rattles of the Wassambe, Bambara, and Malinke peoples; a boy's helmet mask of the Bayaka; a *dea* mask of the *toro* society of the Dan people; Pende masks; Kisi stone figures; animal masks of the Bobo-Fing, Bobo-Ule, Kurumba, Wasalunke, and others; *gelede* masks, *ibeji* twin dolls, *ife* divination boards, and *shango* dance wands of the Yoruba; a wide range of fabrics—a Peul *khasa* blanket, Yoruba *adire* cloth, and Bambara *bokolanfini* or mud cloth; Senufo, Dogon, Pilewo, and Bambara musical instruments; and weapons of the Kikuyu, Masai, Turkana, and Dorobo. All convey the variety and continuity of African cultures across the spectrum of media. Possibly Auntie Em and Uncle Henry weren't the only reasons Dorothy wanted to return to Kansas.

ELLSWORTH

Ellsworth County Historical Museum

104 West South Main Street, Ellsworth, KS 67439
(913) 472-3059
Hours: Tue.–Sat., 9 A.M.–12 P.M. and 1 P.M.–5 P.M.; Sun., 1 P.M.–5 P.M.
Admission: Free; donations encouraged

This museum has remnants of the 19th-century civilian black presence in the vicinity of Fort Harker. (See entry on p. 381.) At one point in the late 19th century, perhaps 100 black families lived here. They are long gone; but they left behind the Second Baptist Church. Built in 1886, the frame church now stands on the grounds of the museum, complete with its original pews, piano, and Bible. Inside the museum visitors can gain a sense of a vanished black community from the photographs of the Wayman Chapel A.M.E. Church.

FORT RILEY

United States Cavalry Museum

Building 205, P.O. Box 2160, Fort Riley, KS 66442-0160
(913) 239-2737
Hours: Mon.–Sat., 9 A.M.–4 P.M.; Sun., 12 P.M.–4:30 P.M.
Admission: Free

At the United States Cavalry Museum, two display cases are devoted to the two black cavalry regiments that comprised 20 percent of America's mounted forces in the latter half of the 19th century. These forces saw repeated action against the Cheyenne, Arapaho, Comanche, Kiowa, Apache, and other Indian tribes, as well as against Pancho Villa's raiders from Mexico and the Spanish forces on Cuba. Few artifacts from the 9th and 10th regiments remain. An 1888 dress helmet; a buffalo coat, a muskrat hat, and bearskin gauntlets, all of which were issued to the troops; a 10th Cavalry guidon of the Spanish-American War period; and photographs are complemented by text that provides an overview of an experience that traditionally is portrayed as involving only white and red folk.

FORT SCOTT

Fort Scott National Historic Site and Museum
Old Fort Boulevard, Fort Scott, KS 66701-1471
(316) 223-0310
Hours: Memorial Day–Labor Day: daily, 8 A.M.–6 P.M. Rest of year: daily, 8 A.M.–5 P.M.
Admission: Ages 13–62, $2; others, free

Perhaps because he was a free-soil leader and a U.S. senator prior to his resignation to accept a commission as a brigadier general, James H. Lane paid scant heed to the federal prohibition against black troops in the Union army. As early as the summer of 1862, according to the *Fort Scott Bulletin*, Lane's efforts to transform "contraband" (slaves who had fled their masters since the opening of the war) into soldiers were under way, encouraged no doubt by a U.S. Congress that in July had authorized Lincoln to arm African Americans. Conscious that such a move as yet lacked broad public support, Lincoln deferred. Lane did not. Twice notified by the War Department that he lacked the authority to proceed, Lane proceeded without authority. Thus when Lane marched into Missouri in October 1862, approximately 250 men of the 1st Kansas Colored went with him, seeing action at Island Mound near Butler. This was the first recorded action by African-American troops in the Civil War.

The 1st Kansas Colored Regiment claims to be the first black regiment of the war, though this claim is somewhat cloudy and depends on definition. In the spring of 1862 General David C. Hunter raised, through methods that recalled the press-gangs of the British navy of earlier times, a unit of at least company strength on St. Simon's Island off of Georgia's coast, though it saw only garrison duty. Hunter was replaced by Brigadier General Rufus Saxton and his project to arm liberated slaves was turned over to the New England abolitionist clergyman Colonel Thomas W. Higginson. Higginson raised the 1st South Carolina, which saw limited action (unless, of course, you were killed; in which case the action was really rather major) on coastal raids just weeks after the 1st Kansas clashed at Mound Island. Also in the spring of '62, General Butler in Union-held New Orleans accepted into service an already existing free black militia unit, which had been raised by Louisiana's secessionist government. The commanders of the native Guards were black (for the historical background of free black militia units in Louisiana, see Chalmette Battlefield entry on p. 90) and, upon occasion, themselves owned slaves. By the time the 1st Kansas Colored got around to being formally mustered into the United States Army at Fort Scott on January 13, 1863, it was the fifth black Civil War regiment to enter the service, taking in December 1864 the unit designation 79th United States Colored Troops.

To date, the Fort Scott National Historic Site and Museum does not have an exhibit on the 1st Kansas Colored, nor on the 2nd, which also was recruited in eastern Kansas and mustered into the Union army at Fort Scott. This lacuna is largely a function of the fort's interpretive framework, which centers on the Indian frontier from 1842, when the fort opened, through 1853, when the fort closed for the first time and saw its buildings sold at public auction. However, the museum does have an exhibit on slavery and "bleeding Kansas," which is particularly interesting because the old fort and Fort Scott town (like most frontier forts, Scott was not stockaded, resembling instead a planned community built around a parade ground) embraced all the contradictions and violence of the period. The old fort and the town were pro-slavery; the surrounding farmers championed free soil and free labor. At the north end of officer's row in the old fort stood Fort Scott Hotel, commonly referred to as Free-State Hotel, while across the parade ground in an old barracks was the Western Hotel, called the Pro-Slavery Hotel. In the town as in the countryside, mayhem and murder flourished. Since the courts and the sheriff in Fort Scott were pro-slavery, the abolitionist "Self-Protective Company" under the violent and vituperative "Captain" Montgomery ran their own kangeroo courts. Though wearing badges, the sheriff's force were simply border ruffians, whose violence was answered in kind. Finally, just days before Christmas 1857, the army—answering ultimately to President Buchanan, who was widely seen as acquiescing in the corrupt attempt to admit Kansas to the Union as a slave state—moved back into Fort Scott to quell the violence. Instead, it found itself caught up in it, under attack particularly from free-state thugs such as Montgomery and John Brown, whose differences with the murderous, pro-slavery William Quantrill were as wide on the issues as they were narrow in field of the application of terror. In addition to the museum, the fort has about 20 restored buildings, living history and audio-visual programs, and a visitor center.

HAYS

Historic Fort Hays
1472 Highway 183 Alternate, Hays, KS 67601
(913) 625-6812
Hours: Sun.–Mon., 1 P.M.–5 P.M.; Tue.–Sat., 10 A.M.–5 P.M.
Admission: Free

Though the 9th and 10th Cavalry were stationed at Fort Hays, no exhibit recalls their presence. However, in following the footsteps of the buffalo soldiers, Historic Fort Hays comes close to being unique, for it commemorates the black 38th Infantry Regiment, which existed for only three years before it and the 41st were compressed into the now-famous 24th Regiment. The 38th was the first unit to occupy Fort Hays. Among its assignments was protecting the stagecoach route that ran along the nearby Smoky Hills Trail. Members of the regiment would ride atop the coach hoping to deter or, failing that, defeat Indian attacks on the main public transportation link heading west. Visitors to Historic Fort Hays will see a photograph of such an escorted stagecoach at one of its stops, the men of the 38th perched atop it.

Visitors also will see paintings and sketchings of the Battle of Beecher Island, including one that shows the black cavalry relief column that rescued the trapped scouts. (See Beecher Island entry on p. 495.) From Fort Hays, an officer of the 9th Cavalry, George Forsyth, who in the Civil War had served as General Sheridan's aide-de-camp, was ordered to experiment with civilian scouts who, it was hoped, would prove better adapted to plains warfare than the average soldier. Detached from the 9th, Forsyth, a Lieutenant Beecher, a surgeon, and about 50 scouts (many of them hangers-on around Fort Hays and Fort Harker rather than experienced frontiersmen) moved west after the Cheyenne and Sioux. Passing through Fort Wallace in western Kansas, the men rode into Colorado. There they found the Cheyenne—and battle. Waking up from a bivouac on the Arikaree River to find themselves confronted by Roman Nose's Cheyenne, the scouts fled with their horses to the only nearby defensible position, a small sandbar out in the river. Having already lost their pack mules, food supplies, medicine, and boxed ammunition, the scouts saw their horses killed within the first few minutes of combat, Forsyth thrice wounded, and Beecher and their surgeon killed. After enduring a nine-day siege shielded behind the bloated and stinking corpses of their horses, the exhausted scouts were rescued by the black troopers of the 10th Cavalry, whose timely arrival later would have inspired Hollywood had it made movies with black folks wearing blue rather than white uniforms and hats rather than hankerchiefs.

The only item the Fort Wallace Museum (Wallace, KS, 67761; 913 891-3564) contains relating to the Beecher Island/Fort Wallace story is a journal reprinting some of the fort's records.

KANOPOLIS

Fort Harker Museum
Wyoming Street, Kanopolis, KS 67454
(913) 472-5733
Hours: Tue.–Sun., 1 P.M.–5 P.M.
Admission: Free; donations encouraged

From Fort Harker in the late 1860s and early '70s buffalo soldiers rode out to provide protection from the Plains Indians to the Irish and Chinese laborers who built the Union Pacific Railroad. Today the Fort Harker Museum, located in the old fort's stone guardhouse, has only one object that recalls the black presence in the American West. A picture of the 10th Cavalry's Lieutenant Henry O. Flipper, who paid in full the tax America levies on African-American men (see Fort Davis entry on p. 161), stands in for the numerous black bodies that helped shoulder the load of closing down Eden and opening up new congressional districts.

LARNED

Fort Larned National Historic Site and Museum
Route 156, Larned, KS 67550
(316) 285-6911
Hours: Daily, 8:30 A.M.–5 P.M.
Admission: Adults (17–61), $1, with a maximum of $3 per family-car load

Fort Larned was constructed in 1860 to serve as the northern anchor of the line of forts defending and defining the southwestern military frontier. From Kansas through Indian Territory (Oklahoma) and into Texas, a string of forts guarded the Santa Fe Trail, over which annually traveled several million dollars' worth of goods and thousands of settlers and traders. From 1867 through 1869, Larned was the base of Company A of the 10th Cavalry, the first unit of buffalo soldiers to be assigned field duty. In these years Company A patrolled and escorted along the Santa Fe Trail, engaging in sundry minor skirmishes but no major battles with the Cheyenne, Arapaho, Kiowa, and Comanche who began to raid in 1868 in violation of the Treaty of Medicine Lodge, which had been signed in 1867. The black troops skirmished as well inside Larned, where they met with repeated incidents of racial harassment. The petty insults and fistfights culminated in the burning of the 10th's stables in January 1869, which resulted in the loss of 39 horses and considerable equipment. As an officer was responsible for his men's gear, Captain Nicholas Nolan—who unsuccessfully denied that his men had set fire to their own stables in anger or in protest—faced a major bill and a blot on his record. Nolan's experience was one reason many ambitious officers' declined to serve with the black regiments. Only years later did the War Department reverse the verdict and reimburse Nolan, who spent most of his military career with the 10th.

Today at Fort Larned National Historic Site and Museum, visitors are introduced to the buffalo soldiers. The ten-minute audio-visual show that makes mention of the 10th and a life-size mannequin of a fully equipped Company A trooper, complete with a cavalry Spencer rifle, and his properly accoutred horse greet the visitor. There is also a living history interpreter dressed as a 10th trooper who provides a fuller explanation of the experiences of the typical African-American soldier in the years following the Civil War. Of course, there also are a number of buildings, sites, and exhibits that interpret the fort from a broader perspective and that will interest the visitor.

LAWRENCE

Museum of Anthropology
University of Kansas, Spooner Hall, Jayhawk Boulevard, Lawrence, KS 66045
(913) 864-4245
Hours: Mon.–Sat., 9 A.M.–5 P.M.; Sun., 1 P.M.–5 P.M.
Admission: Voluntary donations requested

While its significant holdings of Chokwe and Yoruba masks, sculpture, thrones, and carved fetish objects do not distinguish this Museum of Anthropology from its counterparts, its systematic holdings of Baggara household artifacts do. The traditionally nomadic Baggara, a Sudanese tribe extending across Kordofan province, provided the largest single component of the Mahdi's troops that slew Hicks and Gordon, captured Slatin, and drove the Egyptians from Sudan in the late 19th century. The Baggara collection, which dates to the 1980s, is backed up by photographs and other documentation that establishes the whole of the material culture of a household of pastoral nomads. The museum also has small collections of objects of material culture from southern Africa, particularly the beadwork of the Ndebele, and eastern Africa.

Spencer Museum of Art
Kansas University, Lawrence, KS 66045
(913) 864-4710
Hours: Tue.–Fri., 8:30 A.M.–5 P.M.; Sun., 12 P.M.–5 P.M.
Admission: Free; donations encouraged

When one tires of Lawrence as the centerpiece of "bleeding Kansas," there is always Lawrence as Africa (the Museum of Anthropology) and Lawrence as contemporary African-American art. This last expression—from the gelatin silver prints of Gordon Parks through the lithographs of Jacob Lawrence (see Lawrence Home entry on p. 279 and Museum of Modern Art entry on p. 304), to the acrylics of Sam Gilliam and John Newman—may be found at the Spencer Museum of Art.

Quantrill Raid Monument
Oak Hill Cemetery, 14th Street and Oak Hill Avenue, Lawrence, KS 66044
Hours: Daily until sunset
Admission: Free

On August 20, 1863, the murderous Confederate guerilla leader William Clarke Quantrill called the roll of his men at Lone Jack, Missouri. "Bloody Bill" Anderson, Dick Yeager, the 20-year-old Frank James, the 19-year-old Cole Younger, and 290 other men and boys answered. That evening they crossed into Kansas and headed toward Lawrence, center of the antislavery struggle of the 1850s and very soon to be the site of the greatest massacre of civilians perpetrated during the Civil War. Entering the town from the southeast, Quantrill's force surprised the 22 young recruits of the 14th Kansas Regiment, who had not yet been equipped with arms. As they rose from their beds, the slaughter began. Within a minute 17 of the recruits were slain. From New Hampshire Street, Quantrill moved to Massachusetts Street and the Eldridge House Hotel. Here the provost marshal of the state hung out a white sheet signifying surrender. After sacking the hotel, the men were given the command: "Kill every man and burn every house." Hannah Oliver, a small child in 1863, later recalled:

> Then my mother saw a fearful sight: She saw a troop of guerillas ride up to the Griswold gate. She saw four men who lived in D. Griswold's house come out at the front door, pass through the gate, and then start in single file toward the town. Then she heard the shots of the guerillas and saw the men fall, in the order in which they had been walking. The four men lay in the fierce heat of the sun and the burning houses. A little later another posse rode up and shot them again. . . . We went into the Methodist Church, at 724 Vermont Street. Here the bodies of the dead from that part of town had been quickly collected and were lying in rows on the floor in pools of blood. Women were searching among them for their loved ones and finding them with pitiful wailings. . . . Looking down Massachusetts Street we saw the smoking heaps of smouldering debris and shattered walls. We smelt the mingled smell of burning wood and lime and of flesh of the bodies that were burning in the ruins.

Today visitors to Lawrence can view several sites connected to the events of the town's first decade of existence and the struggle against slavery. The historical plaque on Shunganunga Boulder (near 6th and Massachusetts streets) commemorates the founding of the town by the antislavery activists of the New England Emigrant Aid Company. In Oak Hill Cemetery visitors will find both the grave of James H. Lane, who raised the 1st Kansas Colored Infantry Regiment, the first black unit to see combat in the Civil War, and the Quantrill Raid Monument, recalling the town that paid its antislavery dues in blood. (Visitors to the cemetery also may wish to pay their respects at the grave of Lawrence-native George Walker, half of the famous, turn-of-the-century black comedy duo Williams and Walker.)

Elizabeth Watkins Community Museum
1047 Massachusetts Street, Lawrence, KS 66044
(913) 841-4109
Hours: Tue.–Sat., 10 A.M.–4 P.M.; Sun., 1:30 P.M.–4 P.M.
Admission: Free

Though founded by antislavery activists, much of Lawrence's post–Civil War history is of the Jim Crow variety. In the 1950s, though the city's schools were integrated, the racial boundary centered on swimming pools, with four local referenda being held in an attempt to integrate them. Much of the town's local history can be discovered at the Elizabeth Watkins Community Museum. In it is a statue of the 13-year-old Langston Hughes, the town's most famous 20th-century resident. Most of the buildings associated with Hughes are gone, but St. Luke's A.M.E. Church, which like much of his Lawrence experience is rendered in disguise in his largely autobiographical novel, *Not Without Laughter,* still stands at the corner of 9th and New York.

LEAVENWORTH

Buffalo Soldier Monument
Fort Leavenworth, Grant Avenue, Leavenworth, KS 66027
Hours: Daily until sunset
Admission: Free

When Colonel Henry Leavenworth established a fort in 1827 to oversee the Santa Fe and Oregon trails, he laid the foundation for what is now America's oldest active military post west of the Mississippi. Fort Leavenworth also is the site of the activation of the 10th Cavalry Regiment, the first all-black unit to see action in the years following the Civil War and the unit to which first was applied the colloquial designation "buffalo soldiers." Aptly, the fort now is the site of the recently installed Buffalo Soldier Monument, which pays tribute to the African Americans in uniform who helped secure the western frontier in the latter part of the 19th century. The 9th and 10th Cavalry and the 24th and 25th Infantry regiments bore a disproportionate share of the hard duty assignments of those years, for which they were rewarded with anonymity. Today that anonymity has been conquered—though far more slowly than the black troops conquered their foes. In the summer of 1992 the sculpture appropriately was dedicated by General Colin Powell, America's first black chairman of the Joint Chiefs of Staff, who had pushed for such a monument since his days a decade earlier as the post's deputy commanding general. Oddly, however, this monument to America's black soldiers owes its greatest debt to a black officer of the U.S. Navy, Commander Carlton Philpot, whom Powell called in his dedication speech "our champion."

COURTESY FORT LEAVENWORTH

In the Indian Wars of the late 19th century, America's black troops gained fame and a name, the "buffalo soldiers."

Frontier Army Museum
Gibbon and Reynolds avenues, Leavenworth, KS 66027
(913) 684-3191
Hours: Mon.–Fri., 9 A.M.–4 P.M.; Sat., 10 A.M.–4 P.M.; Sun., holidays, 12 P.M.–4 P.M.
Admission: Free. Voluntary donations requested

At the Frontier Army Museum, the African-American military experience on the western frontier is treated in chronological detail in a permanent exhibit that relies primarily on graphics. From an introduction that traces the black military role prior to the 1866 formation of the buffalo soldier units, through their organization and training and their duty assignment roles both as protectors of western expansion and as combat forces in the various campaigns against the Plains Indians, to their contribution to the border campaign against Pancho Villa's early-20th-century depredations, the museum details the life of black troopers in the West. Photographs, maps of duty posts and of clashes with Indians, equipment and artifacts of the men of the 9th, 10th, 24th, and 25th regiments are available to museum visitors. A walk around nearby Fort Leavenworth National Cemetery underscores another aspect of military service.

OSAWATOMIE

John Brown Museum
John Brown Memorial Park, Tenth and Main streets, Osawatomie, KS 66064
(913) 755-4384
Hours: Tue.–Sat., 11 A.M.–5 P.M.; Sun., 1 P.M.–5 P.M.
Admission: Free

A series of murderous reprisals characterized "bleeding Kansas" in the mid-1850s, and few men were better suited for such business than John Brown, who would later go on to fame (and his death) as the author of the raid on the federal arsenal at Harpers Ferry. (See Harpers Ferry entry on p. 207 and Kennedy Farmhouse entry on p. 257.) Brown believed himself divinely appointed to chastise the wicked slavers. During the Kansas border warfare, he led a militia band and made his headquarters in Osawatomie, where he stayed with his half sister and her husband, the Reverend Samuel Adair. Determined to protect the unofficial antislavery government that had arisen in protest against the fraudulently elected, pro-slavery territorial government, Brown's band engaged in a series of running battles with its pro-slavery counterparts. One outrage followed another. After the free-state capital of Lawrence was sacked, Brown and his men (including four of his sons) massacred five pro-slavery settlers in cold blood, hacking the men (none of whom owned slaves) to death in a fashion that befit Old Testament violence.

Today visitors to Osawatomie have access to several sites that recall Kansas's violent past and the part played in that by the martyr of Harpers Ferry. A life-size John Brown Statue stands at the entrance to John Brown Memorial Park. The park occupies the site of the August 1856 Battle of Osawatomie, where five of Brown's men were killed. The nearby Soldier's Monument at the corner of 9th and Main pays homage to the men killed in that encounter. The log cabin Adair Home, where Brown lived during these years, is the centerpiece of the John Brown Museum. The cabin's interior remains much as it was when Brown paced its floor reading the Bible and denouncing the wicked.

TOPEKA

Convention & Visitors Bureau
120 Southeast Sixth Street, Suite 100, Topeka, KS 66603
(913) 234-1030
Hours: Mon.–Fri., 8 A.M.–5 P.M.

Kansas Fever Committee
3730 Truman, Topeka, KS 66609
(913) 267-5381
Hours: Mon.–Fri., 5 P.M.–9 P.M.; Sat.–Sun., 9 A.M.–9 P.M.
Admission: Free

For some years now, Topeka's and Kansas's black heritage have found no more prominent exponent than the Kansas Fever Committee, which has been responsible for spreading the good news of the African-American contribution far and wide. In addition to promoting several annual African-American festivals, Kansas Fever offers informal tours of local black heritage sites, several of which (such as the Elmer Jackson Bridge, which honors one of three victims of a 1920 lynching in Duluth, Minnesota) are marked only because of the committee's efforts to recover a past that had been whitewashed.

Sumner Elementary School Historical Marker
330 Southwest Western Avenue, Topeka, KS 66606
(913) 357-5328
Historical marker mounted on the exterior wall at the right of the front entrance
Hours: Daily until sunset
Admission: Free

It was more than the racial insult and the annoyance that four safe blocks from their home was Sumner Elementary School. It was more than the mile-long bus ride home from Monroe Elementary School, though like most parents, Oliver and Leola Brown were not keen on having children bused away from their neighborhoods solely to satisfy the demands of public policy—particularly a policy as odious as segregated schooling. Beyond the abstractions, Linda Brown's parents were upset that once their daughter was dropped off at the corner of 1st and Kansas Avenue, she had to walk six blocks home through the railroad tracks listening carefully for the whistles that proclaimed an approaching train. But in Topeka, Kansas, of the 1950s, that was the *safer* side of the street—the fields and derelict buildings on the other side sheltered transients.

Oliver Brown, on whose name fame would fall for purely alphabetical reasons, was a 32-year-old welder in the Santa Fe Railroad yard in Topeka, an assistant pastor and sexton of St. John A.M.E. Church, the father of three girls, and one of 13 plaintiffs in a NAACP law suit that would bear his name though he was not a member of the organization. That case, known to history as *Oliver Brown*, *et al. v. Board of Education of Topeka*, was the most significant U.S. Supreme Court ruling of the 20th century. The ruling did more than overturn the precedent of *Plessy v. Ferguson*, which for more than half a century had provided the legal underpinning for the "separate but equal" doctrine employed to justify segregation. It also effectively overturned the social policy of segregation itself, though the policy would die a very lingering death and would require a decade of African-American activism and sacrifice to kill the monster and close the coffin lid.

(In the 1896 *Plessy* case, the Supreme Court on a 7-to-1 vote upheld the "separate but equal" doctrine of a Louisiana law that required racially exclusive railroad accommodations, denying that the doctrine violated the 13th or 14th amendments. The sole dissent was registered by Justice John Marshall Harlan, a former slave owner from Kentucky. Harlan condemned the ruling because it did not merely register the fact of white supremacy, but actively enabled states "to place in a condition of legal inferiority a large body of American citizens." His broader assessment proved prescient: "The judgment this day rendered will, in time, prove to be quite as pernicious as the decision made by this tribunal in the Dred Scott case. The thin disguise of equal accommodations . . . will not mislead anyone nor atone for the wrong this day done." Ironically, this historic case originated with Homer Plessy, to all appearances white but known to have had a black great-grandmother, who objected to being compelled by the Louisiana law to ride in the black rail car.)

Though Kansas had been settled in the 1850s by antislavery activists and initially had welcomed the Exodusters, the flood of black immigrants that moved to the state in the years after the Civil War, an opposition to bondage did not imply an urge toward social equality. As early as 1879 the Kansas legislature granted cities with populations in excess of 15,000 the authority to segregate *elementary* schools, which they quickly did. Two decades later, when William Reynolds, an African-American resident of Topeka, brought suit against the city's Board of Education for denying his son entrance to a white school, the Kansas Supreme Court, citing *Plessy v. Ferguson*, ruled against him. For the next 50 years Topeka's elementary schools remained segregated. (Secondary school classrooms were integrated, though extracurricular activities such as sports teams and dances were segregated.) In the 1950s the town of 100,000 had a black population of about 7,500; 18 white and four black elementary schools; one black hotel; and strictly segregated cinemas, parks, and swimming pools. Except at work, the races lived in separate worlds—a separation undergirded by the U.S. Supreme Court.

Then, in 1951, suit was filed in the U.S. district court for Kansas, bearing the title *Brown v. Board of Education*, challenging the constitutionality of the segregation of Topeka's elementary schools that then was entering its eighth decade. A year later the U.S. Supreme Court had on its dockets five such cases: from Kansas, Virginia, South Carolina, Delaware, and the District of Columbia, all of them orchestrated by the NAACP in pursuit of a two-decade-old strategy to overturn the consequences if not the case of *Plessy v. Ferguson*. Significantly, in several of these cases there was no dispute about the facts: The black education provided was equal regarding all tangible factors with that offered in white schools. What was at issue were intangibles and the U.S. Constitution. The NAACP's lawyers—James Nabrit, Jr., George E. C. Hayes, and Thurgood Marshall—prepared their strategy: to challenge directly the constitutionality of the separate but equal doctrine, not its application. In December 1952 the Supreme Court heard the oral arguments in the cases. The young African-American attorney Robert Carter argued *Brown*. Ten months later, with no ruling yet handed down, the chief justice of the Court, Fred Vinson, died. Earl Warren was confirmed in his place. In December 1953 the attorneys returned to court to respond to the questions justices had posed after the initial arguments. In May 1954 the unanimous Warren Court handed down the 20th century's most significant ruling, holding that school segregation inherently violated the 14th Amendment. (By this time Linda Brown was 11 years old and entering the seventh grade of an integrated Topeka junior high school. Contrary to conventional wisdom, she never attended Sumner Elementary School.)

Today, almost four decades later, Sumner Elementary School—in front of which is a historical marker—and Monroe Elementary School, which saw three generations of the Browns enrolled, are formally registered as National Historic Sites.

State Capitol
Tenth and Harrison, Topeka, KS 66612
(913) 296-3966
Hours: Tours (beginning at Rotunda): Mon.–Fri., 9 A.M., 10 A.M., 11 A.M., 1 P.M., 2 P.M., 3 P.M.; Sat., 9 A.M., 11 A.M., 1 P.M., 3 P.M.
Admission: Free

Kansas's State Capitol displays the famous J. S. Curry mural depicting John Brown as a fiery Old Testament abolitionist, gun and broadsheet in hand, standing against a background in which African Americans largely are portrayed as the victims of Brown's foes. Also found in the Capitol is a portrait of Edward McCabe, the first African American to be elected to a statewide office in Kansas. McCabe was elected state auditor in 1882 and 1884 before going on to found an all-black town in Oklahoma (see Langston entry on p. 454) as a first step toward his dream of a black-majority state. Finally, the clash at Beecher Island (see Historic Fort Hays entry on p. 380 and Beecher Island entry on p. 495), which was ended by the arrival of the black troopers of the 10th Cavalry, is recorded—though the painting catches the desperate band of surrounded U.S. army scouts prior to their rescue and hence lacks African Americans.

Topeka Public Library
1515 Southwest Tenth Avenue, Topeka, KS 66604-1374
(913) 233-2040
Hours: Mon.–Fri., 9 A.M.–9 P.M.; Sat., 9 A.M.–6 P.M.; Sun., 2 P.M.–6 P.M.
Admission: Free

Dominated by the gold weights of the Akan peoples and leavened by *ibeji* figures of the Yoruba and masks from many of the peoples of West Africa, the African collection is one of the surprises of the Topeka Public Library. Be forewarned, however: The collection of several hundred pieces is often in storage due to the rival claims upon scant space. If you call ahead, occasionally it is possible to see the pieces even if they are not in the display cases.

WABAUNSEE

Beecher Bible and Rifle Church
Highway 18, 5 miles southwest of Wamego, Wabaunsee, KS
No postal address
No phone
Hours: Daily until sunset
Admission: Free

In the 1850s a group of Connecticut abolitionists, who had come to Kansas to keep it a free state, founded the First Church of Christ in Wabaunsee. The character of the congregation can be gauged by the church's colloquial designation, the Beecher Bible and Rifle Church. It was an appropriate name, for before the New Haven colonists of the Connecticut-Kansas company had left their homes they had raised money for weapons: The prominent abolitionist and Brooklyn minister Henry Ward Beecher (see entry on p. 290) had promised that his congregation would donate funds for 25 Sharps rifles if the crowd would match his gift. Beecher soon forwarded $625 for the guns, along with 25 Bibles. Today the stone building is the sole surviving church in the state from the era of "bleeding Kansas." For much of the 20th century, the church was kept alive by a congregation that was substantially African American, but today those folks have moved on and the area is largely white. Visitors to the Beecher Bible and Rifle Church view a historical marker and may collect a small pamphlet that outlines the church's origin and history.

WICHITA

Holmes Museum of Anthropology
Wichita State University, McKinley Hall, 17th and Hillside, Wichita, KS 67208
(316) 689-3195
Hours: Mon.–Fri., 12 P.M.–5 P.M.
Admission: Free

Straddling the northern parts of Togo and Benin is the Tamberma people, whose material culture and spiritual expression is explored through their masks, weapons, jewelry, and fetish objects at the Holmes Museum of Anthropology. Also on view is a general exhibit of masks from around the world, among which are several representative samples from the Yoruba, Bamana, Mende, Bena Lulua, Mangbetu, Ashanti, Masai, Turkana, and Pende.

MICHIGAN

Michigan Travel Bureau
Department TPM, P.O. Box 30226, Lansing, MI 48909
(800) 543-2937; (517) 373-0670
Hours: Mon.–Fri., 8 A.M.–5 P.M.

ADRIAN

Laura Haviland Statue
Main Street, Adrian, MI 49221
Hours: Daily until sunset
Admission: Free

In the early 1830s, as Michigan's Quakers deliberated at length whether actively to oppose slavery outside the state's boundaries, two women acted. Elizabeth Chandler and Laura Haviland launched Michigan's first antislavery society. By 1834 Chandler was dead, but Haviland's work was gathering strength. In 1839 the Quaker woman opened Raison Institute for the education of African Americans, who shared classes with white students in the state's first integrated school. She already was active in aiding runaway slaves, work that provoked the wrath of the slave-owning John P. Chester and his son Thomas, who printed and distributed copies of Haviland's correspondence to them with a handbill offering a $3,000 reward for her arrest attached. During the Civil War Haviland traveled south to work as a nurse, a journey she repeated after the war as an active member of Detroit's Freedmen's Relief Association. Two monuments to her exist: her autobiography, unfortunately entitled *A Woman's Life Work* rather than *Critique of Pure Raison,* and the Laura Haviland Statue on the main street of her hometown, across from the town hall.

Lenawee County Historical Museum
110 East Church Street, P.O. Box 511, Adrian, MI 49221
(517) 265-6071
Hours: Tue.–Sat., 1 P.M.–5 P.M.
Admission: Free

In the late 19th century Adrian was Michigan's second-largest town. As a railroad center, it drew in substantial numbers of African Americans—enough that in 1895 two black entrepreneurs published the *Afro-American Journal and Directory of Adrian, Michigan* and distributed a copy to each black resident. It was also the home town of the Page Fence Giants, a black baseball team sponsored by a local fence company. These Giants claimed to be America's best black baseball team, a claim disputed by the far better known New York Cuban Giants, who in 1896 traveled out to Michigan to resolve the matter on diamonds around the state. The New Yorkers should have stayed home. Today visitors to Lenawee County Historical Museum can view photographs of the Page Fence Giants, the 1895 directory of black residents, and other artifacts that touch upon local black history.

AUGUSTA

Unknown Black Soldier's Grave
Fort Custer National Cemetery, 15501 Dickman Road, Augusta, MI 49012
(616) 731-4164
Hours: Daily until sunset
Admission: Free

The 1st Michigan Colored Infantry mustered into service in Detroit in February 1864, departing the state a month later for Annapolis, Maryland, where it was inducted into the Union army as the 102nd United States Colored Troop Regiment. The 102nd primarily saw action in South Carolina. Today one of its nameless dead lies in the Unknown Black Soldier's Grave in Fort Custer National Cemetery.

BATTLE CREEK

Kimball House Museum
196 Capital Avenue, NE, Battle Creek, MI 49017
(616) 965-2613
Hours: Tue.–Sat., 12:30 P.M.–4:30 P.M.
Admission: Adults, $2; students, $1

Three generations of Kimball doctors lived in the Victorian era, Queen Anne mansion that now sees service as the Kimball House Historical Museum. Full of period furnishings and utilitarian objects offering insight into upper-middle-class life in 19th-century Michigan, the museum also has an exhibit on Sojourner Truth and her role in the abolitionist and women's movements. Clothing worn by Truth, a small piece of wood from her old local home, photographs of her, a holograph representing her attempt to write her name, and other artifacts recall the 19th-century champion of God, African Americans, and women.

Sojourner Truth Memorial
Oak Hill Cemetery, 255 South Avenue, Lot #634, Battle Creek, MI 49017
(616) 964-7321
Hours: Daily until sunset
Admission: Free

COURTESY NATIONAL PORTRAIT GALLERY

In order to support herself and the struggle for African-American advancement ("the substance"), Sojourner Truth sold photographs ("the shadow") of herself.

In 1856 the Quaker Henry Willis arranged for Sojourner Truth to speak in Battle Creek, where one of her daughters lived. Truth soon bought a home nearby and more or less settled in a nearby spiritualist community, becoming—thanks to articles written by Harriet Beecher Stowe—Battle Creek's most famous citizen. Here she stayed until midway in the Civil War. After taking the Thanksgiving Day dinner prepared by the town to the 1st Michigan Colored Infantry training at Fort Ward near Detroit, Truth moved to the Washington, D.C., area and aided the many thousands of African Americans who had fled there from slavery. There she ran into trouble for interfering with slave owners from Maryland who sought the return of their property, to whom the terms of the Emancipation Proclamation did not apply. (See Antietam entry on p. 256.) She continued her relief efforts after the war on behalf of the Freedmen's Bureau, before returning to Battle Creek, where she died in her home in 1883. She was buried with members of her family in Oak Hill Cemetery, where today visitors will find a monument that inaccurately suggests Truth was "aged about 105" at her death. It bears the simple inscription that repeats Truth's famous and entirely rhetorical question to a Frederick Douglass who was advocating the necessity and righteousness of violence: "Is God dead?" In fact, Truth's renowned rejoinder to Douglass—like her equally famous "Ain't I a woman" phrase (see Sojourner Truth entry on p. 253)—was never uttered by her, at least in the form in which it has come down to us via an article written in 1860 by Harriet Beecher Stowe. Stowe's phrase, however, is based on a real 1852 encounter between Douglass and Truth.

A final local stop for those interested in Truth is the Michigan Legal Milestone Marker at the Battle Creek Hall of Justice (67 Michigan Avenue East), which pays tribute to "one of America's most influential crusaders for justice."

Underground Railroad Monument
1 Michigan Avenue East, Battle Creek, MI 49017
(616) 968-1611
The monument is on the grounds of the Kellog Foundation, not far from Kellog House
Hours: Daily until sunset
Admission: Free

Courageous but rightly fearing pursuit, moving by night into an unknown world, determined but left vulnerable by ignorance and illiteracy, torn between relying upon themselves or entrusting their lives and those of their loved ones to strangers, the typical experience of a fugitive slave was fraught with anxiety. Yet whether fleeing from the overseer's lash or toward a liberty America proclaimed but denied to them, slaves in their thousands headed north, preferring the perils of an uncertain future and the penalty for recapture to bondage, dispossession, and degradation. Virtually everywhere they fled in the North, they found some white folk willing to lend a helping hand despite the existence of the fugitive slave laws. Black initiative, white support, and a moral penumbra to good works in violation of the law, the Underground Railroad was the 19th century's equivalent of the civil rights struggle of the early 1960s.

In the 1840s Battle Creek, Vandalia, Climax, Albion, Marshall, and other Michigan towns were centers of the "Quaker Route" of the Underground Railroad and saw thousands of runaway slaves pass through on their way to a Canadian freedom. In 1847, when Kentucky slave catchers rode into Marshall to reclaim human property, they found a town broadly united in forestalling their aim. (See Crosswhite Boulder entry on p. 407.) In Marshall, Zachariah Shugart and nine companions aided their fugitive black neighbors to flee to Battle Creek. Forty-five men, women, and children crossed over Battle Creek's Main Street Bridge (now Michigan Avenue West) on a moonlit night as that town's folk—alerted and organized by Erastus Hussey—turned out to welcome them. The next morning the group was on its way to Canada. (The families of William Casey, Perry Sanford, Joseph Skipworth, and Thomas Henderson stayed behind, making Battle Creek their home.)

Today the Underground Railroad, 19th-century America at its best, is recalled in a new, massive (seven-ton, 28-foot-long, 14-foot-high) memorial created by the well-known sculptor Ed Dwight. Placed not far from the old Hussey property that sheltered runaways, the Underground Railroad Monument, in Dwight's words, "dramatize[s] figures from two major historical scenarios. On one side, I have depicted the use of the river as a means of slave movement to the North. Adjacent to the river, I tried to show slaves emerging cautiously from the cover of the forest. Here, Harriet Tubman is depicted in her role as the 'black Moses,' leading her people out of bondage. On the other side, the memorial features a wagon train and focuses on the Hussey family as 'conductors,' with the wife, Sarah, ushering [fugitives] into a cellar and Erastus leading the movement."

CASSOPOLIS

Chain Lake Missionary Baptist Church Historical Marker
16853 Chain Lake Street, Cassopolis, MI 49031
(616) 476-2661
Hours: Daily until sunset
Admission: Free

If the wind rustling through the pine and cedar trees standing amid the Chain Lake Baptist Church Cemetery could carry the tales of those interred, another chapter in America's largely lost black history could be recovered. Buried here are people who sought freedom—and found allies. Manumission papers—and even free black birth—were no guarantee of liberty anywhere within reach of slavery and its agents, with the result that the far Midwest saw a significant influx of African Americans in the mid-19th century. The Chain Lake Baptist Church Historical Marker compresses the story of a local black community formed of the interaction of free blacks, runaway slaves, and white Quakers:

> "In the 1830s southern runaway slaves bound for Canada came into Michigan near Cassopolis. In 1840, Cass County's Quaker community, which provided a haven for the fugitives, became an integral part of the Underground Railroad. Many free African Americans also settled permanently . . . [and in] 1838, Cass County's first African-American church was organized here. In 1853 the Michigan Antislavery Baptist Association, later renamed the Chain Lake Baptist Association, was formed.

DEARBORN

Henry Ford Museum & Greenfield Village
20900 Oakwood Boulevard, Dearborn, MI 48124
(313) 271-1620
Hours: Daily, 9 A.M.–5 P.M. Building interiors closed Jan. 2–Mar. 16
Admission: Adults, $10.50, over 62, $9.50; ages 5–12, $5.25. Extra charge for museum

In antebellum Savannah, as elsewhere throughout the South, enslaved, skilled black laborers, many of them working under purely nominal white supervision, built barns, homes, and bridges, kept the books, and otherwise designed, directed, and then raised structures contracted for by white construction firms.

A still larger number of less skilled slaves lacked only freedom and wages of pennies a day to distinguish them from poor white nonfarm laborers—or from their own sons of the next generation. Not only black oppression existed on both sides of the dividing line of emancipation, so too did black autonomy and a poverty almost matched by many poor whites. The paradoxical result for black families was that both the good and bad aspects of life under formal freedom—which at all times was devoutly desired—did not always represent such a sharp break with the slave past. Both change and continuation are highlighted by a stroll through the Hermitage Slave Houses and Mattox House, which explore enslaved and free black life in coastal Georgia in the 19th and 20th centuries at the Henry Ford Museum & Greenfield Village.

Hermitage was an *industrial* plantation, with steam-powered saw and planing mills, a rice barrel factory, Savannah's largest brick works, and 201 enslaved men, women, and children who among other labors produced more than 60 million handmade bricks. Though by no means unusual in antebellum America, industrial slavery is an experience rarely highlighted in the 20th-century portrayal of the life of the disenfranchised, which until recently focused almost exclusively on the unskilled field hand, the whip and chains—which is all the more reason to visit an 81-acre, indoor-outdoor museum that hosts more than 80 buildings and spans more than three centuries of American history. The two small, gray-brick, one-story, 16-foot-square slave houses, originally raised at Hermitage between 1820 and 1850 and then transported to the museum in the 1930s, now host exhibits that feature the testimony of slaves who gained their freedom and later wrote books about their experiences; reproductions of period beds, tables, benches, and cookware of an enslaved skilled carpenter and his family; and exhibits that focus on the culture that Africans brought with them and its transformation in the cauldron of slavery.

Nearby is the Mattox House built in 1879 on 522 acres in Savannah's neighboring Bryan County by Amos Morel, a formerly enslaved African-American steam engineer who after emancipation became a land-owning farmer and a leader of Bryan's black community. The one-and-a-half-story, two-room, frame farmhouse has been restored to its 1930s appearance and furnished with the original possessions of and an exhibit about the Morel and Mattox families. Through period rooms, graphics, artifacts, audio recordings, and staff presentations, visitors to these adjacent buildings gain a sense of the complexities of southern black life in a span of three generations that separated late antebellum and depression-era America. Greenfield's two other major African-American exhibits focus on the life and career of George Washington Carver—whose cabin birthplace has been reconstructed and whose innovative agricultural research is explored—and on the Maryland plantation house of the slave-owning Carroll family. Henry Carroll, his wife, six children, and the children's English tutor lived in the Susquehanna Plantation house, which now sits in Michigan. A tour of this house is enlightening because it defies the popular conception of a palatial plantation mansion (an image deriving from the Deep South homes that arose from the explosive financial success of nouveau riche cotton magnates). The Carrolls employed 74 slaves on the wheat and tobacco fields that adjoined their upper-middle-class home, and Greenfield interprets for visitors the interdependence of the estate's free and enslaved communities.

DETROIT

Convention & Visitors Center
Two East Jefferson Avenue, Detroit, MI 48226-4328
(313) 567-1170
Hours: Sept.–Mar.: daily, 9 A.M.–5 P.M. Oct.–Apr.: Mon.–Fri., 9 A.M.–5 P.M.; Sat.–Sun., 10 A.M.–4 P.M.

Ask for the "Detroit's African-American Points of Interest" brochure, and for the "Black Historic Sites in Detroit" booklet and the "Doorway to Freedom: Detroit and the Underground Railroad" pamphlet produced by the Detroit Historical Department.

Detroit Institute of Arts
5200 Woodward Avenue, Detroit, MI 48202
(313) 833-7900
Hours: Tue.–Sun, 9:30 A.M.–5:30 P.M.
Admission: Voluntary donations requested

Both in the ancient world and thousands of years later following the collapse of Roman power, African kingdoms were the engine of civilization. Egypt in both periods and the kingdoms of Africa's Mediterranean coast under the guiding influence of Islam in the later period conserved and expanded the realm of knowledge—and provided the social stability necessary to secure its transmission to succeeding generations. More than 3,000 objects at the Detroit Institute of Art testify to this achievement. The institute's Ancient Egypt Collection embraces the Predynastic through the Roman and Coptic periods, with its greatest strengths in Middle and Late Kingdom sculpture and Coptic textiles. The institute's Islamic North Africa Collection examines the Abbasid Period (A.D. 750–1258) and the Fatimid (A.D. 969–1117) and Mamluk (A.D. 1250–1517) dynasties of Egypt and is particularly strong in Abbasid textiles, Mamluk glass, and Moroccan illuminated manuscripts, rugs, and clothing. The institute also holds more recent objects traditionally associated with African collections. Sub-Saharan Africa is represented by sculpture, decorative arts, and textiles from West and Central Africa. Figural sculpture and masks from the BaKongo, Yaka, Bena Lulua, and other peoples are complemented by the metalwork of the Akan peoples and the bronzes of Benin.

Elijah Muhammad Temple No. 1
(Now called Masjid Wali Mohammed Mosque)
11529 Linwood Avenue (Elijah Muhammad Boulevard), Detroit, MI 48206
(313) 868-2131
Hours: Mon.–Sun., 10 A.M.–4 P.M.
Admission: Free

Georgia has given America many prophets, including George Baker (Father Divine), Richard Penniman (Little Richard), and Elijah Poole (Elijah Muhammad). When W. D. Fard, author of *Teaching for the Lost-Found Nation of Islam in a Mathematical Way,* disappeared, the Nation of Islam was a small sect with no discernible future. In depression-era Detroit, and in faith, Elijah Muhammad in 1931 helped establish Temple No. 1, the first of many structures that testify to his enduring impact on 20th-century black America. The century's most powerful formal articulation of black self-affirmation is only partially obscured by the nonsense of the "big-headed scientist," Mr. Yacub, genetically deconstructing blacks and separating and letting loose the blue-eyed white half of evil and weakness, which would rule the world for 6,070 years, tormenting full—that is, black—human beings until 1984. In 1940 the Nation of Islam moved from its storefront to a building of its own on Linwood Avenue.

Dr. Ossian Sweet House
2905 Garland Street, Detroit, MI 48214
Hours: Daily until sunset
Admission: Not open to the public. Exterior viewing only

Few know that the NAACP's Legal Defense Fund, famous for its role in *Hocutt v. the University of North Carolina, Alston v. School Board of the City of Norfolk, Brown v. Board of Education*, and sundry other challenges to segregated America, began as an outgrowth of the 1925 murder and conspiracy charges leveled against Dr. Ossian Sweet. One night the black doctor and his family, who had moved into the white neighborhood two days earlier, were confronted with a large and hostile mob in front of their house. Shots fired from inside the doctor's house—which he had fortified and filled with guns and ammunition—killed a resident of Garland Street, who was standing on his own front porch across from the Sweet home, and wounded a member of the mob. When the defendant is innocent, any Perry Mason will do; but in a city hostile to black men, particularly those who have the temerity and funds to move into white neighborhoods, the not unambiguously innocent needed Clarence Darrow.

The trial was a tabloid's dream: Held amid Detroit's mayoralty election and accompanying Klan campaigning and confronting America's most famous defense attorney with one of his most difficult cases, it offered daily opportunity for inflammatory headlines and racial diatribes. Darrow, true to tradition of his trade, scrupulously avoided unfortunate irreducible facts—such as the corpse across the street—and instead focused on that which supported his client: discrepancies in the police account, his own rhetoric, and Dr. Sweet's testimony. Sweet's testimony was compelling: "When I opened the door and saw the mob, I realized I was facing the same mob that had hounded my people through its entire history. In my mind, I was pretty confident of what I was up against. With my back against the wall, I was filled with a peculiar fear, the kind no one could feel unless they had known the history of our race. I knew what mobs had done to my people before." The prosecution's case was not strengthened by its inability to establish who had fired the shots from the house (11 adult African Americans were inside Sweet's home at the time of the affray) or in what particular circumstances, and the trial ended in a hung jury. In the circumstances, this was a remarkable achievement by Darrow and Sweet, and testimony of some sort to either the empathy or the malleability of the jury.

Sweet, who never stood trial again, remained in his house for another two decades. In the waning days of the Eisenhower administration, despondent over his failing practice, he killed himself. Today Sweet's home, the site of the events that spawned the most effective black civil rights legal organization in our nation's history, still stands on Garland Street. It is now a *private residence not open to the public and lacks any historical marker.* There is, however, a Sweet case historical plaque on the Frank Murphy Hall of Justice, a Detroit criminal court building located at the corner of Gratiot and St. Antoine streets. Named after the judge who presided over the Sweet trial in a fashion that won the approval of the black community—and who went on to serve as governor of Michigan, attorney general of the United States, and a U.S. Supreme Court Justice (1940–1949)—the building has never seen an attorney as effective as Darrow—and only rarely a defendant with as good a case as Sweet's.

Graystone International Jazz Museum, Jazz Hall of Fame
1521 Broadway, Detroit, MI 48226
(313) 963-3813
Hours: Mon.–Fri., 10 A.M.–5 P.M.; Sat., 11 A.M.–4 P.M.
Admission: Adults, $2; children and tour groups of 10 or more, $1 per person

Life is short, art is long. Much has passed since American troops sailed home from World War I. Prohibition has come and gone, segregation has gone, the Graystone Ballroom—in 1922, Detroit's hot spot for an evening's entertainment—is no more, the automobile may in the not too distant future follow suit, but jazz metamorphoses and endures. Both that which has changed and that which abides in America's most distinctive contribution to world culture can be found in memorabilia from the "Jazz Age" to the present at the Graystone International Jazz Museum. Scads of photographs of the old greats; artifacts from the Graystone Ballroom; the instruments of Ellington, Basie, J. C. Heard, Perry Pollard, Tito Puente, and others; an extensive collection of videos of modern-era performers; and guided tours of the place are available to those who walk through the doors.

Institute of African-American Arts
2641 West Grand Boulevard, New Center-West, Detroit, MI 48208
(313) 872-0332
Hours: Daily, 10 A.M.–10 P.M.
Admission: $2

In the 1960s, when Berry Gordy, Jr., ran the Motown label from his house, the producers, technicians, artists, and worker bees of the company had a day-care center for their kids across the street. Today that small house—which now is across the street from the Motown Museum—serves as the Institute of African-American Arts, paying tribute to recently deceased local artists and offering exhibition and performance space for the up-and-coming. The institute's main gallery showcases the work of the late LeRoy Foster, mentor to many Detroit artists. The small Oscar Graves Gallery exhibits a handful of the works of the black sculptor, including his bust of Malcolm, while the Jimmie Wallace–James Lee Gallery pays tribute to the memory of two of Detroit's prominent local painters by offering exhibition space for contemporary black artists. On weekends the institute hosts music, drama, and dance performances. It's not often that one can get a sense of the history both of popular culture and of a town's lesser-known creative energy on one small residential street, so if you're in the neighborhood to see Motown, look both ways and cross the street.

Joe Louis Arena
600 Civic Center, Detroit, MI 48226
(313) 567-6000
Hours: Not open to the public, except for persons paying to see arena events

Joe Louis "Boxing" Sculpture
Cobo Convention Center, Detroit, MI
3 blocks from "The Fist," via Jefferson Avenue
Hours: Daily until sunset
Admission: Free

Joe Louis "Fist" Sculpture
Woodward and Jefferson avenues, Detroit, MI 48226
At the foot of Detroit's main street, Woodward Avenue, at the corner of Jefferson Avenue
Hours: Daily until sunset
Admission: Free

On the night of June 22, 1937, deep in the hard years of the depression, African Americans across the country were glued to radio sets, hoping that a son of Alabama sharecroppers would do what no black man had done since Jack Johnson: claim the world heavyweight boxing crown. When the 23-year-old Joe Louis knocked out Jim Braddock in the eighth round of their title bout, black America went wild with joy and crowned a new hero. The following year, in a contest anxiously watched by all America as a symbol of good versus evil, Louis annihilated the German Max Schmeling, whom racist and antidemocratic Nazi Germany had promoted as a emblem of the Aryan Superman. With his triumph over "evil"—though Schmeling was not a Nazi—Louis took a step beyond being a hero for black America. He became an American icon, reassuring the country that its power was second to none. (Louis's reassuring black American triumph over racist Nazi Germany mirrored that of another son of Alabama sharecroppers, Jesse Owens, whose four gold medals in the 1936 Olympics in Berlin brought him fame—but not the right to use "whites-only" drinking fountains and toilets in his native state.) While it loathed Jack Johnson, who paraded his white wives and flaunted his challenge to racist expectations, white America was happy to see in Louis a symbol both of racial humility and of the link between it and racial progress. During World War II Louis continued his iconic function, identifying uncritically with the country and serving as an athletic instructor in the Air Corps, which then awarded him the Legion of Merit for his "incalculable contributions to the general morale" and now makes the exhibit on him one of the highlights at the United States Air Force Museum. (See U.S. Air Force entry on p. 441.)

Louis's ring successes continued after the war, though age began to exact its toll. Long after his 1949 retirement and his later failed comeback bouts with Ezzard Charles and Rocky Marciano, Louis retained America's affection. Increasingly, however, this was because in an era of rising African-American demands, he was seen as undemanding. Both white and black America united in overlooking Louis's flagrant appetite for adultery (which eventually cost him his wife and anchor) and gambling, his financial irresponsibility (which included his warm and excessive support of charities), his alcohol and drug problems, and his limited ability to function independently in the world. Had he not been Joe Louis, he might have ended as his father did, confined to a mental institution. Instead, Louis ended his real life as a house "shill" for a Las Vegas casino. His life as an American icon is fittingly symbolized not only in his burial in Arlington Cemetery, but in the fact that the principal arm of government power, the IRS, in the face of intense political pressure, forgave Louis's mountain of back taxes. No typical American, white or black, certainly not Jack Johnson, and not even a mere American hero would have seen the IRS capitulate to pressure and forgive anything.

In the city where he grew up after migrating from Alabama, "the Brown Bomber" is honored with an arena; with a massive, 24-foot-long sculpture of his arm and fist, which inaptly recalls the clenched-fist, black-power salute; and with a more conventional sculpture poised in the boxing stance that was the expression of his genius and the means of his rise.

Motown Museum
2648 West Grand Boulevard, Detroit, MI 48202
(313) 875-2264
Hours: Tue.–Sat., 10 A.M.–5 P.M.; Sun., 2 P.M.–5 P.M.; other times by appointment
Admission: Adults, $3; under 12, $2

Berry Gordy, Jr., moved from the shop floor of a Detroit auto plant in the mid-1950s to the boardroom of a multimillion-dollar business in the early 1960s. So why isn't he a case study in more graduate business schools? Why can't the man get more Respect? Gordy had to build his own business and boardroom to get there, of course; by dint of imagination and drive he could break into the record industry—he never could have broken into the boardroom of a white company. As everywhere in life, luck and timing played a part: Gordy elbowed his way into

COURTESY MOTOWN MUSEUM

The "Motown Sound" started here, in what was the home of Berry Gordy, Jr.

the record industry as black music was crossing over and as the industry and radio stations were running scared from the "payola" scandal, in which the major labels bribed DJs to play their songs. Gordy also just happened to have this songwriting-looking-to-be-a-singer friend . . . who went by the name of Smokey Robinson. Please, Please, Please—everyone should be so lucky, crying Tears of a Clown all the way to the bank. Gordy's Motown label, initially headquartered in his two-story home that prophetically proclaimed "Hitsville U.S.A.," rained Supremes throughout the 1960s. With his dreams, it's no Wonder that Gordy felt the Temptations of Los Angeles, to which he departed in the early '70s. He left behind his old home, which now serves as the Motown Museum. There's no need to Shop Around: With restored studios and exhibits on the major singers, writers, and musicians of the Motown label, this place is the Tops (all Four of them) for lovers of the Sound.

Museum of African-American History
301 Frederick Douglass Street, Detroit, MI 48202
(313) 833-9800
Hours: Wed.–Sat., 9:30 A.M.–5 P.M.; Sun., 1 P.M.–5 P.M.
Admission: Tours, free. Donations encouraged

Though Michigan's role in the Underground Railroad forms the centerpiece of the permanent exhibit at Detroit's Museum of African-American History, the wider slave experience provides a surrounding context. From the shores of West Africa, through the Middle Passage (interpreted through a full-scale mock-up of the cargo hold of a slave ship), to colonial and antebellum America, slavery's long night is detailed. Two-dimensional explanatory panels predominate in the museum, though some period artifacts, including letters of Frederick Douglass and Booker T. Washington and photographs of stalwarts of the antislavery movement, also are on display. In addition, the museum hosts temporary exhibits that touch upon the artistic expression and historical experience of African Americans. In August of each year, the museum sponsors its Africa World Festival, which draws a huge crowd.

National Museum of the Tuskegee Airmen
6325 West Jefferson, Detroit, MI 48209
(313) 843-8849
Hours: By appointment
Admission: Free

For African-American fighter pilots the path into and through World War II air combat proceeded in stages: ground school; primary flight training at Moton Air Field at Tuskegee Institute; transition to combat type aircraft and advanced flight training at nearby Tuskegee Army Air Field; overseas assignment; P-40s, P-39s, briefly into P-47s and finally, toward the middle of 1944 at the base in Ramitelli, Italy, P-51 Mustangs. Though less well known—because they never saw combat—African-American bomber pilots of twin-engine craft also trained at Tuskegee, as did flight engineers, gunners, armorers, and mechanics. To a degree difficult to appreciate today, the Army Air Corps (an institutionally independent U.S. Air Force did not come into existence until after the war) was seen—or promoted by its leaders—as an elite organization, whose members were more intelligent, highly trained, and representative of the modern, technological age than America's other warriors. Thus an all-black combat unit of flyers betokened an acknowledgment of racial equality of ability more clearly than did an equivalent ground or naval unit. The Tuskegee experiment, as the U.S. War Department termed its foray into segregated flight training (see U.S. Air Force Museum entry on p. 441), was the prime symbol both of white America's acceptance of African Americans and of the black combat contribution to the defeat of European fascism.

Today that symbol and the reality that underlay it, at least regarding flight training and combat operations, is explored at the National Museum of the Tuskegee Airmen. This quite small museum displays memorabilia of the black airmen, including flying suits, a mock-up of the operations area of Moton Field, paraphernalia of World War II aircraft, and models of some planes flown by the Tuskegee airmen. Be forewarned: The museum is housed within Historic Fort Wayne, most of whose facilities have been closed due to Detroit's financial woes; however, the Tuskegee Museum and a museum of Native American material are still open.

Second Baptist Church
441 Monroe Street, Detroit, MI 48226
(313) 961-0920
Hours: Historical marker: Daily until sunset
Admission: Free

Detroit's first black Baptist church dates back to 1836, when 13 former slaves withdrew from the white First Baptist Church. Not until 1857 did the black congregation raise sufficient funds to construct a church building. Six years later, in 1863, Detroit's black community gathered at the Second Baptist Church in January to celebrate Lincoln's Emancipation Proclamation; then in October black volunteers gathered at the church to form the 1st Michigan Colored Infantry. In 1914 the original structure burned to the ground and the congregation moved to its present address. Here, a little more than a century after Lincoln's Proclamation, President Lyndon Johnson dedicated a historical marker recalling the original celebration.

FRANKENMUTH

Michigan's Own Military & Space Museum
1250 Weiss Street, Frankenmuth, MI 48734
(517) 652-8005
Hours: Mon.–Sat., 10 A.M.–5 P.M.; Sun., 12 P.M.–5 P.M.
Admission: Adults, $2.50; seniors, $2; students under 18, $1

In bleak Camp #5, where Communist North Korea stashed many of America's prisoners of war, Sergeant James Thompson earned a reputation for recalcitrance, repeatedly refusing to encourage his men and others to collaborate with the enemy. The African-American veteran of World War II was judged incorrigible by the North Koreans, who sentenced him to three years in prison to be served after the war ended. Though the terms of the armistice negotiated at Panmunjom precluded Thompson's being held beyond the war's end, the North Korean regime made sure he was the last black man released in the prisoner-of-war exchange. Chief Steward's Mate Emmitt Bowen also spent a long time in a hard camp; he was the first African-American captured in World War II. Caught in a Japanese bombing raid on Manila, Bowen was wounded and ended up in a local hospital rather than back on his submarine. In January 1942 he fell into the hands of the Japanese troops that swiftly occupied the Philippines. Bowen spent the next three and a half years eating rice—when he was fortunate—before returning to Detroit and a new career as a schoolteacher. Michael Washington rose to the top—or rather dove to the bottom—of his military speciality, becoming the first black master diver for the navy's elite SEALs and the fourth master chief diver in the U.S. Navy's history. Rated for unlimited depths, Washington is but one of the black (and white) Michigan veterans whose contributions to the nation are highlighted at Michigan's Own. Rather than weapons, this military and space museum focuses principally on the uniforms and decorations that trace the state's veterans through six wars—from the Spanish-American War through Desert Storm. The museum also has the space suits of Michigan's nine astronauts, six of whom have already made the journey into space.

JACKSON

Ella Sharp Museum
3225 Fourth Street, Jackson, MI 49203
(517) 787-2320
Hours: Tue.–Fri., 10 A.M.–5 P.M.; Sat.–Sun., 12 P.M.–5 P.M.
Admission: Adults, $2.50; seniors, $2; children under 12, $1

If you can't be an artist and you want your work to last, be a stonemason. In the 1860s the noted black stonemason George Brown was brought from New York—after considerable contractural negotiations that included specifying whom he would bring as assistants and that he would not work in the rain—to build without mortar a wall at the Hillside Farm. The farm now serves as the Ella Sharp Museum—and the wall, which won a silver medallion from the Michigan State Agricultural Society, still stands. Brown's work is now the centerpiece of the museum's interpretation of local black history.

LANSING

Malcolm X Homesite Historical Marker
4705 South Logan Street, Lansing, MI 48910
Hours: Daily until sunset
Admission: Free

Lansing proved to be an extraordinarily traumatic town for the young Malcolm Little. In the space of a few years the child was exposed to repeated racial attacks on his family, the mysterious death of a father whom he revered, the birth of his mother's illegitimate child, his mother's swift descent into insanity, the breakup of the Little family, and his own first brushes with the police, reform school, and racial barriers to self-advancement.

Earl and Louise Little and their children moved to Lansing when the future Malcolm X was only four years old. Trouble began immediately, for the home Malcolm's father purchased was covered by a "whites-only" covenant and the Littles' white neighbors were determined to keep the neighborhood segregated. Two weeks later the house burned to the ground in mysterious circumstances. The family moved across town, only to come under racial attack again. Once more they shifted quarters. In these years Earl Little was often away from home, preaching the gospel of the Universal Negro Improvement Association, Marcus Garvey's black nationalist organization. (See Garvey and Malcolm X entry on p. 197.) The young Malcolm often heard his father address crowds of African Americans, stressing the need for the diaspora to unite and uplift itself. Then, one evening when Malcolm was six, the police brought news that his father had been run over by a trolley car and killed. Deprived of a husband and an income, Malcolm's mother moved the family to South Logan Street. Young Malcolm lived here for several years before his mother was committed to the Kalamazoo State Mental Hospital and her children placed in different foster homes. "We wanted and tried to stay together," Malcolm wrote years later in his celebrated autobiography, "but the Welfare, the courts, and their doctor, gave us the one-two-three punch."

Then began Malcolm's roller-coaster years: reform school, seventh-grade class president, work in the local Shop Rite Supermarket, Boston, hustling on the streets—and prison. Malcolm Little entered prison shortly before his 21st birthday, before he'd even begun to shave. He spent long years inside, years put to good purpose, conquering first himself and then the English language. H. G. Wells, W.E.B. Du Bois, Alfred Toynbee, Schopenhauer, Kant, Nietzsche, Spinoza, Milton, and other giants of western philosophy and literature prepared him for a career he could not yet foresee. Of greater importance still, in prison he not only conquered, he submitted—to the teachings of the Honorable Elijah Muhammad and the Nation of Islam. (See Muhammad Temple entry on p. 397.)

Emerging from prison a new man, Malcolm Little shed his slave name and as Malcolm X became the Nation of Islam's principal proslytizer. Detroit, Boston, Philadelphia, and then New York City were his vineyards. He spent a decade articulating the full force of black rage and his resolute refusal to accept white America's image of and future for African Americans. His voice was heard on the streets, in the temples of the Nation of Islam, in the newspaper columns he wrote for the black press, in *Muhammad Speaks*—the Nation of Islam's newspaper that he founded—and finally on television. By the close of the 1950s, Malcom X had become a force in the African-American community. Soon he would be nationally known as an excoriating critic of black leaders from A. Philip Randolph (see entry on p. 202) through Roy Wilkins (see entry on p. 412) and Martin Luther King, Jr. Not long afterward he was a target of FBI investigation, an apostate to the Nation of Islam, a pilgrim to Mecca, penultimately a martyr, and finally—after his assassination in Harlem's Audubon Ballroom (see entry on p. 299)—a work of fiction and commerce, with "X" marking the spot of buried treasure.

Malcolm's life path—including his self-mastery, his bearing witness to the "truth," his bold challenge to white supremacy, his regeneration of the link between Africa and black America, his exposé of the "religious faker" who had been his guide and anchor since his days of incarceration, and his martyr's death—is the stuff of more than legend. His sinking into a regenerative self-loathing ("only guilt admitted accepts truth") that underscored his father's Baptist beliefs, his overdetermined commitment to a fundamentalist cause that kept his doubts and desires at bay, his affirmation of his worth as a (black) man, and his successive redefinitions of himself—culminating in an autobiography that transmuted facts and self-deceptions into myth—ironically made Malcolm's life stereotypically American. This conclusion would have been easier to grasp at the time if he had been white. Being black—that is, lacking full humanity in America—Malcolm was treated by white America as mere symbol, which validated his critique of the denial of humanity to African Americans.

Today the self-made man whose strength, commitment, and contributions to the affirmation of black America brought him love, respect, fame, and death is honored with a historical marker at the site of the childhood home in which his family was "destroyed."

MARSHALL

Crosswhite Boulder
Michigan Avenue at Mansion Street, Marshall, MI 49068
Hours: Daily until sunset
Admission: Free

Politicians can be expected to support their constituents, and Henry Clay was no exception. An early proponent of colonization schemes designed to remove blacks from America, Clay was no ardent proponent of slavery. However, when his constituents' slaves fled north and they themselves were arrested when attempting to secure their chattel's return, Clay championed the property rights of Kentucky slave owners. The Crosswhite family had fled Kentucky slavery for freedom in Michigan, where they were discovered several years later. In 1847 four Kentuckians rode into Marshall to reclaim runaway property. When they attempted to seize the Crosswhites, town officials arrested them on attempted kidnapping charges and aided the family in their flight to a Canadian haven. The outraged slave hunters, who were promptly released after the Crosswhites had fled, brought suit against town officials.

Incidents like this provoked the Fugitive Slave Act, the most controversial element of the Compromise of 1850 and a leading cause of sharpening regional antagonisms around the issue of slavery. The act drove slavery into the consciousness of the North, which now was expected actively to collaborate in the capture and return to bondage of thousands of longtime state residents who had fled their masters. The act was even more politically than legally injudicious—which was saying a great deal in view of the fact that under its provisions alleged runaways could be identified on the basis of a mere affadavit of their putative owners; were denied a jury trial; were denied the right to testify in their own behalf; and faced commissioners whose fee for each case was $10 for returning fugitives and $5 for freeing the "innocent."

Clay, who made reference to the Crosswhite incident in his support of the Fugitive Slave Act, lived long enough to see the North erupt in fury at the new law and at the South. Mobs in several cities battered federal marshals and commissioners and forcibly released black detainees, and several states passed personal liberty laws preventing state officials from enforcing the law. Ever able to win short-term victories (the Crosswhites' owner won a court judgment of almost $2,000) to its long-term detriment, the South continued to perceive itself the victim of everybody and everything except ill-judgment. A decade later the conjunction of self-pity and ill-judgment would put paid to slavery—and to the life of more than 100,000 white southerners, the vast majority of whom possessed no soul but their own.

Today visitors to Marshall view the Crosswhite Boulder, which marks the spot where the Kentucky slave hunters were arrested and the town gained its 15 minutes of fame.

MUSKEGON

Jonathan Walker Memorial
Evergreen Cemetery, 1400 Kenneth, Muskegon, MI 49442
(616) 724-6783
Hours: Daily until sunset
Admission: Free

In 1844 the abolitionist Jonathan Walker was caught off the Florida coast with seven fugitive slaves on board his ship. Following his conviction in federal court, Walker had the letters "SS"—slave stealer—branded into his hand, prompting John Greenleaf Whittier to pen his ode, "The Man with the Branded Hand." Today visitors to Walker's grave pass a memorial that serves notice to the wary that history has a way of overturning verdicts that rest on nothing more than power.

MINNESOTA

Minnesota Office of Tourism
100 Metro Square, 121 East Seventh Place, St. Paul, MN 55101
(800) 657-3700
Hours: Mon.–Fri., 8 A.M.–5 P.M.

MINNEAPOLIS

Convention & Visitors Association
1219 Marquette Avenue, Suite 300, Minneapolis, MN 55403
(612) 348-4313
Hours: Mon.–Fri., 8 A.M.–5:30 P.M.

Minneapolis Institute of Art
2400 Third Avenue South, Minneapolis, MN 55404
(612) 870-3131
Hours: Tue.–Thu., 10 A.M.–9 P.M.; Fri., 10 A.M.–5 P.M.; Sun., 12 P.M.–5 P.M.
Admission: Free

"Trade follows the flag" is the historical cliché, though at least in regard to European intervention in Africa, the process was rather the reverse. In any event, trade precedes art. The diaspora reached Minnesota at least as early as the latter part of the 18th century in the form of fur traders, such as Pierre Bonga.

Today the art of the continent has followed suit and finds a home in the far north. The creative expression of the Baule, Asante, Bambara, Djenne, Benin, Dogon, Yoruba, Chokwe, Kuba, Lega, Lwena, Pende, and Songye cultures, among others, can be examined at the Minneapolis Institute of Art. From high art directly tied to spiritual purposes to material objects that are articulated with beauty, from wooden, metal, and ivory sculpture to textiles and pottery, the institute's collection speaks clearly of Africa's artistic potency. Though small, the collection embraces a notable range and includes a sampling of Ligbi, Teke, Yombe, Lovale, Tabwa, Makonde, Zulu, and other works. If you don't live in Minneapolis, you will probably find the ambient temperature a trifle chilly; if you step inside the institute, you can open your coat and your eyes.

St. Peter's A.M.E. Church
401 East 41st Street, Minneapolis, MN 55409
(612) 825-9750
Hours: Mon.–Thur., 9 A.M.–2 P.M.
Admission: Free

Minnesota's African-American population has never been large. Barring a few black fur trappers and traders, such as Pierre Bonga and his son George, the latter born in 1802 near modern Duluth, and slaves attending southern officers stationed at Fort Snelling in the first half of the 19th century, the state was virtually absent the diaspora. Indeed, when Minnesota officially was organized in 1849, its census revealed the presence of only 40 free persons of African descent, most barbers and cooks. Despite this small presence and despite the fact that adult black male literacy was almost 100 percent, free African-American males were barred from voting in congressional, territorial, county, and precinct elections—a prohibition extended in 1851 to village elections and in 1853 to town meetings! On the eve of the Civil War, the state had only 259 black residents, which makes its black Union troop contribution of 104 men the more impressive. Following the war, state referenda in 1865 and 1867 failed to amend the constitution so as to remove the racial prohibition against voting. (A referendum in 1868 succeeded in this aim.) By 1870 the black population had almost tripled from a decade previously and first St. Paul and then, after 1910, Minneapolis developed small but coherent black communities. By 1869 St. James A.M.E. Church was founded in southeast Minneapolis. In little more than a decade, the congregation split and a group seeking a downtown place of worship withdrew to found St. Peter's A.M.E. Church, in front of whose present building sits a two-foot-square foundation stone that survives from its original structure.

ST. PAUL

Convention & Visitors Bureau
101 Norwest Center, 55 East Fifth Street, St. Paul, MN 55101-1713
(612) 297-6985
Hours: Mon.–Fri., 8 A.M.–5 P.M.

Dred Scott Memorial
Historic Fort Snelling State Park and History Center, Highways 5 and 55, St. Paul, MN 55111
(612) 726-1171
Hours: Park: May 1–Oct. 31: Mon.–Sat., 10 A.M.–5 P.M.; Sun., 12 P.M.–5 P.M. History Center: May–Oct.: daily, 9:30 A.M.–5 P.M. Nov.–Apr.: weekdays, 9 A.M.–4:30 P.M.
Admission: Park: adults, $3; ages 6–15, $1. History Center: free

The Dred Scott ruling made the names of two men. It brought a slave fame, a Chief Justice of the Supreme Court notoriety, the Court itself disrepute, and the Civil War closer. Throughout it all, the slave was only a pawn in the game. Indeed, except for the fact that he never captured a piece, Dred Scott may be said to have entered history the way he lived his life—*en passant*.

Born as the property of Peter Blow in the late 18th century in Southampton County, Virginia, some 35 years before Nat Turner (see entry on p. 171) briefly turned it upside down, Scott was almost 40 and living in St. Louis, Missouri, when he started the voyage that carried him to the Supreme Court and into American history. That voyage began up the Mississippi River, first to Illinois and then to Fort Snelling, in what was then the Wisconsin Territory. Both stops were free territory. In the winter of 1838, after five years of living in free territory, Scott and his owner returned to St. Louis, where the latter died and the former passed to master's widow, Irene Sanford Emerson. In the mid-1840s Mrs. Emerson moved to New York City, leaving Scott in the charge of the sons of his original owner and planting the seeds of a political and legal cause célèbre. Henry Blow, a lawyer, railroad and mining operator, and rising political figure, was an opponent of slavery. Seeing in Scott a landmark test case, Blow helped finance a lawsuit in a Missouri court seeking Scott's freedom on the basis of his having lived in a free territory. The Missouri lower court accepted the argument and ruled that Scott was a free man. Naturally the case was appealed, which suited all the parties (excepting the hapless Scott), whose real interest was a ruling at the highest judicial level on the issue of the implications of the Missouri Compromise, which forbade slavery north of the latitude 36 degrees, 30 minutes. Finally, in 1852, six years after the case first came to trial, the state supreme court ruled that Scott, as a resident of Missouri, was a slave. (To date, Scott had yet to taste freedom, being loosely supervised and his labor hired out by the county sheriff.)

Not only had time passed, things had changed—Mexico, for example, suddenly had gotten substantially smaller and America bigger as a consequence of a war. The addition of new American territory threatened the rough national equilibrium of free and slave states and intensified the political significance of slavery's expansion. This significance grew greater still with the passage in 1854 of the Kansas-Nebraska Act, which extended the doctrine of popular sovereignty—each territory deciding whether to enter the Union as a free or slave state—north of 36 degrees, 30 minutes. This act effectively canceled the

Missouri Compromise and heightened the tensions associated with the admission of new states. Contextually, Scott again proved useful, and "his" case was resurrected. As ownership of Scott had been deeded to John Sanford, Mrs. Emerson's brother in New York, the case was transferred to the federal circuit docket. For Scott to sue in federal court, he had to establish that he was a Missouri citizen—that is, that the case involved *citizens* of different states. Sanford's lawyers argued that as a slave, Scott was not a citizen of Missouri and thus lacked standing to sue in federal court. In 1856—as Kansas lay bleeding and a presidential campaign got under way involving a new, antislavery, Republican Party—the circuit court ruled in Scott's favor and the matter was sent to the U.S. Supreme Court on appeal.

While few cared about Scott, everyone cared about a case that potentially raised the explosive issue of whether the U.S. Congress could prohibit slavery in a territory. This issue could have been finessed by the Supreme Court, five of whose nine members were from slave states. Instead, the newly elected President Buchanan announced in his inaugural address that the question of slavery's expansion was a judicial issue and one that soon would be comprehensively and finally settled. The court issued a broad 7-to-2 ruling whose basic conclusions were that Scott was a slave and hence could not sue in federal court and that Congress had no power to restrict slavery in territories. The decision effectively overturned both the Missouri Compromise and the popular sovereignty doctrine, the successive formulations that had enabled the country to bridge the ever-widening political chasm separating free and slave states in the Union. Chief Justice Roger B. Taney's formulation of the decision was particularly sweeping, boldly stating the view that, he claimed, underlay the Founding Fathers' constitutional thinking: African Americans were "beings of an inferior order, and altogether unfit to associate with the white race, either in social or political relations; and so far inferior that they had no rights which the white man was bound to respect." President Buchanan proved wildly mistaken. Rather than lay the issue of slavery to rest, the ruling heightened slavery's political significance even as it undercut the institutional channels to alleviate its pressure.

About the only thing the ruling did that was final was to indirectly free Dred Scott. When in March 1857 the highest Court conclusively foreclosed any political avenue to freedom, his usefulness as pawn ended and his masters declared him free. Little more than a year later, worn by six decades of slavery, Dred Scott died. The man was finally free; but his usefulness as a symbol, which had kept him enslaved an extra decade, remained to stir the passions of a nation sliding toward the precipice of war.

Today visitors to the restored Historic Fort Snelling pass a Dred Scott Memorial as they enter the fort's main gate. Visitors also are exposed to other African-American aspects of the fort's past; although the fort's interpretive framework centers on the 1820s and its role in maintaining peace on the Indian frontier, the all-black 25th Infantry Regiment was stationed here from 1882 through 1888. Perhaps half the regiment—15 to 20 officers, 250 to 300 enlisted men—

was regularly at the fort, with companies assigned escort duties to the outlying forts of the Dakota territories. During these years approximately 80 percent of the fort's inhabitants were black. Today a few photographs of the men of the 25th, a mannequin of a regimental member in dress uniform, and African-American living history interpreters in various roles, slave and free, remain to reflect this presence.

Minnesota Museum of Art
Kellogg Boulevard at St. Peter Street, St. Paul, MN 55102
(612) 292-4355
Hours: Tue.–Wed., 10:30 A.M.–4:30 P.M.; Thu., 10:30 A.M.–7:30 P.M.; Fri., 10:30 A.M.–4:30 P.M.; Sat.–Sun., 1 P.M.–4:30 P.M.
Admission: Free

From a 46-inch-high Bobo headdress associated with maternity rites through carved wooden Bambara doors, Dogon metalwork and masks of the Baga, Senufo, Dan, and other West African peoples, the Minnesota Museum of Art historically has explored the art and the material culture of the Mother Continent. Those considering a visit, however, should be aware that the museum is reconsidering its purpose and focus, which may well shift toward contemporary American (including African-American) art. A telephone call prior to a visit is advised for those primarily interested in the museum's African holdings, which may not be on display.

Roy Wilkins Bust and Auditorium
St. Paul Civic Center, 143 West Fourth Street, St. Paul, MN 55102
(612) 224-7361
Hours: Open only to viewers who pay for performances
Admission: Varies by event

Though born in St. Louis, Roy Wilkins was raised by an aunt in St. Paul after his mother died while he was quite young. From his days as a college student at the University of Minnesota, Wilkins was active in the NAACP and as a journalist, editing the black weekly *The St. Paul Appeal* and serving as the secretary of the local NAACP chapter. Following graduation in 1923, he returned to Missouri, serving both as managing editor of the Kansas City black newspaper, *The Call*, and as secretary of the local NAACP chapter. In 1931 Wilkins joined the NAACP's national secretariat. The following year, disguised as an itinerant, unskilled laborer, Wilkins traveled the Mississippi Delta, investigating working conditions of black laborers on federal flood-control projects. His reports sparked a Senate investigation and led to improved conditions. Shortly thereafter he replaced W.E.B. Du Bois as editor of *Crisis*, the NAACP's magazine. Upon the death of Walter White in 1955, Wilkins became the leader of America's most prominent civil rights organization, just as the struggle shifted from the courts to direct action. A major force in the institutionalization of black progress over the next two decades, Wilkins found himself under increasing attack by younger and more militant activists, none of whom had labored as long, as hard, or as successfully in the vineyards of the struggle against white supremacy. Today the town in which Wilkins grew up honors his years of heavy lifting with an appropriately larger–than–life-size bust in the Civic Center that also houses the Roy Wilkins Auditorium.

MISSOURI

Missouri Division of Tourism
P.O. Box 1055, Jefferson City, MO 65102
(800) 877-1234; (314) 751-4133
Hours: Mon.–Fri., 8 A.M.–5 P.M.
Ask for "A Guide to Missouri's African-American Heritage" brochure.

CANTON

Lincoln Colored School
Martin Park, U.S. Highway 61 (Business), Canton, MO 63435
Hours: Daily until sunset
Admission: Not open to the public

The mythical one-room Douglass School for black children and the town of Nutbrush, Missouri, made famous in the young adults' and children's stories of Eleanora Tate, derive from the real one-room Lincoln Colored School in the tiny Mississippi River town of Canton, Missouri. Flooded almost yearly by the Mississippi River that ran three blocks east of it, Lincoln School is one of the very few one-room 19th-century midwestern schools still standing. Also to be seen in Canton and appearing in her books are the Second Baptist Church (a.k.a. "Nubia Missionary Baptist Church") and the A.M.E. Church.

COLUMBIA

Museum of Art and Archaeology
University of Missouri-Columbia, One Pickard Hall, University Avenue at 9th Street, Columbia, MO 65211
(314) 882-3591
Hours: Tue.–Fri., 9 A.M.–5 P.M.; Sat.–Sun., 12 P.M.–5 P.M.
Admission: Free

Figurative sculpture dominates the small (50 to 60 pieces) African collection of the Museum of Art and Archaeology at the University of Missouri-Columbia. The collection is well situated from an interpretive perspective, emphasizing the functional rather than aesthetic drive behind the creations, which never were intended to stand alone as objects of art. Particularly interesting are the pieces that play against the common and potentially self-indulgent "Africa's influence on the West" theme. A seated female figure carved by an Ashanti craftsman and a seated male figure of the Ogoni show the western impact on African culture: Both are seated on European-style furniture, the former wearing fine jewelry, the latter a top hat. For the creators, this external impact in no way lessened the functional validity of the pieces, which represent spirits of high prestige and continued (prior to their removal to a museum) to serve as agents of communication between the world of the living and that of the spirits. Also on view are Ashanti *akua'ba*, summations of Ashanti ideals of feminine beauty that are carried by infertile women as a means to elicit spiritually sponsored conceptions; Yoruba *ere ibeji* figures; two sets of Senufo male-female pairs, the larger carried by women at funerals and the smaller part of a diviner's paraphernalia; and a variety of 19th-century weights that were part of gold-weighing kits that also included scales, spoons, pans, and touchstones.

DIAMOND

George Washington Carver National Monument
V Highway and Country Road 16-Q, Box 38, Diamond, MO 64840
(417) 325-4151
Hours: Visitor Center: Memorial Day–Labor Day, daily, 8:30 A.M.–7 P.M. Rest of year: daily, 8:30 A.M.–5 P.M. Grounds: open until dusk. Group tours: by appointment, 4 to 6 weeks in advance. Auditorium films: continuously during Visitor Center hours
Admission: Apr. 1–Oct. 31: adults 17–61, $1; school groups and others, free. Nov. 1–Mar. 31: free

The babe who became George Washington Carver entered the world deprived of liberty and a surname, the former inherent and the latter not uncommon for slaves. Within days, however, his traumas were more individualized. The child was born frail—and, following a fatal accident, soon was fatherless as well. Before this had time to register, he, his mother, Mary, and perhaps a sister were carried off to Arkansas by slave raiders, who left behind his tortured master, Moses Carver, strung up to a tree by his thumbs and bearing on his body the marks of their whips and on his feet the blisters raised by the hot coals with which he had been burned. When Carver had been cut down, he offered a local bushwhacker named John Bentley 40 acres of land and a racehorse named Pacer to recover the woman and her child (or children). Bentley returned with the boy only, and kept the horse as recompense for his efforts. The child's mother—and his sister if she too existed and had been stolen—were never seen again, and with the later death in his teens of his older brother, James, the boy was left without relatives. Though home, the child was far from safe, being near death with whooping cough. He survived, but the cough had torn his vocal cords, leaving a high-pitched voice that he carried to his grave. The sickly child stammered and did not walk until he was three. Fortunately, the Carvers raised him as one of their family, keeping him from the fields where labored Moses and James, who now, following the conclusion of the Civil War, was free. From Susan Carver, George learned the household skills and handicrafts that later in life he would use to find employment with white and black families.

His talent tending plants, for which he early won renown, he learned on his own, through patient observation and some inexplicable innate empathy.

> Day after day, I spent in the woods alone in order to collect my floral beauties, and put them in my little garden I had hidden in brush not far from the house, as it was considered foolishness in the neighborhood to waste time on flowers. And many are the tears I shed because I would break the roots or flowers of some of my pets while removing them from the ground. . . . Rocks had an equal fascination for me and many are the basketfull that I have been compelled to remove from the outside chimney corner of the old log house, with the injunction to throw them down hill. I obeyed but picked up the choicest ones and hid them in another place. . . .

Flowers, rocks, and education constituted Carver's secular childhood trinity. "From a child, I had an inordinate desire for knowledge," he later recalled. Barred from the local church school because of his color, George left the security of the Carvers (carefully wrapping his choicest rocks in a handkerchief for the journey) for nearby Neosho, where at the Lincoln School for Colored Children he had seen for the first time a black man teaching black children. Perhaps unwittingly, he had launched himself on life. He still lacked a name, stammering in response to the question from one of his new Neosho mentors, the black couple Mariah and Andrew Watkins (it was with Mariah that Carver bonded, as he had to Susan Carver and would again to maternal figures, white and black), that he was "Carver's George." In exchange for household chores, George moved in with the childless couple, heeding the first instruction from "Aunt Mariah": "Don't ever again say your name is Carver's George. It's George Carver." As he had with the Carvers, with whom he stayed in loving touch, George worked hard at home, but played little with his peers, instead sitting off in a corner drawing upon his slate.

When he had reached the limits of a Neosho education, Carver moved on—on to other places and other families but to the same household chores and for the same purpose, further education. Fort Scott was his first stop. Work as a cook and then as a launderer provided enough money to eat occasionally, buy books, and pay his school fees. Carver left Fort Scott two years later, immediately following his shocked horror at witnessing an African American dragged from jail and lynched. By the spring of 1885, after more years of study and after taking a middle name, George Washington Carver had set himself up for his life's next trauma, acceptance into Highland University, a small Presbyterian school in northeast Kansas and then sudden rejection upon the school's discovery that he was black. (See Carver Museum entry on p. 370.)

Today at the George Washington Carver National Monument, visitors tour the environment that contributed to the development of the 20th century's most famous botanist. Open for inspection are the Carver birth site, a one-room cabin where he, his mother, and his brother lived briefly prior to the kidnapping from which his mother never returned; a statue of Carver as a boy tending his plants; a springhouse from which Carver had to fetch water as one of his household chores; the 1881 house built by Moses and Susan Carver, to whom Carver returned before entering college; the Carver family cemetery; a visitor center and a museum with exhibits on Carver, including a recording of the man's last speech; and a demonstration garden that suggests the range of his practical accomplishments. (See Tuskegee University entry on p. 31.)

JEFFERSON CITY

Lincoln University
820 Chestnut Street, Jefferson City, MO 65101
(314) 681-5000
Hours: Mon.–Thu., 8 A.M.–11 P.M.; Sat., 1 P.M.–5 P.M.; Sun., 3 P.M.–11 P.M. Tours available
Admission: Free

Led by some of their officers, the men of the 62nd and 65th Colored Infantry regiments gathered around campfires at Fort McIntosh, Texas, in January 1866. The men, who soon would be mustered out of the service, considered their future. After hearing one officer of the 65th advise them to buy land rather than hire themselves out for wages, the men heard a First Lieutenant of the 62nd, Richard Baxter Foster, raise the issue of education. From that campfire discussion arose Lincoln Institute. Started with $6,000 raised by the officers, men, and other interested military personnel, the school for freedmen opened in the fall of that year with two pupils and a principal—former First Lieutenant Baxter. From that date until *Brown v. Board of Education* almost nine decades later, Lincoln remained in the forefront of black education in Missouri. In 1921, aided by Walthall M. Moore, Missouri's first black state legislator, the school became a university; in 1939, after a U.S. Supreme Court ruling arising from the case of a Lincoln graduate, Lloyd Gaines, a school of law was added; and in 1940, following another refusal by the University of Missouri to admit an African American, a school of journalism was added. Though the *Brown* ruling ended its enforced racial character, Lincoln University remains a historically black college. In its new alumni hall, visitors will find an exhibit honoring the founding of the school by the men of the 62nd and 65th USCT regiments.

KANSAS CITY

Convention & Visitors Bureau
1100 Main Street, Suite 2550, Kansas City, MO 64111
(800) 767-7700
Hours: Mon.–Fri., 8:30 A.M.–5 P.M.

Nelson Atkins Museum
4525 Oak Street, Kansas City, MO 64112
(816) 561-4000
Hours: Tue.–Sat., 10 A.M.–5 P.M.; Sun., 1 P.M.–5 P.M.
Admission: Adults, $3; ages 6–18, $1; free on Sunday

In the Nelson Atkins Museum, one of stunning breadth of beauty, two galleries are devoted to the art of Africa. Unlike the museum's extraordinary Asian collection, the range and depth of the African material is rather limited. The sculptural art of Mali, Nigeria, and Zaire predominates, with the masks, standing figures, and thrones of Dogon, Bamana, Benin, Yoruba, Lege, Songye, and Hemba cultures featured. The museum's range allows sculptural comparisons across many cultures, from the significant outdoor pieces of Henry Moore through the works of South America, Oceania, and Asia. If you're in Kansas City and have an interest in high culture, the Nelson Atkins Museum is your destination.

Black Archives of Mid-America
Fire Station 11, 2033 Vine Street, Kansas City, MO 64108
(816) 483-1300
Hours: Mon.–Fri., 9 A.M.–4:30 P.M.; Sat.–Sun. by appointment
Admission: 50 cents

For the past half century, the center of Kansas City's black community has been 18th and Vine. Housed in an old fire station near that intersection is the Black Archives of Mid-America, an institution dedicated to making the city an intellectual center for the study of African-American history. Visitors will find oral histories, exhibits, workshops, storytelling, and artifacts and documents exploring and explicating that heritage. While the Black Archives' display on the buffalo soldiers is easily rivaled at various midwestern and western forts, few institutions can challenge its portrayal of the Kansas City contribution to jazz. Considerably less well known as a jazz town than New Orleans, the Missouri River city produced leading exponents of swing and some of the critical energy behind the bebop revolution.

LeRoy "Satchel" Paige Memorial Tombstone
Forest Hill Cemetery, 6901 Troost Avenue, Kansas City, MO 64131
(816) 523-2114
Hours: Daily until sunset
Admission: Free

Leroy "Satchel" Paige came out of Mobile, Alabama, passed through a brief career as a redcap (collecting his nickname in the process because, said one observer, he "looked like a walking satchel tree"), and then burst upon the black baseball world as arguably its greatest pitcher and certainly its greatest storyteller. Many would contend that the adjective "black" in the preceding sentence is an unnecessary qualification on both counts. Paige was an even better pitcher than he was promoter of an image; indeed, he was an even better pitcher than he was copy—which is saying a great deal, for Paige was up there in both categories with Dizzy Dean and Lefty Gomez, back in the days when wildness and weirdness were authentic aspects of country folk culture, as snake-oil remedies were endemic. Paige's so-called hesitation pitch, his outrageously tall tales (particularly about James "Cool Papa" Bell's speed—so fast he could turn out a light and jump into bed before the room got dark), and his record against (white, of course) major league all-stars in exhibition games all seemed equally unlikely. From his rookie year in baseball with the Birmingham Black Barons through his rookie year in the major leagues more than two decades later, Paige had lost a little speed but none of his puckish humor. His talent was sufficiently indisputable that he is one of 11 African Americans inducted into the Baseball Hall of Fame at Cooperstown on the basis of his career in the Negro Leagues. There he shares space with his few peers. In the Forest Hill Cemetery he has more company, but no peers; there visitors will find the Satchel Paige Memorial Tombstone.

Mutual Musicians Foundation
1823 Highland Street, Kansas City, MO 64117
(816) 421-9297
Hours: Mon.–Fri., 11 A.M.–6 P.M. Late-night jam sessions: Fri.–Sat.
Admission: Voluntary donations requested

Garvin Bushell, who recorded with Sam Wooding, Cab Calloway, Chick Webb, John Coltrane, and scores of other jazz greats, recalled that Ben Webster "was a typical product of Kansas City of that time [1930s]. Kansas City was a fast town where the people were on top of everything—in the line of music, gambling, hustling, and all that. Some of the sharpest characters in the world came from there." Some of the greatest music too, much of it at one time organized around the bands of Jay McShann and Count Basie. Both Lester Young and Herschel Evans, two of Basie's soloists, were from Kansas City, as was McShann's alto saxman, Charlie Parker. They and George and Julie Lee and Bennie Moten are among the local greats whose lives and careers are recalled at the Mutual Musicians Foundation. Once the headquarters of the black musicians' union and an after-hours gathering place for itinerant artists, the foundation is now a National Historic Landmark and a private jazz club; but visitors can tour a photo exhibit that underscores the city's great jazz heritage.

Those interested in pursuing the subject should *not* expect to find anything at the frequently mentioned International Jazz Hall of Fame. This project has yet to get off the ground and has lost the backing of the Charlie Parker Foundation, which secured the original support of Dizzy Gillespie, Count Basie, and others and which owns the International Jazz Hall of Fame trademark name. However, the city has plans to proceed with a jazz museum.

Negro Leagues Baseball Museum
1601 East 18th Street, Suite 260, Kansas City, MO 64108
(816) 221-1920
Hours: Mon.–Fri., 9 A.M.–5 P.M.
Admission: Free

COURTESY NEGRO LEAGUES BASEBALL MUSEUM, INC.

John "Buck" O'Neil (left) was a star of the Negro Baseball Leagues, a manager of the champion Kansas City Monarchs, and then the first African American to coach in the major leagues (with the Chicago Cubs).

Long before Jackie Robinson, there were black baseball stars—they simply couldn't play against their white peers (except in exhibition games, where their record was so good that in the 1930s the commissioner of major league baseball forbid the exhibition teams to have more than three white stars playing for them, thus invalidating comparisons). Instead, they played against each other in a black league organized in a Kansas City YMCA in 1920. Oddly, for today's youth, Josh Gibson, "Satchel" Paige, "Cool Papa" Bell, and "Pop" Lloyd may be better known than Rogers Hornsby and Carl Hubbell. But few know that in the first decade of the century, there was a black women's baseball team, the St. Louis Black Bronchos, or that 65 years before Robinson, Moses Fleetwood Walker negotiated the hostile terrain of a white sport. Far fewer still know that what the signing of Jackie Robinson heralded was the death of black *ownership* of professional baseball teams. From Walker to Robinson, from owners to stars, the African-American heritage in the national pastime in past times when segregation prevailed is on view at the Negro Leagues Baseball Museum. The names, the uniforms, the teams, the trophies, the records, the stats that define achievement, photographs, bats, balls, and gloves—it's all there. To this joy is added a bonus: The chairman of the museum's board is John "Buck" O'Neil (.345 in 1940 and the first black major league coach, with the Cubs in 1962), and one of the board's members is Ernie Banks (twice the National League's most valuable player and a feature at Cooperstown).

The great "Satchel" Paige was a major leagues rookie in his 40s.

COURTESY NEGRO LEAGUES BASEBALL MUSEUM, INC.

Charlie Parker Gravesite
Lincoln Cemetery, 8604 East Truman Road, Kansas City, MO 64126
(816) 252-8175
Hours: Daily until sunset
Admission: Free

Born in 1920 in Kansas City, Kansas, Charlie Parker in his youth hung out around the many jazz clubs of the contiguous and more famous city of the same name just across the state line in Missouri. By the age of 15 he had left school to make a living playing the alto sax. After a few years of gigs in the Midwest, Parker joined the big band of pianist Jay McShann. A few more years found him fully matured as a musician and known for a breakneck tempo, double-time lines, and uniquely accented notes. When he combined with trumpeter Dizzy Gillespie, who had been heading in much the same direction, a critical mass was achieved and bebop was born. His music was as cranked up as his life was slowed down by an addiction to heroin. In 1946 he crashed. Seven months in a clinic left him with greater control over his habit—but without a band. Moving on to stays with the bands of Erroll Garner, Dizzy Gillespie, and Woody Herman, Parker emerged with a series of his own groups, whose players included Max Roach and Miles Davis, and his own compositions. Briefly a living cult figure, "Bird" had clubs named after him in New York and Chicago before his early death at the age of 35. Today his memory is recalled in a recent award-winning biographical film directed by Clint Eastwood and more lastingly preserved at the Charlie Parker Gravesite.

MONROE CITY

St. Peter's Brush Creek Catholic Church
Rural Road 2, Brush Creek area, Monroe City, MO
Hours: Plaque and cemetery: Daily until sunset
Admission: Free

The Civil War broke up the Tolton family. The patriarch, Peter Paul Tolton, fled his Hager master and joined the Union army, in whose service he died. Martha Tolton, who had been freed by her owners, the Elliotts, had no security in a nonseceding slave state and crossed into Illinois with her three children, among them the seven-year-old Augustus, who would go on to become the first American of fully African descent to be ordained a Catholic priest. (See Tolton statue entry on p. 358.) Today, still nestled among the trees shading a gravel road not far from the Florida, Missouri, birthplace of Mark Twain, visitors will find St. Peter's Brush Creek Catholic Church. In May of 1859, in a wooden building that three years later was replaced by the present church structure, Augustus Tolton was baptized into a congregation that dated back to 1844. Today a bronze plaque commemorating Father Tolton is attached to the church. Behind the church lies a cemetery among whose weathered grave markers will be found the names Hager and Elliott.

ST. CHARLES

DuSable Grave
St. Charles Borromeo Cemetery, Randolph Street near Blanchette Park,
St. Charles, MO 63301
(314) 946-1893
Hours: Daily until sunset
Admission: Free

The final years of the founder of Chicago, Jean Baptiste Pointe DuSable (see DuSable marker entry on p. 345), were full of betrayal and poverty. Upon leaving the Great Lakes area around 1800, DuSable moved to St. Charles to live with his son. After his son's death in 1814, the former fur merchant moved in with his granddaughter, to whom he deeded his house in exchange for her caring for him. She took the property and shed the responsibility, and her pauper grandfather found little in his last year of life except a grave in the local Catholic cemetery. Today visitors to the DuSable Grave, which bears a small historical plaque commemorating the "Founder of the City of Chicago," may reflect upon how a man who avoided the keen edge of Indian hatchets fell victim to something sharper than a serpent's tooth.

Lewis and Clark Center
701 Riverside Drive, St. Charles, MO 63304
(314) 947-3199
Hours: Daily, 10:30 A.M.–4:30 P.M.
Admission: Adults, $1; students and children, 50 cents

In May 1804 a party of nearly 50 men left St. Louis for an exploration of uncharted lands in the Northwest at the headwaters of the Missouri River. More than two years passed before they returned from the Pacific Ocean. Led by Meriwether Lewis, President Jefferson's private secretary, and William Clark, this expedition returned with the first appreciation of the vast territory acquired in the Louisiana Purchase and of what remained beyond the purchase's boundary but well within the designs of the new republic. Though the expedition's best-known guide-interpreter proved to be the Shoshone woman Sacagawea, who joined the party when it wintered the first year near modern-day Bismarck, North Dakota, another key figure as porter-facilitator was Clark's young African-American slave, York. Despite York's "bad French and worse English," his initiative aided his masters and his novelty intrigued the Indians with whom he dealt. As Clark noted of the Arikara Indians, "Those people are much pleased with my black servant." Almost two centuries later, most of the Shoshone, Arikara, and Mandan and most of the elk, bear, and salmon are gone, but at the Lewis and Clark Center, visitors can see a mannequin of York, gun in hand, and a brief text identifying him as the first African American to journey through the American Northwest.

ST. LOUIS

Convention & Visitors Bureau
10 South Broadway, Suite 300, St. Louis, MO 63102
(800) 325-7962
Hours: Mon.–Fri., 8:30 A.M.–5 P.M.

While in St. Louis, forget the blues; ask for "The African-American Heritage of St. Louis: A Guide" brochure.

"Black Americans in Flight" Mural
Lambert–St. Louis International Airport, St. Louis, MO 63145
(314) 426-8000
Hours: Daily, 24 hours
Admission: Free

From Eugene Bullard, who flew for the French in World War I because a white-skin requirement prevailed for American combat pilots (see U.S. Air Force entry on p. 441); through the Tuskegee Airmen of World War II; and on to Guion Bluford, Dr. Mae Jemison, and the late Ronald McNair, three black astronauts, 75 African Americans prominent in American aviation history claim center stage in the "Black Americans in Flight" Mural.

First Baptist Church
3100 Bell Avenue, St. Louis, MO 63106
(314) 533-8003
Hours: Sat., 9 A.M.–1 P.M. and by appointment
Admission: Free

The first black pastor of the First Baptist Church was the Reverend John Berry Meachum (1789–1854), who had purchased himself and his family out of slavery. Meachum operated a clandestine school for African Americans at the church, which was erected in 1825. Known as "Candle Tallow School," this enterprise was closed by Missouri authorities, prompting the resourceful Meachum to reopen the school on a boat anchored in the middle of the Mississippi River, which was under federal jurisdiction. An architect of the Underground Railroad in St. Louis and a founder of the Negro National Convention, Meachum today is represented by a painting at the church whose congregation he pastored a century and a half ago.

56th U.S. Colored Infantry Memorial
Jefferson Barracks National Cemetery, Interstate 270 at Telegraph Road, St. Louis, MO 63125
(314) 263-8691
Hours: Wed.–Sat., 10 A.M.–5 P.M.; Sun., 12 P.M.–5 P.M.
Admission: Free

The difference between mere tragedy and true disaster is illustrated in the fortunately not twin fates of the Civil War's 56th Colored Infantry Regiment and the city of St. Louis. Traveling in the summer of 1866 by steamer between Helena, Arkansas (see Phillips County Museum entry on p. 36), and their mustering-out point in St. Louis, Missouri, the veterans of the 56th saw some of their comrades die on board before the unit reached Quarantine Grounds. Passing quarantine inspection, the steamers continued on to St. Louis, which they reached in the evening. The men were kept aboard ship till the morning, at which time several clear cases of cholera were revealed. Immediately ordered back to Quarantine Grounds, the unit was devastated, losing 178 men and one officer to the deadly disease within a matter of weeks. St. Louis, however, escaped an outbreak. Today, at marker section 57, grave 15009, of the Jefferson Barracks National Cemetery, the 56th U.S. Colored Infantry Memorial pays tribute to men who fell to the number-one killer of the Civil War: disease.

Jefferson National Expansion Memorial
11 North Fourth Street, St. Louis, MO 63102
(314) 425-4465
Hours: Courthouse: daily, 8 A.M.–4:30 P.M. Museum of Westward Expansion: Memorial Day–Labor Day: daily, 8 A.M.–10 P.M.; rest of year: 9 A.M.–6 P.M.
Admission: Courthouse, free. Museum of Westward Expansion: ages 17–61, $1; other ages free; admission fee will not exceed $3 per family

Just a few steps west of St. Louis's soaring 630-foot Gateway Arch commemorating America's westward expansion is a fitting symbol of the show-me state, the Old Courthouse. Its dome predates that on the U.S. Capitol in Washington, D.C., and when it was first proposed doubting local officials refused to proceed until a 13,000-pound scale model had been constructed to prove that the dome's weight could be borne. For years the courthouse was the political center of the city: Emigrants bound for the Oregon Territory gathered here, rallies to raise volunteers for the Mexican War were held here, antiabolitionists met here "to devise ways and means to protect their slave property," and slave sales were held here—the last in 1861 when a crowd of 2,000 jeering abolitionists shouted down the auctioneer and precluded any transactions. Here too in a first-floor west wing courtroom were held the opening trials of the notorious and politically critical Dred Scott case. (See Dred Scott entry on p. 410.)

Today the Jefferson National Expansion Memorial, whose centerpiece is the Old Courthouse, commemorates the Scott case with daily tours of a courtroom restored to its 1850s appearance. (The room in which the Scott case twice was heard no longer exists.) Visitors to the restored courtroom will occasionally find school groups on educational tours acting out the Scott proceedings as a learning exercise. Also, temporary exhibits (particularly during February) focus on other aspects of local African-American heritage, such as the "Freedom Schools" that sought to circumvent the 1847 law prohibiting schools "for the instruction of free negroes and Mulattoes . . . in this State." (Two years before the passage of this law, the Sisters of St. Joseph of Carondelet had begun to teach courses to black girls, but eventually a mob destroyed their convent. Earlier still a school for black children with a biracial teaching staff had seen its white teacher carted off to jail. Finally the Reverend John Berry Meachum, a former slave, built a floating school anchored in the middle of the Mississippi River, which brought it under federal jurisdiction and exempted it from Missouri law.)

Meanwhile, the Museum of Westward Expansion, which is part of the Jefferson Memorial, interprets America's 19th-century drive toward the Pacific with exhibits on the Lewis and Clark expedition—incorporating the role of Clark's slave, York—the farmers who plowed and settled the prairie, the Plains Indians, and the African-American experience, such as the Exoduster movement. Both the courthouse and the museum have guided tours, programs, exhibits, and films.

Scott Joplin House State Historic Site
2658 Delmar Boulevard, St. Louis, MO 63103
(314) 533-1003
Hours: Mon.–Sat., 10 A.M.–4 P.M.; Sun., 12 P.M.–6 P.M.
Admission: Adults, $2; children under 12, $1.25

At the close of the 19th century, there was no more vibrant and commercially powerful Mississippi River city than St. Louis. The town teemed with speculators, salesmen, gamblers, migrants heading for the still-open West—and entertainers. Naturally, the future "Father of Ragtime," Scott Joplin (see Joplin marker entry on p. 41 and Sedalia Ragtime Archives entry on p. 427) found his way here, plying his trade in the 1890s in saloons, brothels, pool halls, restaurants, and theaters and at picnics and fairs. For more than a decade Joplin bounced back and forth between St. Louis and Sedalia, Missouri, finally settling in St. Louis in 1900, immediately after the phenomenal success of his "Maple Leaf Rag" and his marriage.

His sojourn from 1900 through 1903 in a flat on Morgan Street (now Delmar Boulevard) proved to be the most stable and productive period of his short life.

COURTESY ST. LOUIS CONVENTION AND VISITORS BUREAU

Scott Joplin, the "Father of Ragtime," returned to poverty in his obsessive pursuit to see his opera *Treemonisha* performed.

Here he composed "Elite Syncopation," "March Majestic," "Ragtime Dance," and "The Entertainer" (which seven decades later renewed his fame when it served as the theme song for the hit movie *The Sting*). Here too he composed his lost opera, *A Guest of Honor,* which was but one indication that Joplin regarded himself as more than an itinerant piano player and his music fit for more than saloons and bordellos. During these years Joplin largely abandoned performing, concentrating instead on teaching and on compositions, working on the latter under the direction of Alfred Ernest, the leader of the St. Louis Choral Symphony Society. His growing interest in "serious" music, however, did not find an audience, and Joplin faced much the same fate as Paul Laurence Dunbar when the poet sought to shift away from dialect idiom and black themes. When he took *A Guest of Honor* on a tour, he met with scant success; a similar fate awaited the minstrel show that he formed.

The death of his child and the breakdown of his marriage led the composer to abandon St. Louis, first for Chicago and then for New York City. There he married again, published only half a dozen rags, and became obsessed with seeing his new 230-page opera, *Treemonisha,* performed. His obsession was supported by his second wife, who according to historical accounts quoted by the Scott Joplin Foundation, "descended to running the[ir] house as a brothel" to raise money for production of the opera. Finally, in desperation in 1915, Joplin rented a hall in Harlem and presented an unstaged performance of *Treemonisha* with himself playing the piano. The audience was unmoved—and Joplin was crushed. Descending into serious depression, the composer was taken to a mental hospital in the fall of 1916, from which he never emerged. Just days before

America's entry into World War I, Joplin died and was buried in St. Michael's Cemetery in Brooklyn.

Today Joplin's various St. Louis residences and the once-famous Rosebud Café, which stood next to St. Louis's Union Station and where Joplin and other composers such as W. C. Handy often tried out their latest works before appreciative audiences, have fallen to dust. Only his Delmar Boulevard residence still stands, and here visitors will find the Scott Joplin House State Historic Site. Joplin's turn-of-the-century home has been restored and houses exhibits on the composer's life and works, on other St. Louis ragtime figures such as Tom Turpin, and on African-American history. In the background, a player piano plays authentic rolls of Joplin's music.

Dred Scott Grave
Catholic Cemeteries, 5239 West Florissant, St. Louis, MO 63115
(314) 381-1313
Hours: Daily until sunset
Admission: Free

Little more than a year after he was freed by his master following the Supreme Court's controversial ruling that as a chattel slave he was beyond the reach of Congress to free, Dred Scott was dead, worn out by more than 60 years of bondage. He'd spent the last decade of his life serving the antislavery cause—and though the cause was one dear to him, he was not exactly a volunteer. (See Dred Scott Memorial entry on p. 410.) Rather, Scott was kept in bondage in order to establish that he *should* be free. Only in the grave did he find final escape from a white society that used him throughout his life either as a laborer or as a symbol.

Shelley House Historical Marker
4600 Labadie Avenue, St. Louis, MO 63115
Hours: Daily until sunset
Admission: Historical marker: Free. House: Not open to the public. Exterior viewing only

The Shelley House Historical Marker recalls a monster, one created by racism rather than by Dr. Frankenstein. Sales-to-whites-only residential covenants helped structure the pattern of segregated housing that enabled segregated schools to last long beyond the 1954 *Brown* Supreme Court ruling. In St. Louis such covenants helped create "the Ville," the center of local African-American community. When the Shelley family sought after World War II to move into a white neighborhood, they ran smack up against the whites-only covenant. Though blockwide covenants had been declared unconstitutional as far back as 1917, the ruling did not apply to individual properties. However, after the Shelleys' lawsuit reached the Supreme Court in 1948, the Court ruled that though covenants might be legal, local governments could not enforce them. This ruling left neighborhoods at the mercy of individual homeowners, who might simply decide with impunity to ignore the racially exclusive agreements they had signed upon purchase of their homes, and it thus began the process of undermining legally enforceable residential segregation. Today the old Shelley property is *a private residence not open to the public*, but the historical marker may be found in front of the house.

Shrine of St. Joseph
220 North 11th Street, St. Louis, MO 63101
(314) 231-9407
Hours: Tours: Mon.–Fri., 9 A.M.–3 P.M.; Sun., at 12:15 P.M.
Admission: Free

Peter Claver (1581–1654) arrived in Central America as a Jesuit priest in 1610 and dedicated his life to the service of slaves stolen from Africa. He was canonized in 1888 and in 1896 was declared the patron saint of all Catholic missions among the diaspora. One of the two "authenticated miracles" that are required for canonization occurred at the Shrine of St. Joseph, where a relic of Claver's body is kept beneath the church altar. In 1861 a tubercular soap factory worker was blessed with the relic and miraculously restored to full health.

St. Louis Walk of Fame
6504 Delmar Boulevard, St. Louis, MO 63130
Hours: Daily until sunset
Admission: Free

Josephine Baker, Scott Joplin, Tina Turner, Chuck Berry, Miles Davis, and black baseball legend James "Cool Papa" Bell are among the 30 St. Louis residents honored in the St. Louis Walk of Fame. Each has a bronze star bearing his or her name imbedded in the sidewalk of the delightful City Loop neighborhood.

COURTESY ST. LOUIS CONVENTION AND VISITORS BUREAU

St. Louis–born Josephine Baker traveled far, taking Paris by storm.

SEDALIA

Sedalia Ragtime Archives
State Fair Community College, Clarendon Road, Sedalia, MO 65301
(816) 826-7100
Hours: Mon.–Fri., 9 A.M.–5 P.M.
Admission: Free

Scott Joplin arrived in Sedalia in 1893, at the age of 25. Here he attended the George R. Smith College for Negroes, where he studied composition, advanced harmony, and musical notation. Here too he published his first work, "Original

Rags," in March 1899. Joplin continued to compose and continued to perform at the Maple Leaf Club in the railroad town's notorious brothel district on Main Street. Soon the club would be famous, as Joplin's "Maple Leaf Rag," after initially slow sales, became the first piece of sheet music to sell a million copies. Joplin's contract with John Stark, his publisher for the next nine years, gave the composer a penny a copy, enough money to get married and follow Stark to St. Louis. Today visitors to the Sedalia Ragtime Archives view Joplin memorabilia and rare original sheet music (including the original score of his opera *Treemonisha* and piano rolls) and hear taped conversations with some of ragtime's leading exponents, such as Eubie Blake. (See entry on p. 241.) The Maple Leaf Club Historical Marker at the corner of Main and Lamine recalls the Father of Ragtime, as does the annual June Ragtime Festival.

NEBRASKA

Division of Travel & Tourism
700 South 16th Street, Lincoln, NE 68509
(800) 228-4307
Hours: Mon.–Fri., 8 A.M.–5 P.M.

CRAWFORD

Fort Robinson Museum
Fort Robinson Park, Box 304, Crawford, NE 69339
(308) 665-2852
Hours: Apr. 1–Nov. 1: Mon.–Sun., 8 A.M.–5 P.M. Rest of year: Mon.–Fri., 8 A.M.–5 P.M.
Admission: Museum: Adults, $1; children, free

It was a bad time to draw a bad detail. Two days after the 7th Cavalry wreaked revenge on their old opponents from the Battle of the Little Big Horn (see entry on p. 497) by provoking sufficient resistance from the dissident Sioux encamped at Wounded Knee to justify in their own minds the slaughter that ensued, the black troopers of the 9th Cavalry rode 104 miles in 24 hours through a northern plains winter to register America's presence on America's aboriginal people. The 9th rode to the Pine Ridge Reservation, where the Oglala Sioux, convinced that their Ghost Dance ritual could restore their warriors' supremacy on the plains and bring back the buffalo on which they depended, were staging their final resistance to America's suppression of the old ways. When the 9th's buffalo soldiers arrived, they found a detachment of the 7th Cavalry pinned down not far from the Holy Rosary Mission. (See entry on p. 516.) Corporal William Wilson of the 9th won the Medal of Honor for his role in extricating the 7th troopers. The black soldiers spent much of the winter of 1890–1891 out at the Pine Ridge Agency. The assignment was part and parcel of life at Fort Robinson, which served as the regimental headquarters of the 9th from 1887 through 1898. It was here that the second and third black graduates of West Point, John Alexander and Charles Young (see Greene County Historical Society entry on p. 451), first were assigned upon graduation. It was here too that the buffalo soldiers of the 10th made their regimental headquarters in the years 1902 to 1907. In 1906 the 10th's show of force quelled the so-called Ute uprising. Their act of deterrence was the final action of U.S. soldiers against the northern Plains Indians. Today visitors to Fort Robinson Museum can follow the story of the 9th and 10th's service at the fort, view photographs of the buffalo soldiers, examine a few artifacts that directly are tied to the regiments and others that were the standard cavalry equipment that the black troops would have used, and walk about the restored officer's quarters that the troopers of the 9th constructed in 1887. Living history interpreters, stagecoach rides, and nature excursions are other good reasons to visit the fort.

LINCOLN

Nebraska State Museum of History
1500 R Street, Lincoln, NE 68501
(402) 471-4754
Hours: Mon.–Sat., 9 A.M.–5 P.M.; Sun., 1:30 P.M.–5 P.M.
Admission: Free

While the African-American impact on Nebraska may be limited, it exceeds that of its representation at the Nebraska State Museum of History. Barring temporary exhibits that treat the state's black heritage, African Americans are represented by a reference to York, a participant of the Lewis and Clark expedition, by a display on the black homesteaders of Custer County, by an account of the abolitionist movement and of the extremely rare presence in the state of slavery, and by the odd photograph or two. However, this situation is a consequence not of lack of interest but of the museum's process of reinstallation and reinterpretation of its permanent exhibits. To date, the process has gone only as far as Nebraska's admission to the Union in 1867 and thus has yet to reach the Exoduster movement that first brought substantial numbers of black folk to the prairie. Look for black heritage to be far more extensively interpreted beginning in 1995. Connected to the museum is the Nebraska State Historical Society Archives, which has a substantial holding of photographs and documents that highlight local black heritage.

NEBRASKA CITY

John Brown's Cave and Museum
20th Street and Fourth Corso, Nebraska City, NE 68410
(402) 873-3115
Hours: Late Apr.–Oct.: Mon.–Sat., 10 A.M.–5 P.M.; Sun., 12 P.M.–5 P.M.
Admission: Adults, $4; children under 12, $2

The man-made cave in which runaway slaves hid extended from beneath the welcoming house to the bank of a nearby ravine. Slightly protruding from the ravine bank was the camouflaged end of a long hollowed-out log ventilator, which drew in air for the shelter's inhabitants. The cave's arched ceiling was several feet underground, propped up by strong timbers. It was crude—but in the 1850s the Missouri River port of Nebraska City was a rough-hewn frontier town. The fugitives' stay would be brief. Soon they were escorted to Lickskillet (now Knox), Iowa, and another step closer to a freedom that was not in immediate jeopardy. Their Nebraska City hosts were the Mayhews, whose one-room log cabin, built in 1851, is the oldest building in the state. In the cabin lived the Mayhews, their six young sons, and Mrs. Mayhew's brother, John Henry Kagi, who served briefly as John Brown's secretary of war before dying in the raid on Harpers Ferry. Brown himself made at least five documented visits to Nebraska City, and his name, perhaps because it is more famous than Kagi's or the Mayhews', graces the John Brown's Cave and Museum. Visitors to the museum stand in Nebraska's oldest building, view household implements of a frontier settlement and an exhibit on the days of slavery, and tour the cave that provided refuge. Nearby are Mt. Zion A.M.E. Church, one of the first black churches west of the Mississippi, a one-room log school, and several period homes of a more refined nature than that of the Mayhews.

OMAHA

Great Plains Black Museum
2213 Lake Street, Omaha, NE 68110
(402) 345-2212
Hours: Mon.–Fri., 8:30 A.M.–5 P.M.
Admission: $2 per person

The "Exoduster movement"—the massive post–Civil War black migration from the South to the Midwest—was driven by more than the crushing of Reconstruction. It was the lack of black capital and land, the only real sources of autonomy for a people daily exposed to violence and a vicious credit system, that combined to restore an insidious and unwelcomed bondage. And so, beginning in the late 1870s, African Americans fled Kentucky, Tennessee, Texas, Alabama, Louisiana, and Mississippi by the thousands, headed toward the promised land of Kansas and Nebraska. It was the first major free African-American immigration in history. When the wave receded, its ebb revealed the white supremacy that had provoked its flow. The migrants did not find the free land many had been promised, but they did find somewhat greater opportunity than they had possessed on tenant farms and city slums throughout the South. Many tried their luck at homesteading, but it was a hard row to hoe without money, teams, and equipment. By 1890 there were only 114 black farming families in Nebraska. A decade later that number had fallen to 77, of whom only 47 owned their farms. By the onset of the Great Depression, there were but 41 black farming families—and this after the "Second Great Black Exodus" following World War I brought the state's African-American populace to 17,000. The story of the black experience in Nebraska—

and that throughout the West—is told at the Great Plains Black Museum, the largest African-American historical museum west of the Mississippi. Three homesteader rooms, exhibits on black cowboys and black women of the prairie, a display on the buffalo soldiers, an account of the Exodusters, a music room with African and African-American instruments, artifacts and busts of black abolitionists such as Frederick Douglass, Sojourner Truth, and Harriet Tubman, and an exhibit on Malcolm X, who was born in Omaha, convey the truth that there is no part of this country that was not touched and transformed by the diaspora.

Malcolm X Home Historical Markers
3448 Pinkney Street, Omaha, NE 68111
Hours: Daily until sunset
Admission: Free

In his own mind, in any event, Malcolm X's (see Audubon Ballroom and Malcolm X entries on pp. 299 and 405) life was overdetermined by race and the value of racial purity even before his conception. His "very black," Georgia-born father, Earl Little, and his West Indian–born mother, who "looked like a white woman," were married in 1919—the year of the 20th-century America's greatest race riots. (See 1919 Race Riot entry on p. 350.) Later, in Omaha, where Earl Little led the chapter of Marcus Garvey's black nationalist Universal Negro Improvement Association, Malcolm himself (at least in his own accounting) faced racial attack even before his birth: "When my mother was pregnant with me . . . a party of hooded Ku Klux Klan riders galloped up to our home in Omaha . . . brandishing their shotguns and rifles . . . shattering every window pane with their gun butts."

In 1925 Earl and Louise Little brought their son Malcolm home from the hospital to a frame house on Pinkney Street, where they lived for the next three years. Today two historical markers recall the first steps of the man who became the leading exponent of African-American self-reliance, the prime symbol of the modern era's black nationalist movement, and a hero to African Americans born long after his assassination in 1965. One marker was erected by the state, the other by the black community.

OHIO

Division of Travel and Tourism
600 West Spring Street, Columbus, OH 43215
(800) BUCKEYE
Hours: Mon.–Fri., 9 A.M.–5 P.M.
Ask for the "Crossroads" brochure, which details Ohio's African-American historical and cultural sites.

AKRON

John Brown House

514 Diagonal Road, Akron, OH 44320
(216) 535-1120
Hours: Tue.–Sun., 1 P.M.–5 P.M.
Admission: $3 (includes admission to the Perkins Mansion, home of Akron's founder)

In the mid-1840s, long before the raid on the arsenal at Harpers Ferry (see entry on p. 207) brought him fame and death rather than the destruction of slavery as he intended, John Brown lived in Akron, where he raised sheep and was a partner in a wool business. The business did not do well, and Brown moved on to other endeavors and other towns. In these years his attention was devoted far less to abolitionism than to sheep, with the result that of all the museum homes devoted to the peripatetic Brown, the John Brown House in Akron is the most unusual. It centers not on the antislavery zealot but on the author of the piece on proper sheep-washing in the March 1, 1847, issue of *The Ohio Cultivator*.

Sojourner Truth Monument

37 North High Street, Danner Press Building, Akron, OH 44308
Hours: Tue.–Sun., 1 P.M.–5 P.M.
Admission: Free

Sojourner Truth (see entry on p. 253) was seen as genuinely strange—as most ill-educated, six-foot-tall, gaunt black women who have lived on utopian communes and receive direct communication from God in visions and then speak about them in a heavy Dutch accent are wont to be. She may have appeared strange; certainly she was extremely moving in her fervent defense of her race and her gender. Her most notable feminist address was made to the second National Woman Suffrage Convention held in Akron in 1852, where she tore into the views ventured by male speakers, who emphasized their responsibilities to the movement in light of female helplessness. Jumping to her feet in unplanned protest against the slander of women's weakness, Truth launched into an account of her trials and triumphs as a female slave. Her impromptu oration roused her sisters and quelled the jibes directed at the strange black woman:

> That man over there says that women have to be helped into carriages and lifted over ditches and to have the best places everywhere. Nobody ever helped me into carriages or over mud puddles or gave me any best place. And ain't I a woman? Look at me! Look at my arm! I have plowed and planted and gathered into barns and no man could beat me—and ain't I a woman? I could work as much and eat as much as a man, when I could get it, and bear the lash as well—and ain't I a woman? I have borne thirteen children and seen most of them sold off into slavery and when I cried out with a mother's grief none but Jesus heard—and ain't I a woman?

This, in any event, is the "history" that prevails and that today is honored with a Sojourner Truth Monument on the site—now occupied by the Donner Press Building—of her famous "Ain't I a woman" address. Although Truth was a forceful advocate of black and women's rights and undeniably merits the honors paid her, each detail of this story is in all probability false. Not only did Truth not employ the expression "ain't" (saying instead "ar'n't"), she almost certainly did not use her famous phrase at all at this meeting (if indeed ever), at least to judge by the fullest contemporary account (*Anti-Slavery Bugle*, June 21, 1851). Nor was she heckled by men nor quelled their disruption with her passionate defense of women's strength. Nor did she bear 13 children, all of whom were sold away from her. She bore five, from only one of whom (Peter) she was separated. And Peter was returned to her from Alabama (scarred physically and mentally from brutal beatings) after a court ruled that he had been illegally transfered south in the period of New York's gradual abolition of slavery. Nor, finally, did she cry out for help and have only Jesus hear her. In fact, she received the assistance of many in her campaign to secure Peter's return, some of whom the illiterate Truth names in her *Narrative of Sojourner Truth*. The "Ain't I a woman" tale as it has entered popular history is based on a "faint sketch" of the Akron convention, written by one of its leading (and literary) participants 12 years after the events described, and is nowhere else supported (indeed its corroborating details are contradicted) in the several contemporary accounts, published and private, of the convention. (One final note: Contrary to popular history—and to the inscription on the monument above her grave in Battle Creek, Michigan—neither did Truth ever say "Frederick [Douglass], is God dead?").

CANTON

Pro Football Hall of Fame
2121 George Halas Drive, Canton, OH 44708
(216) 456-8207
Hours: Memorial Day–Labor Day: daily, 9 A.M.–9 P.M. Rest of year: daily, 9 A.M.–5 P.M.
Admission: Adults, $4; seniors over 65, $2; ages 5–13, $1.50

African Americans reentered the ranks of the National Football League at about the same time they entered baseball's major leagues—just after World War II, when the Los Angeles Rams signed Woody Strode and Kenny Washington. Today the Pro Football Hall of Fame is full of African Americans, including Jim Brown, Gale Sayers, Joe Greene, and Walter Payton. The museum also has a special exhibit on black players in the era prior to the 1920 formation of the NFL. Featured here are four African-Americans, including Charles Follis, "the Black Cyclone," who in 1904 played for the Shelby Blues. In the first 14 years of the NFL, 13 black players sporadically took the field—including Fritz Pollard and Paul Robeson, both of whom were named to unofficial all-league teams, and

Duke Slater, who thrice was selected all-NFL. Then, for reasons never secured by scholarship, African Americans were absent from the professional game until after the war.

CINCINNATI

Cincinnati Convention & Visitors Bureau
300 West Sixth Street, Cincinnati, OH 45202
(513) 621-6994
Hours: Mon.–Fri., 9 A.M.–5 P.M.

Cincinnati Art Museum
Eden Park, Cincinnati, OH 45202-1596
(513) 721-5204
Hours: Tue.–Sat., 10 A.M.–5 P.M.; Sun., 1 P.M.–5 P.M.
Admission: Adults, $5; seniors and students, $4; children under 18, free; free to all on Saturday

With its acquisition in 1890 of the encyclopedic collection of Central African artifacts assembled by Carl Steckelmann during his 1880s safari in the Belgian Congo, the Cincinnati Art Museum broke new ground, bringing the culture of the Mother Continent to the Midwest. Today the Steckelmann material remains the centerpiece of the museum's holdings and comprises the best representation of Vili basketry, mats, and carved ivory tusks in the nation. The museum also possesses pieces more commonly displayed in West African exhibits, including Senufo, Dan, Mossi, Mende, Ashanti, Kota, and Kuba masks, carvings, fetish figures, and so forth.

Harriet Beecher Stowe House
2950 Gilbert Avenue, Cincinnati, OH 45206
(513) 632-5120
Hours: Tue.–Thu., 10 A.M.–4 P.M.
Admission: Free

In 1832 the Beechers moved from Connecticut to Cincinnati, where the Reverend Lyman Beecher became president of Lane Theological Seminary. Here, just the other side of the Ohio River from the slave state of Kentucky, Harriet Beecher received her first direct exposure to slavery—and to its fervent apologists and its activist opponents. Cincinnati, one of the first northern stops on the Underground Railroad, was sharply and volubly divided on the issue of slavery and provided fertile ground for the future novelist. When in 1834 many of Lane's abolitionist faculty offered black students opportunities for advanced training by opening a mission school, opposition from townfolk, who saw the seminary as a breeding ground for a still-unpopular movement, forced its closure. Here too Beecher met the Reverend Rankin, the abolitionist Presbyterian pastor who flagrantly encouraged slaves to flee their masters (see Rankin entry on p. 447) and whose account of a fugitive named Eliza who braved the thawing ice of the Ohio River in the course of her escape provided Beecher with a central scene almost two decades later in *Uncle Tom's Cabin*. From her parents' home on Gilbert Avenue, the young writer visited a friend in Kentucky (see Slave Market entry on p. 84), observing firsthand the horrors of slave sales. Today the Beecher's two-story Cincinnati home is the Harriet Beecher Stowe House and serves both as a community cultural center and as a vehicle for promoting black history. Downstairs, period furniture yields a sense of what the family parlor looked like, though in fact little of the furnishings actually come from the Beechers. Also on view are photographs of the family and other abolitionists; a manuscript page from *Uncle Tom's Cabin*; a photograph of Josiah Henson (see Uncle Tom entries on pp. 253 and 549), generally considered a model for Uncle Tom; 19th-century abolitionist newspapers; and manumission documents.

Taft Museum
316 Pike Street, Cincinnati, OH 45215
(513) 241-0343
Hours: Mon.–Sat., 10 A.M.–5 P.M.; Sun., 12 P.M.–5 P.M.
Admission: Requested contribution: adults, $2; seniors, students, children, $1

The African-American landscape artist Robert Scott Duncanson was born in 1821 and moved to Cincinnati to establish himself as landscape and portrait painter. His choice of venues was a wise one, for the frontier town was both supportive of the arts and sufficiently new and fluid as to permit him to mix with white artists on terms of ease if not of equality. Still, Duncanson's early years as an artist were difficult ones. He was fortunate to be supported (as were other black artists) by the Anti-Slavery Society, which helped him travel abroad for study before the Civil War. Some years prior to his departure, Duncanson was commissioned to paint a suite of murals for a Cincinnati home that is now the Taft Museum. Here he executed eight landscape compositions, each of which measured 9½ by 6 feet, making them one of the largest domestic mural schemes in America and certainly Duncanson's most ambitious attempt to frame the American frontier in a classical perspective. Later in life Duncanson lost his own perspective, descending into mental collapse and a Detroit asylum, in which he died in 1872.

CLEVELAND

Greater Cleveland Visitor Information Center
3100 Terminal Tower, Cleveland, OH 44113
(216) 621-4110
Hours: Mon.–Fri., 8:30 A.M.–5 P.M.

African American Museum
1765 Crawford Road, Cleveland, OH 44106
(216) 791-1700
Hours: Mon.–Sat., 10 A.M.–5 P.M.; Sun., 1 P.M.–5 P.M.
Admission: Adults, $2.50; seniors and children, $1.25

If Cleveland's African American Museum were a contemporary message-sweatshirt, it would read "Black museum with an attitude." As its brochure states, "It is not in the history books! [But] African people were the originators of the calendar, the clock, mathematics, astronomy, medicine, architecture, religion, philosophy, law, chemistry, writing and much more." What "much more" than religion, law, philosophy, mathematics, and writing might be is unclear—perhaps the tango and bingo. Believing with Bishop Henry M. Turner that "a man must believe he is somebody before he is acknowledged to be somebody," this small museum fosters knowledge about black inventors, scientists, and artists whose contributions to the world certainly did not bring them more fame for their being black.

Visitors view three permanent exhibits: a pictorial and photographic survey of the artifacts and monuments of Egypt, the African source of much of the world's original knowledge; a brief history of the works and significance of Russia's greatest poet, Alexander Pushkin (1799–1837), who was justly proud of his descent from an Ethiopian prince who had served as a tsarist general; and a display on the career and the various patented devices of the Cleveland-based inventor Garrett A. Morgan. (See entry on p. 83.) Except for his race, Morgan might have been the stereotypical Yankee tinkerer. His inventions range from the now ubiquitous red/yellow/green traffic light (though it seems that only the red is ubiquitous), to a belt fastener for sewing machines. Morgan was more than merely inventive, he was also notably courageous, civic-minded, and sensitive. His invention of a smoke mask won a gold medal in 1914, though its utility remained in some doubt until two years later when a gas explosion in an excavation under Lake Erie trapped workers and brought the fire and police departments to the scene. It also brought Morgan, his invention, and his brother to the scene. Confident in his design, Morgan donned his mask, entered the fume-filled tunnel, and, with his brother's aid, dragged six men to the surface. Though Cleveland's citizenry was generous with its acclaim of Morgan's courage, what the inventor most clearly remembered years later was not his triumph but "the men curled up in that death chamber." The museum displays one of Morgan's original traffic signal lights and an original 1914 smoke mask. The museum also mounts temporary exhibits of the art and history of the diaspora.

Cleveland Museum of Art
11150 East Boulevard, Cleveland, OH 44106
(216) 421-7340
Hours: Tue.–Fri., 10 A.M.–5:45 P.M.; Wed., 10 A.M.–9:45 P.M.; Sat., 9 A.M.–4:45 A.M.; Sun., 1 P.M.–5:45 P.M.
Admission: Free

The Cleveland Museum of Art has a small collection of African objects and art that concentrate on West African cultures, such as the Yoruba, Senufo, Balue, Akan, Benin, and Ekoi. Most of the few hundred pieces on display are carved wood, though pottery, baskets, bronze, and ivory objects also figure. The collection trisects its presentation of Africa into the world of the living, which explores material culture; the spiritual realm; and the masked mediators—objects, divinities, and personages that unite or at least bridge the palpable and the transcendent.

Karamu House
2355 East 89th Street, Cleveland, OH 44106-9990
(216) 795-7070
Hours: Mon.–Fri., 9 A.M.–5 P.M. Performances: Thu.–Sat., 8 P.M.; Sun., 3 P.M.
Admission: Free to the center; theater, varies with performance

"Karamu" translates from Kiswahili as "place of joyful gathering." While there now are numerous entities in America calling themselves karamu, ujamaa, harambee, and so forth, only one can trace its Africentric name back more than half a century and its existence back more than 75 years. In 1915, as Germany sank the *Lusitania,* Booker T. Washington died, and Einstein postulated his General Theory of Relativity, the Playhouse Settlement was established amid the 15,000 African Americans and the many Austrians, Chinese, Russians, Syrians, and Jews of sundry nationalities living in Cleveland's insalubrious "Roaring Third" precinct. Equally committed to art and to a multicultural perspective, the community center rapidly won national recognition both for its productions and for its social services. The ensuing decades brought a massive immigration of rural southern blacks, altering the racial mix of the Roaring Third and leading the Playhouse Settlement to change its name to Karamu House just before bombs fell on Pearl Harbor. In that year Karamu's fund-raising effort not only received support from the Rockefeller Foundation and from small, local contributors across Cleveland's racial spectrum, it also received large contributions from Hollywood stars such as Katherine Hepburn, Gregory Peck, and Rosalind Russell. Today Karamu retains its national recognition and continues its multicultural artistic exploration of America. From drama through the plastic arts and photographs, from theater workshops through musical study, from dance through chamber music, from crafts through summer camps, Karamu translates as community and culture.

Harriet Tubman Museum
9250 Miles Park, Cleveland, OH 44128
(216) 341-1202
Hours: Tue.–Thu., by appointment; Sat. and Sun., 1 P.M.–4 P.M.; guided group tours by appointment
Admission: Adults, $3; children, $2

Though it has few objects that immediately tie it to its namesake, the Harriet Tubman Museum is well worth a visit for those interested in the African-

American experience. Slave deeds, chains, abolitionist newspapers and broadsides, and signed books and artifacts from abolitionist clubs (which produced for sale facsimiles of slave paraphernalia as fund-raising devices) introduce antebellum America. Included here is a percussion pistol allegedly owned by Tubman—but you wouldn't want to bet your home on its provenance. The museum also displays an immense collection of sheet music, phonograph records, and a comprehensive catalog of photographs, brochures, and posters of the spiritual choir Wings Over Jordan. In addition to statues of prominent African Americans, exhibits on Cleveland's influential African Americans, busts of African women, and African sculpture, the museum has two collections of less commonly seen material that tie in directly to the black experience of the late 19th and early 20th centuries: The outstanding Marcus Garvey Collection embraces letters, souvenir brochures, financial records, and flags of this century's most influential black nationalist organization; this collection is complemented by an exploration of another aspect of black unity, self-help, and colorful display—the uniforms of the Black Masonics, the Eastern Stars, and the early Nation of Islam.

COLUMBUS

Columbus Museum of Art
480 East Broad Street, Columbus, OH 43215
(614) 221-6801
Hours: Tue.–Fri., 11 A.M.–4 P.M.; Sat., 10 A.M.–5 P.M.; Sun., 11 A.M.–5 P.M.
Admission: Free to permanent collection. Nominal charge for traveling exhibitions. Group discounts available

Understanding his mission, to testify to God's power and purpose, Elijah Pierce carved the good news and the admonitions of the Bible for the edification of humankind. Artist, barber, and lay preacher, Pierce felt himself surrounded by the signs and symbols of heaven and hell. Deeply concerned with the hereafter and salvation, Pierce, through faith, negotiated and transformed his anxieties into art, carving into wood what God had carved into his heart. For the last 60 years of his life, the Mississippi-born Pierce lived and carved in Columbus. Today the Columbus Museum of Art has the nation's largest collection of his work, which alone justifies a visit for anyone in the vicinity of Ohio. Those

COURTESY COLUMBUS MUSEUM OF ART

Elijah Pierce, a major presence in 20th-century American art, is represented at the Columbus Museum of Art.

who trek to the museum also will find a small collection of contemporary paintings by regional artists, many of them black, and a small collection of African art and artifacts, including a Baganda drum, a M'Pongwe mask, a Malume xylophone, and a M'Kushiji wooden sculpture. Be forewarned: The museum is small, and although the Pierce pieces are always on display, the African objects are not.

Frank Hale Black Cultural Center and the King Arts Complex
Ohio State University, 153 West 12th Avenue, Columbus, OH 43210-1389
(614) 292-0074
Hours: Mon.–Fri., 8 A.M.–10 P.M.; Sat.–Sun., 11 A.M.–7 P.M.
Admission: Free

More than 160 pieces of African artifacts and African-American artwork are on display in the Richmond Barthé and Elijah Pierce galleries of the Frank Hale Black Cultural Center. The Benin, Yoruba, and Dogon cultures are highlighted, primarily through wood carvings of masks, sculpture, and fetish figures, but also in the form of basketry, ceramics, and jewelery. Also in Columbus is the King Arts Complex (867 Mt. Vernon Avenue; 614 252-KING), which provides a forum for the performing and the visual arts, speakers, and exhibits that reflect African-American heritage.

DAYTON

Dayton Art Institute
Forest and Riverview avenues, P.O. Box 941, Dayton, OH 45401-0941
(513) 223-5277
Hours: Tue.–Sun., 12 P.M.–5 P.M.
Admission: Adults, $3; seniors and students, $2; under 18, free

Perhaps 30 West African pieces, principally small wooden sculptures but also including a few bronze and terra-cotta objects, can be found in the Dayton Art Institute. Fetish objects, masks, medicine staffs, male and female figures, and ritual and utilitarian objects of the Ligbe, Mbole, Mama, and Bena Lulua as well as of the more commonly represented Dan, Dogon, Yoruba, Ashanti, Senufo, and Bale peoples are on display,

Paul Laurence Dunbar House
219 North Summit Avenue, Dayton, OH 45407
(513) 224-7061
Hours: Memorial Day–Labor Day: Wed.–Sat., 9:30 A.M.–5 P.M.; Sun., 12 P.M.–5 P.M. Labor Day–late Oct.: Sat.–Sun. only
Admission: Adults, $2.50; children, 6–12, $1

In de dead of night I sometimes,
Git to t'inkin of de pas'
An de days w'en slavery helt me
In my mis'ry—ha'd an' fas'.

Dough de time was mighty tryin',
In dese houahs somehow hit seem
Dat a brightah light come slippin'
Thoo de kivahs of my dream . . .
We would gethah daih at evenin',
All my frien's 'ud come erroun'
An' hit wasn't no time, twell, bless
you,
You could hyeah de banjo's soun'.
You could see de darkies dancin'
Pigeon wing an' heel an' toe—
Joyous times I tell you people
Roun' dat same ol' cabin do'.

COURTESY OHIO HISTORICAL SOCIETY

Despite his talent, Paul Laurence Dunbar never escaped the confines of dialect poetry.

Though Paul Laurence Dunbar's poetic talent was undeniable, his literary success arguably owed as much to his apparent adoption of stereotypical white views of black folk. Born in Ohio to a father who had escaped slavery in Kentucky and fled to Canada before returning to the U.S. to serve in the 55th Massachusetts Regiment and to a mother who had been enslaved in the Deep South, Dunbar was the star of his high school debating team, the president of its literary society, the editor of its newspaper, and the school's sole African American. In days when even the great majority of white folks couldn't afford college, Dunbar's scholastic success yielded only a job running an elevator in his hometown. With borrowed money, Dunbar published his first collection of poetry, *Oak and Ivy*, when he was 21. The borrowed money—which he promptly repaid from the book's sales—typified an important aspect of the poet's life. Everywhere he went he found assistance from men of standing in the community—from his Dayton friends Wilbur and Orville Wright, who printed the *Dayton Tatler* that Dunbar edited; from his mentor Frederick Douglass, who employed him at the World's Columbian Exposition held in Chicago in 1894; from William Howells, dean of American literary critics, whose 1896 rave review of Dunbar's second book, *Majors and Minors*, made the poet's career; from the socially prominent John Hay, the U.S. ambassador to the Court of St. James, who escorted the poet during Dunbar's hugely successful visit to London during Queen Victoria's Diamond Jubilee; and from President Theodore Roosevelt, whose campaign poem Dunbar authored. Howells's endorsement of "Paul Dunbar . . . the only man of pure African blood and of American civilization to feel the Negro life aesthetically and express it lyrically" enabled the poet to find a wide (white) audience, with the result that he became and remained until his death at 34 one of America's most famous men of letters. To his intense dissatisfaction, however, he also became and remained a captive of his dialect voice, despite publishing several novels (including in 1898 *The Uncalled*, all of whose characters are white), a collection of magazine articles, play librettos, and scripts and collections of "straight" poetry.

Dunbar's prolific writing—which left little time for relaxation—the failure of his marriage, tuberculosis, alcoholism, and his lament that "I'm tired of dialect but the magazines aren't" drove him into an early grave. Though now a victim of the cheerful darky dialect poetry (which remains far better known than poems such as "We Wear the Mask" and the antilynching "The Haunted Oak") that was the foundation of his career, Dunbar was acknowledged by James Weldon Johnson, Langston Hughes, and Claude McKay to have been a major influence on their work. As late as 1924, almost two decades after his death, Dunbar was voted one of the ten greatest African Americans by poll of the American Federation of Negro Students. Today visitors to the Paul Laurence Dunbar House, which was paid for with the profits of his third book of poetry, see his home virtually as he left it, complete with his desk, typewriter, books, personal belongings—including the ceremonial sword presented to him by President Roosevelt and the bicycle given to him in friendship by the Wright brothers—and many of the original manuscripts of his poems.

U.S. Air Force Museum
Gate 28B on Springfield Pike, Dayton, OH 45431
(513) 255-3284
Hours: Daily, 9 A.M.–5 P.M.
Admission: Free

In June of 1940, as the German army flooded into France, an American living in Paris for the preceding 20 years prepared to flee. Exactly two decades earlier, Eugene Jacques Bullard of Columbus, Georgia, had been described as follows: "His black tunic, excellently cut and set off by a fine figure, was decorated with a pilot's badge, a *Croix de Guerre*, the *fourragère* of the Foreign Legion, and a pair of enormous wings, which left no possible doubt, even at a distance of fifty feet, as to which arm of Service he adorned. There was scarcely an American at Avord who did not know and like Bullard. He was a brave, loyal and thoroughly likable fellow." Bullard's French decorations and residence were clues to his color. Racially barred

U.S. AIR FORCE

Eugene Bullard, African-American combat pilot during World War I, had to fly for the French rather than the United States because he was not white.

from army flight training in America during World War I, Bullard had joined the French Foreign Legion, been seriously wounded as an infantryman, and then in November 1916 had transferred to the French Air Service. After flight training, he flew over the Western Front, winning the *Croix de Guerre* with Star and becoming the first African-American combat pilot. Rebuffed in his attempt to transfer to America's Air Corps after we entered the war, Bullard stayed in a French uniform. The black sergeant pilot did not, however, keep his wings: A racial insult led to a quarrel with a French officer and blows, following which Bullard was transferred back to the infantry.

Decades later, after Bullard fled his Paris home and the U.S. again found itself in a world war, not much had changed regarding African Americans and the U.S. Air Corps. But in July 1942 the "Tuskegee Experiment," as the War Department termed its groundbreaking segregated effort to train black air crew, opened in Alabama. Before the war was over 992 men graduated from its pilot training, 450 of whom found themselves with overseas combat assignments. Tuskegee's first graduates were assigned to the 99th Fighter Squadron, where on his eighth mission First Lieutenant Charles B. Hall shot down a Focke-Wulf 190, becoming the first African American to score a verified kill since Bullard 27 years earlier. Initially Hall and his comrades flew air cover missions for the B-25s of the 310th Bomb Group of the 12th Air Force, whose crews referred to them as the black Red Tails because of the identifying red paint on their tail assemblies. (A clearer means of identification were the P-40s the 99th flew: At this stage of the war, they had the only P-40s on the Mediterranean's western littoral—and hence above 9,000 or so feet were easy prey for the few Me-109s and FW-190s the Luftwaffe brought into play.) In the course of more than 15,000 missions over Italy, Germany, and Eastern Europe, the Red Tails destroyed 261 enemy aircraft, lost 66 pilots to aerial combat, and saw another 32 shot down and captured. Before war's end, the 99th was incorporated into the all-black 332nd Fighter Group commanded by Lieutenant Colonel Benjamin O. Davis, Jr., who would go on to become the first Tuskegee graduate to reach the rank of general. (Davis was the son of the first African American to become a U.S. Army general.) The 332nd Fighter Group reached the Italian combat front in February 1944 and flew cover missions for the 15th Air Force, never losing a bomber to enemy fighters (which at this stage of the war rarely were seen).

After the war, most of the 332nd was deactivated, with only the 99th Squadron surviving. Its all-black character lasted until June 1949, when desegregation finally reached the military service. All of this black history and more—including the induction of the heavyweight boxing champion Joe Louis (see entry on p. 400) into the Air Corps and the career of Daniel James (see entry on p. 53), a combat veteran of three wars and the first African-American general to wear four stars—can be seen at the U.S. Air Force Museum. As might be expected, the museum highlights the good news: Judge Hastie's 1943 resignation from the War Department, which if not the proximate cause of, was at least swiftly followed by, the assignment of the 99th Squadron to combat duty, is passed over; the 99th's troubles with its parent unit, the 33rd Fighter Group, are ignored; and the initial combat shortcomings of the 99th pilots pass unmentioned. Though weaker as a critical examination of the black experience in America's air arm, the museum's African-American Heritage Tour is an outstanding success in trumpeting the first-class patriotism of second-class citizens. That patriotism is best represented by Lieutenant General James's observation: "I've fought in three wars and three more wouldn't be too many to defend my country. I love America and as she has weaknesses or ills, I'll hold her hand."

GALLIPOLIS

Emancipation Celebration
Gallia County Fairgrounds, 384 Jackson Pike, Gallipolis, OH 45631
(614) 446-4120 (Fairgrounds); (614) 245-5418 (Celebration committee)
Hours: Third weekend in September
Admission: Free

With the exception of 1887—when fear of racial troubles intervened—an Emancipation Celebration has been held annually in Gallia County every year since President Lincoln's Proclamation following the Battle of Antietam. (See entry on p. 256.) Parades, gospel music, baseball, sack races, greasy-pole climbs, and bake-offs have drawn crowds for 130 years. In times past the celebration was a one-day affair held on September 22 and was recognized as an unoffical black holiday. Businesses understood that their black employees would load their families into wagons and buggies and head out for the gathering. For some years now Gallipolis has been the site of the celebration, whose highlight is the Sunday morning countywide church service. All the county's churches close their doors on the Sunday closest to September 22 and their congregations gather at the fairgrounds for a shared service. Though the now two-day, weekend event is full of fun and games, the celebration takes place in a religious atmosphere and the sponsoring organization is explicitly Christian. Recently as many as 4,000 people have been in attendance, some from as far away as California, and the gathering has taken on the overtones of a people's homecoming.

MOUNT PLEASANT

Mount Pleasant Historical Society Museum
Union and Concord streets, Mount Pleasant, OH 43939
(614) 769-2893
Hours: May–Sept.: Sun., 1:30 P.M.–5 P.M.; otherwise by appointment
Admission: One building: adults, $2; children, $1. Six buildings: adults, $6; youths, $3; small children, free

In the 19th century the small Quaker village of Mount Pleasant was deeply involved in the abolitionist movement, providing shelter and guided passage to fugitive slaves and operating a free-labor store, where customers could be assured that nothing sold had been made by enslaved labor. Today, in a town composed of fewer than 500 souls, the Mount Pleasant Historical Society Museum and five associated buildings offer a glimpse into a way of life and a time now vanished. All six structures lie within a two-block area, and anyone in the town can direct you to them and to the local volunteers who operate them. The museum has a map of the Underground Railroad routes that led through Mount Pleasant north to Steubenville and a map of the local houses that provided shelter to runaway slaves. Photographs, pictures, and artifacts of the antislavery movement complement the maps. Nearby is the local abolitionist printing press, the free-labor shop, two period general stores, a 19th-century tin shop, the local mansion, and the Friends Yearly Meeting House, the first Quaker meeting house constructed west of the Allegheny Mountains. A tour around the aptly named Mount Pleasant is an enjoyable and enlightening trip into the past.

OBERLIN

Allen Memorial Art Museum
Oberlin College, Oberlin, OH 44074
(216) 775-8665
Hours: Tue.–Sat., 10 A.M.–5 P.M.; Sun., 1 P.M.–5 P.M.
Admission: Free

Perhaps a score of ethnographic and art objects from West Africa and a similar number of paintings by African-American artists can be found at the Allen Memorial Art Museum on the campus of Oberlin College. West African textiles and wooden carvings of the Dan, Senufo, Guro, Pende, and Baga dominate the former, while the works of Richmond Barthé, Romare Bearden, and Horace Pippin stand out in the latter.

John M. Langston House
207 East College Street, Oberlin, OH 44074
Hours: Daily until sunset
Admission: Not open to the public. Exterior viewing only

The son of a Virginia planter and a freedwoman of African and Indian ancestry, John Mercer Langston (1829–1897) was freeborn. (See Virginia State University entry on p. 183.) Provided for in his father's will, Langston and his brother were educated at Oberlin College. John was admitted to the Ohio bar in 1834—after the bar association determined that he had more white than black blood in his ancestry. A year later he was elected the clerk of a Ohio township, becoming the first black elected official in America's history. Langston later recruited troops for black Civil War regiments, served as the inspector general of the Freedmen's Bureau, headed Howard University's law school, was U.S. Minister to Haiti, served as president of Virginia Normal and Collegiate Institute, and was elected to the U.S. House of Representatives in 1888 as the state's first African-American congressman. Today the John Mercer Langston House in

Oberlin, a National Historic Landmark that is *not open to the public,* recalls the life of a man whose endeavor took him, as the title of his autobiography proclaims, *From the Virginia Plantation to the National Capitol.*

Oberlin and Oberlin College
Carnegie Building, 101 North Professor Street, Oberlin, OH 44074
(216) 775-8121
Hours: Tours: Mon.–Fri., 10 A.M., 12 P.M., 2:30 P.M., 4:30 P.M. During academic year there are also tours on Sat. at 10 A.M. and 12 P.M.
Admission: Free

The town and college of Oberlin were conceived in 1833 as Christian bodies—in the words of their founder, the Reverend John Jay Shipherd, they were places "to live together in all things as brethren, and to glorify God in our bodies and spirits, which are His." The college was the first in the United States to admit women (1833) and one of the first to admit African Americans. (The prominent New York abolitionist activist Arthur Tappan provided funds for the college on the condition that blacks be admitted and that designated antislavery professors join the faculty.) It was this last that determined the town's history. In February 1835 the college's board of trustees was deadlocked 4 to 4 on the admission of blacks when its chairman, the Reverend John Keep, cast the deciding and favorable vote. From that point through the remainder of the century, Oberlin was the leading institution of higher education for African Americans—and as such the college and community found themselves intimately involved in the antislavery struggle. Virtually the entire community supported the effort, and fugitive slaves who got as far as Oberlin could be assured of passing on to Huron or Sandusky and then on to freedom in Amherstburg, Ontario, in Canada. Oberlin's communal defiance of the Fugitive Slave Act was flagrant: When John Price, an 18-year-old fugitive slave seized by slave catchers and a U.S. Marshal, sat in the nearby Wellington train station awaiting transportation back to slavery, 200 to 300 Oberlin citizens and students, black and white, forcibly removed the youth. Twenty Oberlin men later stood trial in Cleveland for this act; as part of the defense, the town brought kidnapping charges against the slave catchers. Among those arrested was Lewis Leary, one of three Oberlin African Americans who died in the raid on Harpers Ferry led by John Brown. Still standing are the First Church, site both of the Oberlin Anti-Slavery Society meetings and the memorial service for John Copeland, a black martyr of the Harpers Ferry raid; Keep Cottage, which honors the man who cast the deciding vote for the original admission of African Americans to the college; Finney Chapel, named for the abolitionist activist and second college president, who had joined the faculty at Tappan's behest; the Evans House, home of two African-American brothers arrested as a consequence of their participation in the rescue of John Price; and the Monroe House, home of yet another abolitionist activist who served on the college faculty. Other African-American heritage sites include the Shurtleff Statue, which pays tribute to Colonel Giles Shurtleff, commander of Ohio's first black Civil War regiment; the Underground Railroad Monument on South Professor Street; Tappan Square; and Martin Luther King, Jr. Park, which is graced by three statues—one of Dr. King, one commemorating the Oberlin-Wellington rescue, and one honoring the three African Americans from Oberlin who died on the Harpers Ferry raid.

PIQUA

Rossville Museum
8250 McFarland Street, Piqua, OH 45356
(513) 773-6789
Hours: Academic year: Tue.–Fri., 10 A.M.–5 P.M.; Sun., 1 P.M.–5 P.M.
Admission: Free

People come and go; torts are damn near immortal. In 1833 William Randolph, great-great-grandson of the founder of the College of William and Mary and descendant of one of Virginia's most influential families, died. His final will provided for the manumission of his slaves, some of whom were his offspring. The will directed his estate's executor, Judge William Leigh, to purchase land for the slaves in the North, which Leigh did in Ohio. Unfortunately for the slaves, Randolph had left three wills (freeing his slaves in all three) and died addicted to the opium prescribed for his chronic and ultimately fatal tuberculosis. Naturally, the family challenged his last will, which finally was upheld 13 years after Randolph's death. Thus in 1846, 383 survivors of the extended court case shed their status as property and headed for their 3,200 acres in Ohio—only to find that the land had been settled by German immigrants who had no intention of moving on. Instead, it was the newly freed who moved on, to the outskirts of Piqua, where they settled en masse. Sixty years later their descendants took the land dispute to the Ohio courts, where after a mere decade, the state's Supreme Court ruled against them. Today visitors to the Rossville Museum—housed in the 1873 home of the former Randolph slave York Rial and run by Rial's great-great-niece—can trace the peregrinations, legal and otherwise, of Randolph's slaves. From a list of the 383 souls through their African roots traced as far back as the 1700s; from their artifacts through their burial in the local graveyard; from a slide presentation of this particular history through a wider examination of black history in Cincinnati and Ohio, the museum pays tribute to a people who shared at least one common American experience: the courts as Calvary.

PUT-IN-BAY

Perry's Victory and International Peace Memorial National Monument
Bayview Drive, Put-in-Bay, OH 43456
(419) 285-2184
Hours: Mid June–Labor Day: daily, 9 A.M.–6 P.M. Labor Day–late Oct., late Apr.–mid-June: 10 A.M.–5 P.M.
Admission: Adults, $1; seniors over 61 and youth under 17, free

Except for America's naval power, the War of 1812 was almost uniformly disastrous. (See Chalmette entry on p. 90.) One of the war's few bright spots for the United States occurred on the waters of the Great Lakes, where Captain Oliver Hazard Perry ("We have met the enemy and they are ours") won fame. Perry's ships were crowded with black sailors and gunners when they clashed with and captured the British fleet in October 1813 at the Battle of Lake Erie. Initially Perry was less than thrilled with the reinforcements sent him by Commodore Chauncey, writing that he had been sent "a motley set, blacks, soldiers and boys." Though Chauncey's retort—"I have yet to learn that the color of the skin, or the cut and trimmings of the cut, can affect a man's qualifications or usefullness"—places him in a splendid contemporary light, it may have been somewhat self-serving: There is a long military tradition of commanders holding on to their best men and offering their second-echelon troops as reinforcements to other commanders. In any event, six weeks later victory rather than the anxieties of command prior to crucial battle led Perry to a different view. In his letter to the secretary of the navy, Perry praised his African-American sailors—who made up one-fourth of his ships' crews—for their good conduct and bravery. Now visitors to Perry's Victory Monument view a granite column 352 feet high, floodlit at night. Carved into the walls of the rotunda at the base of the column are the names of the dead and wounded from one of America's most crucial naval clashes.

RIPLEY

John Rankin House State Memorial

1824 Liberty Hall, Ripley, OH 45167
(513) 392-1627
Hours: Memorial Day–Labor Day: Wed.–Sun., 12 P.M.–5 P.M. Labor Day–Oct.: weekends, 12 P.M.–5 P.M.
Admission: Adults, $1; children, 50 cents

Nearer and shining more brightly than the North Star for Kentucky slaves seeking freedom was the bedroom window lantern in the Reverend John Rankin's bluff-top home. The lantern was both guiding beacon and, when extinguished, warning of prowling slave catchers along a six-mile stretch of the Ohio River that divided a slave state and the first stop on a flight to Canada. It also was John Rankin's flagrant provocation of slave owners and an unmistakable statement of his life's purpose. Finding scant success preaching abolition in Tennessee in the years after the War of 1812, Rankin moved to Ripley, Ohio, in 1822, living on Front Street, which overlooked the Ohio River. Deciding that his proximity to the river left him vulnerable to raids by Kentucky slave catchers, Rankin and his equally pro-abolitionist wife, Jean, moved to the top of nearby Liberty Hill in 1828, where they continued their antislavery work in the years before the founding of the American Anti-Slavery Society. In four decades of labor, the Rankins aided the escape of approximately 2,000 souls. Despite the

Presbyterian minister's open avowal of his activity, no fugitive who passed through his hands was captured.

African-American visitors of today need not limit themselves to the cellar dug beneath the barn or to the hideyhole in the attic of the John Rankin House State Memorial. Instead, they may tour his former home, view photographs of the Rankins, examine period furniture, and listen to the guided tours offered by local history enthusiasts clothed in mid-19th-century dress. They may also stop in at the nearby Presbyterian Church on Third Street, which was built by Rankin, and at Maplewood Cemetery. Located in the middle of town, the cemetery contains the graves of the Rankins and a memorial bust placed by descendants of a couple who found time, while raising 13 children, to help others.

UPPER SANDUSKY

John Stewart Grave and Memorial Marker

Wyandotte Indian Mission Church, 200 East Church, Upper Sandusky, OH 43351
(419) 294-4841
Hours: Marker and grave: Daily until sunset. Church: irregular visiting hours. Call in advance
Admission: Free

Redemption from "demon rum" and a turn toward religion is an old American story, frequently played out on the frontier as the nation moved west. In 1814 a former alcoholic freeborn African American, John Stewart, who had turned from rum to Methodist gospel, found himself seriously ill out in Ohio and promised God his service if he were spared. From the Northwest came an answering message: "Declare My counsel faithfully." The surviving Stewart upheld his end and—taking the message literally—set out northwest to propagate the Word. His journey took him across the path of the Delaware, a Christianized tribe who pointed him farther on toward the heathen Wyandotte. By 1816 Stewart had reached Upper Sandusky, where he found another African American, Jonathon Pointer. Pointer, a slave in Kentucky, had been seized there by a Wyandotte raiding party and raised among them.

Using Pointer as an interpreter, Stewart preached the gospel to the Wyandotte. Tradition recounts that Stewart's splendid singing voice caught the attention of the Wyandotte, who stayed to listen to ensuing preaching. It's a fine tradition, but whether it was his voice, his sincerity, his message, or the overarching culture he represented, Stewart enjoyed success. At his death seven years later, he left a flock as well as a tribe. In 1824, a year after their mentor's death, the Wyandotte had a mission church. When the U.S. government in 1843 dispossessed the Wyandotte and moved them to Kansas, the tribe insisted that the mission remain under the authority of the Methodist Church, which since has designated the Wyandotte Indian Mission Church a shrine. Today's visitors to the old Northwest Territory view a small, one-room mission church and cemetery situated amid three acres. At the entrance to the cemetery is a memorial marker honoring the first Methodist missionary to the American Indians; in the cemetery are the graves of the Wyandotte, their ministers, and a redeemed African American, John Stewart.

WESTERVILLE

Benjamin Hanby House

160 West Main Street, P.O. Box 1063, Westerville, OH 43081
(614) 891-6289
Hours: May–Oct.: Sat., 10 A.M.–4 P.M.; Sun., 1 P.M.–5 P.M.; otherwise by appointment for groups of five or more
Admission: Adults, $1.50; ages 6–12, 50 cents

In the days before the book became the musical and the musical the movie, the tuneful counterpart to the antislavery emotionalism of *Uncle Tom's Cabin* was "Darling Nelly Gray," a lover's lament sung as its namesake is sold South beyond his reach. The song's composer was Benjamin Hanby, a young theological student who with his parents aided the Underground Railroad. Rather than theology, Hanby should have studied law. When the song became popular, Hanby wrote the publisher inquiring about royalties. The publisher replied, "Nelly Gray is sung on both sides of the Atlantic. We have the money and you have the fame: that balances the account." Eventually Hanby hired an attorney, who secured a $100 settlement, $50 of which he kept for legal services rendered.

Today the Benjamin Hanby House has been restored to its 1850s appearance, when fugitive slaves were hidden in its nearby barn and in its backyard leather shop. Though a stop on the Underground Railroad, the house principally interprets Hanby's musical career (he also wrote "Old Shady, or the Song of the Contraband" and "Up on the Housetop") rather than the family's involvement in the effort to assist fugitive slaves. Period furniture, the flute Hanby purchased at the age of nine, his cloak, sheet music, and presents received at his 1858 wedding are complemented by some of the surviving artifacts of the leather shop. Visitors interested in the African-American link should seek information from the volunteer guides.

WILBERFORCE

National Afro-American Museum and Cultural Center

1350 Brush Row Road, P.O. Box 578, Wilberforce University, Wilberforce, OH 45384
(513) 376-4944; (800) BLK-HIST
Hours: Tue.–Sat., 9 A.M.–5 P.M.; Sun., 1 P.M.–5 P.M.
Admission: Adults, $3.50; children and students with I.D., $1.50

African-American life in the two decades between the end of World War II and the passage of the Voting Rights Act is the theme of the National Afro-American Museum and Cultural Center's permanent exhibit, "From Victory to Freedom." Popular culture is the crux of the exhibit, with photographs and artifacts highlighting the worlds of black business, education, religion, fashion, and music. In addition, temporary exhibits profile African-American artists, history, political activists, and scholars. The museum's holdings recently expanded with the acquisition of some of the belongings of Dr. Carter G. Woodson (1875–1950), founder in 1915 of the Association for the Study of Negro Life and History, editor of the *Journal of Negro History*, and the "Father of Black History." (See Carter G. Woodson House entry on p. 204.) The museum also offers a venue for lectures, films, and workshops on themes that explore black America.

Wilberforce University
1055 North Bickett, Wilberforce, OH 45384
(513) 376-2911
Hours: Mon.–Fri., by appointment
Admission: Free

Seven years after its 1856 founding by the A.M.E. Church, Union Seminary merged with another church-run school in Ohio and adopted the name of Britain's leading abolitionist and the driving force behind the British navy's African interdiction of slave ships. Wilberforce University is America's oldest black-owned and operated coeducational college, and its history can be traced through its archives in the library.

XENIA

Blue Jacket Drama
Caesar Ford Park Amphitheatre, Xenia, OH 45385
(513) 376-4318
Hours: Second weekend in June–Labor Day, 8:00 P.M.
Admission: Adults, $10; children under 13, $6

In the late 1760s—not long after the Ottawa warrior Pontiac led "his" so-called conspiracy of Ottawa, Delaware, Shawnee, and Miami against British overlordship of the western Great Lakes—western Pennsylvania was frontier territory. Somewhere in that time and place, Marmaduke and Charles van Swearingen stumbled across a party of Shawnee. Marmaduke, who was then about 17 years old, spoke enough Shawnee to communicate his willingness to go with the party if they permitted his younger brother to return home. Less than a decade later, so the story goes, Marmaduke was the Shawnee war chief Blue Jacket and a thorn in the side of those to whom Daniel Boone, Simon Kenton, and other white trailblazers were heroes. (Boone was captured by Blue

Jacket in 1778 and "adopted" by a leading Shawnee war chief, Black Fish, from whom he escaped in time to lead the defense of Boonesboro, which would propel him to fame.) Aided by a runaway slave named Caesar, whose death in battle some years later would leave its trace in the naming of Caesar's Creek, Blue Jacket and the various Shawnee *septs* (bands) fought to keep Ohio red. A price was exacted by both sides during the clashes of the 1770s and '80s: More than 1,000 settlers died, as did hundreds of Shawnee—including, in 1777, the murdered Mequashake Shawnee chief Cornstalk, who had been friendly toward the Americans since the Camp Charlotte peace conference in 1774. The end of the Revolutionary War brought relative peace, as British agents were withdrawn from Detroit, from which they had encouraged the western tribes to raid America's frontier settlements. But the peace could not last long. In the face of encroaching white settlements, the Shawnee sought allies among the Delaware, Miami, Ottawa, Mingo, and Wyandotte, all of whom (along with those who did not resist) ultimately were vanquished, dispossessed, transported, and destroyed in order to make Ohio safe for the Cleveland Indians and the nation's capital safe for the Washington Redskins. But before this security was achieved, a good deal more blood was shed. In 1786, 1787, and 1789 Kentucky militiamen raided Shawnee settlements in Ohio. In 1790 Little Turtle of the Miami routed General Josiah Harmar's force after it had burned towns of the Shawnee, Miami, and Delaware. A year later Kentuckians raided Miami towns during the summer, while General Arthur St. Clair's force of 1,400 was annihilated in November by Indian contigents, including Blue Jacket's *sept*, led by Little Turtle. Less than two years later General Anthony Wayne's force of 2,000 regulars and 1,000 Kentucky militiamen retaliated, scoring a decisive victory against Blue Jacket's Shawnee at Fallen Timbers. The Battle of Fallen Timbers put an end to large-scale Indian resistance until the War of 1812 facilitated the rise of the Shawnee Tecumseh's northwest Indian confederation.

Today a commercial enterprise in Xenia commemorates Ohio's Indian heritage in an unlikely fashion: Rather than celebrating the courage, vision, and determination of Little Turtle or Tecumseh, or the courage, vision, and determination of Boone or George Rogers Clark, it recounts the epic of Blue Jacket and Caesar. Today, on the ground crossed by Caesar's Creek, 50 actors armed with flintlock guns and flaming arrows take part in the "Blue Jacket Drama," reenacting the struggle to keep lacrosse America's national pastime.

Greene County Historical Society Museum
74 West Church Street, Xenia, OH 45385
(513) 372-4606
Hours: Tue.–Fri., 9 A.M.–12 P.M. and 1 P.M.–3:30 P.M. Also Sat.–Sun., 1:30 P.M.–4 P.M. from June to August
Admission: Researchers, free; tours, $2

Jim Crow could have been President Woodrow Wilson's middle name. As the U.S. entered World War I, it had one black graduate of West Point as a field officer. Lieutenant Colonel Charles Young spoke Latin, Greek, French, Spanish, and German; had secured recognition for his successful training, organizing, and disciplining efforts of the raw recruits of the 9th Ohio Volunteer Infantry in the earlier Spanish-American War; and was a combat veteran of Pershing's expedition into Mexico. (See Columbus Museum entry on page 503.) Young, who was scheduled to assume command of the renowned 10th Cavalry, saw his career crushed by Wilson's direct and personal intervention. When a white officer of the 10th expressed his dislike of taking orders from a black man, Secretary of War Newton Baker first thought he should "either do his duty or resign." But Wilson, alerted to the issue by a Mississippi senator, presidentially suggested to his war secretary that the officer be transferred. Soon other politicians followed suit, and Baker had Young placed on the retired list on medical grounds. In response, Young rode horseback 500 miles from Wilberforce, Ohio, to Washington, D.C., to establish that he was not medically unfit for service. Perhaps it is indeed better to travel than arrive, for Young's ride was in vain. He could lead black troops in action but not white troops to the mess hall, and certainly he could not *order* a white officer and gentleman to do an officer's duty. Not until five days before the signing of the armistice was Young readmitted to the service and placed in command of a training camp in Indiana.

COURTESY UNITED STATES ARMY

West Point graduate Charles Young as a major during the United States Army's chase after Pancho Villa.

Young earlier had served as America's first black military attaché—to Haiti and Liberia, of course. After the war he again served as military attaché—to Liberia. While on leave during his second African tour of duty, he traveled to Nigeria, where he contracted the tropical fever that soon would kill him. Biographical information on Young and on other prominent local African Americans can be found at the Greene County Historical Society Museum. Nearby in Wilberforce is the Charles Young Home, which is about ½ mile west of the National Afro-American Museum on Route 42 between Brush Row Road and Stevenson Road (1120 U.S. Route 42 East, Wilberforce, OH 45384). Scheduled to open at least intermittently to the public in 1994, the home will offer a glimpse into Young's life and exhibits on the black military contribution to our nation. Also nearby is the Martin Delany Grave (Tarbox Cemetery, Tarbox Road off of Highway 42 about 5 miles east of the museum). (See Delany entry on p. 321.)

OKLAHOMA

Oklahoma Department of Tourism & Recreation
2401 North Lincoln Boulevard, Suite 505, Oklahoma City, OK 73105
(800) 652-OKLA; (405) 521-3981
Hours: Mon.–Fri., 8 A.M.–5 P.M.

BOLEY

Boley Historic District
c/o Boley Chamber of Commerce, 125 South Pecan Street, Boley, OK 74829
(918) 667-3477
Hours: Daily until sunset
Admission: Free

Like Mound Bayou, Mississippi (see entry on p. 105), Boley was an all-black town that began life as a railroad-spawned refuge from white (and in Boley's case, red as well) America. Located near the terminus of the line running from Fort Smith, Arkansas, to Gutherie, Oklahoma, Boley drew its original settlers from the descendants of slaves held by the Creek Indians who had been moved in the early 19th century from their southeastern homeland into what was then the Oklahoma Indian Territory. When Booker T. Washington visited Boley in 1905, two years after its founding, the town was "little more than a name." By 1908 it was "a thriving town of 2,500 inhabitants, with two banks, two cotton gins, a newspaper, a hotel, and a 'college,' the Creek-Seminole College and Agricultural Institute." It was also a town "where, it is said, no white man has ever let the sun go down upon him." The mayor (born a slave in Kentucky) was black, the city council members were black, the sheriff was black, the bankers were black. Today the black past of the American West can be partially retraced in Boley Historic District, a National Historic Landmark, and in the annual Black Rodeo held on Memorial Day weekend.

DOAKSVILLE

Fort Towson Historical Marker
Off Highway 70, about ¾ of a mile from the fort in the old Doaksville cemetery, Doaksville, OK 74735
(405) 873-2634
Hours: Daily until sunset
Admission: Free

The Civil War in what is now Oklahoma was an incredibly confusing affray when viewed from the perspective of racial participation, as white, black, red, and various "mixed-race" men fought on both sides of the conflict. As early as the attack on Fort Sumter, major elements of the Choctaw and Chickasaw had signed treaties with the Confederacy. They soon were followed by Creeks, Seminoles, and Cherokees. Indian (most prominently the Creek chief Opothle Yahola), black, and mixed-race members of all these and other tribes who favored neutrality or the Union slowly fled toward Kansas, suffering attack and the loss of life and property (including their slaves) along the way. Upon arrival in Kansas, many of the black refugees were recruited into a regiment led by a former U.S. senator from Kansas, Jim Lane. Without authorization Lane sent them into battle in Missouri in October 1862, several months before the Union accepted African-American volunteers.

The Cherokee leader Stand Watie became a Confederate general of truly remarkable tenacity. He was the last Confederate general to surrender, doing so in June 1865. Watie's surrender to Lieutenant Colonel Asa Mathews's Union force, which included African-American units, is recalled at a historical marker.

KINGFISHER

The Old Chisholm Trail Museum
605 Zellers Avenue, Kingfisher, OK 73750
(405) 375-5176
Hours: May–Oct.: Tue.–Sat., 9 A.M.–5 P.M.; Sun., 1 P.M.–5 P.M. Nov.–Apr.: Wed.–Sat., 9 A.M.–5 P.M.; Sun., 1 P.M.–5 P.M.
Admission: Free

After the Civil War whites, blacks, and Indians drove cattle from Texas to Kansas along the Chisholm Trail. The Old Chisholm Trail Museum recounts the life of these cattle drives, though it fails to note the African-American presence. The museum does feature photographs and an account of the "Apostle" Paul Sykes, a local black preacher who founded The Straight Gate Church, a place of worship for Kingfisher's African Americans in the late 19th century.

LANGSTON

Langston and Langston University
Highway 33, Langston, OK 73050
(405) 466-2231 (University)
Hours: Mon.–Fri., by appointment
Admission: Free

Shortly after the 1889 settler stampede into the newly opened Oklahoma, an enterprising African American, who had behind him two terms as the state auditor of Kansas and a brief career as a gold prospector in California, purchased 320 acres of land and sent agents into the Deep South to recruit black settlers.

Edward P. McCabe, freeborn in New York in 1850, had large ambitions—and they weren't confined to money. McCabe (see State Capitol entry on p. 389) hoped to settle enough African Americans to make Oklahoma a black-majority state. He named his first town Langston, in honor of John Mercer Langston (see Virginia State University entry on p. 183), who entered the U.S. Congress but a month before the Oklahoma "Sooners" land rush. McCabe's Langston recruiters had a compelling promotional ploy: railroad tickets to nearby Gutherie and titles to land on which no white could ever reside or conduct business. Within a few years Langston had more than 2,000 residents—none white—and by 1897 the territorial legislature had granted the town 40 acres for Langston College, a land-grant agricultural and mechanical school. While McCabe's vision was never to be realized, Langston University still remains. At its Black Library in Sanford Hall can be found traces of a people's effort to build an economic and social basis for political power in a white world.

LAWTON

Fort Sill Military Museum
437 Quanah Road, Old Post Building, Lawton, OK 73503
(405) 351-5123
Hours: Daily, 9 A.M.–4:30 P.M.
Admission: Free

Before joining the 9th Cavalry in Texas in the mid-1870s, the buffalo soldiers of the 10th Cavalry patrolled the Indian Territory (Oklahoma), Kansas, and Colorado, clashing with Comanche, Cheyenne, Kiowa, Ute, and other Plains Indians. In Oklahoma the 10th constructed a series of forts, including Fort Sill (1869), from which they sortied throughout the Red River campaign that lasted until 1875. Today the Fort Sill Museum recalls early frontier garrison duty, with several of its displays highlighting the role of America's buffalo soldiers.

MUSKOGEE

Five Civilized Tribes Museum
Honor Heights Park, Drive Agency Hill, Muskogee, OK 74401
(918) 683-1701
Hours: Mon.–Sat., 10 A.M.–5 P.M.; Sun., 1 P.M.–5 P.M.
Admission: Adults, $2; seniors, $1.75; students, $1

In the years following the War of 1812, the recently settled southeastern frontier of the United States was populated by Creek, Cherokee, Choctaw, Chickasaw, and Seminole Indians, many of whose leaders were the offspring of white traders affiliated with the tribes. Though these tribes had adopted white cultural patterns sufficiently to be collectively referred to as the "Five Civilized Tribes," the white settler population wished their land, not their partial emulation. With the Indian Removal Act of 1830, and more specifically at the determined insistence of President Andrew Jackson, these tribes were compelled to exchange their land for portions of what is now Oklahoma. While the process was one of dispossession and death, it was not uniformly so. The Choctaw acceded first, departing peacefully in 1831 and suffering through a terrible winter. The Chickasaw were next (1832 and 1834) and had a less harsh experience. The Creeks had already surrendered two-thirds of their land following General Jackson's 1813–1814 campaign that culminated in the Battle (and subsequent Treaty) of Horseshoe Bend, and had little effective military capacity left to resist the land transfer of President Jackson's administration. The Seminole, who had suffered in the First Seminole War—in a sense an extension of Jackson's earlier campaign against the Creeks—departed from 1835 to 1842 as a consequence of the Second Seminole War. (See Dade Battlefield entry on p. 42.) The Cherokee, who were perhaps the southeastern tribe most integrated with white America (and who under mixed-blood leaders were already raising cash crops on large farms worked by slaves and publishing a newspaper and books in their own alphabet), attempted negotiation, winning a Supreme Court case against the state of Georgia in 1832. Their court victory proved in vain, however, as Jackson refused to enforce it. The tribe split politically, with the vast majority rejecting both removal and war against the whites. Jackson simply refused to acknowledge this majority's existence and dealt with the rump that was willing, though grudgingly to be sure, to accept what was on offer. Thus, in the fall and winter of 1838–1839, perhaps 15,000 Cherokee were rounded up and marched 1,200 miles to their new home. In the concentration camps where they were held prior to the trek and along the "Trail of Tears," about 4,000 died.

Just as the tribes' removal experiences differed in detail, so too did their relations with African Americans, many of whom were held in loose bondage by the Indians. As a generalization, African Americans fared best with the Seminole, intermarrying and rising to positions of power within the tribe. Perhaps 500 of the 3,000 to 5,000 Seminole who left Florida for Oklahoma were black. The black experience with the Creeks was less fortunate; indeed, in Oklahoma the Creek raided the Seminoles for African Americans, whom they would enslave. These variances continued throughout the 19th century: After the Civil War, freedmen of the Seminole, Creek, and Cherokee were more or less readily accepted as such; the Choctaw resisted emancipation for a generation and the Chickasaw did so until the end of the century.

Today, in the Five Civilized Tribes Museum, the history of black slavery is touched upon in exhibits about the tribes' freedmen.

OKLAHOMA CITY

Convention & Visitors Bureau
4 Santa Fé Plaza, Oklahoma City, OK 73102
(405) 278-8912
Hours: Mon.–Fri., 8 A.M.–5 P.M.

National Cowboy Hall of Fame and Western Heritage Center
1700 Northeast 63 Street, Oklahoma City, OK 73111
(405) 478-2250
Hours: May 30–Sept. 7: daily, 8:30 A.M.–6 P.M.; rest of year, 9 A.M.–5 P.M.
Admission: Adults, $4; seniors, $2; ages 6–12, $1.50

Yet another recognition that the history of the American West included black folk can be found at the National Cowboy Hall of Fame and Western Heritage Center. African Americans made their presence felt not only as soldiers, settlers, and working cattle-punchers and ranch hands, but on the rodeo circuit as well. Bill Pickett, who with the black bronc rider Jesse Stahl is in the Cowboy Hall of Fame, is credited by many with originating the sport of bulldogging. Astride his horse Spradley, the five-foot seven-inch Pickett would chase a bull, launch himself from the saddle, grasp the steer's horns, and wrestle the creature to the ground, gracefully avoiding being stomped on by the irate animal—most of the time. In a life that spanned seven decades, Pickett thrilled audiences in North America, South America, and Europe, and won the admiration of colleagues who included Will Rogers and Tom Mix. He also broke just about every major bone in his body in the course of an illustrious career, including his skull in his final and fatal injury suffered at the age of 72 as he tried to break a bronc.

Oklahoma State Museum
2100 North Lincoln, Oklahoma City, OK 73105
(405) 521-2491
Hours: Mon.–Sat., 8 A.M.–5 P.M.
Admission: Free

Oklahoma's black heritage is interwoven throughout the history exhibits of the Oklahoma State Museum. The Civil War Battle of Honey Springs, buffalo soldiers, homesteaders, badmen, the law, and Edwin P. McCabe, among others, are recognized—if not given their due.

Sanamu African Gallery
Kirkpatrick Museum Complex, 2100 Northeast 52nd Street, Oklahoma City, OK 73111
(405) 427-7529
Hours: Mon.–Sat., 10 A.M.–5 P.M.; Sun., 12 P.M.–5 P.M.; closed Thanksgiving and Dec. 25
Admission: To all the complex's attractions: adults, $5; ages 5–12 and over 64, $3; children under 5, free

The Kirkpatrick Center Museum Complex includes the Sanamu African Gallery, which explores the cultures of sub-Saharan Africa through the medium of their traditional arts and crafts. In addition to the gallery's permanent exhibits, seminars, programs, special exhibits, and tour guides promote an understanding of the Mother Continent.

OKTAHA

Battle of Honey Springs Monument
South of Muskogee on U.S. 69 past Oktaha, then ½ mile north of Rentiesville
Hours: Daily until sunset
Admission: Free

The Battle of Honey Springs site contains a monument to and an interpretive marker about the Civil War experiences in Oklahoma of the 1st Kansas Colored Voluntary Infantry. Honey Springs was Oklahoma's largest Civil War encounter. The 1st Kansas saw action (driving a Texas regiment from the field of battle and capturing its regimental colors) the day before the 54th Massachusetts won renown at the assault on Fort Wagner. (See Battery Wagner entry on p. 135.) The black troops would also clash with Stand Watie's Confederates (see Fort Towson entry on p. 453) at the first and second Battles of Cabin Creek. A few days before the second battle, unarmed black Union troops gathering hay near Flatrock Creek were massacred, many after surrendering, at the so-called Hayfield Massacre.

PONCA CITY

Ponca City Cultural Center Museum
1000 East Grand Avenue, Ponca City, OK 74601
(405) 767-0427
Hours: Mon., Wed.–Sat., 10 A.M.–5 P.M.; Sun., 1 P.M.–5 P.M.
Admission: Out-of-town adults, $1; others, free

At their 101 Ranch south of Ponca, the Miller brothers transformed the informal challenges and local competitions between ranch hands into a flamboyant performance art form and a dangerous profession: the traveling rodeo. Among the stars of the 101 shows was Bill Pickett, who later went on to star in two silent-era films and whose death in 1932 prompted Will Rogers to write to *The New York Times*, America's newspaper of record, to alert the nation to its loss. Pickett was buried on the 101 Ranch beneath a marker erected by the Cherokee Strip Cowboys Association. 101's owner Zack Miller wrote a poem for the occasion: "If they check his brand, and I think they will, / It's a runnin' hoss they'll give to Bill. / And some good wild steers till he gets his fill. / With a great big crowd for him to thrill."

Among the less well known of the 101's black performers were Henry Clay, a rope twirler who worked with Will Rogers, and trick rider George Hooker. Still less well known is the fact that among their audiences in the Southwest were a substantial number of African-American cattle punchers. While the region and the occupation may have enjoyed the typical racism of the day, at the level of the working hand the latter was well integrated. If you've an interest in the grand run of the 101 Ranch, check out the show's memorabilia at the Ponca City Cultural Center. If you want to see Pickett's grave, head south of the town toward what is now a National Historic Landmark, the 101 Ranch.

TULSA

Convention & Visitors Bureau
616 South Boston Avenue, Suite 100, Tulsa, OK 74119-2198
(918) 585-1201
Hours: Mon.–Fri., 8 A.M.–5 P.M.

Greenwood Cultural Center
322 North Greenwood, Tulsa, OK 74120
(918) 585-2548
Hours: Mon.–Fri., 9 A.M.–5 P.M.
Admission: Free

TULSA HISTORICAL SOCIETY

In the midst of the racial conflagration of 1921, armed white patrols round up black men, the more fortunate of whom are not wounded.

As May moved into June of 1921, armed bands of whites and blacks confronted each other outside the Tulsa County Courthouse, inside of which a young African-American bootblack was held on charges of assaulting a white female elevator operator. (Specifically, she said that after entering the elevator "he grabbed my arm, I screamed and he fled.") While the police kept an open mind about the allegation—was it mere rudeness? assault? accidental collision? fantasy?—the local white press did not. As the chief of detectives explained, "The police were quietly conducting an investigation of the alleged incident before taking any action. But when the afternoon paper came out with an untrue and colored account . . . we concluded that it would be best for the safety of the negro to place him behind bars." When the sheriff refused to release the accused to the white mob assembled outside the courthouse, their mood grew more raucous. Suddenly, about 10 P.M., shots rang out, and the two armed bands began firing at each other. Once established order broke down, it was a simply question of which side had the more guns, aggression, and race hatred. As the mob of hundreds of lightly armed African Americans were driven back by its heavier-armed white counterpart, all hell broke loose. Soon carloads of armed whites were driving through Greenwood, Tulsa's thriving black district, killing, burning, and looting. Though the Oklahoma National Guard and troops from nearby Fort Sill were called in within hours, by the time they arrived anarchy reigned, with 3,000 armed rioters in open combat, Greenwood in flames, hundreds of African-American refugees fleeing to outlying towns, and at least 31 officially acknowledged deaths (22 black, 9 white).

Prior to the riot, north Tulsa, centered around Greenwood Avenue, was a prosperous district of about 10,000 people. By June 2, 35 blocks of north Tulsa were destroyed, with 1,200 homes, small businesses, and churches in ashes, including the Mount Zion Baptist Church, built for $84,000 and dedicated six weeks before whatever took place on May 30 in that elevator. It took years to fully rebuild a prosperous black community—years and the countless contributions of effort and money by Tulsa's African Americans. Today the Greenwood Cultural Center documents the resilience and contributions of Tulsa's black community with a exhibit of photographs covering almost a century, a gallery of the work of local black artists, the Mabel Little House (a black heritage museum), and an attached Oklahoma Jazz Hall of Fame.

A postscript: The bootblack was acquitted when the elevator operator declined to testify; the surprising result was that Tulsa's last lynching had taken place in 1920—and the victim was white.

Oklahoma Eagle
624 East Archer, Tulsa, OK 74120
(918) 582-7124
Hours: Daily, 8 A.M.–5 P.M.
Admission: Free

The *Oklahoma Eagle* is the oldest African-American newspaper in Oklahoma and the one major black enterprise to escape the flames of the 1921 riot. More than merely the voice of Tulsa's black community, the *Eagle* was one of the driving forces behind the rebuilding of Greenwood.

WISCONSIN

Department of Tourism
123 West Washington Avenue, Madison, WI 53707
(800) 432-8747
Hours: Mon.–Fri., 9 A.M.–5 P.M.

MADISON

State Historical Society of Wisconsin
816 State Street, Madison, WI 53703
Museum: (608) 264-6588. Library: (608) 264-6535
Hours: Museum: Tue.–Sat., 10 A.M.–5 P.M.; Sun., 12 P.M.–5 P.M. Library: Mon.–Thu., 8 A.M.–9 P.M.; Fri.–Sat., 8 A.M.–5 P.M.
Admission: Free

In 1994, the State Historical Society of Wisconsin Museum will open two exhibits that explore aspects of the local African-American experience. A display on heavy industry, which drew black workers to Wisconsin, particularly to Milwaukee, will use photographs and excerpts from oral histories to trace the post–World War I growth of urban black communities. An immigration exhibit will explore the same theme in a state that long has placed a premium on ethnic identification—though in Wisconsin this usually has turned on the differences between those of Norwegian as distinct from Swedish heritage. In addition, the society's library, which has the largest holding on U.S. history in the nation and which serves as the official archives for state papers, is of interest to those exploring Wisconsin's and America's black past. Some years back the library decided to build up a civil rights collection for future scholars. Today the archives of CORE (the Congress of Racial Equality), materials on the Angela Davis trial, the FBI file on Dr. Martin Luther King, Jr., and important documents concerning SNCC (Student Nonviolent Coordinating Committee) and the Mississippi Freedom Democratic Party are available, as are materials pertaining to slavery, the Civil War, and Reconstruction.

MILTON

Milton House Museum
18 South Janesville Street, Milton, WI 53563
(608) 868-7772
Hours: Tue.–Sun., 11 A.M.–4 P.M.
Admission: Adults, $3; ages 5–18, $1.75

Though Wisconsin entered the Union as a territory under the aegis of the Northwest Ordinance of 1787, which expressly prohibited slavery, sundry antebellum censuses record the presence of small numbers of slaves, most of whom belonged either to southern officers stationed at Fort Crawford or to slave holders who had located in the lead-mining section of Grant County. Among the latter was Henry Dodge, Wisconsin's first territorial governor (who in 1838 freed his five male slaves and provided each with 40 acres and a yoke of oxen). Wisconsin's population in 1840 was only 31,000, of whom 200 were black and only 11 enslaved. A decade later the population of the state had increased tenfold, but the African-American presence had yet to reach 700. The twin pressures of the 1850 Fugitive Slave Act, which encouraged runaways to move north and west to escape its effects, and of southern manumission, which usually required in law the removal of the freed, brought the state's black population to just under 1,200 on the eve of the Civil War.

Though the number of black residents was small, Wisconsin saw larger numbers of fugitive slaves cross its territory on the way to Canada, aided by the Underground Railroad. Remnants of the Railroad remain. The Milton House Museum once was a stagecoach inn and an Underground Railroad station connected by a tunnel to a nearby cabin where lived the inn's owners, the Goodriches. The inn's tunnel entrance was in its basement, hidden behind a grain storage bin. Today the 1844 inn, the tunnel, the 1837 cabin, and the family correspondence of its abolitionist owners have been preserved and may be viewed by visitors.

Visitors to the area should note that the Tallman House in neighboring Janesville, which frequently is referred to as an Underground Railroad station and a connecting link to the inn in Milton, evidently did *not* play a role in the effort to aid fugitive slaves. The Tallman House, built in the late 1850s by an abolitionist-minded, wealthy New York immigrant, had running water, central heating, indoor plumbing, and other conveniences not found often in rural Wisconsin. It is well worth a tour for those interested in exploring upper-class existence on the eve of the Civil War; however, its present curators emphasize the lack of any evidence to corroborate its links to the Underground Railroad and severely deprecate the likelihood of such a role.

MILWAUKEE

American Black Holocaust Museum

2233 North Fourth Street, Milwaukee, WI 53212
(414) 264-2500
Hours: Mon.–Sat., 9 A.M.–6 P.M.
Admission: Adults, $1.50; under 12, 75 cents

Focusing on "genocide and the injustices experienced by African Americans," in the words of its director, the American Black Holocaust Museum explores the Calvary of slavery and racism. Books, paintings, photographs of lynchings, and artifacts that trace the diaspora from Africa to victimization underscore its central theme.

Milwaukee Public Museum

800 West Wells Street, Milwaukee, WI 53203
(414) 278-2700
Hours: Daily, 9 A.M.–5 P.M.
Admission: Adults, $4; ages 4–17, $2

The environments, flora, fauna, and cultures of Africa are examined on the third floor of the Milwaukee Public Museum. Four large walk-through dioramas of an African water hole, the savannah, a bamboo forest, and a Masai lion hunt offer a limited but popular perspective on the Mother Continent. The museum explores the cultures of these ecologies and enables children, in particular, to consider the connections between environments and different ways of living, comparing, for example, the settled agricultural experiences of the Kikuyu and Ikoma to those of the pastoral Masai and Turkana peoples. The museum also offers visitors an overview of African art, including wooden masks, brass and bronze sculpture, terra-cotta heads, and ivory carvings, placing its objects in an appropriate cultural context.

WAUKESHA

Underground Railroad Historical Marker

Cutler Park, Waukesha, WI 53186
Hours: Daily until sunset
Admission: Free

Waukesha was on a main line of the Underground Railroad through Wisconsin in the 1850s. From here, fugitive slaves were forwarded to Milwaukee and then on to Canada, as is noted on the Underground Railroad Historical Marker (see Levi Coffin entry on p. 361) in Cutler Park.

Waukesha County Museum

101 West Main Street, Waukesha, WI 53186
(414) 548-7186
Hours: Tue.–Sat., 9 A.M.–4:30 P.M.; Sun., 1 P.M.–5 P.M.
Admission: Research facility, $1; Museum, free

Perhaps it was the straw that broke the camel's back or teenage rage and confusion exacerbated by her strange family position, but when her angry mistress—who also was her aunt—cut off her long hair, the 16-year-old slave Caroline Quarrels lit out for Canada, leaving Missouri, bondage, and her shorn locks behind. Quarrels's flight was aided by the fact that she was an octoroon with blue eyes and light freckled skin and possessed $100 given her by her black grandmother (who had purchased herself out of slavery) and the hand-me-down clothes of her mistress's daughters (who, of course, also were her cousins). With a $300 reward on her head, Quarrels fled through Wisconsin with slave hunters on her heels. In Milwaukee, she made the mistake of placing her confidence in a black barber, a former slave, who sought to turn her in for the reward. Fortuitously escaping the consequences of her error, Quarrels was aided by the Underground Railroad, passed through Waukesha, was taken in hand by Lyman Goodnow, found freedom in Canada, and left in her wake her story. Forty years later, in the 1880s, Quarrels—by now literate and married to a black man in Sandwich, Ontario—wrote Goodnow a letter of thanks. Today the Waukesha County Museum has a reasonably extensive file of local Underground Railroad information, including the details of the Quarrels affair and issues of the Waukesha abolitionist newspaper, the *American Freeman*, but no displays on the subject of abolitionism or the Underground Railroad. In nearby Prarie Home Cemetery (605 South Prarie Avenue; 414 524-3540), the Lyman Goodnow grave site may be found (Section M, block 17, lot 2, grave 3).

THE WEST

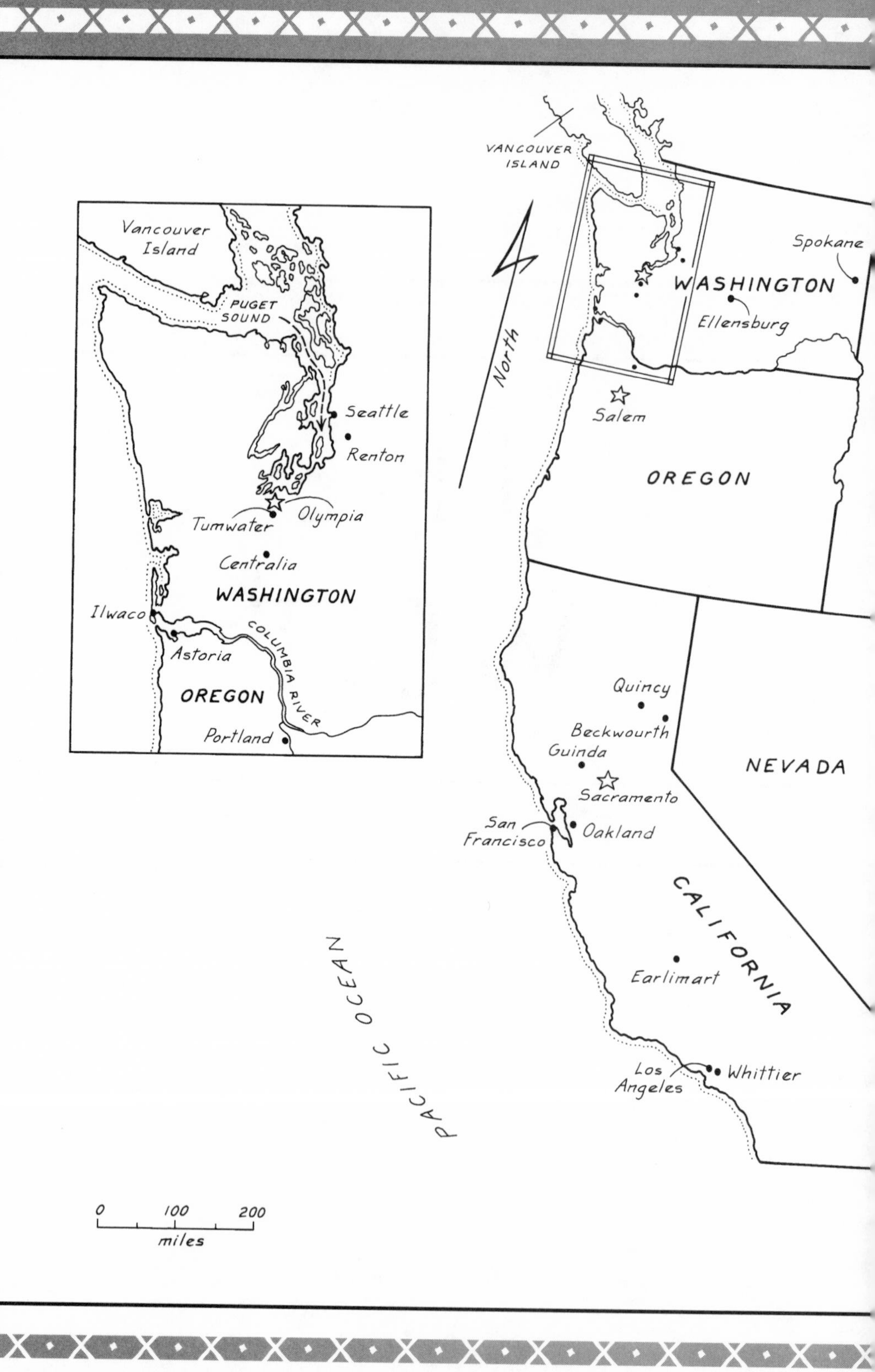

Vancouver Island
PUGET SOUND
Seattle
Renton
Olympia
Tumwater
Centralia
WASHINGTON
Ilwaco
Astoria
COLUMBIA RIVER
OREGON
Portland
VANCOUVER ISLAND
North
Spokane
WASHINGTON
Ellensburg
Salem
OREGON
Quincy
Beckwourth
Guinda
Sacramento
NEVADA
San Francisco
Oakland
CALIFORNIA
Earlimart
Los Angeles
Whittier
PACIFIC OCEAN
0
100
200
miles

MONTANA
Havre
Fort Shaw
Cascade
Missoula
Helena
White Sulphur Springs
Crow Agency
Virginia City
NORTH DAKOTA
Williston
Washburn
Bismarck
SOUTH DAKOTA
Wakpala
MISSOURI R.
Pierre
Fort Meade
Deadwood
Yankton
Pine Ridge
Vermillion
Pickstown
IDAHO
WYOMING
Sheridan
Buffalo
ROCKY MOUNTAINS
Fort Washakie
Fort Laramie
Cheyenne
UTAH
GREAT SALT LAKE
Salt Lake City
Fort Duchesne
COLORADO RIVER
COLORADO
Meeker
Central City
Denver
Wray
Colorado Springs
ARKANSAS RIVER
Pueblo
NEW MEXICO
Folsom
Santa Fe
Watrous
RIO GRANDE
Lincoln
Radium Springs
Bayar
Columbus
ARIZONA
Camp Verde
Fort Apache
Phoenix
Willcox
Tucson
Tombstone
Fort Huachuca
Hereford

THE RAINBOWING OF CALIFORNIA: MOVING FROM THE PAGE TO THE STREETS

ISHMAEL REED

Northern California, and especially Oakland, is the model for the coming rainbowing of America—in all its promise and peril. This multiculturalism looks good on paper, and in Oakland's literary world of Latino, Asian-American, African-American, and Euro-American writers, its promise has already been realized.

Spanish was California's first written language, and the state has boasted a thriving Hispanic theater since the times of Spanish and Mexican occupation. Latino writers have published in Oakland since those early days. More recently, the internationally recognized writer Victor Cruz lived in a Spanish-style apartment building across the street from Oakland's famed Lake Merrit until a few years ago. Today Lucha Corpi and Isabel Allende reside in Oakland. For her mystery novel, *Eulogy for a Brown Angel*, Ms. Corpi won the 1993 PEN Miles Book Award, named for the late poet and professor Josephine Miles. The president of PEN Oakland is the Basque-American Floyd Salas, whose recent novel *Buffalo Nickel* includes riveting scenes of his Oakland childhood.

Toshio Mori, author of *Yokahama California* and one of the first Asian-American authors to be published, was born in Oakland in 1910. Two well-known Asian-American writers whom some critics credit with spearheading the Asian-American renaissance in writing, Frank Chin—whose recent novel *Donald Duk* drew critical raves—and Shawn Wong—whose *Homebase* was published in the late 1970s by Steve Cannon and me—have ties to Oakland. Maxine Hong Kingston, whose latest book is *The Tripmaster Monkey*, still lives in Oakland.

Blacks have influenced writing in northern California directly or indirectly since the day the fabulous James P. Beckwourth, black frontiersman and one-time chief of the Crow Indians, rode into California with a small child named Ina Coolbrith sharing his saddle. Poet and mentor for Oakland's most famous writer, Jack London, Ms. Coolbrith became the first poet laureate of California in 1915. Earlier, in 1856, Mr. Beckwourth's exploits were detailed in *The Life and Adventures of James P. Beckwourth, as told to Thomas D. Bonner*. More recently the late Sarah Fabio, named "Mother of Black Studies" for her pioneering efforts to foster the study of African-American culture, was an Oaklander, as has been—from time to time—Maya Angelou. In 1993 David Hilliard and Elaine Brown, former members of the Black Panther Party, a group originally organized in Oakland to oppose police brutality, published their memoirs, and the Oakland Black Writers Group, headed by Ethel Mae Wilbert, held its annual picnic, at which a number of local poets, including Karla Brundridge, read their works. Oakland's African Americans have produced more than prose and poetry: The Oakland blues sound, influenced by music from Texas and Louisiana, has an international reputation.

Oakland's diverse traditions are most clearly reflected today in the annual PEN Oakland awards ceremony, where Latino, African-American, Asian-American, and European-American writers and their families gather to honor their colleagues' outstanding achievements. Although this rainbowing of Oakland extends beyond the literary world—ethnic people not only live in discrete enclaves but also side by side in the same neighborhood, and in 1993 Oakland was named an All-American City, with its mayor, Elihu Harris, receiving an award on the city's behalf from President Clinton—it remains to be seen whether multiculturalism can be gracefully translated from the page to the streets. If America's economic pie continues to shrink, African Americans, Latinos, Asian Americans, and European Americans may find themselves riven by squabbles over resources and the division of political power. In the last five years alone the city has seen disputes over personnel appointments (in the case of a fire chief, pitting Latinos against the black city manager); construction contracts (in the case of the site of Merrit College, scene of the first organizing efforts of the Black Panther Party, pitting a white feminist councilperson and an Asian-American architectural firm against the efforts of many in the black community); and political redistricting (with Asian Americans—backed by Latinos—carving out a district that made them the majority pitted against the white vice mayor, a black councilperson, and many black residents, who felt the new district would dilute their political clout).

Time magazine's special "California" issue accompanied my article about Oakland with a photograph of Preservation Park and the caption "Capital of Multi-Cultural America?" But it was the article's head, "Bad News for Blacks," that caused offense to some of those devoted to the dream of a multicultural Oakland. However, my observation in that article that 20 years from now blacks will look back to the present as the days when the only racism they had to be concerned about was white racism may not be as far-fetched as it seemed to some readers. This is not a happy prospect. I doubt whether the projects I've been engaged in—the Before Columbus Foundation and PEN Oakland, magazine and small press publishing, and television production—could have been accomplished had I not moved to northern California in 1967.

X·X·X

For more than a quarter of a century, the Pulitzer Prize nominee and National Book Award finalist ISHMAEL REED has lived in Oakland, California, the Black cauldron from which emerged Huey P. Newton, Bobby Seale, and the Black Panther Party. He is the author of more than 20 books, including *Mumbo Jumbo*, *The Terrible Threes*, *Reckless Eyeballing*, *Japanese by Spring*, and most recently *Airing Dirty Laundry*.

ARIZONA

Office of Tourism
1100 West Washington, Phoenix, AZ 85007
(602) 542-8687
Hours: Mon.–Fri., 8 A.M.–5 P.M.

CAMP VERDE

Fort Verde State Historic Park
Hollaman Street, Camp Verde, AZ 86322
(602) 567-3275
Hours: Daily, 8 A.M.–5 P.M.
Admission: Adults, $1; under 18, free

General George Crook added luster to his reputation during Arizona's Indian wars. His winter 1872–73 campaign against the Yavapai and the Tonto Apache drove both peoples onto reservations and somewhat quieted the area around Fort Verde. When the Yavapai Reservation was closed in 1875 and its inhabitants shipped to the San Carlos Reservation, the area became sufficiently a backwater that the army—which was spread incredibly thinly across the Southwest—tried to close the base and consolidate its forces in regions of greater danger. However, local businessman, who had no desire to lose their main market, applied political pressure at the territorial level to keep the fort open. At first it looked like the army would prevail, but with the tragic fiasco of the Cibicue Fight (provoked by a misguided attempt in 1881 to arrest a prominent "medicine man") and the Battle of Big Wash (July 1882), the fort was regarrisoned. It was still open in 1885, when companies I and M of the 10th Cavalry arrived for a three-year stay. For the black troopers, it was a quiet tour of garrison duty. Today Fort Verde's four extant buildings offer an excellent example of a midlevel campaign post from the period of Arizona's Indian wars. (The few other surviving Arizona posts are either reconstructed or were built after the conclusion of conflict.) Fort Verde State Historic Park also has a museum in which post life is interpreted and placed in a context of the Indian wars. Among the displays is a detailed biography of an enlisted black soldier. On file and available upon request are other biographies of the black troops who served at the fort after the flush of conflict had subsided. Names, birth dates and places, career summaries, and postcareer information yield a sense of the individual African Americans beneath the blue uniforms.

FORT APACHE

Old Fort Apache Museum

Log Cabin Road at Fort Apache (San Carlos Reservation), Fort Apache, AZ 85926
(602) 338-4625
On Highway 73, in the heart of the San Carlos Reservation
Hours: Sept.–May: Mon.–Fri., 8 A.M.–5 P.M. June–Aug.: daily, 7:30 A.M.–4:30 P.M.
Admission: Voluntary donations requested

In 1875, as the 9th Cavalry transitioned from Texas to Arizona and New Mexico (see Lincoln County entry on p. 505), government officials decided to abolish four reservations in Arizona and New Mexico and consolidate the Apache at the San Carlos Reservation, a barren and disease-ridden hellhole in the White Mountains overseen by Fort Apache. Trouble was inevitable and would have been both swifter and more intense except that Cochise, the dominant figure among the Chiricahua Apache for decades, had died in 1874 and his people lacked a widely accepted leader. At San Carlos two militant leaders arose: Victorio, a Mimbreño with a following among the Warm Springs Reservation Apache, and Goyahkla, a hitherto unknown and insignificant Chiricahua warrior who enters history under the name Geronimo. In the fall of 1877 Victorio broke out of San Carlos with about 300 Warm Springs followers and a few Chiricahua. In the following spring he surrendered in New Mexico, but only on the condition that he return to the Warm Springs Reservation that the government still wanted to close. Ordered back to San Carlos a year later, Victorio and 80 followers jumped the reservation, seeking to settle with the Mescalero Apache on their reservation. Later that year Victorio raided Warm Springs (see Fort Union entry on p. 507), killing several troopers of Company E of the 9th Cavalry before being tracked to the Chihuahua wastelands, where he was killed by the Mexican army.

Geronimo rode with the Nednhi band of Chiricahua, who made their home in the Sierra Madre in Mexico. He used the Warm Springs and San Carlos reservations as rest areas from and recruiting grounds for his raids. In the spring of 1877 John Clum, the renowned Indian agent, later founder and editor of the *Tombstone Epitath* and ancestor of my fifth-grade teacher, was ordered to Warm Springs to oversee the removal of 400 Chiricahua and Warm Springs Apache to San Carlos. He was supposed to be backed up by eight companies of the 9th Cavalry. When Clum arrived at Warm Springs, the 9th was absent; instead he found Geronimo stirring up trouble. Backed only by the reservation police, Clum arrested Geronimo and 16 other warriors, keeping them under close guard until the 9th rode up two days later. Geronimo was transferred to San Carlos, from which he jumped a year later, only to return in 1880.

At this juncture—tragedy having yielded to farce and farce to cliché—yet another Indian prophet arose, this one called Nakaidoklini. Promising the resurrection of the dead and the return of the halcyon days of raiding and killing, Nakaidoklini proved only half accurate, being himself killed in a reservation clash with U.S. Army troopers in 1881, shortly before Naiche (the son of Cochise), Juh (the Nednhi chief), a Chiricahua leader named Chato, Geronimo, and 74 other warriors jumped the reservation for Mexico. They returned to Arizona on raids, in 1882 killing between 30 and 50 white settlers. They also killed the police chief at San Carlos Reservation and compelled 300 Warm Springs Apache to follow them south. (The following year the new chief of police at San Carlos also was killed when the White Mountain Apache briefly rose up and avenged Nakaidoklini's death.) By March 1884 Geronimo, Chato, and the Warm Springs Apache were back on the San Carlos Reservation and at peace. In May 1885—just after the 10th Cavalry arrived in Arizona—Geronimo and Naiche again bolted the reservation. As always with the Indian wars, the cost of the army's operations was enormous, particularly measured against the few numbers of hostile Indians. The final operation (March–August 1886) against Geronimo had as its goal tracking down a total of 33 people—of whom 13 were women. Another measure of the same disparity (and of the extent to which a small group seizes the attention of folk history while an entire people is overlooked) is that with Geronimo's final surrender in August 1886, the Chiricahua were transported east en masse—all 498 of them—escorted to Florida by the 10th Cavalry. They moved to Oklahoma in 1894. As a tribe, they have never been permitted to return to Arizona: After 1913 they were allowed to move west—but only as far as the Mescalero Reservation in New Mexico.

Today visitors to the Old Fort Apache Museum get a comprehensive picture of the Apache experience, including a broad look at their cultural underpinning, the tension between acceptance and opposition to the reservation system, and their pivotal role as U.S. Army scouts who tracked down their raiding kindred. Incorporated in this interpretation is a review of the U.S. Army at Fort Apache, including displays about and photographs of the buffalo soldiers.

FORT HUACHUCA

Fort Huachuca Museum
Fort Huachuca Military Base, Fort Huachuca, AZ 85613
(602) 533-5736
Hours: Mon.–Fri., 9 A.M.–4 P.M.; Sat.–Sun., 1 P.M.–4 P.M.
Admission: Free

The largest African-American U.S. military base during World War II, Fort Huachuca housed the 92nd and 93rd divisions as well as units of the black Women's Army Corps (WACs). In one sense, the site was appropriate, for the fort earlier (1913–1931) had served as the regimental headquarters of the buffalo soldiers of the 10th Cavalry and (after 1931) the 24th Infantry. The past of America's major segregated black military post of the 20th century is still, if tenuously, on view at the fort. From the base's front gate, near which stands an

COURTESY FORT HUACHUCA MUSEUM

At Fort Huachuca, the black buffalo soldiers are honored for their role in the Indian wars of the 19th century.

eight-foot bronze statue of a 19th-century 10th Cavalry trooper, to the Fort Huachuca Museum, slices of the African-American military experience in the last century are explored. At the museum, visitors will find dioramas with life-size mannequins; photographs of black troopers; a World War II exhibit (with more focus on the 92nd Division, which saw service in Italy, than on the 93rd, which served in the Pacific); a small exhibit on the general history of buffalo soldiers, black troops in the military, and the diaspora in the Southwest; original 19th-century uniforms and equipment; and an exhibit on General Pershing, who served with the black troopers of the 10th Cavalry.

HEREFORD

Coronado National Memorial

East Montezuma Canyon Road, Hereford, AZ 85615
(602) 366-5515
22 miles south of Sierra Vista, by way of Highway 92 and a park road
Hours: Visitor Center: daily, 8 A.M.–5 P.M.
Admission: Free

One of the greatest stories of escape, endurance, and exploration began in the New World in the spring of 1528, when the ill-fated expedition of Pánfilo de Nárvaez arrived to explore Florida. Within months the expedition collapsed into a chaotic attempt to survive. Building five crude boats, the explorers left the west coast of Florida and drifted to the mouth of the Mississippi River and then to present-day Galveston, Texas, where a few men got ashore and were succored by the Karankawa Indians. Soon the survivors had been reduced to four, all of whom were enslaved by the local Indians. Among the four was Estevan, usually referred to by a diminutive that probably owed more to his status—born in Morocco, he was a slave of Andres Dorantes—than his size. After six years Estevanico and his three white companions fled their from captors—and after another two years of wandering through a land no European or African had ever seen, they reached refuge with the Spanish in Mexico. The account of their incredible trek written by their leader Álvar Núñez Cabeza de Vaca records a physical and spiritual journey and arguably represents the first piece of American literature. Certainly it ranks with Cortés's five letters to the emperor as must reading for European man's initial encounters with aboriginal America. (As well as being less self-justifying than Cortés's letters, de Vaca's account inspired one of 20th-century literature's most overlooked achievements, Haniel Long's *The Marvelous Adventures of Cabeza de Vaca*.)

Of Estevanico, who learned the rudiments of six Indian languages, de Vaca wrote: "[He] was our go-between; he informed himself about the ways we wished to take, what towns there were, and the matters we desired to know." It was a role the Moroccan would continue after safety was reached, for while the three white men sailed away to safer harbors, Estevanico was sold by his master and fellow survivor Dorantes (whose cupidity and ingratitude clearly knew no bounds) to the viceroy of New Spain, who used the African as his guide to the farther reaches of his uncharted land. In 1539 Estevanico led Father de Niza's expedition in search of the fabled Cibola, or "The Seven Cities of Gold." It was a journey from which he would not return—and in part it was his fault, for his accounts embellishing Indian tales that the four escapees had heard on their two-year trek had helped spark gold fever. (Also stimulating the viceroy was the exploration launched from Florida by Hernando de Soto; each New World proconsul or conquistador feared that the last great golden city would fall to a rival.)

Estevanico's exploration and his life reached beyond the Sierra Vista pass through the Huachuca Mountains and into New Mexico—and the Zunis of Pueblo Háwikuh. His death and the failure of the de Niza expedition were mere prelude for the more famous exploration of Francisco Vásquez de Coronado, an expedition of 300 armored soldiers, 800 Indian allies, and a traveling party of pigs, chickens, and cattle. Coronado, married to the daughter of an illegitimate son of Spain's first king, Ferdinand, and a man whose sole previous military experience was crushing a black slave rebellion in Amatepeque, relied on the maps produced by the first nonaboriginal to stride through the wasteland of Arizona into New Mexico. Today visitors to Coronado National Memorial are offered an interpretation of the first organized exploration of the American Southwest. Only in the visitor center video is any mention made of the de Niza expedition and Estevan; if you ask one of the staff, more details will be provided. (Though there are no details at the site, those who wish to stand on the spot where Estevanico met his death may visit Zuni, New Mexico. South of Zuni Pueblo, one will find the Háwikuh ruins, where the bones of an African explorer turned to dust and were blown across a land that would give scant recognition to its first recorded explorer.)

PHOENIX

Arizona State Capitol
1700 West Washington, Phoenix, AZ 85007
(602) 542-3701 (research library)
Hours: Mon.–Fri., 8 A.M.–5 P.M.
Admission: Free

One of the eight panels of the "Pageant of Arizona Progress" mural that graces the third-floor research library of the Arizona State Capitol portrays Estevanico, the African guide of the de Niza expedition that laid the groundwork for Coronado's subsequent exploration of the Southwest. (See preceding entry.) Estevanico, who earlier had been one of the few survivors of the Nárvaez expedition through Florida, entered modern-day Arizona in May 1539 through the Huachuca Mountains. He continued north and east along what is now called the Coronado Trail and entered modern-day New Mexico, where he met his death at the hands of the Háwikuh Zuni. Born in Morocco, Estevanico spent most of his life in slavery, which perhaps accounts for why a man with only a retinue of Indians, a pair of greyhounds, and a hell of a nerve became the first non-aboriginal to blaze a path across Arizona and yet has to defer in the history books to a man who followed his trail with an escort of 300 armored soldiers.

TOMBSTONE

Boot Hill Cemetery
Highway 80 West, Tombstone, AZ 85638
(602) 457-3348
Hours: Daily, 7:30 A.M.–6 P.M.
Admission: Voluntary donations requested

In 1945 Tombstone's Boot Hill Cemetery had a new resident, John Swain Slaughter, 99 years and nine months old. Born into slavery, Swain traveled west with his former masters, the Slaughters of Georgia, after the Civil War. Most of the family settled in Texas, but John Slaughter continued on to New Mexico and then Arizona, where he purchased a ranch and served as sheriff of Cochise County from 1887 through 1890. Swain stayed with John Slaughter and served as his ranch hand. Swain's burial was a civic event, celebrating the last survivor of the legendary mining town's wild days. Over his grave on row 11, the city erected a special marker to a "worthy pioneer."

TUCSON

Pima Air & Space Museum
6000 East Valencia Road, Tucson, AZ 85706
(602) 574-0646
Hours: Daily, 9 A.M.–5 P.M.
Admission: Adults, $5; seniors and military, $4; ages 10–17, $3; ages 9 and under, free

COURTESY PIMA AIR & SPACE MUSEUM

Janet Harmon Bragg (second from right), both as an African American and as a woman, was a pioneering pilot.

"It was *my* plane—and I was sharing it with them" was the answer the Georgia-born African-American pilot Janet Harmon Bragg gave when years later she was asked how male pilots at the racially segregated flying classes where she earned her wings in the 1930s responded to her presence. Bragg's career in aviation, which included a role in getting the support of then Senator Harry S Truman for the Tuskegee Airmen Experiment, is one of the highlights of the African-American exhibit at the Pima Air & Space Museum. Material on the Tuskegee airmen; on Captain Lloyd "Fig" Newton, the first African-American member of the Air Force's acrobatic flying team, the Thunderbirds; and on the black contribution to America's space effort complement the host of aircraft and other exhibits available for viewing.

WILLCOX

Rex Allen Museum
155 North Railroad Avenue, Willcox, AZ 85643
(602) 384-4583
Hours: Daily, 10 A.M.–4 P.M.
Admission: Individual, $2; couple, $3; family, $5

An exhibit on the Caleb Martin family, Arizona's most successful African-American ranching family of the early 20th century, will be found at the Rex Allen Museum. The reality of photographs and artifacts, including one of the ranch's branding irons, complements the museum's theme—the life and career of the Hollywood singing cowboy Rex Allen. The films of Allen, a slightly less well-known version of Gene Autry and Roy Rogers, range from the mid-1940s through the 1960s and now serve to mark both a time that never was and one that has passed. Yippee ki ay!

Chiricahua National Monument
Faraway Ranch, Dos Cabezas Route, Box 6500, Willcox, AZ 85643
(602) 824-3560
Hours: Park: 24 hours. Visitor Center and Faraway Ranch: daily, 8 A.M.–5 P.M. Tours: Sat.–Sun., 1 P.M.
Admission: Park: $4 per car, $1 per person on tour bus. Faraway Ranch and tours, free

All 12 companies of the 10th Cavalry left Texas in 1885 for Arizona, arriving in April, less than a month before Geronimo and about 150 Chiricahua jumped the San Carlos Reservation. The army quickly established a line of temporary encampments from Patagonia to the Rio Grande. In August Company E moved into temporary camp at Bonita Canyon, where they later were replaced by Company H and then I. To pass the time, the troops would collect, polish, and then inscribe stones with their names, units, and the date. Eventually these stones formed the blocks of a three-tiered monument to the late President Garfield, who had been assassinated in 1881 by a crazed religious fanatic. Reared in rural poverty, from which he escaped via education and the Disciples of Christ Church, Garfield became the youngest major-general in the Union army during the Civil War. During the war he commanded black troops and fought for their right to equal pay. The buffalo soldiers of the 10th, the lineal descendants of the men Garfield had commanded and supported, had not forgotten what few Americans now know. Nor, evidently, had they forgotten their regimental history, for among the stones inscribed, one bore the name of Henry O. Flipper, the first black graduate of West Point and a former 10th officer who had taken part in the campaign against Victorio and then been dishonorably discharged largely on racial grounds. (See Fort Davis entry on p. 161). (Flipper, apparently a poor record keeper, had been charged with embezzlement; a court martial properly found him innocent on this charge but decided, quite possibly correctly, that he had lied in an attempt to gain time to sort out his books and that this constituted "conduct unbecoming an officer and a gentleman.") Flipper had an exceptionally distinguished career after leaving the 10th, among other things serving as the editor of a Nogales, Arizona, newspaper in the 1880s, a translator for the Senate Committee on Foreign Relations, and a special assistant to the secretary of the interior.

In time, the Garfield monument collapsed and the inscribed stones were used for the chimney and fireplace of the Faraway Ranch. The ranch is now part of the Chiricahua National Monument and may be toured by visitors, who will still be able to read the names of the black troopers. Also available are tours of the park that include a summary of a trooper's day and visits to the remnants of the tent sites, sentry posts, and campgrounds of companies E, H, and I of the 10th. (Not too far away are the ruins of old Fort Bowie. The site sometimes is mentioned as having a connection to the buffalo soldiers; in fact, there is no record that they were ever stationed here, though some of their individual companies reported to the officer commanding Fort Bowie.)

CALIFORNIA

Office of Tourism
801 K Street, Suite 1600, Sacramento, CA 95814
(916) 322-2881
Hours: Mon.–Fri., 8 A.M.–5 P.M.

BECKWOURTH

Beckwourth Pass, Marker and Cabin
Cabin: Rocky Point Road, Beckwourth, CA 96129
(916) 283-6320
On Highway 70, 1½ miles east of Chilcoot
Hours: Daily until sunset
Admission: Free

"Some men rob you with a six-gun and some with a fountain pen" was a truth the black explorer, trapper, trader, and speculator James Beckwourth (see El Pueblo Museum entry on p. 494) learned long before Woody Guthrie wrote "The Ballad of Pretty Boy Floyd." In 1851 Beckwourth discovered what was then the lowest and least precarious pass through the Sierra Nevada Mountains. The Beckwourth Pass crossed the middle fork of the Feather River and headed down into Marysville, the pathway to California's northern goldfields. Almost immediately, the explorer lost money on his discovery. On the promise of payment by the Marysville town government, Beckwourth & Company constructed through the pass a wagon road that served as the main emigrant trail into the region. Judged by the August 13, 1853, issue of the *Marysville Herald*, Beckwourth never got paid despite repeated attempts to collect the money owed. Undaunted, he settled in the valley and became an innkeeper and trading post manager, all the while continuing to lead wagon trains over the pass. Clearly, he understood the principle of synergy—or at least of monopoly: The wagon trains he led stopped for rest and provisions at the first ranch on the California side of the pass. Here, on his property, he built a series of cabins. In 1855, in the third Beckwourth Cabin, he dictated his memoirs, which were published the following year by Harper & Row as *The Life and Adventures of James P. Beckwourth.* Today a historical marker will be found on the California side of the pass about 1.5 miles east of Chilcoot on CA. 70. The Beckwourth Cabin, which was moved to its present site in 1985, cannot be entered; it lies midway between Portola and the town of Beckwourth. (Also see Plumas County Museum entry on p. 488.)

COURTESY PLUMAS COUNTY MUSEUM

James Beckwourth, displayed at the Plumas County Museum in Quincy, California.

EARLIMART

Colonel Allensworth State Historic Park

Star Route 1, Box 148, Earlimart, CA 93219
(805) 849-3433
8 miles west of Earlimart on California 43 between Fresno and Bakerfield
Hours: Visitor Center: daily, 8 A.M.–4 P.M. Museum: daily, 10 A.M.–3 P.M. Park: daily, 8 A.M.–4:30 P.M.
Admission: Visitor Center and Museum: Free. Park: per vehicle, $3; camping fee, $8

The adage is wrong: Prophets are honored in their own country—just not in their own time. Born into slavery in Kentucky in 1842, Allen Allensworth learned the rudiments of reading while playing with white companions. He paid for his audacity by being sold south at the age of 12. Passing through the hands of various dealers, he ended up in New Orleans, the property of Fred Skruggs, whom he later remembered as "the nicest of all" his masters. Skruggs let the lad learn to read and trained him to be a jockey. Returning later with his new master to Kentucky for some horse races, Allensworth seized the opportunity of the Civil War to flee to Union forces, to which he first attached himself as a nurse.

In 1863 he entered the U.S. Navy as a wardroom steward. Discharged a year later, he already had attained the rank of first-class petty officer. After the war he opened two restaurants in St. Louis with his brother, before heeding the call to become a Baptist minister. In 1886 he successfully applied to become the chaplain of the 24th Infantry, one of the four African-American regiments then maintained on the U.S. Army's rolls. Traveling with the 24th troopers from Fort Supply, Indian Territory (Oklahoma), to Fort Huachuca, Arizona (see entry on p. 474), and Fort Douglas, Utah (see entry on p. 520), and on through the campaign in the Philippines, Allensworth rose in rank, retiring in 1906 as a lieutenant colonel. At the time that was the highest rank ever attained by an African American.

Though 64, Allensworth was just beginning his real life's work. After touring the country preaching a black self-help philosophy, Allensworth put his teachings into practice. In conjunction with William Payne and three other black men equally determined to escape the constraints of white America, he established an African-American community in California. Located in Tulare County near a railroad depot and several artesian wells, a new all-black town of Allensworth sprang up, centered squarely in the tradition of Boley and Langston, Oklahoma; Mound Bayou, Mississippi; and Nicodemus, Kansas. The town of Allensworth prospered. Homes, farms, a school, a church, a library, and then a post office arose, as did a hotel, a machine shop, and several stores. A debating team, a children's glee club, and a drama club offered opportunities to the town's 300 residents, who included Joshua Singleton, the son of Benjamin "Pap" Singleton, the "father" of the Kansas Exoduster movement. In 1914 the town precinct became a judicial district and a justice of the peace and a constable were elected, the first African Americans to hold the offices in California's history.

The year closed on a more ominous note, however. The state legislature killed Allensworth's dream of locating an all-black state vocational school in the town—a dream opposed by the black community of Los Angeles, which favored integration over separation. Then in September Allensworth traveled to the Monrovia suburb of Los Angeles to preach. Stepping down from a streetcar, he was struck fatally by a motorcycle. Thereafter the town declined. The very success of California's farming depleted the water table, the railroad moved its depot, and the depression struck. World War II supplied the coup de grâce, the burgeoning shipyards and defense industries sucking whole populaces into the cities. Oakland swelled; Allensworth's bubble burst and the town withered and died.

Today the townsite is the Colonel Allensworth State Historic Park and serves as a monument to the man and to the African-American contribution to California. Visitors may tour the park daily; a telephone call in advance yields a guided tour with explanations and historic notes. Of the restored buildings, the most significant is the schoolhouse, which now is furnished as it would have been on a school day in 1915. Push a button and you hear an audio presentation. Audio presentations are available also at Grosse's Drug Store and the Singleton General Store. Colonel Allensworth's home is furnished in the period of 1912 and contains memorabilia from his life in the ministry and the army. The visitor center offers a 30-minute video presentation, "The Spirit of Allensworth."

GUINDA

"Owl Rock"
Off CA. 16, Guinda, CA 95637
Hours: Daily until sunset
Admission: Free

Nigger Hill, the black settlement's name on the maps of the day, tells you a great deal about the times and the people but little about the location: The place name was as common in America as the colloquial parlance. In Yolo County, California, it referred to the turn-of-the-century black homesteads overlooking the town of Guinda. High above the valley, remote and inaccessible from transportation, the county seat, and white folks, black ranchers and farmers strove to make a living on undesirable land, the only land readily available to them. On what once was the main road leading to the summit, the African-American residents (and others) etched their names in a large sandstone boulder, leaving mute testimony to their presence, to their marginalization, and to the fact that no matter how high you go, you're still black. Today "Owl Rock," somewhat defaced over the years, remains the sole physical evidence of the early black settlement. Although the forthright use of the pejorative Nigger Hill indicates that the black settlement's founding dates back to earlier days, those days were within the 20th century: Until 1900, California's homestead laws required a homesteader to be a white citizen. On the boulder, look for the names Logan, Simpson, Campbell, Haskell, and Hickerson, all of whom were among the pioneer settlers.

LOS ANGELES

Convention & Visitors Bureau
685 South Figueroa Street, Los Angeles, CA 90017
(213) 689-8822
Hours: Mon.–Fri., 8 A.M.–5 P.M.; Sat., 8:30 A.M.–5 P.M.

Afro-American Art Collection
Golden State Mutual Life Insurance Company, 1999 West Adams, Los Angeles, CA 90018
(213) 731-1131
Hours: Tours by appointment (groups of 30 and under): Mon.–Thu., 9 A.M.–4 P.M.; Fri., 9 A.M.–11 A.M.
Admission: Free

In the past—to somewhat arbitrarily select among the three tenses—African Americans found it difficult to get insurance and impossible to do so at nondiscriminatory rates. Expressly created to respond to this situation, the Golden State Guarantee Fund Insurance Company of Los Angeles was chartered in

1925. Today its headquarters is a showcase for an Afro-American Art Collection. Black pioneers of the West, and particularly of California, figure in two historic and historical murals executed by Hale Woodruff and Charles Alston, respectively. Estevan (see Coronado Memorial entry on p. 475); Jim Beckwourth (see El Pueblo Museum entry on p. 494); William Leidesdorff, the state's first black millionaire (see Leidesdorff Grave entry on p. 489); Mary Ellen Pleasant, an early civil rights activist; and a host of black soldiers, miners, and settlers claim the attention of those who seek attention for their claims.

California Afro-American Museum
600 State Drive, Exposition Park, Los Angeles, CA 90037
(213) 744-7432
Hours: Tue.–Sun., 10 A.M.–5 P.M.
Admission: Museum: free. Parking: $3 per vehicle

The art, history, and culture of African Americans and the heritage of the diaspora in the New World form the frame on which hang the sundry temporary exhibits of the California Afro-American Museum. Retrospectives of black artists, the history of blacks in the state, and the impact of Africa on Brazil, Mexico, and the rest of Latin America and the Caribbean are explored through paintings, sculpture, photographs, and artifacts.

Los Angeles County Museum of Art
5905 Wilshire Boulevard, Los Angeles, CA 90036
(213) 857-6000
Hours: Tue.–Thu., 10 A.M.–5 P.M.; Fri., 10 A.M.–9 P.M.; Sat.–Sun., 11 A.M.–6 P.M.
Admission: Adults, $6; seniors and students with I.D., $4; children, $1

Though its collection of sub-Saharan art is limited, the Egyptian material at the Los Angeles County Museum of Art is extensive and significant and ranges from pre-Dynastic through Roman eras. Particularly interesting is the 21st-dynasty sarcophagus decorated with vignettes from *The Book of the Dead,* which offers the viewer a slice of life, as it were, following the end (20th dynasty) of the New Kingdom. Deities of the 26th dynasty (663–525 B.C.), who evidently blessed Psamtik II—invader of Kush—recall the brief revival Egypt enjoyed following Kushite overlordship and Assyrian occupation, a revival soon cut short by the rise of Persia. Among the sub-Saharan pieces, the Benin bronze plaque, the Yoruba ancestral figure, the Senufo fetish figure, and the Bamana headcrest stand out.

Los Angeles County Museum of Natural History
900 Exposition Boulevard, Exposition Park, Los Angeles, CA 90007
(213) 744-3414
Hours: Tue.–Sun., 10 A.M.–5 P.M.
Admission: Adults, $5; seniors and students, $3.50; ages 5–12, $2; under 5, free

In 1521 a small band of virile, violent, and voracious Spaniards overthrew the century-long Aztec despotism and set in motion the mass importation of

African slaves to work Mexico's fields and silver mines. Though Hernán Cortés and his colleagues justly won recognition for their courage and skill and though the culture of the southern half of the New World is termed Hispanic, it was primarily African, not European blood that mixed with the aboriginal population and formed the multiracial and multicultural mélange that is Mexico. Just 125 years after Cortés's conquest, the 1646 census of Mexico City counted 36,000 African slaves and 115,000 persons of African descent; the same census recorded the presence of 14,000 Europeans. The disparity would have been far greater in the silver-mining areas that cut a swath across central Mexico in the present-day states of Jalisco, Michoacán, and Guanajuato.

Little more than a decade after the first Hispanic settlement near San Diego in 1769, recruitment for a settlement in Alta California got under way in the Pacific Coast state of Sinaloa. The offer of free land under the protection of a nearby military garrison appealed to the poor and the ambitious of Rosario village, two-thirds of whose inhabitants the census labeled as mulatto, and 44 settlers arrived in present-day Los Angeles in 1781. Though estimates vary, the burden of scholarship suggests that 26 of Los Angeles's founders were partially or wholly of African descent. Today one of the dioramas at the County Museum of Natural History depicts the founding of Los Angeles by a party substantially reflecting the diaspora's presence in the New World.

Museum of African-American Art
4005 Crenshaw Boulevard, Third floor of the May Co. store, Los Angeles, CA 90008
(213) 294-7071
Hours: Wed., Fri., Sat., 11 A.M.–6 P.M.; Thu., 12 P.M.–6 P.M.; Sun., 12 P.M.–5 P.M.
Admission: Free

While working as a janitor, Palmer Hayden took first prize in the Harmon Foundation painting exhibition of 1927. First oriented toward a greenish-gray palette and sailing boats in harbor or at sea, Hayden shifted to satirical portraits of Harlem life, earning—or in any event, provoking—the criticism of James A. Porter, whose 1943 work, *Modern Negro Art*, was the first serious study of African-American art history. (Though best known as the unofficial "Father of African-American Art History," Porter himself was a black artist of note and won honorable mention in the 1930 Harmon Foundation Exhibition.) For decades a leading light of the Harlem Renaissance, Hayden today finds his most comprehensive portrayal at the Museum of African-American Art. Probably the only museum located within a department store, this museum boldly, if prescriptively, proclaims creative endeavor and its appreciation as aspects of daily life. The Palmer Hayden Collection and Archives is the museum's most notable feature and is complemented by paintings, sculptures, masks, carvings, and ceremonial objects from Africa. The art of the diaspora in the United States, the Caribbean, and Latin America also find a home here.

El Pueblo de Los Angeles Historic Park
Sepulveda House Visitor Center, 622 North Main Street, Los Angeles, CA 90012
Hours: Tue.–Sat., 10 A.M.–4 P.M.
Admission: Free

Today, in the heart of downtown Los Angeles, El Pueblo de Los Angeles Historic Park consists of the restored historic buildings and cultural exhibits associated with the founding and early days of Los Angeles. Included here is the not-yet-restored hotel of Pio Pico, a mulatto who served as the last Mexican governor of California and who sought to transfer the state capital to the city of angels. (See Pio Pico State Park entry on p. 490.) On the south side of the plaza is the Founders Plaque, which lists the names, genders, ages, and racial backgrounds of the 11 families that first settled here in 1781. Visitors will note that more than half of the city's founders were of African extraction.

OAKLAND

Convention & Visitors Bureau
1000 Broadway, Suite 200, Oakland, CA 94607
(510) 839-9000
Hours: Mon.–Fri., 8:30 A.M.–5 P.M.

Ebony Museum of Art
30 Alice Street, Oakland, CA 94607
(510) 763-0141
Hours: Tue.–Sat., 11 A.M.–6 P.M.; Sun., 12 P.M.–6 P.M.
Admission: Free

Knives and other weapons, household implements, items of personal adornment, and the art of a wide range of African peoples are on display at the Ebony Museum of Art. Shedding light on the diaspora's experience in America are artifacts from the era of slavery; everyday items of the early 20th century, such as cookie jars, cards, and posters, that portray African Americans in a disparging manner; memorabilia of the local black community; and an exhibit on African-American foods. Completing the Ebony Museum's offerings are changing exhibits of contemporary African-American art.

Northern California Center for Afro-American History and Life
5606 San Pablo Avenue, Oakland, CA 94612
(510) 658-3158
Hours: Tue.–Fri., 12:30 P.M.–5 P.M. Research hours: by appointment
Admission: Free

The focus of the museum and research library of the Northern California Center for Afro-American History and Life is narrow—it deals only with black history in California. Consequently, it is positioned to explore its subject in depth. Rather than another superficial exhibit on acknowledged African-American heroes such as Frederick Douglass, Harriet Tubman, the buffalo soldiers, or the Tuskegee airmen, the center alerts visitors to the lives and work of, among others, C. O. Dellums, the leading figure in the West Coast black trade union movement and a power on the Fair Employment Practices Commission; Bryon Rumford, author of the Fair Housing Act that bears his name; and Frederick Madison Roberts, the first African American to serve (1916) in the California legislature and a descendant of Sally Hemings—and thus conceivably of Thomas Jefferson. The center's archive is full of photos, manuscripts, records of black organizations, and oral histories. If it's not on display, ask to see it; chances are you'll find what you want.

Oakland Art Museum
1000 Oak Street, Oakland, CA 94607
(510) 238-3005
Hours: Wed.–Sat., 10 A.M.–5 P.M.; Sun., 12 P.M.–7 P.M.
Admission: Free

Measured from the earliest days of nonaboriginal exploration and settlement through the present, California's history is streaked with black. From the 1774 de Anza expedition, which was accompanied by a substantial number of soldiers and servants of partial African extraction, and the founding of Los Angeles in 1748 by 44 settlers, of whom 26 were black or mulatto, through the rise of the Black Panther Party, California's African-American history is interpreted through artifacts and wall text in the Cowell Hall of the Oakland Museum of Art. Photographs of Pio Pico, one of California's two black governor's during the Mexican period, and of the black explorer James Beckwourth are balanced by artifacts similar to those that they would have possessed and used in the course of their widely divergent careers. Photographs of African-American miners drawn to California during the gold rush are complemented by the ivory-handled walking stick, captain's license, and family photograph of William Shorey, possibly the only 19th-century black sea captain on the Pacific Coast. The 19th-century struggle against the state's racial restrictions is represented by artifacts of and text about the black Franchise League, four Conventions of Colored Citizens of the State of California, and the black newspapers of the period. The struggle for civil rights and economic advancement also dominate the museum's exploration of the 20th century, which uses photographs, artifacts, and explanatory text to traverse the experiences of trade unionism and its racial exclusions, the rise of defense industries and of government employment as avenues of opportunity, the Watts riot and various expressions of black nationalism, and the emergence of a black political elite occupying senior city and state positions. If you don't go, you won't know. If you do go, you also get to see a wide range of contemporary African-American paintings, many of them by nationally prominent Oakland artists such as Raymond Saunders and Robert Colescott.

QUINCY

Plumas County Museum
500 Jackson Street, Box 10776, Quincy, CA 95971
(916) 283-6320
Hours: May–Oct.: Mon.–Fri., 8 A.M.–5 P.M.; Sat.–Sun., 10 A.M.–4 P.M. Rest of year: Mon.–Fri., 8 A.M.–5 P.M.
Admission: Voluntary donations requested

The black explorer and scout James Beckwourth (see Beckwourth Pass entry on p. 480 and El Pueblo Museum entry on p. 494) is the center of attention at the Plumas County Museum, though there is some doubt that all the objects to which his name is attached were really his. The daguerrotype is certainly of Beckwourth, as are the reproductions of the photographs of him. The documents are soundly attributed and include Beckwourth's agreement with the author of his biography, mortgages, and a suit Beckwourth filed in court alleging the theft of a wagon and grindstone. The Beckwourth artifacts—a pair of wooden stirrups, a table from his cabin, and a bullet mold—are less certainly his, but the claims regarding them have the merit of dating back to the 19th century, when there was less charm in possessing the remnants of a life of a black man. In any event, we know enough of the real Beckwourth to be confident of his response to the possibly incorrect attributions—a crow of laughter.

SACRAMENTO

St. Andrew's A.M.E. Church
2131 Eighth Street, Sacramento, CA 95818
(916) 448-1428
Hours: Exterior viewing: Daily until sunset
Admission: Free

St. Andrew's A.M.E. Church is the lineal descendant and current designation of what was the first A.M.E. church on the Pacific Coast. Formed in 1850, the congregation built its first frame structure and was admitted into A.M.E. membership a year later. The frame building was the site of the first organized activity by California's African Americans, hosting in 1855 and 1856 the first two conventions of the Colored Citizens of the State of California. In 1855 this organization created a discretionary fund of $10,000 to wage a statewide campaign against the statutory disenfranchisement of African Americans. In the church's basement the first school for blacks, Indians, and Asians was opened. Present-day St. Andrew's is not located on the original church site, nor does it have a historical marker proclaiming its significance—an absence more surprising when one examines the Sacramento County chapter of *California Historical Landmarks*. If the California Almond Growers Exchange Processing Facility, the site of the first county library branch in California, the commercial Overton Building, and the site of the first Jewish cemetery (Chevra Kaddisha), among many others, merit mention, how is it that either the original site (which is now county property) of what was then Bethel A.M.E. Church or present-day St. Andrew's remains unmarked? In addition to being unmarked by the state, St. Andrew's itself has yet to display visible evidence of its historic past.

SAN FRANCISCO

Convention & Visitors Bureau
Powell and Market streets, San Francisco, CA 94102
(415) 391-2000
Hours: Mon.–Fri., 9 A.M.–5:30 P.M.; Sat., 9 A.M.–3 P.M.; Sun., 10 A.M.–2 P.M.

Leidesdorff Grave and Street
Misión San Francisco de Asís (Mission Dolores), 16th and Dolores streets, San Francisco, CA 94110
(415) 621-8203
Hours: Daily, 9 A.M.–4:30 P.M.
Admission: Suggested donation, $1

The interior of Misión San Francisco de Asis, California's sixth mission, dedicated by Father Junípero Serra in 1776, holds but six honored graves. One, the William Leidesdorff Grave, commemorates the founder of the city's public school system, a benefactor to freed slaves, and a locally prominent commercial and political figure during the transition from Mexican to American rule. Born in 1810 to a Danish father and a mulatto mother on the Virgin Islands, then a Danish possession, Leidesdorff arrived in the village of San Francisco in 1841. By the time of his death seven years later, he had made a fortune, received a substantial land grant from Mexico, launched the first steamboat in the San Francisco Bay, sat on the city council and the city's school committee, and served as the vice-consul to Mexico under Commodore Stockton's military rule of California during the Mexican War. Following his untimely death the city fathers gave him an impressive funeral. The following year the California legislature, sitting in its first session, enacted laws that barred African Americans from voting, testifying in court against a white person, receiving a public education, or homesteading on public lands. Today there is no statue to a man who assisted black (and other) folks trying to establish themselves in small businesses in the days before the gold rush widened opportunities; instead there is Leidesdorff Street, a lane as narrow as some folks' thinking.

San Francisco African-American Historical and Cultural Society
Buchanan Street at Marina Boulevard, Fort Mason Center, Building C, Room 165, San Francisco, CA 94123
(415) 441-0640
Hours: Wed.–Sun., 12 P.M.–5 P.M.
Admission: Adults, $2; children, 50 cents

Photographs and artifacts of Mary Ellen Pleasant, a leading 19th-century supporter of the struggle against slavery and for citizen rights for blacks in free states, the paintings of Sargent Johnson, and West African wooden and soapstone carvings and baskets are the centerpieces of the San Francisco African-American Historical and Cultural Society.

WHITTIER

Pio Pico State Historic Park
6003 South Pioneer Boulevard, Whittier, CA 90606
(310) 695-1217
Hours: Wed.–Sun., 10 A.M.–5 P.M.
Admission: Free

Among the ancestors of the last Mexican governor of California were a minor Italian count of the 17th century, a mulatto grandmother, and mestizo parents who were among the original Sinaloa colonists of Los Angeles. After a career of pressing the republican claims of his fellow Californios against the departmental government run by Mexico (and the claims of southern Californios against their politically dominant northern counterparts), Pico rose to the governorship in 1845—just in time to see the Americans assume control of the territory. Fleeing to Mexico to avoid American capture, Pico returned to California following the Treaty of Guadalupe Hidalgo. Long respected by the Americans, he easily shifted gears, becoming a successful businessman and a member of the Los Angeles City Council, before dying in 1894. Today the Pio Pico State Park pays homage to the last Mexican governor of California, a man, the photographs confirm, manifestly of African descent. Visitors to the park have access to the last home in which he lived. The adobe mansion was representative of the structures wealthy southern California dons built for themselves on their ranchos. Its present condition, however, does not reflect its status during Pico's residence, though some of the rooms in which he lived are intact and still convey the look and feel of his life in the latter half of the 19th century. Currently undergoing restoration, the house is open by appointment only.

COLORADO

Tourism Board
1625 Broadway, Denver, CO 80202
(800) 433-2656
Hours: Mon.–Fri., 8 A.M.–5 P.M.

CENTRAL CITY

Clara Brown Chair
Central City Opera House, Eureka Street, Central City, CO 80427
(303) 582-5202
Hours: Tours: Memorial Day–Labor Day, daily, 9 A.M.–5 P.M.; rest of year, Sat.–Sun., 9 A.M.–5 P.M.
Admission: $3.50

The West was wildest not in cattle towns such as Dodge City (which was run by a clique of saloon-brothelkeepers who took turns as mayor) but in mountain mining towns. Gold or silver fever suddenly brought thousands of fortune seekers to places that were little more than unsupervised mining camps, each of whose rugged residents had a belief that he would strike it rich quickly. When gold was found in Gregory Gulch, Colorado, in 1859, it launched several new towns (and the careers of the state's first senators) and drew to the area Clara Brown. A former slave, Brown arrived in Central City and forsook the get-rich mentality for the more assured income of a laundress, patiently saving enough to purchase her kin from slavery in Missouri. When the Civil War released her people, she brought them out west and devoted the rest of her life to good works in the town. Central City briefly blossomed and soon spawned the need for appropriate cultural trappings. In this spirit, in 1878, an opera house was raised. The year before, Brown had died and been buried with official honors by the Colorado Pioneers Association. Half a century later, when efforts were under way to save and restore the old opera house, someone came up with the notion of raising money by selling memorial chairs commemorating Central City's founders and finest, one of whom proved to be Brown. Today's visitors to the opera house will still find the Clara Brown Chair, commemorating the first recorded African-American woman in Colorado.

COLORADO SPRINGS

Pro Rodeo Hall of Fame
101 Pro Rodeo Drive, Colorado Springs, CO 80919
(719) 593-8847
Hours: Memorial Day–Labor Day: daily, 9 A.M.–5 P.M. Rest of year, daily, 9 A.M.–4:30 P.M.
Admission: Adults, $4; seniors, $3.75; ages 5–12, $1.25

Bill Pickett earned a permanent exhibit at the Pro Rodeo Hall of Fame. A plaque, a photograph, and accompanying text outlining the career of a headliner of the 101 Ranch and the originator of bulldogging (see Ponca City entry on p. 458 and National Cowboy Hall of Fame entry on p. 457) greet the visitor. Pickett's repeated brain-jarring falls may account for his death—or in any event for his fatal decision at the age of 72 to try to break one more bronc.

DENVER

Convention & Visitors Bureau
225 West Colfax Avenue, Denver, CO 80202
(303) 892-1112
Hours: Mon.–Fri., 8 A.M.–5 P.M., Sat., 9 A.M.–1 P.M.

Black American West Museum
3091 California Street, Denver, CO 80205
(303) 292-2566
Hours: Wed.–Fri., 10 A.M.–2 P.M.; Sat., 12 P.M.–5 P.M.; Sun., 2 P.M.–5 P.M.
Admission: Adults, $2; seniors, $1.50; ages 12–17, 75 cents; under 12, 50 cents

From soldiers to Indians, sheriffs to rustlers, ranch hands to sodbusters, miners to mail-order brides, preachers to prostitutes, the West was full of black folk—including the occasional doctor. Dr. Justina Ford settled in Denver in 1902. Over the next half century she delivered more than 7,000 children. Specializing in gynecology, obstetrics, and pediatrics, Ford first practiced out of her home—because as a black woman she was denied hospital privileges for a number of years. Today in her old home the Black American West Museum tells a story too long hidden. Photographs underscore both the wide range of African-American activities in the old West and the quotidian nature of the black experience. Ranch hands, lacking the gun belts with which Hollywood invested them, lounge astride horses or swell themselves up for the camera; families in all-black towns such as Deerfield sit stiffly for portraits; and weary miners stare back at the camera with a look that suggests that, at least momentarily, the mines were more tiring than the burden of blackness in a white world. In the museum visitors will find a replica of Dr. Ford's office; artifacts of black cowboys, homesteaders, and soldiers—including spurs, wagon wheels, and clothing; miners' accoutrements such as helmets, lamps, and tools; and temporary exhibits that highlight a black past. The museum also explores atypical examples of the black West, such as the former slave Nat Love, who transformed his 1876 sharpshooting victory at the July 4th celebrations contest in Deadwood, South Dakota, into a sobriquet ("Deadwood Dick"), a career as a self-promoter, and an autobiography. (See Adams Memorial Museum entry on p. 513.)

Colorado Historical Society Museum
1300 Broadway, Denver, CO 80203
(303) 866-3682
Hours: Library: Tue.–Sat., 10 A.M.–4:30 P.M. Museum: Mon.–Sat., 10 A.M.–4:30 P.M.; Sun., 12 P.M.–4:30 P.M.
Admission: Adults, $3; seniors and children, $1.50

The black presence in Colorado is incorporated at the Colorado Historical Society Museum in the decade-by-decade exhibits of the state's 20th-century history. Photographs predominate in the interpretation and are complemented by newspaper headlines, records of black organizations, and memorabilia of notable

COURTESY BLACK AMERICAN WEST MUSEUM

The Parker brothers owned a ranch in what is now one of the most exclusive areas on Cherry Creek, in Denver, Colorado. They were the sons of Rebecca Parker.

African-American figures. The museum also has the Robert Lindneux painting of the Battle of Beecher Island (see entry on p. 495), in which the 10th Cavalry (which is not portrayed in the painting) played a decisive role.

Denver Art Museum
100 West 14th Avenue, Denver, CO 80204
(303) 575-2295
Hours: Tue.–Sat., 10 A.M.–5 P.M.; Sun., 12 P.M.–5 P.M.
Admission: Adults, $3; students, $1.50; under 6, free

A modest African collection in which the sculpture of the Yoruba, Ibo, Ibibio, Bamana, and Yaka predominates can be found at the Denver Art Museum. Masks, standing pieces and doors, a few bronzes and stone pieces, textiles, basketry, and some beadwork combine to offer the viewer a small window onto the art and material culture of parts of sub-Saharan Africa.

MEEKER

Thornburgh Battlefield Monument
Meeker, CO 81625
17 miles northeast of Meeker on Thornburgh Road, 9 miles from the junction of Colorado 13 and 789
Hours: Daily until sunset
Admission: Free

Hey, it's women's work! The Ute warriors were not interested in planting but in the typical Indian male activities of hunting, horse racing (and horse stealing), and religious ritual and spiritual speculation. When the Indian agent at the White River Ute Indian Reservation, Nathan Meeker, plowed up land on which they pastured their ponies and tried to turn them into farmers, trouble could be expected. But when he ran irrigation channels across their racetrack and then requested a military guard on the reservation, trouble was assured. Meeker's request was the result of one of his staff being killed and another fired upon, and it brought Major T. T. Thornburgh and about 160 men of the 4th Infantry from Fort Steele in Wyoming to the reservation. After crossing Milk Creek, Thornburgh's way was barred by Chief Douglass and his band, who warned the major to stay off the reservation. When the warning went unheeded, the command was ambushed by about 300 warriors. Thornburgh and nine of his men were killed immediately. Another four died and 23 were wounded in the six-day siege that ensued along the Milk River. (Meeker and nine male agency personnel were killed elsewhere on the reservation.) First riding to the rescue of the trapped white troopers were the 44 men of Captain Dodge's Company D of the 9th Cavalry. (See Fort Union entry on p. 507.) (Remington's famous painting, "Captain Dodge's Colored Troops to the Rescue," takes some license with the mundane truth: Dodge's men slipped into the 4th's lines at night; most of their horses were killed the following day, but the additional troops provided enough support to withstand the Utes for three more days until Colonel Wesley Merritt's force arrived and drove them off.) This battle was the high point of the Ute War of 1879 to 1881, a war that saw the Utes removed from western Colorado. Today visitors to the Milk Creek Valley find the entire 1,600 acres largely unchanged from the days of the battle, except for the presence of a battlefield monument that pays tribute to the troops, including a specific mention of Company D of the 9th Cavalry, and a more recently erected monument that commemorates the Ute dead.

PUEBLO

El Pueblo Museum
324 West First Street, Pueblo, CO 81003
(719) 583-0453
Hours: Mon.–Sat., 10 A.M.–4:30 P.M.; Sun., 12 P.M.–3 P.M.
Admission: Adults, $2.50; seniors and children 6–16, $2; under 6, free

Jim Beckwourth made a lot of boastful claims—by no means all of them false. A noted explorer, fur trapper, army scout, and an adopted member of the Crow, Beckwourth spent almost 40 years on the frontier after fleeing the constraints of a blacksmith apprenticeship in St. Louis. The son of a Virginia Revolutionary War veteran and a slave, the young Beckwourth took part in the Rocky Mountain Fur Company's exploration of the upper Missouri River in the 1820s, served as the American Fur Company's key agent to the Crow (see Fort Union entry on p. 510), and knew a true freedom long since lost—joining several of the Rocky

Mountains rendezvous of fur trappers such as Jedediah Strong Smith, Jim Bridger, and Kit Carson. Beckwourth later served as an army scout during the Third Seminole War and then as a guide to John C. Fremont, who thanks to Carson, Beckwourth, and their like acquired the sobriquet "The Pathfinder." Still active despite his advancing years, Beckwourth took part in the Bear Flag Rebellion—which in 1846 sought to split California from Mexican dominion—and in 1851 secured himself a place in western history by discovering a pass through the Sierra Nevadas. (See Beckwourth Pass entry on p. 480.)

Beckwourth wandered all over the western plains in the days before the prairie grass that stood taller than men was trampled by wagons. In 1842, along the Arkansas River that served as the boundary first between Spain and France and then between Mexico and the United States, Beckwourth and others founded a trading post that in time would become Pueblo, Colorado. A century and a half later visitors to the El Pueblo Museum find a historical interpretation of Beckwourth and a survey of the sequential cultures at the "Crossroads of the Arkansas." The former is rare, for Beckwourth has long been denied his share of fame, in part because his character—unlike Smith's and, to a lesser extent, Carson's—was no better than the frontier norm and in part because his blackness raised some difficulties given that the western canon is white. (In the 1951 movie *Tomahawk*, Beckwourth is portrayed by Jack Oakie. Hollywood thus got wrong the explorer's color, which was clearly "black"; body type, Beckwourth was angular and wiry; and facial features, Beckwourth's were *more* aquiline than Oakie's!) But at least Beckwourth has been better served by history than Edward Rose, a black/white/red guide, hunter, interpreter, and Indian fighter who in 1806–7 helped Manuel Lisa establish Fort Manuel at the mouth of the Big Horn River and for the next four decades was a noted presence on the frontier. However, since few Americans any longer know the names and exploits of Jedediah Strong Smith, Manuel Lisa, and John Colter, ignorance of Beckwourth and Rose is understandable.

WRAY

Beecher Island Battlefield Monument
Highway 53, 17 miles south of Wray, CO 80758
Hours: Daily until sunset
Admission: Free

Hollywood would have loved it: the swirl of Cheyenne led by Roman Nose, the surrounded scouts—their ammunition depleted, both their surgeon and the second in command (Lieutenant Beecher) killed, and most everyone else wounded—the sun-bloated and stinking corpses of horses, the swarm of flies, the crescendo of doom-laden music . . . but hark! in the distance a cloud of dust, a faint echo of a bugle, the first glimpse of, yes! *blue, by God!* . . . The cavalry to the rescue! The Indians flee, the desperate men breathe a sigh of relief, and on the cavalry troopers, wide grins break out across . . . *black* faces?! Cut!

The frequent presence of the buffalo soldiers at major clashes with the Plains Indians is not surprising: Only the cavalry had the mobility to serve as a tactical interdiction force, and in these years one-fifth of the U.S. Cavalry was black. Into this equation, factor the truth that the black regiments typically were assigned to the most isolated posts and most arduous tasks, and the resulting strong African-American accent to the story of the Plains Indians wars reflects not an Afrocentric bias but rather the unvarnished truth. It is a truth that would have been well understood by Lieutenant Colonel Forsyth's men, who woke up one morning from their bivouac on the Arikaree River to find themselves about to be attacked by Cheyenne and a small complement of Oglala Sioux and Arapaho. (See Historic Fort Hays entry on p. 380.) Their pack animals killed or run off, the men retreated to a small island in the middle of the river, where they hastily entrenched themselves. Almost immediately, their horses were killed and saw service as barricades. Repelling several Indian charges, the men endured a nine-day ordeal, besieged by a foe that held the banks of the river and kept the scouts pinned down. (Contrary to some accounts, Roman Nose was *not* killed in the first charge, depriving the Indians of leadership. In fact, he did not enter the battle for some time, as earlier in a Sioux camp his food had touched iron and thus his "medicine" had been broken.) The heat, the lack of ammunition, the absence of any food except the gradually rotting horse flesh that surrounded them, the death of their surgeon and second in command, and the wounding of Forsyth left their prospects bleak indeed. Riding to their rescue was a detachment of the black 10th Cavalry stationed at Fort Wallace in Kansas.

The best account of these years from the Cheyenne perspective is provided by George Bent, the mixed-blood son of the trader William Bent. George, whose mother was Cheyenne, lived and fought with his mother's people—he was present, for example, in Black Kettle's camp along the Sand Creek at the time of Chivington's berserk massacre and had his hip broken by a soldier's bullet—and his letters offer real insight into the Cheyenne, their male military societies, such as the Dog Soldiers, and the Sand Creek Massacre. (George's brother Charles went wholly Cheyenne, living a life of such consummate savagery—including an attempt to murder his white father and sundry abominable tortures of his white captives—as even to raise the eyebrows of the Dog Soldiers he led.)

Today Beecher Island cannot be found—a flood in 1934 washed away what was little more than an obscure sandbar on which no more than five people were killed. But visitors to eastern Colorado can view the Beecher Island Battlefield Monument, which recalls an episode that supplies true meaning to the cliché "clash of cultures" and underscores how deeply and intrinsically a part of the dominant American culture were the people the Indians called "black white men" and most whites called "black savages." Erected early in the 20th century, the monument makes no mention of the 10th.

A postscript: The small complement of Oglala Sioux would have cause to rue the 10th's intervention, for Forsyth went on to lead the 7th Cavalry. In the harsh winter of 1890–91, Forsyth was the senior commanding officer at the "Battle" of Wounded Knee (see Holy Rosary entry on p. 516 and Fort Robinson entry on p. 428), where a band of desperate Sioux were provoked into firing on the 7th, who soon pushed the resulting pile of Sioux corpses into a mass grave, essentially ending the Plains Indians wars.

MONTANA

Travel Promotion Division
1424 Ninth Street, Helena, MT 59620
(800) 541-1447
Hours: Mon.–Fri., 8 A.M.–5 P.M.

CASCADE

Mary Fields Grave
Hillside Cemetery, St. Peter's Mission Road, P.O. Box 314, Cascade, MT 59421
(406) 468-2808
¼ mile west of town on St. Peter's Mission Road
Hours: Daily until sunset
Admission: Free

A black woman far afield from her community, Mary Fields led a varied life and counted the famous among her acquaintances. Tiring of life as a nurse for the Ursuline nuns, Fields hauled freight, drove a stagecoach in her 60s, and ran a restaurant before settling down in her 70s as a laundress in Cascade. Evidently, she remained vigorous in her old age, collecting a long overdue laundry bill—and more notoriety—by catching a deadbeat customer on the streets and punching his lights out. A hometown boy, the noted western artist Charles M. Russell, sketched Fields, and the actor Gary Cooper, who visited relatives in Cascade as a child, recalled her presence there. Today's visitors to Cascade can find the Mary Fields Grave at the Hillside Cemetery.

CROW AGENCY

Little Bighorn Battlefield National Monument
Interstate 90 at Highway 212, Box 39, Crow Agency, MT 59022
(406) 665-2060
Hours: June–Aug.: daily, 8 A.M.–8 P.M. Sept.–May: daily, 8 A.M.–4:30 P.M.
Admission: Per vehicle, $4; per person, $2

As the sun rose on June 25, 1876, General George Armstrong Custer and the 600 men of the 7th Cavalry located the Sioux and Cheyenne encampment in the valley of the Little Big Horn River. Evidently underestimating the number of his foe—the 1,000 lodges held the largest gathering of Plains Indians ever assembled—Custer divided his force, in the afternoon sending Captain Frederick W. Benteen and three companies to scout the bluffs to the south and ordering Major Marcus Reno and his three companies to cross the river and strike the upper end of the camp, where the Hunkpapa Sioux of Gall, Crow King, and Sitting Bull were lodged.

Custer's fate is well known; Reno's is not. The major quickly found himself faced by a superior Sioux force, which flanked his line of battle and compelled the troops to retreat pell-mell for the river and the bluffs overlooking it. Here he and his men defended themselves until about 4:00 P.M., when the Indians mysteriously vanished. Soon Reno was reunited with Benteen, who was hurrying forward in response to Custer's written order: "Come on; Big village, be quick, bring packs." Having distributed ammunition, Reno ordered the companies toward the sound of firing to the north. Arriving on a high hill overlooking the Custer battlefield, the troops saw nothing of their comrades, nor did they any longer hear the sounds of battle. Suddenly confronted by a large force of Indians, the men were compelled to retreat back to the bluffs, where they entrenched themselves and endured a siege through the remainder of that day and the next before being rescued by the approach of General Alfred Terry's force. In this, the Plains Indians' greatest triumph, Custer lost about 225 men, all of companies C, E, F, I, and L; Reno and Benteen saw 47 of their men killed.

Among the latter was Isaiah Dorman, an African-American interpreter married to a Santee Sioux. Dorman, who carried the Sioux name "Teat," died early, in the initial retreat from the village. Much of "pop" black history portrays Dorman's fate after the battle as unique, claiming that his being both an acquaintance of the Sioux and black—and hence, like the buffalo soldiers, more respected as a foe because the black troops purportedly were less cruel than whites—forestalled his being scalped or mutiliated. Typically, each aspect of this claim is nonsense. Lieutenant Bradley, who had discovered the aftermath of the Custer battlefield and led Benteen and two other officers to the site, wrote a letter a month afterward to the Helena, Montana, *Herald* in an attempt to correct the anti-Indian hysteria sweeping the country. He noted, "Of the 206 bodies buried in the field, there were very few that I did not see, and beyond scalping, in possibly a majority of cases, there was little mutiliation. Many of the bodies were not even scalped, and in the comparatively few cases of disfiguration, it appeared to me the result rather of a blow with a knife, hatchet, or war club to finish a wounded man, rather than deliberate mutilation." According to one account, Dorman "was found with many arrows in his body and head, and badly cut and slashed." The last clause really identifies *where* he was found, for most of the bodies that were disfigured were found from Reno's group that fell near the camp, that is, within range of the women and children. As Kipling wrote in another context: "When you're left wounded and lying on Afghanistan's plains / And the women come out to cut up what remains / Roll to your gun and blow out your brains / And go to your God like a soldier."

Today's visitors to the Little Big Horn Battlefield National Monument will find a battle monument honoring Custer's men (Dorman, who was not listed among the casualties in the Bismarck *Tribune Extra* issue on the battle, is listed on the monument only as "Isaiah"); a museum; a visitor center; a cemetery; a Reno-Benteen Entrenchment Trail; a documentary film; a slide program; interpretive programs on the Plains Indians, the U.S. Cavalry, and the battle itself; and guided tours of the battlefield.

FORT SHAW

Fort Shaw Historical Marker
Highway 200, northwest of the town, Fort Shaw, MT 59443
Hours: Daily until sunset
Admission: Free

Perhaps it was the army's way of saying: Don't complain. For the 25th Infantry exchanged the searing heat of Texas for the 20-degree-below-zero winters of the northern plains. Fort Shaw was yet another of the remote postings in harsh environments that seemed to be the fate of America's buffalo soldiers. Here, in a fort named after the commander of the Civil War's most famous all-black regiment, the 54th Massachusetts (see Robert Gould Shaw and 54th Regiment entry on p. 263), black troopers of the 25th Infantry made their regimental headquarters from 1888 through 1891. By this time the troops' main activities were maintenance of the fort and the telegraph lines to Fort Benton. Field exercises occupied the remainder of their energies. Today three adobe buildings dating to the late 1860s remain, two on the old officer's row and one from the stable/barn complex. On the parade ground visitors will find a historical marker that recounts the career of the commander of the 54th Massachusetts Regiment. No members of the 25th are to be found in the nearby restored military cemetery, which like the fort's remains owes much to the local historical society and nothing to the federal government.

HAVRE

Fort Assiniboine Marker
c/o H. Earl Clack Museum, Hill County Fairgrounds, Highway 2 West, Havre, MT 59501
Museum: (406) 265-9913
Hours: Museum: daily, 9 A.M.–9 P.M. Fort tour: Sat.–Sun., 5 P.M.
Admission: Museum: free. Fort tour: adults, $2; children, $1

After he gained fame as the commander of American forces in World War I—during which campaign he had scant use for black troops (see Victory Monument entry on p. 351)—General John Pershing recalled, "It has been an honor which I am proud to claim to have been at one time a member of that intrepid organization of the Army which has always added glory to the military history of America—the 10th Cavalry." Pershing's tour with the 10th included a stay at Fort Assiniboine, the regimental headquarters from 1893 through 1898. From this post the 10th left for Cuba and the Spanish-American War, where the regiment garnered five Medals of Honor—the last to be awarded to African-Americans until the Korean War. Eighteen brick buildings still stand at the old fort, including the remains of the officer's quarters, the guardhouse, the stables, and the post trader's complex, but there are no interpretive markers, nor can the site be toured except under the aegis of the local historical society. A diorama of the fort grounds will be found at the H. Earl Clack Museum, through which one arranges tours of what remains of the old fort. South of town on U.S. 87 at milepost 107 is the Fort Assiniboine Historical Marker.

HELENA

Montana Historical Society Museum
225 North Roberts Streets, Helena, MT 59601
(406) 444-2694
Museum: (406) 444-1645. Library: (406) 444-2681
Hours: Memorial Day–Labor Day: Mon.–Fri., 8 A.M.–6 P.M.; Sat.–Sun., 9 A.M.–5 P.M. Rest of year: Mon.–Fri., 8 A.M.–5 P.M.; Sat., 9 A.M.–5 P.M.
Admission: Free

The famous Charles M. Russell painting of York, the slave member of the Lewis and Clark expedition, standing in a Mandan lodge as a warrior vainly attempts to rub the black color off his skin; turn-of-the-century broadsides and tickets from the St. James A.M.E. Church in Helena; artifacts of Taylor Gordon, the Harlem Renaissance author; and photographs of black soldiers and cowboys and of Taylor Gordon and his family and associates constitute the African-American holdings of the Montana Historical Society Museum. The society's archives include the Fort Assininboine records that establish the tenure there of the 10th Cavalry, records of the Montana Federation of Colored Women's Clubs, and original manuscripts of Taylor Gordon.

State Capitol
Sixth and Montana streets, Helena, MT 59620
(406) 444-2654
Hours: Mon.–Sat., 8 A.M.–5 P.M.
Admission: Free

Charles M. Russell's large canvas portraying the meeting between the explorers Lewis and Clark and the Flathead chiefs, in which York—the resolute slave member of the expedition—is prominently depicted, covers the entire wall behind the speaker's desk in the State House of Representatives. Also in the

State Capitol is the E. S. Paxon mural, "Lewis and Clark at Three Forks," where again York is depicted. In the Gallery of Outstanding Citizens, Mattie Castner, a black woman, and her husband are honored for founding the mining town of Belt, Montana, in 1888.

MISSOULA

Fort Missoula Historical Museum
Building 322, South and Reserve streets, Missoula, MT 59801
(406) 728-3476
Hours: Memorial Day–Labor Day: Tue.–Sat., 10 A.M.–5 P.M.; Sun., 12 P.M.–5 P.M. Rest of year: Tue.–Sun., 12 P.M.–5 P.M.
Admission: Free; donations encouraged

UNIVERSITY OF MONTANA, MANSFIELD LIBRARY

The all-black 25th Infantry tested bicycles as a means of military transport.

Anyone who has served in the army will understand: Mountainous Montana was selected as the location for the experimental use of bicycles by the U.S. Army. The black troopers of the 25th Infantry got the dubious privilege of conducting the experiment, one detachment pedaling 1,000 miles from its headquarters in Fort Missoula to Yellowstone Park and back, and then doubling that journey the next year with a trip to St. Louis. The story of an exercise ahead of its time is told at the Fort Missoula Historical Museum. Photographs and accompanying text about the Bicycle Corps interpret one of the weirder experiences of the buffalo soldiers. In addition, there are photographs depicting barracks life and artifacts of the black troopers, who also are mentioned in the museum's slide show.

VIRGINIA CITY

Thompson-Hickman Library/Thompson's Museum
200 block of Wallace Street, Virginia City, MT 59755
(406) 843-5346
Hours: May 15–Oct. 15: daily, 10 A.M.–5 P.M.
Admission: Voluntary donations requested

Booming mining towns and far-flung ranches once attracted a notable black presence to Montana, but those days have passed and now little trace is left of the community's material culture. Black cattle punchers and miners active in the heyday of Virginia City can still be seen, however, in the fading photographs of the Thompson-Hickman Library and Museum.

WHITE SULPHUR SPRINGS

Castle Museum
310 Second Avenue, NE, White Sulphur Springs, MT 59645
(406) 547-3370
Hours: May 15–Sept. 15: daily, 10 A.M.–6 P.M.
Admission: Adults, $3; seniors and children, $2

Family photographs and artifacts of Taylor Gordon, the prize-winning black author of the 1920s and '30s, can be found at the Castle Museum. *Born to Be* and *The Man Who Built the Stone Castle* made the reputation of a man who grew up in White Sulphur Springs.

NEW MEXICO

Tourism Division
The Joseph Montoya Building, Box 20003, 1100 St. Francis Drive, Santa Fe, NM 87503
(800) 545-2040
Hours: Mon.–Fri., 8 A.M.–5 P.M.

BAYARD

Fort Bayard
N.M. 180, P.O. Box 219, Bayard, NM 88036
(505) 537-3302
Hours: Daily until sunset
Admission: Free

It was Apache country and it was mid-August, neither adding up to a splendid duty assignment, though the area was beautiful and the elevation high enough to limit the agony of summer. Company B of the 125th U.S. Colored Infantry had yet to be mustered out of its Civil War service and spent the summer of 1866 living in canvas tents while constructing Fort Bayard. It was close to Silver City and, more important, to the Gila Wilderness, whose natural springs were—and are—the area's main water supply. Five years later the "Post [was] everything undesirable. Huts of logs and round stones, with flat dirt roofs that in summer leaked and brought down rivulets of liquid mud; in winter the hiding place of the tarantula and centipede, with ceilings of 'condemned' canvas . . . low, dark, and uncomfortable." But by 1879 there were vegetable gardens and attractive quarters. Present were one brevet lieutenant colonel, a major, four captains, 11 lieutenants, 325 enlisted men (companies A, B, and G of the black 9th Cavalry and Company E of the white 15th Infantry), 25 Navajo scouts, 14 laundresses (frequently something of a misnomer), 14 civilian employees, 280 horses—and it was still Apache country. Following the death of Victorio, Nana took up the fight, leading a particularly devastating raid in the summer of 1881. Eight times in this summer troopers from the 9th based in Fort Bayard clashed with Nana's band. Today many remnants of the fort remain, including officers' quarters and 48 outbuildings, and are utilized as administrative quarters for the state hospital that now occupies the site. Visitors may drive or walk (much the better choice) by the buildings—those choosing the latter mode will gain a good sense of the basic layout of the 19th-century fort. Those strolling the full 480 acres of the complex may turn up arrowheads, horseshoes, and shards of pottery. Whichever mode is selected, be sure to stop by the old parade ground, where you will find a life-size statue of a former fort resident, Corporal Clinton Greaves of the 9th, who won a Medal of Honor for his action on patrol against the Chiricahua Apache in the Florida Mountains in January 1877.

COLUMBUS

Columbus Historical Museum
Junction of N.M. 11 and 9, P.O. Box 27, Columbus, NM 88029
(505) 531-2620
Hours: May–Aug.: Sun.–Fri., 1 P.M.–4 P.M.; Sat., 10 A.M.–4 P.M. Sept.–Apr.: daily, 10 A.M.–4 P.M.
Admission: Voluntary donations encouraged

March 9, 1916, long would be remembered by the surviving residents of Columbus, New Mexico, for before dawn the American citizens woke up to find their country invaded and their homes under attack by a foreign power. Pancho Villa, at a disadvantage in the three-cornered struggle for power occasioned by the Mexican Revolution of 1910, sought to internationalize the domestic upheaval. Toward that end, he sacked Columbus. As the Villistas rode out of town, they left American corpses strewn in its streets, eight of them civilian and seven of them soldiers. A week later General John Pershing, at the head of 5,000 men, rode into Mexico tasked with tracking Villa through the Chihuahua wasteland. Pershing spent 11 largely futile months south of the border. He never ran down Villa (indeed, most of Pershing's skirmishes were with the Mexican army), but he did deter further incursions. During this time his force grew to 15,000 and included the 10th Cavalry, with whom he had served earlier both in the West and in the Spanish-American War, and the 24th Infantry. In Mexico as an officer with the 10th was Charles Young (see Greene County Historical Society Museum entry on p. 451), the third African-American graduate of the U.S. Military Academy at West Point. The 10th saw action in several skirmishes, rescuing units of the 13th Cavalry trapped at Santa Cruz de Villegas and clashing with a Federal Mexican force at Carrizal, and lost upward of a dozen men. (In June 1919 Villa's next sortie near the U.S.—his raid on Juarez, across the Rio Grande from El Paso, during which he fired into American territory—brought a rapid response from the black 24th Infantry, who in conjunction with cavalry units crossed into Mexico behind a line of howitzer fire and easily dispersed the Villistas.) Today Columbus is secure from Villa, who was assassinated in 1923, and visitors may tour the Columbus Historical Museum without peril. Inside they will find photos of the town before and after the raid and of Villa, a map of the route Pershing's force followed, and other interpretive material. They will not, however, find any specific mention of the role of the 10th Cavalry. For that, travelers will need to view the free visitor center video at the nearby Pancho Villa State Park (505 531-2711), which is located right across the street from the museum and is open daily from 10:00 A.M. to 4:00 P.M.

FOLSOM

Folsom Museum
Junction N.M. 456 and N.M. 325, P.O. Box 317, Folsom, NM 88419
(505) 278-2122
Hours: Memorial Day–Labor Day: daily, 10 A.M.–5 P.M. May and Sept.: Sat.–Sun., 10 A.M.–5 P.M.; otherwise by appointment (call 505 278-2477 or 278-3616)
Admission: Adults, $1; children 6–16, 50 cents; under 6, free

It's hard for an amateur to convince professionals, and it doesn't help if the amateur is a cowboy—and black to boot. Born a slave in Texas in 1851, George McJunkin first earned recognition from his cowboy peers in New Mexico as a survivor of the Great Blizzard of 1889—after two disorienting days of being caught outside in the storm with a herd, lost and half frozen, he led 14 other cowboys to safety at the Harvey Bramblet ranch, where they holed up for 13 days as the devastating blizzard raged. Later he was the foreman of the Crowfoot Ranch near Folsom and something of an amateur archaeologist. When a major flood in 1908 uncovered bones in an arroyo back in the hills, McJunkin judged them to be prehistoric—and he had the wit to leave them in place. His restraint later enabled archaeologists to authenticate the presence on the North American continent of early humans, a presence the prevailing scientific establishment denied. (A previous find near Midland, Texas, had been scientifically corrupted by the removal of human implements from the uncovered bones, which broke the chain of evidence.) For years McJunkin attempted to interest authorities in his discovery, to no avail. Finally, in 1926, a University of Colorado dig at the McJunkin site uncovered the remains of 23 bison and 19 implements/projectiles and pushed back the authenticated presence of early humans in North America. Unfortunately, George McJunkin had died five years before his efforts bore fruit. While the scientific endorsement of his judgment probably would not have carried as much weight with his comrades as the memory of his courage and composure during the Great Blizzard, nor even of his day-to-day competence as the Crowfoot's foreman, it's difficult to believe that it would not have greatly pleased the amateur archaeologist. Today the Folsom Museum has a board display on McJunkin and the Folsom Man site as well as literature on the subject. It does not, however, have any of the original projectiles or bones. Just west of town on top of a hill will be found the Folsom Cemetery in which McJunkin lies, his bones, unlike the bisons', undisturbed.

LINCOLN

Lincoln County Heritage Trust Historical Center
U.S. Highway 380, Lincoln, NM 88338
(505) 653-4025
Hours: Mother's Day weekend–Sept. 30 (all museums: Historical Center, Old Courthouse Museum, Dr. Wood's House, and the Tunstall Store): daily, 9 A.M.–6 P.M. Rest of year (Historical Center and Old Courthouse Museum only): daily, 9 A.M.–5 P.M.
Admission: Mother's Day weekend–Sept. 30 (combination ticket for all museums): adults, $4.50; children, free. Rest of year (Historical Center and Old Courthouse Museum): adults, $4; children, free

Across time and space, one can trace the Indian threat pattern by the presence of the black cavalry—the two track closely. The mid-1870s saw the end of the Comanches as a hostile force. The sad process revealed all that was pathetic about the Plains Indians: Courage could never compensate for a complete absence of strategic vision, poor tactical use of force, inept shooting, lack of sustained action, an anarchic individualism, and, most telling of all, an embracing superstition that only later etiolated generations of the victors would label as a philosophy uniting all living things in a harmonious circle of creation—or some such nonsense. Among the Comanches, the Kwahadi stood out as supremely untamed—though not entirely uncivilized, as they were shocked by the cannibalism of their Tonkawa foes. Led by Quanah "Parker"—who was fully Comanche despite the fact that his mother was Cynthia Ann Parker, a white who had been abducted by the tribe when she was nine—the Kwahadi decided in 1874 to put an end to a buffalo hunters' camp at Adobe Walls, Texas. The camp had been raised in contradiction to U.S. government promises, and it heralded the end of the southern Plains Indians, who had seen Kansas turned into a mound of buffalo bones. Still another Indian man of "vision" arose, the prophet Isatai, who promised that he had been taken into the spirit world and vouchsafed a vision and great power, including the power magically to render enemy bullets harmless and confer immunity upon warriors. Provisionally secure in this promise, perhaps 500 to 700 Comanche and Kiowa warriors rode toward Adobe Walls, led by the justly renowned Quanah and accompanied by Isatai, the latter stark naked except for a small cap of sagebrush stems that marked his magic powers. In the ensuing battle, which Isatai sat out communing with the Great Spirit, 26 men and one woman withstood the initial Indian rush, after which the Comanche settled down to the desultory sort of siege that ensured defeat.

Adobe Walls marked the opening of the Red River War of 1874–75, a war culminated on the Staked Plains, where the Comanche, Kiowa, and Cheyenne learned anew the lesson they repeatedly forgot: Unlike them, the U.S. Army did not fight skirmishes and then go into winter quarters; it waged *war.* The famous 4th Cavalry, led by the renowned Colonel Ranald Mackenzie, who earlier in his career had commanded the black 41st Infantry Regiment, rode into the Palo Duro Canyon, over which, typically, the Indians had not stood guard even though they knew troopers were in the vicinity, and systematically destroyed the encamped Indians' ability to survive the harsh plains' winter. Tepees, cooking implements, food, clothing, weapons, and 1,400 ponies—all were destroyed. It was scarcely necessary to kill people. Within weeks the tribes started to come in to make their peace—which was the signal for the 9th Cavalry to move from the now-secure Texas into New Mexico and Arizona.

Units of the 9th would be based at Fort Stanton for much of the next decade, years during which the Apache would be the threat. During their New Mexico service, troopers of the 9th would earn seven of the 11 Medals of Honor secured by the regiment. The 9th (companies F and M) also played a role in quelling the so-called El Paso Salt War of 1877. They sortied from Fort Stanton to quell the violent protests of some Mexican salt merchants who had been displaced by Americans, who bought salt wells that previously had been exploited but not owned. Today the state uses Fort Stanton as a hospital, and although the exteriors of the old quarters may be seen, for an interpretation of its 19th-century role visitors must journey to the nearby Lincoln County Heritage Trust Historical Center. Here—in an area made famous by the insignificant Billy the Kid and a minor range war—one will find an exhibit on the buffalo soldiers in general and the 9th Cavalry in particular. The exhibit includes a campaign medal of a 9th trooper, a mannequin in an NCO in dress uniform, uniform headgear and gloves, two carbines, photographs and other artifacts, and an account of the 9th's campaign against the Mimbreño Apache chief Victorio and of their role in the Lincoln County War that brought notoriety to the Kid.

RADIUM SPRINGS

Fort Seldon State Monument
NM 157, P.O. Box 58, Radium Springs, NM 88054
(505) 526-8911
Hours: Summer: daily, 9:30 A.M.–5:30 P.M. Winter: daily, 8:30 A.M.–4:30 P.M.
Admission: $2.10; under 15, free

Life at Fort Seldon, where companies of the 9th Cavalry were stationed in 1877 and 1880–81 (during the campaign against Victorio), is interpreted at this state monument through a photographic exhibit on the 9th Cavalry and a more general video on the buffalo soldiers.

WATROUS

Fort Union National Monument
P.O. Box 127, Watrous, NM 87753
(505) 425-8025
Hours: Memorial Day–Labor Day: daily, 8 A.M.–6 P.M. Rest of year: daily, 8 A.M.–5 P.M.
Admission: $3 per car, $1 per person

Four companies (D, E, K, L) of the 9th Cavalry moved into Fort Union in 1876 to take up garrison duties in an environment far less onerous than the searing West Texas plains with which they had become all too familiar. At first their duties were light, consisting of protecting the Sante Fe Trail and making forays throughout Colfax County to ensure public order during the bitter land disputes then prevailing. But soon there was trouble at the Warm Springs (Ojo Caliente) Apache Reservation (located not far from the Zuni Háwikuh ruins where Estevanico met his death—see Coronado Memorial entry on p. 475). Late in 1877 the Mimbreño Apache chief Victorio and 300 of the Ojo Caliente folk, including a few Chiricahua, fled the reservation. Two of the 9th's Fort Union companies spent the next several months in the field before Victorio returned of his own volition to Warm Springs. It wasn't the last they would hear of the Mimbreño leader or of Ojo Caliente. Two years later Victorio and 60 warriors attacked Company E at the Warm Springs Reservation, killing eight troopers and stealing 46 ponies. An influx of Mescalero Apache brought Victorio's strength to about 150 and also brought several U.S. Army units into the field after him. They tracked him into the wastes of Chihuahua before being warned off by the Mexican army, which put an end to Victorio in 1880. Also dispatched from Fort Union in 1879 was Company D. Led by Captain Francis Dodge, the black troopers rode to the rescue of Major T. T. Thornburgh's forces pinned down by the Utes along the Milk River in Colorado. (See Thornburgh Monument entry on p. 493.) Today's visitors to Fort Union National Monument will find the adobe ruins of the old fort spread over 70 acres and an exhibit on the 9th Cavalry, including a mannequin of a trooper, photographs, and text interpreting the role and the exploits the black cavalry regiment.

NORTH DAKOTA

Tourism Promotion Division
Liberty Memorial Building, 600 East Memorial Building, Bismarck, ND 58505
(800) 437-2077; (701) 224-2666
Hours: Mon.–Fri., 8 A.M.–5 P.M.; Sat., 9 A.M.–5 P.M.; Sun., 11 A.M.–5 P.M.

WASHBURN

Fort Mandan
Rural Route 1, Washburn, ND 58577
(701) 462-8129
2 miles west of town on RR 1
Hours: Visitor Center: Mid-Apr.–mid-Oct: Tue.–Sun., 1 P.M.–5 P.M.
Fort: daily, daylight hours
Admission: Free

The overland journey from St. Louis, Missouri, to Bismarck, North Dakota, is now a matter of a day. For Meriwether Lewis and William Clark and the men of their expedition in 1804, it was nearer half a year before they camped at a Mandan village near the juncture of the Knife and Missouri rivers north of modern Bismarck. Here, huddled in cottonwood cabins the explorers hastily had constructed, they endured a northern plains winter—five months of blizzards, biting wind, and sullen skies. Here too they were joined by Sacagawea, the Shoshone woman who would serve as guide and interpreter for part of the journey to the Missouri headwaters, the Rocky Mountains, and the Salmon, Snake, and Columbia rivers. (Sacagawea's role was limited. She spoke almost no English or French. She translated Shoshone into Hidatsa. Outside of her Lehmi-Shoshone country, she could not serve as guide; indeed, even in that country, old Toby, a local Indian guide, and his sons had to be hired to lead the expedition west through the passes of the Bitterroots.) It was during the stay with the Mandan that Clark's slave York first emerged as a center of attraction and a useful emollient for cross-cultural encounters. Clark's diary recorded how he ". . . ordered my black Servant to Dance which amused the crowd very much, and Somewhat astonished them, that So large a man should be active &c, &c." York, who stood more than six feet tall and weighed more than 200 pounds, made a sufficient impression on the Mandan that years later the noted western artist, Charles M. Russell, would capture the encounter in a famous painting depicting York in a Mandan lodge permitting an Indian to attempt to rub off his black color. (See Montana Historical Society Museum entry on p. 500.)

Today's visitors to the reconstructed Fort Mandan will find historical markers recounting the Lewis and Clark expedition but little to recall York. Nor will they find the original fort, which was buried by the Missouri River. The closest one will come to the original fort is the Fort Mandan Historical Marker, which lies not far from nearby Fort Clark, an American Fur Company trading post established in 1830. While Fort Clark is rather barren, with only self-guided tours of the remains of a Mandan earth lodge and the foundations of two forts built on the site, the journey is through beautiful country and brings one close to Knife River Indian Villages National Historic Site, a marvelous interpretation of the culture of the Three Affiliated Tribes—Mandan, Hidatsa, and Arikara. Of the last tribe's response to York, Clark's journal recorded, "Those people are much pleased with my black servant." Knife River also takes note of Lewis and Clark, but its principal focus is on the native tribes. Though one may have seen before the Bodmer painting of the Mandan chief Mato-Tope, a visit to Knife River will allow one to comprehend the significance of his notched, tufted, split, and painted feathers, which respectively indicate cutting the foe's throat and taking the scalp, first coup, arrow injury, and killing the foe. It's the sort of detail that allows one to appreciate—as Clark did, no matter that its expression in his journal reflects a context of mastership—York's ability to ease the passage of the expedition through the territory of warrior societies. Both Fort Clark (701 794-8832; Apr.–Oct., 8 A.M.–5 P.M., Thu.–Sun; free) and Knife River (P.O. Box 9, Stanton, 58571; daily, 8 A.M.–6 P.M. in summer and 4:30 P.M. other seasons; free) are located near Stanton, North Dakota.

WILLISTON

Fort Buford State Historic Site Museum
Route 1, Box 57, Williston, ND 58801
(701) 572-9034
About 20 miles southwest of Williston on Highway 1804
Hours: Museum: May 16–Sept. 1: daily, 9 A.M.–6 P.M. Rest of year: by appointment only
Admission: Adults, $2; ages 6–15, $1; under 6, free

In the 1890s troopers of the 10th Cavalry and 25th Infantry were stationed on the upper Missouri River at Fort Buford in the Badlands above the Black Hills. This was the land of the Assiniboine, Cree, Crow, and—after 1847—Sioux. Though the fort had been established in 1866 near the confluence of the Missouri and Yellowstone rivers as a consequence of Sioux participation in the Minnesota Uprising of 1862, by 1890 the Plains Indians' day was past. The main function of the resident black troopers was maintenance of the fort and patrols of deterrence. Today, on land nearly as beautiful as it then was, visitors to Fort Buford State Historic Site Museum will find themselves greeted by a life-size cutout of the 25th's Carter Huse. Little else at the museum specifically deals with the black troopers, but the general interpretation of a frontier fort, complete with the artifacts of a soldier's existence, yields an accurate impression of what wearing a blue uniform in the waning days of the frontier entailed.

Fort Union Trading Post National Historic Site
Buford Route, Williston, ND 58801
(701) 572-9083
A few miles from Fort Buford. About 20 miles southwest of Williston on Highway 1804
Hours: Memorial Day–Labor Day: daily, 8 A.M.–8 P.M. Rest of year: 9 A.M.–5:30 P.M.
Admission: Free

"A craftsman or workman receives $250 a year . . . a hunter receives $400 . . . an interpreter without other employment, which is seldom, gets $500. Clerks and traders who have mastered [Indian languages] . . . may demand from $800 to $1,000. . . ." So reported a clerk at Fort Union Trading Post in 1851. For much of the early 19th century, the fur trade was one of the country's major enterprises and one in which African Americans participated, though in very small numbers. In its heyday Fort Union, an outpost of John Jacob Astor's American Fur Company, employed up to 100 men. Almost without exception, the men were resourceful, profane, violent, and hard-drinking. They also were not always white—or American. Russians, Germans, Spaniards, Italians, African Americans, and their Indian "wives" and their mixed-blood children could be found at the fort. John Brazeau served Astor's company for some years and was remembered as "a full-blooded Ethiopian, apparently, of small stature and intelligent, though not handsome, face. . . . He enunciated his English well and had a good command of it for an uneducated man. He spoke French better than most Canadians; also Sioux and other Indian languages." Brazeau probably went west as a servant or slave, but such was not the case for the resourceful, entrepreneurial, and by no means entirely scrupulous James Beckwourth, fur trapper, explorer, and son of a Revolutionary War officer from Virginia and a slave woman. (See El Pueblo Museum entry on p. 494 and Beckwourth Pass entry on p. 480.) In the 1830s the fort's founder and first superintendant, Kenneth McKenzie, personally selected Beckwourth to handle the company's Crow "account."

Like most institutions that interpret the fur trade, the Fort Union Trading Post National Historic Site has no material that directly reflects the African-American component of that experience, which was but a very small aspect of a largely white endeavor. However, in addition to Fort Union's reconstructed walls, stone bastions, Indian trade house, and superintendant's house, its museum sells an abridged edition of Charles Larpenteur's *Forty Years a Fur Trader*, from whence comes our knowledge of Brazeau, whose final fate it describes:

> About 1868, the company he had been working for at Fort Berthold sold out to an opposition concern, which had houses outside the fort. The

> people of the latter firm moved in and turned all the old hands out, including Brazeau, who was too old, feeble and rheumatic to work. He was literally turned out to die; no white man offered him anything. Then the Indians took pity on him and gave him such shelter and food as they could afford; but they were, themselves, very poor at this time. Hearing of this I had him conveyed 14 miles to Fort Stevenson, where I was then serving . . . One morning, when the attendant brought him his breakfast, Brazeau was found kneeling at the side of his bed, dead.

The museum has books that relate the life of Beckwourth, who would remain an independent actor on the frontier for some decades after his employment at the fort. The museum also has an excellent array of period artifacts that contrast the material cultures of the Indians and the trappers. Guns, traps, knives, clothing, and trade merchandise are on display. The last items, including German silver and Italian beads, emphasize the fur industry's international character and the extent to which Assiniboine and Crow had been brought within the international economy.

OREGON

Department of Tourism
775 Summer Street, NE, Salem, OR 97310
(800) 547-7842
Hours: Mon.–Fri., 8 A.M.–5 P.M.

ASTORIA

Fort Clatsop National Memorial
Route 3, Box 604-FC, Astoria, OR 97103
(503) 861-2471
Hours: Mid-June–Labor Day: daily, 8 A.M.–6 P.M. Rest of year: daily, 8 A.M.–5 P.M.
Admission: Adults 17 and older, $2; families, $4; seniors (U.S. citizens) 62 and older, free

"Great joy . . . the roaring . . . made by the waves breaking on the rocky shores . . . may be heard distinctly," wrote William Clark in his journal entry of November 7, 1805. The Pacific Ocean had been reached after a journey of more than 600 miles down the Snake and Columbia rivers and after more than a year and a half of travel from St. Louis. It's hard to believe the joy lasted long, for soon it was time to go into winter quarters once again. In December a fort was constructed on the south side of the Columbia River mouth near the Clatsop Indians. For the next 106 days the men endured a hard winter. Cold, damp, rheumatism, and rain were constant companions—indeed, it rained for all but 12 of the days. Clothing rotted and fleas abounded in the furs and hides of the bedding, so much so that in their journals all members of the group complained of loss of sleep. On March 23, 1806, Clark wrote a telling journal entry, though of course to him it was mere dry commentary: "At this place we . . . wintered and remained from the 7th Decr. 1805 to this day and have lived as well as we had a right to expect." Clearly, limited expectations of comfort should be a criteria for selecting members of exploration parties. Among the suffering members was York, Clark's slave.

Today Fort Clatsop National Memorial offers a more comfortable venue for an interpretation of the American government's first formal exploration of the land that separated the English and Spanish colonial possessions on the North American continent. A visitor center and the fort, the latter reconstructed from the floor plan drawn by Clark on the elkhide cover of his field book, are the principal venues for interpretation, though they are complemented by the spring from which the explorers drew water, the canoe landing site where the party stepped ashore, the salt-making camp, and a living history program in which park staff dressed in period clothing demonstrate frontier skills. Visually, York's role figures most prominently at the visitor center museum, while at the fort he is mentioned in the interpretive presentation given by park guides. Nearby at Fort Stevens State Park are camping facilities—did I mention the rain?

PORTLAND

Convention & Visitors Bureau
26 Southwest Salmon, Portland, OR 97204
(503) 275-9750
Hours: Mon.–Fri., 8:30 A.M.–5 P.M.; Sat., 9:30 A.M.–3 P.M.

Children's Museum
3037 Southwest Second Avenue, Portland, OR 97201
(503) 823-2227
Hours: Tue.–Sat., 9 A.M.–5 P.M.; Sun, 11 A.M.–5 P.M.
Admission: Voluntary donations requested

Beginning in 1994, "Omokunle Village," a Yoruba setting with a marketplace, chief's house, schoolhouse, and central village tree, will be on display at the Children's Museum. Meanwhile, the museum's permanent collection embraces 31 objects from Zulu daily life, including clothes, utensils, instruments, household goods, and toys.

Portland Museum of Art
1219 Southwest Park at Jefferson Avenue, Portland, OR 97223
(503) 226-2811
Hours: Tue.–Sat., 11 A.M.–5 P.M.; Sun., 1 P.M.–5 P.M.; first Thu. 11 A.M.–9 P.M.
Admission: Adults, $3; students and seniors over 62, $1.50; ages 6–12, free. Free first Thursday of each month

The art and artifacts of the Tikar, Bamum, Manbila, and other peoples of Cameroon find one of their most comprehensive expressions in America at the Portland Museum of Art. Chiefs' stools and tapestries, masks, ancestral figures, house posts, woven bags, pipes, jewelery, footrests, fly whisks, drinking cups, and other objects convey the immense range of creative expression compressed in the relatively small area of the Cameroonian grasslands. Wood predominates as a medium, though brass masks and figures, ivory and horn carvings, and objects sculpted out of the pith of the raffia palms also will be found.

SOUTH DAKOTA

Department of Tourism
Capitol Plaza, Pierre, SD 57501
(800) 843-1930; (605) 773-3301
Hours: Mon.–Fri., 8 A.M.–5 P.M.

DEADWOOD

Adams Memorial Museum
54 Sherman, Deadwood, SD 57732
(605) 578-1714
Hours: May–Sept.: Mon.–Sat., 9 A.M.–6 P.M.; Sun., 9 A.M.–5 P.M. Oct.–Apr.: Tue.–Sat., 10 A.M.–4 P.M.; Sun., 12 P.M.–4 P.M.
Admission: Voluntary donations requested

Photographs of black cowboys, miners, and residents of Deadwood and surrounding towns and the grave marker of "Aunt Sally" Campbell, a cook for an officer of the 7th Cavalry and the first nonaboriginal woman to walk the Black Hills, are the African-American highlights of the Adams Memorial Museum. Pictured among the African-American cowboys is Nat Love. Born in a slave cabin in Tennessee in the 1850s, the teenage Love lit out for Kansas in 1869, later earning the sobriquet "Deadwood Dick" for his triumphant feats in the July 4th celebration shooting and roping contests held here in 1876. He treasured his triumph, setting his nickname in type as the subtitle of his 1907 autobiography. The book is a triumph of good-natured self-promotion, absurd braggadocio, and racist claptrap applied to Indians and Hispanics. Alleged friend of Bat Masterson, Jesse James, and Billy the Kid, Indian fighter extraordinaire, and dandy companion of sundry women, the "heroic" Love culminated his western career as a porter on the railroads that ran the cattle punchers off the range. Also at the museum is a small collection of West African artifacts, principally items of personal adornment. Deadwood has other tourist sites, such as Boot Hill, for those interested in the Wild West; but except for the public library at 435 Williams Street, which has articles on Love and Campbell, the Adams Museum is the sole place in town to incorporate the African-American presence out where the cattle and Indians roamed.

COURTESY BLACK AMERICAN WEST MUSEUM

Nat Love, or "Deadwood Dick," was one of the few cowboys to publish his autobiography.

FORT MEADE

Fort Meade Museum
Highway 34 East; P.O. Box 164, Fort Meade, SD 57741
(605) 347-9822
Hours: June–Aug.: Mon.–Sat., 8 A.M.–7 P.M.; May and Sept., Mon.–Sat., 9 A.M.–5 P.M.
Admission: Adults, $2; under 12, free

Companies A, D, H, and K of the 25th Infantry arrived at Fort Meade in 1880 and spent the next eight years there, leaving 13 of their comrades in the cemetery. One, Corporal Ross Hallon of Company A, died the victim of a lynching—and perhaps of a macabre pun. Hallon's death symbolized the 25th's less-than-sterling relations with the nearby town of Sturgis. Though the facts are not absolutely beyond dispute, the burden of evidence establishes that Hallon murdered a local doctor, H. P. Lynch, who had advised Hallon's battered mistress, Minnie Lewis, to press charges against the trooper. Following testimony by two of his Company A comrades, Hallon was detained in the city jail on a murder charge. Two days later he was dragged from the jail to a tree west of town by the Catholic Church and hanged. The tree was "semiofficial," having a year earlier supported Alex Fiddler, a white thief who had robbed an immigrant. Officially the army listed Hallon's death as of "natural causes," though whether this was to protect his good name or the regiment's—or because the army perceived lynching as a natural death for African Americans—remains unclear. Scarcely had the town calmed down before there was more trouble between the white civilians and the black troopers. Again a white civilian was killed, though this time accidentally in the course of repeated assaults by some black troopers on a black-owned and staffed brothel. (Western white communities used these crude "hog ranches" as their "respectable" explanation for why black troopers should be assigned elsewhere.) Though four troopers were indicted for manslaughter, the townspeople petitioned for the removal of all the black troops. The commanding officer of Dakota Territory, General Alfred Terry, rejected the petition, and the 25th remained at Fort Meade until 1888. Today's visitors to Fort Meade Museum will find some photographs of the 25th's troopers and a small display on the buffalo soldiers. In general, the museum's focus is on life at the fort, rather than on particular units. The cemetery where Hallon and his comrades lie also is open to visitors, but neither there nor at the museum will one find an account of the friction between the town and the black troops.

PICKSTOWN

Historic Fort Randall
P.O. Box 109, U.S. Army Corps of Engineers, Pickstown, SD 57367
(605) 487-7845
Hours: Lake Visitor Center: Memorial Day–Labor Day: daily, 8 A.M.–6 P.M. Dam Visitor Center: Memorial Day–Labor Day: daily, 8 A.M.–5 P.M. Historic fort site: daily, daylight hours
Admission: Free

The land was Ponca and Teton Sioux territory, and in the 1860s and '70s there were frequent skirmishes. But by 1880, when the black troopers of the 25th Infantry arrived at Fort Randall, the last link in a chain of forts that guarded the overland route along the Platte River and the first fort in a chain along the upper Missouri River, the western frontier had passed by and life was a little quieter. For the majority of soldiers at the fort, life was a tedious round of drilling, maintenance chores, road-repairing, and target practice, made the more dreary by the long winters. Band concerts, baseball games (the fort's O'Reillys regularly challenged the Yankton Coyote Ball Club), military balls, and skating parties in the winter and picnics in the summer were instituted to enliven existence. Also enlivening existence from 1881 to 1883 was the imprisoned Sitting Bull, whose band of 158 Hunkpapa Sioux camped south of the fort. Today none of the fort's buildings remains, but visitors to Historic Fort Randall take a self-guided tour around the foundations of the fort's structures. Frequent interpretive markers make mention of the black troops, whose presence also is recalled by a couple of photographs, including one of the assembled band and one of Company B on the parade ground. There also are two nearby visitor centers, one at the dam that towers above the fort site and one overlooking the lake. Both contain artifacts from the fort and photographs of the troops that served there prior to its closure in 1892.

PINE RIDGE

Holy Rosary Mission
Pine Ridge Indian Reservation, U.S. 18, Pine Ridge, SD 57770
(605) 867-5821
Hours: Daily until sunset
Admission: Free

When the detachment of the 9th Cavalry from Fort Robinson (see entry on p. 428) arrived at Pine Ridge in the waning days of 1890, they found their comrades from the 7th pinned down not far from Holy Rosary Mission, a building for which the Oglala Sioux Ghost Dance warriors had scant use. Driving the Sioux from the ridges overlooking the white troopers, the 9th won its last Medal of Honor from the Plains Indian wars. Corporal William Wilson collected the 11th such award won by the unit in two decades. Today at the church, historical markers recount the violent conclusion to a true clash of cultures and recall the role of "black white men" in suppressing the final gasp of a defeated people.

VERMILLION

Shrine to Music Museum
414 East Clark Street, Vermillion, SD 57069
(605) 677-5306
Hours: Mon.–Fri., 9 A.M.–4:30 P.M.; Sat., 10 A.M.–4:30 P.M.; Sun., 2 P.M.–4:30 P.M.
Admission: Free

There's an African beat in a South Dakota town whose name recalls the body adornment of Masai warriors (*moran*). *Sansas* ("thumb pianos") from Central Africa, "talking drums" (Nigeria), bowl lyres (Sudan, Ethiopia, Uganda), xylophones (Sierra Leone), tuned sets of large drums (Uganda), arched harps (Zaire), and gourd rattles (Botswana) grace the Shrine to Music Museum. These are complemented by samples from Egypt, including single- and double-reed wind instruments (which in Europe would become oboes and clarinets, respectively) and small frame drums with cymbals attached (which in Europe emerged as tambourines). The bowl lyres are particularly interesting for Afrocentrists whose museum experiences have included a survey of ancient Greek vases. At the museum the continuum of the African musical tradition is traced through the diaspora. Samples of slave stringed instruments will be found in the American Folk Instrument Collection, and there are exhibits on the emergence of ragtime and jazz.

WAKPALA

Arikara Village Historical Marker
Wakpala, SD 57658
North from Wakpala on Highway 1806 about 12 miles, then east on a gravel road for 2 miles or so, then south for about 4 miles
Hours: Daily until sunset
Admission: Free

One good thing about visiting the Arikara Village Historical Marker outside Wakpala is that it is located sufficiently far from civilization to give one a sense, even though attenuated, of the difficulties faced by Lewis and Clark and their comrades. When the expedition arrived here in October 1804, it found "a collection of conical lodges made of willow wattles covered with straw and five or six inches of mud, some of them fifty feet in diameter." The Arikara, who had seen white traders before, were startled by York, who, according to Clark, proceeded to tell them that "he had once been a wild animal, and caught, and tamed by his master; and to convince them showed them feats of strength which, added to his looks, made him seem more terrible than we wished him to be." The Dakotas' beauty compensates the hardy traveler who wishes to trace York's journey; however, only the foolhardy will attempt to locate this marker without asking directions in Wakpala.

YANKTON

Allen Chapel A.M.E. Church
508 Cedar Street, Yankton, SD 57078
(605) 665-1449
Hours: Tours by special arrangement
Admission: Free

It was a long journey from Alabama to South Dakota, but to some in the 1880s the Black Hills seemed preferable to the Black Belt after the crushing of Reconstruction. Shortly after their arrival in Yankton, the terminus of the steamboat line, the African-American community raised the Allen Chapel A.M.E. Church. It still stands not far from the old Fort Randall, which once served as a duty station for buffalo soldiers of the 25th Infantry. This is the oldest black church in the state and one of the farthest reaches of the diaspora's wave.

UTAH

Utah Travel Council
Council Hill, Capitol Hill, Salt Lake City, UT 84114
(801) 538-1030
Hours: Mon.–Fri., 8 A.M.–5 A.M.; Sat.–Sun., 10 A.M.–5 P.M.

FORT DUCHESNE

Fort Duchesne Historical Marker
Uintah and Oray Indian Reservation Tribal Headquarters, P.O. Box 190,
Fort Duchesne, Utah 84026
(801) 722-5141 (Mon.–Thu. only)
Hours: Daily until sunset
Admission: Free

In August 1886, amid reports of disputes among the White River, Uncompahgre, and Uintah bands of Ute Indians and between the Utes and their American overseers, companies B and E of the 9th Cavalry and four companies of the white 21st Infantry arrived on the Uintah frontier to establish Fort Duchesne. The only thing historically unusual about the assignment was the major commanding the two companies of black troopers. Frederick W. Benteen was tarred, unfairly to be sure, for having not gotten himself and his command killed at the Battle of Little Big Horn. (See entry on p. 497.) Now, 20 years after having declined a promotion to major and service with a black regiment (see Fort Davis entry on p. 161), Benteen had both—the latter, he believed, because of his "failure" at Little Big Horn. (In 1866 Benteen declined to serve with the 10th Cavalry, choosing instead to remain with the 7th as a captain. He saw his service with the 9th as a form of punishment, believing, as he wrote following his retirement, that "it was not proper to remain with a race of troops that I could take no interest in and this on account of their 'low-down' rascally character.")

Except for six months in 1898—when the black troopers fought in Cuba during the Spanish-American War—Fort Duchesne was garrisoned entirely by the 9th's buffalo soldiers for almost a decade. (This assignment gave Uintah County the second largest black population in the state.) Two of the first three black graduates of West Point, John Alexander and Charles Young (see Greene County Museum, entry on p. 451), served at Fort Duchesne. Both drew the typical post assignments of their rank: leading patrols, directing fatigue details, and attempting to keep the Utes on and the whites off the reservation. Perhaps the most significant event of their stay here was that Young's tenure overlapped with that of then Sergeant Benjamin O. Davis, whom he tutored for his commissioned officer's examination. Davis, of course, went on to become the first African American of general rank in the United States Army, while his son became the first black graduate of West Point since Charles Young.

For the troopers of the 9th, Fort Duchesne (unlike Fort Douglas) was an unpleasant assignment: Torrid in summer and frigid in winter, the fort's location had little to recommend it. Isolation and loneliness were interrupted but scarcely assuaged by reveille, fatigue, school, drills, dinner, and tattoo. Not even drinking and visits to "the Strip," an insalubrious, off-post refuge of bars and brothels, offered much break to the routine. Typical assignments included escort duty, maintenance of the post sawmill, maintaining the telegraph line between Fort Duchesne and Price, Utah, and keeping a lookout on the reservation. Sitting for days at a time at "Devil's Playground," one unknown company of the 9th constructed a large dirt mound in the shape of a heart. About 25 feet by 25 feet, the mound was identified with rocks that spelled out "9th CAV." Today little remains to recall this past except a historical marker, which specifically mentions the 9th Cavalry. The heart mound also remains, though its condition has deteriorated considerably. Finally, there is a tribal museum, but its operation is on-again, off-again.

SALT LAKE CITY

Convention & Visitors Bureau
180 South West Temple, Salt Lake City, UT 84101
(801) 521-2822
Hours: Mon.–Fri., 8 A.M.–5 P.M.; Sat., 9 A.M.–4 P.M.

Brigham Young Monument
Main Street at Temple, Salt Lake City, UT 84101
Hours: Guided tours: May–Sept., daily, 8 A.M.–10 P.M.; rest of year, daily, 9 A.M.–9 P.M.
Admission: Free

Only in their racial perspective could the founders and early adherents of the Church of Jesus Christ of Latter-day Saints (the Mormons) be called orthodox. Their other views—God as a personal being, Jesus as his literal son, the inspired character of the golden tablets of Moroni, the postdeath saving of one's ancestors, polygamous marriages—long forced them to the geographical and cultural periphery of America. But their support of slavery and their refusal up until 1970 to accept that African Americans were ready to be "given the right to hold the priesthood" helped their integration into a society that otherwise regarded them as a bizarre cult.

Although a peripheral element of a peripheral American experience, African Americans have been connected to the Mormons from their early days, before their 1847 trek to the Great Basin (the 19th-century wilderness of Utah and Nevada). When the founder of the church, Joseph Smith, and his brother Hyrum were martyred by a mob in the Carthage, Illinois, jail, Isaac Manning, an African-American servant of the Mormon prophet, rescued their bodies and secretly buried them. Then, as the Mormons prepared to abandon their Illinois base for the far West, at least three African Americans—Green Flake, Hark Lay, and Oscar Crosby, all of whom bore the last names of white members, suggesting at least a prior condition of slavery—joined the original party of 148 settlers led by Brigham Young. The task of these African Americans was to prepare comfortable quarters for their masters—Flake, for example, had a cabin nicely prepared for the John Flake family of North Carolina when they arrived in October 1848. Green Flake was a busy man, for also in 1848 he returned east to escort a party of Mississippi Mormons, 34 of whose 91 members were black. (Or in any event, 34 of the group were black; most were slaves of the whites and hence their religious affiliation was simply presumed.)

Today inscribed on the base of the Brigham Young Monument are the names of the founding party of settlers, including those of Flake, Lay, and Crosby. Their names also will be found on the "This Is The Place" Monument east of the city at the mouth of Emigration Canyon, which again honors the founding party of settlers. Flake's grave will be found in Union Cemetery, while that of Isaac Manning and of Elijah Abel—an African-American undertaker in Illinois who converted to the church in the 1840s and became the only black man to be given a function in the Mormon ecclesiastical hierarchy prior to 1970—will be found in the Salt Lake Cemetery.

Calvary Baptist Church
532 East 700 South Street, Salt Lake City, UT 84102
(801) 355-1025
Hours: Mon.–Fri., 9 A.M.–2 P.M.; Sat. hours vary; Sun., 8 A.M.–1 P.M. and 7 P.M.–8:30 P.M.
Admission: Free

Calvary Baptist Church is the oldest black Baptist church in Utah. Though the congregation dates to 1892, the present church structure is neither the original nor located on the original site. On permanent display is a gallery of African-American art and artifacts; most of the former center on religious themes; most of the latter reflect the development of black fraternities and sororities.

Fort Douglas Museum
32 Potter Street, Fort Douglas, Salt Lake City, UT 84113
(801) 588-5188
Hours: Tue.–Sat., 10 A.M.–12 P.M. and 1 P.M.–4 P.M.
Admission: Free

In Utah the army confronted two adversaries—the Utes and the Mormons: one red, one white; one anarchic, one emphatically not. One was unwilling to change, while the other was open to apparent concessions to conformity. Today one has virtually disappeared, the other effectively runs the state. If you won't learn, or least conform, you *will* get run over—especially if you're not white.

The Mormons found opposition everywhere they went, being driven from New York, to Ohio, to Missouri, to Illinois, to Utah—even figuring as a pejorative object of depravity in the Sherlock Holmes story "A Study in Scarlet." Hoping—like McCabe in Oklahoma (see Langston entry on p. 454)—to found a state in which they would predominate, they instead saw the U.S. Congress establish the Utah Territory, which the U.S. Army then occupied. Not for four decades would Utah be permitted to enter the Union, and then only after the Mormons had agreed to refrain from performing plural marriages, had disbanded their political party, and had separated the church from its effective control of the economy. (It was an interesting deal: The U.S. government flagrantly interfered with the rights of the Mormons and the Mormons pretended to acquiesce; the power of both was flaunted.) The Utes were rather less cohesive and astute than the Mormons and were simply crushed.

Both the 9th Cavalry and the 24th Infantry spent years in Utah dealing with one or the other of the army's adversaries. Units of both buffalo soldier regiments spent time at Fort Douglas, where today at the Military Museum visitors will find exhibits on the black troops and a self-guided tour of the fort. Ten companies of the 24th (26 officers and 486 enlisted men) were stationed at the fort from the fall of 1896 until the spring of 1898, when they left for combat in Cuba. Today they are represented by two mannequins, one in a uniform of the 1870s, the other in a uniform of the 1890s. Panels of text tell their story—and that of the 9th, which spent most of its time at Fort Duchesne, where they were commanded by Major Benteen of Little Big Horn notoriety. Photographs of the 9th troopers and artifacts and monographs on the buffalo soldier regiments complete the African-American aspect of the museum. Nearby, at the Fort Douglas Cemetery, visitors will find the graves of 9th and 24th troopers.

Trinity A.M.E. Church
239 East 600 South Street, Salt Lake City, UT 84102
(801) 531-7374
Hours: Mon.–Fri., 9:30 A.M.–12 P.M.
Admission: Free

The congregation of Trinity A.M.E. Church erected the first African-American church in Utah. The present building, to which the state has attached a historical marker, dates to 1907.

University of Utah Library
400 South and University streets, Salt Lake City, UT 84102
(801) 581-8864; (801) 581-8863
Hours: Mon.–Fri., 8 A.M.–5 P.M.; Sat., 9 A.M.–5 P.M.
Admission: Free

African-American oral histories, photographs of early black residents, microfilm of the 1895–1901 black newspaper *Broad Axe*, and documents detailing the relation between the Mormon church and African Americans will be found at the University of Utah Library.

WASHINGTON

Tourism Division
101 General Administration Building, AX-13, Olympia, WA 98504-0613
(800) 544-1800
Hours: Daily, 7 A.M.–9 P.M.

CENTRALIA

George Washington Grave, Park, and Plaque

Grave: Washington Lawn Cemetery, Washington Avenue, Centralia, WA 98531
Park: Pearl and Harrison streets, Centralia, WA 98531
Hours: Daily until sunset
Admission: Free

Never advance goods on credit if you lack legal standing in the courts. In the 19th century the civil rights priority of free blacks was not the right to vote but rather the right to testify in court. Failing that right, no man's property (or person) was secure against the arbitrary exercise of power or racial privilege.

The Missouri legislature's 1843 gift of extensive though incomplete civic rights to George Washington underscored the tangled ramifications and limitations of African Americans' legal status without constitutional protection. Born in Virginia in 1817, Washington's background is somewhat uncertain—usually he is referred to as a slave to whom legend attributes a white mother and a slave father, though clearly the two statements are mutually exclusive. In any event, shortly after his birth, Washington was adopted by a childless white couple, James and Anna Cochran, who moved to the Missouri frontier, where years later they secured partial civic rights for their adopted son. Washington ran a sawmill in St. Joseph, where he also ran into a legal roadblock, being unable in federal court to prosecute an out-of-state customer because he lacked standing as a citizen. Heading west with his adoptive parents in 1850, Washington found in the Oregon Territory (which included present-day Washington state) that which he had fled, repressive antiblack laws. Unable to purchase land, Washington in 1852 accepted land deeded to him by the Cochrans, to whom he paid $2,000, repeating the procedure a few years later. This was the beginning of his landed wealth, which rose in value in 1872 when the Northern Pacific Railroad decided to lay tracks across his property. It was also the beginning of the town of Centralia, which grew rapidly, aided by Washington's willingness to sell 2,000 lots of property at $5 each, provided that the new owners raised houses valued at $100 or more. Washington donated land for a park, which now bears his name, a cemetery, in which he now rests, and for churches, in one of which his funeral service was held. On his death in 1905, the town closed down for a day of mourning for its founder and benefactor.

Today George Washington's Grave will be found in the Washington Lawn Cemetery. Near George Washington Park is the Timberline Library—which has a significant collection of material on the town's father—and a historical plaque honoring a black pioneer of the far Northwest.

ELLENSBURG

Ellensburg Public Library

209 North Ruby Street, Ellensburg, WA 98926
(509) 962-7252
Hours: Mon.–Fri., 10 A.M.–8:30 P.M.; Sat., 10 A.M.–5 P.M.; Sun., 1 P.M.–5 P.M.
Admission: Free

Today Roslyn, Washington, is best known as the location on which *Northern Exposure* is filmed—hence the sign "Roslyn Cafe" by which the moose strolls. (The moose is an imported background artist.) But in the early years of the century, the area was known for its coal and gold mines—and its black miners. Today the Ellensburg Public Library maintains a permanent collection of photographs, newspaper clippings, articles, and books on African-American mining life in the nearby community of Roslyn. Entitled "Through Open Eyes: 95 Years of Black History in Roslyn," the exhibit is not always on display, but the folks at the library are happy to make it available if you ask to see it.

ILWACO

Lewis and Clark Interpretive Center
Fort Canby State Park, Ilwaco, WA 98624
(206) 642-3029
Hours: May 7–Sept. 30: daily, 10 A.M.–5 P.M.
Admission: Free

As you walk down the ramp at the Lewis and Clark Interpretive Center, you trace the path of the expedition, gradually ascending until you see the Pacific Ocean, which marked the farthest boundary of their exploration. Along the way, wall text of the explorers' journals, paintings, and doll figures in a camp setting make reference to York, Clark's slave who served as a figure of interest and ingratiation with the Indians. Both the video program at the center and the audio buttons that one encounters along the ramp offer running commentary from the journals and historical explanations that include the role of York.

RENTON

Jimi Hendrix Grave
Greenwood Memorial Park Funeral Home, 350 Monroe Avenue, NE, Renton, WA 98056
(206) 255-1511
Hours: Daily, 8 A.M.–4:30 P.M.
Admission: Free

Are you experienced? Talk about crossing over! The greatest rock guitarist in the age of acid was African American. The only thing black he lacked was an audience. The time has come today, as the Chambers Brothers might say, to pay tribute to Jimi Hendrix, who grew up and went to high school in Renton, Washington. After high school came a tour of duty with the U.S. Army paratroopers. It was only after leaving the service that Hendrix spent time flying, finally crashing and burning—dead of a heroin overdose—in 1970 at the age of 27. Before his sordid death, the man did more things with a guitar—and with "The Star-Spangled Banner"—than anyone before or since. Beyond his command of the instrument, which he could make weep, scream, and moan, Jimi Hendrix was one of the dominant visual images of '60s' youth culture. His untamed hair and flamboyant clothes served notice that he played the guitar and lived life with abandon. He not only played with abandon, he played with his teeth! There was little he could not do with a guitar—and little that he did not do with drugs.

Today over the Jimi Hendrix Grave lies a flat, bluish-gray stone marker in which is etched a guitar. Jimi Hendrix is etched in history in all the colors of the rainbow. Hey, Joe, Renton's not huge, so you won't find much Crosstown Traffic on the way to the cemetery; once there, you'll hear the wind cry Jimi.

SEATTLE

Convention & Visitors Bureau
Washington State Convention Center, 800 Convention Place, Seattle, WA 98101
(206) 461-5840
Hours: Mon.–Fri., 8:30 A.M.–5 P.M.
Ask for the "Multi-Ethnic Guide to Seattle–King County" brochure.

Mt. Zion Baptist Church
1634 19th Avenue, Seattle, WA 98122
(206) 322-6500
Hours: Mon.–Sat., 9 A.M.–5 P.M.
Admission: Free

Though the congregation dates back to 1890, the most striking feature of the Mt. Zion Baptist Church is far more recent. Outside and inside, the church has an Afrocentric accent. Colors, shapes, forms, figures, and symbols recall the Mother Continent and the diaspora. Unfinished beams support the structure and are intended to convey the notion of African Americans as an unfinished people. Carvings in the pulpit and the offering table have an African resonance and require a closer inspection, unlike the stained glass windows, which proudly portray a descent from Prince Hall, Nat Turner, Sojourner Truth, Paul Laurence Dunbar, Mary McLeod Bethune, Martin Luther King, Jr., and a black pioneer of Washington, George Bush (see Henderson Museum entry on p. 525), among others.

Seattle Art Museum
100 University Street, Seattle, WA 98101
(206) 654-3100
Hours: Tue.–Wed. and Fri.–Sun., 10 A.M.–5 P.M.; Thu., 10 A.M.–9 P.M.
Admission: Suggested donation: Adults, $6; seniors and under 12, $4

The 16th-century ivory salt cellars of the African Collection of this museum were among the first works of commissioned tourist art produced for Europe in sub-Saharan Africa. Modeled on their metal counterparts possessed by Portuguese sailors, the ivory pieces added forms of adornment never seen before in Europe—for example, carved crocodile snouts with jaws agape—making the household objects the talk of Lisbon upon the sailors' return. Though far from the collection's most significant works of art, the Afro-Portuguese ivory objects offer a useful glimpse into the cultural exchange that took place in the wake of the voyages of exploration sponsored by Prince Henry. Africa in the 16th century is also represented by Benin metal and ivory pieces of deeper indigenous roots and higher artistic aspiration. With 2,000 or so African objects in its possession, the museum is well placed to traverse the continent's artistic and material production. Among the stronger holdings are West and Central African objects of adornment. Textiles, jewelery, and household implements are held in large quantity, though the high art end of the spectrum is not slighted. Yoruba, Bamana, BaKongo, Dan, Senufo, Ibo, and Luba objects abound, while the Kom kingdom of Cameroon also is featured. Metal objects are rare in this collection, with one prominent exception, weaponry—so many kids will refrain from clamoring to go elsewhere.

SPOKANE

Henderson House Museum
602 DesChutes Way, Spokane, WA 98501
(206) 753-8583
Hours: Thu.–Sun., 12 P.M.–4 P.M.
Admission: Voluntary donations requested

Simmons Party Memorial
Tumwater Falls Historical Park at the foot of Grant Street, Tumwater, WA 98502
Hours: Daily until sunset
Admission: Free

Tumwater Pioneer Cemetery
Little Rock Road, Tumwater, WA 98501
(206) 753-8583
Hours: Daily until sunset
Admission: Free

Where're you gonna run to—and what will you do if you can't phone ahead? Born free in Pennsylvania, the son of a black sailor and an Irish housemaid, George Bush left home at the age of 18 to take part in the War of 1812. After venturing west and making a stake in the fur trade, he settled in Missouri. His farm and cattle-trading business near St. Louis prospering, Bush married Isabella James and raised five sons. Despite being mulatto, well-to-do, and married to a white woman, as a free black he found limited acceptance. When the Missouri legislature prohibited further free-black entry to the state, Bush decided to head west again. His goal was the virtually unsettled Northwest Territory, whose ownership was still being disputed between the U.S. and Britain.

Joining (and probably partially financing) a party of white acquaintances led by Michael Simmons, Bush and his family in 1844 ventured along the Oregon Trail. Bush had been this way before as a trapper and was a welcome addition for more than financial reasons. His advice to his companions was pithy: "It's a hard country . . . anything you see as big as a blackbird, kill and eat it." Their journey took seven months—and when they arrived at the Hudson Bay Trading Post on the Columbia River, they learned that the Oregon "Provisional Government" had passed a law precluding black residence! Bush wasn't even street legal where he stood. So he and Simmons and a few others pushed on north toward Puget Sound, an area effectively governed by Britain and hence lacking black codes. Here they hacked out a 35-mile wagon trail and settled at Tumwater Falls.

The hospitality of the Bushes over the ensuing years figures prominently in the pioneer diaries of those who followed them. People were fed and sheltered, the women and children often for weeks as their menfolk went ahead to arrange the prospective farm sites. No one was asked to pay and no one was turned away. Bush established the first school and the first grist and saw mills in the area, and he and his son William brought the first reaper to Washington. He did well, but he was better known for doing good. Perhaps he was best known for refusing amid a general drought to sell his grain to speculators, instead selling it to those in need at cost. But he was still black and when America and Britain settled their boundary dispute, drawing the U.S.-Canadian border at the 49th parallel, what is now the state of Washington briefly became part of Oregon Territory and Bush again was an illegal resident. (Ironically, it was the presence of Bush, Simmons, and others that justified the American claim of what became the state of Washington.) At this juncture, Michael Simmons and other Tumwater residents successfully petitioned the Territorial Legislature of 1849 for a special exemption authorizing Bush's residence, a procedure that was followed in 1854 in the newly established Washington Territorial Legislature. This in turn led to an act by the U.S. Congress granting Bush and his heirs civic status in the territory and the 640 acres of land due the family under the terms of the old Oregon Territory's Land Donation Act. Bush was still black, though—some things never change—and never got the right to vote, dying in 1863. His son William saw better days and was elected to Washington's first state legislature.

Today George Bush is honored, particularly in Tumwater, as one of Washington's pioneers. The Henderson House Museum has a permanent exhibit on the man who gave his name to the Bush Prairie, while the Simmons Party Memorial has inscribed on it the names of Tumwater's founders, prominently including George Bush's. Finally, George and Isabella Bush, Michael Simmons, and others of that original party are buried in the Tumwater Pioneer Cemetery.

WYOMING

Division of Tourism
I-25 at College Drive, Cheyenne, WY 82002
(800) 225-5996
Hours: Mon.–Fri., 8 A.M.–5 P.M.

BUFFALO

Gatchell Memorial Museum
100 Fort Street, Buffalo, WY 82834
(307) 684-9331
Hours: May–Sept.: daily, 9 A.M.–9 P.M.
Admission: Free

It was another clash of cultures in the West, this time between free-range cattle barons and settlers, and it wasn't settled by Shane of movie fame but by the buffalo soldiers of the 9th Cavalry. The influx of homesteaders—and their damned barbed wire—into Johnson County in the last decade of the 19th century ended the open range on which major beef businessmen depended. Six men died in the two years preceding the so-called Johnson County War, all of whom, swore the Wyoming Stock Growers Association, were rustlers—but then the cattle barons identified all "nesters" as rustlers. In 1892 the cattle interests imported a private army to run off the homesteaders. Telegraph wires were cut to isolate the county, and two men were killed at the KC Cabin. The sheriff from Buffalo then raised a posse and surrounded the cattleman and their gunmen at the TA Ranch. By this time the news had reached the state capital, and the army was ordered to intercede. The 9th Cavalry then rode in and arrested their private sector counterparts—who would not surrender to the sheriff's posse, fearing swift retribution—ending the war. For a more detailed account of the range war and the role of the buffalo soldiers, visit the Gatchell Memorial Museum, which holds a couple of photographs of the black troopers and a table and chair stenciled with "9th Cav." Also stop by the Johnson County Library. (See next entry.) Just outside of Buffalo on Highway 16, visit the remains of old Fort McKinney, which now serves as a Wyoming Veterans' Home and which has a Fort McKinney Historical Marker on its grounds.

Johnson County Library
117 North Adams, Buffalo, WY 82834
(307) 684-5546
Hours: Mon.–Sat., 10 A.M.–5 P.M.
Admission: Free

Here you will find copies of the records of nearby Fort McKinney, where companies of the 9th Cavalry were stationed, and contemporaneous newspaper accounts of the war and its aftermath, the Suggs incident. In Suggs—modern-day Arvada—northwest of Buffalo, a couple of troopers from the 9th were killed in a racial brawl, sparked by a freed cattleman who wished to provoke martial law and centered on a dispute over a prostitute. This incident, of course, violates the western canon, in which there are white hats and black hats, but not white guys and black guys.

FORT LARAMIE

Fort Laramie National Historic Site and Museum
Fort Laramie, WY 82212
(307) 837-2221
Hours: June 1–Labor Day: daily, 8 A.M.–7 P.M. Rest of year: daily, 8 A.M.–4:30 P.M.
Admission: Adults, $1

Fort Laramie, which began in 1834 as a small stockaded trading post of the Rocky Mountain Fur Company, was the first garrisoned army post in Wyoming and the single most critical post of the emigrant trail heading west. Between Fort Laramie in eastern Wyoming and South Pass in the central part of the state, all the trails came together: the Oregon, Mormon, and California trails; the overland stage route; the Pony Express route; and the overland telegraph lines all funneled through the North Platte Valley guarded by the fort. Fort Laramie saw the defeat of the Plains Indians, the growth of the open range cattle industry, the coming of homesteaders, and—with the 1894 passage of the Carey Act, written by Wyoming's U.S. senator Joseph M. Carey, which made a million acres of cheap land and water for irrigation available to homesteaders—the closing of the frontier. Through Fort Laramie passed African Americans known—George Bush (see Henderson Museum entry on p. 525), George Washington (see entry on p. 522), Green Flake (see Brigham Young Monument entry on p. 519)—and unknown. Unfortunately, none of the four black regiments of the Plains Indians wars were stationed here. Their absence, coupled with the relatively few black migrants to the far West, leaves the Fort Laramie National Historic Site and Museum without an impetus to interpret the black presence in the West. This situation is the more regrettable because the fort's history and its operation by the always outstanding National Park Service interpreters makes it well worth a visit.

FORT WASHAKIE

F. E. Warren Museum
P.O. Box 9521, F. E. Warren Air Base, Fort Washakie, WY 82514
(307) 775-2980
Hours: Memorial Day–Labor Day: Wed.–Sat., 1 P.M.–4 P.M. Rest of year: Wed., Fri., Sat., 1 P.M.–4 P.M.
Admission: Free

From 1887 through 1916, units of the 9th, 10th, and 24th regiments served at Fort D. A. Russell (now F. E. Warren Air Force Base). Though there are few buffalo soldier artifacts at the F. E. Warren Museum, there are photographs of the black troops, including one of the 24th Infantry marching on the parade grounds. The centerpiece of the buffalo soldier exhibit is a uniform from the 1920s, a period little interpreted in the military histories of the African-American troops since there were no armed clashes to occupy their attention and the cavalry was coming under scrutiny in the aftermath of World War I.

SHERIDAN

Fort McKenzie
VA Medical Center, Fort Hill Road, Sheridan, WY 82801
(307) 672-3473, ext. 3642
Hours: VA voluntary services tours by appointment
Admission: Free

Fort McKenzie is a tribute to congressional representation, being built in 1899, long after the threat of a Plains Indians uprising had receded. Following the appeal of Congressman H. A. Coffeen, who petitioned Senator F. E. Warren and the Committee on Military Affairs for a military post at Sheridan to "protect the community from Indians," the U.S. Congress appropriated $100,000 (and in the nature of things, spent $364,629) for Fort McKenzie. Thus in 1899 the black troopers of the 25th Infantry moved to the foothills of the Big Horn Mountains and began construction of temporary wooden buildings that would house a small detachment of the 1st Cavalry. By 1903 work on brick buildings began, doubtless to the satisfaction of companies G and H of the 10th Cavalry, who arrived the same year. Not once in any report from 1899 through 1916 are Indians mentioned, and the men garrisoning the fort spent most of their time at target practice, marching, maintaining the fort, and playing baseball. Today most of the fort is still intact and serves as a Veteran's Administration Hospital. Barracks, officers' quarters, and stables—the last with the engraved names of the horses still visible on the walls—may be viewed by visitors, who also have access to a library with archival material and photographs. Although little remains that is specifically African American, don't cavil: While you're hunting for the black remnants of a relatively easy duty station, look up—towering 10,000 feet above the 3,800-foot elevation where you are standing is the snowcapped, highest peak of the Big Horn Mountains.

CANADA

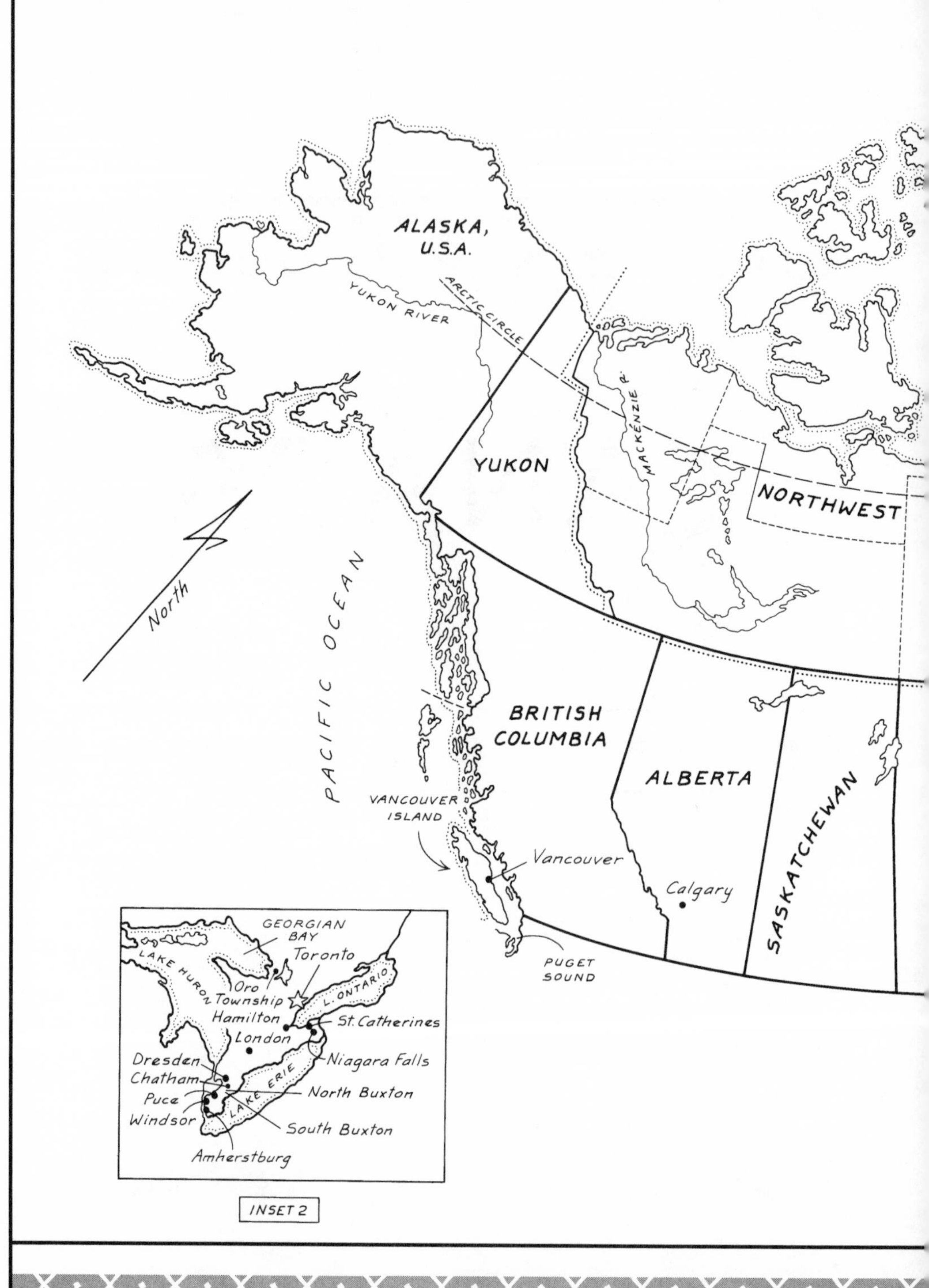
ALASKA, U.S.A.
YUKON RIVER
ARCTIC CIRCLE
YUKON
MACKENZIE R.
NORTHWEST
North
PACIFIC OCEAN
BRITISH COLUMBIA
ALBERTA
SASKATCHEWAN
VANCOUVER ISLAND
Vancouver
Calgary
PUGET SOUND
GEORGIAN BAY
LAKE HURON
Toronto
Oro Township
L. ONTARIO
Hamilton
St. Catherines
London
Niagara Falls
Dresden
Chatham
LAKE ERIE
North Buxton
Puce
Windsor
South Buxton
Amherstburg
INSET 2

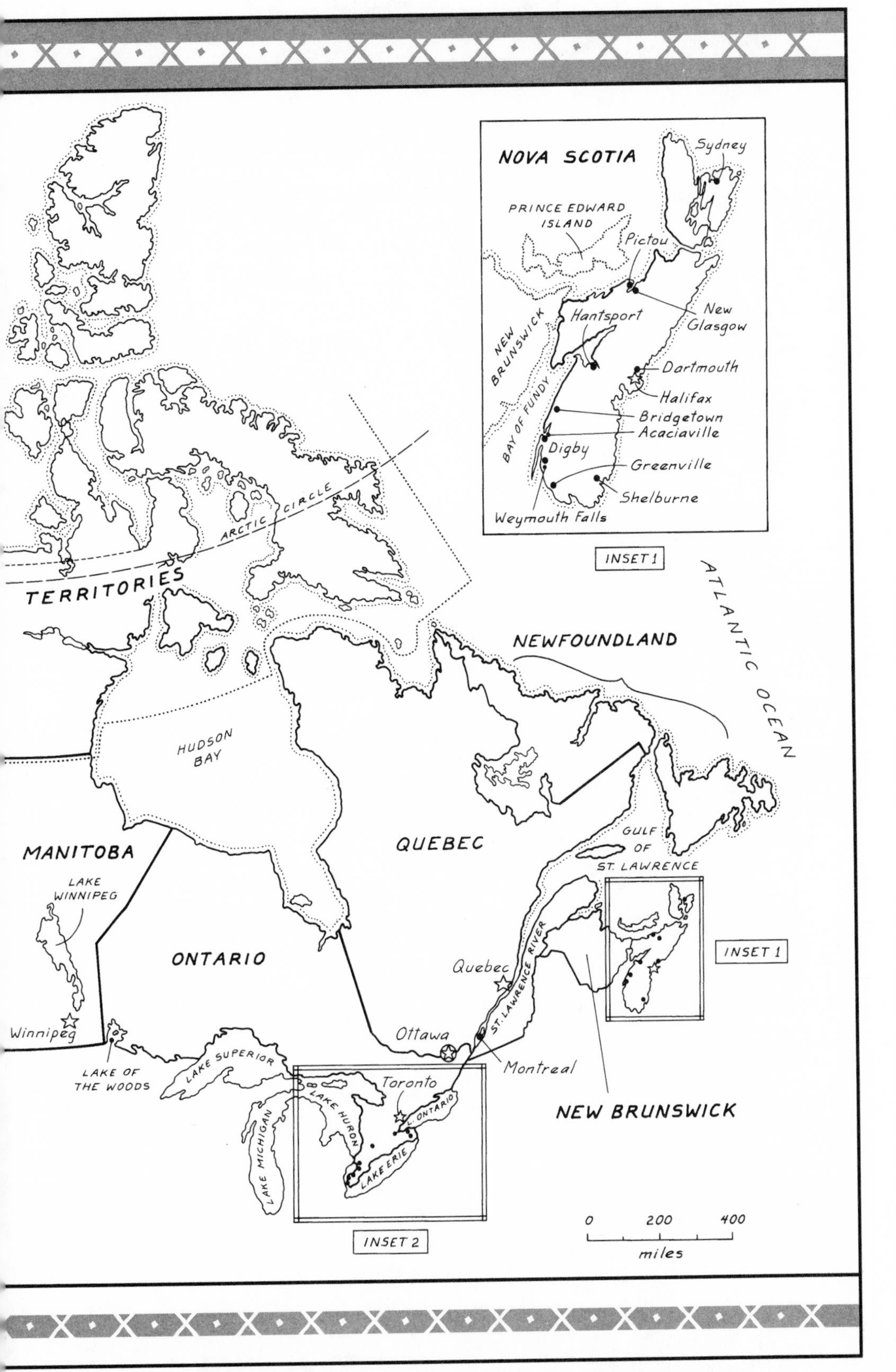
NOVA SCOTIA
Sydney
PRINCE EDWARD ISLAND
Pictou
NEW BRUNSWICK
Hantsport
New Glasgow
Dartmouth
Halifax
BAY OF FUNDY
Bridgetown
Acaciaville
Digby
Greenville
Shelburne
Weymouth Falls
INSET 1
ATLANTIC OCEAN
ARCTIC CIRCLE
TERRITORIES
NEWFOUNDLAND
HUDSON BAY
MANITOBA
QUEBEC
GULF OF ST. LAWRENCE
LAKE WINNIPEG
ONTARIO
INSET 1
Quebec
ST. LAWRENCE RIVER
Winnipeg
Ottawa
Montreal
LAKE OF THE WOODS
LAKE SUPERIOR
Toronto
LAKE HURON
L. ONTARIO
NEW BRUNSWICK
LAKE MICHIGAN
LAKE ERIE
INSET 2
0
200
400
miles

FOLLOW THE NORTH STAR

FREDERICK IVOR CASE

I live in Canada—by choice. This vast land is staggeringly beautiful—criss-crossed by hundreds of rivers, segmented by soaring mountains, beaten by oceans' surf, and bejeweled with thousands of lakes. I live in Ontario, the wealthiest, most dynamic, and most populous of Canada's ten provinces. Across this land, Ontario is despised, envied, and emulated. I live in Toronto, Ontario's proud and orderly capital and the country's principal magnet attracting people young and old, aboriginal, black, white, Chinese, and Somali. The United Nations recently judged Toronto to be the safest and most cosmopolitan city in the hemisphere. In a beautiful land, I live in the western hemisphere's safest and most cosmopolitan city. And yet . . . I live with fear: Fear that my children, too, will pay the violent tax levied on those of African descent . . . levied by the uniformed police, levied by the expanding Klan and neo-Nazi movements, levied in less violent form by every figure of authority who resents the coloring of Canada. When my sons, in their early 20s, go out in the evenings I have more fear of the police than of the thugs who are not in uniform.

When I arrived here in the late 1960s as part of a wave of black immigrants from Europe, I was struck by the existence of a vibrant, indigenous African-Canadian population. The descendants of Canadian slaves, the offspring of fugitive slaves from the United States, later immigrants from the Caribbean and still more recent arrivals from the Mother Continent had all left an imprint. Today our community not only is larger, it also is far more diverse. Africans from all corners of the world live here, some 300,000 strong, speaking many languages. Our presence is heard on the streets—and on the airwaves. In our diversity, the black community mirrors the nation. And yet we are a widely dispersed racial group without power and without a voice. We have no credible national organization and no identifiable national leaders. Sometimes I feel that we are as unknown to the outside world as are the Africans of Pakistan.

To escape the harsh realities of racism in Toronto, I go north, frequently to Sudbury, where my mother and eldest brother live amid the largest population of African Canadians in the north of Ontario. On the way to Sudbury I pass through the Georgian Bay area, which has long been the choice summer retreat for Canadians. Here are breathtaking scenes of lakes, rivers, and forests. Even in the heart of winter there is splendid beauty and contentment about this place. Though the night temperature regularly dips below 40 degrees Celsius, my greatest pleasure (not shared by the rest of my family!) is taking a brisk walk beside a solidly frozen lake not too far from my brother's home.

Much farther northeast are Moosonee and Moose Factory. To reach these locations on James Bay, I take the Ontario Northland train from Toronto to Cochrane, overnight there, and leave the next morning by the Polar Bear Express to my destination. Moosonee is on the mainland and Moose Factory is an island that is reached by motorized canoe. The two communities are in fact a Cree reserve, and here Cree is the language most commonly heard and seen. But even in these marvelously out-of-the-way places, there are a few black members of the community. Indeed, in every part of this country to which I have traveled, I have found people of African heritage.

In one sense, this black presence should elicit no surprise, for there were blacks in Canada before the English colonies in North America were ever established. The first known African in Canada was an interpreter named Mathieu da Costa, who arrived in 1604 with the French explorer Samuel de Champlain. He spoke French and the language of the Mic Mac people of the Maritime coast. About 20 years later the first known African slave arrived in Quebec City and was given the name Olivier Le Jeune. He and a native Canadian boy became the first students of the first school set up by the Jesuits in North America. Olivier was but the start of a long procession of slaves, freedmen, and fugitives from south of our border.

Indeed, for me, one of the pleasures of traveling about Canada is its black heritage. On my family's visits to Montreal, Quebec, the Old City is a regular place of pilgrimage. Here the principal tourist attraction is a magnificent cathedral church; but few people realize that in 1734, in the old parish church on this site, a black slave, Marie-Joseph-Angelique, was executed. Having learned that her mistress was about to sell her, Marie set fire to the house in which she was working. That was the start of the famous fire of Montreal about which all Canadian children read in their history books—though they rarely learn that the fire was set by a black slave trying to save herself and her children; nor that this slave paid for her audacity at the executioner's block before the parish church of Montreal. There is no plaque or statue to Marie-Joseph-Angelique—only our memory preserves her.

More joyfully, Montreal, the birthplace of Oscar Peterson, is the site of a marvelous annual jazz festival during the first two weeks of July that brings in performers from all corners of the earth. This celebration segues into a festival of African music that takes place in the streets and parks of the city.

In my hometown of Toronto, I stroll along Eglinton Avenue west of Oakwood, drawn by the variety of shops and businesses owned by African Canadians, or wander the west side of Bathurst Street north of Bloor, where there is also a small concentration of black-owned businesses. A stroll farther north to 942 Bathurst Street brings me to Third World Books and Crafts, one of the major African-Canadian institutions of the city. Toronto is the home of three prestigious universities and a wide variety of annual festivals, exhibitions, and sports events. On any given weekend, I might take in a Sikh parade, an Eritrean celebration, a Nigerian festival, a Brazilian triumph, and during the last weekend of July that great Toronto extravaganza—Caribana! Caribana regularly attracts more than 1 million spectators to the biggest street party in North America. The music and the weather entice; the atmosphere is usually terrific. Caribana—for one day of the year we live in the illusion of happiness as our people bring in tens of millions of tourist dollars to a city in which we do not even own a modest cultural center.

Canada's major cities are not the only destinations in which to find our heritage. In the Windsor area of Ontario there are small towns and villages that still reflect their original settlement either by black Empire Loyalists (those who, either freely or in bondage, came north in the wake of the victorious American Revolution) or later by African Americans using the Underground Railroad to flee oppression. Within easy reach of Windsor there is Dresden. My children have always enjoyed the visits there to the settlement and the vocational school founded by the fugitive slave Josiah Henson, whose life partially inspired Harriet Beecher Stowe's *Uncle Tom's Cabin*. Nearby, North Buxton, the site of another all-black fugitive slave settlement, annually holds a homecoming during the Labour Day weekend, and local museums and archives contain much important information on the African Canadians who settled and farmed this region.

Despite the legends of the Underground Railroad organized by courageous heroes such as Harriet Tubman, it is essential to bear in mind that racial oppression existed in Canada, slave catchers operated here, and many of the white population wanted—and still want—us out. Significantly, prior to 1831 there were several attempts to escape slavery in Canada by fleeing to those northern states in the U.S. that had abolished it. Indeed, after the fire Marie-Joseph-Angelique fled Montreal for New England, where she was captured. Later still, many African Canadians who fought in the American Civil War stayed south of the border, judging that there they would be better able to ensure the education and future of their children.

Periodically, I find it necessary to remind my children and other young African Canadians that we are not beggars in this land. We have paid our dues and continue to do so. African Canadians have fought in every major international conflict involving their country, including the War of 1812, which found us in conflict with the continent's major slave power, the United States of America. (Amherstburg, a few miles from Windsor, was a major African-Canadian community and is worth visiting for its reputation for resistance to the American invasion.) During World War I, African Canadians were greatly humiliated in their attempts to be recruited and in the tasks given to them once their sole segregated unit was established. It was only during World War II that we fought not merely along with but in the same desegregated ranks as our white compatriots. African Canadians have also served in our peacekeeping forces around the world. Since 1945 about a dozen African-Canadian soldiers have risen to the rank of lieutenant-colonel, including my eldest brother, a veteran of the Royal Navy from 1939 to 1945. One measure of progress that is dear to me is that he has served as commander-in-chief of a vast region comprising northern Ontario and northwestern Quebec. We are all very proud of him. But a measure of how far we have to go is that despite his past achievements and failing health, he finds it necessary to continue service as an elected school board trustee in Sudbury, where he lives. The education system, our main medium for advancement, remains the principal arena in which opposition to the presence of African Canadians (and other peoples of colour) is expressed. And thus I return on my journey to my home and to my fear. Not long ago, a cross-burning took place outside of London, Ontario, and while the Ku Klux Klan reportedly is strong in heavily white Alberta and Saskatchewan provinces, virulent white supremacist groups also abound in Ontario, even in Toronto high schools. *Plus ça change, plus c'est la même chose.*

However, among the things that have remained unchanged is our presence here in Canada since the days of Mathieu da Costa and Olivier Le Jeune, a presence that testifies that we live here by choice. If the struggles for equality and progress never really end, neither do Canada's pleasures—pleasures of nature and of man. From calm lakes to lively multicultural cities, from historical sites that underscore Canada's black heritage to museums that reveal Africa's ancient Nubian kingdoms, Canada remains—particularly for our cousins south of the border—North America's great unexplored territory. Follow the North Star. You'll find Canada—and unread chapters of our heritage.

X·X·X

FREDERICK IVOR CASE is principal of New College, at the University of Toronto. He is the author of *Racism and National Consciousness* and *Crisis of Identity*, among other titles. As a scholar and academic administrator, he is one of the foremost authorities on African Canadians.

NOVA SCOTIA

Department of Tourism and Culture
Cornwallis Place, 1601 Lower Water Street, P.O. Box 456, Halifax,
Nova Scotia B3J 2R5, Canada
(902) 424-5000; (800) 565-0000
Hours: Mon.–Fri., 8:30 A.M.–4:30 P.M.

Ask for the "Nova Scotia Black Heritage Trail" brochure produced by the Black Cultural Centre for Nova Scotia.

ACACIAVILLE

Acaciaville United Baptist Church
Acacia Valley Road, Acaciaville, Nova Scotia
Mail: c/o Cherry Paris, P.O. Box 275, Digby, Nova Scotia B0V 1A0, Canada
No phone
Acaciaville, Jordan, and Conway are all on the outskirts of Digby
Hours: Daily until sunset
Admission: Free

Born to a Yoruba clan, abducted from Africa and renamed in America, where he labored in slavery, Thomas Peters came of age during the American Revolution, during which he sided with the British in exchange for the promise of freedom. A skilled carpenter, Peters joined a pioneer battalion, was twice wounded, and rose to the rank of sergeant. Withdrawn with other African-American Loyalists following the British defeat, Peters and his family (and many of his compatriots) settled in Brindleytown, Nova Scotia, where land grants were offered. Believing that he had not received all that he had been promised, Peters petitioned the Canadian government. After six years of his protests did not yield satisfaction, Peters sailed to England for redress. There he met John Clarkson, the noted abolitionist and proponent of African immigration schemes. Peters returned to Canada with Clarkson, where they promoted the new Sierra Leone colony. In 1792 Peters and David George (see Shelburne Museum entry on p. 544) led the massive African-American exodus from Canada to Sierra Leone. There Peters died within months of his arrival, having in his lifetime journeyed from freedom in Africa to slavery in America and back home in freedom again.

Today the original 1853 Acaciaville United Baptist Church is the center of the remnants of three small black villages—Jordan, Conway, and Acaciaville (then called Brindleytown)—that formed the heart of one of the African-Canadian Loyalist settlements. A stroll around the three communities lying on the outskirts of Digby reveals their African-Canadian past—and provides the opportunity to enjoy the clams and scallops for which the town is famous.

BRIDGETOWN

African United Baptist Association Commemorative Cairn

Inglewood Baptist Church, RR 2 (Inglewood Road), Bridgetown, Nova Scotia B0S 1M0, Canada
No phone
Hours: Daily until sunset
Admission: Free

Under the leadership of the Reverend Richard Preston (see Cornwallis Church entry on p. 542), 14 black churches across Nova Scotia gathered together in 1845 to form the African United Baptist Association (AUBA). Probably the first major black organization in Canada, AUBA is certainly the oldest existing African-Canadian group. Today the founding of this group is honored with a commemorative cairn at the Inglewood Baptist Church in Bridgetown.

DARTMOUTH

Black Cultural Centre for Nova Scotia

Highway 7 at Cherrybrook Road, Box 2128, East, Dartmouth, Nova Scotia B2W-3Y2, Canada
(902) 434-6223
Hours: Mon.–Fri., 9 A.M.–5 P.M.; Sat., 10 A.M.–4 P.M.
Admission: Museum: Adults, $1 Can.; families, $5 Can.; under 5, free

Jutting into the Atlantic, Nova Scotia is more famed for fishing villages and farms than for Afro-Canadians, but it too has been shaped in some measure by the presence of the diaspora, which first arrived in large numbers in the wake of the Loyalist exodus from the triumphant American Revolution. The largely hidden black heritage of Canada's principal Atlantic peninsula is explored in the museum of the Black Cultural Centre for Nova Scotia. Canada's World War I, white-officered, all-black construction battalion, more than half of whose members were Nova Scotians, finally gets its due in an exhibit built around photographs, memorabilia, and artifacts. Birchtown, a black Loyalist community established in 1783, is explored through the medium of 19th-century photographs. Nova Scotia's black contribution to the world of boxing is traced through the careers of two paladins, George Dixon and Sam Langford. Born in the Africville district of Halifax, Dixon (see Boxing Hall of Fame entry on p. 292) spent a decade as world champion, first as a bantamweight and then as a featherweight. As a black man, he found more problems out of the ring, particularly after marrying a white woman, and died addicted to opium at the age of 39. Langford is judged to have been one of the ten greatest boxers of all times, though he never held a major title—in part because fighters, including Jack Johnson, ran away from contests with him and in part because he regularly fought above his weight. Finally, organized religion (Protestant until the early 20th-century influx of Catholic West Indians) as the prime vehicle for Afro-Canadian expression and advancement is traced through artifacts, memorabilia, and photographs of ministers, choirs, and congregations. Museum visitors also have access to temporary exhibits that explore other aspects of the diaspora's experience in the far North. **Note:** Ask for the "Nova Scotia Black Heritage Trail" brochure produced by the center.

GREENVILLE

Greenville United Baptist Church
Greenville Road, Greenville, Nova Scotia B5A 4A8, Canada
No phone
Hours: Historical markers: Daily until sunset
Admission: Free

Perhaps the first race riot in North America occurred in July 1784 in Nova Scotia. It resulted in the dispersal of many inhabitants of the black Loyalist settlement of Birchtown, which was located within the township of Shelburne. Many fled to the smaller black Loyalist settlement near Greenville. The descendants of that settlement raised two churches in the mid-19th century, African Bethel (1849) and Salmon River (1853). Today the graveyard of the former is

COURTESY PHOTOGRAPH COLLECTION, PUBLIC ARCHIVES OF NOVA SCOTIA AND BOB BROOKS

Though lacking running water and sewage facilities even as late as the 1960s, Africville was a vibrant community for more than a century.

located close to Greenville United Baptist Church, which is the lineal descendant of the Salmon River Church. The exterior walls of Greenville United hold two historical plaques outlining the church's history; the interior walls boast one plaque and old photographs of the local black community.

HALIFAX

Africville Memorial Cairn

Seaview Memorial Park, Barrington Street North, Halifax, Nova Scotia, Canada
Hours: Daily until sunset
Admission: Free

In the 1960s the vibrant Africville settlement of Halifax, which dated back to the 1840s, contained perhaps 400 families of African descent—and no running water or sewage facilities. The area was "redeveloped" and the property-owning residents compelled to leave their homes. Today many of the former residents live in projects, which have turned into high-crime zones. All that remains of Africville are memories, reunions held at Seaview Memorial Park, a song and an album entitled *Africville* by the African-Canadian singer Faith Nolan, and a memorial cairn that recalls the community of the past and the peril of "progress."

Cornwallis Street United Baptist Church

5457 Cornwallis Street, Halifax, Nova Scotia B3K 1B1, Canada
(902) 429-5573
Hours: Daily until sunset
Admission: Free

Presided over by the Reverend Richard Preston at the time he inspired the formation of the African United Baptist Association (AUBA), Canada's first all-black organization, Cornwallis Street United Baptist Church (1832), is considered the AUBA's mother church and as such is now a listed Heritage Property Site. A historical plaque on the church's exterior wall outlines the work of Preston, who is also mentioned on the church's foundation stone.

HANTSPORT

William Hall Commemorative Cairn

Hantsport United Baptist Church, Main Street, P.O. Box 35
Hantsport, Nova Scotia B0P 1P0, Canada
(902) 684-9265
Hours: Daily until sunset
Admission: Free

In the midst of the Sepoy Rebellion—a mid-19th-century nationalist eruption against Britain's rule of India—William Hall, a black Nova Scotian serving in the Royal Navy, volunteered for a mission to retake Lucknow in India's interior and was assigned to an artillery task. In the course of the battle outside the city, all his comrades servicing the cannon saving the commander, Lieutenant Young, were killed. Hall and Young thereupon serviced the gun themselves, pushing the 300-pound cannon into place and lifting and loading each 24-pound ball, eventually breeching Lucknow's walls and enabling the royal marines to retake the city and release the surviving British hostages.

COURTESY PHOTOGRAPH COLLECTION, PUBLIC ARCHIVES OF NOVA SCOTIA

William Hall was the first black man, and only the third Canadian, to be awarded the coveted Victoria Cross, Britain's highest medal for military valor.

For their efforts, Hall and Young were awarded the Victoria Cross for valor. Hall was the first Canadian sailor (and only the third Canadian), the first Nova Scotian, and the first person of African descent to win the coveted medal. Upon his return home, he received neither credit nor recognition for his deed and was buried in an unmarked grave in his hometown of Lockerville. Years later, thanks to the Canadian Legion, his remains were disinterred and prominently reburied on the lawn of the United Baptist Church in nearby Hantsport.

Today a 12-foot-tall commemorative cairn, adorned with a plaque, recalls an African-Canadian who justifiably took pride in his accomplishment on behalf of an empire crushing a popular revolt by a people of color against foreign rule and ways. Visitors should be forewarned: Nothing on the cairn alerts one to Hall's racial heritage. Of course, perhaps this is because his compatriots viewed him simply as Canadian—though one somehow worthy of being interred originally in an unmarked grave. The Hantsport Historical Society (Community Centre, Main Street, c/o P.O. Box 35, B0P 1P0; 902 684-9257; summer: daily, 9 A.M.–6 P.M.; other months, by appointment; free) has photographs and newspaper clippings that detail Hall's life and his reburial.

NEW GLASGOW

Second United Baptist Church

340 Washington Street, New Glasgow, Nova Scotia B2H 3M1, Canada
(902) 752-1360
Hours: Tue.–Wed., 8:30 A.M.–11:45 A.M. and 1:30 P.M.–3:30 P.M.;
Thu.–Fri., 8:30 A.M.–11:45 A.M.
Admission: Free

Born in Virginia, W. A. White (1874–1936) arrived in Wolfville, Nova Scotia, to attend Acadia University, a well-reputed Baptist seminary. Staying on in Nova Scotia, White preached at Zion Baptist in Truro and then in Halifax. Commissioned a chaplain in the all-black No. 2 Construction Battalion (see next entry) during World War I, White saw service from 1916 through 1920, becoming—it is believed—the first black captain in the armies of the British Empire. Of more lasting significance, White founded in New Glasgow the Second United Baptist Church, which still serves a congregation that has not forgotten the Virginian. **Note:** There is neither a historical marker nor other interpretive material on White at the church.

PICTOU

No. 2 Construction Battalion Memorial

Market Wharf, Pictou, Nova Scotia B0K 1H0, Canada
Hours: Daily until sunset
Admission: Free

More than seven decades after African-Canadians' attempts to serve their country in World War I first were turned aside and then channeled into a segregated noncombatant unit, the only all-black Canadian battalion to serve overseas in the Great War has been honored with a battalion memorial. Nineteen officers and 605 other ranks shipped overseas in March 1917 and were attached to the Canadian Forestry Corps. Though black men across Canada and the United States served in the unit, more than half of its members were Nova Scotians. Today, in addition to the granite memorial located near the former site of the battalion's local headquarters, there is a commemorative plaque and interpretive panels that make clear that Canada's second-class citizens resolutely sought to serve their country.

SHELBURNE

Shelburne County Museum

Maiden Lane and Dock Street; P.O. Box 39, Shelburne, Nova Scotia B0T 1W0, Canada
(902) 875-3219
Hours: Oct. 15–May 15: Mon.–Sat., 9:30 A.M.–12 P.M. and 2 P.M.–5 P.M.
May 16–Oct. 14: Daily, 9:30 A.M.–5:30 P.M.
Admission: Voluntary donations requested

David George led a life of adventure and purpose. Born into slavery in Virginia in 1742, he fled to the wilds of South Carolina, attaching himself first to the Creek chief Blue Salt and then to the Natchez chief King Jack, the latter of whom sold him back into slavery not far from Augusta, Georgia. Awakened to the Baptist faith by a slave, and to literacy by his master's children, George preached at the Silver Bluff Baptist Church (see entry on p. 133 and see Acaciaville United Baptist Church entry on p. 539), arguably the first black church in America, before moving to Savannah, Georgia (and freedom), in the chaos of the American Revolution. There George joined George Liele and Andrew Bryan (see First African Baptist Church entry on p. 75 and First Bryan Baptist Church entry on p. 75) to form the most potent pre-Federal trinity of black preachers in America and the foundation of Baptist missions to Africa.

Following the war George departed to Nova Scotia with many other black Loyalists, where they founded the Birchtown settlement near the harbor of Shelburne. In Shelburne he met with white (and doctrinal) opposition ("they came one night and stood before the pulpit and swore how they would treat me if I preached again") in the course of preaching to biracial congregations that gathered in the local Anglican church. Undaunted, George founded the first Baptist church in Shelburne ("we baptized almost every month"), which soon was housed in a small frame building ("by mid-summer we had a roof, but still no pulpit or pews"). George remained desperately poor and managed at one point to feed his family only through the assistance of a white Baptist couple who arrived from London. In time, Birchtown's black veterans became despondent over the lack of land grants on arable land and the absence of racial equality. And so in 1792 George joined with Thomas Peters (see Acaciaville United Baptist Church entry on p. 539) to lead more than 1,200 African Americans to the Sierra Leone colony, where he introduced the Mother Continent to Baptism.

Today visitors to the Shelburne County Museum view a permanent exhibit on the Birchtown settlement, which survived in attenuated form into the 19th century. The museum also has considerable archival material on George (including his brief autobiographical account), who in Africa carved out a Baptist missionary path just as his former colleague Liele would do in Jamaica.

SYDNEY

St. Philip's African Orthodox Church
34 Hankard Street, Sydney, Nova Scotia B1N 2C2, Canada
(902) 567-1220
Hours: By appointment
Admission: Free

Early in the 20th century, West Indian (principally Barbadian) immigrants were brought to Cape Breton to work the steel mills and coal ovens. They followed on the heels of an earlier importation—of black steel workers from Alabama. Fewer than 100 Alabamians arrived and most—but not all—left after passing on their knowledge. But between the two groups, Cape Breton found itself with a substantial black presence. Responding to the discrimination they found (or felt) in the local Anglican, Baptist, and Catholic churches, the immigrants in 1921 communicated with Marcus Garvey's Universal Negro Improvement Association (UNIA) (see Marcus Garvey and Malcolm X entry on p. 197) and requested a UNIA chaplain. This is the origin of Canada's sole African

Orthodox Church. Today St. Philip's African Orthodox Church is a listed Canadian Heritage Property Site. Inside the church is an old photograph of the church's first building, a former tool shed of the British-American Steel Company.

WEYMOUTH FALLS

Sam Langford Memorial Plaque
Langford Community Centre, RR 4, Weymouth Falls, Nova Scotia B0W 3P0, Canada
(902) 837-4004
Hours: Daily until sunset
Admission: Free

Sam Langford (1886–1956) was one of the toughest boxers ever to enter the ring. Standing five feet, six inches tall and weighing between 150 and 185 pounds, depending on the match (Langford fought in more different weight classes than anyone in history), he frequently boxed as a heavyweight—and this in the days when bouts would go 50 to 80 rounds. In more than 600 professional engagements lasting into his late 30s (by which time he was blind in one eye!), Langford won a reputation for ferocity and endurance. In 1906, before Jack Johnson became the world heavyweight champion, he fought Langford. Although he outweighed the Canadian by 49 pounds and had a far greater reach, Johnson barely won a split decision and refused ever after to enter the ring with the man to whom he allegedly had promised a title match should he become champion. (Langford never forgave Johnson for running away from the promised title bout; thus during the famous Johnson-Jeffries title fight, Langford worked with the Jeffries camp.) Born in Weymouth Falls, the underweight Langford only held one official heavyweight championship crown—Mexico's. Dying in Boston virtually penniless and blind in the 1950s, Langford paid the price of a lifetime's battering and bad management. Today in his hometown, the man is honored with a Langford Community Centre, outside of which is a memorial plaque.

ONTARIO

Ministry of Culture, Tourism and Recreation
77 Bloor Street West, Toronto, Ontario M7A 2R9, Canada
(800) 668-2746
Hours: Mon.–Fri., 9 A.M.–8 P.M.; Sat.–Sun., 10 A.M.–6 P.M.

Ask for "The Road That Led to Freedom: An African-American Heritage Tour" brochure.

AMHERSTBURG

North American Black Historical Museum and Cultural Centre
277 King Street, Amherstburg, Ontario N9V 2C7, Canada
(519) 736-5433
Amherstburg is 18 miles south of Windsor
Hours: Apr. 18–Nov. 30: Wed.–Fri., 10 A.M.–5 P.M.; Sat.–Sun., 1 P.M.–5 P.M.
Admission: Adults, $3 Can.; seniors and students, $1 Can.; families, $7 Can.

The Upper Canada Abolition Act of 1793, which placed limited constraints on existing slavery and which established that any slave *newly* entering the province, whether with his or her master or in flight from bondage, would be deemed legally free, was enacted the same year the U.S. Congress passed its first Fugitive Slave Law. Two decades later African Americans' knowledge of a Canadian haven grew as a consequence of the War of 1812 and the attendant Cochrane Proclamation. This proclamation sought to undermine the American economy and war-fighting potential by disrupting through the promise of freedom and sanctuary a slave-based economy and by compelling the United States to divert military resources to maintain control systems for a social order built on bondage. (See Chalmette Battlefield entry on p. 90.) By the time the first black national convention met in Philadelphia in 1830, Canada was well known as a refuge for escapees, and convention delegates approved of migration there even as they decisively rejected a homeland in Liberia. Migration north accelerated in the 1830s as restraints on free-black existence in America were intensified and as Benjamin Lundy's *The Genius of Universal Emancipation* reported on the greater racial equality north of the border. (During Lundy's Canadian visit of 1832, he found more than 300 African Americans living in Amherstburg, "a considerable settlement" at Chatham, several hundred souls near London, and distinct black districts at Woolrich and Oro Township. Though some of these black communities dated back to the Loyalist exodus following the Revolutionary War, most were more recent and reflected African Americans' point of entry into Canada: Those entering through Niagara settled there or moved on to St. Catherines and Hamilton; those entering from Detroit settled in Windsor, Amherstburg, and Sandwich, or moved on to Chatham and London.) The constraints on free-black existence and their relation to migration were significant: The early 20th-century African-American historian Carter G. Woodson estimated that 15,000 of the 40,000 antebellum black residents of Canada had been freemen in the United States, searching in Canada for equal rights rather than fleeing southern plantations and their overseers.

All this history and more is explored at the North American Black Historical Museum and Cultural Centre. Though the museum covers black history from Africa to the present, its focus is on the Underground Railroad and the black settlements of southwestern Ontario. Slave sale bills, maps of fugitive routes, contemporaneous newspaper accounts of black settlements, a log cabin circa 1855, a small genealogical file, and black-oriented videotapes offer visitors a window onto a world of which most North Americans, on both sides of the border, are unfamiliar. Adjacent to the center is Nazery A.M.E. Church, whose congregation was the point of origin for the museum and cultural center. Dating back to the 1850s and still attended by descendants of the escaped slaves who founded it, the church offers additional testimony to the determination, drive, and concerns of the diaspora.

CHATHAM

Kent-Chatham Tourist Bureau
233 King Street West, Chatham, Ontario N7M 1E6, Canada
(519) 354-6125; continental U.S., (800) 561-6125
Hours: Mon.–Fri., 9 A.M.–5 P.M.

Ask for their "Follow the North Star" brochure, which outlines the more prominent African-Canadian heritage sites of the county.

John Brown Meeting House Historical Marker
First Baptist Church, 135 King Street East, Chatham, Ontario N7M 3N1, Canada
(519) 352-9553
Hours: Marker: Daily until sunset. Church interior: By appointment (519 354-6125)
Admission: Free

In May of 1858 John Brown—soon to be famous for his raid on the U.S. federal arsenal at Harpers Ferry—and various associates, white and black, arrived in Chatham, Canada, to hold a convention to form a government-in-exile and lay the foundation for an insurrection leading to the establishment of a revolutionary regime on liberated territory in the United States. Chatham, a principal terminus of the Underground Railroad, held the promise of safety as fully one-third of the community was black and many were fugitive slaves. In the guise of a fraternal meeting, 35 African Americans and 12 whites first gathered at the British Methodist Episcopal Church on Wellington Street East to adopt a constitution. When the pastor, the Reverend Toyer, learned of the meeting's real purpose, he forbade them the church's grounds. The conspirators moved next to the King Street School and then to the First Baptist Church, which had been constructed by fugitive slaves. Among those present were the prominent black nationalist and future Union Civil War officer Martin Delany, who then lived in Chatham on the corner of Murray and Adelaide streets; the Reverend W. C. Munroe, a black minister from Detroit, who was elected chairman of the gathering; John Henry Kagi, who was elected secretary of war; Brown's sons, Owen and John (the former of whom would survive the raid on Harpers Ferry and die in California in 1891); Isaac Shadd and the husbands of Julia and Mary Ann Shadd (see Uncle Tom entry on p. 549); Addison Smith, an escaped slave whom Brown tried to persuade to return to the South to win recruits to the cause; Osborne Perry Anderson, who would escape Harpers Ferry and write about the raid in Mary Ann Shadd's newspaper, *The Provincial Freeman;* and the Reverend T. W. Stringer, a freeborn mulatto who served in the Mississippi legislature after the Civil War and earned a reputation for political eclecticism.

Today, outside the First Baptist Church, a historical marker commemorates the final gathering place of the conspirators, only five of whom (Brown and his two sons, Kagi, and Anderson) would ride into Harpers Ferry in October of 1859. (See Kennedy Farm entry on p. 257 and Harpers Ferry entry on p. 207.) Inside the church, founded in 1841 by escaped slaves, is the table around which Brown, Delany, Kagi, and others plotted to overthrow slave rule in the United States. **Note:** Excepting church services, access to the church interior and the table is by appointment; interested visitors should contact the Kent-Chatham Tourist Bureau (519 354-6125).

DRESDEN

Uncle Tom's Cabin Historic Site
Kent County Road 40, R.R. 5, Dresden, Ontario N0P 1M0, Canada
(519) 683-2978
Dresden is located on Highway 21, off of Highway 401 (the main road linking Detroit and Toronto)
Hours: Victoria Day Weekend (third weekend in May)–last Sun. in Sept.: Mon.–Sat., 11 A.M.–5 P.M.; Sun., 1 P.M.–5 P.M. Rest of year: closed. Group tours, by appointment
Admission: Adults, $3 Can.; seniors and students 12–18, $2.50 Can.; children 6–11, $2 Can.; under 6, free; families, $10 Can.

In 1830 Josiah Henson loaded his family into a small boat and crossed the Ohio River, leaving Kentucky and bondage behind and setting out on the frightening road of a freedom still in jeopardy from slave catchers. For two weeks the family traveled by night and hid by day. Their experiences were representative of the Underground Railroad, which was more a series of routes utilized by individuals who had taken destiny into their own hands than an organized enterprise with "stations" and "conductors." Upon reaching Cincinnati, they found assistance. In Sandusky, Ohio, a sympathetic ship's captain accepted Henson's labor in exchange for the group's passage to Buffalo, whence they crossed into Canada. Once in Canada, Henson settled down to providing for his family, though much of his time was devoted to assisting fugitives.

In 1841 Henson and other former slaves and white abolitionists, prominently including Hiram Wilson of Ohio, purchased 200 acres of land near Chatham with money largely donated by British church groups. Here they established the British-America Institute, an agricultural and manual labor training school for freedmen and fugitives, as the nucleus of Dawn, a black cooperative settlement.

Dawn arose six years after the collapse of Wilberforce, Canada's first formal all-black cooperative settlement, and sought to learn from the errors of its predecessor by emphasizing education and manual training. Soon a saw and grist mill, a brickyard, and a church were erected, and approximately 500 souls settled in an expanding black community. Six years later Henson stepped on to the world's stage in a small way with the publication of his *The Life of Josiah Henson, Formerly a Slave, Now an Inhabitant of Canada*. Three years later, with the publication of Harriet Beecher Stowe's *Uncle Tom's Cabin* (see First Parish Church and Stowe House entries on p. 236), Henson's role on that stage would assume larger proportions and the man would be forever diminished, subsumed within the identity of Uncle Tom. While this identity conferred benefits—it was, for example, certainly the basis of his visit to Britain, during which he met with Queen Victoria—it made it all the harder to hide when the Dawn community collapsed amid scandal and charges of fraud.

The preeminent source exposing the corruption inside the Dawn community was Mary Ann Shadd's *The Provincial Freeman*. Shadd (1823–1893) was born into a large free-black family whose patriarch, Abraham, was a leader of the black convention movement, an opponent of African colonization schemes, and an early adherent of the American Anti-Slavery Society. After an education in Quaker schools and a career as a teacher in black schools, Mary Ann Shadd in 1849 published *Hints for the Colored People of the North*, which detailed the economic mechanisms by which free states constrained African-American financial and economic development. Following the 1850 Fugitive Slave Act, Shadd, her father, and her brother Isaac moved to Windsor, Canada, where she opened a school for African Americans and in 1852 wrote *Notes on Canada West*, a guide to aid black immigrants' absorption into a new life. The following year she and Samuel Ringgold Ward published *The Provincial Freeman*, making her the first black female newspaper editor in the history of the western hemisphere. Shadd used the paper to pursue her lifelong commitment to black self-sufficiency within integration and her staunch opposition to black self-segregation. Her paper also campaigned against the corruption she found within the abolitionist and fugitive movements—though, to be sure, she viewed the black movement's tendency continually to solicit white funding as corrupt per se. This assessment and her rejection of all-black communities, coupled with the fund-raising activities of Henson and John Scoble, Dawn's superintendent, which continued unabated even as the community's facilities sank into ruin, provided the grounds for one of the 1870s' major intrablack feuds, a feud that left Henson's reputation somewhat tarnished. Henson survived the criticism and lived on, dying in 1883, the same year the 60-year-old, still-active Shadd graduated from Howard University Law School.

Today visitors to the old Dawn settlement will find Uncle Tom's Cabin Historic Site. The house in which Henson lived, the cemetery in which he's buried, the community-erected church in which he preached, the building in which fugitive slaves first were housed upon their arrival at Dawn, an agricultural building complete with period implements, some of the original school buildings, a Henson memorial plaque, and a museum with modest holdings (period furnishings, slave handcuffs and chains, and a first edition of Henson's 1849 autobiography) interpret the man and the all-black community that provided refuge to fugitives from slavery. The site is run by Henson's great-great-granddaughter. Henson is not alone in having descendants still living in Canada's historically black communities—Shadds too will be found throughout southwest Ontario.

NIAGARA FALLS

Nathaniel Dett B.M.E. Memorial Chapel
5674 Peer Street, Niagara Falls, Ontario L2G 1X1, Canada
(416) 358-9957; (416) 354-9470
Hours: By appointment
Admission: Voluntary donations requested

The Methodist Mission, as it was originally known, dates back to 1814. In that year the battles of Chippewa and Lundy's Lane on the Niagara frontier found African Americans—some the descendants of slaves brought to Canada by Loyalists fleeing the American Revolution, some freemen, and some fugitive slaves—fighting in the Canadian ranks and cheering the victories that ensured that slave power (as distinct from slavery, which still existed in attenuated form in Canada and would until 1833) would stay south of the border. (Of course, African Americans also manned the American ranks in this war; see Perry's Victory entry on p. 446 and Chalmette Battlefield entry on p. 90.) In 1836 fugitive slaves associated with the Methodist Mission built a meeting place on the bleak and windy Murray Hill in Niagara Falls. Two decades later that church was rolled on logs to its present site, to land donated by Oliver Pannall, a fugitive slave who had swum the Niagara River to freedom. The same year the British Methodist Episcopal Church Conference of Canada was formed in Chatham, Ontario, and this church joined as one of the founding members. Now known as the Nathaniel Dett B.M.E. Memorial Chapel, the century-and-a-half-old frame building still stands. In addition to worship services, the church houses the Norval Freeman Johnson Heritage Library, which offers access to 300 volumes that touch upon the diaspora's experience in North America.

Canada's and Niagara's Underground Railway Tours
Niagara Falls Tours, Box 385, Niagara Falls, Ontario L2E 6T8, Canada
Canada: (800) 263-2542. U.S.: (800) 263-5701

Canada's and Niagara's Underground Railway Tours explore the African-American heritage north of the border.

NORTH BUXTON

Raleigh Township Centennial Museum
County Road 6, North Buxton, Ontario N0P 1Y0, Canada
(519) 352-4799; (519) 354-8693
In the village of North Buxton, 10 miles south of Chatham
Hours: May–Sept.: Wed.–Sun., 1 P.M.–4:30 P.M.; other times, by appointment
Admission: Per person, $3 Can.; families, $10 Can.

Even as the Dawn colony sank into acrimony and dispute, another black settlement was demonstrating that African-American cooperative colonies could prosper—albeit at the initial expense of paternalistic white leadership. William King arrived in Canada in 1846 as a reverend, a widower, and an abolitionist with a past—as an Irish immigrant to America he had married into a slave-owning Louisiana family and himself purchased a slave. Shortly after his arrival in Canada he was working with fugitive slaves. Inheriting human chattel upon the death of his father-in-law, King resolved to free them and establish them and other black refugees on a Canadian colony near Chatham. His proposal was not welcomed by many local residents. The *Chatham Journal* asked whether

> the intelligent, honest and industrious citizens of any township in Canada would submit to having 1,000 coloured paupers introduced into their community, to have the whole township government controlled and its officers selected by them, to have their sons and daughters educated under the same roof with a Black man for a teacher. . . . Let Walpole Island be purchased from or an exchange made with the Indians, and let the African be as nearly by himself as possible. . . .

Despite these reservations, the Canadian government, headed by Lord Elgin, supported King's effort, and an association was charted by an act of Parliament in 1850 to purchase a tract of land. Among the new settlement's first colonists were the various slaves King had acquired through or in connection with his first marriage, two of whom went on to fight in the Union ranks during the Civil War. The Elgin Settlement required settlers to purchase rather than rent or sharecrop land (though it could be purchased in installments) and construct a cabin to minimum specifications—18 by 24 feet, four rooms, adjoining garden, and picket fence. Liquor was forbidden in the settlement, and a court of arbitration ruled on any disputes that arose. The education offered at Elgin was demanding, which attracted additional colonists. Henry Johnston enrolled his son in King's school, explaining that while he had "left the States for Canada for rights, freedom, and liberty, I came to Buxton to educate my children." (Three generations of Johnstons still can be found in the Buxton area.) This was no mere mechanical and agricultural trade school. Latin and Greek prepared the students for college, and all of the school's first graduating class went on to higher education.

Today North Buxton, as the area of the old Elgin Settlement is now known, is a middle-class black community. Its residents, many descendants of the original colonists, justifiably take pride in their heritage, much of which can be traced at the Raleigh Township Centennial Museum. Here visitors view a slide presentation outlining the history of the Elgin community, artifacts and diaries of the colonists, artifacts and the papers of King, census data from 1851, and family trees that trace yet another achievement of the diaspora. Part of the museum complex is the adjacent old Second School (1861) and the old settlement cemetery (1857). Nearby are the B.M.E. Church (1855) and the First Baptist Church (1883), which testify to the 19th-century growth of a black community in Canada.

ORO TOWNSHIP

Slave Settlement Memorial Cairn
A.M.E. Church, Third Line, County Road 11, Oro Township, Ontario
LOL 2XO, Canada
(705) 487-2171 (Township clerk)
Hours: Daily until sunset
Admission: Free

The remnants of Canada's first fugitive slave settlement still can be seen in Oro Township. Near the restored and no longer utilized old log A.M.E. Church is a half-acre graveyard filled with the mortal remains of men and women who followed the North Star to freedom. Next to the church stands a memorial cairn, while about two miles down County Road 11, surrounded by a protective fence, are three graves (lot 11, concession 5) of former residents of the settlement.

PUCE

John Freeman Walls Historic Site and Underground Railroad Museum
Puce Road, Puce, Ontario, Canada
(519) 727-6555; (519) 258-6253
In Maidstone Township, 8 miles east of Windsor-Detroit border; take Puce exit off of Highway 401, then travel 1 mile north.
Mail: Proverbs Heritage Organization, 1307 Pelissier Street, Windsor, Ontario N8X 1M4
Hours: July 1–Labor Day: daily, 10 A.M.–5 P.M. Groups, by appointment
Admission: Adults, $3 Can.; children, $2 Can.; group rate, $2 Can. per person

In 1846 the escaped North Carolinian slave John Freeman Walls and his wife, Jane King Walls, constructed a log cabin on land purchased from the Refugee Home Society, a Canadian group whose leaders included two fugitive slaves, Josiah Henson and Henry Bibb (founder and publisher of the black newspaper *Voice of the Fugitive*). The Puce River settlement subsequently grew to almost 100 families, and the Wallses' cabin served as an Underground Railroad terminus and as the first meeting place of the Puce Baptist Church. Following the Civil War many of the settlement's former slaves returned to the United States, but Walls and his wife stayed on in Canada. Today the descendants of John and Jane Walls operate the John Freeman Walls Historic Site and Underground Railroad Museum. The museum is housed in the restored log cabin built in 1846, on whose walls one can still see inscribed the initials "J.W." These Walls have voices, which they use to speak about the slave trade, tracing the diaspora's experience from Africa to Canada. A pathway has been carved through the site's 22 acres and is used to simulate a slave's journey north. Tape recordings of barking dogs and burbling streams add an element of verisimilitude to the journey, which concludes with your arrival at the 1846 cabin in which John and Jane Walls found freedom and built a future for themselves and their descendants.

SOUTH BUXTON

St. Andrew's Presbyterian Church and Reverend King Crypt
c/o Raleigh Township Centennial Museum, RR5, Merlin, South Buxton, Ontario N0P 1W0, Canada
(519) 352-4799; (519) 354-8693
Hours: By appointment
Admission: Free

The Reverend King's Elgin Settlement attracted many prominent guests. Frederick Douglass visited—which was entirely appropriate, as he had helped William Parker make his way there after the African American had fled his Christiana, Pennsylvania, home following the killing in his front yard of Edward Gorsuch, a Maryland slave owner attempting to reclaim his human chattel. Benjamin Drew (*Narratives of Fugitive Slaves*), the black abolitionist Samuel Ringgold Ward (who wrote of Elgin in his autobiography), the Quaker abolitionist Samuel May, William Lloyd Garrison, John Brown, Harriet Beecher Stowe (whose second novel, *Dred of the Dismal Swamp*, is said to be based on King's life), and Samuel Gridley Howe, who was sent by the Freedmen's Bureau to write a report for Lincoln's secretary of war, all came away favorably impressed with the settlement. But those most impressed with the settlement were the African-American refugees in Canada West, as southwestern Ontario was then called, and their brethren in America. Significantly, however, Elgin did not prosper for long after the Civil War and the passage of the 13th, 14th, and 15th amendments. By 1870 King reported that Buxton had seen 700 of its men and women return to America.

While North Buxton today retains many remnants of its black past, old South Buxton has few. One of its most prominent is St. Andrew's Presbyterian Church. Still hanging in the church's steeple is a bell inscribed "Presented to the Rev. William King by the coloured inhabitants of Pittsburgh [USA], for Academy at Raleigh Canada West." The 500-pound bell originally was set in King's garden and, in accordance with the request of its black donors, was rung at dawn and dusk to remind the Elgin brethren of their liberty. Today access to the bell is difficult, necessitating a climb up a ladder that is not likely to encourage repeat visits. King left $100 to a similarly named church in nearby Chatham, St. Andrew's United (85 Williams Street South), for the maintenance of the Reverend King Crypt, which today can be visited at Maple Leaf Cemetery (Maple Leaf Drive—stop first at nearby office, 445 Park Avenue East—Chatham; 519 354-2060; daylight; free).

ST. CATHERINES

Anthony Burns Grave and Historical Marker

Victoria Lawn Cemetery, Queenston Street, St. Catherines, Ontario L2R 7K6, Canada
(416) 682-5311
Enter through the main gate on the south side of Queenston Street. The historical marker is by the office at the main gate. The grave is in section "G"; a black and green stake on the cemetery's internal drive directs one to the grave. For further directions, ask at the office
Hours: Office: daily, 8:30 A.M.–4:30 P.M.; closed 12 P.M.–1 P.M.
Admission: Free

Born into slavery in Virginia in 1834, Anthony Burns spent a not atypical slave youth, being hired out by his master to serve both as a domestic and as a laborer, secretly learning to read and affiliating with the Baptist Church. In 1854 Burns stowed away on a ship bound for Boston, where he found employment and assistance from the city's abolitionists. A month later his Virginia master arrived, obtained a federal warrant for his arrest, and seized him in accordance with the provisions of the Fugitive Slave Law. Upon the failure of the Boston Vigilance Committee to free him by legal means, a biracial mob of 2,000 people, led by Lewis Hayden, a prominent black abolitionist (see Faneuil Hall entry on p. 262), and Thomas Wentworth Higginson, a white parson, activist, and subsequent Civil War commander of black troops (see Fort Scott entry on p. 379), attempted forcibly to free Burns from the courthouse in which he was being held prior to his return south. One person was killed in the melee, and the state was compelled to call out 22 militia companies to maintain order. After the mob's failure to free Burns, he was marched down to Boston's docks along streets thronged with 50,000 peaceful citizens shouting "Shame!" Burns was transferred to the slave pens of Norfolk, Virginia, where he eventually was purchased. One year after his bid for freedom, Burns was repurchased and freed by the congregation of Boston's Twelfth Baptist Church, where he had worshipped during his brief interlude of freedom. He then was sponsored to study at Oberlin College and at a theological school. Afterward he briefly pastored a black congregation in Indianapolis before fleeing the constraints of a free-black existence in the North for the haven of Canada. Burns served the Zion Baptist Church in St. Catherines from his Canadian arrival in 1860 until his death two years later. The man who was at the center of one of the most celebrated anti–Fugitive Slave Law riots in the North found his final resting home at Victoria Lawn Cemetery, where today visitors will find his grave and a historical marker.

Harriet Tubman/Underground Railroad Historical Marker
Salem Chapel British Methodist Episcopal Church, 92 Geneva Street, St. Catherines, Ontario L2R 4N2, Canada
(416) 682-0993
Hours: Daily until sunset
Admission: Free

Harriet Tubman's headquarters for the Canadian end of her fugitive slave operation was the British Methodist Episcopal Church in St. Catherines, which was located just around the corner from the North Street boardinghouse that she ran from 1851 to 1858. Most of her colleagues in Canada shared with her a background of slavery, a personal initiative that propelled them to freedom, and a passion for the cause of their brothers and sisters still held in bondage. Today, outside the 1857 church structure raised by fugitive slaves, a historical marker recalls the first gathering place in freedom for runaways who had crossed into Canada via Niagara. (As with Shadd, Henson, and Johnston, many of Tubman's descendants today live in Ontario.)

Not far away, in the Lock 3 Complex on the Welland Canal (P.O. Box 3012; L2R 7C2), is the St. Catherines Museum (416 984-8880; daily, 9 A.M.–5 P.M. or 9 P.M., seasonally; adults, $3 Can., seniors and students, $2 Can.), whose archives has information on local black heritage.

TORONTO

Ontario Black History Society
Ontario Heritage Centre, 10 Adelaide Street East, Suite 202, Toronto, Ontario M5C 1J3, Canada
(416) 867-9420
Hours: Tours: by appointment, with 48 hours' notice
Admission: Adults, $20 Can.; seniors, $15 Can.; children under 12, $12 Can.

A nonprofit organization formed in 1978, the Ontario Black History Society offers three-hour tours of Toronto's black heritage sites. Stops include the building in which Mary Ann Shadd edited and published *The Provincial Freeman;* the hall in which was held the First North American Convention of Coloured Freemen, one of whose principal organizers was Henry Bibb; the headquarters of the Toronto chapter of Marcus Garvey's Universal Negro Improvement Association; and the hotel owned by J. Mink, one of Canada's wealthiest black men in the 1840s—who was perhaps best known for having offered $10,000 for "a respectable white husband" for his daughter. He only got half of that for which he bargained: The white and unrespectable husband, on the pretext of a honeymoon in the United States, sold Mink's daughter into slavery! History records that she was rescued from her predicament, and one presumes the precipitating act provided grounds for annulment.

FURTHER READING

The past three decades have seen an unprecedented exploration of different realms of the African-American experience. Ranging from the earliest days of North American settlement through the historic civil rights struggle of the 1960s, the texts suggested below supply information, insight, controversy, perspective, and pleasure. This list is illustrative rather than comprehensive, and necessarily slights both fine scholars and general works.

From Slavery to Freedom: A History of Negro Americans, John Hope Franklin (Knopf, 1987). Franklin's career as a historian spans half a century and this work, first published in 1947, demonstrates anew both his passion and his adamant commitment to scholarship.

White over Black: American Attitudes Toward the Negro, 1550–1812, Winthrop D. Jordan (Norton, 1977). An accessible landmark study that continues to inspire detailed rebuttal and endorsement by Jordan's peers in the field of black studies.

"Myne Owne Ground": Race and Freedom on Virginia's Eastern Shore, 1640–1647, T. H. Breen and Stephen Innes (Oxford University Press, 1980). A large subject explored in a small place, this book offers an account of the extraordinary period before race and slavery dominated the American experience.

The Black Presence in the Era of the American Revolution, Sidney Kaplan and Emma N. Kaplan (University of Massachusetts Press, 1989). Popular history of an unpopular subject; the African-American role in tending liberty's garden and advancing American culture.

Climbing Jacob's Ladder: The Rise of Black Churches in Eastern American Cities, 1740–1877, Edward D. Smith (Smithsonian Institution Press, 1988). The church was the principal vehicle of expression for the African American people, and Smith explores its urban development from colonial times to the crushing of Reconstruction.

Segregated Sabbaths: Richard Allen and the Rise of Independent Black Churches, 1760–1840, Carol V. R. George (Oxford University Press, 1973). Though

Nat Turner, Gabriel Prosser, and Denmark Vesey seize the imagination of the public, Richard Allen, founder of the Free African Society and the African Methodist Episcopal Church, was the most historically significant black man ever to walk this land.

Blacks in Early Canada: The Freedom Seekers, Daniel G. Hill (Irwin, 1981). Canada was the destination for many who followed the North Star, and the lives they made there are traced by Hill.

North of Slavery: The Negro in the Free States, 1790–1860, Leon F. Litwack (University of Chicago Press, 1965). Though published in the year the Voting Rights Act passed, Litwack's book treats a subject *still* largely ignored by popular history: northern white supremacy and the substantial legal, social, and political impediments to racial equality in states that condemned the South for slavery.

The Underground Railroad, Charles L. Blockson (Prentice Hall, 1987). Black leaders, white allies, and moral fervor; the Underground Railroad was 19th-century America's great clandestine experience.

The Negro's Civil War: How American Blacks Felt and Acted During the War for the Union, James M. McPherson (Ballantine Books, 1991). First published in 1965, but still the best popular summary of black voices speaking out in the years 1861–1865.

Reconstruction: America's Unfinished Revolution, 1863–1877, Eric Foner (Harper and Row, 1988). A magisterial account that reflects Foner's dominance of the material, the period, and the craft of history.

Exodusters: Black Migration to Kansas after Reconstruction, Nell Irvin Painter (Knopf, 1977). A survey of the post-Reconstruction period from the perspective of the black masses, *Exodusters* provides an account of the first major migration of free African Americans.

Strength for the Fight: A History of Black Americans in the Military, Bernard C. Nalty (Macmillan, 1986). The great bulk of Nalty's work focuses on the African-American military contribution in the century following Lee's surrender at Appomattox.

Dark Journey: Black Mississippians in the Age of Jim Crow, Neil R. McMillen (Illini Books, 1990). The hangman's noose encircled more than simply scores of black men—though only African Americans died, an entire society was choked.

Eyes on the Prize: America's Civil Rights Years, 1954–1965, Juan Williams (Viking Press, 1986). An excellent introduction to the tumultuous era that opened with the Supreme Court's *Brown* decision and closed with the passage of the Voting Rights Act.

Parting the Waters: America in the King Years, Taylor Branch (Simon & Schuster, 1988). The movement, the man, and the moment met, and America was changed.

When Harlem Was in Vogue, David Levering Lewis (Oxford University Press, 1989). Brilliantly interweaves anecdote and scholarship to explore the lives of the artists, philosophers, and players at the heart of black society.

INDEX